D0712883

Never Let a Serious Crisis Go to Waste

Never Let a Serious Crisis Go to Waste

How Neoliberalism Survived the Financial Meltdown

Philip Mirowski

VERSO

London • New York

First published by Verso 2013
© Philip Mirowski 2013

1 3 5 7 9 10 8 6 4 2

Verso
UK: 6 Meard Street, London W1F 0EG
US: 20 Jay Street, Suite 1010, Brooklyn, NY 11201
www.versobooks.com

Verso is the imprint of New Left Books

ISBN-13: 978-1-78168-079-7

British Library Cataloguing in Publication Data
A catalogue record for this book is available from the British Library

Library of Congress Cataloging-in-Publication Data
Mirowski, Philip, 1951–
Never let a serious crisis go to waste : how
neoliberalism survived the financial meltdown / Philip
Mirowski.
pages cm
Includes bibliographical references and index.
ISBN 978-1-78168-079-7 (pbk. : alk. paper)
1. Neoliberalism. 2. Economic policy. 3. Financial
crises. 4. Global Financial Crisis, 2008–2009.
5. United States— Economic policy— 2009– I. Title.
HB95.M57 2013
320.51'3— dc23
2013013476

Typeset in Bembo by Hewer Text UK Ltd, Edinburgh
Printed in the US by Maple Vail

To neoliberals of all parties

Contents

List of Tables

List of Figures

One More Red Nightmare:

The Crisis That Didn't Change Much of Anything

Conjure, if you will, a primal sequence encountered in B-grade horror films, where the celluloid protagonist suffers a terrifying encounter with doom, yet on the cusp of disaster abruptly wakes to a different world, which initially seems normal, but eventually is revealed to be a second nightmare more ghastly than the first.[1] Something like that has become manifest in real life since the onset of the crisis which started in 2007. From the crash onward, it was bad enough to endure house prices sinking under water, dangling defaults and foreclosures, the collapse of what remained of manufacturing employment, the reduction of whole neighborhoods to bombed-out shells, the evaporation of pensions and savings accounts, the dismay of witnessing the hope of a better life for our children shrivel up, neighbors stocking up on firearms and people confusing bankruptcy with the Rapture. It was an unnerving interlude, with Nietzschean Eternal Return reduced to an Excel graph with statistics from the Great Depression of the 1930s.

Fast forward to 2011. Whether it was true or not, people had just begun to hope that things were finally turning around. Moreover, journalists in mainstream publications bandied about the notion that academic economics had failed, and hinted that our best minds were poised to rethink the doctrines that had led the world astray. Yet, as the year grew to a close, it slowly dawned upon most of us that the natural presumption that we were capable of rousting ourselves from the gasping nightmare, that we might proceed to learn from the mistakes and fallacies of the era of Neoliberal Follies, was itself just one more insidious hallucination. A dark slumber cloaked the land. Not only had the sense of crisis passed without any serious attempts to rectify the flaws that had nearly caused the economy to grind to a halt, but unaccountably, the political right had emerged from the tumult stronger, unapologetic, and even less restrained in its rapacity and credulity than prior to the crash.

In 2010, we were ushered into a grim era of confusion and perplexity on the left. It took a rare degree of self-confidence or fortitude not to gasp dumbfounded at the roaring resurgence of the right so soon after the most dramatic catastrophic global economic collapse after the Great Depression of the 1930s. "Incongruity" seems too polite a term to describe the unfolding of events; "contradiction" seems too outmoded. Austerity became the watchword in almost every country; governments everywhere became the scapegoats for dissatisfaction of every stripe, including that provoked by austerity. In the name of probity, the working class was attacked from all sides, even by nominal "socialist" parties. In the few instances when class mobilization was attempted by trade unions to counterattack, as in the recall petition for Scott Walker in the state of Wisconsin, the birthplace of American progressivism, it failed. The pervasive dominance of neoliberal doctrines and right-wing parties worldwide from Europe to North America to Asia has flummoxed left parties that, just a few short years ago, had been confident they had been finally making headway after decades of neoliberal encroachment. Brazenly, in many cases parties on the left were unceremoniously voted out because they had struggled to contain the worst fallout from the crisis. By contrast, the financial institutions that had precipitated the crisis and had been rescued by governmental action were doing just fine—nay, prospering at precrisis rates—and in a bald display of uninflected ingratitude, were intently bankrolling the resurgent right. Indeed, the astounding recovery of corporate profits practically guaranteed the luxuriant postcrisis exfoliation of Think Tank Pontification. Nationalist proto-fascist movements sprouted in the most unlikely places, and propounded arguments bereft of a scintilla of sense. "Nightmare" did not register as hyperbolic; it was the banjax of the vanities.

The Winter of Our Disconnect

I remember when I first felt that chill shiver of recognition that the aftermath of the crisis might be suspended in a fugue state far worse than the somnolent contraction itself. I was attending the second meeting of the Institute for New Economic Thinking (INET) at Bretton Woods in New Hampshire in April 2011.[2] There probably would have been better places to take the temperature of the postcrisis Zeitgeist and observe the praxis of the political economy than up in the White Mountains, but I had been fascinated by the peccadilloes of the economics profession for too long, and anyway had felt that the first INET meeting at Cambridge University in 2010 bore some small promise—for instance, when protestors disrupted the IMF platitudes of Dominique Strauss-Kahn in Kings great hall, or when Lord Adair Turner bravely suggested we needed a much smaller financial sector. But the sequel turned out to be a profoundly more unnerving and chilly affair, and not just due to the caliginous climate. The nightmare scenario began with a parade of figures whom one could not in good conscience admit to anyone's definition of "New Economic Thinking": Ken Rogoff, Larry Summers, Barry Eichengreen, Niall Ferguson, and Gordon Brown. Adair Turner was summoned for a curtain call, reprising his previous year's performance, but offered only tired bromides on "happiness studies" and rationality. The range of economic positions proved much less varied than at the first meeting, and one couldn't help notice that the agenda seemed more pitched toward capturing the attention of journalists and bloggers, and those more interested in getting to see some star power up close than sampling complex thinking outside the box. It bespoke an unhealthy obsession with Guaranteed Legitimacy and Righteous Sound Thinking. But, eventually, even the journalists and the bloggers sensed the chill in the proceedings. Here were a few contemporary responses:

> University economists, of the sort gathered at Bretton Woods, are now under relentless pressure to conform to a narrow, established paradigm. Inexplicably most supporters of that paradigm also feel that the crisis confirmed its validity.[3]

> The last great crash caused a revolution in economics. Why hasn't this one? . . . None of those theories appears to have appreciably shaped the economic policy proposals coming from the White House or Congress, where lawmakers draw much of their economic inspiration from think tanks built on dogma . . . Neither party seems keen to search for orthodoxy-challenging economic answers.[4]

> The weight of the 1920s-decorated rooms, and the grey presence of so many headliners of the economics profession (which we are making the most of with the interviewing) is creating great confusion about what is "new" in New Economic Thinking. One line is nostalgia and it began with the opening session when Rogoff recalled with regret and humor how as a young man he was

unengaged by Charles Kindleberger's teachings . . . In a trope that I saw repeated thrice, it was said that economics is at a stage where a Copernican revolution has occurred but one needs still to use Ptolemaic cosmology for a few decades more, for policy advice . . . None of this is new, and worse still, none of it is very critical. New Economic Thinking is hard to win. For nearly a century philanthropic money tried to steer economics into interdisciplinarity and social and historical consciousness, in the 1970s they gave up. And because change is so hard, there is a danger that INET gives up, and becomes a left of center think tank to argue the policy wars. The task of producing knowledge against the grain requires imagination. I would have wished to see the big headliners back to back with some new ideas from INET grantee portfolio. I would have wished more collaborative work and less staging [sic] speeching. I would have wished more time for debate and critique. I would have wished less farce and more tragedy.[5]

Unlike Gordon Brown, Mr. Summers portrayed himself in the role of a Chinese mandarin tired at the world daring to challenge his mandate from heaven. For example, when the irrepressible Yves Smith asked Larry Summers about whether banking risks in the United States could not be helpfully diminished if its large institutions were run (read: compensated at the top) more like utility companies, he immediately aborted any effort at an intellectually honest answer by making it sound as if she were proposing to bring state socialism to banking. A man who reportedly earned millions for having advised hedge funds one day a week for a year shortly before serving in the Obama Administration (and who is quite likely, now that he's out, to do so again), he ought to have been patriotic and intellectually honest enough to provide a real answer.[6]

The most interesting moment at a recent conference held in Bretton Woods, New Hampshire—site of the 1945 conference that created today's global economic architecture—came when *Financial Times* columnist Martin Wolf quizzed former United States Treasury Secretary Larry Summers, President Barack Obama's ex-assistant for economic policy. "[Doesn't] what has happened in the past few years," Wolf asked, "simply suggest that [academic] economists did not understand what was going on?" . . . For Summers, the problem is that there is so much that is "distracting, confusing, and problem-denying in . . . the first year course in most PhD programs." As a result, even though "economics knows a fair amount," it "has forgotten a fair amount that is relevant, and it has been distracted by an enormous amount." . . . [Unlike Summers,] it is the scale of the catastrophe that astonishes me. But what astonishes me even more is the apparent failure of academic economics to take steps to prepare itself for the future. "We need to change our hiring patterns," I expected to hear economics departments around the world say in the wake of the crisis.[7]

Many at the conference confessed their perplexity as "The crisis is over, but where was the fix?" The political debacle of the "rescue package" promulgated throughout the West was acknowledged by all and sundry, although accounts concerning the nature and causes of the failure would have drawn much less consensus. Some suggested that the immediate imperative of being seen to act (by the Federal Reserve, or the Treasury, or the ECB, or other authority) had preempted the equally necessary stage of reflection and reform. Yet the nightmare cast its shroud in the guise of a contagion of a deer-in-the-headlights paralysis: beyond their pretense of expertise, no one who fancied themselves opposed to neoliberal decadence really possessed solid convictions concerning where the intellectual failure behind the crisis should have been well and truly situated. They seemed united by nothing more than a vague disaffection from the status quo in economics. And worse, while the authorities dithered, the Ghoulish Creatures of the Right had gotten back up, dusted themselves off, and discovered renewed strength. Economists such as Ken Rogoff and Carmen Reinhart had the audacity to stand up at INET and treat the contemporary world crisis as just another ho-hum business cycle: nothing untoward or unprecedented had happened here. Thus doctrines concocted at the American Enterprise Institute and the Cato Institute began their slow seepage back into respectability. The INET crowd kept trying to wake up from—what?—neoclassical microeconomics, rational expectations, the efficient markets hypothesis, Black-Scholes, the Coase theorem, faux-Keynesian macroeconomics, optimality, public choice theory, baroque fiduciary mathematics, the end of history—what exactly? How could you even know if the fix was in or not, if you weren't even sure about where one needed to look for conceptual guidance?

Now, the reader may cavil I just had myself to blame for my little nightmare scenario; for, after all, whyever would a shindig produced and paid for by George Soros actually conjure up any authentic New Economic Thinking?[8] True to form, there was almost no serious debate of any sort at Bretton Woods, nary even an impressionistic summary of possible alternative paths for economics; there was, however, a nostalgia so thick it curdled the sumptuous desserts, sustained by a motley scrum of B-list celebrities (since no economist after Keynes would ever attain the cultural name recognition of an Arnold Swarzenegger, or a Bob Dylan, or even a Malcolm Gladwell) hoping to enjoy a frisson of safe transgression; their jollity tempered by a caution that it was prudent to downplay any concrete divergences from the economic orthodoxy that, after all, had granted them their modicum of fame in the first place. None of the participants evinced the slightest unease in their embrace of the dogma that *nothing* that had transpired in the last seventy-five years had moved the goalposts of allowable economic controversy away from those supposedly positioned by John Maynard Keynes and Friedrich Hayek. Many speakers openly delighted in conjuring the Shade of Maynard in those hallowed halls. Surely it had been fatuous of me to hope INET might have provided a platform for any authentic divergent strains of economic thought, given that those glitterati would have avoided the conference like the plague if it had been stocked up with post-Keynesians, Regulation School representatives, Institutionalists, and Minskyites, much less Chinese-style Marxists.[9]

But the nightmare scenario was not confined to INET or George Soros. It turns out to have been far more pervasive than that.

From the White Mountains to Mont Pèlerin

On March 5–7, 2009, the Mont Pèlerin Society (MPS) held a special meeting at Ground Zero of the global economic meltdown, New York City, to discuss the implications of the tremors for their political project. Around a hundred members and an additional hundred guests convened under the banner "The End of Globalizing Capitalism? Classical Liberal Responses to the Global Financial Crisis." Back then, many titular heads of the neoliberal movement were dreading the possibility that the snowballing crisis might just be their own worst nightmare. After all, the prime event that had originally prompted the organization of the nascent Neoliberal Thought Collective [NTC] was the Great Depression of the 1930s. The initial motley crew of Friedrich Hayek, Ludwig von Mises, Lionel Robbins, Milton Friedman, and all the rest had endured the horror of being ridiculed and lambasted for their responses to the Great Contraction, relegated to the margins of discourse by the sheer misfire of the Economic Engine of Human Progress. They had huddled at Mont

Pèlerin in 1947 to try and figure out how to intellectually redeem themselves. In many ways, the first generation had spent the rest of their lives living down the shame that had accompanied their disenfranchisement and defeat at the hands of John Maynard Keynes, FDR, scientists such as J. D. Bernal, a phalanx of market socialists such as Oskar Lange and Jacob Marschak, and a host of European political thinkers. So it was not pitched beyond the realm of possibility that, with the benefit of hindsight, the Third Generation Neoliberals would be in for a rough ride in 2009.

Once upon a time, such an emergency executive committee meeting of the NTC might have been the occasion for truly imaginative blue sky thinking, forging an optimal response to the impending collapse of their cherished worldview. Perhaps, in a rerun of the 1940s, the neoliberals in 2009 might have come up with some transformative new ways to think about the market, stealing some of the thunder of the left by combining previously statist concepts with a novel revision of the True Nature of market activity. To a historian, it is striking the extent to which the neoliberals have repeatedly taken ideas from the left over the last half of the twentieth century and twisted them to their own purposes. Perusing the papers from the New York conference, however, one finds instead mostly predictable platitudes and tired retreads about the wicked government causing the crisis.[10]

Deepak Lal raised an interesting question in his keynote address: why did the crisis occur when so many "Friends of the MPS" like Alan Greenspan and Jean-Claude Trichet were in charge of the world financial system, and hinted they may not have leaned sufficiently in favor of "Sound Money." Niall Ferguson rallied the troops with the catechism that it must have been regulation that caused the crisis, and not some failure of the market economy, while also exploring his personal theme that somehow China might be to blame. Gary Becker floated the opinion that it might be better to do nothing in response to the crisis, rather than flail about with all manner of government remedies. (This book refutes that canard, when it comes to the neoliberals.) It seems the general mood of the conference was that neoliberals (the "classical liberal" moniker was a smokescreen to be discussed in later chapters) should pretty much keep doing what they had been doing all along, even if the crisis appeared a little scary. Other observers of the neoliberals noticed this soon thereafter: "And just like that, the idea-intoxicated American right vanished . . . Instead of reckoning with a starkly transformed global economy, conservative thinkers are reviving seventy-odd-year-old talking points from the Liberty League."[11]

For some on the left, this betokened evidence of relative decline of the MPS from its postwar heyday, or perhaps the participants had been just caught unawares, like most professional economists. Nevertheless, three years on, it now looks as though the neoliberals have come through the crisis unscathed. Far from the economic crisis constituting the invigorating jolt of the 1930s redux for the Neoliberal Thought Collective, early returns seemed instead to have ratified their intransigence, repetitiveness, and lack of imagination. Now it confirms that they were right to stick to their guns, because, contrary to every expectation, nothing much has been changed by the crisis. But the neoliberals have not won by default—that would be a sorry interpretation of events. Neoliberals don't let a serious crisis go to waste. Instead, the thought collective subsequently made a number of moves that cemented their triumph. This book aims to document the strategies, and survey their successes. Many of these activities involved the economics profession.

Ranging from the White Mountains to Mont Pèlerin, economists have proven exceedingly shopworn and hackneyed in their responses to the crisis. This opinion has congealed into conventional wisdom. However, this coagulation has had an asymmetrical effect upon the two ends of the political spectrum. Monotonous repetition seems to have fortified the right admirably well in weathering the crisis, whereas by contrast, it has delegitimated the left to an even greater degree than its rather parlous status during the decade of the Great Bubble. Beyond the tendering of excuses, there hovers the open question of to what extent the unexpected resurgence of the right after the crisis has grown out of the stock of neoliberal cultural infrastructure built up over the period from 1980 till 2008, and conversely, to what extent the left has been the author of its own rout. This phenomenon, I will suggest, needs to be examined much more closely.

Nothing substantial has been altered in the infrastructure of the global financial system from its state before the crisis.[12] Government "reforms" have proven superficial at best in both Europe and the United States. Further post-2008 evidence of debilities, such as the "flash crash" of May 2010, the epic failure of the BATS IPO in March 2012, and the Knight Capital meltdown in August 2012 passed without serious concerted response, even though they suggest that market malfunctions run deeper than the conventional fixation over mortgage securitization and banking fraud. The coincidence of employment stagnation and persistent inflation has resurfaced for the first time in three decades, although the responsible agencies persist in obscuring the evidence. Bubbles have returned with astounding rapidity in commodities speculation (especially in oil) and in initial public offerings (such as LinkedIn and Fusion-io). The predominant focus upon government austerity programs as the central response to the crisis demonstrates that public discourse has degenerated to an analytical level that one would have recognized in the early 1930s. The MPS apparently has not suffered the ignominy of dramatic falsification of its cherished economic ideas; rather, it has been its opponents situated on the "level-headed left" that have collapsed instead. Given the palpable absence of innovative neoliberal analyses, one is hard-pressed not to suspect that one major source of weakness inheres in what passes for interventionist economic doctrine among the professional economic orthodoxy. But perhaps the debility runs even deeper than that.

Where There's Smoke, There's Toast

There subsists a surfeit of books and articles dedicated to covering the crisis. Many people who rushed to read them in 2009–10 have ended up feeling less informed than before they started. Furthermore, as if that weren't bad enough, no one volunteers to relive a nightmare; what they want is to be rousted back to the comforts of consciousness. The latter-day appeal of these crisis books seems to have become limited to those who harbor a penchant for crunch porn. By 2012, it seems most people had begun to tune out most serious discussions, and flee the tsunami of l'esprit de l'escalier.

There was a short interlude when editorial cartoonists and TV comedians tried to turn the whole thing into a joke, portraying how buffoon bankers bemoaned that the restive public just could not understand that they were the only ones who could clean up the godawful mess they had made, and proved petulant and unrepentant when Uncle Sam unloaded truckloads of money to pay them to do just that. As usual, reality outpaced satire when the former CEO of AIG, Hank Greenberg, brought suit against the U.S. government for not bailing out AIG at a sufficiently munificent rate.[13]

Bitter comic mordancy can be ripping fun; but a nagging voice whispers: isn't it just *too easy* to make fun of the Invisible Hand? Isn't there something *lazy* about Stephen Colbert and Jon Stewart? Is the right response to the nightmare of crisis fatigue to laugh it off? What if the people who helped bring on the crisis were quite literally laughing all the way to the bank as the financial system approached the precipice? Gales of merriment apparently rocked the meetings of the Federal Reserve Open Market Committee, as revealed by a tabulation of all the recorded instances of stipulated "[laughter]" in meetings transcripts from 2001 to 2006, reproduced in Figure 1.1.[14]

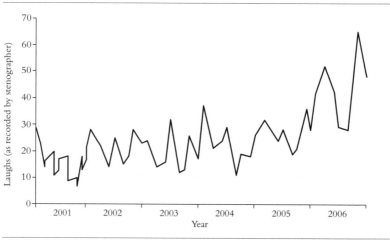

Figure 1.1: Hilarity at the Federal Reserve

Source: Federal Reserve FOMC Transcripts, Graph created by Daily Stag Hunt

Sometimes the best response to crisis fatigue is not an injunction to recover your flagging sense of humor, or to aspire to the status of he who laughs last. Levity might not be a universal nostrum.

The filmmaker Adam Curtis has written in disgust, "Despite the disasters we are [still] trapped in the economists' world."[15] Yet it will become necessary for us to differentiate the world of the economists and the world of the neoliberals. This conflation is an affliction of many on the left. A major sticking point here is that neoliberals themselves generally do not believe in the comic-book version of laissez-faire sometimes promoted by the economists. They may profess it to the masses; they may even propound it in Economics 101; but it does not characterize their sophisticated internal discussions, and is belied by their political activities.

Moreover, advocacy of economic inequality can lead to parallel advocacy of epistemic inequality: this is something we will probe in depth in chapter 2. Readers of Foucault and his followers are familiar with the idea that neoliberalism involves a reconstruction of the ontology of what it means to be a person in modern society; where some

Foucauldians have fallen down, I propose, is that they have neglected to plumb the symmetrical ontological transformation of what it means for a "market" to even exist.

Maureen Tkacik caught a glimpse of what is disturbing about the plenitude of Monday-morning quarterbacking:

> What was easy to convey was that something about the past ten years had been unsustainable. But the truth—that an *entire ideology* had been unsustainable—is one that we have not yet grasped. And that is why so many journalists, economists, intellectuals and financiers now scramble to churn out books that for the most part read like the memoirs of people trying to make themselves feel less stupid. The current financial system was constructed to make us all feel stupid, and in the process of building it the architects allowed themselves to become stupid as well.[16]

The crisis has not only wrought the economic insult mutely suffered by so many; it has also inflicted a breakdown in confidence that we can adequately comprehend the system within which we are now entrammeled. It has been de rigueur to denounce the antics of groups like the Tea Party, Golden Dawn, the True Finns, and the Front National; but can the left really claim it has been all that more sober, thoughtful, and incisive since 2007? The problem I grope toward in this volume is: How can people dismayed at the unexpected fortification of the Neoliberal Ascendancy feel less stupid? What would a useful intellectual history of the crisis and its aftermath look like?

Everyone seems to champion their own personal favorite candidate for Nostradamus of the Crisis—and I will deal with this whole vexed issue of "prediction" in chapter 5—but here I want to consider those on the nominal left who long ago discarded the Marxist eschatology of the Collapse of Capitalism and the Transition to Socialism, only now to retreat to a position of unabashed professions of ignorance. To pick on one journalist at random (I will deal with the economists later), I here point at Ezra Klein:

> "Inside Job" is perhaps strongest in detailing the conflicts of interest that various people had when it came to the financial sector, but the reason those ties were "conflicts" was that they also had substantial reasons—fame, fortune, acclaim, job security, etc.—to get it right.
>
> And ultimately, that's what makes the financial crisis so scary.

The complexity of the system far exceeded the capacity of the participants, experts and watchdogs. Even after the crisis happened, it was devilishly hard to understand what was going on. Some people managed to connect the right dots, in the right ways and at the right times, but not so many, and not through such reproducible methods, that it's clear how we can make their success the norm. But it is clear that our key systems are going to continue growing more complex, and we're not getting any smarter.[17]

The fact that some representatives of the "level-headed left" have felt compelled to attack the popular documentary *Inside Job* is itself a token of just how dire things have gotten in the interim; even more telling is the way in which fundamental neoliberal precepts concerning episte-mology and the sociology of knowledge are baldly taken as presuppositions. After the crisis, professional explainers from all over the map were throwing up their hands and pleading that the economy was just *too complex* to understand. Better to treat the Great Recession like an Act of God, and simply move on. This is a *cultural* debility that predated the crisis but has worked wonders in immobilizing responses to the debacle. As described in chapters 2 and 3, and anatomized in chapter 6, the neoliberals have developed a sophisticated position with regard to knowledge and ignorance; getting a grip on how they manage to deploy ignorance as a political tool will go some distance in dispelling the onus of having been transparently duped. It may also suggest that the time has come for the left to reinvent its own plausible sociology of knowledge.

The first step toward a history and sociology of knowledge about the crisis is to acknowledge that the intellectual response has occurred on a range of different levels, with counters situated at each level sometimes diverging in content and timescale, but eventually achiev-ing rendezvous and resonating in such a manner as to stymie any political responses not controlled by the banks and financial sector. One must be nimble to manage these variant levels. There is the level of the culture at large, where entrenched neoliberal images of human flourishing had to confront the palpable onset of collapse of a whole way of life. There is the level of public elite wisdom, momentarily blindsided, in tandem with the Mont Pèlerin Society, which found itself enjoined to improvise new understandings of the outpouring of academic chatter concerning the world turned upside down. There is (I will insist) a general Neoliberal Playbook as to how to strategically respond to really big crises. And then there was the economics profession. While not the only priesthood brandishing the key to something they diffidently called "the economy," it turned out that academic economists have played a critical role in the aftermath to the crisis, in a manner I believe has been poorly appreciated by both insiders and the general public. The neoliberal resurgence after the crisis has been heavily reliant upon the interplay of contemporary orthodox economists with the other levels of cultural response and elite generalist knowledge, even though no one tradition could be reduced to any other. Neoclassical economics was not intrinsically neoliberal over its entire one-and-a-half-century history; but it sure looks like they are working in tandem now. That is why this volume, in chapters 4 and 5, devotes a fair proportion of attention to what economists have said and done after 2007.

When considering the relationship of formal economic knowledge to social movements, it has become commonplace for pundits to quote the dictum of John Maynard Keynes in the *General Theory*: "Practical men who believe themselves to be quite exempt from any intellectual influence, are usually the slaves of some defunct economist. Madmen in authority, who hear voices in the air, are distilling their frenzy from some academic scribbler of a few years back."[18] However stylish was Keynes's prose, the rudimentary sociology of knowledge propounded therein has turned out badly flawed. Far from ectoplasmic missives from the late lamented, a simulacrum of a genteel Edwardian séance, the injection of economic ideas into quotidian politics has been conducted in ways both more concrete and yet more convoluted than is suggested by this rather tendentious bit of economists' self-flattery.

Economic doctrines rise to dominance because they have been built up from compelling intellectual trends located elsewhere in the culture, and often, in other sciences; and, in turn, depend upon promoters and funders to impress their importance upon other economists, and thenceforward the larger world. Ideas may be retailed, but they are not simply marketed, whatever the neoliberals insist otherwise. As with history, men make ideas, but not as straightforwardly as they please. Ideas have a nasty habit of transubstantiating as they wend their way throughout the space of discourse; sometimes proponents do greater harm to their integrity than do their opponents. Other times, people seem congenitally incapable of grasping what has been proffered them; and creative misunderstanding drives thought in well-worn grooves. In a riot of Dubious Signifiers, the Big Lie is king; but that does not preclude the fact that the juddering call and response strewn around it can be regularly bent to political ends. Furthermore, whenever basic notions are treated as colorless and transparent, the more they can serve as political ramparts to channel history in only one direction. When doctrines persist against all odds, say, in a world-wide economic crisis; when knowledge and power converge in stasis, then surely there is something that demands explication.

Do Zombies Dream of Eternal Rest?

In the throes of the red-misted nightmare, it looks as if the crisis, other-wise so virulent and corrosive, didn't manage to kill even one spurious economic notion. This is not exactly news. John Quiggin has enter-tainingly dubbed the phenomenon *Zombie Economics*, and deserves kudos for stressing this point. Incongruously, Friedrich Hayek's *Road to Serfdom* has returned to best-seller lists after a long hiatus. Even Ayn Rand has apparently enjoyed a new lease on (undead) life. One can readily agree with Colin Crouch: "What remains of Neoliberalism after the financial crisis? The answer must be 'virtually everything.'"[19] Similarly, a glut of crisis books has been pouring from every possible digital delivery system of publishers. They fall from the presses, not stillborn, but clone-dead. The cynic might say: Leave it to academics to turn a pervasive human disaster into another unsustainable growth industry. What could be the purpose of yet another jokey variation on the metaphor of the "Invisible Hand" on the cover of some text that purports to convince us that a very few select events or principles (usually a prime number) constitute the Rosetta Stone for decoding recent events? The distance from self-help books (*Six Things Momma Taught Me to Succeed When Good People Do Bad Things*) to crisis prescrip-tion books (*Dunk That Invisible Hand in Talcum Powder and Snap on the Handcuffs*) and get-rich-quick books (*Who's Afraid of the Big Black Swan?*) narrows precipitously in the modern marketplace of ideas.

Rest assured this will not be another of those books "about the crisis," in the sense of purveying yet one more play-by-play account of who did what to whom. Indeed, some of the best-detailed accounts of the economic history of the contraction of 2007–9 are freely available online; the problem seems to be, rather, that no one cares enough anymore to expend the effort to read them.[20] There is even a superb film that lays out the basic sequence of breakdown in an admirably clear way for a general audience: I refer to the movie *Inside Job* (2011). It even comes with an equally insightful follow-up book (Charles Ferguson's *Predator Nation*). In an ideal world, as a service to tyros, there would be a YouTube link to it right here in the text. Of course, the film is weak on intercalated structural causes, elides nonfinancial considerations, and tends to fall down on international developments; and it has that bad American habit of needing to finger the stick-figure "bad guys." Of course, such *son et lumière* pageants are no replacement for detailed indispensable sources of financial defalcations, quantifornication, legal sabotage, and twisted crisis particulars. But there is something else: while the film stands as an unprecedented indictment of the economics profession, it rather incongruously gives ideas a wide berth. It is skeptical of economists, but discordantly, takes no position on *economics*. This book therefore seeks to supplement it along a crucial dimension: it explores the economic crisis as a social disaster, but simultaneously a tumult of intellectual disarray. If the references hadn't been so egregiously obscure, I toyed with the prospect of calling the book *The Goad to Neoliberal Serfdom*. Avoiding that gaffe, it may nevertheless transpire that we can recognize our predicament as a conceptual debacle, and perhaps then, in retrospect, the crisis will not go down in history as such a pathetic waste.

Beyond that, I will endeavor to make use of the crisis as a pretext and a probe into the ways in which neoliberal ideas have come to thwart and paralyze their opponents on the left. The ongoing crisis is a political watershed; keeping that conviction front and center turns out to be much more difficult than one might initially think. And by "the left," I do not mean those benighted few, those Revenants of the Economic Rapture, who were certain that only complete and utter breakdown of capitalism would pave the way for a transition to the political ascendancy of the proletariat. History has already been unkind to them. I aspire to a different, more general audience. The Great Contraction has completely wrong-footed people who used to be called "socialists" or "progressives," confounding every expectation that they had finally achieved some small measure of vindication for their understanding of the economy. It ushered in a mongrel regime leaving them baffled and bewildered, such that one frequently heard them wonder out loud whether there was any left left.[21] It is those people who have taken it as a fundamental premise that current market structures can and should be subordinate to political projects for collective human improvement whom I seek to address here. Such like-minded compatriots are legion, but I fear their understanding of markets and societies has fallen into dire intellectual desuetude.

Let me draw one example from the film I have just praised, *Inside Job*. There and elsewhere in the aftermath of the crisis, one heard that the neoliberals were primarily responsible for the disaster because they imprudently deregulated markets, or else because they undermined existing regulation. I witnessed this proposition rolled out repeatedly at INET, for instance, and from people in Washington. Without a doubt, there had been important alterations in regulatory structures since 1980, and I will point to some of them in this book; but in no sense were they a simple *removal* of strictures that could or should be reinstated in any sense. To accept the language of "deregulation" is to become ensnared in a web of concepts that serves to paralyze political action. The neoliberals have openly expressed contempt for their opponents' easy appeals to "reregulation"; and I think the time has come to take them far more seriously.[22]

The nostrum of "regulation" drags with it a raft of unexamined impediments concerning the nature of markets, a dichotomy between markets and governmentality, and a muddle over intentionality, voluntarism, and spontaneity that promulgates the neoliberal creed at a subconscious level. This, I believe, has been one major symptom of the endemic failure of economic imagination on the left. Phalanxes of political theoreticians before me have repeatedly insisted that the neoliberal project primarily *reregulates* and institutes an alternative set of infrastructural arrangements; it never ever wipes the slate clean so that it gets closer to the tabula rasa of laissez-faire. Neoliberalism has never been especially enamored of the Eden of right-wing folklore, a paradise that never existed anywhere, anytime. I cannot exaggerate the myriad times this point has been made over the last century,[23] and yet there perdures a dizzy distracted air about the culture of late modernity that keeps ignoring it, repeatedly embracing the Dumb Dichotomy every time the politics heats up. This paramnesia is far too convenient for one side of the political spectrum to chalk up to ambient Alzheimer's or inept journalists. Appeals to "free markets" treat both freedom and markets as undefined primitives, largely by collapsing them one into another. It takes substantial theoretical sophistication to keep this fact front and center in the political disputes of the modern era; both neoclassical and Marxian economics have not proven salutary in this regard. This book aims to remind us that economics turns out to be good to forget with; one prophylactic will be recourse to a different approach to economics, one that is antithetical to core neoliberal tenets at its ontological base.

There is another way Team Regulation inadvertently capitulates to Team Greed. Team Regulation often has quipped a quick one-liner justification for its prescription: there were no financial crises (often left unstated: *in the United States*) from the 1940s to the mid-1980s;

therefore, all we need do is reset all the dials back to that Golden Era. In subscribing to this notion, the left unconsciously accepts the key notion of the populist right and the neoclassical orthodoxy, that "nothing is substantially different between then and now." Markets are timeless entities with timeless laws, they insist. Indeed, this is the identical premise of some of the most popular crisis books of the last few years, from Kenneth Rogoff and Carmen Reinhart's *This Time Is Different* to David Graeber's *Debt: The First 5,000 Years*.[24] Yet that is precisely where the polemical divergence should originate on the left. Things *are* profoundly different about the economy, the society, and in the global political arena than they were during the Cold War: some recent neoliberal innovations have lent the current crisis its special bitter tang; understanding precisely how and where they are different is a necessary first step in developing a blueprint for a better world. The neoliberals divested themselves of their nostalgia[25] for a Golden Age long ago; it is high time their opponents on the left did likewise. There is one very basic example how Team Regulation has served to betray the left, a lethal dynamic that has played out in the previous three decades. When financial crises erupted, first in peripheral countries, and then increasingly in the metropoles, technocratic economists in alliance with the neoliberals claimed they could contain it and "clean it up" by substituting sovereign state debt and rich-country guarantees for the insolvency of private actors; hence, when the Big One hit in 2007–8, responses reverted to the standard scenario. The mantra had always been to have the government in question "rescue" the collapsing sectors by shoring up their balance sheets, through the instrumentality of taking more debt onto its own accounts; and then purportedly when the worst had finally passed, subsequent efforts could be devoted to addressing any structural flaws, perhaps with more regulation. Imprimatur was sought indifferently from both Milton Friedman and John Maynard Keynes for this practice. Yet I shall argue in chapter 6 there was something new and sinister about the way the "rescue" was prosecuted, so as to prevent any return to older structures. The "level-headed" response turned out to be a shell game, with much of the mechanics of the rescue handed over to private interests, and where so much sovereign debt was being piled on over time that the backstop character of state fiscal authority was undermined; private sector insolvency had infected state solvency. In other words, recurrent banking crises revealed the basic incapacity of the Keynesian state to immobilize and rectify endemic macroeconomic crises, rendering "regulation" a hazy memory. Indeed, by 2012, people were actually forgetting that this was at base a crisis of capitalism, and only deriva-tively a fiscal crisis of the state. Sovereign debt looked as wobbly as private bank debt. This dynamic was avoidable because it was entirely predictable.

If you don't have a working comprehension of how the economic system failed—and a major thesis of this book is that most economists did not understand the economy's peculiar path prior to the crisis, and persisted in befuddlement in the aftermath—then the notion that one could impose some one-size-fits-all format of rational regulation is a vain delusion. This catastrophic intellectual failure of the economics profession at large should quash wistful evocations of Cold War versions of "regulation" on the left, and further, frame the implosion of things such as the Dodd-Frank initiative and Basel III. The intel-lectual wing of the neoliberal movement had actually long made this argument concerning easy appeals to regulation many times before; the difference is that they currently preach that all and sundry conse-quently should simply capitulate to their natural state of ignorance, and give up most (but not all—an important caveat) attempts at steer-ing the economy. Conspicuously, the neoliberals themselves do not themselves practice what they preach; and it is incumbent upon the left to develop an alternative framework to explain that fact, as part of a project to build an economy that conforms to open advocacy of a roster of social goals.

Reusing Old Graves with Tombstones Marked "Neo"

I earlier mentioned John Quiggin's *Zombie Economics*; our two books share more than a few common concerns; and it so happens that the current book will also touch upon a few of the same technical concepts found therein. Quiggin and I both propound the thesis that our culture is held in thrall to dead and rotten ideas concerning the economic crisis. Suspended in a gauzy red nightmare, it can be hard to discrimi-nate zombies from mere bit players; I think Quiggin is also right to suggest that it is the economists who are the ambient zombies, and *not* the neoliberals (yet another reason it is indispensable to keep neoclas-sical economics and neoliberalism separate and distinct as analytical categories).[26] Treating everything that moves as malignant and menac-ing is almost as big a mistake as treating all markets as operating alike. Quiggin provides a nice overview of the state of play of orthodox macroeconomic theory circa 2008 for the noneconomist, thus absolv-ing me (for the most part) of having to initiate you into the intricate mysteries of the same. I will often have occasion to point to his concise and brave diagnoses of where mainstream economics has gone astray. This is one way of saying his book is indispensable collateral reading.

However, I am equally going to take that book as exemplary of the kinds of thinking that have inadvertently consigned the left to passive ineffectual resistance to neoliberalism in the current crisis. Reprising his undead trope, it seems Quiggin believes that the best way to coax a zombie back into the grave is to reason with him. If only it were so easy to recycle old graves. Quiggin has done us the favor of boiling down his basic approach to political economy to a few pithy paragraphs on the popular blog *Crooked Timber*.[27]

> Although I'm clearly to the left of most people in the economics profession (including a fair number who would call themselves heterodox), I'm happy to identify myself with the mainstream research program in economics. The first reason for this is one of personal/political strategy. Starting from broadly social-democratic premises about the way the world works, I'm concerned to identify and advocate policies that will lead to better outcomes for society as a whole and particularly for the working class and the disadvantaged. Mainstream economics provides a set of tools (the theory of public goods, externality and market failure, taxation and income distribution) to do the analysis and a widely-understood language in which to express the results. No existing alternative body of thought in economics comes close to this.
>
> By attacking the logical foundations of this simple model, heterodox economists may undermine faith in the policy conclusions derived from it. But this doesn't get you very far. Even if you regard economic arguments for laissez-faire as worthless, this does not establish any positive case for alternative policies.
>
> More generally, I don't find the whole idea of orthodoxy and heterodoxy, or the related notion of schools of thought, particularly useful. It seems to me to imply a kind of intellectual ancestor-worship which is of no use to anybody. It goes with debates about what Keynes or Commons or Hayek really thought, which seem to me to be almost entirely pointless. In most cases, if their ideas were good ones, they will have been adopted by at least some people in the mainstream, and tracing their intellectual ancestry is of at most second-order interest.
>
> This goes with a judgment that most of the concerns* that are commonly raised against simple-minded versions of economics can

be addressed without throwing out the whole system and starting from scratch. If you don't believe in the perfectly rational economic man (sic), there's a huge body of work on behavioral economics, bounded rationality, altruism and so on. If you don't like simplistic competitive models, the shelves are groaning with books on strategic behavior and game theory.

I am sure Quiggin didn't intend it, but this came too perilously close to Margaret Thatcher's "There Is No Alternative" for comfort. These notions that serious intellectual work outside well-worn paths sanctioned by the established disciplines has often proven ineffectual when it comes to political rough and tumble; that every valid critique of neoclassical economics has already been made by someone else long ago and, furthermore, has been adequately absorbed by the cognoscenti; that you must voluntarily shackle yourself to the tropes of the modern economic orthodoxy if you have pretentions to be taken seriously; and that every doctrine should be judged in a cod–John Dewey fashion by its immediate proximate uses—all constitute major impediments to understanding how the left has failed in the current crisis.

Quiggin's book illustrates the disturbing conundrum of how difficult it can be for him, or indeed any other critic internal to the orthodoxy, to certify that he is not already infected with the zombie virus (a standard conundrum in zombie movies), and therefore deserves some culpability for their recrudescence. The first rule of nightmares is that sniping at zombies does not often stem their tide. For instance, Quiggin argues at one point, "The appealing idea that macroeconomics should develop naturally from standard microeconomic foundations has turned out to be a distraction"; but it is a distraction he himself cannot resist, relying as he does on neoclassical notions of "market failure," natural monopoly, absence of Arrow-Debreu contingent commodities, information as a public good, and conventional definitions of risk to motivate his version of "real-world" economics. At another juncture, he admits that a relevant macroeconomics "is not simply a matter of modifying the way we model individual behavior," but as he repeatedly conjures "behavioral economics" as the font of deliverance, he has nothing else on offer. In chapter 5 we suggest that behavioral economics has been a sink of despair. Quiggin frequently wishes for a "newer Keynesianism," but has to concede that the neoclassical synthesis was "not particularly satisfactory at a theoretical level, but it had the huge practical merit that it worked."[28] Time and again he signals that he is aware that neoclassical economics frustrates and confounds intellectual deliverance from the morass of zombie ideas; but nevertheless, he cannot seriously countenance the possibility that the solution to logical incoherence involves its repudiation. The result is that Quiggin repeatedly contradicts himself, and perforce treats it as a virtue. This is itself a pungent symptom of zombie thought, and is widely found across the board of the "legitimate left" of the economics profession, from Paul Krugman to Joseph Stiglitz to Adair Turner to Amartya Sen to Simon Johnson. Paul Krugman, feeling secure in his status, has conveniently confessed to the derangement:

> The brand of economics I use in my daily work—the brand that I still consider by far the most reasonable approach out there—was largely established by Paul Samuelson back in 1948, when he published the first edition of his classic textbook. It's an approach that combines the grand tradition of microeconomics, with its emphasis on how the invisible hand leads to generally desirable outcomes, with Keynesian macroeconomics, which emphasizes the way the economy can develop magneto trouble, requiring policy intervention. In the Samuelsonian synthesis, one must count on the government to ensure more or less full employment; only once that can be taken as given do the usual virtues of free markets come to the fore.
>
> It's a deeply reasonable approach—but it's also intellectually unstable. For it requires some strategic inconsistency in how you think about the economy. When you're doing micro, you assume rational individuals and rapidly clearing markets; when you're doing macro, frictions and ad hoc behavioral assumptions are essential. So what? Inconsistency in the pursuit of useful guidance is no vice.[29]

I do not wish to suggest one should never, ever simultaneously entertain A and Not-A. There is a grain of truth to this: quantum mechanics has been deemed inconsistent with classical mechanics and macro-scale theories such as relativity at various points in its history; it is possible for a science like physics to operate for a while with conceptual schizophrenia. Indeed, sometimes it may be a necessary prerequisite to come to understand the full nature and character of the submerged contradiction. However, the historical divergence comes with neoclassical economics in that most other sciences do not then banish their members who point out the inconsistencies and worry over their meaning. Nor do they simply expel the proponents of one side of the theory in order to maintain doctrinal purity, as happened with the rational-expectations movement and its epigones.

During the Cold War, the economics profession was growing more exclusive, but was not completely intransigently intolerant of rival doctrines, for reasons of ideological appearances. For instance, evidence from the Paul Samuelson archives suggests he really did nominate Joan Robinson for the Bank of Sweden economics "Nobel."[30] Things really ratcheted upward in terms of imposed conformity only after the Fall of the Wall, for equally obvious political reasons. However, the apogee of denial of divergent thought occurred during the Great Bubble. A very strange literature sprang up in the early 2000s, asserting that there was no such thing as neoclassical economics anymore, in the sense that the legitimate orthodox economics profession had explored every possible analytical divergence from the rigid Walrasian general equilibrium model of days past, and someone, somewhere, sometime had built formal models addressing the previously heterodox concerns.[31] Rationality? Who needs it? Equilibrium? We can do without it! Maximization? We can get around it! Individual greed? Just read Amartya Sen! Supply and demand? That just gets fed to people insufficiently mathematical to grasp the latest interpretation of the Sonnenschein-Mantel-Debreu theorems! Bubbles? We got 'em, hot, foamy, and rational. Complexity? How much can you handle? And so on and so on. Point to anything you may not find salubrious, and we've got a "not-so-new" model (and maybe a bridge) to sell ya. And yet, all this putative open-minded tolerance and catholic heedfulness was accompanied by bald attack on and excommunication of any last vestige of heterodox economics in top-ranked universities throughout the world, and the redoubled exclusivity of top-ranked economics journals. History of doctrines was banished, and scattered ghettos of heterodox thought were unceremoniously leveled. Even European holdouts were vigorously routed in their national contexts. For those on the front lines, it was wrenching to witness this contradiction up close.

I believe it was no accident that all manner of otherwise tolerant eclectic people started claiming that heterodoxy in economics was finally a thing of the past precisely during the Bubble run-up to 2007; perhaps we can now appreciate it as the twin offspring of the neoliberal herald of the "end of history," akin to the "Great Moderation," only now in the precincts of intellectual endeavor. The profession had been rendered starkly more homogeneous in outlook and training, not least through graduate recruitment of tyros with no undergraduate degree in economics, which had significant consequences for the bumbling responses of economists when the crisis hit. Training and backgrounds had grown so narrow that the newer generation had no idea there had ever been anything alien to their tradition, and hence their impressions of intellectual freedom were simple artifacts of their ignorance. Things had gotten so bad that some heterodox holdouts felt they had fallen victim to an elaborate fraud themselves: "There is nothing more frustrating for critics of neoclassical economics than the argument that neoclassical economics is a figment of their imagination."[32] No purge is more insidious than that which comes cladded with plausible deniability.

There are many different ways to understand how Big Brother managed to accrue a reputation for political neutrality and an open mind; and this book is an attempt to look at that phenomenon from a number of different perspectives. It is a bit more of a stretch to see how that reputation has been maintained (albeit under persistent duress) throughout the drubbing that the economics profession has suffered in the aftermath to the crisis; that also is the concern of this volume. It seems clear that the faux-tolerance of the "End of Neoclassical Economics" movement in the new millennium actually has made the response to the crisis by economists even more addled than it might have been otherwise.

However, there is one concise explanation of this history that no PhD economist would deign to entertain, although we shall insist it be kept on the table for the duration of this book. It is the proposition that Quiggin turned out to be half-right: it is not just that a few component models found in economics are zombiefied; rather, it is the neoclassical tradition as a whole that is approximating the walking undead, and has been lurching around that way for a while. Patently, this begins to get at why no amount of heterodox brickbats (or incisive reasoning) can halt its inexorable march. Before my audience dismisses this notion out of hand as too draconian, consider the following.

Let us provisionally take the proponents of the dissolution of the neoclassical program at face value. First off, it seems we have arrived at the historical epoch where academic neoclassical economics no longer strives to explain "the economy," because for sophisticated economists, there is no such thing. Critics who prattle on about "real-world economics" merely flaunt their naïveté to the quiet disdain of the gatekeepers of expertise. Rather, card-carrying neoclassical economists come convinced they possess a Theory of Everything at the End of History, and apply their so-called economic approach to everything great and small under the sun: life and death, sex, neurons, nations, language, knowledge, science itself, personal identity, evolution, aesthetics, global environmental disruption, even human virtues such as dignity.[33] Through prestidigitation, a theory of trade has morphed into a "theory of choice"; and choice is everywhere. After all, isn't that the central message of *Freakonomics,* the best-selling book of the Great Moderation: that wicked rebel (yet safely orthodox) economists can explain sumo wrestlers, teen homeboys, girls' first names, and crime statistics? Yet explanatory hubris brings its own special tragedy: it is a philosophical commonplace that a doctrine that nominally explains "everything" in fact explains nothing at all. Everything can potentially be portrayed by neoclassical economists as the orderly product of disembodied "self-interest" as long as the "interest" is defined in a sufficiently post hoc manner, order is conflated with the status quo, and the ontology of the "self" changes from one application to the next. As with all good zombies, there is something missing where a brain should be. Neoclassical economics resembles a catechism for the undead who have palsied difficulty counting to ten.

The unbearable lightness of the economy within neoclassicism is only the tip of the iceberg. Let us look more closely at the practical mechanics of orthodox contemporary "economics imperialism." While gleefully encroaching upon the spheres of interest of other disciplines, orthodox economics has also freely appropriated formalisms and methods from those other disciplines: think of the advent of "experimental economics" or the embrace of magnetic resonance imaging, or attempts to absorb chaos theory or nonstandard analysis or Brownian motion through the Ito calculus. Indeed, if there has been any conceptual constant throughout the history of neoclassical theory since the 1870s, it has been slavish attempts to slake its physics envy through gorging on half-digested imitations of physical models. A social science so promiscuous in its avidity to mimic the tools and techniques of other disciplines has no principled discrimination about what constitutes just and proper argumentation within its own sphere; and this has only become aggravated in the decades since 1980. Economics, seemingly so powerful because so ubiquitous, parlously teeters on the edge of fragmenting into a pointless succession of whatever turns out to be fashionable in other scientific disciplines, which at least possess the virtue of having intellectual agendas that spawn novel practices and techniques.

Third, it would appear that the corporeal solidity of a live intellectual discipline would be indicated by consensus reference texts that help define what it means to be an advocate of that discipline. Here, I would insist that undergraduate textbooks should not count, since they merely project the etiolated public face of the discipline to the world. But if we look at contemporary orthodox economics, where is the John Stuart Mill, the Alfred Marshall, the Paul Samuelson, the Tjalling Koopmans, or the David Kreps of the early twenty-first century? The answer is that, in macroeconomics, there is none. And in microeconomics, the supposed gold standard is Andrew Mas-Collel, Michael Whinston, and Jerry Green (*Microeconomic Theory*), at its birth a baggy compendium lacking clear organizing principles, but now slipping out of date and growing a bit long in the tooth. Although often forced to take econometrics as part of the core, there is no longer any consensus that econometrics is situated at the heart of economic empiricism in the modern world. Beyond the graduate textbooks, the profession is held together by little more than a few journals that are designated indispensable by some rather circular bibliometric measures, and the dominance of a few highly ranked departments, rather than any clear intellectual standards. Indeed, graduates are socialized and indoctrinated by forcing them to read articles from those journals with a half-life of five years: and so the disciplinary center of gravity wanders aimlessly, without vision or intentionality. The orthodoxy, so violently quarantined and demarcated from outside pretenders, harbors a vacuum within its perimeter.

Fourth, and finally, should one identify specific models as paradigmatic for neoclassical economics, then they are accompanied by formal proofs of impeccable logic which demonstrate that the model does not underwrite the seeming stolidity of the textbooks. Neoclassical theory is itself the vector of its own self-abnegation. If one cites the canonical Arrow-Debreu model of general equilibrium, then one can pair it with the Sonnenschein-Mantel-Debreu theorems, which point out that the general Arrow-Debreu model places hardly any restrictions at all on the functions that one deems "basic economics," such as excess demand functions. Or, alternatively, if one lights on the Nash equilibrium in game theory, you can pair that with the so-called folk theorem, which states that under generic conditions, almost anything can qualify as a Nash equilibrium. Keeping with the wonderful paradoxes of "strategic behavior," the Milgrom-Stokey "No Trade theorem" suggests that if everyone really were as suspicious and untrusting as the Nash theory makes out, then no one would engage in any market exchange whatsoever in a neoclassical world. The Modigliani-Miller theorem states that the level of debt relative to equity in a bank's balance sheet should not matter one whit for market purposes, even though finance theory is obsessed with debt. Arrow's impossibility theorem states that, if one models the polity on the pattern of a neoclassical model, then democratic politics is essentially impotent to achieve political goals. Markets are now asserted to be marvelous information processors, but the Grossman–Stiglitz results suggest that there are no incentives for anyone to invest in the development and refinement of information in the first place. The list just goes on and on. It is the fate of Delphic oracles to deal in obscurity.

Returning to our point of departure in this section, it really will turn out to be of paramount importance to keep the thought collectives of "neoclassical economics" and neoliberalism separate and distinct, for analytical purposes of understanding the nightmare of the current crisis.[34] Neoclassical economics as a theory long predated the Neoliberal Thought Collective; it is only lately that it has shown signs of morbidity. As we shall argue, it has fallen to neoclassical economists to swarm over and incapacitate most serious attempts to isolate and diagnose why the crisis came as a shock and an enigma to those tasked with its understanding. The economists have haunted our dreams with their half-coherent struggles to describe and analyze the creeping dread. Yet it has been the neoliberals who have served as the advance shock troops for the zombie hordes, reconnaissance parties deploying their shock doctrines and shock therapies that rally the walking dead in their wake.

Once summoned, lurching across the landscape, scaring the populace with their bad haircuts, dull, staring eyes, and adamantine cries, neoclassical economists became the major enablers of the Neoliberal Resurgence across the land. As Quiggin confessed, "I underestimated the speed and power of Zombie ideas."[35] We need to see why.

2

Shock Block Doctrine:

Neoliberalism as Thought Collective and Political Program

There are many ways that social theory operates in a modality different from the natural sciences; but one standout characteristic is that when it comes to the Big Notions that really matter, the social disciplines often find their acolytes proclaiming the "Death of X" contemporaneously with commensurate authorities insisting that X never really existed. In physics, for instance, analysts might want to claim that Ptolemaic astronomy or aether theory or cold fusion was "dead" for the modern profession, but never go so far as to assert that the theory or concept had historically just been a figment of the imaginations of people who should never have been taken seriously all along. By contrast, this happens all the time in social thought: social theorists often attempt the torturous straddle of denying that some widespread concept ever really existed, while pronouncing last rites over the ectoplasmic corpse. No wonder we have become ensnared in zombie nightmares, as glimpsed in the last chapter. It may be symptomatic of an endemic wobbly sense of ontology, or perhaps a deficiency in sense of decorum for the dear departed, or maybe something worse, but it nonetheless is an occupational hazard that renders debate treacherous.

The theoretical entity "neoliberalism" has suffered this straddle over the unfolding of the current crisis. A chorus of think tanks trumpeted its negligibility, while a smaller choir chanted its dirge. All manner of commentators, including, significantly, no small number of neoliberals, have insisted that the theory behind the label never really existed;[1] if they happen to be preternaturally pugnacious, they tend to dismiss it as a swearword emitted by addled denizens of the left. The confusion was then confounded by an outbreak of premature rumors of the Demise of Neoliberalism, when people were suggesting that the economic crisis had finally sealed its fate. The impression back then was so vivid for some that they could practically hear the worms feasting on the carcass of the still-warm ideology. The purpose of chapter I was to suggest that a few subsequent years' experience has vexed and discomfited almost everyone involved, and that political progress demands that this calamity be better understood. It may be the case that even those who feel they have a good working knowledge of political theory need to revisit the entire question of neoliberalism, if only to better focus upon the incongruity of the neoliberals coming out of the crisis stronger than when they were paving the way for its onset. It is one thing to glibly appeal to a nefarious "Shock Doctrine" (see Naomi Klein), it is another to comprehend in detail how the reckoning was evaded: something here dubbed the "Shock Block Doctrine." Neoliberalism is alive and well; those on the receiving end need to know why.

Questions as to its existence, its efficacy, and its vulnerability to refutation lie at the heart of the concerns that motivate this chapter. Neoliberal initiatives and policies still carry the day, and more to the point, most people still understand their own straitened circumstances through the lens of what can only be regarded as neoliberal presumptions. Can it be chalked up to confusion, or sour grapes, or a gullible temperament? Was it due to the intersection of some otherwise uncorrelated historical tendencies, like the provocation of immigrant labor, the weaknesses of the governmental structures of the European Union, or heavy state dependence on the financial sector? In writing the history, many local conjunctures must be acknowledged, but none of them really get at the Intellectual Teflon: the way the crisis did not provoke any fundamental revision of prior political catechism.[2] The most likely reason the doctrine that precipitated the crisis has evaded responsibility and the renunciation indefinitely postponed is that neoliberalism as worldview has sunk its roots deep into everyday life, almost to the point of passing as the "ideology of no ideology."

Indeed, at this late hour, the world is still full of people who believe that neoliberalism doesn't really exist. I run into them every day. Mitchell Dean nicely captures this attitude: "Neoliberalism, it might be argued, is a rather overblown notion, which has been used, usually by a certain kind of critic, to characterize everything from a particular brand of free-market political philosophy to a wide variety of innovations in public management."[3] For such skeptics, it is inconceivable to them that contemporary political economy displays any kind of structure, outside of some vague notions of supply and demand. Most people, it seems, have never even heard of the Mont Pèlerin Society, which at one time in its history was the premier site of the construction of neoliberalism. Liberalism, neoliberalism, conservatism, libertarianism . . . at least in America, they are all just a blur. People who live elsewhere in the world have little feeling for the American cultural drumbeat that keeps insisting politics has no theoretical grounding—it is only something dubbed "human nature" that can be theorized. America, that fabled Land of Neoliberalism in European parlance, soldiers on, blissfully unaware that it is neoliberal. One temptation might be to attribute this to some notorious Anglophone allergy to abstract political analysis; but that would be too hasty. Part of the blame might be laid at the door of the neoliberals themselves: as I document below, even though the members of Mont Pèlerin Society initially used the term "neoliberal" to refer to themselves in the early 1950s, by the 1960s they had backtracked, trumpeting the ambagious notion that their ideas all could be traced back to Adam Smith, if not before. But an equal moiety of blame should be dished out to their opponents on the left, who often bandy about attributions of "neoliberalism" as a portmanteau term of abuse when discussing grand phenomena often lumped together under the terminology of "globalization" and "financialization" and "governmentality." The Washington Consensus, the death of the welfare state, the risk society, the wars in Iraq and Afghanistan, European (dis)integration, the ascendancy of China, and the outsourcing of manufacturing all portend cosmic themes, mostly of interest to those who regard themselves of taking the broad view of power politics.[4] But broad characterizations of contemporary political events should not be mistaken for the painstaking construction of political doctrines to motivate organization in the long run, however much they may be related. Abstract dreadnoughts battling in the hyperspace of concepts, as with nationalisms clashing in the dead of night, have done little to illuminate the nature of neoliberalism for the average person, alas. And then there are those who insist it is really all about "economic theory," which is guaranteed to make most people want to pass it by as quickly as possible.

The clarification of the neoliberal program is first and foremost a historical inquiry: much of the preliminary spadework unearthing its lineage and development has already been performed. We shall have occasion to reference this body of work over the rest of this volume.[5] But rather than simply recapitulating that historical narrative here, this chapter will approach the role of neoliberalism in the crisis in a more analytical register: first by documenting the ways that it was anticipated that the crisis would purportedly change the intellectual landscape; then by summarizing commonplace misconceptions about the core doctrines of neoliberalism which serve to reinforce its longevity; following that up with the indispensable characterization of the "double truth" of neoliberalism; and ending up with one of the major reasons neoliberals have come through the crisis unscathed, as rooted in their approach to knowledge itself. Fortified with this understanding of the political background, we can then turn directly to issues of the conceptual unfolding of the crisis itself in the rest of the volume.

Don't Look Back

There can be no joy in pointing out just how wrong people have been about the intellectual consequences of the crisis. I recall myself entertaining the notion back in 2008 that perhaps, finally, we just might dispense with some of the rubbish that had sullied a political economy orthodoxy over my lifetime. Apophenia cascades at epidemic proportions when the sky seems to be falling.

In August 2007, the *Guardian* columnist George Monbiot wrote, "We are all neoliberals now."[6] Now, five years later, Monbiot's claim must seem eerily prescient. Things were not always thus. In the midst of the downdraft of 2008–9, I remember people saying to me: Yes, it's been awful, but maybe the trial by fire will cleanse as well as sear. As Jenny Turner reminisced in the *London Review of Books*, "People imagined that a crash, when it came, would act like Occam's Razor, cutting out the hedge funds and leaving the world a little saner . . ." Who among us back then did not suspect that the collapse of Bear Stearns, Lehman Brothers, AIG, Northern Rock, Lloyd's Bank, Anglo Irish Bank, Kaupthing, Landsbanki, Glitnir (and a parade of lesser institutions) would at least cut through the smarmy triumphalism of those who claimed to fully comprehend the workings of the globalized economy? Such a simultaneous worldwide collapse, first of finance, then of the rest of economic activity, had up till then been the hallmark of conspiracy theorists, apocalypse mongers, and some unreconstructed historical materialists. As the world witnessed the meltdown in dazed disbelief, it was not so outlandish to imagine that epochal events so seared into everyone's consciousness could not help but prompt them to reevaluate their previous beliefs. How could anyone deny something had gone badly awry? The next step in the syllogism, but the link fated to fail, was that everyone would perceive that the prior bubble was the direct consequence of certain modes of thought, and thus, it was these doctrines that would be refuted. Collect those doctrines together under the umbrella term "neoliberalism," toss into the mix a Little Bo Peep falsificationist psychology, and there materialized the widespread perception that we were living through the demise of an entire way of thinking:

> The first intellectual consequence of the economic crisis was to undermine Neoliberalism—or the belief in the sufficiency of markets to secure human welfare—as the age's default ideology.[7]

> The free market project is on the ropes. Never before has the question of neoliberalism's political, economic and social role—culpability might be a better word—been debated with such urgency, so globally, in such a public manner.[8]

> Neoliberalism has self-destructed. The thirty year long global march of free market ideology has come to an end.[9]

> Today there has been a partial awakening . . . A striking number of free market economists, worshippers at the feet of Milton Friedman and his Chicago colleagues, have lined up to don sackcloth and ashes and swear allegiance to the memory of John Maynard Keynes.[10]

> The crisis revealed the strategy's unsustainable character, leading to what can be denoted as the "crisis of neoliberalism" . . . No distinction is made between hegemony and domination as in approaches of Gramscian inspiration.[11]

> The promises of neoliberalism are revealed for what they were: a sham. An ideology that seduced most of the population is broken. The psychic and political consequences are incalculable.[12]

> The fall of Wall Street is to neo-liberalism what the fall of the Berlin Wall was to communism.[13]

This naturalization of market logic (or "values," to use Massimo de Angelis's language) was nothing more than a spell. This spell was broken in 2008, a year after *The Beginning of History* was published. The point of all this: When I argue that we now live in a postneoliberal world, I do not mean that its practices or program have ceased (Ireland, Greece, and Portugal make it loud and clear that it's alive and kicking), but that the narrative of the market's universality is no longer unchallenged. The market is not the one and all; it has an outside, it has a limit.[14]

Just so it doesn't appear that I am unfairly taking advantage of a certain class of people who might have been overly inclined to jump the gun, let's sample some people closer to the orthodoxy in American economics like, say, Joseph Stiglitz:

> Neo-liberal market fundamentalism was always a political doctrine serving certain interests. It was never supported by economic theory. Nor, it should now be clear, is it supported by historical experience. Learning this lesson may be the silver lining in the cloud now hanging over the global economy.[15]

In an interview with the *Berliner Zeitung*, Stiglitz was quoted as saying, "Neoliberalism like the Washington Consensus is dead in most western countries. See the debates in South America or other countries. The U.S. has lost its role as the model for others. Everyone only laughs when U.S. technocrats give lectures in other countries and say: 'Do as we do, liberalize your financial markets!'"[16] Stiglitz, as one of the few neoclassical economists who has periodically attempted to intellectually refute neoliberalism over the course of his career, should therefore be regarded as someone who had significant credibility tied up in expressing his conviction that the demise of neoliberalism was at hand.

Or, alternatively, suppose we consult an eminent proponent of globalization analysis, Saskia Sassen, prognosticating "The End of Financial Capitalism": "The difference of the current crisis is precisely that financialized capitalism has reached the limits of its own logic."[17] David Harvey more tentatively and cautiously asked whether it was "really" the end of neoliberalism.[18] Some members of the faculty at Cambridge and Birkbeck declared, "The collapse of confidence in financial markets and the banking system . . . is currently discrediting the conventional wisdom of neo-liberalism."[19] Various politicians temporarily indulged in the same hyperbole: Prime Minister Kevin Rudd of Australia openly proclaimed the death of neoliberalism, only to succumb to his own untimely political demise at the hands of his own party; Senator Bernie Sanders prognosticated that as Wall Street collapsed, so too would the legacy of Milton Friedman. Yet, unbowed, the University of Chicago solicited $200 million in donations to erect a monument in his honor, and founded a new "Milton Friedman Institute."[20] "Wakes for Neoliberalism" were posted all about the

Internet in 2008–9; a short stint on Google will provide all the Finnegan that is needed.

More elaborate analyses of the unfolding of the crisis by academics on the left followed suit. John Campbell, for one, has argued that the financial meltdown was itself a manifestation of the crisis of neoliberalism, in that defective understanding of markets led to the loosening of financial regulation and other trickle-up government policies—that ideas were just as important as the inertia inherent in institutions.[21] Of course, Campbell tempers the analysis with the warning, "Despite theoretical arguments about the moment of crisis triggering radical change, many scholars now recognize that institutional change tends to be much more incremental even at historical junctures like this one." Others were a bit less cautious. Yet, whether circumspect or perfervid, each crisis diagnostic held fast to the syllogism that people can learn from their mistakes; the deep contraction and financial breakdown stands as irrefutable evidence that neoliberalism is false; and therefore, neoliberalism must be on its last legs. That credo was the fuel of the machine that churned out reams of crisis commentary from 2008–10; it put the hi-fi in early litanies of financial reform. One encounters this admonitory approach to the death of neoliberalism in the most diverse accounts of the crisis.[22] It could even be found in authors who would not themselves otherwise be caught dead using the term "neoliberalism" in elevated company.

While it would be a digression to plunge into the bramble thickets of formal epistemology in a book about the crisis, there was at least one major flaw in all these prognostications that needs to be taken into account here. Social psychology, the history and philosophy of science, and the sociology of knowledge all combine to instruct us that people don't generally behave like that. Only the most ersatz Popperian believer in the awesome power of local falsificationism would begin to presume that some finite observation would immediately impel people to cast their most cherished beliefs into doubt and reconsider long-held ideas that anchor much of their worldview. Such conversions have been known to happen, but they have been few and far between. Predominantly, the long history of schooling, socialization, and past experience induces a stubborn inertia into cognitive processes. More commonly, people react to potential disconfirmation of strongly held views by adjusting their own understandings of the doctrine in question to accommodate the contrary evidence; this has been discussed in the social psychology literature under the rubric of "cognitive dissonance," and in the philosophy literature as Duhem's Thesis. Cognition sports an inescapable social dimension as well: people cannot vet and validate even a small proportion of the knowledge to which they subscribe, and so must of necessity depend heavily upon others such as teachers and experts and peers to underwrite much of their beliefs.[23] And then there is a second major consideration relevant to our current conundrum, namely, the issue of whether most people who may subscribe to something like neoliberalism actually understand it to be constituted as a coherent doctrine with a spelled-out roster of propositions, or instead treat their notions as disparate implications of other beliefs. As we have already intimated, many people still have no clue what neoliberalism is, much less harbor opinions about how their own thought processes might relate to it. In other words, how could they come to reject something which for them putatively lacks spatio-temporal solidity, or at minimum, must they themselves consciously understand their beliefs as part of a coherent intellectual tradition?

This volume is dedicated to exploring the ways in which the crisis has not yet served as an exemplary instance of falsification of much of anything; it explores various defense mechanisms of critical groups such as orthodox economists and members of the Neoliberal Thought Collective; the intention is to clear a path to some potential remedy to that situation. However, in order to reach that point, it is first necessary to become better acclimatized to the notion that a burst of bad news does not generally bring a dogma crashing down of its own accord. It takes a whole lot more than that; and thus a preliminary admonition of epistemic caution is the touchstone of the current chapter. The rest of this section is devoted to a quick sketch of the sobering lessons of social psychology for the premature expectations of the demise of neoliberalism; whereas the next section is devoted to the difficult question of whether neoliberalism could or should be considered a tolerably coherent phenomenon that has exhibited sufficient integrity over past decades for any refutation to have something to stick to.

What happens when a seductive synoptic ideology suffers "breakage," as our commentators have it? It would be odd if this had not been a major topic of exploration, since it speaks so directly to our images of ourselves and others. While there have been many modes and idioms in which the question has been broached, for the sake of brevity we shall describe but one: the attempt to comprehend these responses as a case study in the social psychological problem of cognitive dissonance. The father of "cognitive dissonance theory" was the social psychologist Leon Festinger. In his premier work on the subject, he addressed the canonical problem situation which captures the predicament of the contemporary economics profession:

> Suppose an individual believes something with his whole heart . . . suppose that he is then presented with unequivocal and undeniable evidence that his belief is wrong: what will happen? The individual will frequently emerge, not only unshaken, but even more convinced of the truth of his beliefs than ever before. Indeed, he may even show a new fervor about convincing and converting people.[24]

This profound insight, that confrontation with contrary evidence may actually augment and sharpen the conviction and enthusiasm of a true believer, was explained as a response to the cognitive dissonance evoked by a disconfirmation of strongly held beliefs. The thesis that humans are more rationalizing than rational has spawned a huge literature, but one that gets little respect in economics.[25] Cognitive dissonance and the responses it provokes venture well beyond the literature in the philosophy of science that travels under the rubric of Duhem's Thesis, in that the former plumbs response mechanisms to emotional chagrin, whereas the latter sketches the myriad ways in which auxiliary hypotheses *may* be evoked in order to blunt the threat of disconfirmation. Duhem's Thesis states that there are an infinite number of auxiliary hypotheses that may be invoked to explain why an empirical event did not actually impugn the target doctrine at risk: instead, uncontrolled factors intervened. Philosophy of science revels the ways in which it may be rational to discount contrary evidence; but the social psychology of cognitive dissonance reveals just how elastic the concept of rationality can be in social life.

Leon Festinger and his colleagues illustrated these lessons in his first book (*When Prophecy Fails*) by reporting the vicissitudes of a group of Midwesterners they called "The Seekers," who conceived and developed a belief that they would be rescued by flying saucers on a specific date in 1954, prior to a great flood coming to engulf Lake City (a pseudonym). Festinger documents in great detail the hour-by-hour reactions of the Seekers as the date of their rescue came and passed with no spaceships arriving and no flood welling up to swallow Lake City. At first, the Seekers withdrew from representatives of the press seeking to upbraid them for their failed prophecies, but soon reversed their stance, welcoming all opportunities to expound and elaborate upon their (revised and expanded) faith. A minority of their group did

fall away; but Festinger notes they had tended to be lukewarm peripheral members of the group before the crisis. Predominantly, the
Seekers never renounced their challenged doctrines, as reported by
Festinger. At least in the short run, the ringleaders tended to redouble
their proselytizing, so long as they were able to maintain interaction
with a coterie of fellow covenanters.

In a manner of speaking, the legacy of renunciation of philosophy
and methodology in graduate education led much of the orthodox
economics profession, and many of the denizens of the neoliberal
world of think tanks and media outlets, to behave from 2008 onward
in ways rather similar to the Seekers. The parallels between the Seekers and the contemporary economics profession, on the one hand,
and the Neoliberal Thought Collective, on the other, are, of course,
not exact. The Seekers were disappointed when their world didn't
come to an end; economists and neoliberals were convinced their
Great Moderation and neoliberal triumph would last forever, and
were disappointed when it did appear to come to an end. The stipulated turning point never arrived for the Seekers, while the unsuspected
turning point got the drop on the economists. The Seekers garnered
no external support for their doctrines, indeed, quitting their jobs
and contracts prior to their fated day; the economists, and more
clearly, the Neoliberal Thought Collective, persisted in being richly
rewarded by many constituencies for remaining stalwart in their
beliefs. The public press was never friendly toward the Seekers; it
turned on the economists only with the financial collapse. (There are
now plentiful signs it has been reverting to its older slavish adoration,
however.) But nonetheless, the shape of the reactions to cognitive
dissonance turned out to be amazingly similar. The crisis, which at
first blush might seem to have refuted almost everything that the
NTC and the economic orthodoxy stood for, was in the fullness of
time more often than not trumpeted from both the left and the right
as reinforcing their adherence to, respectively, neoclassical economic
theory or the neoliberal tradition.

In the last few years, there may have opened up a divergence
between the explicit behavior of professional economists and that of
other groups who may have displayed some allegiance to neoliberal
doctrines. This distinction, insisted upon in chapter 1, now begins to
bite. The difference comes with the economists readily accepting that
they do share some common doctrines and intellectual orientations.
Their PhD from a ranked institution does double duty as a membership card; few of them spend any time doubting whether "economics"

as a body of doctrine exists. Thus it will prove relatively straightforward to demonstrate that they have not revised their erstwhile doctrines dating from before the crisis. But the denizens of the think tank planisphere and journalists and political actors in these contentious times may not subscribe so intently or openly to a fixed, discrete set of doctrines in quite the same unself-conscious manner. (Indeed, chapter 6 will propose a stratified spectrum of crisis response under neoliberalism.) Consequently, demonstration of the fundamental premise of cognitive dissonance theory—that people don't shift allegiances in the throes of contravening evidence—will require more elaborate documentation for the neoliberals. Once again, the imperative to treat both groups separately will prove clarifying.

Does Neoliberalism Really Exist?

The really fascinating battles in intellectual history tend to occur when some group or movement goes on the offensive and asserts that Something Big really doesn't actually exist. A short list of blasts from the past would include: the earth-centered universe, God, the Philosopher's Stone, atoms, the vacuum, the divine right of kings, perpetual motion machines, evolution, a formally complete axiomatic system, aether, global warming, society, and human consciousness. As chapter 1 noted, we have just passed through a period when a substantial cadre were insisting that orthodox neoclassical economics didn't exist. Nothing gets the blood roiling like the assertion that we have been arguing over nothing. Whatever the eventual outcome, these negations are the flash points that tend to force thought out of its complacent ruts and tend to mark periods of lush proliferation of theoretical and empirical innovation. I would like to explore the possibility that we might approach the concept "neoliberalism" with the same appreciation. In order to accomplish this, a certain modicum of intellectual history is indispensable.

We elect to start with the manifest phenomenon that most people whom outsiders would identify as neoliberals would reject the label outright, and indeed, deny the position exists as a coherent doctrine. For them, it is just another swearword bandied about by their opponents, rather like "fascism" or "equality." Some go further, adopting the nominalist position that if "we" refuse to call ourselves neoliberal, then no one else has the right to do so, either. More recently, one can find certain authors on the left advocating that the doctrine is so ephemeral and diffuse that it displays insufficient quiddity for analysis.

The nominalist position can be rapidly dispensed with. As my collaborators and I have insisted elsewhere, the people associated with the doctrine *did* call themselves "neo-liberals" for a brief period lasting from the 1930s to the early 1950s, but then they abruptly stopped the practice.[26] In the early phases, various figures such as Alexander Rüstow vied for bragging rights in coining the term.[27] Others simply acknowledged its currency. To give one pertinent example from many, Milton Friedman wrote in the Norwegian journal *Farmand* in 1951:

> A new ideology . . . must give high priority to real and efficient limitation of the state's ability to, in detail, intervene in the activities of the individual. At the same time, it is absolutely clear that there are positive functions allotted the state. The doctrine that, on and off, has been called neoliberalism and that has developed, more or less simultaneously in many parts of the world . . . is precisely such a doctrine . . . But instead of the 19th century understanding that laissez-faire is the means to achieve this goal, neoliberalism proposes that *competition* will lead the way.[28]

Friedman was still flirting with something like the label as late as 1961, in an early draft of what later became *Capitalism and Freedom*:

> This use of the term liberalism in these two quite different senses renders it difficult to have a convenient label for the principles I shall be talking about. I shall resolve these difficulties by using the word liberalism in its original sense. Liberalism of what I have called the 20th century variety has by now become orthodox and indeed reactionary. Consequently, the views I shall present might equally be entitled, under current conditions, the "new liberalism," a more attractive designation than "nineteenth century liberalism."

In another historical phenomenon that I feel has not received sufficient attention, soon after many of the neoliberals renounced the label, opponents *to their right* began to resort to it in order to be provocative. Murray Rothbard, from a more libertarian perspective, began to excoriate Friedman for his position. Later classical liberals, dissatisfied specifically with the evolution of the Mont Pèlerin Society, would resort to the term to contrast the position of Ludwig von Mises with what they considered the debased version found in Friedrich Hayek and elsewhere.[29] The question of why the target group in and around Mont Pèlerin invoked a self-denying ordinance in using the label is interesting in its own right, and we will return to it in the next section. But for the nonce, I trust everyone can accept that the nominalist position is flawed: the term was and sometimes still is used in a sensible way on both the left and right, and moreover, the roster of people and institutions referenced is fairly stable over time: members of the Mont Pèlerin Society and their close associates. To a first approximation, the MPS will serve as our Rosetta Stone: any idea or person with membership or strong ties to the organization will qualify as "neoliberal." With further research, we can expand the purview to encompass outer orbits of the Neoliberal Thought Collective.

Anyone who has made a study of politics realizes that the conventional left–right continuum needs to be splintered into numerous subsets and offshoots in order to make any intellectual sense of the cacophony of argumentation to be found therein. This admonition needs repetition in the current context, because of the ubiquitous confusion over the referent and meaning of the term "liberal" in America, even at this late date. Every historian of the New Right in America acknowledges that it is a fractious coalition of groups who may not share much in the way of doctrinal overlap: classical liberals, cultural conservatives, theocons, libertarians, old–school anticommunists, anarchists, classical Burkean traditionalists, ultranationalist neoconservatives, strict construction federalists, survivalist militias, and so forth. A standard narrative of historians of the modern right is that a number of these different factions declared a tentative truce from the 1970s onward under the rubric of "fusionism," and that this détente was a major factor in their resurgence from a low point after the Great Depression.[30] Rather than plow old furrows, we shall provisionally accept this basic account for our own purposes, primarily to insist that "neoliberals" should be approached as one individual subset of this phalanx. Hence we seek to characterize a relatively discrete subset of right-wing thought situated within a much larger universe, although it does tend to stand out as the faction most concerned to integrate economic theory with political doctrine. For that reason alone, it is directly germane to a wider purview of the economic crisis.

Much pandemonium concerning the existence of neoliberalism derives from the fact that outsiders often confuse it with libertarianism or classical liberalism; and this, in turn, is at least partly due to the fact that many key neoliberal figures themselves often conflated one or another alternative position with their own. For instance, Friedrich Hayek notoriously pioneered the notion that his own ideas could be traced in a direct line back to classical liberals such as David

Hume and Adam Smith.[31] Combined with his statement concerning Mont Pèlerin, "I personally do not intend that any public manifesto should be issued,"[32] we can begin to detect a concerted policy to blur the boundaries between factions, itself part of the larger move to impose détente. This becomes more obvious in instances when we witness someone like Milton Friedman interacting with other factions on the right:

REASON In seeing yourself harkening back to 19th-century liberalism, you never became a system-builder like Rand or Rothbard . . .

FRIEDMAN Exactly. I'd rather use the term *liberal* than *libertarian*.

REASON I see you occasionally use the word *libertarian*.

FRIEDMAN Oh, I do.

REASON As a concession to accepted usage?

FRIEDMAN That's right. Because *liberal* is now so misinterpreted . . . My philosophy is clearly libertarian. However, *libertarian* is not a self-defining term. There are many varieties of libertarian. There's zero-government libertarian, an anarchist. There's a limited-government libertarianism . . . I would like to be a zero-government libertarian.

REASON Why aren't you?

FRIEDMAN Because I don't think it's a feasible social structure.[33]

No wonder tyros and outsiders get so flummoxed, when it proves hard to get a straight answer from many neoliberals, even when you profess to be on their side. And the more you become familiar with their writings, it often only gets worse: for instance, it would be a long, thankless task to attempt to extract actual libertarian policy proposals from Friedman's corpus—a complaint one encounters in some actual libertarian writings. They have to avert their eyes from Friedman quotes such as, "You can have a high degree of social freedom, and a high degree of economic freedom without any political freedom."[34] Strident demonization of some bugbear entity called "the government" is not at all the same as rejecting "The State" *tout court*.[35] That is because mature neoliberalism is not at all enamored of the minimalist night-watchman state of the classical liberal tradition: its major distinguishing characteristic is instead a set of proposals and programs to infuse, take over, and transform the strong state, in order to impose the ideal form of society, which they conceive to be in pursuit of their very curious icon of pure freedom. I agree with Wendy Brown that neoliberalism became a "constructivist" project, no matter how much it was a term against which Hayek often railed.[36] That neoliberalism turned out to be very nearly the polar opposite of libertarian anarchism is something that has taken a long while to sink in, but is now becoming widely accepted in circles concerned with political economy.[37] That is why "neoliberalism" is not only a historically accurate designation of a specific strain of political thought, but it is descriptively acute as well: most of the early neoliberals explicitly distanced themselves from what they considered the outmoded classical liberal doctrine of laissez-faire.[38] They sought to offer something newer, and less passive. Later members like James Buchanan were even more frank regarding the neoliberal attraction to the state, at least when addressing the closed meetings of the MPS:

> Among our members, there are some who are able to imagine a viable society without a state . . . For most of our members, however, social order without a state is not readily imagined, at least in any normatively preferred sense . . . Of necessity, we must look at our relations with the state from several windows, to use the familiar Nietzschean metaphor . . . Man is, and must remain, a slave to the state. But it is critically and vitally important to recognize that ten per cent slavery is different from fifty per cent slavery.[39]

Similar sentiments were expressed at other comparable conclaves. For instance, John MacCallum Scott proposed to the 1956 meetings of the Liberal International, "Liberty, too, must be limited in order to be possessed"; the British economist Arthur Shenfield pronounced in a speech to the 1954 MPS conference, "It does no service either to liberalism or to democracy to assume that democracy is necessarily liberal or liberalism is necessarily democratic."[40] Thenceforth, for neoliberals, "freedom" would have to change its connotations.

Thus there are at least two imposing obstacles confronting anyone seeking a deeper understanding of neoliberalism: the fog thrown up around the term "neoliberalism" and attendant doctrines by the participants themselves, in pursuit of their own political unification ambitions and projects with other movements on the right; and the fact that the tenets of neoliberal doctrine evolved and mutated over the postwar period.[41] The ten-plus commandments of neoliberalism were not delivered complete and immaculate down from the Mont in 1947, when the neoliberals convened their first meeting of the MPS. Nor can one reliably reconstruct it from a small set of "Hayekian encyclicals," as Jamie Peck so aptly puts it. In fact, if we simply restrict ourselves to Mont Pèlerin itself (and this is unduly narrow), there rapidly precipitated at least three distinguishable sects or subguilds: the Austrian-inflected Hayekian legal theory, the Chicago School of neoclassical economics, and the German Ordoliberals.[42] Hayek himself admitted this in the mid-1980s, when he warned of "the constant danger that the Mont Pèlerin Society might split into a Friedmanite and Hayekian wing."[43] An impartial spectator could observe ongoing tensions between them, but also signs that they eventually cross-fertilized each other. It takes a rather bulky Baedeker to keep it straight; another thing that surely wards off the merely curious outsider.

It is reasonable to wonder what could have held neoliberalism together under the centrifugal forces threatening to fragment it into factionalism. David Harvey propounds the Marxist position that it is straightforwardly a class project masked by various versions of "free market" rhetoric. For him, the ideas are far less significant than the brute function of serving the interests of finance capital and globalized elites in the redistribution of wealth upward. Michael Howard and James King proffer what they term an historical materialist reading, fairly similar to Harvey, one that "stresses the importance of the contradictions inherent in the institutions prevalent in the postwar era, and the crises these contradictions spawned in the 1970s."[44] Daniel Stedman Jones divides neoliberalism into three phases characterized by dominant political practices: the prehistory up to the first meeting of Mont Pèlerin, a second phase up to the ascendancy of Reagan and Thatcher consisting of a monetarist critique of neo-Keynesianism, and a modern phase since the 1980s.[45] Jamie Peck gives greater weight to ideas, suggesting that the fragmentation is real, but still offset by a shared commitment to an unattainable utopian notion of freedom. Nevertheless, he credits success in infiltrating the state as permitting wide latitude in divergent component theories: "Only with the capture of state power could immanent critique become rolling autocritique."[46] Peter-Wim Zuidhof suggests that the fragmentation is part of a conscious program of rhetoric to empty out any fixed referent for the term "market."[47] Without denying the force of any of these explanations, there are also a few rather more pedestrian considerations of the actual structure of the MPS and its attendant satellite organizations.

I would suggest that the Mont Pèlerin Society evolved into an exceptionally successful structure for the incubation of integrated political theory and political action outside of the more conventional structures of academic disciplines and political parties in the second half of the twentieth century. Perhaps, one day, it will come to be studied as something new in the sociology of knowledge in the twentieth century. It was a novel framework that served to confine any tendencies to intellectual dissolution, holding the three subguilds in productive tension. Hayek in 1946 initially promoted a vision of the MPS as "something halfway between a scholarly association and a political society,"[48] but it evolved into something much more than that. The main reason the MPS should serve as our talisman in tracking neoliberalism is because it exists as part of a rather special structure of intellectual discourse, perhaps unprecedented in the 1940s, one I would venture to propose to think of as a "Russian doll" approach to the integration of research and praxis in the modern world. The project was to produce a functional hierarchical elite of regimented political intellectuals; as Hayek wrote to Bertrand de Jouvenel, "I sometimes wonder whether it is not more than capitalism this strong egalitarian strain (they call it democracy) in America which is so inimical to the growth of a cultural elite."[49] Neoliberals found that Mont Pèlerin was an effective instrument to reconstruct their hierarchy, untethered to local circumstances. Henceforth, I will use the term "thought collective" to refer to this multilevel, multiphase, multisector approach to the building of political capacity to incubate, critique, and promulgate ideas.

The Neoliberal Thought Collective was structured very differently from the other "invisible colleges" that sought to change people's minds in the latter half of the twentieth century. Unlike most intellectuals in the 1950s, the early protagonists of the MPS did not look to the universities or the academic "professions" or to interest-group mobilizations as the appropriate primary instruments to achieve their goals. Those entities were held too in thrall to the state, from the neoliberal perspective. The early neoliberals felt, at that juncture with some justification, that they were excluded from most high-profile intellectual venues in the West. Hence the MPS was constituted as a closed, private members-only debating society whose participants were hand-picked (originally primarily by Hayek, but later through a closed nomination procedure) and which consciously sought to remain out of the public eye. The purpose was to create a special space where people of like-minded political ideals could gather together to debate the outlines of a future movement diverging from classical liberalism, without having to suffer the indignities of ridicule for their often blue-sky proposals, but also to evade the fifth-column reputation of a society closely aligned with powerful but dubious postwar interests. Even the name of the society was itself chosen to be relatively anodyne, signaling little in the way of substantive content to outsiders.[50] Many members would indeed hold academic posts in a range of academic disciplines, but this was not a precondition of MPS membership. The MPS could thus also be expanded to encompass various powerful capitalists, and not just intellectuals.

One then might regard specific academic departments where the neoliberals came to dominate before 1980 (University of Chicago Economics, the LSE, L'Institut Universitaire des Hautes Etudes Internationales at Geneva, Chicago Law School, St. Andrews in Scotland, Freiburg, the Virginia School, George Mason University) as the next outer layer of the Russian doll, one emergent public face of the thought collective—although one rarely publicly acknowledging links to the MPS. Another shell of the Russian doll was fashioned as the special-purpose foundations for the education and promotion of neoliberal doctrines; in its early days, these included entities such as the Volker Fund, the Earhart Foundation, the Relm Foundation, the Lilly Endowment, the John M. Olin Foundation, the Bradley Foundation, and the Foundation for Economic Education. These institutions were often set up as philanthropic or charitable units, if only to protect their tax status and seeming lack of bias.[51] Some of these foundations were more than golden showers for the faithful, performing crucial organizational services as well: for instance, the Volker Fund kept a comprehensive "Directory" of affiliated neoliberal intellectuals, a list that had grown to 1,841 names by 1956.[52] The next shell would consist of general-purpose "think tanks" (Institute for Economic Affairs, American Enterprise Institute, Schweizerisches Institut für Auslandforschung [Swiss Institute of International Studies], the Hoover Institution at Stanford) and satellite organizations such as the Federalist Society that sheltered neoliberals, who themselves might or might not also be members in good standing of various academic disciplines and universities. The think tanks then developed their own next layer of protective shell, often in the guise of specialized satellite think tanks poised to get quick and timely position papers out to friendly politicians, or to provide talking heads for various news media and opinion periodicals.[53]

To facilitate mass production in a transnational setting, neoliberals actually concocted a "mother of all think tanks" to seed their spawn across the globe. The Atlas Economic Research Foundation was founded in 1981 by Antony Fisher to assist other MPS-related groups in establishing neoliberal think tanks in their own geographic locations. It claims to have had a role in founding a third of all world "market oriented" think tanks, including (among others) the Fraser Institute (Canada), the Center for the Dissemination of Economic Information (Venezuela), the Free Market Center (Belgrade), the Liberty Institute (Romania), and Unirule (Beijing).[54] Atlas provided, among other services, one convenient conduit to launder contributions from such corporations as Philip Morris and Exxon to more specialized think tanks promoting their intellectual agenda. Later on, the thought collective began to consolidate a separate dedicated journalistic shell to more efficiently channel the output of inner layers of the Russian doll outward, such as Rupert Murdoch's News Corporation,[55] Bertelsmann AG, and a wide array of Internet blog and social networking sites.

When addressing their venture capital angels, the entrepreneurs of the Russian doll would admit that this interlocking set of institutions should be regarded as an integrated system for the production of political ideas. For instance, Richard Fink, one of the primary protagonists in building up George Mason University as a neoliberal outpost, by linking it directly to the Koch Foundation, of which he later became president, informed his prospective funders:

> The translation of ideas into action requires the development of intellectual raw materials, their conversion into specific policy products, and the marketing and distribution of these products to citizen-consumers. Grant makers, Fink argued, would do well to invest in change along the entire production continuum, funding scholars and university programs where the intellectual framework for social transformation is developed, think tanks where scholarly ideas get translated into specific policy proposals, and implementation groups to bring these proposals into the political marketplace and eventually to consumers.[56]

Although the language dealt in terms of "markets" and "consumers," the reality was a vertically integrated set of operations, whose outlines were apparent by the 1980s. The expansion of the think-tank shell proceeded apace with the expansion of the MPS presence, as revealed in Figure 2.1. One can appreciate the amount of groundwork that had preceded the "breakout" decade of the 1980s for the neoliberal project described by Fink from this and other indicators of the activities of the thought collective.

Figure 2.1: Growth of MPS-Affiliated Think Tanks

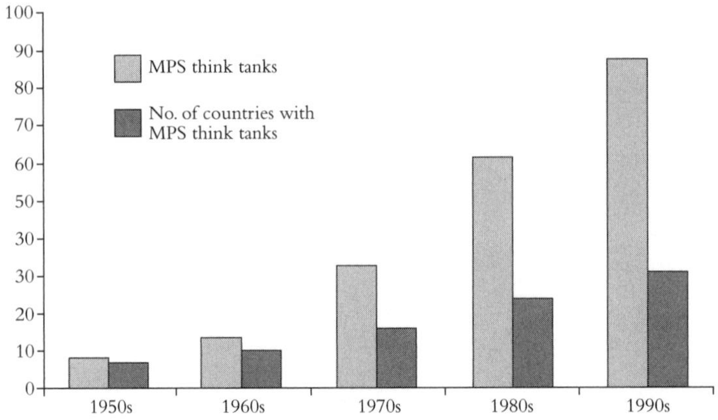

Source: Walpen, Die offen Feinde und ihre Gesellschaft

Further outer shells have cladded and been augmented around the Russian doll as we get closer to the present—for instance, "astroturf" organizations consisting of supposedly local grass-roots members, frequently organized around religious or single-issue campaigns.[57] Some aspects of the so-called Tea Party in the U.S. reveal how the practice of astroturfing has had direct impact upon reactions to the crisis. "FreedomWorks say they hope to turn the inchoate anger of the Tea Party into a focused pro-Hayek movement."[58] Fostering the appearance of spontaneous organization was often just as important for neoliberals as the actual political action that the astroturf organization was tasked to accomplish. Outsiders would rarely perceive the extent to which individual protagonists embedded in a particular shell served multiple roles, or the strength and pervasiveness of network ties, since they could never see beyond the immediate shell of the Russian doll right before their noses. This also tended to foster the impression of those "spontaneous orders" so beloved by the neoliberals, although they were frequently nothing of the sort. Moreover, the loose coupling defeated most attempts to paint the thought collective as a strict conspiracy. It was much beyond that, in the sense it was a thought collective in pursuit of a mass political movement; and in any event, it was built up through trial and error over time. It grew so successful, it soon became too large to qualify.

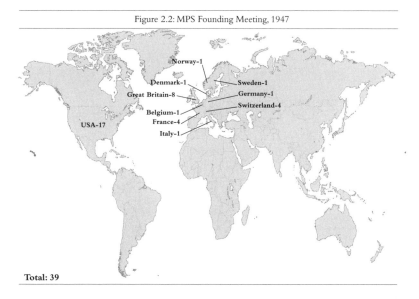

Figure 2.2: MPS Founding Meeting, 1947

Norway-1
Denmark-1
Sweden-1
Great Britain-8
Germany-1
Belgium-1
Switzerland-4
France-4
USA-17
Italy-1

Total: 39

The MPS edifice of neoliberalism was anchored by a variety of mainly European and American keystones, progressively encompassed a variety of economic, political, and social schools of thought, and maintained a floating transnational agora for debating solutions to perceived problems, a flexible canopy tailored with an eye to accommodating established relations of power in academia, politics, and society at large. It was never parochial, and was globally oriented before "globalization" became a buzzword. Max Thurn captured this aspect in his opening remarks to the 1964 Semmering MPS meeting:

> Many of you have been to Austria before. There is little I can tell them about the country that they do not know already. Others have come for the first time. They may like to get a general idea of what this country was and what it is now before the meeting begins. What I can say on this subject has of course nothing to do with the topics of this programme. As members of the Mont Pèlerin Society *we are not interested in the problems of individual nations* or even groups of nations. What concerns us are general issues such as liberty and private initiative.[59]

This division of labor between the global thought collective and the parochial political action rapidly proved a transnational success; and by capping formal membership at five hundred, became another

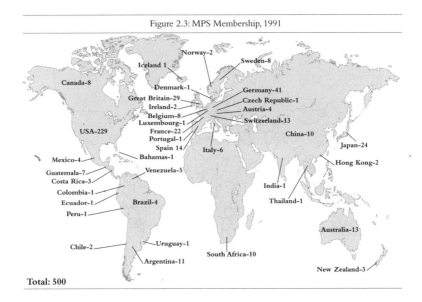

Figure 2.3: MPS Membership, 1991

Total: 500

exclusive mark of distinction for famous right-wing aspirants. The global reach of its membership is displayed in the two maps of membership: at its inception, and then in 1991.

The unusual structure of the thought collective helps explain why neoliberalism cannot be easily inscribed on a set of three-by-five cards, and needs to be understood as a pluralist entity (within certain limits) striving to distinguish itself from its three primary foes: laissez-faire classical liberalism, social-welfare liberalism, and socialism. Contrary to the dichotomies and rigidities that characterized classical liberalism with regard to its proposed firewalls between economics and politics, neoliberalism has to be understood as a flexible and pragmatic response to the previous crisis of capitalism (viz., the Great Depression) with a clear vision of what needed to be opposed by all means: a planned economy and a vibrant welfare state. Contrary to some narrow interests of some corporate captains (including some in the MPS), neoliberal intellectuals understood this general goal to imply a comprehensive long-term reform effort to retat the entire fabric of society, not excluding the corporate world. The relationship between the neoliberals and capitalists was not merely that of passive apologists. Neoliberals aimed to develop a thoroughgoing reeducation effort for all parties to alter the tenor and meaning of political life: nothing more, nothing less.[60] Neoliberal intellectuals identified their immediate targets as elite civil society. Their efforts were primarily aimed at winning over intellectuals and opinion leaders of future generations, and their primary instrument was redefining the place of knowledge in society, which also became the central theme in their theoretical tradition. As Hayek said in his address to the first meeting of the MPS:

> But what to the politicians are fixed limits of practicability imposed by public opinion must not be similar limits to us. Public opinion on these matters is the work of men like ourselves . . . who have created the political climate in which the politicians of our time must move . . . I am sure that the power of vested interests is vastly exaggerated compared with the gradual encroachment of ideas.[61]

The Russian doll structure of the Neoliberal Thought Collective would tend to amplify and distribute the voice of any one member throughout a series of seemingly different organizations, personas, and broadcast settings, lending it resonance and gravitas, not to mention fronting an echo chamber for ideas right at the time when hearing them was most propitious. Not without admiration, we have to concede that neoliberal intellectuals struggled through to a deeper understanding of the political and organizational character of modern knowledge and science than did their opponents on the left, and therefore present a worthy contemporary challenge to everyone interested in the archaeology of knowledge.

Of course, neoliberalism should not then or now be reduced to the MPS and the roster of related think tanks—that would be a travesty of the history.[62] My stress on the MPS and the Russian doll serves to counter the tendency on the left to regard neoliberalism as a hopelessly diffuse and ill-defined movement. In subsequent chapters we will explore how neoliberal ideas have become rooted in the economics profession, as well as in many facets of everyday life, which of course extends outside the narrow circumference of MPS activities. And then there are the consequences of transformation of political parties on the right and left, which tend to occupy much more attention in the existing literature. Nevertheless, at least until the 1980s—when the advance of neoliberal ideas, and thus the success of the original neoliberal networks, led to a rapid multiplication of pretenders to the title of progenitors of neoliberalism—the MPS network can be safely used as cipher to decode with sufficient precision the neoliberal thought style in the era of its genesis.

Of course, such considerations do not have the same salience once we get to the current economic crisis. While the detailed research is yet to be conducted, outsider perceptions of the modern MPS suggest that it no longer serves as the cornucopia of blue sky thinking and rigorous debate which then gets conveyed to the outer shells of the Russian doll in the ways that it did during the 1950s and 1960s. Part of the problem seems to have been that, as neoliberals savored political success, membership in the core MPS came to be just another "positional good" especially prized by the idle rich with intellectual pretensions. As the composition of the membership skewed in the direction of the sort of persons more often found at Davos or the Bohemian Grove, the actual role of the core as a high-powered debating society has tended to ossify. That function, it seems, tended to migrate to outer layers of the Russian doll, such as certain key university centers and the larger established think tanks. When the crisis hit, the first tendency was to attempt a reversion to the older model of a Grand Conclave of the Faithful; but as we observed in chapter 1, the best that was mustered was a reiteration of doctrines developed a half-century previously. However, in chapter 6, we moot the possibility that the outer shells themselves have developed a generic full-spectrum pattern of political response to dire crises. If true, it means that neoliberalism has become *more coherent* in the face of the crisis, not more diffuse, as some authors maintain.

A Short Course in Neoliberal Economic Doctrine

Throughout the second half of the twentieth century, the neoliberal project stood out from other strains of right-wing thought in that it self-consciously was constituted as a multitiered *sociological* entity dedicated to the continued transnational development, promulgation, and popularization of doctrines intended to mutate over time, in reaction to both intellectual criticism and external events. It was a movable feast, and not a catechism fixed at the Council of Trent.[63] Much of the time the litmus test was shared political objectives inculcated through prolonged internship in the thought collective; but infrequently, even that was open to delicate negotiation. Nevertheless, it was a sociological thought collective that eventually produced a relatively shared ontology concerning the world coupled with a more-or-less shared set of propositions about markets and political economy. These propositions are, of necessity, a central focus of a book on the relationship of neoliberals to the crisis. It should be very important to have some familiarity with these ideas, if only to resist simple-minded

definition to throw up their hands in defeat. Disbelievers and skeptics often scoff when they hear about the mutable character of neoliberal doctrine, but I think they ought to pay a little attention to science studies, which seems quite comfortable tracking functional identity-within-change by combining institutional data with a rotating yet finite roster of protagonists, with an old-fashioned history of ideas. For instance, what did it mean to be "doing quantum physics" in the 1960s and '70s? It wasn't just big teams working on solid-state devices plus a few geniuses in pursuit of a Grand Unified Theory. It even extended to hippie communes and New Age consciousness. Or, in another case, the pursuit of cosmological theories has a colorful coherent history, even though it repeatedly transgressed the boundaries of existing sciences, and sometimes had trouble deciding if the object of its attentions typified stark stasis or dramatic metamorphosis.[65] As long as we possess similar multiple markers of participation and discernment of designated doctrines for the Neoliberal Thought Collective, from exclusive organizations like the MPS and certain designated think tanks, to denumerable membership lists to *vade mecum* texts covering keynote ideas and theories, to archival reflections of the principals, then a working characterization of neoliberalism is perfectly possible.

Quite a few perceptive historians of the NTC have worried that this Protean entity might be a little too variable to underwrite serious intellectual analysis.[66] "There may therefore be a certain degree of truth in what might otherwise seem to be a sloppy and unprincipled claim, that neoliberalism has become omnipresent, but it is a complex, mediated and heterogeneous kind of omnipresence, not a state of blanket conformity. Neoliberalism has not simply diffused as a (self-) replicating system."[67] Granted, the ectoplasmic theory of mind control is usually a poor way to contemplate analysis of politics; yet the point remains that the neoliberal ground troops seem to be fully capable of recognizing kindred spirits, fostering intellectual interchange among allies, and more to the point, funding and organizing political movements with stable objectives and repetitive arguments even in the face of the global economic crisis. Here we point to bellwether phenomena to be addressed, from the demonization of Freddie Mac and Fannie Mae to the neutralization of financial reform at both national and international levels, the promotion of class warfare against public employees by "populist" right-wing politicians to the total control over framing the problem of global warming, from the best-sellerdom of *The Road to Serfdom* to the astroturfing of the Tea Party, and, most notably, the pronounced shift of public attention from the culpability of banks and hedge funds to the predominant conviction that the crisis has been attributable to governmental fiscal irresponsibility. These suggest a degree of coherence and stability deriving from both continuity of intellectual tradition and persistence of community boundary work, the sum total of which is capable of supporting analytical generalizations about the movement.

Clearly, neoliberals do not navigate with a fixed static Utopia as the astrolabe for all their political strivings. They could not, since they don't even agree on such basic terms as "market" and "freedom" in all respects, as we shall observe below. One can even agree with Brenner et al. and Naomi Klein that crisis is the preferred field of action for neoliberals, since that offers more latitude for introduction of bold experimental 'reforms' that only precipitate further crises down the road.[68] Nevertheless, Neoliberalism does not dissolve into a gormless empiricism or random pragmatism. There persists a certain logic to the way it approaches crises; and that is directly relevant to comprehending its unexpected strength in the current global crisis.

Under that supposition, we endeavor here to provide a telegraphed and necessarily non-canonical characterization of the temporary configuration of doctrines that the thought collective had arrived at by roughly the 1980s. It transgresses disciplinary boundaries, in precisely the ways the neoliberals have done. Furthermore, the Thirteen Commandments below are chosen because they have direct bearing upon unfolding developments during the period of the crisis from 2007 onwards. To elide issues of who said what to whom, in and out of Mont Pèlerin, we provide the tenets in an abridged format of stark statements, without much individual elaboration or full documentation.[69]

[1] The starting point of neoliberalism is the admission, contrary to classical liberal doctrine, that their vision of the good society will triumph only if it becomes reconciled to the fact that the conditions for its existence must be *constructed*, and will not come about "naturally" in the absence of concerted political effort and organization. As Foucault presciently observed in 1978 "Neoliberalism should not be confused with the slogan 'laissez-faire,' but on the contrary, should be regarded as a call to vigilance, to activism, to perpetual interventions." The injunction *to act* in the face of inadequate epistemic warrant is the very soul of "constructivism," an orientation sometimes shared with the field of science studies, and the very soul of the Neoliberal Thought Collective. Classical liberalism, by contrast, disavowed this precept. As Sheldon Wolin once wrote, classical liberalism "conceived the issue as

one of reconciling freedom and authority, and they solved it by destroying authority in the name of liberty and replacing it by society." The neoliberals reject "society" as solution, and revive their version of authority in new guises. This becomes transmuted below into various arguments for the existence of a strong state as both producer and guarantor of a stable market society. As Peck puts it, "Neoliberalism was always concerned . . . with the challenge of first seizing and then retasking the state." "What is 'neo' about Neoliberalism . . . [is] the remaking and redeployment of the state as the core agency that actively fabricates the subjectivities, social relations and collective representations suited to making the fiction of markets real and consequential."[70]

[2] This assertion of a constructivist orientation raises the thorny issue of just what sort of ontological entity the neoliberal market is, or should be. What sort of "market" do neoliberals want to foster and protect? While one wing of the MPS (the Chicago School) has made its career by attempting to reconcile one version of neoclassical economic theory with neoliberal precepts, other subsets of the MPS have innovated entirely different characterizations of the market. The "radical subjectivist" wing of the Austrian School of economics attempted to ground the market in a dynamic process of discovery by entrepreneurs of what consumers did not yet even know that they wanted, due to the fact that the future is radically unknowable.[71] Perhaps the dominant version at the MPS (and later, the dominant cultural doctrine) emanated from Hayek himself, wherein the "market" is posited to be an information processor more powerful than any human brain, but essentially patterned upon brain/computation metaphors.[72] This version of the market is most intimately predicated upon modern epistemic doctrines, which in the interim have become the philosophical position most closely associated with the neoliberal *Weltanschauung.*

Here we find the first intimate point of connection with the narrative of the global crisis. From this perspective, prices in an efficient market "contain all relevant information" and therefore cannot be predicted by mere mortals. In this version, the market always surpasses the state's ability to process information, and this constitutes the kernel of the argument for the necessary failure of socialism. All attempts to outguess the market, even in the midst of crisis free fall, must fail. But far from a purely negative doctrine, another related version of the efficient-markets hypothesis underwrote much of the theories and algorithms that were the framework of the baroque financial instruments and practices which resulted in the crisis in the first place.

Another partially rival approach to defining the market emanated from German ordoliberalism, which argues that competition in a well-functioning market needs to be directly organized by the state, by embedding it in various other social institutions.[73] Hence, contrary to much that has been written on the beliefs of our protagonists, neoliberals do not speak with one voice on the key concept of the nature of the market. They most certainly do not uniformly subscribe to neoclassical economic theory, nor do they all pledge their troth to the cybernetic vision of the market in lockstep. (This reiterates the analytical separation broached in chapter 1.)

It may seem incredible, but historically, both the neoclassical tradition in economics and the NTC have been extremely vague when it comes to analytical specification of the exact structure and character of something they both refer to as the "market." Both seem overly preoccupied with what it purportedly *does*, while remaining cavalier about what it actually *is*. For the neoliberals, this allows the avoidance of a possible deep contradiction between their constructivist tendencies and their uninflected appeal to a monolithic market that has existed throughout all history and indifferently across the globe; for how can something be "made" when it is eternal and unchanging? This is solved by increasingly erasing any distinctions among the state, society, and the market, and simultaneously insisting their political project is aimed at reformation of society by subordinating it to the market.

[3] Even though there has not existed full consensus on just what sort of animal the market "really" is, the neoliberals did agree that, for purposes of public understanding and sloganeering, neoliberal market society must be treated as a "natural" and inexorable state of mankind. Neoliberal thought therefore spawns a strange hybrid of the "constructed" and the "natural," where the market can be made manifest in many guises.[74] What this meant in practice was that there grew to be a mandate that natural science metaphors must be integrated into the neoliberal narrative. (This is explored further in chapter 6.) It is noteworthy that MPS members began to explore the portrayal of the market as an evolutionary phenomenon long before biology displaced physics as the premier science in the modern world-picture.[75] If the market was just an elaborate information processor, so too was the gene in its ecological niche. Poor, unwitting animals turn out to maximize everything under the sun just like neoclassical economic agents, and cognitive science "neuroeconomics" models treat neurons as market participants. "Biopower" is deployed to render nature and our

bodies more responsive to market signals.[76] Because of this early commitment, neoliberalism was able to make appreciable inroads into such areas as "evolutionary psychology," network sociology, ecology, animal ethology, linguistics, cybernetics, and even science studies. Neoliberalism has therefore expanded to become a comprehensive worldview, and has not been just a doctrine solely confined to economists.[77]

With regard to the crisis, one wing of neoliberals has appealed to natural science concepts of "complexity" to suggest that markets transcend the very possibility of management of systemic risk.[78] However, the presumed relationship of the market to nature tends to be substantially different under neoliberalism than under standard neoclassical theory. In brief, neoclassical theory has a far more static conception of market ontology than do the neoliberals. In neoclassical economics, many theoretical accounts portray the market as somehow susceptible to "incompleteness" or "failure," generally due to unexplained natural attributes of the commodities traded: these are retailed under the rubric of "externalities," "incomplete markets," or other "failures." Neoliberals conventionally reject all such recourse to defects or glitches, in favor of a narrative where evolution and/or "spontaneous order" brings the market to ever more complex states of self-realization, which may escape the ken of mere humans.[79] This explains why the NTC has rejected out of hand all neoclassical "market failure" explanations of the crisis.

[4] A primary ambition of the neoliberal project is to redefine the shape and functions of the state, *not to destroy it*. Neoliberals thus maintain an uneasy and troubled alliance with their sometimes fellow-travelers, the anarchists. The contradiction with which the neoliberals constantly struggle is that a strong state can just as easily thwart their program as implement it; hence they are inclined to explore new formats of techno-managerial governance that protect their ideal market from what they perceive as unwarranted political interference. Considerable efforts have been developed to disguise or otherwise condone in rhetoric and practice the importance of the strong state that neoliberals endorse in theory. As Peck puts it, the pursuit of neoliberal policies is "a self-contradictory form of regulation-in-denial."[80] One implication is that democracy, ambivalently endorsed as the appropriate state framework for an ideal market, must in any case be kept relatively impotent, so that citizen initiatives rarely are able to change much of anything.[81] As Hayek said in an address

before the MPS in 1966: "Liberalism and democracy, although compatible, are not the same . . . it is at least possible in principle that a democratic government may be totalitarian and that an authoritarian government may act on liberal principles . . . [A state] demanding *unlimited* power of the majority, has essentially become anti-liberal."[82] One way to exert power in restraint of democracy is to bend the state to a market logic, pretending one can replace "citizens" with "customers" (see point 5). Consequently, the neoliberals seek to restructure the state with numerous audit devices (under the sign of "accountability" or the "audit society") or impose rationalization through introduction of the "new public management"; or, better yet, convert state services to private provision on a contractual basis.[83] Here again our commandments touch directly upon the crisis. The financial sector was one of the major sites of the outsourcing of state supervision to quasi-private organizations, such as the Financial Industry Regulation Authority (FINRA) or the credit rating agencies such as Moody's, Fitch, and Standard & Poor's.[84] Indeed, the very "privatization" of the process of securitization of mortgages, which had started out in the 1960s as a government function, has become a flash point in explanations of how the financial sector lost its way. The willful blurring of the line between a private firm and a political instrument in the United States in the cases of Freddie Mac and Fannie Mae will be treated in chapter 5.

One of the great neoliberal flimflam operations is to mask their role in power through confusion of "marketization" of government functions with the shrinking of the state: if anything, bureaucracies become more unwieldy under neoliberal regimes.[85] Another is to imagine all manner of methods to "shackle" the state by reducing all change to prohibitive constitutional maneuvers (as with the "public choice" school of James Buchanan). In practice, "deregulation" always cashes out as "reregulation," only under a different set of ukases.

[5] Skepticism about the lack of control of democracy is periodically offset by recognition of the persistent need for a reliable font of popular legitimacy for the neoliberal market state. This is a thorny problem for neoliberals: how to maintain their pretence of freedom as noncoercion when, in practice, it seems unlikely that most people would freely choose the neoliberal version of the state. As Hayek once wrote: "It would be impossible to assert that a free society will always and necessarily develop values of which we would approve, or even, as we shall see, that it will maintain values which are compatible with the preservation of freedom."[86] In one sense, the NTC is itself one

practical political solution to this conundrum: the Russian doll exists, in part, as a conscious intervention to change the culture in a direction more favorable to the neoliberals by disarming political opposition. However, since the very project itself could be regarded as violating a precept of the inviolability of individual volition, the neoliberals also have proposed a conceptual "fix" for the audacity of intervention.

Neoliberals seek to transcend the intolerable contradiction of democratic rejection of the neoliberal state by treating politics *as if* it were a market, and promoting an economic theory of "democracy." In its most advanced manifestation, there is no separate content of the notion of citizenship other than as customer of state services.[87] This supports the application of neoclassical economic models to previously political topics; but it also explains why the neoliberal movement must seek to consolidate political power by operating from within the state. The abstract "rule of law" is frequently conflated with or subordinated to conformity to the neoliberal vision of an ideal market. The "night watchman" version of the state is thus comprehensively repudiated: there is no separate sphere of the market, fenced off, as it were, from the sphere of civil society. Everything is fair game for marketization.

The neoliberals generally have to bend in pretzels to deny that in their ideal state, law is a system of power and command, and is, rather, a system of neutral general rules applicable equally to all, grounded in something other than the intentional goals of some (that is, their own) group's political will. As Raymond Plant explains, for the Rothbard anarchists, this is something like natural law; for the Buchanan-style public-choice crowd, it is contract theory; for Chicago economics, it is a world where the economy is conflated with the universe of human existence; and for Hayek, it is his own idiosyncratic notion of cultural evolution.[88] In everyday neoliberalism, the Chicago story seems to win out. However, in the recent crisis, the evolution story has been brought out of mothballs, as we shall observe in chapter 6.

[6] Neoliberalism thoroughly revises what it means to be a human person. Many people have quoted Foucault's prescient observation from three decades ago: "In neoliberalism . . . Homo Economicus is an entrepreneur, an entrepreneur of himself."[89] However, they over-look the extent to which this is a drastic departure from classical liberal doctrine.

Classical liberalism identified "labor" as the critical original human infusion that both created and justified private property. Foucault correctly identifies the concept of "human capital" as the signal neoliberal departure—initially identified with the MPS member Gary Becker—that undermines centuries of political thought that parlayed humanism into stories of natural rights. Not only does neoliberalism deconstruct any special status for human labor, but it lays waste to older distinctions between production and consumption rooted in the labor theory of value, and reduces the human being to an arbitrary bundle of "investments," skill sets, temporary alliances (family, sex, race), and fungible body parts. "Government of the self" becomes the taproot of all social order, even though the identity of the self evanesces under the pressure of continual prosthetic tinkering; this is one possible way to understand the concept of "biopower." Under this regime, the individual displays no necessary continuity from one "decision" to the next. The manager of You becomes the new ghost in the machine.[90]

Needless to say, the rise of the Internet has proven a boon for neoliberals; and not just for a certain Randroid element in Silicon Valley that may have become besotted with the doctrine. Chat rooms, online gaming, virtual social networks, and electronic financialization of household budgets have encouraged even the most intellectually challenged to experiment with the new neoliberal personhood. A world where you can virtually switch gender, imagine you can upload your essence separate from your somatic self, assume any set of attributes, and reduce your social life to an arbitrary collection of statistics on a social networking site is a neoliberal playground. The saga of dot.com billionaires, so doted over by the mass media, drives home the lesson that you don't actually have to produce anything tangible to participate in the global marketplace of the mind. This is the topic of chapter 3.

The Incredible Disappearing Agent has had all sorts of implications for neoliberal political theory. First off, the timeworn conventional complaint that economics is too pigheadedly methodologically individualist does not begin to scratch the neoliberal program. "Individuals" are merely evanescent projects from a neoliberal perspective. Neoliberalism has consequently become a scale-free Theory of Everything: something as small as a gene or as large as a nation-state is equally engaged in entrepreneurial strategic pursuit of advantage, since the "individual" is no longer a privileged ontological platform. Second, there are no more "classes" in the sense of an older political economy, since every individual is both employer and worker simultaneously; in the limit, every man should be his own business firm or corporation; this has proven a powerful tool for disarming whole swathes of older left discourse. It also appropriates an obscure historical development in

American legal history—that the corporation is tantamount to person-hood—and blows it up to an ontological principle. Conversely, it denies personhood to government: "Government has no economic responsibility. Only people have responsibility, and government is not a person."[91] Third, since property is no longer rooted in labor, as in the Lockean tradition, consequently property rights can be readily reengineered and changed to achieve specific *political* objectives; one observes this in the area of "intellectual property," or in a development germane to the crisis, ownership of the algorithms that define and trade obscure complex derivatives, and better, to reduce the formal infrastructure of the marketplace itself to a commodity. Indeed, the recent transformation of stock exchanges into profit-seeking IPOs was a critical neoliberal innovation leading up to the crisis. Classical liberals treated "property" as a sacrosanct bulwark against the state; neoliberals do not. Fourth, it destroys the whole tradition of theories of "interests" as possessing empirical grounding in political thought.[92]

Clearly, we're not in classical liberalism anymore.

[7] Neoliberals extol "freedom" as trumping all other virtues; but the definition of freedom is recoded and heavily edited within their framework. Most neoliberals insist they value "freedom" above all else; but more hairs are split in the definition of freedom than over any other neoliberal concept. This is probably a necessary consequence of the development of other neoliberal tenets, like that covered in thesis 6. It is a little hard to conceptualize freedom for an entity that displays no quiddity or persistence; and most neoliberal discussions of freedom have been cut loose from older notions of individualism.

Some members of the Neoliberal Thought Collective, like Milton Friedman, have refused to define it altogether (other than to divorce it from democracy), while others like Friedrich Hayek forge links to thesis 2 by motivating it as an epistemic virtue: "the chief aim of freedom is to provide both the opportunity and the inducement to insure the maximum use of knowledge that an individual can accrue." As this curious definition illustrates, for neoliberals, what you think a market really is seems to determine your view of what liberty means. Almost immediately, the devil is secreted in the details, since Hayek feels he must distinguish "personal liberty" from subjective freedom, since personal liberty does not entail political liberty. Late in life, Milton Friedman posited three species of freedom—economic, social and political—but it appears that economic freedom was the only one that mattered. Some modern figures such as Amartya Sen attempt to factor in your given range of choices in an index of your freedom, but neoliberals will have none of that. They seek to paint all "coercion" as evil, but without admitting into consideration any backstory of the determinants of your intentions. Everyone is treated as expressing untethered context-free hankering, as if they were born yesterday into solitary confinement; this is the hidden heritage of entrepreneurialism of the self. This commandment cashes out as: no market can ever be coercive.[93]

In practice, neoliberals can't let others contemplate too long that their peculiar brand of freedom is not the realization of any political, human, or cultural telos, but rather the positing of autonomous self-governed entities, all coming naturally equipped with some version of "rationality" and motives of ineffable self-interest, striving to improve their lot in life by engaging in market exchange.[94] It follows from the human-capital concept that education is a consumer good, not a life-transforming experience. Followers of Foucault are often strongest on the elaborate revision required in cultural concepts of human freedom and morality, although this may be attributed to Foucault's own sympathies for elements of the neoliberal project.[95] Curiously enough, the fact that this version of "freedom" may escape all vernacular referent was noted when an argument broke out within the MPS in the 1970s, with Irving Kristol accusing Milton Friedman and Friedrich Hayek of depending upon a version of "self-realization" as the great empty void at the center of their economic doctrines.[96] You can't realize a Kantian essence that is not there.

Whatever else it betokens in the neoliberal pantheon, it is axiomatic that freedom can only be "negative" for neoliberals (in the sense of Isaiah Berlin), for one very important reason. Freedom cannot be extended from the use of knowledge *in* society to the use of knowledge *about* society, because self-examination concerning why one passively accepts local and incomplete knowledge leads to contemplation of how market signals create some forms of knowledge and squelch others. Meditation upon our limitations leads to inquiry into how markets work, and metareflection on our place in larger orders, something that neoliberals warn is beyond our ken. Knowledge then assumes global institutional dimensions, and this undermines the key doctrine of the market as transcendental superior information processor. Conveniently, "freedom" does not extend to principled rejection of the neoliberal insurgency. Neoliberals want to insist that resistance to their program is futile, since it inevitably appeals to a spurious (from their perspective) understanding of freedom.

[8] Neoliberals begin with a presumption that capital has a natural right to flow freely across national boundaries. (The free flow of labor enjoys no similar right.[97]) Since that entails persistent balance-of-payments problems in a nonautarkic world, neoliberals took the lead in inventing all manner of transnational devices for the economic and political discipline of nation-states.[98] They began by attempting to reintroduce what they considered to be pure market discipline (flexible exchange rates, dismantling capital controls) during the destruction of the Bretton Woods system, but over the longer term learned to appreciate that suitably staffed international institutions such as the WTO, the World Bank, the IMF, and other units are better situated to impose neoliberal policies upon recalcitrant nation-states. Initially strident demands to abolish global financial (and other) institutions on the part of early neoliberals such as Friedman and some denizens of the Cato Institute were subsequently tempered by others—such as Anne Krueger, Stanley Fischer, and Kenneth Rogoff—and as these neoliberals came to occupy these institutions, they used them primarily to influence staffing and policy decisions, and thus to displace other internationalist agendas. The role of such transnational organizations was recast to exert "lock-in" of prior neoliberal policies, and therefore to restrict the range of political options of national governments. Sometimes they were also used to displace indigenous "crony capitalists" with a more cosmopolitan breed of cronyism. Thus it is correct to observe an organic connection between such phenomena as the Washington Consensus and the spread of neoliberal hegemony, as Dieter Plehwe argues.[99] This also helps address the neoliberal conundrum of how to both hem in and at the same time obscure the strong state identified in point 4, above.

The relevance of the rise of the neoliberal globalized financial regime to the crisis is a matter of great concern to the thought collective and to others (such as Ben Bernanke) who seek to offload responsibility for the crash onto someone else. Because there was no obvious watershed linking policy to theory comparable to Bretton Woods, and the post-1980 infrastructure of international finance grew up piecemeal, the relationship between neoliberalism and the growth of shadow and offshore banking is only beginning to be a subject of interest. Evidence, by construction, is often inaccessible. However, the drive to offshore outsource manufacturing in the advanced economies, which was mutually symbiotic with the frustration of capital controls, was clearly a function of neoliberal doctrines concerning the unbounded benefits of freedom of international trade, combined with neoliberal projects to reengineer the corporation as an arbitrary nexus of contractual obligations, rather than as a repository of production expertise. The MPS member Anne Krueger was brought into dialogue with her fellow member Ronald Coase, and the offspring was the flight of capital to countries such as China, India, and the Cayman Islands. The role of China as beneficiary, but simultaneously as part-time repudiator of the neoliberal globalized financial system, is a question that bedevils all concerned.

While freedom of capital flows have not generally been stressed by neoliberals as salient causes of the crisis, they do manage to unite in opposition to capital controls as one reaction to the crisis.

[9] Neoliberals regard inequality of economic resources and political rights not as an unfortunate by-product of capitalism, but a necessary functional characteristic of their ideal market system. Inequality is not only the natural state of market economies from a neoliberal perspective, but it is actually one of its strongest motor forces for progress. Hence the rich are not parasites, but a boon to mankind. People should be encouraged to envy and emulate the rich. Demands for equality are merely the sour grapes of the losers, or if they are more generous, the atavistic holdovers of old images of justice that must be extirpated from the modern mind-set. As Hayek wrote, "The market order does not bring about any close correspondence between subjective merit or individual needs and rewards."[100] Indeed, this lack of correlation between reward and effort is one of the major inciters of (misguided) demands for justice on the part of the hoi polloi, and the failure of democratic systems to embrace the neoliberal state, as discussed in tenet 5, above. "Social justice" is blind, because it remains forever cut off from the Wisdom of the Market. Thus, the vast worldwide trend toward concentration of income and wealth since the 1990s is the playing out of a neoliberal script to produce a more efficient and vibrant capitalism.

Here again we touch upon the recent crisis. This particular neoliberal precept dictates that the widely noted exacerbation of income inequality in the United States since 1980 cannot possibly have played a role in precipitating the crisis in any way.[101] Indeed, attempts by the state to offset or ameliorate the trend toward inequality of wealth—especially through attempts to expand home ownership and consumer credit—become themselves, for neoliberals, major root causes of the crisis.[102] This then gets translated into the preferred neoliberal story of the crisis, which attributes culpability to the Democrats by lodging blame for the housing bubble via securitization with Fannie Mae and Freddie Mac (see chapter 5).

[10] Corporations can do no wrong, or at least they are not to be blamed if they do. This is one of the stronger areas of divergence from classical liberalism, with its ingrained suspicion of power concentrated in joint stock companies and monopoly stretching from Adam Smith to Henry Simons. The MPS set out in the 1950s entertaining suspicions of corporate power, with the ordoliberals especially concerned with the promotion of strong antitrust capacity on the part of the state. But starting with the Chicago law and economics movement, and then progressively spreading to treatments of entrepreneurs and the "markets for innovation," neoliberals began to argue consistently that not only was monopoly not harmful to the operation of the market, but an epiphenomenon attributable to the misguided activities of the state and powerful interest groups.[103] The twentieth-century socialist contention that capitalism bore within itself the seeds of its own arteriosclerosis (if not self-destruction) was baldly denied. By the 1970s, antitrust policies were generally repudiated in the United States, as neoliberals took the curious anomaly in American case law treating corporations as legal individuals and tended to inflate it into a philosophical axiom.[104] Indeed, if anything negative was ever said about the large corporation, it was that separation of ownership from control might conceivably pose a problem, but this was easily rectified by giving CEOs appropriate "incentives" (massive stock options, golden handshakes, latitude beyond any oversight) and instituting marketlike evaluation systems within the corporate bureaucracy, rectifying "agency problems."[105] Thus the modern "reengineering of the corporation" (reduced vertical integration, outsourcing supply chains, outrageous recompense for top officers) is itself an artifact of the neoliberal reconceptualization of the corporation.

This literature had a bearing on the crisis, since it was used to argue against aspersions cast that many financial firms were "Too Big to Bail," and that the upper echelons in those firms were garnishing dangerously high compensation packages. Nothing succeeds like market success, and any recourse to countervailing power must be squelched.

[11] The market (suitably reengineered and promoted) can always provide solutions to problems seemingly caused by the market in the first place. This is the ultimate destination of the constructivist orientation

within neoliberalism. Any problem, economic or otherwise, has a market solution, given sufficient ingenuity: pollution is abated by the trading of "emissions permits"; inadequate public education is rectified by "vouchers"; auctions can adequately structure exclusionary communication channels;[106] poverty-stricken sick people lacking access to health care can be incentivized to serve as guinea pigs for privatized clinical drug trials; poverty in underdeveloped nations can be ameliorated by "microloans"; terrorism by disgruntled disenfranchised foreigners can be offset by a "futures market in terrorist acts."[107] Suitably engineered boutique markets were touted as a superior method to solve all sorts of problems previously thought to be better organized by governments: everything from scheduling space shots to regulating the flow through airports and national parks. Economists made money by selling their nominal expertise in setting up these new markets, rarely admitting up front that they were simply acting as middlemen introducing intermediate steps toward future full privatization of the entity in question. Economists also proposed to fix the crisis by instituting new markets, as we shall discover in chapter 5.

The fascinating aspect of all this is how this precept was deployed in what seemed its most unpropitious circumstance, the erstwhile general failure of financial markets in the global economic crisis. One perspective on the issue is to recall that, in the popular Hayekian account, the marketplace is deemed to be a superior information processor, so therefore all human knowledge can be used to its fullest only if it is comprehensively owned and priced. This was deployed in a myriad of ways to suggest what might seem a string of strident non sequiturs: for instance, some neoliberals actually maintained that the solution to perceived problems in derivatives and securitization was redoubled "innovation" in derivatives and securitization, and not their curtailment.[108] Another variant on the Hayekian credo was to insist that the best people to clean up the crisis were the same bankers and financiers who created it in the first place, since they clearly embodied the best understanding of the shape of the crisis. The revolving door between the U.S. Treasury and Goldman Sachs was evidence that the market system worked, and not of ingrained corruption and conflicts of interest.

[12] The neoliberal program ends up vastly expanding incarceration and the carceral sphere in the name of getting the government off our backs. Members of the Mont Pèlerin Society were fond of Benjamin Constant's adage: "The government, beyond its proper sphere ought

not to have any power; within its sphere, it cannot have enough of it." Although this might seem specious from the perspective of a libertarian, it is central to understanding the fact that neoliberal policies lead to unchecked expansion of the penal sector, as has happened in the United States. As Bernard Harcourt has explained in detail, however much tenet 11 might seem to suggest that crime be treated as just another market process, the NTC has moved from the treatment of crime as exogenously defined within a society by its historical evolution, to a definition of crime as inefficient attempts to circumvent the market. The implication is that intensified state power in the police sphere (and a huge expansion of prisoners incarcerated) is fully complementary with the neoliberal conception of freedom. In the opinion of the MPS member Richard Posner, "The function of criminal sanction in a capitalist market economy, then, is to prevent individuals from bypassing the efficient market."[109]

This precept has some bearing on the unwillingness to pursue criminal prosecution against many of the major players in the global crisis. In this neoliberal perspective, there is also a natural stratification in what classes of law are applicable to different scofflaws: "the criminal law is designed primarily for the nonaffluent; the affluent are kept in line, for the most part, by tort law."[110] In other words, economic competition imposes natural order on the rich, because they have so much to lose. The poor need to be kept in line by a strong state, because they have so little to lose. Hence, the spectacle of (as yet) no major financial figure outside of Bernie Madoff and Raj Rajnarathan going to jail because of the crisis, while thousands of families behind on their mortgages are turfed out into the street by the constabulary, is a direct consequence of this neoliberal precept.

[13] The neoliberals have struggled from the outset to have their political/economic theories do dual service as a moral code. First and foremost, it would appear that the thought collective worshipped at the altar of a deity without restraints: "individual freedom, which it is most appropriate to regard as a moral principle of political action. Like all moral principles, it demands that it be accepted as a value in itself." However, Hayek in his original address to the first MPS meeting said, "I am convinced that unless the breach between true liberal and religious convictions can be healed, there is no hope for a revival of liberal forces." The very first MPS meeting reflected that wish, and held a session called "Liberalism and Christianity"; but it revealed only the antagonisms that percolated just below the surface. As a consequence,

the neoliberals were often tone-deaf when it came to the transcendental, conflating it with their epistemic doctrines concerning human frailty: "we must preserve that indispensable matrix of the uncontrolled and non-rational which is the only environment wherein reason can grow and operate effectively."[111]

The more sophisticated neoliberals understood this was rather thin gruel for many of their allies on the right; so from time to time, they sought to link neoliberalism to a specific religion, although they only ventured to do this sotto voce in their in-house publications:

> All that we can say is that the values we hold are the product of freedom, that in particular the Christian values had to assert themselves through men who successfully resisted coercion by government, and that it is to the desire to be able to follow one's own moral convictions that we owe the modern safeguards of individual freedom. Perhaps we can add to this that only societies which hold moral values essentially similar to our own have survived as free societies, while in others freedom has perished.[112]

Other MPS figures such as Buchanan entertained the notion that a certain specific type of moral order would support a neoliberal state, or that morals could reduce the costs of rent-seeking losers throwing monkey wrenches into government.[113] It took a lot of effort, and a fair bit of pussyfooting around the danger of alienating the partisans of one denomination (often in some other part of the world) by coquetting with different denominations or versions of religion, but the project of intellectual accommodation with the religious right and the theocons within the neoliberal framework has been an ongoing project at the MPS, although one fraught with contradictions that have dogged the liberal project since the Enlightenment.[114]

These thirteen more or less echt-commandments gathered here characterize the rough shape of the program eventually arrived at by the Neoliberal Thought Collective. In this summary, I have sought to highlight the stark divergence from both classical liberalism and libertarianism; further, the individual tenets will also serve as touchstones for our account of the intellectual history of the global economic crisis in subsequent chapters. Yet, having strained to discern unity in what sometimes appears a free-for-all, we should now confront the contrary proposition—that neoliberalism, in some fundamental conceptual sense, does not hang together in actual practice.

Neoliberalism, the Crisis, and the Double Truth Doctrine

All political movements of whatever stripe frequently find themselves in the position of needing to deny something they have affirmed in the past. If politics were the realm of consistency, and consistency the bugaboo of small minds, then zealots would indeed inherit the earth. Acknowledging that, there seems to be nonetheless something a little unusual going on in the Neoliberal Thought Collective, and I think it can be understood, if not entirely justified, by recourse to the doctrine of "double truth."

Just to be clear about the nature of what will be asserted, I am *not* referring here to the Platonic doctrine of the "noble lie," nor the Latin Averroist precepts concerning the tensions between philosophic reason and faith. Neither is it the "doublethink" of Orwellian provenance, which has more to do with the state twisting the meaning of words. It may have some relationship to the thought of Leo Strauss—the herme-neutic awareness that "all philosophers . . . must take into account the political situation of philosophy, that is, what can be said and what must be kept under wraps," as the *Cambridge Companion to Leo Strauss* puts it—but exploring the possible Chicago connections between his writings and the neoliberals would be too much of a distraction, given all the other topics we must cover.[115] What I shall refer to here is the proposition that an intellectual thought collective might actually concede that, as a corollary of its developed understanding of politics, it would be necessary to maintain an exoteric version of its doctrine for the masses—because that would be safer for the world and more beneficial for ordinary society—but simultaneously hold fast to an esoteric doctrine for a small closed elite, envisioned as the keepers of the flame of the collective's wisdom. Furthermore, whereas both the exoteric and esoteric versions would deal with many similar themes and issues, the exoteric version might appear on its face to contradict the esoteric version in various particulars. It will be necessary to explore the possibility that these seeming contradictions are not *cynical* in the modality one often encounters in career politicians, but rather grow organically out of the structural positions that motivate the thought collective.

I don't think it has gone unnoticed that the NTC embodies a budget of paradoxes, to put it politely. It starts with the strange behav-ior we already encountered: the neoliberals had begun acknowledging in the 1930s–'50s that they were in pursuit of something "neo," only to subsequently deny all divergence from an ancient time-honored "liberalism," against all evidence to the contrary. Subsequently, the continuity story became the exoteric stance, whereas the "neo" remained an esoteric appreciation. But then the dichotomy expands into all manner of seemingly incompatible positions. As Will Davies has put it: market competition should stand as a guarantor of democracy, but not vice versa; unimpeded economic activity would guarantee political freedom, but not vice versa. Yet, curiously, this did not apply to Mont Pèlerin itself.[116]

The Neoliberal Thought Collective tamed many of the contending contradictory conceptions of the "good society" documented in this volume by trying to have it both ways: to stridently warn of the perils of expanding purview of state activity *while simultaneously* imagining the strong state of their liking rendered harmless through some instrumentality of "natural" regulation; to posit their "free market" as an effortless generator and conveyor belt of information *while simultaneously* strenuously and ruthlessly prosecuting a "war of ideas" on the ground; asserting that their program would lead to unfettered economic growth and enhanced human welfare *while simultaneously* suggesting that no human mind could ever really know any such thing, and therefore that it was illegitimate to justify their program by its consequences; to portray the market as something natural, *yet simultaneously* in need of solicitous attention to continually reconstruct it; to portray their version of the market as the *ne plus ultra* of all human institutions, *while simultaneously* suggesting that the market is in itself insufficient to attain and nourish transeconomic values of a political, social, religious, and cultural character. "Neoliberal writings on allocation shift back and forth between libertarian and utilitarian vocabularies, with the two sometimes appearing interchangeably within a paper or chapter."[117] This ability to vertiginously pivot between paragraphs should itself be considered a political technology of the NTC.

The proliferation of straddles cannot be chalked up to mere pluralism of voices, inadequate critical attention, or absentmindedness. Few political doctrines have undergone the sustained extent of internal criticism of neoliberalism at Mont Pèlerin. All systems sport a modicum of internal contradictions as they age; but these particular discordances appear to betoken some structural problems within the neoliberal program, which have been dealt with in the recent past through application of the double-truth principle. I opt to cover three such contradictions here, which are arguably central to an understanding of the crisis: (1) that a society dedicated to liberal ideals had to resort to illiberal procedures and practices; (2) that a society that held spontaneous order as the *ne plus ultra* of human civilization had to submit to heavy regimentation and control; and (3) that a society dedicated to rational discourse about a market conceived as a superior information processor ended up praising and promoting ignorance. These, I trust, are stances so incongruous, such howling lapses of intellectual decorum, that one cannot imagine that the protagonists themselves did not take note of them. The historical record reveals that they did.

1. The illiberalism and hierarchical control of the MPS.

Can a liberal political program be conceived and prosecuted by means of open discussion with all comers? Hayek, with his sophisticated appreciation for the sociology of knowledge, thought it should not right from the very beginnings of Mont Pèlerin. In 1946, as he toured the United States attempting to drum up support for his new society, he explicitly stipulated that he was "using the term Academy in its original sense of a *closed society* [my emphasis] whose members would be bound together by common convictions and try to both develop this common philosophy and to spread its understanding."[118] This evocation of Plato's Academy was not harmless, as he doubtless understood; it has been the recourse of other MPS members whenever the closed, secret nature of the society has been raised. Hayek managed to have his way in this regard—from the start, recruitment, participation, and membership in the NTC has always been strictly controlled from within—but this starkly raises the issue of whether the MPS could practice what it nominally preached. This objection was immediately raised in 1947 by one of the more famous members of the collective, Karl Popper.

Popper had just published *The Open Society and Its Enemies* in 1945, attacking Plato, Hegel, and Marx; he was already closely allied with Hayek, who would conspire to bring him to the LSE. Popper notoriously had argued that a regime of open criticism and dispute was the only correct path to political progress; this dovetailed with his influential characterization of science as an ongoing process of conjecture and refutation. Significantly, he pressed this objection upon Hayek almost immediately upon receiving his prospectus for the envisioned organization:

> I feel that, for such an academy, it would be advantageous, and even necessary, to secure the participation of some people who are known to be socialists or close to socialism . . . My own position, as you

will remember, was always to try for a reconciliation of liberals and socialists . . . This does not, of course, mean that the emphasis on the dangers of socialism (dangers to freedom) should be suppressed or lessened. On the contrary . . . It occurred to me that you might ask me for the names of socialists who might be invited; and I must confess I am at a loss.[119]

As it happens, due either to lack of "suitable" candidates, or to Hayek's intransigence on this point, no such diversity of opinion was ever permitted to materialize at the MPS meetings. All discussion was kept within a small circle of political enthusiasm, more often than not held together by what they jointly opposed, rather than some shared Utopia. Popper continued to argue at early MPS meetings against the idea that fruitful discussions of politics required prescreening for ideological homogeneity, or as it was delicately put, "common basic assumptions"; but essentially, he was ignored.[120] Many other participants, rather, expressed concern that ideological agreement was already not being sufficiently policed; a few, such as Maurice Allais, withdrew due to its perceived dogmatism. As he explained his reservations to Hayek:

> The entire issue is to know if the envisioned group wants in the future to coalesce around a rigid dogmatism or if, on the contrary, it wants in its very organization to maintain the principle of liberal thought, of liberal discussion, within the cadre of principles generally accepted by all. Is it a matter of creating a political action group or a society for the defense of private property, or on the contrary, is it a matter of founding a society of thought capable of reexamining without bias all the questions up for debate and of initiating the foundation of a genuine and effective renewal of liberalism?[121]

Hayek clearly opted for having both simultaneously, but to make it work, there had to be high barriers to entry, and a putsch or two along the way.[122] A clash of worldviews on home turf was to be avoided at all costs. For good or for ill, the MPS rapidly evolved into a closed society with a rather stringent ideological litmus test.

This raises the difficult issue of whether the "Open Society" really works the way it was portrayed by Popper, and still sometimes evoked by the NTC when waxing catholic. Many writers have noted in detail how Popper's vision proved incompatible with that of Hayek; many philosophers of science have rejected Popper's vision of how science actually works.[123] But Popper himself at least glimpsed that his youthful exaltation of tolerance for unlimited criticism was unavailing in many circumstances that resembled those the MPS was constructed to counter. For instance, in a long footnote in *Open Society* he grants the plausibility of paradoxes of tolerance ("Unlimited tolerance must lead to the disappearance of tolerance") and democracy ("the majority may decide that a tyrant should rule"), but had little to offer concerning how those paradoxes should be defanged. Yet around the same time, Popper was already flirting with the Hayekian "solution": membership in the Open Society had to be prescreened to conform to a "minimum philosophy": but the principles of selection for that philosophy were never made as explicit as they were by Hayek in practice.[124]

Here, I believe, we can witness the birth of one of the trademark "double truth" doctrines of neoliberalism at the MPS. By professing a continuation of classical liberalism to outsiders, neoliberals lauded a tolerant open society that let all positions have a fair hearing and full empirical test. Hayek's *Road* is written in this register, with its dedication, "To socialists of all parties." Divergent views should compete and be criticized from the opposing camp. Everyone, they said, was welcome to participate. Yet there abided a closed subset of MPS insiders who recognized the force of the paradoxes of tolerance and democracy; and consequently they ran their thought collective as an exclusive hierarchical organization, consisting of members preselected for conformity, which encountered opposed conceptions of the world only in highly caricatured versions produced by their own true believers. Esoteric knowledge was transgressive: a liberalism for the twenty-first century could be incubated and sustained only by an irredeemably illiberal organization. Part of the price of admission was initiation into the double truth of the "minimum philosophy": insiders could learn to live with this esoteric doctrine after a long period of apprenticeship. Outsiders need never know anything about it, and could persist snug in their belief that liberalism meant the tolerant dialogue of the open society; of course, they need never apply to actually enter the MPS.

2. The MPS as regimented controlled society dedicated to the doctrine of "spontaneous order."

As in the previous case, the internal MPS membership themselves were first to comment on the incongruity of this situation. As the house historian of the MPS reports, Milton Friedman joked in a letter to Hayek, "Our faith requires that we are skeptical of the efficacy, at least in the short run, of organized efforts to promulgate [MPS doctrines]."[125] The problem, quite clearly, was if the neoliberal portrait of market order was so overwhelmingly superior, then why hadn't it just naturally come to dominate all other economic forms? Why hadn't it already summoned the spirit of liberalism that would guarantee it to flourish? Who really needed the shock troops of the Neoliberal Thought Collective? Classical liberals had adopted the consistent position either that it already had or would happen inexorably, so just sit back and enjoy the inexorable trend of history. Neoliberals had rejected all that in favor of an activist stance, but then had to face up to the vexatious intellectual lack of consilience between their sneers at the impudence of the will to planning and their own presumption of the utter nobility of their own will to power. In other words, how could they justify the Audacity of Intervention, or as James Buchanan so cagily posed the question by misrepresenting their own program as classically liberal:

> The classical liberal, in the role of social engineer, may, of course, recommend institutional *laissez faire* as a preferred policy stance. But why, and under what conditions, should members of the citizenry, or of some ultimate political decision authority, accept this advice more readily than that proffered by any other social engineer?[126]

As we have now grown accustomed, there existed more than one engagement with this conundrum within the Neoliberal Thought Collective; however, this fact should be understood as intimately entwined with the double-truth doctrine. Although I expect further research will uncover further variants, I will briefly point to three responses within the MPS.

The *first* response was that pioneered by Milton Friedman, and, it so happens, James Buchanan. The story here went that modern government was an aberration in the history of civilization, one that continually sought to leverage its massive power into engrossment of even more power, growing like a cancer on the otherwise healthy body of market society. Friedman in particular took the position that if he could explain this in simple and compelling ways to the public, in short sentences and punchy proposals and catchy slogans, they would respond favorably to his image of natural order, and voluntarily accept the political prescriptions offered them by the NTC.[127] All that was required to offset the wayward course of history was some media coverage of a plucky little David standing up to the governmental Goliath. Friedman was the master of the faux-sympathetic stance, "I just want what you want; but the government never gives it to us. I can."[128] He remained faithful to this prescription to a fault, expending prodigious efforts on popular books, a television series, his *Newsweek* column, and his indefatigable willingness to debate the most diversified opponents on stages all over the world. He even bequeathed his fortune to fund the effort to undermine state-sponsored primary education, since that was where the state had brainwashed the largest number of tender minds. Of course, this notion of expert tutelage constituted the most superficial response that would have occurred to any postwar American economist of whatever stripe, given the presumptive role of the expert during the Cold War era.[129] In that frame, the people were a featureless lump of clay to be molded by the charismatic expert. Friedman did in fact become the public face of the NTC in America from the 1960s to the 1990s; but his position was pitched too far into Pollyanna territory, and gave too many hostages to "democracy," to suit the tougher-minded souls in the MPS.

The second, richer and more complex answer was proffered by Hayek. He did strive to maintain that there was a natural telos driving history in the neoliberal direction (although this surfaced only late in his career), but the obstacle to its realization was the treason of the intellectuals. He notoriously dismissed these "second-hand dealers in ideas," and convened Mont Pèlerin as a countermovement to neutralize them politically in the longer run. This hostility was shared by many other members of the MPS, from Bertrand de Jouvenel to Raymond Aron. However, this set up a dynamic where Hayek eventually felt he had to distinguish between legitimate and fake organizations, or what he called "kosmos" versus "taxis." The taxis, or constructed order, was usually "simple" and intentionally set up to serve a preconceived set of purposes. The kosmos, or spontaneous order, grew up organically without intended purpose, although it would persist due to the fact that it performed certain unforeseen functions in a superior manner. Participants didn't need to know or understand the rules of a kosmos to go with the flow, but generally had to be compelled to follow the rules of a taxis. In his usual subtle manner, after defining it, Hayek invested the notion of taxis with negative connotations, and then equated it with institutions of formal government; whereas the kosmos came endowed with all manner of positive connotations, only to imperceptibly turn into his own neoliberal conception of the market.[130]

All this taxonomizing was fine; but the question that was motivating Hayek, even if he never adequately addressed it directly, was: What sort of "order" was the MPS, and what sort of order was the Neoliberal Thought Collective dedicated to bringing about?[131] The provisional answer began by blurring the boundaries of the sharp distinction he had just wrought: "while the rules on which a spontaneous order rests may also be of spontaneous origin, this need not always be the case . . . it is possible that an order which would still have to be described as spontaneous rests on rules which were entirely the result of deliberate design . . . collaboration will always rest both on spontaneous order as well as deliberate organization."[132] Here he elided acknowledgment that the MPS and the larger NTC did not themselves qualify as a spontaneous order, if only because it was predicated upon stipulated rules that were not the same for all members; nor were they independent of any common purpose. When you unpacked all the shells of the Russian doll, it was just another elaborate hierarchical political movement.

But perhaps this might be mitigated in the instance it could be regarded as a mongrel amalgam of taxis and kosmos. Certainly, intentional stipulation could potentially have unintended consequences, which meant that almost any phenomenon was a mare's nest of both kosmos and taxis elements; but Hayek decided he could not condone such promiscuity:

> [I]t is impossible, not only to replace spontaneous orders by organization and at the same time to utilize as much of the dispersed knowledge of all its members as possible, but also to improve or correct this order by interfering in it by direct commands. Such a combination of spontaneous order and organization it can never be rational to adopt.[133]

Since Hayek's original point had been that no one "rationally" adopts a kosmos, here was where his construct broke down. Either the dividing line between kosmos and taxis was bright and clear, and the MPS was an example of a taxis, which was thus illegitimate by his own lights, or else kosmos and taxis were hopelessly intertwined, but then there was no dependable way in his system to separate "government" from "market," and the politics of the NTC would threaten to become unintelligible. The Hayekian wing of the thought collective has never been able to square this circle, so it has to resort to double-truth tactics. For outsiders, neoliberal thinkers are portrayed as plucky individual rebel blooms of rage against the machine, arrayed against all the forces of big government and special interests, and in a few hyperbolic instances, even against the "capitalists."[134] They are neither sown nor cultivated, but are like unto dandelions after a spring rain, pure expressions of the kosmos. But once initiated into the mysteries of the thought collective, only the organization men rise to the top, and they know it. The Richard Finks, Leonard Reads, and Antony Fishers of the world are the true movers and shakers of the neoliberal movement, not some blogger in a basement. Salarymen are the purest expression of taxis, but must not say so.

In my opinion, the most perceptive and honest attempt to address the straddle between spontaneous order and calculated politics was the legacy of a rather less-cited MPS member (although another winner of the Bank of Sweden Prize), George Stigler. The oral tradition at Chicago had long acknowledged that Stigler's approach to the ultimate purpose of economics was different from that of the others:

> MILTON FRIEDMAN: There's no problem [between their respective approaches]. It's true, that George wanted to change things.
> AARON DIRECTOR: But he preferred to study them, not to change them.
> MF: He preferred to say that he preferred to study them . . . It was partly a long-running difference between him and me . . . And he liked to stress, "I just want to understand the world and Milton wants to change it."[135]

Stigler's self-denying ordinance was not, however, the conventional instance of the reticence and humility of the temperate scholar. He was directly responding to the contradiction lodged in the NTC identified in this section. Stigler understood that the Audacity of Intervention was a consequence of an asymmetry in the neoliberal theory of politics:

> As I mentally review Milton's work, I recall no important occasion on which he has told businessmen how to behave. . . . Yet Milton has shown no comparable reticence in advising Congress and the public on monetary policy, tariffs, schooling, minimum wages, the tax benefits of establishing a ménage without benefit of clergy, and several other subjects. . . . Why should businessmen—and customers and lenders and other economic agents—know and foster their own interests, but voters and political coalitions be so much in need of his and our lucid and enlightened instruction?[136]

Stigler was a true believer in the marketplace of ideas, a neoliberal notion if ever there was one. The public buys the information it wants, and adopts political positions based upon optimal ignorance.[137] For Stigler, there was no necessary historical trend or telos toward the neoliberal market. In his books, Friedman's (and Buchanan's) quest to educate and edify the unwashed was a miserable waste of time and resources, if one were to believe the neoliberal characterization of the market, and of politics as a market phenomenon. But then, what was the putative function of the Neoliberal Thought Collective? Stigler's answer was profound: it was to capture the minds of the crucial elites by innovating new economic and political doctrines that those elites would recognize as being in their interest once they were introduced to them (presumably by the outer shells of the neoliberal Russian doll). The MPS was that most noble protagonist, an intellectual entrepreneur; it came up with products before the clientele even knew they wanted them; and what it sold were the tools for those poised to infiltrate the government and immunize policy from the optimally stupid electorate. Technocratic elites could intently maintain the fiction that "the people" had their say, while reconfiguring government functions in a neoliberal direction. These elite saboteurs would bring about the neoliberal market society far more completely and efficaciously than waiting for the fickle public to come around to their beliefs.[138] Friedman and Buchanan had sailed too close to the wind in not holding democracy in sufficient contempt; what the neoliberal program counseled was a coup, not a New England town-hall meeting. Stigler did want to change the world, but in a manner more Machiavellian than his peers.[139] His was the instruction manual for neoliberals to occupy government, not merely disparage it.

I think that Stigler's construction of the meaning and purpose of the Neoliberal Thought Collective was the version that won out after the 1980s, in part because it openly embraced the double-truth doctrine, rather than uneasily squirming around it, as Friedman had done. The MPS offered its elite recruits one thing, and the outer shells of the Russian doll another. The exoteric knowledge of the spontaneous order of the market was good enough for Fox News and *The Wall Street Journal*; the esoteric doctrine of reengineering government to recast society comprised the marching orders of the NTC. Friedman was the public face, Stigler the clan fixer. For the former, the MPS was just another debating society; for the latter, it was the executive committee of the capitalist insurgency.

3. The MPS as a Society of Rationalists promoting ignorance as a virtue.

Many observers have seen fit to comment that the MPS was not a very open society, in the Popperian sense, and that its regimented character may have appeared a bit incongruous given its professed beliefs; but in my opinion, most analysts have fallen down when it comes to this third straddle[140]. That is a shame, because it will transpire that this particular "double truth" is far and away the most important of the three for understanding how the NTC managed to come through the crisis relatively unscathed.

Hayek is noteworthy in that he placed ignorance at the very center of his political theory: "the case for individual freedom rests chiefly on the recognition of the inevitable ignorance of us all."[141] Most commentators tend to interpret this as an appeal to ignorance as some kind of primal state of mankind; but I think they need to expand their horizons. The distinction begins to bite when we take note that Hayek harbored a relatively low opinion of the role of education and discussion in the process of learning, and notoriously, an even lower opinion of the powers of ratiocination of those he disparaged as "the intellectuals." These, of course, were the mirror image of his belief in the market as a superior information processor:

> Nor is the process of forming majority opinion entirely, or even chiefly, a matter of discussion, as the overintellectualized conception would have it . . . Though discussion is essential, it is not the main process by which people learn. Their views and desires are formed by individuals acting according to their own designs . . . It is because we normally do not know who knows best that we leave the decision to a process we do not control.[142]

For Hayek and other advocates of "emergent" social cognition, true rational thought is impersonal, but can occur only between and beyond the individual agents who putatively do the thinking. As he wrote in *The Constitution of Liberty*, "to act rationally we often find it necessary to be guided by habit rather than reflection." As Christian Arnsperger so aptly put it, for Hayek, "rational judgment can only be uttered by a Great Nobody."[143] That may seem odd in someone superficially tagged as a methodological individualist supporter of freedom; but it just goes to show how far ignorance has become ingrained in American political discourse. The trick lies in comprehending how Hayek could harbor such a jaundiced view of the average individual, while simulta-neously elevating "knowledge" to pride of place in the economic pantheon:

> Probably it is true enough that the great majority are rarely capable of thinking independently, that on most questions they accept views which they find ready-made, and that they will be equally content if born or coaxed into one set of beliefs or another. In any society freedom of thought will probably be of direct significance only for a small minority.[144]

For Hayek, "Knowledge is perhaps the chief good that can be had at a price," but difficult to engross and accumulate, because it "never exists in concentrated or integrated form but solely as the dispersed bits of incomplete and frequently contradictory knowledge which all the separate individuals possess." You might think this would easily be handled by delegating its collection and winnowing to some middle-men, say to academic experts, but you would be mistaken, according to Hayek. He takes the position that all human personal abilities to evalu-ate the commodity are weak, at best. And this is not a matter of differential capacities or distributions of innate intelligence: "the differ-ence between the knowledge that the wisest and that which the most ignorant individual can deliberately employ is comparatively insignifi-cant." Experts are roundly disparaged by Hayek, and accused of essentially serving as little more than apologists for whomever employs them.[145] On the face of it, it thus seems somewhat ironic that Hayek would be touted as the premier theorist of the New Knowledge Econ-omy. But the irony dissolves once we realize that central to neoliberalism is a core conviction that the market really does know better than any one of us what is good for ourselves and for society, and that includes the optimal allocation of ignorance within the populace: "There is not much reason to believe that, if at any one time the best knowledge which some possess were made available to all, the result would be a much better society. *Knowledge and ignorance are relative concepts.*"[146]

What purportedly rescues Hayek's system from descending into some relativist quagmire is the precept that the market does the think-ing for us that we cannot. The real danger to humanity resides in the character who mistakenly believes he can think for himself:

> It was men's submission to the impersonal forces of the market that in the past has made possible the growth of civilization . . . It does

not matter whether men in the past did submit from beliefs which some now regard as superstition . . . The refusal to yield to forces which we neither understand nor can recognize as the conscious decisions of an intelligent being is the product of an incomplete and therefore erroneous rationalism. It is incomplete because it fails to comprehend that co-ordination of the multifarious individual efforts in a complex society must take account of facts no individual can completely survey. And it also fails to see that . . . the only alternative to submission to the impersonal and seemingly irrational forces of the market is submission to an equally uncontrollable and therefore arbitrary power of other men.[147]

There you have Hobson's choice: either the abject embrace of ignorance or abject capitulation to slavery. The Third Way of the nurturing and promotion of individual wisdom is for Hayek a sorry illusion.[148] The Market works because it fosters cooperation without dialogue; it works because the values it promotes are noncognitive. The job of education for neoliberals like Hayek is not so much to convey knowledge per se as it is to foster passive acceptance in the hoi polloi toward the infinite wisdom of the Market: "general education is not solely, and perhaps not even mainly, a matter of the communication of knowledge. There is a need for certain common standards of values." Interestingly, science is explicitly treated in the same fashion: if you were to become an apprentice scientist, you would learn deference and the correct attitudes toward the enterprise, rather than facts and theories. Of course, Hayek rarely capitalizes or anthropomorphizes the Market, preferring to refer instead to euphemistic concepts like "higher, supraindividual wisdom" of "the products of spontaneous social growth." Formal political processes where citizens hash out their differences and try to convince one another are uniformly deemed inferior to these "spontaneous processes," wherein, it must be noted, insight seems to descend out of the aether to inhabit individual brains like the tongues of the Holy Ghost: this constitutes one major source of the neoliberal hostility to democratic governments. But the quasi-economistic language testifies that the nature of the epiphany is not otherworldly but more mundane and pecuniary: "civilization begins when the individual in pursuit of his ends can make use of more knowledge than he himself has acquired and when he can transcend the boundaries of his ignorance by profiting from knowledge that he does not himself possess."[149]

This language of "use and profit from knowledge you don't actually possess" might seem a bit mysterious until we unpack its implications for ignorance *as a status to be produced rather than a state to be mitigated.* I second the analysis of Louis Schneider that Hayek should be read as one of a long line of social theorists who praise the unanticipated and unintended consequences of social action as promoting the public interest, but who take it one crucial step further by insisting upon the indispensable role of ignorance in guaranteeing that the greater good is served.[150] For Hayek, the conscious attempt to conceive of the nature of public interest is the ultimate hubris, and to concoct stratagems to achieve it is to fall into Original Sin. True organic solidarity can obtain only when everyone believes (correctly or not) they are just following their own selfish idiosyncratic ends, or perhaps don't have any clear idea whatsoever of what they are doing, when in fact they are busily (re)producing beneficent evolutionary regularities beyond their ken and imagination. Thus, *ignorance helps promote social order,* or as he said, "knowledge and ignorance are relative concepts."

The major point to be savored here is that individual ignorance fostered and manufactured by corporations, think tanks and other market actors is suitably subservient to market rationality, in the sense that it "profits from the knowledge that the agent does not possess." Paid experts *should* behave as apologists for the interests that hire them: this is the very quiddity of the theory of self-interest. As Schneider explains, "Organic theorists hold that while actors may cojointly achieve important 'beneficent' results, they do so in considerable ignorance and in ignorance of the socially transmitted behavior they are reproducing contains accumulations of 'knowledge' now forgotten or no longer perceived as knowledge."[151] Burkean conservatism revels in the preservation of tradition, the great unconscious disembodied wisdom of the ages. This is why cries of "teach the controversy" in the schoolroom, "sound science" in the courtroom, and stipulations of "balance" in the news media are sweet music to neoliberal ears. That is why, as we shall repeatedly observe in subsequent chapters, and especially chapter 6, neoliberals and economists have served to sow confusion and falsehoods about the causes and consequences of the crisis. Neoliberals strive to preserve and promote doubt and ignorance, in science as well as in daily life; evolution and the market will take the hindmost.

The second salient implication is that, from the neoliberal vantage point, "science" does not need special protection from the ignorant, be they the partisan government bureaucrat, the craven intellectual for hire, the lumpen MBA, the Bible-thumping fundamentalist, the global-cooling enthusiast, or the feckless student. In an ideal state, special institutions dedicated to the protection and pursuit of knowledge can more or less be dispensed with as superfluous; universities in particular must be weaned away from the state and put on a commercial footing, dissolving their distinctive identities as "ivory towers." Science should essentially dissolve into other market activities, with even its "public" face held accountable to considerations of efficiency, profitability, and subservience to personal ratification. "Competition" is said to ensure the proliferation of multiple concepts and theories with the blessing of the private sector. The only thing that keeps us from enjoying this ideal state is the mistaken impression that science serves higher causes, or that it is even possible to speak truth to power, or that one can rationally plan social goals and their attainment.[152] Despairing of extirpation of these doctrines from within the university in his lifetime, Hayek and his confederates formed the Mont Pèlerin Society and then forged a linked concentric shell of think tanks to proselytize for the neoliberal idea that knowledge must be rendered subordinate to the market. Little did he suspect just how successful his crusade would be after his death.

Hayek is sometimes portrayed as a postmodern figure who did not believe in Truth; but again, I don't think that really gets to the heart of the matter. Equally misguided would be the interpretation that Hayek would only promote the production of instrumentally useful knowledge: "Science for science's sake, art for art's sake, are equally abhorrent to the Nazis, our socialist intellectuals, and the communists. Every activity must derive its justification from a conscious social purpose."[153] Instead, I believe he initiated an important neoliberal practice as advocating a double-truth doctrine: one for the masses, where nominally everything goes and spontaneous innovation reigns; and a different one for his small, tight-knit cadre of believers. First and foremost, neoliberalism masquerades as a radically populist philosophy, one that begins with a set of philosophical theses about *knowledge* and its relationship to society. It seems at first to be a radical leveling philosophy, denigrating expertise and elite pretentions to hard-won knowledge, instead praising the "wisdom of crowds." The Malcolm Gladwells, Jimmy Waleses, and James Surowieckis of the world are its pied pipers. This movement appeals to the vanity of every self-absorbed narcissist, who would be glad to ridicule intellectuals as "professional secondhand dealers in ideas."[154] But of course it sports a predisposition to disparage intellectuals, since "knowledge and ignorance are relative concepts." In Hayekian language, it elevates a "kosmos"—a supposedly spontaneous order that no one has intentionally designed or structured *because they are ignorant*—over a "taxis."

Sometimes people are poleaxed by some of the astounding things neoliberals have said (in public, in the media) about the crisis: that it was all the fault of Freddie Mac and Fannie Mae, that China made us do it, that it all was due to a "deficiency of economic literacy" on the part of the lower classes, that investors rationally factored in the threat of the Obama administration taking office by going on an investment strike from 2008 to 2010, that the greatest contraction since the Great Depression is solely to be laid at the door of government debt—and I am not making these up; they will be documented herein. How could people of moderate intelligence and goodwill say and write such things? Here the double-truth doctrine bites hard. *The major ambition of the Neoliberal Thought Collective is to sow doubt and ignorance among the populace.* This is not done out of sheer cussedness; it is a political tactic, a means to a larger end. Chapter 6 makes the argument: Think of the documented existence of climate-change denial; and then simply shift it over into economics. Of course, they can't seriously admit it in public; but years of evidence since 2007 and the esoteric theory of ignorance recounted above unite to buttress the case that this has been one of the main tactics by which the NTC has escaped all obloquy for the crisis. The double truth is: as an insider, you realize that this is a good thing, since it fosters defeat of political opponents, the health of the kosmos, and the victory of the neoliberal market society.

Learning from Carl Schmitt

Perhaps the greatest incongruity of the Neoliberal Thought Collective has been that the avatars of freedom drew one of their most telling innovations from the critique of liberalism that had been mounted by totalitarian German and Italian political thinkers from the interwar period. Although there were a fair number of such writers who were important for the European MPS members, the one that comes up time and again in their footnotes is Carl Schmitt, whom Hayek called "Adolf Hitler's crown jurist Carl Schmitt, who consistently advocated the replacement of the 'normative' thinking of liberal law by a conception of law which regards as its purpose 'concrete order formation'"; another was Bruno Leoni, who posited law as something best fortified as resistant to all popular alteration. It is a watchword among those familiar with the German literature that Hayek reprises much of

Schmitt's thesis that liberalism and democracy should be regarded as antithetical under certain circumstances[155]:

> Liberalism and democracy, although compatible, are not the same ... the opposite of liberalism is totalitarianism, while the opposite of democracy is authoritarianism. In consequence, it is at least possible in principle that a democratic government may be totalitarian and that an authoritarian government may act on liberal principles ... [in] demanding unlimited power of the majority, [democracies] become essentially anti-liberal.[156]

Since the epistemic innovations covered above informed the MPS thought collective that the masses will never understand the true architecture of social order, and intellectuals will continue to tempt them to intervene and otherwise muck up the market, then they felt impelled to propound the central tenet of neoliberalism, viz., that a strong state was necessary to neutralize what he considered to be the pathologies of democracy. The notion of freedom as exercise of personal participation in political decisions was roundly denounced.[157] Hayek insisted that his central epistemic doctrines about knowledge dictated that freedom must feel elusive for the common man: "Man in a complex society can have no choice but between adjusting himself to what to him must seem the blind forces of the social process and obeying the orders of a superior."[158] Paraphrasing Walter Benjamin, citizens must learn to forget about their "rights" and instead be given the opportunity to express themselves through the greatest information conveyance device known to mankind, the market.[159] The Neoliberal Thought Collective, through the instrumentality of the strong state, sought to *define and institute* the types of markets that they (and not the citizenry) were convinced were the most advanced. Hayek's frequent appeals to a "spontaneous order" often masked the fact that it was the NTC who were claiming the power to exercise the Schmittian "exception" (and hence constitute the sovereignty of the state) by defining things like property rights, the extent of the franchise, constitutional provisions that limit citizen initiatives, and the like. As Scheuerman writes about the comparison with Hayek, "For Carl Schmitt, the real question is *who* intervenes, and *whose* interests are to be served by intervention."[160]

In too many ways to enumerate here, the reaction of both economists and the NTC to the global economic crisis is a case study in the applications of Schmitt's doctrine of the exception. All the rationalizations of the Federal Reserve "staying within its legal mandate" went out the window the minute it started to block market verdicts on which banks should fail; the American government followed by deciding which auto firms and insurance companies would live or die; the imperious negation of market diktat continued apace with a stream of further arbitrary decisions. Governors in Michigan began to oust legitimately elected local officials, and replace them with unelected "emergency managers"; mortgage firms set about to ignore long-standing legal restrictions on conveyance and foreclosure. Similar things began to happen within the European Union, with the imposition of unelected prime ministers in Greece and Italy, and the suspension of competition guidelines at the Brussels level. As Will Davies so perceptively noted, "In answer to the question of whether neoliberalism is alive or dead, it seems entirely plausible to speak of an ongoing or permanent state of exception."[161] The NTC has demonstrated that true political power resides in the ability to make the decision to "suspend" the market in order to save the market.

As in so many other areas, they were merely echoing Schmitt's position that "Only a strong state can preserve and enhance a free-market economy" and "Only a strong state can generate genuine decentralization, [and] bring about free and autonomous domains." This was echoed (without attribution) by Hayek: "If we proceeded on the assumption that only the exercises of freedom that the majority will practice are important, we would be certain to create a stagnant society with all the characteristics of unfreedom."[162]

One can therefore only second the verdict of Christi that, "In truth, Hayek owed much to Schmitt, more than he cared to recognize."[163] For Hayek and the neoliberals, the Führer was replaced by the figure of the entrepreneur, the embodiment of the will-to-power for the community, who must be permitted to act without being brought to rational account. While he probably believed he was personally defending liberalism from Schmitt's withering critique, his own political "solution" ended up resembling Schmitt's "total state" more than he could bring himself to admit. If it had been apparent to his audience that he was effectively advocating an authoritarian reactionary despotism as a replacement for classical liberalism, it would certainly have not gone down smoothly in the West right after World War II. Further, there was no immediate prospect of a strong authority taking over the American university system (by contrast with Germany in the 1930s) and sweeping the stables clean. In an interesting development not anticipated by Schmitt, Hayek and his comrades hit upon the brilliant notion of developing the "double truth" doctrine of neoliberalism—namely, an elite would be tutored to understand the deliciously transgressive Schmittian necessity of repressing democracy, while the masses would be regaled with ripping tales of "rolling back the nanny state" and being set "free to choose"—by convening a closed Leninist organization of counterintellectuals. There would be no waiting around until some charismatic savior magically appeared to deliver the Word of Natural Order down from the Mont to the awestruck literati. Intellectual credibility could not be left to the vagaries of "spontaneous order." The constellation of double-truth doctrines enumerated in this chapter are the direct consequence of Schmitt's definition of politics as the logic of the friend/enemy distinction.

This was sometimes admitted by members of Mont Pèlerin in public, but only when they felt that their program was safely in the ascendant:

> Let's be clear, I don't believe in democracy in one sense. You don't believe in democracy. Nobody believes in democracy. You will find it hard to find anybody who will say that if, that is democracy interpreted as majority rule. You will find it hard to find anybody who will say that at 55% of the people believe the other 45% of the people should be shot. That's an appropriate exercise of democracy ... What I believe is not a democracy but an individual freedom in a society in which individuals cooperate with one another.[164]

Christian Arnsperger has captured the double-truth doctrine nicely, by insisting that Hayek had denied to others the very thing that gave his own life meaning: the imprimatur to theorize about "society" as a whole, to personally claim to understand the meaning and purpose of human evolution, and the capacity to impose his vision upon them through a political project verging upon totalitarianism. It was, as Arnsperger puts it, a theory to end all theories; not so different from the "end of history" scenarios so beloved of his epigones. The doctrine of special dispensation for the Elect is one very powerful source of ongoing attractions of neoliberalism, viz., the feeling of having surrendered to the wisdom of the market by coming to know something most of the nattering crowd can't possibly glimpse: freedom itself must be as unequally distributed as the riches of the marketplace.[165]

Of course, any embittered autodidact in his darkened room is "free" to believe that he deserves the same intellectual dispensation as the one eventually granted to Hayek. The world is full of minor Raskolnikovs with their contempt and disdain for the ignorant herd. But therein lies the critical difference, which is the most important fact for understanding neoliberalism: the NTC had been working assiduously to support his (and their) special vision for decades before his own dispensation came to be taken seriously by the larger culture, as demonstrated in Figure 2.4 in tabulated mentions of Hayek in the press and British Parliament.[166] There was always the danger that the masses he had so haughtily disdained would have returned the favor and consigned him to oblivion. The double-truth doctrines we have summarized here did not readily lend themselves to popularization or general acceptance in the postwar milieu. But tremendous effort, team tenacity, and a very timely Nobel Prize revived his prospects.[167] And now, if there was ever a figure who received an intellectual boost from the crisis, it would be difficult for them to claim parity with the revival of Friedrich Hayek

Figure 2.4: Mentions of Friedrich Hayek in Various English-Language Sources, 1931–1991

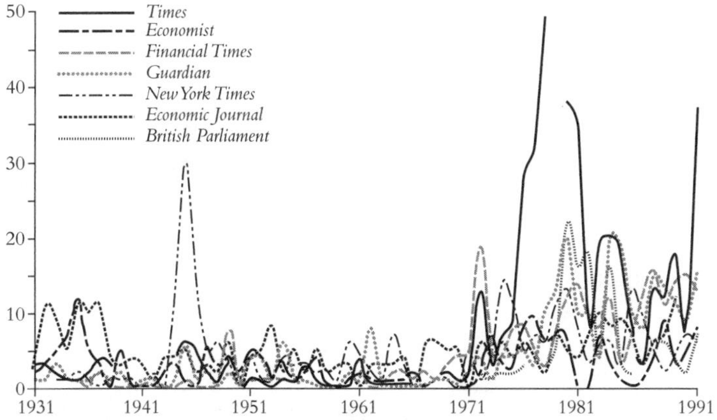

Source: Gilles Cristophe, University of Lille I

In the aftermath of the crisis, Hayek is now treated as a seer of prodigious perspicuity; and at the exhortation of Glenn Beck, his *Road to Serfdom* has been read (or maybe just scanned) by thousands who will never be bothered to delve much deeper into neoliberalism, or come to comprehend the political project that they feel speaks to them. But then again, it may be because the actual dry and stilted Hayekian encyclicals have less to do with all that than the fact that neoliberal images now so pervade cultural discourse that the situation has far transcended explicit political theory.[168]

In the next chapter, we leave the scriptures behind, to begin to contemplate everyday neoliberalism.

3

Everyday Neoliberalism

The mystery is why the right is now where the real energy is in U.S. political life, why the conservative message seems so much more straightforward and stimulating, why they're all having so much more goddamn *fun* than the left . . . That the U.S. left enjoyed this sort of energized coalescence in the 1960s and '70s but has (why not admit the truth?) nothing like it now is what lends many of the left's complaints about talk radio a bitter whiny edge.[1]

And that was *before* the crisis.

Starting from a heightened appreciation for the complexity and double truth of the neoliberal heritage, we can now make a fortified assault on this question: How did neoliberalism apparently come through the crisis unscathed?

Chapter 2 made the case that much hinges upon the interplay of the sociological structure of the Neoliberal Thought Collective built up around the Mont Pèlerin Society and the stratification of esoteric and exoteric doctrines, depending upon one's location within or without the Russian doll. Briefly reiterating, different cadres are supposed to maintain different understandings of the "true" political implications of the neoliberal project, as one of the internal structural aspects of the project. However, I need to emphasize that, while a necessary precondition, this consilience of doctrine and function is not at all sufficient by itself to "explain" the modern success of the movement. All it accomplished was to help us identify its intellectual provenance and genealogy. The tenacity of neoliberal doctrines that might have otherwise been refuted at every turn since 2008 has to be rooted in the extent to which a kind of "folk" or "everyday" neoliberalism has sunk so deeply into the cultural unconscious that even a few rude shocks can't begin to bring it to the surface long enough to provoke discomfort.

The relationship between culture and politics is an age-old topic that rarely commands much assent. Often one reads statements such as "Culture is now saturated with a market-oriented mentality that closes out alternative ways of thinking and imagining"; or, "The most fateful change that unfolded during the past three decades was not an increase in greed. It was the reach of markets, and of market values, into spheres of life traditionally governed by nonmarket norms."[2] That is *not* the claim being argued for in this chapter. Indeed, the impression that there exists a single coherent "market mentality" seeping into every pore turns out to be a big part of the problem. Neither has "governmentality" been as helpful a concept as it might have initially appeared. Martijn Konings has complained about recent work of a "constructivist" orientation that has not altogether escaped the dichotomy between government and a separate "market":

> [R]ecent work in political economy has taken up the theme of social construction in a somewhat abortive manner. Concerned not to end up in the muddy methodological waters of postmodernism, it has generally been reluctant to consider social construction as extending "all the way down" to the basic facts of economic life . . . It has tended to do so by retreating from the explanation of the internal structures and "technical" aspects of markets and focusing primarily on formal regulatory institutions . . . In this way, it has tended to employ a very restricted notion of construction, one that sees it as limited to the organizational environment of markets but does not really see it to be at the core of what our everyday experience of economic life is about. In the end, international political economy still presents us with a world of regulators and markets.[3]

It is not that many of these writers don't realize that neoliberalism has become entrenched at a very personal level of existence: indeed, Foucault is often credited with having insisted upon that very notion. However, the proposition, if contemplated at all, has mostly been explored at an austere level of abstraction—for instance, Foucault himself comments upon the theoretical writings of Gary Becker and the German ordoliberals; he was seemingly uninterested in how the dynamics actually played out at ground level. One might have expected Foucauldians to pursue that option; the next section inquires why this apparently hasn't happened. Consequently, as Konings suggests, it has not been the political theorists or philosophers who have made the greatest strides toward understanding everyday neoliberalism; rather, progress has been made by a motley clique from anthropology, business schools, marketing agencies, law schools, and cultural studies who have explored the contemporary contours of neoliberal consciousness.

It began more than three decades ago with a brace of studies concerned to understand creeping "commodification" of sex, children, body parts, and discourse itself.[4] One strain of this discussion initially lost its way by stumbling onto a quest for some "correct" ontological/moral criteria for the objects in question to qualify for quarantine in "separate spheres" of human existence away from the "market." In seeking to displace the vernacular revulsion concerning market encroachment on the sphere of the sacred with something else, many of these authors sought secular succor in social science, only quickly to encounter an obstacle in the shape of neoclassical economics, which by that time had pretty much dismantled any ontological distinctions between the "market" and the rest of social life. A sort of ineffectual disdain for economists combined with incongruous simultaneous recourse to their neoclassical concepts ("public goods," "efficiency vs. equity") grew up around some quarters, which only further induced ingrained misconceptions concerning political theory; subsequently, attempts to erect citadels against "market logic" then became bogged down and immobilized in the literatures of communitarianism and virtue ethics. I think it fair to say most of this literature had simply turned its back on the pertinence of the phenomenon of neoliberalism, which accounts for much of its ineffectual irrelevance.

Another, more productive line of inquiry eschewed spelunking the ontology of the commodity in favor of Radin's astute observation that questions of commodification would themselves rapidly devolve into questions of the nature of personhood; and this resonated with all manner of feminist scholars, anthropologists, and cultural studies advocates. As this contingent pursued their empirical explorations of recent alterations in what it meant to be a free and autonomous agent in the modern world, they increasingly found themselves brought back into confrontation with neoliberal political economy. Their writing was pitched just about as far from formal disciplinary economics as it is possible to go in the contemporary academy; perhaps it was this fact that allowed them to more directly access accounts of the NTC as germane to their concerns. Once they made the connection, they uncovered all manner of unexpected facets of the new personhood. It is their work that provides the fabric and texture of the current chapter.

They, and we, do not treat this construction of the neoliberal self as a monolithic *Weltanschauung* or cultural iron cage or industrial-scale brainwashing. Many people are sufficiently reflexive that they can and do catch glimpses of worlds outside the neoliberal ambit; they often indulge in bricolage to refurbish neoliberal materials into something else entirely; and of course, not every innovation emitted from the NTC has panned out or avoided intended consequences. Nevertheless, bulletins from the home front of modern agency do suggest we currently inhabit a quintessentially neoliberal era. This is a fact, not some cry of despair. Certainly it would be wrong to retreat to the easy slogan "there is no alternative," although the possibility of dereliction on the left is entertained later. Rather, we shall attempt in this chapter to explore the accretion of neoliberal attitudes, imaginaries, and practices that have come to inform everyday life in the first few decades of the new millennium.

It is predominantly the story of an entrepreneurial self equipped with promiscuous notions of identity and selfhood, surrounded by simulacra of other such selves. It tags every possible disaster as the consequences of risk-bearing, the personal fallout from making "bad choices" in investments. It is a world where competition is the primary virtue, and solidarity a sign of weakness. Consequently, it revels in the public shaming of the failed and the hapless. It replaces the time-honored ambition to "know yourself" with the exhortation to "express yourself," with everything the bunco shift in verbs implies. It counsels you to outsource the parts of your life you find irksome. The effect of this congeries of technologies, entertainments, mobilizations, and distractions has been first and foremost to reinforce the exoteric version of the neoliberal self, but more important, has served to so addle and discombobulate the populace that they end up believing that adoption of neoliberal notions constitutes wicked rebellion against the powers that be, corporations, and a corrupt political class. The nimble trick of portraying a neoliberal world as an insurgency always on the edge of defeat, a roiling rage against the system, the rebel bloom of dissent from a stodgy cronyism of corporate and government governance, not to mention the epitome of all futuristic hope, is the secret weapon of the Russian doll structure, deflecting the gale-force winds of prolonged economic contraction. It offers more, better neoliberalism as the counter to a sputtering neoliberalism, all the while disguising any acknowledgment of that fact. It is the promotion of ignorance as the neoliberal first line of defense.

Discipline and Furnish: Foucault on Neoliberalism

One of the better ways to become aware of everyday neoliberalism is to approach it from a slightly oblique angle. Many works of art have set out to do just that; one of my favorites is Gary Shteyngart's popular novel *Super Sad True Love Story*. The overarching narrative line of this vaguely futuristic novel involves the political collapse of the "American Restoration Authority" and a coup by a for-profit security firm, backed by Chinese investors in American government debt. But the author is less fixated upon such macro-level political science fiction than his plausible exaggerations of trends in the organization of everyday life. For instance, urban streets are equipped with "Poles" that give instant LED readouts of your credit ranking as you pass by, accompanied by personalized investment advice; the protagonist works for the Post Human Services Corporation, which provides unspecified rejuvenation services to those of advanced age (that is, over thirty) by means of prostheses. Everyone wears a device called an "apparat," which continually streams data between people in near proximity, and allow the user to FAC (Form a Community) on the fly by scanning a standardized set of statistics concerning compatibility, income, and history:

> Streams of data were now fighting for time and space around us. The pretty girl I had just FACed was projecting my MALE HOTNESS at 120 out of 800, PERSONALITY 450, and something called SUSTAINABILITY at 630. The other girls were sending me similar figures . . . The bar was now utterly aflash with smoky data spilling out of a total of fifty-nine apparati, 68 percent of them belonging to the male of the species. The masculine data scrolled on my screen. Our average income hovered at a respectable but not especially uplifting 190,000 yuan-pegged dollars. We were looking for girls who appreciated us for what we were.[5]

This might sound like a slightly less gloomy version of the Panopticon of Foucauldian fame; but in the novel, everyone just treats it as uninflected second nature, a logical pedestrian response to a set of desires that would naturally arise in any social setting. People are "free" to use the apparat or not; people are free to alter their personal peccadilloes that factor into the statistical summaries; people are even free to dissimulate and misrepresent their "true" selves, whatever those might be. Politics has become so outré that the possible impending collapse of the government is itself reduced to a set of abstract statistics, which the individual feeds into his strategic risk calculations on the apparat. Revolution is just another occasion for disaster porn and reshuffling the portfolio, rather than a transformation of history. Shteyngart does mention a few characters who recoil from using the apparat, but they are portrayed as backward Russians whose quaint obsessions date from a bygone era of buggy whips and communism.

I can imagine my reader poised to retort, "That was precisely Foucault's point!" Power is not simply exercised between the ruler and the ruled; it has been integrated directly into the makeup of modern agency, it fills up the pores of our most unremarkable day; it is the default option of our reflex assumptions about what others think and do. It gets under our skin; which is one way to try to understand what Foucault meant by his seductive term "biopolitics."[6] Yet, as I have already hinted, leaning on Foucault as a guide to everyday neoliberalism can be a treacherous proposition, at best.

First, let us accord him his due. Foucault read some of the most important members of the NTC, from the ordoliberals to Gary Becker, when it was highly unfashionable to do so. He did not simply recapitulate their writings, but rather drew out a range of stunning implications that ventured far beyond the exoteric knowledge then being broadcast by the collective. Accomplishing this back in 1979, he was the first to appreciate the vaunting ambition of neoliberals to recast not just markets and government, but the totality of human existence into a novel modality, to be disciplined and punished by structures of power/knowledge. He also insisted, contrary to their deceptive assertions, that it was no "return" to classical liberal principles: "Neoliberalism is not Adam Smith; neoliberalism is not market society."[7] He transcended the moralism of those who denounced the commodification of everyday life. The fact that he pursued these insights in lectures that were not further developed into full-blown texts before his death in 1984 accounts for the long delay in cognizance of that fact. (The current Foucault renaissance dates from posthumous publication of the Collège de France lecture transcripts over the past decade.) His perspicuity takes on greater significance in retrospect, since it is conventionally said that the political ascendancy of the neoliberals dates from the early 1980s. Figure 2.4 in chapter 2 also demonstrates that interest in the neoliberals (outside of the thought collective itself) was not widely common prior to that date. Thus, Foucault was reconnoitering a development in its infancy, one that most people in his circles had up till then ignored, and which has since proven to be far more consequential than it was in his own lifetime.

Let us venture even further in giving him his due. Foucault appears to have been the trailblazer when it came to insisting that power operates on the microlevel through the production of subjectivity in the multitude. He highlighted a number of phenomena characteristic of the neoliberal project that have since been topics of frequent commentary, when not taken as obvious. A short list (with citations to his lectures) would include:

> *A) The fragmentation of identity is attendant upon*
> *an entrepreneurial version of the self.*

The individual's life must be lodged, not within a framework of a big enterprise like the firm, or if it comes to it, the state, but within the framework of a multiplicity of diverse enterprises connected up to and entangled with each other . . . [It] must make him into a sort of permanent and multiple enterprise.[8]

> *B) An entrepreneurial regimen for the self will eventually extend*
> *the purview of its calculus to every conceivable social activity,*
> *and not just those narrowly oriented to pecuniary profit.*

This happens *because* it renders persons more susceptible to control, and not simply due to the profit motive. As Foucault put it, one extends the "grid, the schema, and the model of *Homo economicus* to not only every economic actor, but to every social actor in general inasmuch as he or she gets married, for example, or commits a crime, or raises children, gives affection and spends time with the kids . . . *Homo economicus* is someone who is eminently governable." Entrepreneurship was insensibly downgraded as a narrow societal function and redefined as a set of character traits.[9]

> *C) A stance of cold calculation of interest will eventually be*
> *reprocessed as a new, warm, soulful form of moral economy.*[10]

Quoting Margaret Thatcher: "Choice is the essence of ethics; good and evil only have meaning insofar as man is free to choose." In the neoliberal imagination, "faith-based charities" "were crowded out by the rise of the welfare state and would grow again . . . if government were to reduce its profile or remove itself entirely."[11]

> D) *"The malleability of the self presumed by the theory of human*
> *capital investment will extend down to the most basic corporeal level,*
> *which will eventually mean investment in genetic manipulation."*[12]

Foucault was the first to insist that Becker's "human capital" was a first move in the neoliberal disintegration of the self. This race to the empty bottom is the terminal meaning of "biocapital."

> E) *"The Entrepreneurial self cannot be passive, but must move strategically*
> *in a world rife with risk. Hence, reward and punishment are accepted by the*
> *agent as the outcome of calculated risks, not as the dictates of 'justice.'"*[13]

Casinos are not cynical scams taking advantage of the naïve and improvident; they are the practice tables for life. Risk is the oxygen for the entrepreneurial self, but also the means through which failure is leached of its political valence. The failed should accept the verdict of the market without complaint or pleas for help. Insecurity is the incubator for risk-loving behavior. The birth of actuarial tables is the death of tragedy.

> F) *Ignorance is the natural state of mankind, and the guarantor of*
> *neoliberal order. The neoliberal self is comfortable with this ignorance.*

"Everyone must be uncertain with regard to the collective outcome if this positive collective outcome is really to be expected. Being in the dark and blindness of all the economic agents is absolutely necessary ... Invisibility is absolutely indispensable. It is an invisibility which means that no economic agent should or can pursue the collective good. But we must no doubt go further than economic agents; not only no economic agent, but also no political agent ... You cannot because you do not know, and you do not know because you cannot know."[14] Ignorance as the linchpin of the neoliberal project was already stressed in the previous chapter. These quotes reveal that Foucault got there first.

There are undoubtedly further observations on the neoliberal approach to everyday life salted throughout the lectures; but these will suffice to demonstrate that Foucault was poised to elucidate the microstructures of a new sort of power. He was fascinated with the prospect that the classical liberal notion of a governmentalized "population" in a designated "territory," the very calling card of the prince, was being downsized and recast by neoliberalism through its transformation of the disciplined body into an autogoverned federation of temporary investments. However, in stark contrast to his previous writings, he was not teasing out the operation of power on the ground and under the skin, so to speak; instead, he was extrapolating certain trends from the theoretical writings of some of the most prominent members of the Neoliberal Thought Collective. These lectures did not resemble his prior texts, usually amply stocked with anthropological nuggets from archival sources. The shift in register was a little odd. It was as if he had taken in his waning years to writing the ethnography of the twenty-second century by reading H. G. Wells's *The Time Machine*.[15] Or, to clumsily switch metaphors in midstream, it was as if Foucault were thumbing through an IKEA catalog, trying to decide what sort of deck chairs to order, without paying any attention to whether the furniture would come assembled, or indeed, whether he was furnishing the deck of the *Titanic* or the *QE2*. (Foucault compares governmentality to the piloting of a ship in *The Birth of Biopolitics*.)

I am not the first to demur that Foucault's treatment of neoliberalism leaves something to be desired. It seems that a few scholars are coming around to the position that Foucault managed to be so very prescient with regard to everyday neoliberalism precisely because he took on board such a large amount of the neoliberal doctrine as a font of deep insight into the nature of governmentality. Although he would never have openly adopted the normative stance, he was converging on the assessment that it was "right," at least as description of the contemporary *dispositif*.[16] Again, to be clear, I am not accusing Foucault of being a member of the Neoliberal Thought Collective—an absurd counterfactual—but rather, suggesting that he shared quite a bit of common ground with their doctrines, and was coming to appreciate that incongruous fact toward the end of his life.

The main common denominator of the later Foucault and the neoliberals was located in the attitude toward economics. Earlier, in *Les Mots et les Choses*, Foucault had treated political economy as just another epiphenomenon of the episteme, on a par with philology and natural history.[17] By the time we get to *The Birth of Biopolitics*, somehow the economy had become elevated as the privileged locus of the "site of truth": the Archimedean point that allows a critique of autocratic state power. "The possibility of limitation and the question of truth are both introduced into governmental reason through political economy . . . it was political economy that made it possible to ensure

the self-limitation of governmental reason." And not just any old political economy. Supposedly lacking a market, Foucault denied that
socialism had ever possessed its own governmentality or governmental
rationality. It was not Marx, but Adam Smith and Röpke and Hayek,
that Foucault identified as the key tradition in governmentality.[18]

One way to interpret this is to say that the cast of historical figures
in capitalist societies operated within a regime of truth that elevated
the construct identified as "the economy" to pride of place in their
exercise of power; and further, the appeal to self-limitation was a
means to their expansion of power; but that does not correspond to
what appears in the lectures. Rather, Foucault seeks to interrogate
government as the assemblage of techniques, beliefs, practices, and
excuses that try to maintain order; but he leaves "the economy" as the
independent Representative of the Real, a placeholder without inter-
rogation or even any description. The market as portrayed by Foucault
in his late lectures on neoliberalism is the *sole legitimate site for the production of indubitable knowledge of the whole*; in other words, an absent deity
rendered in a manner no different from Hayek or Stigler or Friedman
or Buchanan. The "market" (always referenced as a monolithic entity)
provides the boundary condition for governmentality, because it alone
knows things we can never know. It offers nonstop cogent critique of
the pretensions of the state. Far from a ramshackle Rube Goldberg
device, it is instead constituted as the Delphic Oracle, capable of interpreting our every dream. Apparently, by 1979 Foucault had abstained
from casting his characteristic gimlet eye on the historical constructs
that give our life meaning, at least when it came to the economy.

If I had to summarize where the otherwise prescient Foucault took
a wrong turn, it was in too readily swallowing the basic neoliberal
precept that the market was an information processor more powerful
and encompassing than any human being or organization of humans.
What Foucault missed were the critical notions of double truths
outlined at the end of the last chapter. The neoliberals preach that the
market is the unforgiving arbiter of all political action; *but they absolve
themselves from its rule*. They propound libertarian freedoms but practice the most regimented hierarchy in their political organization; they
sermonize about spontaneous order, while plotting to take over the
state; they catechize prostration of the self before the awesome power
of the knowledge conveyed by the market, but issue themselves sweeping dispensations. Most significantly, they reserve to themselves the right
of deployment of the Schmittian exception. Their version of governmentality elevates the market as a site of truth *for everyone but themselves*.

If Foucault had taken this to heart, he would have had to revise his portrait of how regimes of truth validate power.

I leave it to others to sort through the biographical record to try to figure out the motives and considerations that may have steered Foucault in the direction of the neoliberals.[19] In this book, Foucault's acquiescence in the neoliberal doctrine of the market as über–information processor renders him pretty useless for our discussions of the crisis. The point of relevance for our present concerns is that Foucault's lectures reproduced an asymmetry between the "state" and the "market" that smacks far more of the exoteric caricature promoted by Mont Pèlerin, rather than its internal esoteric understanding. We who acknowledge his acuity and foresight should nevertheless doubt his understanding of everyday neoliberalism, precisely because of this drawback. As Tellmann puts it, in a further play on Foucault's own evocation of the "invisible hand":

> Only that which does not exhibit its particularity can be assumed to be universal; only an invisible market can promise viable sight. The . . . invisibility of the market is directed against the very analytical perspective Foucault typically assumes, one aimed at detecting the instruments, positions and architectures that produce epistemological claims and privileges. A more typical Foucauldian approach would commence to undo the invisibility of the economy and the market as an invisible "telescope" and "information machine." This would mean rendering visible the market's own "machine of seeing," rather than seeing like the unseen market itself. [20]

This is how I would suggest we should read the disdain of authors like Clive Barnett concerning the way Foucault has been frequently married to critiques of neoliberalism in countless screeds.[21] As we have observed, many authors of a Marxist bent want to portray neoliberalism as the simple deployment of class power over the unsuspecting masses, but encounter difficulty in specifying the chains of causality stretching from the elusive executive committee of the capitalist class down to the shopper at Wal-Mart. To paper over the gap, many reach for Foucault and "governmentality" to evoke how shifts from state to market are modulated in the microcontexts of everyday life. But of course, the later Foucault abjured their Marxism; and furthermore, his own appeals to the hard discipline of the market merely recapitulated the invisible hand jive of the neoliberals themselves. The incompatibility with Marxism should have been blindingly obvious, since dissolving all labor into entrepreneurialism of the self thoroughly undermines any Marxist concepts of exploitation and surplus value, and therefore, much else besides. In any event, Foucault disavowed any such use of his work for most of his career: "We must cease once and for all to describe the effects of power in negative terms: it 'excludes,' it 'represses,' it 'masks,' it 'conceals.' In fact, power produces reality; it produces domains of objects and rituals of truth."[22] By the time of *The Birth of Biopolitics*, Foucault denied any efficacy to the modern conscious intent on the part of anyone to exert political power, because the market effectively thwarts it.[23] This comes dangerously close to subsequent platitudes that the crisis was no one's fault, because it was everyone's fault. That train of thought just paralyzes analysis.

There is even a deeper reason to hesitate when it comes to biopolitics. Foucault also declines to allow that agents are somehow bamboozled by power/knowledge, since the market is posited to exist in a privileged epistemological space with special position in the regime of truth. The fact that neoliberal concepts such as human capital seep into the daily lives of those perched outside the NTC is just evidence that the entire system of power/knowledge works: autogovernance of the entrepreneurial self is not a puppet show, but rather the wherewithal of how modern agents bring the truth of the world into their own lives. Paraphrasing Walter Benjamin, modern neoliberal citizens must learn to forget about their "rights" and be given free rein to "express themselves," especially through the greatest information-conveyance device known to mankind, the market. This is very nearly what Foucault himself believed:

> People rebel, that is a fact. In this way subjectivity (and not just that of great men but of any given person) enters into history and breathes life into it. A prisoner sets her life against excessive punishment. A mentally ill person does not want to be incarcerated and robbed of rights. A people sets itself against a regime that oppresses it. In this way, the prisoner does not become innocent, the mentally ill person does not become healthy, and the people do not take part in the promised future. And no one must show solidarity with them. No one must believe that these voices might sing more beautifully than others and pronounce the final truth. It is enough that they are there and that everything attempts to silence them in order that it becomes meaningful to want to listen to them and understand what they say . . . Because such voices exist, the era of humans does not have the form of evolution, but of history.[24]

It is not so much that resistance is futile for Foucault, as it is that the audience for leftist rebellion is fickle. Truth is a mobile army of metaphors. Empathy has the half-life of the time it takes to click the remote control. And for recovering post-structuralists, things don't really change.

Our approach in this volume will be different. We shall maintain there is no such thing as "the market" as monolithic entity, and in any case, it does not come equipped with supernatural powers of truth production. Markets don't "validate" truth; rather, markets are the product of struggles over the truth. Furthermore, Foucault was just dead wrong about neoliberalism as fostering the autolimitation of state power. He bought into the exoteric doctrine that the market is the backstop of the state, keeping it in check. The state has not been limited in purview by the neoliberal response to crisis, but instead, has greatly expanded its role, in finance, in "picking winners," and in the discipline of citizens through the further injection of neoliberal themes into everyday life. The Schmittian usurpation of power has been formidable. The jumble that gets lumped together as "the market" is constructed on the fly in such situations; and it is as much a bricolage as its counterpart, the neoliberal construct of the self. Both are not constructed top-down, from blueprints kindly supplied by Mont Pèlerin, nor bottom-up through the aimless evolution of the kosmos, but rather outward, in trial-and-error mutual adjustment of the politically fortified market and the everyday entrepreneurial self.

We take as our fugleman not Foucault but rather people such as Martijn Konings, Carolyn Sissoko, Yves Smith, and Christopher Payne, who insist that the crisis was not some aberration due to over-enthusiastic deregulation, but instead the expression of intrinsic system pathologies. This chapter explores the way those pathologies were embedded in the very everyday neoliberalism that has become so prevalent since the 1980s. Foucault's concentration on micropower had an unfortunate tendency to keep the noses of his followers too close to the ground, and hence to ignore how the entrepreneurial self was then recruited into all sorts of innovations that took place on the phenomenological level of markets. Exquisite discipline of the self was treated as hapless if it did not make money for someone even more entrepreneurial than you. The mechanisms that culminated in the crisis were built upon foundations of the entrepreneurial self, from exhortations to surrender to the risk of thrill-ride mortgages, capitulation to the financialization of everyday life, participation in virtual selves wending their way through the "weight-less economy" on the Internet, day trading like the big boys, getting your information from Facebook and Fox and talk radio, to the indulgences of entertainment theology as Ponzi scheme, and recruit-ment into astroturfed politics to assist you in expressing your smoldering yet underappreciated individuality. Everyone strove to assume a persona that someone else would be willing to invest in, all in the name of personal improvement.

Found yourself in trouble? You could always sell a kidney or enroll in a drug trial . . . Maybe you could rent your body as surrogate mother, or maybe resort to just a little strategic intimacy, with discreet recompense on the side[25] . . . Wait! Someone from India is already calling you on the phone to offer you an even more outrageously far-fetched baroque loan! And there's an app for that . . . Just make the leap of faith . . . Make some money in your spare time! Unemploy-ment is an unbidden golden opportunity to start anew with an entirely different life! Don't let the moochers and complainers drag you down! Become your own boss, after you embrace the power of positive thinking . . . Didn't you always want to start your own business, after working a quarter-century for corporations?

We will close with the ultimate in solipsism in promotion of every-day neoliberalism: Don't like the way things are looking? Has the state of the world got you down? Then create your own personal solipsistic economy, a fit virtual abode for your own fragmented entrepreneurial identity.[26] That's the ultimate in self-reliance.

Mine Eyes Have Seen the Glory of the Coming of the Galt

Foucault refuses to allow that people may be mired in "false conscious-ness," or to concede that there are means by which they may become instilled with systematically distorted beliefs about both themselves and their place in the social order, distractions that work in regular ways against their own interests and welfare. There have been a fair number of writers who assert the contrary; one worth considering because he has been specifically concerned with political develop-ments in the last three decades in the United States is Thomas Frank. In his breakthrough book *What's the Matter with Kansas?* he posed the question in a rather American idiom: Why had the blue-collar work-ing class abandoned the Democratic Party in favor of voting for snake-oil neoliberal salesmen who had demonstrated open contempt for their welfare? Or as he himself put it:

All they have to show for their Republican loyalty are lower wages, more dangerous jobs, dirtier air, a new overlord class that comports itself like King Farouk—and of course, a crap culture whose moral free fall continues, without significant interference from the grandstanding Christers whom they send triumphantly back to Washington every couple of years.[27]

Frank's answer to his own question was, crudely, a version of "bait and switch" that subsequently gained a fair level of acceptance among circles of the U.S. left, at least before the crisis. He suggested that the working class had gotten distracted by a constant harping on a broad range of cultural and religious issues, fired up through talk-radio raving and local pulpits, and thus overlooked or displaced their more direct economic concerns: they were mesmerized by "cultural wedge issues like guns and abortion and the rest whose hallucinatory appeal would ordinarily be far overshadowed by material concerns." In this diagnosis, the median voter mistook the froth of "values" for denunciation of sharp dealing dedicated to stealing away their livelihoods.[28]

There are all manner of reasons to be skeptical of the bait-and-switch account of "false consciousness" when it comes to the triumph of neoliberalism. The least of these caveats came when economists were promptly scandalized by the very notion that *Homo economicus* could ever suspend his assiduous calculation of economic advantage under any circumstances whatsoever, and therefore proceeded to deny there was any phenomenological world of values outside of the political marketplace; some rather unimaginative souls consequently engaged in all manner of statistical wizardry to demonstrate that true-blue American agents had never once disregarded their legitimate "economic" interests.[29] Another, more pertinent complaint against Frank would be that the simplistic dichotomy of Republican vs. Democratic parties did not begin to capture the phenomenon beating at the heart of the transformation; Frank had himself admitted elsewhere that party affiliation does not easily translate into what he calls "market populism," which has infected both parties (*One Market Under God*). The obsession with Red/Blue scores inside the Beltway tends to diverts us from the real issue of the cultural framing of political consciousness. And then there was the onset of the crisis itself: here was an economic catastrophe so great that no one, no matter how beguiled and hornswoggled, could long avert their eyes. And yet, with their minds focused forcibly on economic matters, still the electorate was persuaded to respond to it in ways reminiscent of the earlier decade: great masses of voters under the sway of the putative Tea Party had in 2010 voted in the most neoliberal Congress of all time.

Probably the best indication that the crisis has deep-sixed most simple "bait and switch" accounts of the success of neoliberalism is that Tom Frank himself had to walk back his earlier thesis in his postcrisis book *Pity the Billionaire*. By that, I do not intend to suggest Frank openly admitted he was wrong in *Kansas*, but rather, he did rather concede that the Tea Party and other redoubts of revanchism were avoiding issues of social conservatism in favor of defending "freedom" against creeping socialism. Frank in effect had to face up to the fact that his earlier book was incapable of addressing the nagging question that is also the topic of the current chapter: "What kind of misapprehension permits the newest Right to brush off truths that everyone else can see so plainly?"[30]

The problem with bait-and-switch accounts is that they compartmentalize everyday experience in a way that utterly misconstrues how neoliberalism works. Tom Frank in an earlier incarnation had seemingly understood this: "Making the world safe for billionaires has been as much a cultural and political operation as an economic one"; it was only when he artificially set them at odds that he attained best-sellerdom with *Kansas*, but at the price of losing his way. The core insight of the Neoliberal Thought Collective was that the cultural and the economic should not be treated as substitutes, much less discrete spheres of experience, but rather, as integrated into a virtuous whole: surrender your selfish arrogance and humbly prostrate yourself before the Wisdom of the Universe, as nurtured and conveyed by the market. "Be all you can be" had jettisoned the injunction to "know yourself" and replaced it with "Start your own business!" even if it only meant homeschooling your children. As religion took on more of the trappings of just-in-time provision of entertainment services, and "values" assumed the mix-and-match character of Do It Yourself bricolage, the materiality of rock-solid "interests" melted into thin air. After all, neoliberals deny that you are the unimpeachable judge of your own welfare, however much they worship at the altar of Freedom. The more the line between "The Sphere Previously Known as the Economic" and culture or religion was progressively obscured and erased, the more irreversible the neoliberal long march. Conversely, if citizens believed that the game was rigged and the fix was in, now the only way they could manage to express it would be with variants upon the dogma that the Government was encroaching upon the ever-flexible and blameless Me. Collective nouns were being slowly leached from usage in the language. The ideal neoliberal agent was a person who didn't even need to know she was neoliberal, because the various aspects of her selfhood were conceived as being in natural harmony with the totality of the kosmos, whether she consciously aspired to be wicked vanguard rebel or placid conformist. As Foucault so aptly summarized it, "There is no first or final point of resistance to political power other than in the relationship of self to self."[31]

This may explain why Frank's *Pity the Billionaire* comes off as such a letdown: he senses that something deep and structural is permitting the neoliberals to escape scot-free from the crisis, and it possibly has something to do with general comprehension of everyday life, but the best he can muster is endless sneering jibes launched at Glenn Beck and Ayn Rand. He can't be bothered to immerse himself in what the neoliberal theorists and right-wing economists have written, and consequently misconstrues neoliberalism as the most superficial "roll-back of the state"; in the language of the previous chapter, he never gets beyond the exoteric doctrines of the thought collective. Worse, he then attributes the political strength of the neoliberal resurgence to the superficial facts that many in the Tea Party get their information only from Beck and Fox News, combined with the notion that hoi polloi expected some breast-beating and bankster-roasting after the crisis, but that the Democratic Party declined to provide it. He quotes, but does not take to heart, the ambition of the leader of the Koch-funded Freedom Works, Dick Armey, "not just to learn from their opponents on the left, but to beat them at their own game."[32]

The Rise of the Neoliberal Agent is not very easy to gloss, by any means. Anytime one resorts to Belief/Action scenarios, three centuries of philosophical qualifications loom, not to mention social psychology as indicated in chapter 1, threatening to freeze the argument in its tracks. And then there are the various objections that harry the attempt to draw determinants from political considerations. There is the recurrent unwillingness in giving up hard and fast distinctions between the economy and the world of the spirit, as we have been describing. There is the crucial distinction between the esoteric and exoteric versions of neoliberal doctrine, as outlined in the last chapter. The average person may be encouraged to believe all sorts of things about the government that have no correspondence to the esoteric neoliberal playbook, or untethered from any facts, for instance, and this is a key aspect of the construction of a viable neoliberal self under the sway of the double-truth doctrine. The average citizen severely underestimates the amount of their livelihood that comes from the government; and are utterly deluded about their current place in the distribution of income and wealth. There is the wild card of globalization: How much of the outlines of neoliberal agency has been contingent upon the cultures of the hegemonic centers of capital, curious artifacts of the parochial peccadilloes of its incubators, and how much can be regarded as a new model for cosmopolitan existence in a world that persists in thinking it shrugs off the trappings of the nation-state? There is a literature, located particularly in anthropology, which preaches that cosmopolitan aspirations of neoliberal "reforms" are deceptive, because more often than not they are predicated upon minor reconfigurations of long-standing local practices.[33] And then there is the difficult question of just to what extent these particular innovations in agency are relatively new, and how much they come lumbered with a long, hallowed heritage, which obviously intersects with the question of the extent to which the NTC can legitimately appeal to small-c "conservatism" in its older Burkean sense. Does the neoliberal self have an archetype, or a birthday? With everyone from *Jesus CEO* to the "Founding Fathers" undergoing retreads, facelifts, and résumé rewrites, challenging the historical authenticity of many of the icons of neoliberal selfhood could become a full-time operation on its own.

These questions are all important, and deserve serious consideration, but this chapter is not the place to attempt to settle them. Friedrich Hayek once claimed to be able to separate "true" liberalism from its "false" pretender; I have far less confidence in my own ability to accomplish anything similar for neoliberalism. My more limited goal here is to establish some of the most salient facets of neoliberalism with a human face in the early twenty-first century. It is far too premature to write the definitive biography of the neoliberal self, so in lieu of comprehensive cultural history, perhaps we can peruse a few quotidian snapshots from various angles and profiles. Think of it as Five or So Vignettes on the Life and Times of John Galt.

The proof of the project will not come in adherence to some Identikit notion of accuracy, but rather with personal recognition of the subconscious prompts that lurk in each of our own lives, the attitudes that have grown to be the unremarkable furniture of waking life, and their possible instrumentality when it comes down to acquiescence in the neoliberal wisdom of crowds. The advent of the neoliberal way of being quite literally transforms the subject, and consequently, inhibits all tendencies to interpret the crisis as a system-wide failure of economic organization.

Five Vignettes from the Life of John Galt

A) The Freedom That Comes from Fragmentation.

The Neoliberal Thought Collective, as suggested in the last chapter, interprets freedom in a largely negative fashion, while simultaneously elevating freedom as the ultimate value. While this observation has become commonplace in the literature on political philosophy, that commentary has been strangely silent on how neoliberals have come to abjure or otherwise avoid the salience of positive liberty. The key to comprehension of the neutralization of time-honored traditions of positive liberty comes with the progressive fragmentation of the self, both in economic theory and in everyday life. The moral quest to discover your one and only "true self" has been rendered thoroughly obsolete by the reengineering of everyday life, and that, in turn, is the *fons et origo* of most characteristics of everyday neoliberalism.

I start with the notion that definitions of private property are bound up with the presumed definition of the self. The classical liberal approach to this question has been admirably summarized by Margaret Radin:

> I have used the term "personal property" to refer to categories of property that we understand to be bound up with the self in a way that we understand to be morally justifiable . . . Since personal property is connected with the self, morally justifiably, in a constitutive way, to disconnect it from the person (from the self) harms or destroys the self. The more something takes on the indicia of an attribute or characteristic of the self, or at least the self as the person herself would wish, the more problematic it seems to alienate it . . .[34]

Radin builds upon this observation to argue in favor of imposition of spheres of "incomplete commodification," and to prohibit some markets altogether, such as the selling of human infants. The Rosetta Stone of neoliberalism rejects the basic premise of this version of liberalism, not only by denying that any such spheres should exist, but more important, insisting *there is no self that is harmed by the creation and alienation of private property.* Indeed, one might reasonably wonder if there is much of any Archimedean Self whatsoever in the neoliberal game plan. Absent such a self, there is nothing left of a "positive" notion of freedom to preserve and protect.

This analysis may seem incorrigibly bloodless and abstract, but it is not. The banishment of the core unified self is experienced daily in a thousand different ways by every single person who holds down a job, gets ejected from a job, gets sick, surfs the Internet, sits in a classroom, embarks on a love affair, watches a movie, emulates a celebrity, or starts a family. The news is brought home in most instances wherein someone is forced to juggle multiple roles in social situations, and discovers that the demands of one role contradict or belie those of another. Of course, the insight that the self may be internally conflicted is nowise new or deep; neither is the notion of adoption of multiple personas distinguished by context; nevertheless, the routinization and stand-ardization of denial of a true invariant self has become a hallmark of modern life. It is the sheer ordinariness of the expectation that the self should provide no obstacle to success because it is supple, modular, and plastic that is the germ of everyday neoliberalism. The traces of the vanishing self are of course pervasive in economic life, but are by no means confined to it.

The fragmentation of the neoliberal self begins when the agent is brought face to face with the realization that she is not just an employee or student, but also simultaneously a product to be sold, a walking advertisement, a manager of her résumé, a biographer of her rationales, and an entrepreneur of her possibilities. She has to some-how manage to be simultaneously subject, object, and spectator. She is perforce *not* learning about who she really is, but rather, provision-ally buying the person she must soon become. She is all at once the business, the raw material, the product, the clientele, and the customer of her own life. She is a jumble of assets to be invested, nurtured, managed, and developed; but equally an offsetting inven-tory of liabilities to be pruned, outsourced, shorted, hedged against, and minimized. She is both headline star and enraptured audience of her own performance. These are not effortless personas to be adopted, but roles to be fortified and regimented on a continuous basis. As Foucault insisted, the neoliberal self dissolves the distinction between producer and consumer. Furthermore, there is no preset hierarchy of resident personas, but only a shifting cast of characters, depending upon the exigencies of the moment. The *summum bonum* of modern agency is to present oneself as eminently *flexible* in any and all respects.[35]

This kind of everyday wisdom is so pervasive that one tends to notice it only in cases of extreme parody, such as that reported by Siva Vaidhyanathan:

In his manual for a better (or, at least, for his own) life, *The 4-Hour Workweek: Escape 9–5, Live Anywhere, and Join the New Rich*, self-help guru and Silicon Valley entrepreneur Timothy Ferriss outlines his secrets to a productive and wealthy life. One of the book's central tenets is to "outsource everything." Ferriss suggests we hire a series of concierges to triage our correspondences, arrange travel and restaurant reservations, contact old friends, and handle routine support tasks in our lives. Ferriss contracts with concierge companies in India to handle much of his data flow. He suggests we hire local people to take our clothes to the cleaners, scrub our floors, and cook for us.

Ferriss has become a guru to the geek set, as I witnessed at the book-signing event for his hefty fitness manual, *The 4-Hour Body*, at the 2011 South by Southwest Interactive meeting in Austin, Texas. A line of more than one hundred remarkably unkempt, unfit young men waited to shake Ferriss's hand and thank him for releasing them from the bonds of the full-time working grind. They can't all be working four-hour weeks, I thought. My understanding of work life in the tech sector leads me to believe that retrieving the *forty*-hour week would be a major personal, if not indeed a political, victory. Ferriss greeted fanboys for more than an hour that day, leaving him a mere three more hours of actual work before the fun began. As if to emphasize his mastery over his life and the better times he had waiting for him upon his release from the event, Ferriss held hands with a striking young woman who looked as if she could not wait to be relieved of this duty to dazzle young men with whom she would rather not make eye contact. It was not clear if that young woman was part of Ferriss's outsourced personal labor force. But she certainly did not seem thrilled to be part of his commercial branding effort.

Ferriss's life is his brand, his data, his evidence, his project. In his books he shares—no, sells—every feature of his daily life, including details of ejaculations and defecations. Every aspect of Ferriss's life is on the market, just as he engages with market transactions to advance many of his professional and personal aims.[36]

This was a quantum leap beyond the social psychology of an Erving Goffmann, merely the age-old challenge of the staged presentation of the self in everyday life. Living in the material world these days means that one must maintain a rather strained, distanced relationship to the self, since one must be prepared to shed the current pilot at a moment's notice. Due to the shifting cast of characters with their complements of accessories, technologies, and emotional attachments, it is never altogether clear whom precisely is managing the menagerie. Outsourced components of the self still need to report to something more than a post office box on some distant offshore platform.[37] Integration and coordination may sometimes need to take a backseat to innovation and appropriation. Self-care must be balanced against the dictum that bygones are bygones, or in more economic terms, sunk costs should never be entered into calculation of expected future revenues. The weight of history is more often than not considered a burden of little consequence for the entrepreneurial agent, something that can be repudiated and reversed. The stipulation of flexibility militates against treating any aspect of the self as indispensible; taken to extremes, this can resemble out-of-body experience or asomatoagnosia.

Ethnographers of everyday life have noted these effects in societies that have been severely disrupted by economic downsizing and roiled by neoliberal modernization. For instance, those seeking employment must learn to regard themselves as a "bundle of skills" for which they bear sole responsibility. Over time, the language of "skills" has transmigrated away from older notions of craft mastery, and toward a vague set of "life skills," "communication skills," and a range of related euphemisms for amenability to enter into temporary alliances with others, and to accept all forms of supervision. "Soft skills discourses are largely about persuading workers that these skills are what they are made of." One no longer simply contracts to supply quantities of abstract labor; rather, one commits to a willingness to alter one's very quiddity in an ongoing adjustment of agency to the requirements of social and physical adaptability to shifting market forces. Emily Martin has demonstrated how such techniques are inculcated in management training, while Barbara Ehrenreich documents the ways that the recently unemployed are exhorted to forget their past and become a different person. The mortal sin denounced by unemployment counseling is to blame your status on some immotile attribute of the self, even one that might seem impervious to change, such as chronological age. She quotes the counselor at a boot camp for the white-collar unemployed: "It's all internal—whether you're sixty-two or forty-two or twenty-two . . . It's never about the external world. It's always between you and you." Unless you can be split in twain and still discern your center of gravity, the "internal" threatens to become unmoored from any coordinates whatsoever.[38]

In Alcoholics Anonymous, one is taught to chant: "God, give us the grace to accept with serenity the things that cannot be changed, courage to change the things which should be changed, and the wisdom to distinguish the one from the other." Neoliberals go Niebuhr one better by deleting the first and last clauses as superfluous. This is illustrated by interviews conducted with corporate counselors by Elaine Swan:

> I don't think there is such a thing as a false self . . . It's [instead] expanding their choices and options. So there's no false self. There's just limited awareness and the options we have at any one time . . . It's not false, it's out of date. So they just come in for an upgrade. My job is to create an upgrade of their life that is structured in such a way—if I use that computer metaphor—that it will have an inbuilt self-updating ability.[39]

These technologies of the self are drilled into every supplicant from something as small as how you arrange your dress and grooming to something as large as how you "choose" to invest your life with meaning. A major technology for self-constitution can be something as simple as how you dress: "Proper management of one's external appearances simply signals to one's superiors that one is prepared to undertake other kinds of self-adaptation." At the other end of the scale, espousal of a religion of well-entrenched denomination is treated as one of the best techniques for demonstrating self-care and willingness to refashion one's identity. One of the most effective means of networking with other itinerant entrepreneurial selves is through vaguely denominational prayer meetings for businessmen. As for laborers in the service sector, the "feminization" of the workforce through part-time casualized work with erosion of seniority and benefits has been recast as a "blending of service, shopping and religion"; the imposition of personal flexibility in organizations such as Wal-Mart is rendered bearable as a commitment to "family values." Rehab, retreats, and five-step programs are on offer for people who lose their bearings in juggling and altering their multiple selves, as we will observe below. The most common prescription for identity breakdown is—what else?—yet more intensified entrepreneurialism of the self.[40]

The plasticity of the self is not only demonstrated in employment settings, but also in the so-called private sphere of everyday life. Arlie Hochschild describes a smorgasbord of possibilities in her *Outsourced Self*. Some more entertaining examples of self-outsourcing include:

hiring a "nameologist" so you won't inadvertently give your offspring monikers that condemn them to lives of "weight problems" or "poverty syndrome"; spending dough on a "coordinator" for your child's fifth birthday party so kindergartners won't get bored; paying a "wantologist" to help you align your perceived needs to what you can afford; and handing over $2,000 to a consulting outfit called Family/360 that rates your parenting skills on a scorecard and then draws up an action plan of "best practices" to help you create more positive "family memories" for your children. You can pay someone to look in on your elderly father at the nursing home, and you can pay someone else to provide a personally tailored funeral for him after he goes—such as a Nascar-themed casket "or a biodegradable one, for the environmentally conscious." Too busy or too lazy to scatter your departed father's ashes into the ocean yourself? Maritime Funeral Services on Long Island will do that for you. But these still reside in the more conventional realm of the service economy.

One of the most studied examples of the rise of neoliberal agency is the behavior of people while surfing the Internet. The popular press has been besotted with notions that the Web has turned the provision of information upside down, and in the process has altered our humanity. Horror stories of online characters misrepresenting their identity are rife in our culture; but one needs to get past the simplistic moralism to discover that the Internet has become a testbed of simulation practice for the modern fragmented self. It is not just that on the Web no one knows whether you're a dog; it is that most people have embraced this technology to give them the sense of what it feels like to mimic a convincing canine. Starting with rudimentary chat sites, and moving on to the Game of Life, Second Life, Facebook, Twitter, LinkedIn, and the rest, one can experience the thrill and the danger of tailoring one's identity to the fleeting demands of the moment.[41]

There are so many different instrumentalities of simulation and dissimulation on the Web that they cannot be comprehensively surveyed here. To offer just a truncated indicator, we can point to the neoliberal technology par excellence, Facebook. Facebook is the ultimate in reflexive apparatus: it is a wildly successful business that teaches its participants how to turn themselves into a flexible entrepreneurial identity. Even though Facebook sells much of the information posted to it, it stridently maintains that all responsibility for fallout from the Facebook wall devolves entirely to the user. It forces the participant to construct a "profile" from a limited repertoire of relatively stereotyped materials, challenging the person to somehow attract "friends" by tweaking their offerings to stand out from the vast run of the mill. It incorporates subtle algorithms that force participants to regularly change and augment their profiles, thus continuously destabilizing their "identity," as well as inducing real-time metrics to continuously monitor their accumulated "friends" and numbers of "hits" on their pages. It distills the persona down to a jumble of unexplained tastes and alliances, the mélange of which requires the constant care and management by an entity that bears some tenuous relationship to the persona uploaded, but who must maintain an assured clear distance from it. Facebook profiles then feed back into "real life": employers scan Facebook pages of prospective employees, parents check the pages of their children, lovers check Facebook pages for evidence of philandering. As the consequences of multiple personas of indeterminate provenance proliferate, the solution for Facebook problems is always more tinkering on Facebook.[42] If you don't like the profile you made, you can attempt to erase it, but with only indifferent success. It is a scale model of the neoliberal self, and most instructively, it makes a profit.

As Turkle so deftly puts it, on the Internet, in solitude, one discovers new intimacy; and in prior intimacies, the Internet offers new solitudes:

> Brad says, only half jokingly, that he worries about getting "confused" between what he "composes" for his online life and who he "really" is. Not yet confirmed in his identity, it makes him anxious to post things about himself that he doesn't really know are true. It burdens him that the things he says online affect how people treat him in the real. People already relate to him based on things he has said on Facebook. Brad struggles to be more "himself" there, but this is hard.[43]

Contemporary fascination with the virtual online world may foster the impression that the neoliberal demolition of the self is primarily notional or psychological, happening only in cyberspace; but that would be an unfortunate error. Modern culture is, if anything, even more obsessed with the reconfiguration and dismemberment of the physical body than it is with the reformation of the soul. The corporeal self should be rendered as plastic and malleable as "skills" or "attitudes" if it is yield to the entrepreneurial gaze. The endless exhortation to undergo self-improvement extends not just to raiment and grooming, but cuts to the corporeal level. Everyone is of course prodded to lose weight and redistribute body mass; but if that isn't sufficient, then there begin the intrusive procedures of liposuction, botox, plastic surgery, and implants. While the quest for a pleasing demeanor is ancient (including piercings and primitive tattoos), and many cosmetic surgical practices were innovated in reconstructive surgery dating from the nineteenth century, the treatment of the body as raw material for the sculptor's knife in pursuit of a different self is relatively recent, and its credibility heavily indebted to neoliberal notions of self-improvement. The inducements to carve the body in the name of speculative enhancement serves to teach many people the basic principles of neoliberalism at a visceral level, people who might otherwise never give a second thought to political theory or economic imperatives. Furthermore, corporeal reconstruction of the self is not skin-deep, but extends down to the organs and very cells, as we discuss in section E. Tom Frank extracted the eventual terminus of this logic from an article in *Forbes*: "Cannibalize yourself."[44]

While we shall indict orthodox neoclassical economics from time to time as having a less-than-sure grasp on phenomena it seeks to portray, it must be said that neoliberal orthodox economists have closely shadowed the phenomenal fragmentation of the everyday self in their theoretical lucubrations. Starting with the MPS member Gary Becker's *Human Capital* (1964), these economists have decentered the supposedly rock-solid *Homo economicus* as avidly as the Internet has decentered the coherence of *Homo sapiens*. Since 1870, there had been a long history of identification of the integrity of the individual with the invariance of the so-called utility function (with many detours into various notions of consilience of this formalism with neoclassical economists' imperfect understanding of various psychological theories, all of which we can thankfully avoid here); but with the advent of Becker's human-capital theory, it became permissible to blur the boundaries of the "individual" by incorporating all manner of variables representing other "people" into the utility function, and more pertinent, to begin manipulating variables representing "embodied" personal attributes also within this rapidly ballooning utility function. Once the original integrity of the utility function was breached, then effectively anything became fair game as occasion for legitimate agent self-alteration; and voilà, the agent in formal economics submitted to fragmentation as intense as that experienced by the denizen of Late Neoliberalism. Economics ceased to be concerned with conventional economic questions, and claimed purview over any and all attempts of the agent at self-fashioning: drug addiction, marriage, divorce, suicide, gender bending, religion, theology, abortion, changes in preferences, and eventually, the names one chooses to designate oneself.[45]

Curiously enough, just as the fragmented personality in everyday neoliberalism experiences some difficulty in specifying who or what remains at the helm of agency, elaborations upon and extrapolations of the Incredibly Promiscuous Utility Function eventually led formal economic theory to unrestrained Bedlam.[46] *Homo economicus* was not so much "atomistic" as atomized in the mathematics. The conceptual problem with human capital was that the purely plastic self could hardly be asserted to exhibit self-identity. To solve some technical problems, economists began to write down models with "multiple selves" collated into a single mega-utility function. This, in turn, led to Sissyphyssian task of shoring up whatever was left of the concepts of "agency" and "preference." For some, identity came from imposition of further variables of "self-confidence" and self-reputation read through the eyes of others—neoliberal prescriptions par excellence (see Benabou and Tirole). Another economist we shall encounter later in our survey of crisis theories, George Akerlof, purported to concoct a neoclassical theory of identity by stuffing the utility function with even more arbitrary variables. This version of the "individual" seeks to reduce anxiety-creating cognitive dissonance induced by the behavior of others whose actions don't conform to the social categories assigned to them—it smacked of nothing more than teen angst blown up to grand levels of utilitarian generalization, an infantilization of *Homo economicus*. When agents are endlessly desperate to refashion themselves into some imaginary entity they anticipate that others want them to be, the supposed consumer sovereignty the market so assiduously pampers has begun to deliquesce. It is a mug's game to trumpet the virtues of a market that gives people what they want, if people are portrayed as desperate to transform themselves into the type of person who wants what the market provides.[47] There were of course many other versions within the economic orthodoxy of the fragmentation of *Homo economicus*.[48] One might have expected that this constituted the revenge of social psychology on the profession, were it not that neoclassical economics had been so tone-deaf on the subject for so long. But economists were bereft of the capacity to entertain the notion that their own local obsessions were an epiphenomenon of a larger social transformation.

The ceremonial "economics of identity" was the investiture of the central ethos of everyday neoliberalism into the heart of the neoclassical agent.

B) There Is No Class but the Middle. There Is No Life Without Risk.

Another critical aspect of defining selfhood is the suitable availability of a repertoire of categories to limn the components of the self. Bending to the persistent reductionist trend of Western thought, the social scientist might seek to resolve the whole individual into its constitutive parts, or at minimum, into some set of classifications that provide the boundaries between one self and the next. Certain categories might be transient, and others more permanent; but nevertheless, the existence of such a menu of components would provide an ontology of self-hood, a polestar to guide the way through attributions of normality, pathology, and onset of Alzheimer's. In some societies the categories might assume the form of castes or "blood"; in others, they might be structured by the notion of an occupation as apprenticeship; in yet others, they might be deployed as psychological theories of "types."

A striking characteristic of the neoliberal approach to selfhood is the intransigent renunciation of most forms of classification of people, and abjuration of the resolution of the self into rigid components. One (older, classical liberal) version of this renunciation is the postulate that all humans are essentially alike, or should be treated as such, displaying equality in fundamental constitution and capacities, but this most emphatically is *not* the strategy adopted by the NTC. "Equality" of any sort releases a bugbear for the neoliberals, the wormhole to the slippery chute to serfdom. Instead, the neoliberal self is regarded as so exquisitely supple, mobile, and plastic that imposition of any categorization is deemed imperious and elitist. Every dedicated follower of fashion has been enjoined to plead, "But you don't know me." To pigeonhole that self with what are deemed to be premature categories is denounced as a basic violation of "freedom." However awkward the image, you are most yourself when you are putty in your own hands. Since only the market can bestow upon people what they reputedly want, all fixed skills or virtues or psychological orientations that can guarantee predestination and salvation are peremptorily banished.

The neoliberal contempt for human categories has become well ensconced in everyday life in the last three decades. Whatever their predicament, whatever their station in life, everyone is encouraged to think they, too, can be Metis, unperturbed (or ignorant) that their fate is to be consumed by Zeus. Time and again, the supposed success of some teen idol or hedge fund manager or sports star is said to illustrate the tired platitude that "you can be anything that you want to be, if you want it bad enough." This presumes a self that can incorporate any attribute, take up any challenge, transcend any limitation, and embody any quality. There are few neoliberal tropes more cynical, or incantations more convenient. This catechism of permanent metamorphosis has spawned a number of cultural devices that structure everyday neoliberalism. Here we will merely touch upon two: the modern disappearance of economic class as a serious taxonomy, and the hollowing out of the notion of "risk" when elevated to a general imperative of agency.

One major cultural development over the last three decades is that the only permissible mention of "class" in the economic sense has been the utterly superfluous habit of treating oneself and others as solidly "middle class." In the late 1990s, in Britain, New Labour proclaimed "We're all middle class now" on the grounds of the evaporation of industrial jobs. In this, they were parroting their putative Tory opponent: "Class is a Communist concept," Margaret Thatcher told Newsweek in 1992. "It groups people together and sets them against each other." In America, every sociological generalization in the mainstream press pontificates on "the middle class," conveying the sense that any other class is negligible in significance. The rich and the poor have become so evanescent as mental categories that they are rarely ever accorded the right to occupy space in the real world. The rich are continually quoted as not feeling "really" rich, while the poor are cued to deny that they are poor, to avoid opprobrium. If they confess to poverty, they are examined for personal failings, rather than class membership. This is patent evidence of a creeping linguistic neoliberalism. The suppression of the obvious point that every "middle" needs two substantial extremes to be legitimate is an artifact of the neoliberal doctrine that *there is no such thing as social class, and most decidedly, "economic" classes (working class, upper class, proletariat) do not exist.* The *only* class in which one can safely profess membership is the "middle class," or the class of no class. But this all-inclusive category is nervously duplicitous, because it really consists of the denial of all personal categories. No one should be definitively tagged with class membership, since every individual is supposedly poised on the brink of becoming someone else.[49]

The abolition of class has been a font of political dividend for the neoliberals, since it has frustrated all attempts to mobilize politics on a class basis. Indeed, one might argue that the defeat and decimation of unions has been intimately involved with the dissipation of class identities. As Owen Jones put it: "A blue-uniformed male factory worker with a union card in his pocket might have been an appropriate symbol for the working class of the 1950s. A low-paid, part-time, female shelf-stacker would certainly not be unrepresentative of the same class today."[50] The extinction of political entities like unions, ethnic clubs, and party affiliations leaves the vast bulk of the working population bereft of communal identities. The mainstream media may sneer at "chavs" or "trailer trash," but never as a functional economic category; rather they serve as a narrative placeholder for people who refuse to remake themselves into someone the market would validate. In this manner, revolts such as the August 2011 English riots were preemptively leached of their political significance, in favor of interpretation as the inchoate tantrums of the undisciplined self. As David Cameron bombinated in Parliament in the 2011 riots' aftermath, "This is not about poverty, it is all about culture." Serried ranks of experts chimed in with the sentiment. Consequently, poverty is first personalized, and then criminalized in neoliberal everyday life.

The neoliberal dismissal of effective social categories has had other consequences. For instance, during the 2008–10 crisis, the Obama administration encountered great difficulty in rolling back regressive tax cuts of the previous administration, because it had equally invested in the ludicrous language of "not raising the taxes of the middle class." They became bogged down in a game of guessing where the upper tax boundary of that elusive middle class might be found: $100,000, $200,000, $250,000, $1 million? This was occurring when the median household income in the United States (2009) was $51,221 and the average per capita annual money income was $27,041; the public discourse was consequently conducted in a pristine fact-free zone.[51] Or in another instance, all social insurance schemes that are necessarily based upon membership in economic classes are undermined by the abolition of class as a voluntary category of self-identity. Pension and Social Security schemes can be personalized and then privatized only when the target population has been stripped of all notions of justice as rooted in class solidarity; once the authority begins to recast its provision of an insurance scheme as a "personal investment," and retreats to justification of such schemes as "getting back what you (alone) put in," then the neoliberals have won half the battle.

The denial of legitimacy of personal categories has also had profound implications for the construction of the keyword "risk" in neoliberalism. The connotations of the term "risk" are treacherous in the modern world. Should one approach risk as an actuarial concept, then the ability to sort individuals into stable categories and identities is the indispensable prerequisite for the application of probability algorithms to what would otherwise be merely the idiosyncratic and incommensurate life trajectories of historical personalities. Classical approaches to risk parlayed stable categories into prudential outcomes. Yet, because of the first commandment of the plasticity of the individual, this is increasingly not how everyday neoliberalism understands risk.

It is commonplace to observe that "risk" is a state of being that the Neoliberal Thought Collective revels in, second only to their prime directive of "freedom." Embracing risk and taking chances is the putative mark of the entrepreneur, the only solid evidence that the agent has been actively engaged in pursuit of self-advantage, as opposed to passively accepting the lot that has been bequeathed him by others. Risk is the archetypal second stage of Aristotelian narratives of the self, leading to the catharsis of validation (or tragedy). But here is the point where "risk" suffers vernacular slippage, since it is not portrayed as actuarial risk, reducible to probabilities and expected values, but rather bald impetuous abandon in the face of an intrinsically unknowable future. Neoliberals, recall, insist upon the thoroughgoing ignorance of everyone in the face of the all-knowing market. Therefore, for them, accepting risk is not the fine balancing of probabilities, the planning for foreseen exigencies and the exercise of prudential restraint; rather, it is wanton ecstasy: the utter subjection of the self to the market by offering oneself up to powers greater than we can ever fully comprehend. It is, quite literally, an irrational leap of faith, with the parallels to religious traditions intentional.

This is one reason that participation in neoliberal life necessitates acting as an entrepreneur of the self: unreserved embrace of (this version of) risk is postulated to be the primary method of changing your identity to live life to the fullest. Contemporary entrepreneurial autobiographies almost always start out with some variation on: "I am not sure what it is about entrepreneurs that makes us risk-taking thrill seekers, but every entrepreneur I know is an adrenaline junkie. We kite board, heli ski, race cars, and keep finding new creative ways to challenge ourselves." Alternatively, anyone who participates in the welfare state is just a dull drone, lost in a vegetative state. They are debased because they expect the state to shield them from risk, when in fact, they should be reveling in the opportunity to remake themselves. "Scientists" then chime in to reiterate that success accrues to those who grasp rashly and imperiously for self-gratification:

The risk-taking, novelty seeking, and obsessive personality traits often found in addicts can be harnessed to make them very effective in the workplace. For many leaders, it's not the case that they succeed in spite of their addiction; rather, the same brain wiring and chemistry that makes them addicts also confer on them behavioral traits that serve them well.[52]

A denizen of modern neoliberal society has not demonstrated real flexibility of personal identity until they have prostrated themselves before the capricious god of risk. Freedom without the uninhibited embrace of risk cannot be experienced as anything other than static mechanical "choice." Any machine can accomplish that. Salvation through the market comes not from solidarity with any delusional social class or occupational category, but instead bold assertion of individuality through capitulation to a life of risk. The heady elixir of distilled risk is hawked as the drug of choice of the modern neoliberal self: just say yes. This, of course, has almost nothing to do with the actual economic history of capitalist business: it is entirely a cultural construct.

Risk is the premier device for combining a supposed instrumentally rational approach to action with a post-hoc moralization of any market outcome whatsoever, and as such, has become central to neoliberal narratives of the crisis. Whenever the market appears to break down, it really boils down to a mistaken apprehension of "risk" on the part of most participants, which in some sense could have been avoided. (This is the cultural importance of such best-sellers as Michael Lewis's *Big Short*.) Taking a risk means that, in the final analysis, you have brought the failure upon yourself; political organization to punish the perpetrators is rendered nugatory. In these periods of cognitive recalibration, the insight that technical models of risk must always fail is treated as some sort of grand epiphany, when in fact it is simply one aspect of the tautology that will always be accessed in a neoliberal world to reduce the experience of calamity to personal moral failure.

> As long as it can be shown that risks *could have been* better managed—by diversification, better models, better rules, better institutions, better professionals—the loss is morally justified. The retrospective argument that risk could have been better managed becomes the moral justification for the losses of everyone involved . . . the risk management discourse enables us to simultaneously celebrate the indeterminacy of outcomes and to

retrospectively moralize these outcomes; to deny a singular causal-ity before an outcome materializes and to attribute a moral causality after an outcome materializes.[53]

Hence the modern culture of risk is the very embodiment of the neoliberal commandment: there is no such thing as commutative justice, and consequently, the participant must simply acquiesce in the verdict of the market. The discourse of risk, which seems to be forward-looking, in fact stands as the post-hoc justification of any outcome whatsoever. "It cleanses the epistemic foundations of the risk order from the shortfalls of performativity, redefining past terminology and categorizations, and realigning past calculations with the world that had in a sense out-performed them."[54]

Before his participation in the MPS, Frank Knight sought to make the stance toward risk the key to economic life in his *Risk, Uncertainty and Profit* (1921). His separation between calculable expected values and true unknowns, while famous, was never able to be incorporated in any substantial way into formal neoclassical economics. By the same token, Knight pointed to risk as the ultimate source of profit, which languished unexplained in full Walrasian general equilibrium theory. (His terminology also never caught on; Knight identified risk with probabilistic calculation, whereas modern neoliberals tend to use it more as the existential state of unknowable loss.) What was missing from his work was this later abrogation of all categories of personhood in the NTC, which perforce undermined all partition-based defini-tion of probabilities for entrepreneurial individuals, effectively collapsing all "risk" into primal "uncertainty." In this, as in other areas, the modern collective ended up repudiating Knight. This curious neoliberal inversion of classical connotations of risk will surface during many postmortems of the crisis discussed in later chapters.

The neoliberal celebration of risk is woven throughout everyday life in the modern era. For instance, this may explain why casino and commercial gambling has made such a comeback in the neoliberal era. There was a time when gambling was regarded as the immoral fleecing of the working man, which motivated many attempts to declare it illegal, or at minimum, confine it to a strictly controlled sphere. A mid-twentieth-century opinion held that it was better to drive it underground than to sanction the bankrupting of people with limited means lacking the fortitude of will to walk away from the racetrack or gaming table. But in the neoliberal pantheon, the person who abjectly submits to risk (even handicapped by house advantage) is a hero, not a weak-willed fool. Hence, in modern life, and in contrast with prior regimes, gambling takes on an aura of moral probity. In a sense, playing slot machines or attending betting parlors or blackjack or roulette tables is not just the privilege of the idle rich, but rather, a mass version of simulated practice for an ideal life. In the neoliberal era, the state went from trying to quarantine gambling to insinuating it into every hamlet, high street, filling station, and Indian reservation. In the United States, individual states have been falling over one another to promote every form of gambling they might tax. Not only was it lucrative, but it taught the precariat to live suspended in a delirium of lottery fever, the better to be distracted from working life.

This elevation of risk as the heightened consciousness of the neoliberal self has direct causal connections to the crisis, as one might expect. This case has been made by Christopher Payne in his *Consumer, Credit and Neoliberalism*. He explicitly documents how various think tanks in the neoliberal Russian doll took it upon themselves to refute the older "paternalistic" Keynesian identity of the "worker-saver" household and replace him/her with the swashbuckling entrepreneur. This multi-pronged offensive united intellectual innovations in Chicago political economy (such as Friedman's reconceptualization of the consumer in his theory of the consumption function) with political interventions on the ground: banking reform was not configured just to unbound Promethean banksters, but to help refashion consumers to be able to manipulate their own balance sheets through assumption of debt. Waves of neoliberals promoted the "enterprise culture" and preached the virtues of undertaking risk in the self-management of one's very own portfolio. Of course, those newbie wizards of personal leverage did not themselves invent or conjure the outlandish mortgages and dubious practices of the debt pushers: that confusion was a slander concocted by some neoliberals.[55] But there is more than a grain of truth in the observation that the personal identity of the consumer had to have been first turned topsy-turvy, such that the grand sausage grinder of securitization could have chewed up such a vast swathe of individually owned owner-occupied real estate.

The makeover of the worker/consumer into daredevil risk-taker turns out to be central to the neoliberal blanket absolution of the financial sector for causing the crisis. In this construct, there can be no such thing as "predatory lending," since any economic transaction, no matter how studded with booby traps, is freely entered into by the ideal entrepreneurial agent, and therefore is prima facie noncoercive or free of exploitation. Since all those "subprime" and "alt-A" mortgages were merely shiny products responding to the desires of all those income-challenged potential home owners (not inconsequentially overrepresented by marginal borrowers from disadvantaged racial and demographic groups), the buck stops with the latter. Because the market is the greatest information conveyor known to mankind, if home owners got the feeling of being bamboozled and hornswoggled, it was entirely due to their own personal mental deficiencies and lack of attention to the cornucopia of choice made available through financial innovations such as adjustable rate, no-documentation, no-down-payment loans. If their optimal stupidity rendered them easy marks, it was their own fault for insufficient investment in human capital.

Of course, the rival critical narrative detects a concerted effort to render the information as deceptive and corrupt as possible, to entrap all those newbie risk-takers:

> Experts often describe the run-up to the financial crisis as a "race to the bottom." In reality it was a veritable track-and-field meet of such contests: some of them played out in the marketplace, others inside the government. Out in the financial marketplace, in the 2000s, opaquely marketed subprime products pioneered by unregulated, fly-by-night, nonbank mortgage lenders began to take off in the mainstream. Much as in the credit card business—where the boldly marketed 4.9 percent teaser rate masks the 18.9 percent rate that will eventually kick in—these were often mortgages that masked exploding costs down the line. Banks and thrifts, in order to hold their own, had to jump in with similar products, lest their plain-Jane fixed-rate mortgages look expensive by comparison. In market after market, hiding the true costs and risks of a product became a requirement for survival.[56]

The naïve Elizabeth Warren–style reaction to this travesty is to enforce bureaucratic simplicity and transparency upon the lenders, perhaps combined with some "consumer education"; but this displays a distressing lack of understanding of the neoliberal mind-set. Banks and other vendors have generations of marketing savvy built into their understanding of the entrepreneurial self, a persona for whom they were instrumental in parturition. They are masters of sales pitches that seem "simple" but in fact are highly manipulative and empty of key information. The nascent Consumer Financial Protection Bureau is only beginning to confront this fact, realizing that the dream of a transparent two-page standardized mortgage agreement is only marginally less prone to manipulation than the balloon-option ARM. If one is serious about countering modern bank practices, then tinkering with legal forms is utterly ineffectual: you have to be willing to muck in and manipulate the entrepreneurial self, as much as or more so than the banks.[57]

This is how neoliberalism works: first it moves heaven and earth to induce you to manage your own portfolio and assume more risk; then it demonizes the victim when the entire structure comes crashing down, as it inevitably must. The most famous (and consequential) attack on the poor for their indebtedness was the rant on the floor of the Chicago Mercantile Exchange by Rick Santelli, which is credited in retrospect with jump-starting the Tea Party in the United States. Santelli was catapulted to instant fame after his five-minute outburst on CNBC in February 2009—where he decried government bailouts, called struggling home owners "losers" and speculated aloud that a new Tea Party might be needed—went viral.[58]

The fallacy with the Tea Party slogan "Your mortgage is not my problem" is that most people are not continually scheming to live beyond their means: they have to be introduced into structures and schemes larger than themselves that are constructed precisely to attain that end. To attribute the crisis to the profligacy of the average person presumes a level of understanding that is otherwise denied to the individual in the neoliberal era. As John Lanchester put it: "From the worm's-eye perspective which most of us inhabit, the general feeling about this new turn in the economic crisis is one of bewilderment . . . People feel they have very little economic or political agency, very little control over their own lives; during the boom times, nobody told them this was an unsustainable bubble until it was already too late."[59]

Neoliberal risk has turned out to be very much a one-sided phenomenon in practice, however. The proliferation of risk revelers required a parallel counterposed infrastructure of staid for-profit organizations to monitor the risk-taking of the population of these neoliberal subjects; and incongruously, these firms have made their money by automating the pigeonholing of selves in the moments of their assumption of risk; but they do not themselves endorse or conform to the same wanton notions of risk inculcated in their subjects. When providing their services, they structure their data collection back into the older actuarial definitions of risk, by sorting all those hapless selves back into arbitrary impersonal categories of income, parentage, race, gender, health, education, age, and so forth. As we have come to expect with neoliberalism, the despised bureaucratic iron cage of rationality is situated just in the background, lightly camouflaged. While the entrepreneurial selves of neoliberal folklore have been busy audaciously making themselves anew, concurrently, the various actuarial firms retort that they are stereotypical protagonists living out the same old pedestrian story. While the agents congratulate themselves that they have been busy bursting their notional fetters of identity, these surveillance firms persist, hard at work enforcing their personal identities through time and space.

Technologies for both facilitating and taking advantage of personal "failures of plasticity" have proliferated in the neoliberal era; here we simply opt to describe two colorful examples that tend to impinge upon much everyday life: the market for viatical settlements, and the uses and enforcement of FICO credit scores.

Life insurance is of course very old, and was often tied to state-sponsored lotteries and tontines from the seventeenth century until the nineteenth century. However, from the eighteenth century onward, various schemes were devised to pool mutual payments into burial societies, and from the nineteenth century onward, dedicated life insurance policies were often sold as methods to make provisions for descendants and other assignees in case of early death. To distinguish it from stigmatized wagering on the demise of some arbitrary policy-holder, various prohibitions were instituted against purchase of insurance on the lives of unrelated strangers. In other words, life insurance was successfully rendered palatable for mass market purchase by presenting it as a product whereby you might "personalize" your prudence with regard to those closest to you, most generally, bereaved family members. But once life insurance had become a mass commodity, then the standardized narrative unraveled.

In the neoliberal era, life insurance has become "securitized" in much the same way as most other personal income streams have been financialized. Specialized firms have arisen to purchase life insurance policies from the late 1980s onward from people in extremis, and in particular (then) HIV-positive persons, for a lump-sum cash settlement. The more that retirement provisions and social insurance schemes have been hollowed out, the more this market grew. The new owner of the insurance contract assumes the premium payments, wagering that the impending death minimizes the cost relative to the policy payoff: these are known in the trade as "viatical settlements." This secondary market has grown dramatically over the last three decades.[60] Policies purchased are often bundled together, and turned into derivative asset-backed securities that are then retailed to all manner of institutional investors, often ignorant of the underlying unsavory ghoulish trade. Hence, contrary to economic pundritry, ABSs, CDOs, and CDSs were not just the narrow preserve of Wall Street, but reached down into the very recesses of everyday life (and death). In this instance, we observe that the terminally ill are exhorted to redouble their "entrepreneurial" efforts regarding their dwindling assets, while the firms that securitize the policies and exercise surveillance (aka deathwatch) do not assume neoliberal risk, but operate solely in the realm of actuarial categories and fixed client identities. This asymmetry with regard to risk and identity is a characteristic symptom of everyday neoliberalism. What appears to the agent as recognition of his or her own special personal needs, an appreciation of openness to change in the face of adversity, and validation of idiosyncratic predicaments of the self, are treated by firms as new occasions to turn misfires of entrepreneurial activity into cold hard cash through reimposition of impersonal actuarial fixed categories. In later chapters, again and again we will encounter similar vultures of distress swooping down upon souls disenfranchised by the crisis, offering indigents more neoliberal markets to ameliorate the disappointments and defeats delivered by existing neoliberal markets. As one lawyer dealing with viaticals was quoted in 2005:

> It's a receivable, just like credit card receivables and movie royalties. Whatever. I really see it from a capital market perspective. It's an income-producing asset that just doesn't mature until there's a death . . . [People] have an asset called their insurability and that translates into a financial product.[61]

Consumer debts are yet another major area where the everyday "risks" embraced by entrepreneurial selves are regimented, reinterpreted, and repackaged to produce dependable actuarial profits. For now, we merely seek to illustrate how the frisky freedom of entrepreneurial selves is asymmetrically offset by the for-profit imposition of fixed class categories.

It does not come as news that the working class has been lumbered with all manner of debt in the last three decades as one effective way to divert attention from flat personal income receipts, not to mention to otherwise soften the blow of a steadily worsening distribution of income in the United States, Britain, and the peripheral EU states.

The standard sales pitch that promoted this trend was the stereotypic neoliberal exhortation to joyfully embrace risk through assumption of loans in order to transform the self in a more market-friendly direction, be it through student loans, credit card debt, mortgage debt, or more exotic arrangements. But while all the little entrepreneurs were assiduously busy striving to morph into Galateas exquisitely engineered to succeed without really trying, special panopticons had to be erected to maintain actuarial notions of class membership and fixed identity. Credit proliferation required concerted management; liabilities had to be recurrently affixed to a vigorous continuous human identity; and an augmented scale of loan activity required further standardization of the entities that would be granted this credit. In the crisis literature, most attention has been focused on the transition from an "originate and hold" model of granting of loans to consumers (where the lender keeps possession of the loan) to a model of "originate and distribute," facilitated by the process of securitization. This watershed was preceded by another just as critical: the extraction of judgments of creditworthiness out of a web of local personal relationships and the consequent injection of automation of judgment in the format of uniform quantitative indices provided by for-profit firms. For corporations, these services had been provided by the "Big Three" ratings agencies; for consumers, these were constructed as the FICO® scores from an algorithm invented by Fair Isaac and Company.[62]

Fair Issac introduced the generalized FICO score in 1987; by 1995, it was incorporated into Freddie Mac rules for the standardization of underwriting mortgage loans in the United States. By construction, the FICO score ranges between 300 and 850, exhibiting a right-skewed distribution, with 60 percent of scores to the right between 650 and 799. According to Fair Isaac, the median score in 2006 was 723.[63] What is fascinating is the extent to which this seemingly neutral technocratic number, initially retailed to banks to automate their credit card retail operations, soon burst its boundaries to become the statistic of choice to track the neoliberal self. Insurance firms now monitor credit histories to set premiums. Companies now frequently pull credit reports as part of their background checks of prospective employees. Retailers analyze FICO scores to find lucrative neighborhoods for new stores. And in recent years Fair Isaac has marketed other esoteric models to help casino operators predict which customers are likely to be the most profitable, and even to health insurers to predict which patients are least likely to take their medications. The neoliberal self lives in an invisible grid of FICO gradients. Yet, just as it was becoming more

Protean, the number on the dial of your own personal success meter, it was becoming unmoored from its putative original function, which was to provide a dependable predictor of the probability of personal default—and that was before the crisis (Foust and Pressman, "Credit Scores"). In fact, the crisis revealed that FICO was not so much a prospective predictor of much of anything, as it had become another cross-firm tool for surveillance and control of the identity of the shape-shifting neoliberal self. Rather than base economic decisions on old-fashioned notions of "character" or "integrity," FICO was a retro-spective dog tag that forced a human being to bear the consequences of his entrepreneurial risk sprees as a member of a class of stereotypical consumer types superimposed by Fair Isaac. All that was solid about personal identity melted into thin air. Martha Poon has flagged this watershed as a shift from "credit-control-by-screening" to "credit-control-by-risk-category";[64] we just designate it "neoliberalism," the latest installment in the surveillance of the modular entrepreneurial self. Indeed, by the late 1990s, FICO scores had become all-purpose quantitative proxies for your "worth" as a human being, rendering your debts comparable with those of a million others, incorporated directly into the models that served to justify stratification into the various trenches of the mortgage-backed securities that were one direct cause of the crisis. The Panopticon of FICO turned out to be a necessary prerequisite for the bubble to inflate.

Even though the Panopticon was conveniently privatized, neither Fair Isaac nor the credit raters were held to be responsible for "risk" created by their own activities offloaded onto their subjects, unlike the neoliberal selves that they kept under close surveillance. This again illustrates the sharp asymmetry of neoliberal concepts of "risk." Should the chains of identification be breached in FICO, say, by "identity theft" or "data errors" or "computer glitches," these firms did not bear the responsibility of making the person whole; no, that devolved to the frantic individual in extremis to somehow "correct" or otherwise rectify their deviance from the imperatives of actuarial accuracy. It should be noted that the credit raters did not make rectification easy. An elaborate secondary market grew up in service providers who themselves charge the agents to monitor the records of the consumer credit-rating firms, in order to flag any divergence of the surveillance dossiers from the notional identity that the entrepreneurial self enter-tained about his own autobiography. This nicely illustrated the key neoliberal precept that any "problems" generated by neoliberalism could be adequately addressed by a redoubled bout of entrepreneurial innovation and further market activity. Unfortunately, that particular neoliberal precept was embarrassed by the further breakdown of the whole credit-scoring edifice in the crisis of 2008. And yet, just as in so many other instances, the entrenched character of FICO scores in everything from credit cards to background checks, plus their purported "convenience," prompts them to live on, unfazed by their tenuous connection to reality.

C) Everyday Sadism

When a limo cruises New York City, the financial capital of the world, equipped with a massive sign painted on the side reading "Kill the Poor," is this "irony" or is it something else altogether?[65] When Ted Nugent conducts a "Trample the Weak" rock tour, what kind of person attends the concert?[66] Is this intended as "entertainment" or as agitprop? Since 2008, we might want to consider whether the answer has taken on new significance. In order to shift the frame away from offhand dismissal of some trifling stunt to something a bit more profound, I would like to quote the premier philosopher of cruelty on the wellsprings of that urge:

> An equivalence is provided by the creditor's receiving, in place of the literal compensation for injury, a recompense in the form of a kind of *pleasure*—the pleasure of being allowed to vent his power freely upon one who is powerless, the voluptuous pleasure *de faire le mal pour le plaisir de la faire*, the enjoyment of violation. This enjoyment will be the greater the lower the creditor stands in the social order.[67]

Friedrich Nietzsche derived the will to punish from the world of debt obligations, and not vice versa. If one were to take this version of psychology seriously, it suggests that the exacerbated asymmetry between imperious creditors and distressed debtors that has widened since the crisis has freed up an antagonistic field of cruelty that may have festered in a more repressed state during more prosperous times. Clearly, by this late date everyone is aware of the multitudes unceremoniously turfed out of their underwater houses mortgaged beyond all rescue, the one in five children reduced to poverty in the United States, the newly disenfranchised filling the homeless shelters and Wal-Mart car parks at night, the mute beggars standing at street corners with their crude handmade cardboard signs, the sheepish families crowding the food pantries, the superannuated, the forlorn, the downwardly mobile. One way to live in this grim harsh world would be to tell yourself that all these people are just collateral damage, and that no one bears them any particular animus for it, that it is just the unfortunate result of transpersonal forces: in Rawls-speak, there but for the grace of God go I. Such would run the exculpation of the classical liberal.

This, I would suggest, is not now the predominant mind-set in our neoliberal era. Instead, the culture of everyday neoliberalism tends to foster a set of attitudes reminiscent of Nietzsche's creditor psychology, and has plumped for a different morality: it extends beyond a defensive schadenfreude of the Great Contraction, if only because it predates the crash. Since the 1990s, not just the rich, but almost everyone else who still has a job has been galvanized to find within themselves a kind of guilty pleasure in the thousand unkind cuts administered by the enforcers of trickle-down austerity. Since, as we argued above, the poor no longer are held to exist as a class, it is easier to hate them as individuals. They are the detritus of the market. Those wretched souls subsist at our munificence, it is hinted; therefore it is the indigent who owe us, it is implied; hence we qualify as the righteous and willing audience at the theater of cruelty. Through this guilty pleasure, people of modest means are ushered into the vicarious experience of what it feels like to be extravagantly rich in an era of decline. For a brief moment, the working class can empathize with the imperious creditor, even though they lack the assets to maintain the charade. In a sense, one might approach this phenomenon as an elaboration of Thorstein Veblen's basic insight in his *Theory of the Leisure Class*: "An invidious comparison is a process of valuation of persons in respect to worth."[68] The theater of cruelty becomes an emporium of conspicuous consumption.

But beyond a little virtual reality, the normalization of everyday sadism fulfills deeper functions as well. The "double truths" of neoliberalism outlined in the last chapter cannot be permanently confined within the ambit of the NTC, but tend to leak out as barely repressed contradictions in quotidian life—between populism and plutarchy, between freedom and control, between smug ignorance and fervent conviction, between Christian theology and norms of efficiency, between kosmos and taxis, between the enjoyment of pleasure and the deployment of pain. These contradictions could not be confronted directly by the larger populace without fomenting utter disenchantment with the promises of neoliberal order. To get around the cognitive dissonance, cultural outlets square the circle by staging little neoliberal allegories in the public sphere, directing anger away from intractable predicaments in the political sphere and toward the victims. As one analyst put it, every system of cruelty requires its own theater.[69]

In the neoliberal theater of cruelty, one torments the poor or indigent precisely *because* they are prostrate. Everyday sadism of this sort is enshrined in every crisis-porn news story that dupes the victims into "sharing their feelings" over their eviction notices and job losses; it reared its head when the Nebraska attorney general un-self-consciously compared recipients of unemployment benefit with "scavenging raccoons";[70] it is there in the ridiculous obligatory "upbeat" ending to every failure narrative so as not to unduly derange our complacent spectatorship. It is rampant in every suggestion that relief offered by religious charities (accompanied by the obligatory sectarian message) renders the predicament of the downtrodden and disenfranchised bearable. It underpins the argument that the poor must of necessity bear the brunt of austerity now, because it will only get worse for them later if they do not.[71] As a political ploy, right-wing think tanks began their counteroffensive against a rising chorus pleading taxation of the rich in 2011 by disingenuously twisting the evocative rhetoric of "equality" in pointing out (in a fit of indignation) that a large proportion of the poor do not "pay their share" of income taxes (viz., none at all) and thus lacked "skin in the game"; this echo chamber of contempt ricocheting throughout the news media was so extravagantly over the top that it became the target of satire on many of the usual cable outlets, such as Jon Stewart and Stephen Colbert.[72]

In the current climate, it seems there is almost nothing you could do to the poor that would earn you opprobrium and ostracism from polite company, (maybe) short of sexual molestation of children. Prior to the 1980s, the practice of "salary purchase," aka "payday loans," had been outlawed; but a concerted effort beginning at the state level progressively legalized this particular form of predatory lending. As of 2008, there were more payday lender outlets in the United States than there were McDonald's and Burger King restaurants combined, with turnover that dwarfed casinos, the other major poverty vampire operation.[73] What is astounding about such operations is that they are no longer treated as reviled bottom-feeders by both the media and politicians, but rather as exemplary of the types of legitimate businesses that provide opportunity and salvation in the current contraction. Given the vast hollowing out of the income distribution, it makes sense that the working poor constituted one of the only substantial customer segments that left any room for expansion:

> Jared Davis [CEO of Check 'n Go] . . . pulls in around $20 million a year making loans of $300 or $400 or $500 a year to the working poor but he had brought his brother into the business and it was his father's money that had gotten him started. "I don't consider myself wealthy," he tells me . . . There were photos around his office of him shaking hands with George W. Bush and John McCain and behind his desk hung stylish black-and-whites of his young children blown up so large that they were distracting. I watched the YouTube videos made by former Davis employees who felt horrible about how they made their money ("I resigned because I could no longer stomach the lies, and I could no longer continue exploiting customers, making hard lives even harder," one said), I had spent the better part of a day with a former store manager who had saved some of the crass directives she had received from management (lend "to anyone getting social security," one read, even if a customer only had "one dime to their name"). I only got to spend two hours with him before I was shown the door—barely enough time to even get into the lawsuit his father has filed against his two sons charging them with bilking him out of money . . . A district director who used to work for him called a press conference a few years back to talk about the company's methods for choosing new store locations. "I have been responsible for selecting sites for new stores in D.C. and northern Virginia," he said—and to those who claim the company doesn't target minority communities, "I can tell you emphatically that it does."[74]

The mantra "your debt is not my problem" has permitted other bottom-feeding organizations like personal debt collection agencies to revive the once-banned practice of debtor prisons.[75] As people fall behind in their debts and are often unaware of being subject to lawsuits, any arrest whatsoever now can trigger jail time, often for sums as small as five hundred dollars. Hundreds of fly-by-night firms scoured databases to find those falling behind in their mortgages, and hired offshore phone banks to endlessly call and promise false hope, only to swindle them with false stories of help with principal reductions, stealing from them fees they could ill afford. Yet no major media outlet has mustered even a scintilla of outrage for what is, at bottom, cheap illegal ways to harass and torture debtors.

How has this theater of cruelty been made to seem so unexceptional?

Martijn Konings has pointed out that the dark underbelly of the bright shiny neoliberal self is the daily spectacle of the public put-down.[76] Not only must the truly entrepreneurial life embrace the risk and insecurity of a constantly revised self tossed hither and yon by market forces beyond our ken; the fundamental narcissism encouraged by neoliberalism demands that we participate in an active externalization of the experience of insecurity and vulnerability to revaluation. The complement to a culture of celebrity has become therefore the unabashed theater of cruelty, the public spaces where we gaze upon the half-speed car wrecks of the lives of others in the throes of failure, Nascar for the politically challenged. In one sense, this programming of everyday sadism explicitly aimed at the poor and distressed is so ubiquitous that one need hardly recite the titles: *The Jerry Springer Show, Dr. Phil, The Apprentice, Shattered, Unbreakable, Big Brother, Hell's Kitchen, Survivor, American Idol*—it is hardly worth the minor effort that it takes to disparage it. A moment's reflection reveals it is pervasive in American culture. Unremarkable people, desperate for some sort of acknowledgment and validation, yearning for some promise of escape from the stale and commonplace, offer themselves up on the altar of abject humiliation to an audience of millions; smarmy celebrities berate them to their face; and the spectacles proliferate because they are cheaper for the networks to program than either scripted fiction or news. In many instances, the audience is even encouraged to pay to "vote" for those to ostracize and banish—a clear simulacrum of the neoliberal marketplace. Game shows used to reflexively reward the poor; now pay-to-play reality TV crushes them. Computer gaming used to be about triumphs of virtuosity; now, as in *Grand Theft Auto*, it is all about debasement of the losers. Rather than engage in the kabuki of high dudgeon, it might be worthwhile to meditate briefly on the possibility that this genre is indicative of some relatively new lifestyle under everyday neoliberalism.

One rather common approach is to describe this theater of cruelty as essentially a ruse: it diverts attention from the real forces at work in the impoverishment of people, set in train by the three decades or more of increasing inequality and wage stagnation in the West. This might be construed as a somewhat kindred version of the "bait and switch" argument of Tom Frank, only now with the theater of cruelty as stand-in for the culture and religious themes he identified as weapons of mass distraction. This appears to be the position taken by Konings:

> The culture of self-help that is so crucial to neoliberal governmentality involves a dialectic of continuous affirmation and rejection, seduction and denial . . . Neoliberal governmentality involves the creation of chains of disciplinary pressures, networks composed of acts of everyday sadism and expressions of judgment that serve to distract us from the resentment provoked by our submission to authority structures we do not fully understand and experience as oppressive and constraining. This re-direction of our anger and discontent serves to . . . contort our notions of self-realization and responsible living in such a way that we end up ascribing a spiritual dimension to balancing the household budget.[77]

Just as in the case of Frank, while this may sound plausible on its face, it too readily partitions the landscape into a self-regulating economy as separate from hierarchical structures and cultural epiphenomena that putatively merely surround it. The spectacle of shaming is not merely a lightning rod for burning resentment; nor is it just an inconsequential occasion for rubbernecking by people with truncated attention spans; it is also a technology for recasting economy and society. After all, what is the vast industry of "job retraining" than a government-subsidized walk of shame? The economy and the theater of cruelty have been merged into a vertically integrated conglomerate. It is a parable of the droves and the wishes. It can be deployed in a myriad of ways under a variety of circumstances; the question here is whether there is some special common denominator in the ways it has been used in a didactic sense in the last three decades. Shock jock or shock doctrine, it cannot be written off as merely a surefire expedient to divert attention. To paint it prematurely as cynical sideshow forecloses the option that everyday sadism is not just some facile prestidigitation of the hand invisible, but serves other more targeted purposes, such as teaching techniques optimized to fortify the neoliberal self.

I expect many readers will immediately object: stylized sadism as extravaganza is nothing new, and therefore (it will be said) bears no necessary relationship to neoliberalism. Spectacles of cruelty are literally timeless. Of course, much art aestheticizes violence, as does much politics; but this line of argument tends to deflect the inquiry into areas irrelevant to neoliberalism. Perhaps the reflex dismissal of anything distinctive about the modern theater of cruelty seeks to appeal to putative distinctions between high and low culture: low-culture violence tends toward the literal, whereas high-culture violence is symbolic or allegorical, and thus subject to critical interpretation. Greek tragedy linked sadism and fate, but attempted to draw lessons from it concerning the defects of the virtues. Likewise, the highly stylized middlebrow theater and film of Lars von Trier and Neil La Bute are notorious for their fascination with evil as an abstract category, and debasement as a form of salvation, but that also ends up being beside the point. None of these constitute bona fide instances of the neoliberal theater of cruelty. Moreover, we are not talking about satire here (interestingly, mostly a non-American phenomenon, such as *How to Get Rid of the Others* or *Un Mundo Maravilloso*). Everyday sadism within the theater of cruelty in the neoliberal era has been crafted into a much more finely tuned and precisely targeted instrument, providing a necessary counterbalance to the proleptic upbeat stress on the magic of self-fashioning transformation. It is not so much that explicit portrayals of violence or aggression need to be paraded (although the entertainment values cannot be discounted), as it is that pageants of the ostracized appear to accept the dictates of the market as final, and also in the audience coming to appreciate that it is legitimate for themselves and others to take advantage of those who fail.

The modern neoliberal theater of cruelty does not seek to plumb any deep pathologies of the human psyche, precisely because it does not endorse any solid notion of an invariant persistent self. Typically, it is uninterested in depth characterization of personality, dealing instead with the most superficial stereotypes. In this way, it departs from the anatomy of shaming inscribed in most self-conscious art. *Pace* the acolytes of Adam Smith, neither is it concerned with interpersonal empathy, nor evocation of the impartial spectator; it is unconcerned about any glue to bind society together. To recapitulate Nietzsche, it deals in the pleasure derived from gazing upon those reduced to helplessness by their overwhelming pecuniary obligations or failure in their quest to fashion a pleasing persona. The allure of the neoliberal theater of cruelty derives from the essential distancing of the audience from the spectacle: becoming complicit with the cruelty merely by being willing spectators, deriving pleasure from the wretchedness of the scapegoat; throughout the experience, the actual onus for the pain is inevitably diverted onto faceless collectives—this is the simulacrum of capitulation to the wisdom of the market. Furthermore, the audience is guaranteed to shed any residual guilt they might feel in their enjoyment at the distress of the unsuccessful and the destitute through reification of the invisible fourth wall; the lesson reiterated is that it is fine for the audience to bear witness to distress, because the mark entered the arena "voluntarily," and the verdict was delivered through the "wisdom of crowds," and in the last instance, there is money to be made and gratification to be experienced at the expense of the loser. Their shame in abject failure becomes a fungible commodity, albeit one of the least rare commodities on the planet. Defeat is not stoic nobility planted on this stage; it is instead the human compost of conspicuous destitution, the fertilizer of economic growth. Losers must learn to let their defeat be turned by others into something that will, at minimum, make money for third parties. Soylent Green *is* people!

Antonin Artaud wrote in *The Theatre and Its Double*, "Without an element of cruelty at the root of every spectacle, the theatre is not possible. In our present state of degeneration it is through the skin that metaphysics must be made to re-enter our minds." Artaud probably did not mean to preach actual torture or cruel affrontery in his text; but the neoliberals do. Their dramaturgy is that the castaways should not affront us; rather, we should affront them. Staged acts of everyday sadism do not seek to confront the audience with an inconvenient truth they refuse to recognize; rather, they promote the reign of a double truth by appealing to a convenient rationalization that the audience can feel under its skin: If the losers, the poor, the lost, the derelict, and the dissolute would only exit the stage after their fifteen seconds of notoriety, having abjectly accepted their status, never to be heard from again, the world would seem a much better place, wouldn't it?

To drive these lessons home, a spectacle must be made out of random outbreaks of misfortune. Thus the erstwhile war on poverty has become a guerrilla war on the poor in the contemporary theater of cruelty. Past standard harassment, there really would otherwise be very little point in subjecting the destitute to further irrational punishment, unless, of course, the purpose of the exercise was instead to exemplify, titillate, and instruct an audience. We need to feel their pain, but only in an abstract vicarious fashion. It is all the more poignant when administered through an absentminded procedure. One index is the willful catch-22 character of the official determinations tendered along with the torment:

> In Colorado, Grand Junction's city council is considering a ban on begging; Tempe, Arizona, carried out a four-day crackdown on the indigent at the end of June. And how do you know when someone is indigent? As a Las Vegas statute puts it, "an indigent person is a person whom a reasonable ordinary person would believe to be entitled to apply for or receive" public assistance. One person who fits that

description is Al Szekeley. A grizzled sixty-two-year-old, he inhabits a wheelchair and is often found on G Street in Washington, D.C.—the city that is ultimately responsible for the bullet he took in the spine in Phu Bai, Vietnam, in 1972. He had been enjoying the luxury of an indoor bed until December 2008, when the police swept through the shelter in the middle of the night looking for men with outstanding warrants. It turned out that Szekeley, who is an ordained minister and does not drink, do drugs, or cuss in front of ladies, did indeed have one—for "criminal trespassing," as sleeping on the streets is sometimes defined by the law. So he was dragged out of the shelter and put in jail. "Can you imagine?" asked Eric Sheptock, the homeless advocate (himself a shelter resident) who introduced me to Szekeley. "They arrested a homeless man in a shelter for being homeless?"[78]

The sheer cantankerousness of the torment of the poor for the edification of the comfortable shows up in a thousand little ordinances and prohibitions found in every small town and suburb across America, like the one in Fresno, California, that specifically prohibits the homeless from panhandling on median strips of roads, while explicitly permitting richer people to solicit contributions for their "good causes" on the very same strips.[79] The confrontation with losers in the neoliberal sweepstakes must necessarily be tightly scripted and closely supervised in the neoliberal theater of cruelty; it cannot be left willy-nilly to those spontaneous orders that the NTC loves to extol.

We would be remiss if we did not point out that the theater of cruelty sometimes is staged in an actual theater. One of the more bizarre developments of the post-2007 crisis is that filmmakers have sought out terminal urban dereliction and poverty to serve as backdrops for their popcorn epics, lending a special frisson of revulsion. Graffitti-defaced walls and garbage-strewn streets are no longer sufficient to signify destitution, since they are literally a dime a dozen, ubiquitous in urban experience. Consequently, some dying cities, such as Detroit and Gary, Indiana, are exhorted to parade their squalid decay and long-abandoned structures to satisfy an aesthetic of grunge porn cultivated among the prosperous in search of an "edgy" experience.[80] Locals are employed to offer themselves up for a pittance to lend authenticity to the postapocalyptic landscapes. No film company or photographer thinks to offer to clean up any sites after they have finished their shoot, it seems. And as one now expects, Gary does not even have one functioning movie theater to show the films that have used it as gruesome backdrop.

One of the most commonplace entryways into the theater of cruelty is the ambuscaded introduction to debt peonage. These days, young people are involuntarily initiated into its mysteries when they are offered student loans to attend university in the U.S. (and increasingly, other countries). The expansion of university attendance for the poor has been inflated in much the same way as the earlier mortgage bubble, but with one big difference. Student loans stipulate posting neoliberal human capital as collateral, and legally define it as something that can never be repudiated, reversing centuries of bankruptcy reform. More astoundingly, in 2005 the provision was extended to for-profit companies who make student loans. Over the last two decades, student loans have been retrofitted to enforce a pitiless twenty-first-century version of indentured servitude. Even if disease strikes you blind after graduation, existing law forces you to run a gauntlet of one degrading court appearance after another, to see if you might possibly qualify for a standard called "certainty of hopelessness"; and even then, there is only a slim chance to have the debt repudiated.[81] I cannot think of a more depraved and decadent theater of cruelty than having to repeatedly prove before an audience and some smug judge that your life has become "hopeless."

> With mortgage defaults, banks seize and resell the home. But if a degree can't be sold, that doesn't deter the banks. They essentially wrote the student loan law, in which the fine-print says they aren't "dischargeable." So even if you file for bankruptcy, the payments continue due. Hence these stern words from Barmak Nassirian of the American Association of College Registrars and Admissions Officers. "You will be hounded for life," he warns. "They will garnish your wages. They will intercept your tax refunds. You become ineligible for federal employment." He adds that any professional license can be revoked and Social Security checks docked when you retire. We can't think of any other [debtor] statute with such sadistic provisions.[82]

What better way to have the university teach the home truths of neoliberal life?

D) You Can Pay to Feel as Though You Are Opting Out. Murketing Is Ubiquitous.

The lowest common denominator of everyday neoliberalism is the act of being sold on something. It is one index of the blatant irrelevance of neoclassical economic theory that, in general, no one in the model is portrayed as being "sold on something," because consumers supposedly already know what they desire, and anyway, they are presumed to be "sovereign" in the marketplace. They just go out and buy what they always already want, presuming someone conveniently has it on offer. "Taste changes," should they exist, sport the divine aspect of being uncaused first causes. Hence, the vast effort dedicated to everything from persuasion to advertising to marketing to con artistry is left out of the account as irrelevant.[83] The fact that appreciable sums of money are spent in the pursuit of these activities is left to the purview of the denizens of marketing departments in business schools, exiled beyond the realm of economics proper.

Once upon a time, this oversight was deemed a devastating criticism of orthodox economics. In a sense, this was the original accusation of the bait-and-switch complaint, now blown up to system level: what goes on in markets is not primarily the conveyance of goods and services to those in need, but rather the conjuring of symbols and the fabrication of felt needs. The market, it was said, is not your humble servant, but rather a Svengali or a Stromboli. This point was popularized by John Kenneth Galbraith in his *New Industrial State*:

> Most goods serve needs that are discovered to the individual not by the palpable discomfort that accompanies deprivation, but by some psychic response to their possession. They give him a sense of personal achievement, accord him a feeling of equality with his neighbors, divert his mind from thought, serve sexual aspirations, promise social acceptability, enhance his subjective feeling of health, well-being or orderly peristalsis, contribute by conventional canons to personal beauty, or are otherwise psychologically rewarding.[84]

This approach to the economic agent as dupe never caught on, either within economics or in vernacular discourse. Leaving neoclassical economics aside (because it could never condone pervasive massive disconnect between purchases and ends), it is of some interest to explore why average people in pursuit of everyday ends could not be brought to entertain the idea that much of the economy was devoted to the manipulation of their beliefs and actions, in the face of overwhelming empirical evidence. The answer has something to do with another neoliberal technology, this one bound up with the innovation of "murketing."

It goes without saying that no one in their right mind would willingly concede that they were a hapless dupe of remote powerful economic interests. It would be a denial of a fundamental sense of autonomy, and abdication of personhood. Even Galbraith acknowledged this: "It is true that the consumer may still respond to his own view of his satisfactions. But this is superficial and proximate, the result of illusions created in connection with the management of his wants."[85] The response of most people (as opposed to economists) to such assertions is twofold: first, I feel free to ignore or otherwise negate any message beamed in my direction, thus my ability to resist is at least as strong as their ability to woo; and second, if Galbraith were right, then no product line would ever fail to find a clientele. I have a mute button on my remote control, and use it. Ad campaigns fail: QED. Latter-day followers of Galbraith bring various counterexamples to the table, such as the recent policy to suppress cigarette advertising in the United States, but to no avail.[86] Curiously enough, given that it bulks so large in everyday life, the average person still ardently believes that all that expenditure and all that effort to manage their desires is essentially impotent, and by implication, wasted.

Neoliberals, as one might expect, have come to concoct a much more plausible justification of the phenomenon. They have carefully read and absorbed their leftist critics, from Thorstein Veblen to Naomi Klein, and far from rejecting them outright, they openly use their ideas to render the process of persuasion both more unconscious and more effective.[87] Neoliberals have pioneered the signal innovation of importing the double-truth character of their project into the everyday lives of the common man. The modern hidden persuaders have gladly nurtured the conviction of the average person that he is more clever than those who seek to manipulate him in order to render him all the more open to that manipulation; the set of techniques predicated on this inversion has been dubbed "murketing." As usual, David Foster Wallace put it best: murketing is "a tongue-in-cheek pseudo-behind-the-scenes Story designed to appeal to urban or younger consumers' self-imagined savvy about marketing tactics and objective data and to flatter their sense that in this age of metastatic spin and trend and the complete commercialization of every last thing in their world they were unprecedentedly ad-savvy and discerning and canny and well-nigh impossible to manipulate."[88]

The primary technique of murketing is to blur the boundaries between branded entities and the rest of everyday life, and then proceed to engage the frank complicity of the consumer in embracing branded pecuniary culture while believing they are immune to it. It is symptomatic of the dramatic shift in conceptualization of the market away from mere conveyance of commodities and toward the neoliberal framing of the market as uniquely omnipotent information processor. It is intimately conjoined to the neoliberal project of the permanent revolution of the self: by constantly conjuring the magic of self-transformation through purchases, one must understand one's projects as subverting all external attempts by the powers that be to impose conformity to external manufactured identities. It incites the targets to believe that they can "see through" and comprehend all the brands, the con artistry, the flimflam, the propaganda, the logos, and marketing culture, all the while easing their acquiescence into that very same culture. It is another manifestation of the neoliberal promotion of ignorance, covered in the last chapter.

Murketing takes on a political dimension because it is always concerned with defining personal activity with regard to rebellion and resistance. Older muckraking work about the nefarious "hidden persuaders" would point toward clumsy techniques of subliminal appeal, like subconscious messages or sex appeal, as though we were still trapped in Orwell's Ministry of Truth. These techniques existed to get around the fundamental contradiction that some product could help you express your cherished individuality only if the corporation behind it could afford the ads by selling it to millions of people. Of course, those apparati are still in the toolbox, but the modern neoliberal murketer is far more sophisticated, because his major occupation is to replace lived experience with prefabricated "lifestyles," always seeking to move beyond the intrinsic contradiction between "belonging" and assertion of individuality. What murketing always promises to provide is the experience of thrilling rebellion from conformity, but safely nested within a popular shared script. Apostasy takes on a cozy air; insurrection is hardly distinguished from playtime. It takes what could potentially become the spark of political activity and turns it into another occasion for shopping. Murketing is therefore one of the prime defenses against actual political mobilization in the modern polity.

Although the topic deserves a tome unto itself, given our current purposes, we shall provide two short examples of the role of neoliberal murketing in everyday life.

1) Snapprenticeship. One of the most fascinating technologies of faux rebellion in the modern neoliberal murketing toolkit is the construction of situations in which the mark is led to believe she has opted out of the market system altogether. There is no better simulation of contumacy than the belief that you have removed yourself from the sphere of the market, itself then subordinated to the process of market engagement. Rob Walker supplies one of the more stunning versions of murketing, wherein a new breed of ad agency recruited unpaid volunteers to talk up products with which they were unfamiliar among their friends and acquaintances, according to sheets of talking points supplied by the agency. It is essentially the process of astro-turfed political mobilizations, pioneered by the NTC, taken to the next higher level of a marketing campaign. From the perspective of standard economic theory, "the number of individuals willing to market products they had previously never heard of, frequently for no money at all, is puzzling to say the least"; but clearly, not to the neoliberals. They know that people might feel more viscerally empowered if they have occasion to project what they conceive to be their own personality onto others, with some help from shadowy murketing agencies. The result nicely combines rebellion and conformity. Ignorance is enabling, or as one ad executive put it, "It doesn't matter if you know what you're talking about, as long as you are willing to talk a lot."[89] As the neoliberals have gleaned from the Internet, their media affiliates, and their political mobilizations, a burst of well-placed buzz tends to set the agenda, at least over the short horizon. The important thing is to coordinate the early echo-lalia, and then come prepared to ride the Gompertz curve. It helps if the initiating guerrilla cadres sport an edgy character, mime disdain for their clients, and wax ironic about their faux rebelliousness, with names like BzzAgent, the Ministry of Information, Bold Mouth, and Girls Intelligence Agency.

What is striking is the resemblance of such promotional techniques to those of the open-source movement. There also, people are recruited to provide the fruits of their labor gratis in the guise of a rebellion against the market system, which is then reprocessed by other parties into fungible commodities. Although promoted under the banner of "freedom" the process is much more attuned to fostering the self-image of the insolent anarchic hacker culture, while averting participants' gaze from the sheer amount of hierarchical coordination that is required to invest any such project with a modicum of persist-ence and continuity. Their work is cherished as direct expression of their individuality, but assumes significance only when folded into a well-integrated scheme of insiders and outsiders. The consciousness of participants is so thoroughly socialized that many of them voluntarily become avid acolytes of Hayek and his notions of spontaneous organization, without detecting the possibility of their own personal collapse of kosmos into taxis.

This strange hybrid of voluntarily unpaid labor and hierarchical control and capitalist appropriation has become so prevalent in the current neoliberal era that some have suggested it actually constitutes a novel form of economic organization, or incipient mode of production, if they indulge in Marxist terminology.[90] Perhaps it deserves to be called "unprimitive accumulation," or better, snapprenticeship. As a snapprentice, you demonstrate your willingness to serve as a neoliberal agent by voluntarily forgoing all recompense while providing something of value to others, unconcerned that they may in turn commodify its consequences or derivatives in pursuit of a profit. Snapprenticeship is very different than charity, which prides itself in bypassing the market nexus in providing eleemosynary benefit. Snapprenticeship also differs from older apprenticeship in that there are absolutely no promises or obligations bequeathed to the recruit. Snapprenticeship seeks to simulate the warm glow from giving in the indigent peon, while making sure it is a corporation that is on the receiving end.

The spread of the Internet has proven a technological boon to snapprenticeship, as well as third-party valorization of freely provided labor. Not just open-source projects, but vanity sites such as MySpace and Facebook and Google aggregate information provided gratis into databases and derivative formats that can be sold to advertisers or other aggregators. Reviews and ratings provided for free may appeal to the vanity of autodidacts, but they play a major marketing role in the business plans of sites such as Amazon and Netflix. Software that is thrown open to "beta testing" in fact confiscates all matter of quality-control stress testing that constitutes unpaid labor for the corporations that then turn around and sell the revised source code. Alternatively, websites that aggregate the voluntary unpaid contributions of bloggers are then capitalized and sold to information conglomerates. A little appeal to vanity has been leveraged into massive appropriations of unpaid labor time in the online world.[91]

The dispersed character of the Internet would seem ideally apportioned to summon forth this profusion of free labor; but old-fashioned face-to-face labor has also experienced the redoubled cultivation of snapprenticeship as a cost-saving device. Indeed, students made desperate by the dearth of employment available for new job entrants since the crash of 2008 have flooded into "internships," even to the extent of paying for the opportunity to provide free labor on a temporary basis to some of the largest and richest corporations in existence. In the ultimate neoliberal inversion, a business enterprise now exists to auction off internships, so that hapless selves desperately seeking upgrading can actually pony up serious money to work for nothing.[92] Vague promises of getting one's foot in the door and spinning networking connections rarely materialize, while the overeducated supplicant performs the most menial of tasks for less than a pittance.

As if getting domestic college students to work for free were not sufficiently cost-saving, one firm has taken the notion of international student exchange programs and turned it into a cheap way to recruit and sell temporary manual labor. Come to America and immerse yourself in the culture!

> That's the pitch on the flashy CETUSA website recruiting young college students from around the globe to work shit jobs in the US, on J-1 visas ostensibly for cultural exchange. In this case, CETUSA [Council for Educational Travel in the U.S.] delivers the students to SHS Onsite Solutions, a temp agency furnishing workers to Exel North American Logistics Inc. The latter, a subsidiary of Deutsche Post DHL, manages all the labor and operations at the big Hershey warehouse, packing and distribution center. The students pay around $3,000 to get into the program, then earn around $8 an hour, from which exorbitant rent and other fees are docked till they get down to somewhere between $140 and $40 PER WEEK of intense factory labor.[93]

This situation appeared in the *New York Times* after an organized walk-out from the indentured student workers at Hershey. CETUSA then decided to retaliate, and terminated the visas of some of the ringleaders, effectively getting them deported. The subcontracting arrangement allowed them to claim plausible deniability about the labor practices. Similar programs then came to light at other employers, because the larger program run by the State Department had placed 130,000 students in jobs during 2011.

The poor clients of CETUSA did get an education in "neoliberalism for dummies" for their trouble, although it may not have been the one they bargained for. The main lesson of snapprenticeship is that murketing works.

2) Buycotting. The second great neoliberal innovation in murketing is the creation of the phenomenon of "buycotting," or as it is sometimes called, "ethical consumerism" (Yates, "Critical Consumption"). Instead of seeming to bypass the market altogether, as in the first case, here everyday participants are enticed to believe that it is possible to mitigate some of the worst aspects of market organization by paying an "ethical premium" for particular commodities and helping to make the world become a better place. Previous generations had sought to punish firms that were perceived to violate ethical norms by boycotting them, viz., organizing the wholesale withdrawal of purchasing power from the products of the targeted firm. In the current neoliberal era, people have been weaned off the notion that concerted political abdication from market behavior can ever succeed in its objectives, and instead have been seduced into believing that the market itself can offer sufficient choice in expression of political programs along the entire spectrum. Worried about global warming? Imaginative entrepreneurs have endeavored to purvey "carbon offsets" to consumers. Want to help African AIDS patients? Get yourself an AMEX Red Card. Want to support small independent producers in underdeveloped countries? Other entrepreneurs have conveniently developed "fair trade" brands for coffee, textiles, glass, and other imports.[94]

The intellectual defenses surrounding the phenomenon of buycotting are especially instructive concerning the ways that the NTC has managed to neutralize its political opponents through the techniques of murketing. It is one of the neoliberal commandments that innovations in markets can always rectify any perceived problems thrown up by markets in the first place. Thus, whenever opponents on the nominal left have sought to ameliorate some perceived political problem through direct regulation or taxation, the Russian doll of the thought collective quickly roused itself, mobilized to invent and promote some new market device to supposedly achieve the "same" result. But what has been often overlooked is that, once the stipulated market solution becomes established as a live policy option, the very same Russian doll then also rapidly produces a harsh critique of that specific market device, usually along the lines that it insufficiently respects full market efficiency. This seemingly irrational trashing of a neoliberal policy device that had earlier been emitted from the bowels of the NTC is not evidence of an unfortunate propensity for self-subversion or unfocused rage against government, but instead an amazingly effective tactic for shifting the universe of political possibility further to the right. For buycotting always constitutes a tactical half-measure within the neoliberal project: one observes this in the initial promulgation and subsequent scuppering of carbon cap-and-trade schemes (described in chapter 6), including consumer purchase of "carbon offsets"; one observes it again in the imposition of "health insurance mandates" as a preemptive substitute for the single-payer system found in Europe, and then followed rapidly with the subsequent sabotage and rebellion against them in the United States, once they became the "centrist" approach to health care reform. The same dynamic has now has been kicking in with some forms of ethical consumerism. Buycotting exists to lull the uncommitted into belief that they can reconcile their skepticism of market results with redoubled participation in market purchases; only then to reprimand them for failing the efficiency test in the sphere of their ethical purchases.

This buycott dynamic is played out at a homely level in everyday life with one commodity many people swear by: the cup of coffee from the local barista. Coffee is the second most valuable basic commodity exported from developing countries, just after petroleum. Subsequent to the failure of an attempted OPEC-style coffee cartel in the 1980s, the organization Fairtrade Labeling Organizations International (FLOI) was created to define and organize a subset of the coffee market, combining certification of origin of the coffee in specially designated producer cooperatives, a fixed price floor to be paid to these producers, and branding as "fair trade coffee." This FLOI version of fair trade coffee accounts for approximately 4 percent of the "specialty coffee" market in 2009;[95] other branding initiatives run by large conglomerates (such as Starbucks' "Conservation International") offer some category vaguely approximating "fair trade" but with much-curtailed restrictions on the growers and price floors, which ends up being "FLOI-lite." Customers rarely have the time or patience to pay much attention to such subtle distinctions.

Customers buycotting fair trade coffee often pay a premium, and feel they are striking a blow for the faraway small producer vis-à-vis the globalized mass product. Fair Trade USA produces advertising to foster this impression; it suggests on its website:

> Instead of creating dependency on aid, we use a market-based approach that gives farmers fair prices, workers safe conditions, and entire communities resources for fair, healthy and sustainable lives. We seek to inspire the rise of the Conscious Consumer and eliminate exploitation.[96]

However, the results have been less than unequivocal. For instance, while branded fair trade coffee may indeed come from sanctioned cooperatives, it may also be packaged by prison labor or used to launder drug money. Furthermore, the majority of fair trade planters manage to sell only around 20 percent of their output to fair trade markets, so on balance, the brand has had little impact upon poverty at the ground level.[97] The commodification of "social justice" tends to be a dicey proposition even predicated upon the best of intentions, but in this instance there is constant pressure on FLOI to loosen its definitions and slacken its demands for certification throughout the commodity chain. In practice, the FLOI system is devised to make it possible for coffee consumers to "express themselves" through purchases, more than it is about changing the supply chain; this is a signal characteristic of neoliberal life, as we have argued.

However, now that fair trade coffee has achieved a substantial presence in the marketplace, along comes a concerned member of the Neoliberal Thought Collective just in time to insist that you only hurt yourself by purchasing fair trade coffee.[98] Primarily, the critique rests upon a standard neoclassical economic argument about misaligned "incentives": it is asserted that whenever prices rise, co-ops sell their inferior beans to the FLOI system and reserve their quality stock for the utterly free market in specialty coffees—in other words, the fair trade brand dupes clueless café liberals into paying more for a crappier cup of coffee. Unabashedly taking a page from the left, this critique also suggests that the FLOI funds don't really trickle down to a substantial degree to the peasant level, and that free trade has proven little more than a marketing ploy that channels much of the profits back into advertising. It is not that these questions have been settled by concerted empiricism—they have not—but the payoff comes in the moral of the story: if you had capitulated to the wisdom of the totally free market in the first place, everything would have worked out just fine.

Ultimately, buycotting exists to preempt state regulation of working conditions, product standards, best practices, and the like by inserting brands where conscious intervention would normally be imposed. It takes as its inspiration the neoliberal doctrine that the state is in many respects indistinguishable from a market, except in its handicapped ability to provide "services." This has been taken to an extreme in Sicily:

> Proponents of buycotting see these premiums as pure political expression . . . Some even argue that cash-voting goes further than ballot-casting: we buy, and therefore incentivize producers, every day; but we vote far less often. "We are convinced that how people

buy can be more effective than how they vote," said Francesco Galante, director of Comitato Addiopizzo, a civic group in Palermo, Sicily, that has taken on the mafia using an analogue of fair-trade labeling. In 2004, some volunteers in Palermo decided to bypass politicians: they approached local businesses, many of which paid the mafia 'pizzo,' or bribes, and asked them to certify that they paid pizzo no longer; in exchange, the Comitato brought them business from pizzo-averse Sicilians. Today 400 businesses and 9,000 customers have joined, even though products from the law-abiding companies often cost more.[99]

E) Biopolitics Is Here to Stay.

One of the oddities of contemporary everyday neoliberalism is that people rarely get worked up anymore when encountering overt cruelty to the poor or murketing or endless scams consisting of privatized schemes of self-improvement, and seem to have passively capitulated to fallout from the crisis, but do tend to get distinctly queasy when entrepreneurialism of the self digs down deep into the corporeal. Somehow, that pound of flesh is deemed all the more offensive or transgressive when it really is a pound of flesh traded in the marketplace. There is something about the experience that seems to trigger a gag reflex, piercing the complacency of all the other encounters that demand acquiescence in the worldview descended from Mont Pèlerin. Perhaps the only thing that keeps us from being permanently nauseated is that we ply our trades believing most corporeal enhancements and fungible soma to be merely science fiction conceits; they resemble the implausible cyborgs that populate late-night reruns. We are irreducibly intact at the cellular level; that is our rock-bottom quiddity; no one can take that away.

This abiding somatic integrity of the self is the last great double truth of the neoliberal era. It is the rock-solid foundation of our freedom, and yet the fleeting evanescent product of the imperative of flexibility. It is a myth promoted by the orthodox neoclassical economist, if only because dispelling it would reveal the great gaping emptiness of their entire edifice:

> Should we bar people from improving a very bad economic lot because it requires a deprivation of their personhood? Justice may not be "served by a ban on desperate exchanges" as, for example, selling human organs . . . An immediate reaction might well be to

let each individual decide what is essential to his or her self-constitution and act accordingly . . . To put the matter another way, who is to decide what is essential to the constitution of the self other than the self?[100]

Who or what indeed, once we start swapping out body parts, neural transmitters, biological components, and somatic identities? This breathtaking interpretation of "freedom" has not in fact been passed down through the annals of legal or institutional tradition; rather, it has been the catalytic agent in many recent interventions to render the fleshy body better tuned to respond to the exacting demands of the marketplace. The self, inevitably, takes the hindmost.

Legal systems have sought to draw bright lines where identity begins and ends, although this has come under increasing pressure in the last three decades. The universe is conventionally divided up into three big categories: items and bodies that are prohibited in every instance; items and bodies that are deemed inalienable; and items and bodies that are both legal and alienable, but where exchange under the profit motive is banned or limited. The Thirteenth Amendment of the U.S. Constitution prohibits both slavery and sale of military conscription, moving these phenomena into the second category from prior full commodity status. Sale and commercial possession of babies was subsequently presumed to occupy the first category, although we shall observe that this is rapidly eroding. Various drugs of potency in altering mental identity have been allocated to categories one and three. Steroids and other muscle enhancements in certain professional sports are relegated to category one, but for everyone else they fall into category three. The sale of human organs and gametes was long presumed to fall into the third category, but that, too, is changing. The outsourcing of certain bodily functions, such as the carrying of a human embryo to term, used to fall into category two, but that has lapsed into commodity status. Categories can sometimes differ across geographic boundaries: European law often prohibits the outsourcing of surrogacy. The fact that somatic selfhood can be sliced, diced, and reshuffled in such dramatic fashion in a relatively short time frame only goes to show that once we submit to a regime of entrepreneurship of the self, then the Archimedean fulcrum of personhood starts to slip rather perilously.

Because each of these corporeal phenomena threatens to sport a sensationalistic aura, the literature on this particular aspect of everyday neoliberalism has enjoyed somewhat better coverage than in our previous four instances of the neoliberal lifeworld. Pop culture in particular has been endlessly fascinated with the conundrums of somatic identity and emotional selfhood, so we can here rapidly point to relevant academic writings on these topics. Some Foucauldians have also been active in exploration of the topic.[101] All that has been missing in the hubbub has been exposition of the explicit links to the neoliberal project.

Outside of the obvious corporeal interventions in self-enhancement such as plastic surgery and liposuction, many of the earliest experiments in neoliberal self-alteration came out of the drug culture of the 1960s. While drugs such as caffeine, amphetamine, and Benzedrine had long been used to boost awareness, experimentation in the 1960s with drugs such as LSD, peyote, and psilocybin was oriented to subvert and otherwise alter mental identities in the user. Whereas the hippie drug culture was notionally an artifact of a rebellious counterculture, in fact the experience of taking these psychotropic hallucinogens provided one of the early testbeds for the discipline of the neoliberal transmogrification of the self. Some of the drugs heightened the experience of being a spectator at one's own performance, while others fostered dissociation from past behavior; endless analysis of trips after the fact reinforced belief in the plasticity of the self.

From this baseline, all that was required to activate the neoliberal playbook was to reorient these attitudes and practices from a feckless narcissism to a conviction that one was engaged in concerted self-modification to propitiate a market rationality far more omnipotent than anything promoted by any counterculture. One way this happened was a progressive shift in emphasis to the image of a "neurochemical self," itself a bubbling brew of neurotransmitters and electrolytes, which required pharmaceutical management and enhancement.[102] Both pharmaceutical companies and the neuroscience community promoted a doctrine of the brain as the primary corporeal organ responsible for conferring identity and selfhood. This heightened academic activity in turn attracted the attention of the economics profession, always on the lookout for any nouveau trend in the physical sciences to co-opt and absorb (not to mention new funding sources to tap). Hence another neoliberal development has been the rise of subfields of "neuroeconomics" and behavioral economics, which purport to reconcile the insistence of older neoclassical economics upon the irreducible rationality of the self with the newer neoliberal imperative to optimize the self on a daily basis.[103] For some, this suggested that the solution to the economic crisis could be outsourced to an alliance of Big Pharma and some Internet startups, recapitulating the neoliberal commandment that the solution to any market problem is redoubled market innovation:

> Perhaps one day investors and traders will have a biometric contraption connected to their computers. It could scan the prefrontal cortex of the brain, determine testosterone levels and measure sweaty palms in microseconds before warning you not to make a trade. Or today's research could result in drugs that make people more rational. "Within a few decades, performance-enhancing drugs will be part and parcel of our world," says Hersh Shefrin, a professor of behavioral finance at Santa Clara University. "Right now it's science fiction, but science fiction often becomes science."[104]

But of course, not everyone is a Wall Street trader or a major-league baseball player; but conveniently, the average person doesn't need to wait around for such science fiction scenarios to come to fruition. Performance enhancement is already part and parcel of our world. Existing neuroenhancers, from the prescription serotonin selective reuptake inhibitors (Prozac) to the off-label uses of drugs such as Ritalin, Adderall, modafinil, or Provigil, are widely used as neuroenhancers by those with access to compliant physicians, to give the lagging brain that extra kick. "Daddy's Little Helpers" have found a wide market as cognitive enhancements, when mere "human capital" can't do the trick. And they have received the endorsement of the tributaries of the Neoliberal Thought Collective:

> [The think tank employee Nicolas Seltzer said that using neuroenhancers] "is like customizing yourself—customizing your brain . . . It's fundamentally a choice you're making about how you want to experience consciousness." Whereas the 90s had been about the "personalization of technology," this decade was about the personalization of the brain . . . I asked him if he had any ethical worries about smart drugs. After a pause, he said that he might have a concern if somebody popped a neuroenhancer before taking a licensing exam that certified him, say, as a brain surgeon, and then stopped taking the drug. Other than that, he couldn't see a problem. He said that he was a firm believer in the idea that "we should have a fair degree of liberty to do with our bodies and our minds as we see fit, so long as it doesn't impinge upon the basic rights, liberty and safety of others." He argued, "Why would you *want* an upward limit on the intellectual capacities of a human being?"[105]

This enchantment with the freedom to cannibalize the self is the signal characteristic of everyday neoliberalism. As Talbot says, "It's not the mind-expanding sixties anymore. Every era, it seems, has its own defining drug. Neuroenhancers are perfectly suited for the anxiety of white-collar competition in a floundering economy."[106] Enhancement and alteration are the duty of every entrepreneurial agent in a world of unremitting competition and product uncertainty.

Once the body is analogized to a firm, then every so often it needs to be reengineered like a firm, rendering it more lean and mean, which includes takeovers (hostile or otherwise), mergers, spinoffs, divestments, and "going public." Mergers under this regime look like implants, transplants, and other surgical enhancements; divestitures look like the sale of organs, blood, and gametes. Of course, the neoliberals had nothing to do with developing the actual physical/medical processes, which long predated Mont Pèlerin; where the thought collective has made its crucial contribution has been through its insistence upon submission of these activities to dedicated market considerations, and in promotion of a proactive ethic of remaining open to elective amputation, extraction, and prosthesis. Entrepreneurial selves are far more likely to submit to corporeal alteration if they don't feel stigmatized by the asymmetric sacrifices made by those corresponding bodies undergoing divestment. Dependence upon Titmuss-style "gift economies" is therefore stridently derided, and dark hints have been routinely mooted that attempts to build reconstructive institutions upon "altruism" only make things worse—say, blood contamination during the early phases of the HIV crisis. Conversely, the destitute are praised as prospective "professional donors."[107]

The ultimate in corporeal spinoffs is the parturition of a new child; but in the neoliberal era the process has been segmented, streamlined, and outsourced in order to produce a more flexible bodily experience. The old-fashioned intimacy of the sexual act can be separated as much as the self wishes from the mechanics of reproduction: one can purchase sperm and/or eggs optimized for genetic excellence; one can dispense with copulation through in vitro fertilization; one can even outsource the carrying of the child to term through contract surrogacy.[108] What better index of the fragmentation of the self than to open up biological reproduction to a ménage à trois (or à quatre or cinq)! The oldest profession and the newest are joined in the upending of the most basic building block of cosmology in human societies: that of matrilineal or patrilineal descent. Surrogacy plays havoc with the whole idea of kinship or genealogy, creating all sorts of virtual relationships for which the language lacks common nouns.[109] As in so many other instances, what the neoliberal self loses in continuity, it gains in convenience. This is not some unfortunate by-product of technological development, it is a direct consequence of the neoliberal fragmentation of the self; and neoliberals have rushed to incorporate all the corporate innovations crash-tested elsewhere into the surrogacy relationship. For instance, the fastest-growing segment of the surrogacy market is offshore outsourcing of the carrying of embryos to wombs for rent in developing countries. Furthermore, "major lenders have begun to enter the parenthood market, offering separately tailored products to those seeking infertility treatments . . . the entrance of repeat-payer lenders offering specialized fertility credit products is likely both to increase the size of the parenthood market and alter the market's structure."[110]

The market for organs and surrogacy already exists; but the beauty of the long march of neoliberalism is that it transforms the push for its expansion into a permanent revolution of the self. In the ethics community, there has been much hand-wringing over the idea that, as genetic testing and manipulation improve, one can anticipate that customers will combine their flexible gestational activities described above with detailed genetic engineering of human children, leading to a world of designer offspring. All the palaver about healing disease and human suffering is a sideshow compared with the real objective of commercialized science, which is to empower the affluent to play God in defining their own pedigree to accommodate their individual tastes. But the beauty of twenty-first-century neoliberalism is that it thinks not one, but three moves ahead in the game of custom-made selves. As has been recently pointed out, designer children are only an imperfect way station on the path to a perfectly flexible self.[111] Why lock those children into a corporeal cage that they may themselves not like, or themselves seek to transform according to good neoliberal entrepreneurial imperatives? The ultimate goal of genetics is therefore a DNA upgrade: the ability to freely alter yourself at will at the ribonucleic level.

> An artificial chromosome could be loaded with chemical switches that allowed specific genes to be turned on or off at will, simply by taking a pill containing the right chemical trigger for activation or deactivation. In addition, the entire chromosome could itself be designed in such a way as to allow it to be turned off selectively in a

person's sex cells—thereby insuring that the construct would not be passed on to the next generation . . . One would get the best of both worlds: genetic alterations that affected all cells within a person's body, but that could still be tinkered with or completely shut down at any point in a person's lifetime.[112]

This is the true terminus of the neoliberal self: to supplant your own mother and father; to shrug off the surly bond ratings of earth; to transform yourself at the drop of a hat or the swallow of a pill; to be beholden to no other body but only to the incorporeal market. It doesn't matter if the procedure actually lies within the bounds of contemporary scientific possibility, because it is the apocalypse and the Rapture of the neoliberal scriptures.

Where's the Rest of Me?

Not many people can be bothered to actually read Hayek or Buchanan or Milton Friedman or (even) Ayn Rand; but a whole lot more people drink fair trade coffee from time to time, watch *Big Brother* or Jerry Springer; have a Facebook page they desultorily update; contemplate whether to buy insurance; find themselves short until payday; are worried enough to check their FICO score; spring for a lottery ticket at the checkout; feel conflicted at the sight of a scruffy panhandler; worry about the foreclosure sale down the street; commiserate with friends over what to think about the British summer of riots in 2011; take medication to lose weight; or anguish over whether to visit a fertility clinic. In these thousand and one little encounters spread over a lifetime, the average person begins to absorb a set of images, causal scenarios, and precepts that begin to add up to something approaching a worldview. What is significant about these brushes with neoliberalism on a granular scale is that one need not be affluent, nor have a college degree or be an autodidact, to become infused with a vision of the self that is besotted with the narcissism of a thoroughly unmoored personality, unhinged aspirations oblivious to layers of social determination. Indeed, the modern conception of agency bequeathed by the Neoliberal Thought Collective has become so intently self-centered that it has a tenuous grasp upon the very existence of something called "the economy," which assumes the divine attribute of being simultaneously everywhere yet, in practice, nowhere. We are encouraged to believe we are so "free" that no one can really control our lives, and yet the terminus of this freedom is a peculiar sort of solipsism. As one famous neoliberal economist put it:

> There has been a fundamental shift in the balance of power between consumers and salesmen over the last generation and it points in the direction of consumers. The quality and quantity of "interior" pleasures is higher than ever before, so many people shift more toward these very cheap entertainments. Because of this rise of interiority, we're saving money on our learning and entertainment and we're also telling ourselves more stories . . . If you are looking to create your own economy, what role should stories play in the process?[113]

Clearly, the role of all the stories is to keep your attention acutely focused upon *yourself*. The worse things get, you must not engage in rage, remonstration, or "stoicism," much less communal support; instead, the space spanned by your consciousness becomes the perimeter of the "economy," which is no longer about what you may make, but consists exclusively of the stories you tell about yourself. Your vigilance must never waver from its focus upon the center of your own little universe. If you encounter some difficulty in comfortably inhabiting your own little cubbyhole, there is always someone else who will tell you how to succeed at it, for a modest fee. Conjure the confidence fairy! The contemporary financial crisis collapses to a temporary aberration between your ears. Let them buy cake! If only you, the consumer, would rouse yourself to spend more! (How many times have you heard that?)[114]

This has to be one major reason the neoliberals have emerged from the crisis triumphant.

4

Mumbo Jumble: The Underwhelming Response

of the Economics Profession to the Crisis

In the aftermath to the worst economic crisis of capitalism since the Great Depression, many people understandably have grown weary of accounts concerning recent forms of suffering visited upon various categories of the populace. Some disgruntlement can be attributed to the influence of the neoliberal theater of cruelty described in the last chapter, though one cannot altogether discount garden-variety disaster fatigue. More than four years out, what seems really to have captured the imagination of the general public are instead ripping sagas of those intrepid souls who managed to come through the crisis unscathed, impervious to the damage done all around them. One nice example is Michael Lewis's *The Big Short*, which Amazon at one time listed as one of the top best-selling books on the crisis:[1] therein he relates the stories of a bunch of misfits and contrarians who managed to make substantial fortunes by betting against the securities derivatives that everyone else had found so seductive in the run-up to 2007. If Lewis's plucky Boys Behaving Badly could have bucked the headwinds so handily, then why not the rest of us?

I would like to explore a different, but similar saga of another band of brothers who appear to have emerged from the crisis unscathed, even though their behavior before and after the crisis was less than exemplary. This particular clan did not exactly get rich off the crisis, but contrary to all rational expectations, did not suffer from it, either. They appear to have evaded all responsibility for having fostered the conditions for the crisis to materialize, and subsequently have been upheld in much of the public press as solid repositories of wisdom, or at least prophets of prosperity. The group I scrutinize here is the contemporary orthodox, or "neoclassical," economics profession. Although its intellectual center of gravity can be found in the U.S., the story I impart has turned out to be more or less global in scope and character. The economic orthodoxy is (still) strikingly intellectually homogeneous across Europe and the Americas, even though it now recruits from a much more diverse geographical catchment area. Neoclassical economists, having worked hard to convince the world that everything was hunky-dory circa 2005, and concurrently having invented the rationales and the theories behind the financial time bombs that went off across the landscape, don't seem to have suffered one whit for the subsequent sequence of events, a slow-motion train wreck that one might reasonably have expected would have rubbished the credibility of lesser mortals. Individually and collectively, they have only become more dominant in academia and in government. No one among their number was fired for incompetence; no one was forced to endure status degradation ceremonies. Economists were not drummed out of their government posts. No departments of economics were closed as cost-saving measures. You have to hand it to the *New York Times*—their reporter sensed there would be no reprisals and no mass recantations among the elect as early as March 2009.[2] Indeed, contrary to all initial expectations, neoliberal economists have only elevated their public profiles and consolidated their occupation of the glittering heights since 2007. The 2011 Bank of Sweden Prize bestowed upon Thomas Sargent and Christopher Sims was exemplary of this particular culture of effrontery, this hegira from all reckoning, a big middle finger brandished at anyone who dares disparage orthodox macroeconomics. This looks like the sort of invincibility that makes for really popular comic book heroes, or embattled dictators who pronounce from the parapet that "there is no alternative."

But wait: escaping scot-free is not equivalent to having evaded all controversy and condescension along the way. The task in the next few chapters is to explore this tepidly tempestuous phenomenon within the contemporary economics profession: professing a fairly narrow set of doctrines with zero tolerance for heterodoxy before the crash, and then appearing clueless during the crash, they set upon one another with a barely restrained nastiness in the immediate aftermath. Once that grew old, instead of calling a truce and opening up their intellectual horizons by entertaining alternative accounts in reaction to events, they hastily reinstated the status quo ante and closed ranks after an interregnum, only to emerge with their positions and authority relatively unscathed.[3] Granted, there have been one or two concessions to the squaminous mobs outside the gates, but they were so minor as to pass almost unnoticed. It has been a thrill ride worthy of a quick-tempo disaster movie (think *Speed* or

Black Hawk Down), and topped only by the Houdini-esque escape of the bailed-out bankers.

Although it is usually a travesty to distinguish sharply between socio-logical and conceptual issues when seeking to comprehend a thought collective, for purposes of exposition we shall imperfectly divide our inquiry into issues of professional and personal behavior of the econom-ics profession in this chapter, and postpone consideration of specific doctrinal claims that were made in the heat of the crisis to the next chapter. While generic denunciations of economists after the crisis are a dime a dozen, we shall break ranks to go out of our way here to name names, disclose affiliations, and recount statements that the protagonists may now wish they had never uttered. We shall scour their vitas and interrogate their employers as well. It will not be unexpected that our rogues' gallery will be built upon a subterranean connection between the Neoliberal Thought Collective and the economics profession.

Churls Gone Wild

Economists did not manage to comport themselves with much dignity during the crisis.[4] Normally so quick off the mark to ferret out and expose irrationality in others, they have conspicuously been loathe to recognize a pandemic of bizarre behavior within their own ranks. One could evoke the untenable straddle of economists through the crisis by pointing to an incident that may also have occurred at a university near you, and juxtaposing it to some later developments. I have been informed of a (tenured) professor of economics at my own school, the University of Notre Dame, who, while teaching advanced macroeconomics in spring 2009, was importuned by some of his students to discuss the crisis that was then breaking out all around. After all, if you can't examine and debate a current economic crisis in a macro class, then wherever should you expect to learn about it in a modern university? Yet the students were curtly informed that it wasn't on the syllabus, and there was noth-ing about it in the assigned textbook, and the instructor therefore did not wish to diverge from the set lesson plan. And he didn't.

Now, contrast this with our predicament in 2012. All around, from the most rabid Hayekian on the right to the polemical Joseph Stiglitz on the "legitimate left," almost every economist enjoying a modest public profile now proclaims that the crisis clearly demonstrated that his own favorite economic theory was right after all, and consequently, there is no need to call for any thoroughgoing revisions to economics.[5] More astounding, the public press and the blogosphere had taken to uncritically repeating this wisdom verbatim, but had begun to have second thoughts. In one high-profile case, the Queen of England felt impelled to query the economists at the LSE in November 2008 as to why no one in the profession had warned of the crisis. After a fluster of indecision, the economists at the British Academy wrote back to the monarch suggesting she was mistaken: they had been on top of events all along, although there may have been a wee failure of imagination.[6] Or in another instance, when I attended the widely reported and lavishly appointed inaugural meeting of the Institute for "New" Economic Thinking, funded by George Soros, in Cambridge in April 2010, I was struck that (by my estimate) roughly 70 percent of all the presentations were devoted to the argument that existing neoclassical economics most emphatically need not be replaced, nor even much revised in dealing with the crisis. No one was caught unawares, they insisted; no one was forced to reconsider their commitments, to hear them tell it now. If this was New Thinking, one trembles to contemplate what Old Thinking had looked like.

Clearly, all these gems of conventional wisdom cannot all be simultaneously correct. Neoclassical economics cannot have been both oblivious to system degradation before the fact, and yet spot-on concerning the crisis all along. Perhaps we should have anticipated this reaction from a profession renowned for predicting fourteen of the last six downturns. But it was not as though some individual members of the profession had not noticed that they had entered treacherous waters when the crisis broke. Something had to give.

The figure of the economist has more often than not served as a butt for jokes or perhaps the template for an unsympathetic protagonist in the larger culture;[7] economists make for lousy celebrities. No one thinks twice about Charlie Sheen when the house lights come back up. The standard stereotype is verbose, dull, and a little oblivious. When Greece and Italy needed faceless technocratic Gray Men to head up their floundering governments in the euro crisis, they short-circuited elections and opted for economists (trained at MIT, no less; and former Goldman employees). Nevertheless, something novel and not a little creepy started to happen in 2008. General-interest magazines, from *Business Week* to *The Economist* to the *New York Times*, which had hitherto volunteered as cheerleaders for the economics profession without encouragement, turned openly hostile in 2008, hectoring whole schools of thought for their failures, grasping randomly for "new paradigms," rooting around for sixth-round draft picks and telegenic wicked rebels to replace their prior stable of catallactic pundits. Lusting for scapegoats, journalists initially scoured the landscape for miscreants like

Bernie Madoff, Dick Fuld, and Joseph Cassano; and then instinctively turned to find their counterparts inside the economics profession. There was even an online ballot for receipt of the Ignoble (or "Dynamite") Prize, to be awarded to three economists deemed to have contributed the most to the global financial collapse. (The winners were Alan Greenspan, Milton Friedman, and Larry Summers.)

Of course, there existed no equivalent of the Justice Department or the Securities and Exchange Commission to actually police the economists, just as there was no phalanx of gumshoes and DAs to do the hard investigative work; and thus it dawned upon some that (unlike medicine, and even sociology) there was not even a professional code of ethics to which bona fide economists were enjoined to subscribe. (We revisit this miscarriage later in this chapter). You can't transgress a ukase that doesn't actually exist. Contrary to first impressions, then, it was going to be a long, hard slog to make any indictments stick. Think-tank ringers (and agents provocateurs from the neoliberal Russian doll) were busy stirring the pot, while remaining hidden in the wings.[8] Furthermore, some of the self-appointed cops (and not a few of the political protagonists) turned out to be card-carrying economists themselves. *Quis custodiet ipsos custodes?*

Hence the jejune American habit of dividing up the dramatis personae into the "good guys" and "bad guys" ran smack dab into the journalists' nightmare, namely, the Sargasso Sea of Ambiguity, where all shadows were gray and all doctrines context-laden. That didn't put a stop to the attacks on economics; but it did encourage certain lazy journalistic practices, like uncritically conflating the Nobel Prize (which, of course, due to its provenance was itself not a fully legitimate Nobel in the first place) with an imprimatur of generic intellectual legitimacy and relevance to issues of crisis. (No journalist would ever be reprimanded by their editor for consulting a Nobel winner, however irrelevant the actual work of the person in question had been to the matters at hand.) Hence, it became a cliché to pit one Nobel economist against another, and to substitute kabuki blood sport for serious thought concerning the really interesting question of the culpability of the existing economics profession in bringing about the current crisis.

Mark Thoma reported on how bootless the unreflexive dependency upon the sanctioned wisdom of Nobel winners had become by 2011:

What caused the financial crisis that is still reverberating through the global economy? Last week's 4th Nobel Laureate Meeting in Lindau, Germany—a meeting that brings Nobel laureates in economics together with several hundred young economists from all over the world—illustrates how little agreement there is on the answer to this important question. Surprisingly, the financial crisis did not receive much attention at the conference. Many of the sessions on macroeconomics and finance didn't mention it at all, and when it was finally discussed, the reasons cited for the financial meltdown were all over the map. It was the banks, the Fed, too much regulation, too little regulation, Fannie and Freddie, moral hazard from too-big-to-fail banks, bad and intentionally misleading accounting, irrational exuberance, faulty models, and the ratings agencies. In addition, factors I view as important contributors to the crisis, such as the conditions that allowed troublesome runs on the shadow banking system after regulators let Lehman fail, were hardly mentioned.[9]

Public disputations on the crisis had begun to take on the air of a bad Rodney Dangerfield film. Paul Krugman had kicked things up a notch with his September 2009 magazine article "How Did Economists Get It So Wrong?" which pointed out the "profession's blindness to the very possibility of catastrophic failures in a market economy," but then attributed it to the bizarre notion that "economists, as a group, mistook beauty, clad in impressive-looking mathematics, for truth." This provoked such a rise out of a number of economists that they promptly left all penchant for beauty behind. People who normally spoke in mind-numbing monotones about optimal monetary rules and time-inconsistent policies suddenly started gettin' up in others' bidness, trash talkin' who be disrespectin' whom, dissing anyone but their peeps. You may think I exaggerate, but do take a moment to check out the level of calumny, defamation, and slander crammed into this single footnote,[10] and then tell me this is circumspect behavior in a science that prides itself in maintaining savoir faire amid dour conformity and dismal prognostications.

After a couple of rounds of this, the disquiet that began to nag at many journalists was: Just how far should we be trusting these guys, anyway? Jamie Galbraith was about the only high-profile economist to echo an attitude that had become commonplace in the blogs:

> Leading active members of today's economics profession . . . have formed themselves into a kind of Politburo for correct economic thinking. As a general rule—as one might generally expect from a gentleman's club—this has placed them on the wrong side of every important policy issue, and not just recently but for decades. They deny the possibility of events that then happen . . . They oppose the

most basic, decent and sensible reforms, while offering placebos instead. They are always surprised when something untoward (like a recession) actually occurs. And when they finally sense that some position cannot be sustained, they do not reexamine their ideas. They do not consider the possibility of a flaw in logic or theory. Rather, they simply change the subject. No one loses face, in this club, for having been wrong.[11]

Economists were not of a temperament to suffer what they deemed the New Disrespect lying down. Anyhow, it was proving galling to turn the other cheek when reputable news outlets were sneering "What Good Are Economists, Anyway?" (Coy) and "What Went Wrong with Economics?" (*Economist*), and books from reputable publishers were quick off the mark trumpeting "The Myth of the Rational Market" (Fox) and "A Failure of Capitalism" (Posner). "Is it fair to attack the economics profession? To a large degree, yes."[12] People were of course always welcome to mock at economists in private, which was nothing new, but this seemed to be a different sort of animal. Remonstrants flocked to the talk shows, the newspapers, magazines, and op-ed pages; but beyond that, they also entered the blogosphere in a big way for perhaps the first time. Not only did a range of hallowed Big Names begin posting regular blogs, but so did some previously unsung economics faculty, and more significantly, tyro students of the subject.[13] Prior to the crisis, economics had been something that the average person had gone out of their way to avoid, rather like a colonoscopy. Suddenly, it seemed like everyone with a Web browser summoned a quick and nasty opinion about what had gone wrong with economics, and were not at all shy about broadcasting it to the world. Consequently, it looked as if the content and significance of modern economics for the crisis had collapsed into an unseemly free-for-all, pitched somewhere between a barroom brawl and a roller derby.

Yet the strangest thing of all about this fracas was that much of it was forgotten almost as soon as the pixels faded. It was as if economists and their critics were no different from the protagonist of the Christopher Nolan film *Memento*: beset with massive memory loss, they forgot what they had just inscribed on their skin last week or last month, condemned to surprise themselves over and over. The contempt of neoclassical economists for the history of economic thought was notorious; but here it was, deployed in real time. One of the ten commandments of neoclassical theory is that bygones are bygones; neoclassical economists trusted that the attention spans of their patrons were so short and flighty that this principle would extend to anything they might have said about the crisis, and one another. And with hindsight, who's to say they were wrong?

One major problem of documenting what actually happened during this melee is that all manner of defenses were being sent up as trial balloons, and just as often rapidly abandoned if they landed with a thud. Some economists coquetted with the idea that the crisis had nothing whatsoever to do with them, as if it had happened in a parallel universe far, far away; like the position of the Notre Dame economist described above. Others assumed the stance that economists should acknowledge the obvious, but that from the tough-minded "only the market matters" perspective, there would be no negative fallout for orthodox economics. Card-carrying members of the NTC were major players in this regard. For instance, MPS member Robert Barro wrote, "Like Bob Lucas, I have a hard time taking seriously the view that the financial and macroeconomic crisis has diminished economics as a field. In fact, the crisis has clearly raised the demand for economic services and economists. There is no more counter-cyclical occupation than economist."[14]

But the standard neoliberal line that eventually won the day, as we should expect, was that any failings, should they have existed, were distinctly personal and idiosyncratic, and that the thought collective *qua* collective was pure and innocent as the driven snow. Raghuram Rajan, a Chicago economist and a major presence on the airwaves because the media anointed him as one of the mainstream "predictors" of the crisis, was point man on this line: "'It was not so much ideology as it was hubris,' Rajan said of conservative economists, Greenspan included." In an op-ed article in the *Financial Times*, Rajan defended the upside of financial speculation, blaming the harmful fallout on the Congress and the Fed for distorting market incentives. Elsewhere, the Stanford economist Gregory Rosston was quoted as saying, "I don't think (recent events are) necessarily a repudiation of the Chicago School of economics as personified by Alan Greenspan, but it definitely shows there is some role for regulation in society." Actually, all that was revealed was the unabashed ignorance of history on the part of Rosston, since Alan Greenspan was never a member in good standing of the Chicago School, but rather an acolyte of the Ayn Rand cult, who had been awarded a belated PhD by NYU in 1977 *after* serving as chairman of the Council of Economic Advisors under Gerald Ford, and who subsequently parlayed numerous right-wing political connections into elevation to his position as chairman of the Federal Reserve from 1987 to 2006. The fact that such an extreme outsider and ersatz economist could have risen to such a pinnacle of prominence was itself testimony to the hold of neoliberals on power, a fact that could never quite sink in for the American news media.[15]

Everyone likes a good catfight, and if that's all there had been to it, then this entire episode could be left to some future cultural historian. But there were two considerations that render the folderol of current interest: one, the effectiveness of neoliberals in stiffening resistance to any and all initiatives to reform the economics profession; and two, the fact evident in retrospect of neoclassical economics sailing through the crisis essentially unscathed in the face of such unseemly behavior. To take but two counterexamples, Freudian psychology and social studies of science have in the recent past been internally roiled and intellectually altered by attacks far less evocative in the way of public embarrassment. Yet here was economics, by contrast, the prodigal profession, rapidly welcomed back to the media and the halls of power with alacrity, patted on the head, and all was forgiven. People began to revert to their general hebetude toward economic theory and economists, and even while the economy further deteriorated, more orthodox neoclassical economists were churned out of academic departments. Barro had been prescient. A few economists noticed and marveled at this.[16] That is how it must feel to be really invincible.

I'm not interested in getting in a few sucker punches of my own; and I'm not congenitally a peacemonger nor conciliator, much less inclined to preach the virtues of a quiet life; but there does seem a modicum of insight in taking a deep breath and surveying the curious predicament of the economics profession, as a preliminary to exploration of how and why it dodged the bullet. Maybe we might extract a few lessons from the fiasco, if only to preserve some small part of the historical record before it is expunged from the collective memory of the profession (a purge that is already under way). Apologists are already hyperventilating that *nothing untoward has happened.*[17]

Four Short Homilies from a Dark Nave

Lesson 1: This is what happens when you banish history and philosophy

The reader may struggle to find it within their own heart to feel sorry for economists in their plight; and it is not my intention to stoke pity or schadenfreude in the audience. Rather, the task is to recount these events as a sequence of otherwise avoidable tragedies, the first of which must be conceded to have been the exile of history and philosophy from any place within the contemporary academic economic orthodoxy. After a brief flirtation in the 1960s and '70s, the grandees of the profession took it upon themselves to express their disdain and scorn for the types of self-reflection practiced by "methodologists" and historians of economics, and to go out of their way to prevent those so inclined from occupying any tenured foothold in reputable economics departments.[18] It was perhaps no coincidence that history and philosophy were the areas where one found the greatest concentrations of skeptics concerning the shape and substance of the postwar American economic orthodoxy.

Top-ranked journals such as the *American Economic Review*, *Quarterly Journal of Economics*, and the *Journal of Political Economy* (the Chicago house organ) declared they would cease publication of any articles whatsoever in the area, after a long history of acceptance. Once this policy was put in place, then derivative journal rankings were used to deny hiring and promotion at the commanding heights of economics to those with methodological leanings. Consequently, the graybeards summarily expelled both philosophy and history from the graduate economics curriculum; and then they chased it out of the undergraduate curriculum as well. This latter exile was the bitterest, if only because many undergraduates often want to ask why the profession believes what it does, since their own allegiances are still in the process of being formed. The excuse tendered to repress this demand was that the students needed still more mathematics preparation, more statistics, and more tutelage in "theory," which meant in practice a boot camp regimen consisting of endless working of problem sets, problem sets, and more problem sets, until the poor tyros were so dizzy they didn't have the spunk left to interrogate the masses of journal articles they had struggled to absorb. How this encouraged students to become acquainted with the economy was a bit of a mystery—or maybe it telegraphed the neoclassical lesson that you didn't need to attend to the specifics of actual existing economies.[19] It was brainwashing, pure and simple, carried out under the banner of rigor. Then, by the 1990s, by construction there was no longer any call for offering courses in philosophy or history of doctrine, since there were no economists left with sufficient training (not to mention interest) in order to staff the courses.[20] Economists would periodically be sounding off in the most illiterate registers concerning Karl Marx, Vilfredo Pareto, Hyman Minsky, Adam Smith, or even John Maynard Keynes, because they were confident no one would ever call them to task on their shallow pretenses.

Consequently, once the Great Mortification followed in the wake of the collapse of the Great Moderation, those occupying the commanding heights of the profession were bereft of any sophisticated resources to understand their predicament. In a pinch, many fell back on the most superficial of personal recollections, or else the last refuge of scoundrels, the proposition that "we" already knew how to handle the seemingly anomalous phenomena, but had unaccountably neglected to incorporate these crucial ideas into pedagogy and cutting-edge research. It takes some thick skin not to cringe at the performance of four famous economists at the January 2010 meetings of the American Economics Association in Atlanta, in a session expressly titled, "How Should the Financial Crisis Change How We Teach Economics?"[21] Three out of the four could not even be bothered to actually address the posited question, so concerned were they to foster the impression that they personally had not been caught with their pants down by the crisis. The fourth thought that simply augmenting his existing textbook with another chapter defining collateralized debt obligations and some simple orthodox finance theory would do the trick. Things got even worse in the subsequent year, with figures such as Alan Blinder and John B. Taylor touting new editions of their undergraduate macrotheory textbooks by reassuring instructors that the crisis did not require them to change anything they had been teaching for years.[22] No second thoughts for us foxes, thank you.

For the ragged remnants of economic methodologists, it was a sorry sight to watch a few older economists rummaging around in the vague recesses of memories of undergraduate courses criticizing Milton Friedman's little 1953 benediction for believing whatever you pleased as long as it was neoclassical, and coming up with nothing better than badly garbled versions of Popper and Kuhn.[23] Of course, quite a few had premonitions that something had gone very wrong, but the sad truth was that they were clueless when it came to analytical deployment of abstract philosophical argument in isolating just where the flaws in professional practice could be traced, and assessing the extent that they were susceptible to methodological remedies. Mired in banality, the best they could manage to prescribe was more of the same. No wonder almost every economist instead took their philosophical perplexity as an opportune occasion to settle internecine scores *within* the narrow confines of the orthodox neoclassical profession: MIT vs. Chicago, Walras vs. Marshall, mindless econometrics vs. mindless axiomatics, New Keynesians vs. New Classicals, Pareto suboptima vs. rational bubbles, efficient markets vs. informationally challenged markets . . . In May 2010, Dominique Strauss-Kahn, still chief at that point of the IMF, insisted that "the crisis is an opportunity"; perhaps even he didn't quite grasp back then that the main opportunity was for revenge (both personal and intellectual).

Lesson 2: Economists lost control of the discussion
of the shape of the crisis early on

Exhibit #1 demonstrating that the economics profession was caught unawares by the meltdown in 2008 was the fact that it rapidly lost any control over how the crisis was discussed in public that year. From the failure of Bear Stearns forward, journalists scrambled to understand how it could be that problems in one sector would ramify and amplify into other sectors, such that the entire financial system seemed poised on the brink of utter failure. There had been bankruptcies and dodgy financial deals before: What was so different this time around? Reporters started out by interviewing the usual suspects (Alan Greenspan, and Ben Bernanke—himself prophet of the Great Moderation), and overwhelmingly, neoliberal economists from gold-plated schools (Martin Feldstein, Gregory Mankiw, Matthew Slaughter, Robert Barro, Glenn Hubbard, Larry Summers, Allan Meltzer, Ken Rogoff), but you could tell that all the tendering of lame reassurances was not holding up against the tsunami of bad news. Of course, the keening public just wanted simple answers and quick fixes, but the economists didn't seem to provide any answers whatsoever. So the journalists, with a little help from the chattering classes, came up with the metaphors which ultimately rose to dominate initial discussions of the crisis in 2008–9.

Upon reflection, it was perhaps not unexpected that the concepts which came to dominate "explanation" in the generalist press were a mélange of biological and religious metaphors: Nature and God usually trump the market in America. Although the actual array of metaphors bandied about back then pose all sorts of interesting questions from a rhetorical point of view (and someday should attract its very own Derrida), the main lesson we shall draw here from our superficial survey is that none of them had anything whatsoever to do with economic theory. They were the flimsiest of jerry-built constructs, improvised on the fly to make someone disoriented by panic believe we could make some instant sense of the crisis.

The first, and most persistent, explanation of the nature of the crisis involved repeated reference to "toxic assets." A quick content search reveals the term first surfacing in the *Wall Street Journal* in January 2004. What started out as a mere figure of speech suddenly blossomed in 2008 to constitute Finance for Dummies in the heat of the crisis—and even seems to have influenced the shape (and title) of the original three-page TARP plan sent to Congress. People liked it because it embodied both a notion of the problem and the cure—if you "ingest/invest" too many "toxic assets" you die, but the way to get rid of poison is to flush it out of your system. Hence the entire crisis was not so different from an outbreak of *E. coli* infesting your spinach: dangerous, to be sure, but definitely not a system pathology. All we had to do was detox and everything would return to health. The beauty of the metaphor was it elided all the hard work of explaining ABSs, CDOs, CDSs, SIVs and nearly everything else that actually caused the crisis. The assets were toxic; we didn't need to know how or why; we didn't stop to think that the financial system might have *intentionally produced them*—raising the prospect that therefore the entire metaphor was wonky at base. (It would be as if a snake naturally produced venom, only to kill itself.)

But more to the point, the metaphor had no basis whatsoever in the orthodox theory of finance, such as it existed in 2008. In that theory, efficient markets are arbitrage-free, and any contingent claim can be reduced to any other contingent claim through some stochastic wizardry (chapter 5 goes into some greater detail on these issues). Hence risk itself can always be commodified and traded away—that is the service the financial sector performs for the rest of the economy. That's just Intro Finance 101, from CAPM to Black-Scholes. In academic doctrine, the system as a whole simply cannot fail to price and allocate risks; hence there is no such thing as virulently "toxic" assets. Crappy assets, junk bonds, dogs with fleas, yes; but inherently "toxic," never.

The other dominant metaphor was the biblical "Day of Reckoning."[24] Americans love a good apocalypse, and journalists found some figures who were willing to deliver it, from Naseem Taleb and his "Black Swan" to Nouriel Roubini as Dr. Doom. The evil will be punished, the last shall be made first, the moneychangers will be ejected from the temple, and the righteous shall triumph. I hope I need not expound upon the fact that there is nowhere to be found such Old Testament reckoning in orthodox economic theory: the market correctly evaluates everything in real time, and no one is really punished, but rather experiences depreciation of their human capital (or something like that). This metaphor lacked staying power, however, once it started to become clear that the putative sinners, the investment bankers, never had to face the music at all. Instead, they were bailed out by the taxpayers, and went on to enjoy their most profitable year in history in 2009. Notoriously, bankers raked in record bonuses. Indeed, profits per employee in all privately held U.S. companies more than recovered by 2011, as revealed in Table 4.1 and Figure 4.1, while employment itself languished.

Apparently all boats were not raised by the profit gusher. Socialism for
the rich seems blatantly antithetical to the Great Reckoning, so we just
stopped hearing about that by roughly mid-2009.

Table 4.1: Average Profits per Employee, U.S. Firms	
Year	Profit per employee (Privately held companies)
2001	$9,998.21
2002	$10,716.71
2003	$10,813.91
2004	$11,663.59
2005	$13,026.41
2006	$13,428.02
2007	$13,638.99
2008	$12,533.96
2009	$10,045.56
2010	$12,488.02
2011	$15,278.72

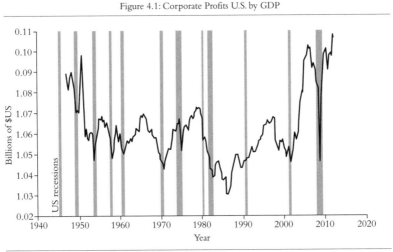

Figure 4.1: Corporate Profits U.S. by GDP

Source: St. Louis Federal Reserve

The last dominant metaphor of desperate resort was the myth of Eternal Return—usually phrased as the question "Is this another Great
Depression?" This was not an attempt to channel Nietzsche as much as
it was a quest to normalize threatening events by suggesting that
however bad things got, it had all happened once before. The

economists Barry Eichengreen and Kevin O'Rourke did some serious work attempting quantitative comparisons (see Figures 4.2, 4.3),[25] but the truth was, after a short interval, the most this trope demonstrated was that no one really had cared very much about the specifics of history. The underlying motivation of journalists had been to recast system breakdown as *repetition*, and therefore unremarkable, something partaking of a modicum of reassurance. Yet the figures revealed that, while the initial contraction was, if anything, sharper than 1929–30, around year two of the crisis, both equity markets and world trade began to turn around in a way they had not in the Great Depression. While both divergences could be traced to specific neoliberal triumphs in the teeth of the crisis—namely, the direct bailouts of large financial firms and their financialized counterparts in other sectors, combined with a ferocious resistance to any controls imposed upon capital flows and international trade—and as such might betoken further weakness down the line, journalists instead rapidly lost interest in the ways in which the current crisis might be "different" than the Great Depression. Indeed, they were rescued from having to seriously confront history by the intervention of a famous Harvard professor, and thus endorsed the convenient Kenneth Rogoff mantra that we could ignore anyone who insisted upon structural specificity in history, because every financial crisis was essentially the same.[26] At that juncture, journalists just lost all interest in the Great Depression.

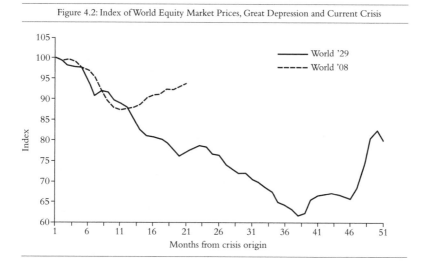

Figure 4.2: Index of World Equity Market Prices, Great Depression and Current Crisis

Figure 4.3: Index Volume of World Trade, Great Depression and Current Crisis

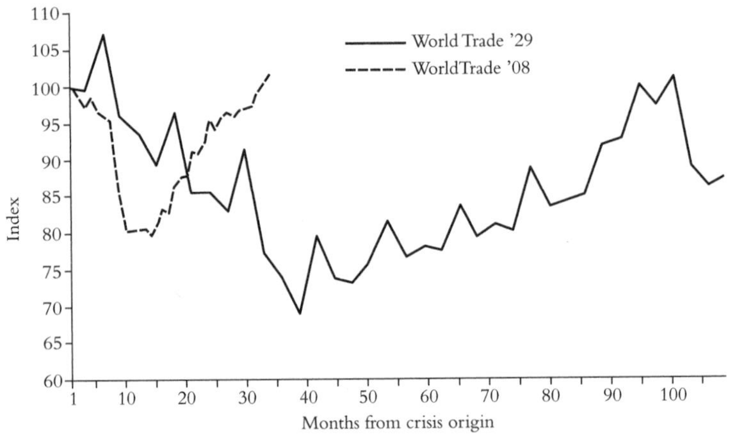

Source: voxeu.org

This blasé line emanating from Harvard and the National Bureau of Economic Research committed the ultimate historical solecism by lumping together two centuries of credit crises as somehow "the same," attempting to reduce them all to a few implausible quantitative indicators of sovereign debt to GNP and a "capital mobility index." Thus was this particular journalists' trope tamed and recaptured by the economics profession, indirectly revealing neoclassical economists' contempt for history. Conveniently, this recapture of crisis discourse turned out also to be the opening salvo of the neoliberal offensive that all attention concerning crisis debilities should be refocused away from the private sector and toward the debt obligations of the state. But economists could not bring themselves to begin to discuss the major structural difference between 1929 and 2008: this time around, professional economists had played a much larger role in producing the conditions leading to systemic breakdown, from theorizing the financial innovations and staffing the financial institutions to justifying the deconstruction of regulatory structures held over from the last Great Depression. The profession did not entirely succeed in distracting public attention from that fact, but history was never a strong suit for Americans, and luckily for the economists, flighty attention spans quickly moved elsewhere.

What is significant in hindsight is that all of this hastily improvised analysis and metaphorical effusion by journalists and bloggers had essentially evaporated by 2010. A net search of Google Trends, inscribed in Figure 4.4, shows just to what extent mentions of "toxic assets" turned out to be just a flash in the pan. The "explanations" concocted by the journalists tended to melt away like the late winter snow as the crisis lengthened, and there exposed were the economists, same as they'd always been, ready to resume their role as high priests of the economy.

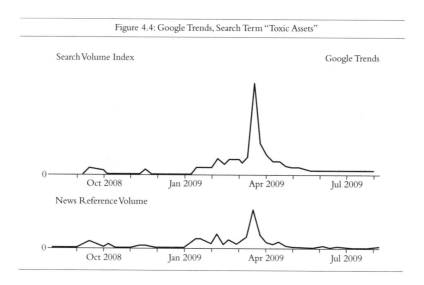

Figure 4.4: Google Trends, Search Term "Toxic Assets"

Somehow, the public managed to forget that economists had been caught clueless in the initial downdraft, and began to play along with the pretence that economists had been on top of things all along.

Lesson 3: Science is part of the problem, not obviously the solution

Whenever economists hit a bad patch, it is inevitable that outsiders will begin to sneer about how economics is not a science, and proceed to prognosticate how "real science" would make short work of the crisis. This is such a tired Western obsession, threadbare and careworn, it is astounding that it has not occurred to critics that such proleptic emotions must have occurred before, and are thus themselves part of a chronic debility in our understanding of economic history. Without going into the issue here, the current author has shown elsewhere in detail how neoclassical economics was born of a crude attempt to directly imitate physics in the 1870s, and that the American orthodoxy was the product of further waves of physicists cascading over into economics in the Great Depression and World War II. It is thus not such a stretch that, for instance, Paul Krugman became an economist because he had fallen in love with science fiction as a child.[27] So, if anything, economics has suffered a surfeit of saviors (and their theories) transported from the natural sciences: the real question should be, why should we expect things to work out any better this time around?

Actually, it is known among the cognoscenti that physicists have again been tumbling head over heels into economics since the 1980s, as their own field experienced severe contraction at the cessation of the Cold War. And where did most of them end up? Why, in the banks, of course, inventing all those ultracomplex models for estimating and parceling out risk. Some of these Exiles on Wall Street bothered to attain some formal degree in economics, while others felt it superfluous to their career paths. In any event, the exodus of natural scientists into economics was one of the (minor) determinants of the crisis itself—without "rocket scientists" and "quants," it would have been a whole lot harder for banks and hedge funds to bamboozle all those gullible investors, not to mention turning privatized trading into a robot operation (Patterson, *Dark Pools*). Everyone since the eighteenth century has sought to leverage their credibility in the history of economics with "science," most frequently through appropriation of mathematical models and/or methods; alas, never has it turned out to be the Philosopher's Stone. So much for the bracing regimen of a background in the natural sciences.

If anything, responses to disparagements of the contemporary profession that tended to pontificate upon the nature of "science" were even more baffling than the original calls for deliverance through natural science in the first place. Economists were poorly placed to lecture others on the scientific method; although they trafficked in mathematical models, statistics, and even "experimentation," their practices and standards barely resembled those found in physics or biology or astronomy. Fundamental constants or structural invariants were notable by their absence. Indeed, one would be hard pressed to find an experimental refutation of any orthodox neoclassical proposition in the last four decades, so appeals to Karl Popper were more ceremonial than substantial. Of course, sometimes the natural sciences themselves encountered something commensurable to a crisis in their own fields of endeavor—think of dark matter and dark energy, or the breakdown of causality in the 1920s—but they didn't respond by evasive maneuvers and suppressing its consideration, as did the economists.

In retrospect, appeals to science will be seen to have proven a bit of a red herring in coming to terms with the current crisis. Physical complexity theory or neuromysticism or dark matter won't save us now. In the heat of battle, economists purported to be defending "science'"when, in fact, they were only defending themselves and their minions.

Lesson 4: The failure of the economics profession is a saga of social disfunction

> The completeness of the [orthodox] victory is something of a curiosity and a mystery. It must have been due to a complex of suitabilities in the doctrine to the environment into which it was projected. That it reached conclusions quite different from what the ordinary uninstructed person would expect, added, I suppose, to its intellectual prestige. That its teaching, translated into practice, was austere and often unpalatable, lent it virtue. That it was adapted to carry a vast and consistent logical superstructure, gave it beauty. That it could explain much social injustice and apparent cruelty as an inevitable incident in the scheme of progress, [with] the attempt to change such things as likely on the whole to do more harm than good, commended it to authority. That it afforded a measure of justification to the free activities of the individual capitalist, attracted the support of the dominant social authority. But although the doctrine itself has remained unquestioned by orthodox economists up to a late date, its signal failure for purposes of scientific prediction has greatly impaired, over the course of time, the prestige of its practitioners. For professional economists . . . were apparently unmoved by the lack of correspondence between the results of their theory and the facts of observation; a discrepancy which the ordinary man has not failed to observe, with the result of his growing unwillingness to accord to economists that measure of respect which he gives to other groups of scientists.

Is this paragraph the writing of some superficial blogger venting intemperate spleen, spitting on economists when they are down? Or perhaps some unreconstructed conspiracy theorist, eager to expose the nefarious plot behind the rise and fall of intellectual orthodoxies? Or instead, is it the rumination of some crude externalist sociologist of science, who can only explain the behavior of intellectuals as sock puppets for the interests they represent? Or yet one more Foucauldian exercise in ferreting out the subterranean connections between power and knowledge? I expect that few will recognize the author as the figure whose stock had briefly risen since 2007, John Maynard Keynes.[28]

In this book, I hold no brief for Keynesian economics as an automatic prescription for whatever ails us in the twenty-first century. Indeed, it has long been argued by an older generation of thinkers[29] that Keynesian economics, or at least the version enshrined in the so-called neoclassical synthesis, has been a self-inflicted wound on the left from the 1950s onward. At minimum, it has been used to promote the short-sighted fallacious doctrine mooted in our first chapter, that financial crises could be unproblematically sequentially repaired by "reflation" and the state backstopping insolvent institutions by assuming their debts. This dogma has been the Achilles heel of otherwise interesting economists commenting on the crisis, from Joseph Stiglitz to John Quiggin to Jared Bernstein. However, leaving that aside for the nonce, it is striking the way that it could be taken for granted in the 1930s that the social position of economists might tend to lead them to exhibit biases in certain predictable directions, and that respected members of the profession could concede that those social structures would mount obstacles to serious analysis of economic breakdown. This was not flaming Marxism; it was just commonsense sociology of knowledge. Yet where are the comparable analyses today? Perhaps because we now have come to suspect that there is no direct lockstep connection between socialization and thought has it been given a wide berth, or is it something far more insidious, like unconscious capitulation to the neoliberal epistemic doctrine of the prevalence of an efficient marketplace for ideas?

As late as February 17, 2010, PBS *Newshour* provided a platform to the Chicago economist John Cochrane to roundly assert that government spending has no net effect on the economy. Insiders to the profession know this as "Ricardian Equivalence," but that is tantamount to insisting, "You can't fool Mother Market." But fooling the market was how the crisis developed in the first place. You should view the segment for yourself to gain an impression of the smug demeanor of someone who has drunk the Kool-Aid a little too avidly. I had to check my browser to make sure I wasn't watching a clip from *The Colbert Report*. Perhaps Cochrane and I had been living in parallel universes over the previous two years. Just one representative quote: "The economy can recover very quickly from a credit crunch if left on its own." Maybe in the Chicago Wormhole Universe.[30]

But then again, maybe not. The *New Statesman* had the brilliant idea of reconnecting with the twenty U.K. economists who had signed an open letter in February 14, 2010, supporting Chancellor George Osborne's strategy of producing growth through fiscal austerity and budget cuts.[31] Since then, Britain had promptly entered further contraction, and the Treasury ended up far exceeding its borrowing limits: so much for deficit reduction. The respondents were astoundingly mealy-mouthed, avoiding comment on their clear error (John Vickers, Kenneth Rogoff) or vaguely distancing themselves from Tory cuts by mumbling about "investments" (Roger Bootle, Danny Quah, David Newbery, Hashem Pesaran, Tim Besley); only two opted for full-throated repudiations of Keynesian stimulus (Christopher Pissarides, Albert Marcet). No mea culpas from that quarter—they thought you ditsy folks had long forgotten that inconvenient letter!

Even a year or two later, it can be readily discerned that Cochrane was baldly in error. However, the question that haunts this chapter is: How can these people maintain such positions? How could 132 economists sign a public petition in November 2011 stating that fiscal austerity by the government will provide more jobs than fiscal stimulus in *both* the short and long term?[32] Does the experience of Greece and Spain mean nothing? To a first approximation, one may subdivide the question in two: what psychological equipment permits people like Cochrane to persist so doggedly in their error; and second, what permits the various gatekeepers of the media and academic journals to continue to promote figures like Cochrane, Michael Boskin, Casey Mulligan and Douglas Holtz-Eakin as people worth reading and listening to? Our brief excursion into historical amnesia and social psychology in chapter 2 proffers a short answer to the first question: it is human nature not to relinquish deeply held beliefs in the face of contradictory evidence, especially if one never knew anything different. Lesson 1 informs us that the modern economist comes equipped with a trained incapacity for historical and philosophical reflection. However, the answer to the second question turns out to be far more complicated, and will connect us up with our primary concerns regarding the Neoliberal Thought Collective.[33] It is insufficient to baldly assert, "Neoclassical economics has won, not because it describes reality accurately, but because it describes a reality which dominant interests want."[34] What sustains their stubbornness? What injects the steel in their steely confidence? That is the topic of the rest of this chapter.

Navigating Denial

I will return shortly to how the economics profession failed the journalists and the general public; but first, I want to insist that, contrary to urban legend, almost no orthodox economists warned how pervasive the crisis would be or the extent of its devastating character beforehand.[35] The reason was simple: the orthodox models taught at the finest universities at their most advanced levels of macroeconomics had no room for fiscal policy or involuntary unemployment or financial crises or system-wide breakdown. Far from an oversight, this was a matter of common knowledge within the profession.[36] Among other features, the economics of John Maynard Keynes had been thoroughly and emphatically repudiated by the orthodox profession since the 1980s. The Bank of Sweden Prize winner Robert Lucas was always good for a quote: "I think Keynes' actual influence as a technical economist is pretty close to zero, and it has been close to zero for 50 years. Keynes was not a very good technical economist. He didn't contribute much to the development of the field."[37] This should prove significant for our subsequent purposes, because some public intellectuals like Paul Krugman and Robert Skidelsky had misleadingly asserted back in 2008–9 that Keynesian theory still enjoyed broad-based theoretical legitimacy within the orthodox economics profession. By 2012 we can observe just how fleeting were Keynes's allotted fifteen minutes of comeback fame.

The consensus macroeconomic model, called the "dynamic stochastic general equilibrium model," could serve no useful function once the crisis hit, because it essentially denied that any such debacle could have materialized. (We document this in chapter 5.) And yet, respected figures within the economics profession could not be embarrassed into acknowledging the deep disconnect between textbook and reality. For instance, Olivier Blanchard, then chief economist at the IMF, pronounced in 2008, "The state of macro is good," and the profession was enjoying "a broad convergence of vision."[38] Even that was not sufficiently ill-timed and imprudent to get him booted from the IMF.

It wasn't just macroeconomists who were living in deep denial. Derivatives such as CDOs and CDSs were based upon a set of normative theories invented by financial economists, which asserted that their purpose was to repackage risk and retail it to those best situated to bear it. This theory was colloquially known as the efficient-markets hypothesis (again covered in chapter 5), and had undergone extensive mathematical elaboration by academics and their acolytes in the banks, known as "quants." The efficient-markets hypothesis claimed to show that all relevant information for all parties to a transaction were already embodied in the market price of a financial instrument. As with the case of the macro models, there was no room for systemic failure in these theories, since they presumed that everything could be subject to insurance due to the stochastic properties of portfolios constructed to mimic the movements of the entire market. Market designers subsequently went to work gilding the lily. Yet economic theory was so central to the construction of financial products that layer upon layer of derivative paper was concocted on top of some original debt instruments based upon nothing more than the scientific promise of the finance theory that underwrote the manipulations.

After the crash, the *New Yorker* reporter John Cassidy made a pilgrimage to the citadel of efficient-markets theory at the University of Chicago, as he said, "looking for apostasy." As a service to the rest of us, he interviewed many of the major economists behind the theory at length, and then posted the verbatim transcripts online.[39] The interviews are so chock-full of juicy quotes and wicked aperçus that it takes superhuman effort not to cut and paste the entire brace here. For instance, when Cassidy asked the father of efficient-markets theory, Eugene Fama, how the theory had fared in the crisis, Fama replied, "I think it did quite well in this episode." When challenged by Cassidy, he responded, "We don't know what causes recessions . . . We've never known." When queried about the seemingly refuted Modigliani-Miller theorem, Fama responded: "The experiment we never ran is, suppose the government stepped aside and let these institutions fail? How long would it have taken to unscramble everything and figure everything out? My guess is we are talking a week or two" . . . Cassidy: *So you would have just let them* . . . Fama: "Let them all fail. (Laughs)." Lucas flat-out refused to talk to him about the crisis. He at least had the presence of mind to realize how outrageous his beliefs would appear to the vast majority of readers. Cassidy then approached John Cochrane to get him to engage in a little unintentional self-examination, asking him what Chicago doctrine remained after the crisis of the efficient-markets hypothesis and the rational-expectations theory. Cochrane answered, "I think everything. Why not? Seriously now, these are not ideas so superficial that you can reject them just by reading the newspaper." When Cassidy began hinting at a certain zombie-like uniformity along the Midway, Cochrane retorted: "This is not an ideology factory . . . The Chicago of today is a place where all ideas are represented, thought out, argued. It is not an ideological

place." Of course, it is easy to cover the notional waterfront if everything else is banished. Cochrane: "Today, there is no 'freshwater versus
saltwater' There is just macro. What most people are doing is adding
some frictions to it."

Cassidy then approached Raghuram Rajan, who was frequently
portrayed by the media as one of the more open-minded economists
at Chicago, given his reputation for warning about bank problems in
2005. Yet beyond ripping tales of an epic clash of Rajan and Lawrence
Summers at the Fed conference at Jackson Hole in 2005, almost no
one had bothered to actually read his academic papers. Perhaps Cassidy
would have been better prepared if he had first perused a paper Rajan
had written back in 1994 suggesting that the Glass-Steagall Act had
constituted unnecessary regulation back in the 1930s, because commingling of investment and commercial banking had *not* ratcheted up the
riskiness of the entire system, and in any event, "We find no evidence
that commercial banks systematically fooled the public securities
markets."[40] Rajan was True Blue Chicago, so of course he defended
the home team to Cassidy: "Forget the public utterances: the research
done at this place was, essentially, right on the ball." When Cassidy
asked about the behavior of the Federal Reserve and the Treasury in
2008, Rajan responded: "One doesn't have to be corrupt or in the pay
of the financial sector to say, hey, wait a minute: it's not as simple as
letting them all go under or taking them all over. That's my rant about
the business sector. By and large, I think we've done all the things that
needed to be done." Thus abides the Socratic diversity, the alpha to
omega of public disputation at that great agora of the search for truth,
that wholly owned subsidiary of the NTC, the University of Chicago
economics faculty.

Actually, I need to credit Rajan with a bit more ingenuity than he
claims for himself in these interviews. His book *Fault Lines* has managed
to amalgamate what had by then become the neoliberals' favorite
stories about the crisis into one neat and tidy package. In caricature, it
combines: fingering the Asian economies for seeking to accumulate
dollar reserves after the Asian crisis of 1997, and therefore creating a
world "savings glut"; luxuriant financial innovation (a phenomenon
that was "natural"), which lulled bankers and others into taking on
"excessive risk"; and technological innovation, which lowered wages
and worsened income distribution in the United States, which in turn
lured the government to ineptly try to counter it by screwing around
with the household mortgage market. The financial sector got frisky,
investors bought it, and the government foolishly sought to lean

against the wind. The beauty of this narrative is that it mentions some of the major bugaboos of the left, but deftly subordinates them to the time-honored litany that the markets worked as they should, and it was all, in the final analysis, the fault of the government.[41] This ingenious commingling of complaints about worsening income distribution and rapacious bankers with what is at bottom a unilateral denial that economists got anything wrong has been so effective that it often has inserted Rajan into critical leftish campaigns where the audience was oblivious to the true character of the analysis.[42]

I don't want to especially pick on Chicago in this book; Berkeley's Christina Romer, Obama's first head of his Council of Economic Advisors, was just as embarrassing.[43] Nevertheless, the sheer density of denial per square economist at Chicago does raise a more interesting issue, given voice by Donald Westbrook and others: "No doubt World War II would have occurred without Martin Heidegger, Carl Schmitt or the other Nazi intellectuals, but it is not so clear that the crisis could have occurred without the Chicago School of neoclassical economics." Far from being the conventional generic blanket disparagement of "freshwater economics" (such as that spread by Paul Krugman, Brad DeLong, George Akerlof, and others), this points to the fact that Chicago was the prime initial incubator for modern finance theory, which has indeed provided direct intellectual inspiration and justification for most of the so-called innovation in financial derivatives and automated equity trading of the last three decades. There is also the Chicago inspiration for the theory of "public choice" and Stigler's theory of regulation, so central in the modern development of government (anti)regulation. In other words, Chicago was the intellectual godfather of modern "securitization" and privatized regulation, among other activities.[44]

Academic economists of a certain persuasion might aver that they and their theories should not be blamed for economic debacles, since they were merely passive observers, and not actually in charge. Economists propose; politicians dispose; or so they say. Furthermore, floor traders flagrantly misuse Black-Scholes option-pricing theory as they employ it. Yet this excuse turns out to be implausible for the profession as a whole; economists had come to occupy many of the commanding heights of the governance of the economy prior to the crisis. Economists didn't simply come up with some speculative ideas; they helped run many of the institutions, both public and private, that ended up being central to the inception and playing out of the crisis. Indeed, just like the notorious revolving door between

Wall Street and the U.S. Government, there has been a twirling door between the economics profession and the large firms and banks that run the economy.[45]

To take just one crucial example: one of their illustrious own was put in charge of the U.S. Federal Reserve Bank precisely because he had expressed a brash confidence in his colleagues' professional mastery, which reflected economists' perceptions of their own powerful mojo just prior to the crash.

Bernanke, the Federal Reserve, and the Great Mortification

Benjamin Bernanke was appointed to the Federal Reserve Bank Board in 2002, and named chairman of the Fed by George Bush in 2005. Bush was persuaded that this avowed follower of Milton Friedman would make a suitable replacement for the previous chair, Alan Green-span. Following his nomination as Fed chairman, Bernanke told the press that, if confirmed, his plan was "to maintain continuity with the policies and policy strategies established during the Greenspan years." Although many are convinced they detect a repudiation of his prede-cessor in his subsequent activities, a case can be made that Bernanke was faithful to his original pledge. Much has been made in the interim that one of Bernanke's academic specialties in his previous life had been the economic history of the Great Depression of the 1930s; but (tedious nag that I am), yet again, few have bothered to actually read his writings and speeches. As late as July 20, 2006, Bernanke was testi-fying before Congress thus: "The best way to achieve good oversight of hedge funds is through market discipline . . . I think that market discipline has shown its capability of keeping hedge funds well disci-plined." The record discloses Bernanke channeling Greenspan with a tonier Ivy League pedigree.[46]

Beyond continuity of approach, another reason for his accession was that Bernanke had begun in 2004 in speeches and writings to proclaim the onset of a "Great Moderation" in the macroeconomy since 1984.[47] Briefly, his was an assertion that economists had attained such an acute understanding of the economy, infused with such subtle perspicuity of analysis, that macroeconomic fluctuations had been tamed relative to previous experience, and consequently, we had entered unto a new era of capitalist stability and prosperity. With the shallow hindsight of seven years, these assertions still hold the power to cause the toughest ortho-dox neoclassicist to cringe with embarrassment:

One of the most striking features of the economic landscape over

the last twenty years or so has been a substantial decline in macroeconomic volatility . . . Three types of explanations have been
suggested . . . structural change, macroeconomic policies, and good
luck . . . My view is that improvements in monetary policy, though
certainly not the only factor, have probably been an important
source of the Great Moderation . . . the policy explanation for the
Great Moderation deserves more credit than it has received in the
literature.[48]

His repeated assertion of this thesis in the intervening years went
some distance in explaining why Bernanke's Fed did essentially nothing to curb the worst financial abuses that led up to the crisis of
2007–8; Bernanke had been insisting throughout that the mortgage
market was sound, hedge funds were "disciplined," and the banks
solid right up to the onset of the failure of Lehman Brothers. This
self-congratulation persisted even though a few inside figures such as
the Fed governor Ned Gramlich (who was forced to resign in 2005)
and the Atlanta Fed president, Jack Guynn, had been sounding the
alarm since 2005. It is difficult to convey in any short space just how
much the orthodox economics profession loved this trope of the
Great Moderation and its ballyhooed prophet; so much so that it
spawned a huge academic literature in its own right. Not only did
highly ranked economics journals continue to publish articles discussing the Great Moderation long after the crash rendered the very idea
ludicrous, but (having no shame) some tone-deaf economists even
argued that the crisis had in no way impugned the existence of a
Great Moderation. And neoclassical economists wonder why outsiders tend to snicker at them behind their backs.[49]

But to return to the Fed: because Bernanke had previously been a
Princeton professor, and had been reappointed by Barack Obama, the
media and the public seemed to conceive of the curious notion that
Bernanke must be some sort of "centrist" or Roosevelt technocrat,
and no shill for neoliberal capitulation to the financial sector. When
President Barack Obama nominated Bernanke for a second four-year
term as chair of the Federal Reserve Board in August 2009, he empha-
sized Bernanke's "bold action and outside-the-box thinking" in
preventing the financial collapse from turning into another Great
Depression. It may have been bold, but the playbook had come directly
from inside the neoliberal box, and anyway, Obama himself had yet to
learn the pitfalls of prematurely calling a game before the score was in.
The orthodox economics profession has been even more effusive; the

neoliberal economist Gregory Mankiw "says there is a bizarre disconnect between the chairman's reputation among experts, who mostly
respect him, and the public's disapproval." Actually, there is a close
affinity between a narrowly defined coterie of "experts" and the Fed;
but that is precisely what requires more intense scrutiny.[50]

One of the great success stories of the NTC has been its ability to
keep close tabs on fellow travelers situated among the heathen, so
when and if the crunch comes, they might end up controlling "both
sides" of any momentous debate. As described in chapter 6, neoliberal politics is generally (at least) a full-spectrum procedure, wherein
a neoliberal-inspired "amelioration policy" is frequently paired with
a harder-right "market solution." Think, for instance, of the American "insurance mandate" paired with full privatization of Medicare.
Indeed, what greater guarantee of control of the parameters of intellectual possibility could follow an Ayn Rand acolyte than a good old
fashioned Friedmanite monetarist?[51] Bernanke began his Fed tenure
by genuflecting to the (by then long refuted) Friedman tenet that
one should try and put the money supply on rule-governed autopi-
lot.[52] Bernanke had been a dedicated follower of the neoliberal
playbook during the crisis as well, as he admitted in the following
testimony to Congress:

> Milton Friedman's view was that the cause of the Great Depression
> was the failure of the Federal Reserve to avoid excessively tight
> monetary policy in the early 30s. That was Friedman and Schwartz's
> famous book [*The Monetary History of the United States*]. With that
> lesson in mind, the Federal Reserve has reacted very aggressively to
> cut interest rates in this current crisis. Moreover, we've tried to
> avoid collapse of the banking system.[53]

What this "rescue operation" amounted to began to emerge only
after an unprecedented lawsuit brought by Bloomberg (with which
the Fed refused to comply) and an act of Congress, which resulted in
the disclosure of 21,000 transactions (but not the totality) from late
2007 through 2009.[54] Indeed, while Bernanke makes great show of
his commitment to "openness," the Fed under his watch has fought
tooth and nail every single attempt to disclose the range of its activities during the crisis, even well after the fact: the Sanders report, the
GAO report, and the Bloomberg Freedom of Information Act
request. While Fed officials trot out the highly misleading assertion
that almost all of the government loans were subsequently repaid and

there have been no losses to the public purse, closer scrutiny of the details suggest taxpayers paid a price far beyond the publicly provided numbers (such as the TARP), as the secret funding helped preserve a broken status quo and enabled the biggest banks to grow even bigger. The Fed has bestowed upon the banks seemingly permanent options to reward executives and shareholders by capping the downside while permitting an unlimited upside. Over the course of the crisis the Fed made loans of over $7 *trillion* to financial institutions at negligible rates of interest, with no quid pro quo. Far from regarding the early Bear Stearns rescue as a flashing warning sign that something was very wrong, Bernanke and Tim Geithner reverted to Mission Accomplished mode, unconcerned over what seemed to be going haywire with all those derivatives. They revealed that during the crisis the Fed had been intently picking and choosing which banks and other financial entities to save and which to let fail (Lehman Brothers the egregious sacrifice here), including foreign banks such as Barclays, UBS, Dexia, and Royal Bank of Scotland.[55] After a round of stress-test theater, the Fed gave the banks permission to pay out dividends and repurchase stock rather than bolster their equity base. The Fed provided billions in bailouts to banks in places like Mexico, Bahrain, and Bavaria, billions more to a spate of Japanese car companies, more than $2 trillion in loans *each* to Citigroup and Morgan Stanley, and billions more to a string of lesser millionaires and billionaires with Cayman Islands addresses. The Fed was also bringing in politically favored individuals and hedge funds to buy derivatives and other securitized debt with government money and government guarantees. Matt Taibbi had some fun pointing out that even wives of the rich and famous were bestowed enormous opportunities to enrich themselves off TALF, a program nominally instituted to support the rancid securities the Fed had permitted to proliferate over the previous decade.[56] But few have acknowledged that this was *precisely* the Depression remedy promoted by Milton Friedman: keep the rich from suffering writedowns or defaulting on their debts so the so-called money supply does not contract inordinately, and everything else will just work itself out fine.

Yves Smith has made the important point that Bernanke tends to justify the sites and instances where the Fed has intervened largely by insisting that private contracts have to be respected; but this is yet another Big Lie from Foggy Bottom. If the contracts favored the banks, such as the credit default swaps written by AIG, then it was permissible to stretch the Fed legal charter by essentially nationalizing an insurance company, or purchasing mortgage-backed securities. (Saving AIG reveals the Bernanke excuse that "we had no legal authority" to save Lehman to be bootless.) However, whenever it was the banks themselves that violated sanctity of contract, from the total travesty of riding roughshod over the chain of title in mortgage securitization, to the defrauding of clients and investors, to reverse long-established principles of creditor hierarchy, then the Fed looked the other way. This was the heart of the Schmittian "exception" explained in the previous chapter. Bernanke is not the great hero saving "capitalism" as portrayed in the many hagiographic accounts;[57] rather, he is dedicated primarily to saving the largest banks at all costs, which is not at all the same thing.

Even more damning details of the so-called rescue by the Fed were buried in a little-read GAO report.[58] During the crisis, the Fed was printing conflict-of-interest waivers almost as fast as it printed money, precisely because many of the identities of the rescued and the saviors were essentially identical. For instance, the New York Fed president William Dudley was issued waivers to keep his AIG and GE investments all the while he was bailing out those firms. But beyond such garden-variety double-dealing, the Fed followed good neoliberal precepts by outsourcing most of its emergency lending programs to private contractors such as JP Morgan Chase, Morgan Stanley, and Wells Fargo *in the form of no-bid contracts*. These favored firms then turned around and were lavishly supported by the Fed with near-zero interest rate loans. So much for the deep reserves of independent economic expertise on tap at the Fed. One gets glimpses of why Bernanke doggedly fought the congressional ukase for even a very limited audit of Fed behavior during the crisis.

Indeed, as time passes, it begins to appear that Bernanke presides over little more than a cabal of bankers using public funds to keep themselves in power and riches. Simon Johnson has highlighted the role of Jamie Dimon as benefiting tremendously from the forced and subsidized purchase of Bear Stearns by JP Morgan while he was on the Board of the New York Fed, which was orchestrating the deal. Senator Bernie Sanders has released a list of eighteen other Fed directors who received substantial funding from the Fed during the crisis.[59] It appears that "saving the economy" was tantamount to flooding their own banks (and pockets) with liquidity. As more details are leaked, it appears Bernanke provides a thin veneer of academic imprimatur to what can only be regarded as a vast morass of insider dealing.

Bernanke's Fed has not suffered from what can only be judged an intellectual imbroglio of epic proportions; this has been one of the most glaring instances of economists getting away with murder. Bernanke assiduously deployed the Fed's prodigious public relations arm and lobbying bench to proclaim that he had taken the extreme but necessary steps in order to keep the Great Recession from turning into another Great Depression; and yet there was very little that was "principled" about this gusher of federal loans and subsidies directed to bail out insolvent organizations headed by people with the right political connections. How was this so very different from the so-called Greenspan put, which had operated the same way with the lesser financial crises during his reign? Yet the orthodox economics profession (including nominally leftist critics, such as Paul Krugman and Joseph Stiglitz) fell right into line, praising the deft perspicuity of the Fed chairman in transforming the Fed into a beacon of financial rectitude and disaster deliverance. Greenspan had made for a convenient pariah once he famously conceded his "error" in congressional testimony of October 23, 2008, but mostly, it served only to divert attention from the even worse behavior of Bernanke.

Ben Bernanke is one major character study in the syndrome of denial that has gripped the orthodox economics profession. All that flimflam about the "Great Moderation" has been blessedly forgotten by the Fed chair, though never actually repudiated. Bernanke insists upon the prodigious intellectual capacity of the Fed to regulate the postcrisis financial sector and the shadow banking sphere, even though he and his former lieutenant at the New York Fed Timothy Geithner had been asleep at the wheel in the run-up to the crisis, and then outsourced much of the bailout. Bernanke has stood in the way of most attempts to restructure the U.S. financial sector, from opposing the Volcker Rule to blocking attempts to break up "too big to fail" firms. Bernanke resisted most attempts to financially penalize banks or hedge funds, with the excuse that they were too fragile to face the music. The Fed's ability to even anticipate contractions had been persistently addled, dating from the onset of the crisis, as demonstrated in Figure 4.5. His grasp on reality has been tenuous: Bernanke himself had insisted that the subprime mortgage crisis was "contained" as late as March 2007.[60] Incredibly, in the face of the mayhem that ensued, Bernanke's Fed has evaded suffering any consequences for its intellectual incompetence; it still does pretty much whatever it pleases, including continued deregulation of the shadow banking sector and frustrating Elizabeth Warren's crusade to set up a fully independent consumer finance protection bureau; and yet, even that Great Bank Amnesty was not enough for Ben Bernanke. He decided he had to get the orthodox neoclassical economists off the hook for any conceptual error, as well.

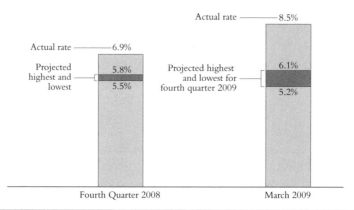

Figure 4.5: The Fed Projection Misses the Mark

Unemployment rates: actual vs. June 2009 projections

Source: Federal Reserve, Bureau of Labor Statistics

On September 24, 2010, Bernanke returned to his home turf of Princeton to pronounce absolution upon the orthodox economics profession and, not incidentally, upon himself. It needs to be quoted *in extenso* in order to convey the hubris of the man:

> [The financial crisis] has not been kind to the reputation of economics and economists, and understandably so. Almost universally, economists failed to predict the nature, timing, and severity of the crisis; and those who issued early warnings generally identified only isolated weaknesses in the system . . . As a result of these developments, some observers have suggested the need for an overhaul of the system as a discipline, arguing that much of the research in macroeconomics and finance in recent decades has been of little value or even counterproductive. Although economists have much to learn from this crisis, I think that calls for a radical reworking of the field go too far. . . .
>
> I would argue that the recent financial crisis was more a failure of economic engineering and economic management than of what I have called economic science . . . although the great majority of economists did not foresee the near-collapse of the financial system, economic analysis has proven and will continue to prove critical in understanding the crisis . . . the distinction between economic science and economic engineering can be less sharp than my analogy may suggest, as much economic research has policy

implications . . . I don't think the crisis by any means requires us to
rethink economics and finance from the ground up . . .

As it was put by my former colleague, Markus Brunnermeier . . .
"We do not have many convincing models that explain when and
why bubbles start." I would add that we also don't know very much
about how bubbles stop, either.[61]

Bernanke then went on to praise various trends in contemporary
neoclassical economic theory, but we cover those in chapter 5, and in
any event, they are superfluous in bearing witness to the contradictions
embodied in this text. First off, note the intemperate conflation of
neoclassical orthodoxy with the totality of "economic theory"—as
though there were nothing but barren desert outside its cool oasis.
Second, if the orthodoxy was bereft of all understanding of "bubbles," as
he confesses, then in what sense did the Fed possess actionable intelligence as to how to comport itself appropriately once the crisis hit? And
third, if all the blame can be lifted from the economics profession and
foisted onto "engineers" and "managers," then where does that leave the
Fed and, in particular, the figure of Ben Bernanke? Was he not financial
manager-in-chief during the late contretemps? The answer to this third,
and most troublesome, question is that Bernanke never once in that
lecture concedes that the Fed did anything wrong before or after the
crisis, and indeed, in a subsequent lecture, attempted to load the blame
on China and the "global savings glut" for the entire episode.[62] Those
"engineers" and "managers" must be slippery, devious fellows indeed,
since they are forever undermining the noble economists, without ever
once leaving a visible calling card or forwarding address.

I have had some economists warn me that *of course* Bernanke had to
say stuff like this: for the sake of political stability, he must hew to the
party line in public. It is just the Fed Chair Pantomime. I find this
implausible, for one major reason: every bit of documentary evidence
points to the conclusion that Bernanke subscribes to one of the two
major neoliberal catechisms on money. One, the one Bernanke rejects,
associated with Hayek and the so-called libertarians like Ron Paul, is
that the Fed is the devil, and that it should be replaced with free banking and pure market control. It would be a little hard to become
chairman of the Fed while toeing that line, so Bernanke endorses the
Friedmanite alternate: the central bank should be "independent" of all
democratic control, preferably run by like-minded neoliberals, but only
the market can recognize a bubble, so don't try to rein in the specula-
tors, but simply clean up afterward by lending freely to the rich people

who created the problem in the first place. It is the old neoliberal two-step all over again: Rick Perry and Ron Paul can offer the groundlings red meat by threatening to beat up on Bernanke, and keep the base rabidly opposed to anything that looks suspiciously like the guv'mint; but the major players understand that they need Bernanke (or someone like him) on the inside to support their remunerative activities and ward off anything that smacks of nationalization. You can remain a neoliberal in good standing quite comfortably without subscribing to the free banking fringe, because you are useful. And it is the economics profession that makes the straddle work on a daily basis.

Here we encounter one of the major pieces of evidence that the Federal Reserve Bank is an avowedly neoliberal institution, and one that relies upon its major symbiotic relationship with the American economics profession to skew its membership in a neoliberal direction.[63] I have just demonstrated that the last two chairmen of the Federal Reserve System were card-carrying neoliberals; but moreover, the entire governance structure of the Federal Reserve has evolved to guarantee responsiveness to its main constituency, the pinnacle of finance. As Dean Baker has written, few realize that "The Fed has been deliberately designed to insulate it from democratic control and leave it instead a tool of the financial industry."[64] The member private banks "own" stock in the regional Feds, and indeed, are paid dividends on their stock.[65] The twelve regional Feds are governed by nine-member boards, six elected by member banks, and the remaining three by the Board of Governors.[66] Each of the twelve regional Federal Reserve Banks is a separately incorporated not-for-profit that is privately owned by the member banks in its district. Further, the entire Fed system is self-funded from its operations, freeing it from the rigors of an external budgetary control or any serious accountability. The Federal Reserve Board of Governors, to be sure, has seven members appointed by the president and confirmed by the Senate for nonrenewable fourteen-year terms; but almost inevitably they are chosen from those with previous experience in the regional Feds, or representatives of the banks or Treasury, although they may have concurrently served as academics. The Fed is technically run by the twelve regional Fed presidents plus the seven-member Board of Governors. Substantial power is vested in the chairman of the board, also appointed by the president for renewable four-year terms. This neither-fish-nor-fowl organization chart dating from 1935 has admirably served to camouflage many of the activities of the Fed in the past.[67] Indeed, the Fed is a bulwark of industry "self-regulation," decked out as government entity dedicated to the public welfare; a sheep in wolf's clothing.

Fed directors typically hold down a full-time job elsewhere, so in practice, most directors are officers of banks, or academics who are somehow connected to them. This level of private control of a central government regulatory agency is rather more extreme in the United States than in other developed countries, where directors are often paid civil servants; but what it accomplishes is an enhanced degree of "self-regulation" of the industry, covered over with a patina of plausible deniability. This is combined with a critical dynamic wherein the Fed has engineered greater concentration in the financial sector over time (through shotgun mergers of failing banks, plus other blandishments), such that there are fewer banks to provide and elect qualified directors, and therefore, the entire system is increasingly being "regulated" by the few oversized firms that conveniently dictate the staffing of the Fed. The most recent history of this unprecedented consolidation is depicted in Figure 4.6. This leads to those very same banks being bailed out in times of crisis, and, not insignificantly, something approaching the Bernanke doctrine. As Donald Westbrook has sagely observed, "Corporations may live globally, but they die—or are rescued—nationally."[68]

The only wild cards that might potentially mitigate this built-in regulatory capture are the residual academic members of the boards, primarily economists. Yet most observers then miss how the Fed system facilitates repeated indelicate liaisons between financial executives and the economics profession, and brings about "cognitive capture" of the discipline. One way this happens is that large financial firms are induced to hire prominent academics, even to the extent of incorporating them onto their own boards, as we shall see below. It thus remains opaque exactly the constituency any given economist actually "represents" while nominally propounding the general welfare. Another significant way this occurs takes place by the Fed itself either hiring or providing contract funding for a substantial proportion of the economics profession concerned with macroeconomics and monetary economics. The following is the result of some underappreciated research by Auerbach, White, and Grim on this issue.[69]

In 1992, testimony provided directly by the Fed listed at least 493 economists employed as "officers, economists and statisticians" and an additional 237 as "support staff."[70] Since about 1,700 members of the American Economics Association listed "monetary and financial theory" as their primary or secondary fields in that year, the Fed was currently employing something like 43 percent of the field. White estimates that there are about 390 economists specializing in money, macro, or banking in the "top 50" graduate departments in the United

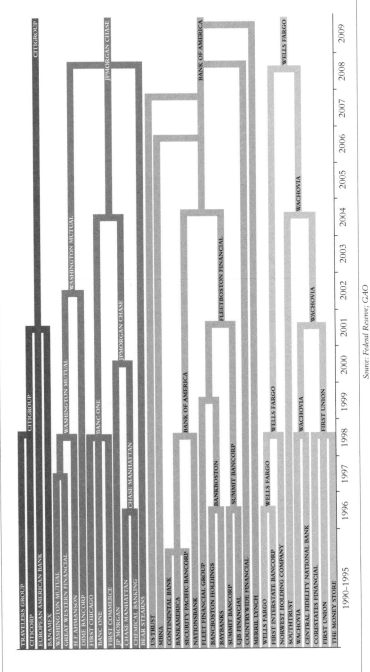

Figure 4.6: American Bank Mergers, 1995–2009

Source: Federal Reserve; GAO

States; so the Fed could easily have employed that totality, or engaged them in some consulting relationship over the course of their careers. White also reports that over a five-year horizon 80 percent of the papers in the *Journal of Monetary Economics* had at least one co-author with a Fed affiliation (not all disclosed in the article, however), whereas in the *Journal of Money, Credit and Banking* it was 75 percent.[71]

The Fed is constructed to evade democratic accountability, and as such, short of a Supreme Court order, it abstains from documentation of its web of support of the modern economics profession. For instance, the Fed declined to report more recent totals of actual employment. Related agencies loom equally large. Depending on how one regards the International Monetary Fund in the financial constellation, that would add roughly another 1,100 economists employed in Washington, D.C., alone. The World Bank refuses to report any breakdown of employment statistics out of its aggregate 10,000 employees worldwide whatsoever. But that was not all. The Fed board plus the twelve regional Feds awarded 305 contracts to other external economists to the tune of $3 million—although some individual economists enjoyed multiple contracts. In 2009, contracts issued for external economic research totaled $433 million. Some high-profile economists are kept on paid retainer, without even having to produce actual reports. Printing your own money means you can afford to cover all relevant bases. It is safe to say that there are few orthodox American macroeconomists who have not enjoyed a subvention from the Fed (or the international agencies) at some time during their career.[72]

There is no doubt that that the Fed system and its international counterparts as a whole either employ or fund a substantial proportion of the economics profession concerned with monetary policy and macroeconomics, and have therefore had an enormous intellectual influence on the profession. Grim reports that every single member of the editorial board in 2009 of the *Journal of Monetary Economics* was or had been affiliated with the Fed, and 54 percent were on the payroll. Of the editorial boards of eight top-ranked economics journals, 84 out of 190 had been affiliated with the Fed at some point in their careers. Indeed, sometimes the connection is even more intimate, with the bulk of the offices of the economics department at the University of Minnesota essentially located to a large degree at the Minnesota Fed.[73] Much of the early and intermediate stages of the "rational expectations revolution" were funded and promoted out of the Minnesota Fed, in a period when it was not yet conventional wisdom, or entirely welcome in some "saltwater" departments. A major pillar of support for the DSGE model (described in the next chapter) originally came from research staffs and contracts of the regional Feds. Moreover, the money, once bestowed, comes with strings. Employees and contractors must sign nondisclosure agreements, and published articles are often vetted by Fed bureaucrats. In the interests of needing to speak with one voice in monetary policy, the Fed regularly imposes the trappings of intellectual uniformity.

It is tempting to describe this situation as "symbiosis" but even that would not manage to capture the unholy alliance of banks, the Fed, and the economics profession. It is an open secret that junior Fed positions are considered consolation prizes within the economics discipline: what you get for a first job if you graduate with a PhD from a top-ranked department in the areas of macro/money, but fail to land an academic post at another top-tier department. The movers and shakers are, rather, given the plum consulting contracts, appointed visiting positions, and other perks. Both are entryways into subsequent work for the financial sector. Hence the Fed manages to curry favor with a number of strata of the profession simultaneously with forging links to the financial sector, building a deep bench for support of the kinds of positions exemplified by Bernanke in this chapter. The net result is an interlocking directorate of the self-defined "orthodoxy," which has been able to recruit, sustain, and promote its members almost on a par with the neoliberal Russian doll itself. Indeed, the Fed and the doll have grown increasingly fond of each other. Since the 1980s, when Ronald Reagan was able to appoint all the Fed governors, the Fed has become an unapologetic openly neoliberal institution; and this has constituted one of the major channels through which the economics profession was shepherded in a more neoliberal direction. One Russian doll mated with another.

The slavish genuflection to the financial sector within modern economics is therefore quite easily understood once a little effort has been devoted to exploring the sociology of the profession. The cognitive capture of the profession by the bankster-regulator industrial complex helped set up the profession for its fall, and is indispensable for understanding the rituals of denial that ensued.

A Potemkin Consensus

The Fed, undeniably a powerful, pervasive patron of professional economists, has not yet ascended to the eminence of the Ministry of Truth, and thus cannot, by itself, fully account for the contours of the entire contemporary economics profession. The brute fact is that it has been unable to completely eradicate dissent concerning the macro-economy, although it has wrought wonders banishing it to the margins of discourse. The mere fact that such a dissenting remnant persists has led in the aftermath of the crisis to yet another symptom of the paralyzing syndrome of denial: the incessant hand-wringing about the extent (or not) of "consensus" within the "legitimate" orthodox economics profession. Famous neoclassical economists love to assure us that "everyone that matters" subscribes to their own favorite roster of shared truths in the profession, no matter how much this proposition has been besmirched by recent events. In their disarray, economists indulged their bad habit of confusing regression to the safe median with an unimpeachable badge of Truth. They seemed incapable of imagining that their glittering prizes (and Fed contracts) may not be much more than signifiers of abject capitulation to sanctioned ideas. Indeed, they often unconsciously channel neoliberal epistemology, as if putting the questions up to a vote (or a market) would somehow manage to extract the dependable "wisdom of crowds," which would naturally endorse the validity of neoclassical economics. Journalists, having had to resort to their own devices in the early stages of the crisis, have also grown solicitous in searching out where that magic consensus might be located, since their own metaphorical flights have come to grief in the interim.

The explicit projects to codify orthodox "consensus" reveal just how difficult it has become for the profession to police its boundaries, and yet also the extent to which neoliberal presuppositions have become second nature in any arena one seeks to frame whatever economists are supposed to know. If one takes the simplest possible proposition—say, that the raising of the debt ceiling by an August 2011 deadline would serve to stave off a disastrous financial crisis and employment contraction pursuant to a technical default of the U.S. Treasury on part of its debt—then it was a snap to get 162 economists, *including two Nobel winners*, to sign a statement denying that proposition.[74] Or take that larger and more contentious issue, the question of whether there was a bubble in housing prices by 2006, and why so few economists were willing to sound the alarm. There is retrospective evidence that a few prominent economists had warned the New York Fed of a housing bubble as early as 2004; in response to one such presentation, Timothy Geithner removed Robert Shiller from the Fed advisory board.[75] But the orthodox profession seems loathe to ever admit knowledge is actively policed

and purged according to a preset script. After the fact, some economists at the Boston Fed decided that, because one would encounter
a range of opinions on that issue before the crisis, there is no justification in blaming the profession for missing the disaster. They
wrote: "Economic theory provides little guidance as to what should
be the 'correct' level of asset prices—including housing
prices . . . While optimistic forecasts held by many market participants in 2005 turned out to be inaccurate" those projections were
not "unreasonable" given what was understood about the economy
and housing market dynamics in the years before housing prices
crashed. "The pessimistic case was a distinctly minority view, especially among professional economists . . . The small number of
economists who argued forcefully for a bubble often did so years
before the housing market peak, and thus lost a fair amount of credibility" in the process. Others spotted a bubble with "arguments
fundamentally at odds with the data" that became available after the
fact. "Academic research available in 2006 was basically inconclusive
and could not convincingly support or refute any hypothesis about
the future path of asset prices."[76]

The "dog ate my homework" level of self-exculpation here is
quite extraordinary, especially coming as it did from within the Fed.
It went: First off, you can't blame us just because the neoclassical
orthodoxy we actively help enforce is pathetically empty in its ability
to discriminate such matters. Moreover, we assert those who were
adamant in sounding the alarm were cranky Cassandras and perennial moaners, which means mostly pariahs exiled outside the
orthodoxy, so we, the Fed, were fully justified in ignoring them.
When in doubt, always err on the side of Pollyanna optimism. Finally,
the supposed consensus enforced at the Fed was clearly not based on
any demonstrable intellectual discernment, so much as herding
behavior and the chairman's visible iron hand, but not to worry,
because it is eminently "rational" to stick with the herd. People
whine about the parade of economists being unable to come to a
conclusion, but soothing their anxieties concerning dissent and
disputation is the main reason we were right to persist in our stubborn errors. We simply channel the cultural zeitgeist.

The chutzpah of economists in their hyperactive attempts at self-
exculpation tended to backfire rather dramatically, but that didn't stop
them coming. One particularly embarrassing Aunt Sally appeared in
the *Financial Times*:

But crises will happen and, even if there is a depressing periodicity to them, their timing, form and provenance will elude prognostication . . . So, if the value of economics in preventing crises will always be limited (although hopefully not nonexistent), perhaps a fairer and more realistic yardstick should be its value as a guide in responding to them. Here, one year on, we can say that economics stands vindicated.[77]

Here, three years on, we can observe that everything faulty with the predictive capacities of the profession became compounded with the exquisitely groundless pomposity that orthodox economics never made anything worse, and so should take credit before the fact for them getting better. The blogs, once again, broke out in an orgy of derision.

Panglossian exercises of this nature were ill-suited to reassure the keening populace, so the more proactive journalists went about seeking to construct a provisionary consensus. The *Economist* decided to ask roughly fifty handpicked economists to identify which economist had been most influential over the past decade, and which had proposed the most important ideas for a postcrisis world. The "most influential" list they compiled was Ben Bernanke, John Maynard Keynes, Jeffrey Sachs, Hyman Minsky, and Paul Krugman; the "most important ideas" roster was Raghuram Rajan, Robert Shiller, Kenneth Rogoff, Barry Eichengreen, and Nouriel Roubini.[78] If you were a member of the orthodoxy back then, it is hard to see how these lists could be anything other than profoundly unsettling; if you are someone reading this book right now, then perhaps you will gaze upon them with existential nausea. That list counts at least three open neoliberals, Bernanke, Rajan, and Rogoff, and one maverick neoliberal, Shiller. Three are rather conventional defenders of the veracity of orthodox neoclassical economics: Sachs, Krugman, and Eichengreen. We have already mentioned the unbearable lightness of the Keynesian rehabilitation within the economics profession. Minsky is nowhere taught in any ranked economics department. Roubini is the odd man out, largely ignored by the profession because of his propensity to cry wolf. The angst comes with the utter void of anything that could charitably be designated "new ideas" in the second list, and the sheer deliquescence of influence of the middle three of the former list for the economics profession. But worse, other than fealty to the home team, there is nothing here which acknowledges that the individual candidates tend to contradict one another in the main. If this be consensus, then sound and fury may be our fate.

Thus recent conatus to make it appear as though there exists some sort of stable "consensus" among economists concerning what to do about the crisis and its aftermath reveals more about the "incentives" to misrepresent the real state of affairs in the postcrisis profession—making it appear to speak with one confident voice—than it has to do with serious reform and repair of the international financial system. Not that some organizations haven't tried. One such attempt to render a motley collection of economic prescriptions seem issued from a professional consensus was *Make Markets Be Markets* (2010) by the Roosevelt Institute, and largely funded by George Soros.[79] It was perhaps most noteworthy for demonstrating a lack of agreement about what "markets" should indeed be and do. Rather, most attention was focused squarely on the regulators, pointing out, for instance, that the United States was unique in having multiple agencies competing as bank regulators within the federal government (but ignoring the structural debilities of the Fed itself as any kind of "regulator" of the financial industry). Frank Partnoy did describe therein how bank balance sheets had become a tissue of lies due to the shadow banking sector; while Rob Johnson insisted that the "too big to fail" problem could not be solved independently of reigning in derivatives. Simon Johnson did mention the "intellectual capture of the economics profession," but nothing further was done with the observation in the way of analysis or empirical confirmation (such as that found in this chapter). One of the more extreme failures of imagination found therein was a proposal to create an analogue of the FDA for new financial instruments; clearly none of the assembled worthies had bothered to dip into the literature concerning the utter abject failure of the pharmaceuticals industry to actually find really new drugs in the last two decades, in part due to capture and corruption of the entire research process overseen by the FDA.[80] But this foray was rapidly overtaken by events, with the passage of the Dodd-Frank legislation.

Another comparable attempt to manufacture a consensus out of unpromising materials, the mysteriously titled *Squam Lake Report*,[81] was even less venturesome in endorsing a potpourri of unrelated yet relatively ineffectual reform proposals. In that case, the quasi-anonymity was more calculated, since some of the members of the group had individually suffered extremely bad press in the period just prior to the release of the report in 2010: Frederic Mishkin and John Campbell had just been exposed to ridicule in the movie *Inside Job*, and John Cochrane has already been mentioned above. The roster also included several other prominent neoliberals, such as Raghuram Rajan, Robert

Shiller, and Matthew Slaughter. However, significantly, the report was widely trumpeted in the press as eminently "nonpartisan," justified by pointing to the inclusion of more "centrist" figures such as Martin Bailey and Hyun Song Shin. Nevertheless, *Squam Lake* turned out to be yet another instance of the "layering" techniques of the neoliberal Russian doll: although publicly promoted out of the supposedly centrist Brookings Institution, the money and organization can be traced back to the Maurice Greenberg Center for Geoeconomic Studies at the Council of Foreign Relations, itself an unabashed neoliberal think tank that boasts staff such as Sebastian Mallaby, Benn Steil, Jagdish Bhagwati, and Amity Shales.[82] Maurice "Hank" Greenberg was the disgraced former chairman and CEO of AIG. If there was a consensus inscribed in the Squam Lake documents, it was less representative of the full economics profession than it was more intently slanted toward codification of the minimum that the banking sector could get away with in the tense political aftermath of the debacle of the crisis, rather than any serious attempt to rethink the financial sector from the ground up.[83] Indeed, the report rarely exhibits the ambition to actually repair much of anything, but instead proposes thin bromides like "more information" or "greater capital requirements," which one reason so much of it ended up looking like much of what eventually became the Dodd-Frank legislation. Of course, greater capital requirements for banks amount to no binding constraint if there is continued enhanced freedom to identify as "capital" almost anything you want (debasing its "quality"), if there is no serious confrontation with the shadow banking sector and especially the plague of repo financing, and nothing whatsoever addresses the virtues of the possibility of separation of banking functions into different insulated institutions, such as the so-called Volcker Rule. Here the British Vickers Report was more venturesome, although also hardly radical.[84]

The one way that the *Squam Lake Report* was revealed as the product of the crème de la crème of the orthodox American economics profession was in its luxuriant excess creativity when it came to inventing new Rube Goldberg devices to "ameliorate" future financial crises, but to no avail. The regimen of constructing little toy models to get published in major journals was now made manifest in extravagant ingenuity in imagining pointless financial contraptions that have never before existed. Further, the Squam Lake group tended to conflate "regulation" with these contraptions. One centerpiece was to require banks to issue newfangled "contingent convertible [CoCo] bonds," which would transform debt into equity given certain stipulated macroeconomic triggers. Much of this excess ingenuity was dead on arrival, due to the fact that the bulk of existing financial innovation that had already occurred in actual markets was concertedly attuned to blur the distinction between debt and equity, in order to evade regulatory strictures. And then there was the cute innovation of requiring "too big to fail" banks to file living wills, as if they could or would voluntarily undergo expedited circumspect bankruptcy in case we had another meltdown. That trifle did make it into Dodd–Frank, and has become probably the only successful permanent make-work program to come out of the Obama administration: unfortunately, the sole beneficiaries have been white-shoe law firms.[85]

The Squam Lake cadre didn't seek to actually rein in unchecked financial innovation; all they wanted to do was to augment it with a little more of their own strategems. But more telling, in question-and-answer sessions at the rollout of that report, one of the authors was forced to admit that orthodox finance theory (in the guise of the "Modigliani–Miller" theorem) actually contradicted a number of their own prescriptions in the report, since the theory deemed that debt/equity ratios did not matter in an efficient market. Here were the crown princes of academic finance conveniently suppressing one of their own key tenets: faithfulness to orthodoxy proved more treacherous than they had anticipated. Their supposed consensus therefore had no intellectual foundations in the canon being taught in most basic economics courses, and in any event, was not politically astute, since once again it entirely ignored the problems of regulatory capture and the Gresham's Law of financial instruments. So much for the consolations of "consensus."

There are many other similar examples from the last few years, but it may be more helpful to tackle the more general issue of the meaning and significance of "consensus" when it comes to the crisis. Much pointless debate emerges from a mistaken impression that, to qualify as a "science," all bona fide members of a profession must be seen to agree on almost all the propositions characteristic of that field. While this tends to be the lay impression, the history of science reveals that there is often substantial room for dissention in real sciences.[86] There abide no stone-scratched Ten Commandments of physics or geology or statistics, however much pedagogy for tyros tends to be prosecuted on that basis. Indeed, the more self-assured the science, the less one finds regularly scheduled expulsion ceremonies for apostates. Instead, one often finds membership in a thought collective correlated with a diverse range of litmus tests: use this model, that empirical technique, this set of subject matters, that rhetorical convention of argumentation, this borrowed bit of theory from a collateral subfield, and so on. Real innovation comes from questioning the full monty in various subtle ways, staying sufficiently within the range of sanctioned methods.

The reason that the economic orthodoxy and journalists had been so obsessively fixated upon the supposed existence of consensus in economics is that many people suspect that economists are little more than crude shills for powerful interests. I doubt that skeptics are as rigidly concerned with logical consistency—since how would that be judged definitively?—as they are with the notion that arguments get repeatedly trumped by instrumental and venal considerations. This is a recurrent topic on blogs, for instance.[87] These people are therefore fixated on the sociology of the discipline, and not so much its intellectual trajectory. Thus, for lay spectators of the economics profession, the degree of dissensus serves as a rough proxy of the weight and resources arrayed for and against a particular issue, which are largely unobservable. The fact that this stance presumes a ground state of no outside manipulation to be indexed by full and sweet concord reveals that the underlying image of science is more than a little bit faulty.

Neoclassical economists attempt to get around this problem by proposing a "rational choice" explanation of their predicament. To quote one of their number, the Princeton economist Alan Blinder and his version of Murphy's Law: "Economists have the least influence on policy where they know the most and are most agreed; they have the most influence on policy where they know the least and disagree most."[88] The problem with this, as with so many other folk generalizations within the neoclassical tradition, is that it has precious little grounding in a body of empirical research. What area of fundamental research has received more attention from economists in the twentieth century than macroeconomic failure and financial crises? And yet, when the time comes to proclaim that there abides a stable corpus of knowledge that constitutes the fruits of all that labor, consensus does not just congeal, but needs to be created from scratch, and shorn up with Sisyphean efforts. And this just as readily occurred in the area that Blinder himself believed was least contentious within the orthodoxy, that is, microeconomics.

The discomposure of dissensus did not end with the subsequent deflation of the bubble. It then broke out in the theoretical area concerning whereof the vast majority of neoclassical economists were most proud: the microeconomics of a fully competitive market.[89]

One of the most worrying heralds of fresh mortification was the so-called flash crash that occurred in New York share markets on the afternoon of May 6, 2010. For twenty minutes, starting at 2:30 p.m., trading volume spiked dramatically as a wide range of shares fell more than 5 percent in a matter of minutes, only to recover equally sharply (Figure 4.7). The same also happened on a number of exchange-traded indexes.

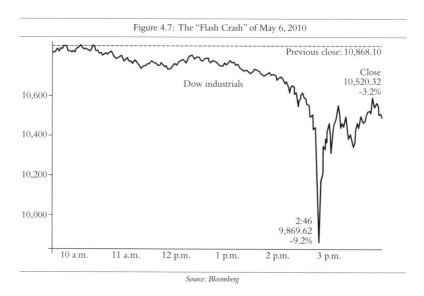

Figure 4.7: The "Flash Crash" of May 6, 2010

Source: Bloomberg

Some individual share prices dropped to mere pennies in price, forc-ing the various exchanges to impose "broken" or canceled trades on something like 27 percent of all transactions. Then many prices immediately recovered, although not all the way to previous levels. Incredulity toward the validity of registered prices struck at the heart of the economists' pretenses to expertise. Such behavior belied all bedrock neoliberal claims of the efficacy of the marketplace in converting information into valid prices. This unprecedented behav-ior was initially attributed by some journalists to "fat finger" computer-entry mistakes, but their trademark attempt to simplify causality through personification of the economy quickly collapsed, as later reconstruction of events tended to reveal that explanation was false. Perhaps more distressing, a month later, the government inves-tigators and financial economists were no more the wiser as to the real causes of the whipsaw movement.[90] What was more disconcert-ing was that a brawl subsequently broke out among economists over which of the myriad "innovations" in trading may have been the culprit: high-frequency automated trading, the dispersal of trades among numerous for-profit exchanges, robo-trading in general, the practice of "stub quotes," the role of exchange-traded funds, and so forth. Other, smaller flash crashes have occurred in financial markets since then, among which may be counted the BATS IPO fiasco and the Knight Capital spasm. Distressingly, no consensus interpretation of the flash crashes has taken hold among economists. While this should give market participants pause, you might have thought it would frighten economists even more, since this phenomenon potentially contradicts everything their core models postulate about market behavior. Neoliberals should equally take umbrage, since the wonderful information processing capacities of the market seem impugned by such events. Furthermore, since it occurred on exchanges that were previously deemed to be relatively open and transparent, so that the concurrent prescription that enforced transparency and exchange listing would be able to somehow "fix" the proliferation of specialty OTC derivatives with their faulty pricing (something that purportedly constituted one of the major causes of the last crash) seemed to be put at risk. That is, if anyone was still concerned with making logical arguments.

Disturbing phenomena such as the low-grade fever of flash crashes in asset markets, which continues intermittently down to the present, should have been taken as a warning that the crisis was slowly undermining neoclassical microeconomics as well; and yet nothing of the sort has transpired. Instead, most economists kept pretending that, should any disconfirmatory experience of the crisis exist, it had remained localized somewhere in the neighborhood of "macroeconomics" alone.[91] One of the strangest aspects of this crisis has been the utter failure of repeated attempts to insist that the orthodox economics profession in the face of crisis hews closely to a solid consensus, anchored to Walrasian general equilibrium theory, combined with the neurotic insistence that the damage has been contained to some relatively small subset of orthodox economic thought. It is astounding that neoclassical economists seem predisposed to accuse everyone other than themselves of something they called "irrationality" in the crisis, when a good working definition of irrational action is the repetition of the same old behaviors in hope of a different outcome.

How Did Neoclassical Economics Dodge the Bullet?

And yet the profession has not really suffered any dire consequences from the litany of embarrassments enumerated above. Economists are still invited to talk shows, profiled in *The New Yorker* and PBS *Newshour* and BBC *Newsnight* and the *Wall Street Journal*, respectfully solicited for their opinions without being ridiculed openly (even on the recurrent occasions when any pair of them sequentially asserts A and not-A with a straight face). Orthodox economists propound a neoclassical orthodoxy awash in waves of willingly submissive students, are paid salaries frequently second only to the research MDs at their universities, and allowed to preach the self-congratulatory proposition that they remain in firm possession of a self-confident science. Under the influence of the brief uprising known as the Occupy movement in 2011, when a group of students noisily walked out of Gregory Mankiw's introductory economics lecture at Harvard, it was treated as some passing undergrad hijinks by the press: Who were they kidding? Economists have been treated with relative impunity even on *The Colbert Report*. They are continually importuned to prophesy: Is the crisis over yet? Will things get better? Where should I park my pitiful 401(k) account? Economists, it appears, have unexpectedly displaced the clergy as the untouchable Delphic oracles in modern society.

There are two rough tacks that one can pursue to try to understand the Teflon ascendancy of the economics profession throughout the crisis. The first is to baldly insist that nothing of substance that has transpired contradicts the intellectual core of the orthodox scriptures. One still infrequently encounters this take-no-prisoners gambit, especially on occasions when some Nobel graybeard is trotted out to defend the profession;[92] but I feel fairly confident that if you have read this far, you will agree that this ploy has been utterly implausible and ultimately unavailing; it may even be suffering diminishing returns as time passes. It is just undeniable that, as the crisis drags on, the pall does tend to besmirch the shiny surfaces of the tablets upon which the neoclassical commandments are inscribed.

The other tactic is to engage in serious sociological examination of the profession and its foibles, as we do here. The economics profession can seem to have escaped scot-free from the crisis only because certain fundamental intellectual trends and supportive institutions conspired to maintain its standing in the face of screaming headwinds. Intellectual orthodoxies never persevere out of pure inertia, not over the long haul; it takes more than a village to keep them on life support.

The armory of defense mechanisms in the particular case of neoclassical economics will become apparent only with the fullness of time and the diligent efforts of future serious intellectual historians of economics; but in the interim, I shall venture to suggest four major sources of the deliverance of economics from its critics.

The Immunity Granted by the Financial Sector and the Fed

We have already encountered the gist of this assertion, but the time has arrived to make it explicit. I have spent inordinate time on the Federal Reserve in this chapter for one very salient reason: If it was indeed the case that the orthodox economics profession was heavily integrated with the formal financial sector, which means *both* the banking and allied spheres *and* the major governmental institutions tasked with their regulation, then in the eventuality that both spheres will have managed to come through the crisis intact, then the economics profession would also be sheltered from the storm. The evasion of consequences from the crisis by the banking sphere, however achieved, translates directly into evasion of contumely by orthodox economists. In a counterfactual world, had the reaction been instead the breaking up of the big banks and cleaning up the shadow banking sector, say by some new resolution authority, not to mention the sweeping purge of the Augean stables at the Fed and (say) the SEC and CFTC and even the IMF, then the economics profession would have acutely discovered a badly exposed and vulnerable flank. Once heads started to roll, the press would have been more inclined to discover economists' craniums skittering hither and yon, and then it would have proven far more difficult to maintain the pretense of serving as detached spectators, guarantors of the public weal.

The interlocking connections between the pinnacles of the economics profession and the glittering heights of the financial sector have been briefly noted in passing, but tended to get lost when many of those firms were rescued or otherwise saved by the Fed. The movie *Inside Job* attempted to foreground the subject of how there must have been something systematic about an entire profession getting paid to be on the wrong side of a degenerating financial infrastructure, and then shielded from audit thereafter; but perhaps predictably, the lesson was rapidly interpreted as concerning the decrepit morality of a few individuals taking a little money "on the side." The riposte was predictable: Defenders were readily recruited to huff, and intone with gravitas:

these people really believed what they preached, were not craven lick-spittles, and could not be corrupted by modest emoluments. One indication that this interpretation was itself faulty was that the amounts of money involved were *many multiples* of their official academic salaries. Another is that the point being made about the Teflon economists has nothing to do with their personal probity or cherished beliefs: rather, it concerns the ways in which these figures led the economics profession to be suborned to the financial sector.

The most famous instance was that of Larry Summers, erstwhile president of Harvard University, and head of the National Economic Council during the first two years of the Obama presidency. Indeed, it was precisely that high-profile government position that forced him to disclose his numerous ties to and payments from the financial sector. When he filed his "Executive Branch Financial Disclosure Report" on January 20, 2009, listing a net worth of $17–$39 million, he prompted a flurry of newspaper and blog accounts of his outsized speaker fees and favors done for the financial sector from the late 1990s onward.[93] Summers has enjoyed an extremely checkered career in many respects, dating from his controversial tenure as chief economist at the World Bank in 1990, but had nonetheless risen to political prominence due to the long-term patronage of Robert Rubin, formerly co-chair of Goldman Sachs, secretary of the Treasury, and later gray eminence at Citigroup and other Wall Street institutions. During the Clinton administration, Rubin and Summers played a now-infamous role in quashing Brooksley Born at the CFTC in 1998 when she proposed reining in the proliferating markets in credit default swaps. Indeed, many of the most significant neoliberal bank deregulations that led up to the crisis happened during the joint watch of Rubin, Summers, and Greenspan. When Rubin left the Treasury in 1999 for Citigroup, he persuaded Clinton to name Summers as his replacement. Rubin lobbied for Summers to be appointed president of Harvard, a term that ended rather inauspiciously in 2006 with accusations of economics faculty fraud from the federal government.[94] Summers did not suffer from these contre-temps, however; he was taken on board at Taconic Capital Advisors, a Goldman alumni hedge fund,[95] and began earning $5 million a year working one day a week at the hedge fund D. E. Shaw, and earning really substantial speaking fees from all the main players in the crisis: $135,000 from Goldman Sachs, $67,000 from JP Morgan, $67,500 from Lehman Brothers, and $45,000 from Merrill Lynch eight days after Obama's election. Much of his wealth appears to have been racked up during this run-up to the crisis. Obama then appointed Summers his top economics advisor, as someone who would serve Solomon-like in helping decide who would be rescued, and who cast into oblivion.[96]

Summers has been contemptuous of the few journalists who have had the temerity to suggest that this revolving door has had any conditioning effect on his behavior in the Obama administration.[97] Although Summers has long been associated with the Democratic Party, he has been an unapologetic neoliberal for most of his career. He wrote:

> If Keynes was the most influential economist of the first half of the 20th century, then Milton Friedman was the most influential economist of the second half . . . Any honest Democrat will admit that we are now all Friedmanites . . . I grew up in a family of progressive economists, and Milton Friedman was a devil figure. But over time, as I studied economics myself and as the world evolved, I came to have grudging respect and then great admiration for him and his ideas . . . Today we take it as given that free financial markets shape finance . . . At the time Mr. Friedman first proposed flexible exchange rates and open financial markets, it was thought that they would be inherently destabilizing.[98]

What confuses people is that Summers apparently understands the true nature of neoliberal policy response to crisis in a way that escapes its rather more literal True Believers.[99] Relace the term "stimulus" with "bank bailouts," and one quickly discerns Summers's Realpolitik:

> "the central irony of financial crises is that they're caused by too much borrowing, too much confidence and too much spending and they're solved by more confidence, more borrowing and more spending." That is profoundly counterintuitive. It makes it difficult to persuade people of the need for more fiscal policy. That's one element.
>
> The second element is that people see economic issues through moral frames and people think there's an extent to which recessions are punishment for sins—mainly sins of excess—and you don't expiate sins by binges. So there's a kind of moral counterintuitiveness that has made it difficult for the public and for political figures to accept stimulus.[100]

Whatever else one might say about Summers, and many have taken their turn,[101] it seems safe to observe that if the banks and hedge funds had been quasi-nationalized or otherwise wound down when they were on the brink of failure, and the financiers consequently demoted to modest roles in the Democratic Party, then economists such as Summers would not have been positioned among the serious candidates to occupy the political stage from 2009 onward; further, his neoliberal credentials might have come in for far more scathing criticism, rendering him persona non grata.

Take another illustrious Harvard economist, Martin Feldstein. Among other ties to the key crisis institutions, he had been on the board of AIG for twenty-two years, only to conveniently resign from his duties on June 30, 2009. He had also been chair of its finance committee and risk management, and therefore was formally directly responsible for the disastrous AIG Financial Products division, whose credit default swaps and other unsustainable derivatives brought down the company. For his services there he accrued more than $6 million, and has apparently never suffered any ostracism for saddling the Treasury with a shell of a remnant of an insurance behemoth that is still hemorrhaging money. Indeed, none of this seemed an obstacle to President Obama appointing him to his Presidential Economic Recovery Advisory Board in 2009, and his Tax Policy task force thereafter.

The AIG stint was only the most high-profile corporate directorship held by Feldstein, disclosed in part because the news media speculated that the reason he was not appointed Federal Reserve chair by George Bush back in 2005 was this politically problematic connection. He has also served as a director of Morgan Guarantee Trust, and in his dual capacity as a health care economist, previously was on the board of HCA Inc., and has been on the board of directors of Eli Lilly since 2002. His annual compensation for the Lilly position alone is $300,000 per year. Feldstein has been a staunch neoliberal his whole life, starting out with a critique of the British National Health Service, and has been credited with transforming the Harvard undergraduate economics curriculum from its prior breadth to a narrow orthodox boot camp with strong neoliberal inclinations. Feldstein served as chair of the Council of Economic Advisors under Ronald Reagan, and took with him as staffers Larry Summers, Gregory Mankiw, and Paul Krugman. His protégés are salted throughout the East Coast economic establishment. He is a master of navigating the interlocking directorates of finance and academia, arranging, for instance, to have the Starr Foundation (controlled by the former AIG CEO Hank Greenberg) to make numerous grants to Harvard and the NBER when he was head of that latter institution.[102]

None of this is mentioned at Feldstein's official Harvard website.

He has explicitly denied on record that the financial industry has had any influence on the economics profession.[103]

Sticking for the moment with AIG, a third Teflon financial action figure is manifest as the Yale economist Gary Gorton. Feldstein may have been formally responsible for the AIG fiasco in his role on the board, but Gorton was substantively responsible. Gorton joined AIG Financial Products as a consultant in 1996, for remuneration that climbed from $200,000 per year at the beginning to more than $1 million per year toward the end. Gorton is reported to have told an AIG shareholders' meeting in 2007, "no transaction is approved by the chief of AIG's financial products unit if it's not based on a model that we built."[104] Gorton provided the intellectual justification (and some of the code) behind AIG's disastrous credit default swaps from 1998 onward that by all accounts caused the company to fail in September 2008.[105]

So, did Gorton suffer any of the consequences of detonating one of the biggest IEDs in the biggest financial crisis since the Great Depression? Apparently not. First off, in May 2008, just as AIG was reporting a massive quarterly loss of $7.8 billion, the Yale School of Management thought it an auspicious occasion to hire Mr. Gorton away from the Wharton School. In August, Mr. Gorton presented a paper to the Fed conference in Jackson Hole on the "Panic of 2007," something with which he presumably had some intimate experience. Chairman Ben Bernanke was so favorably impressed with it that he went around promoting it as the must-read document concerning the crisis for the year 2010. Gorton then turned that paper into a book, graced with the possibly ironic title *Slapped by the Invisible Hand*, which mentioned AIG and his intimate involvement only in one lone sentence: "I also consulted for AIG Financial Products, where I worked on structured credit, credit derivatives, and commodity futures." That's it. This unrepentant practice of mendacity through circumspection is precisely how the economics profession manages to purport to speak for "the public" while functioning as public relations arm for the financial sector. Certainly it seems to have fooled at least one journalist who might otherwise been on the lookout for self-serving narratives concerning the crisis.[106]

Astoundingly, the *Journal of Economic Literature*, the primary reviews journal of the orthodox economics profession, turned to this particular scofflaw, in preference to literally hundreds of other economists who had written about the crisis, to provide a short syllabus for general economists to "get up to speed" on the crisis. Gorton's choice of indispensable texts for crisis hermeneutics was so narrow of scope and devoid of curiosity as to be gobsmacking: Ben Bernanke's testimony before the Federal Crisis Inquiry Commission blaming the whole thing on a spurious "global savings glut"; the Rogoff story that all crises throughout history look alike and involve government overindebtedness;[107] the Shiller index on the housing bubble; his own work on repo; some deadly colorless reports from the IMF; and a couple of papers that suggest banks pulled back on their lending in 2008 because they were "constrained" when their own short-term lending dried up. Nothing untoward or illegal here. Other than insisting that the extent of mortgage defaults in 2008 did not warrant such a drastic contraction—because the magic of high-powered credit securitization models (unstated: flogged by Gorton during his time at AIG) was on the money in retailing risk—the rest of the story comes across so bland and diffuse and colorless that it beggars belief that we have come through the worst economic collapse since the Great Depression. Perhaps it resonated with the implicit requirements of the *JEL* not so much that these texts were baldly *wrong*,[108] but rather that they were strategically superficial, bordering on irrelevance. In Gorton's world, nobody really did anything *wrong*; nothing hints at a system that is self-destructive and unsustainable; the economy hasn't really changed its stripes; all that happened was that garden-variety financial innovation got a little ahead of itself: "The novelty here was in the location of the runs, which took place mostly in the newly evolving shadow banking system . . . This new source of systemic vulnerability came as a surprise to policymakers and economists."[109]

Gorton has only grown bolder in fulfilling the role as apologist-in-chief. In *Slapped*, he described the securitization process as a contraption for reducing the ability to get at underlying fundamentals, and praised it as a good thing. In a subsequent interview he stated: "The term shadow banking has acquired a pejorative connotation, and I'm not sure that's really deserved . . . Banking evolves, and it evolves because the economy changes. There's innovation and growth, and shadow banking is only the latest natural development of banking."[110]

Seemingly perched outside the process, his own interventions obscured, Gorton can paint the current situation as the product of purely "natural" evolution, without once mentioning the role of economists such as himself in juking and splicing the DNA of the evolving entities.[111] If, in some alternative universe, AIG had been wound down in a more rigorous and systematic fashion, with something approaching retrospective full disclosure, would anyone still be listening to Mr. Gorton outside of a Yale classroom?

There is a fourth case, highlighted here not so much because of this figure's intimate direct involvement in the crisis (unlike Summers, Feldstein, and Gorton), but rather because he was the other designated reviewer of a marathon evaluation of twenty-one books devoted to the crisis in the *JEL*.[112] Andrew Lo is the Harris & Harris Group Professor of Finance at the MIT Sloan School of Management and the director of MIT's Laboratory for Financial Engineering. In other words, in the rarefied world of the "quants" who built the models that underpinned most of the complexity in the run-up to the crisis, he was chief guru. The only private affiliation listed on his personal website is as founder and chief scientist at the hedge fund AlphaSimplex, but on its website we learn, "Andrew has 24 years of industry experience. Prior to starting AlphaSimplex, Andrew developed investment strategies and trading technologies as a consultant to a number of prominent Wall Street firms." Professor Lo never lists any of these consultancies on his public papers and appearances, nor does he mention his position at the New York Fed or FINRA, an organization dedicated to the private self-regulation of the securities industry, along the lines of a "Better Business Bureau." But we are getting used to this pattern of strategic silences. Despite all these rather specific commitments, Professor Lo presents himself as an open-minded, impartial arbiter of all things having to do with the crisis, all the while promoting a very specific political set of positions. Not surprisingly, the premier thesis that he never misses an opportunity to roll out is that the quants, and economists in general, should not be saddled with any responsibility for the crisis. (This was probably one of the reasons he was chosen to survey the crisis landscape by the *JEL*.) He opted for this position as early as October 2009, in a public lecture produced by the National Science Foundation (so much for the neutrality of the funders of the natural sciences), which argued that blaming financial engineering for the crisis was on a par with blaming accounting, or the system of natural numbers.[113] There he also mooted a proposition he has returned to repeatedly in the interim, that the causes of the crisis should instead be rooted in individual psychology, such that any blame is diffuse, or "all of us participated to some extent in the crisis." It was rather due to a series of technical glitches, ones that we may be congenitally blind toward as they develop, but that can be diagnosed and fixed by technocrats in retrospect, rather like the National Transportation and Safety Board inspecting a plane crash. (The seductiveness of the metaphor smoothly elides the fact that the NTSB was not tasked with the postmortem of the planes ramming into the Twin Towers in New York.) In his most recent survey, Lo tends to favor neoliberal books on the crisis, such as Rajan's *Fault Lines* and Rogoff and Reinhart's *This Time Is Different*, while disparaging books such as Stiglitz's *Freefall*.[114] Economists on the center left are chided for getting a little testy, whereas books by neoliberals are treated as par for the course. There he also innovates a few more rather contrarian positions on the crisis: that the efficient-markets hypothesis (more on this in the next chapter) did not lead investors astray; that Wall Street compensation packages did not distort incentives and behavior; and finally, that the big investment banks did not become especially highly leveraged in the boom. From the commanding heights of the current pinnacles of finance, what's not to like here?

Other similar cases of repressed allegiances have come to light over the past two years, although perhaps lacking the direct immediacy and audacity of immunity that one detects with a Summers or a Feldstein or Gorton. For instance, much has been made of the testimony of the Stanford economist Darrell Duffie before the Financial Crisis Inquiry Commission concerning, among other things, the culpability of the ratings agencies, while neglecting to mention he was a member of the board of governors of Moody's.[115] At minimum, under pressure, he then disclosed that he did work for at least two hedge funds, and consulted on the winding-up of the Lehman estate. Simon Johnson has noticed that Duffie's work has frequently been paid for by industry interests, but that this is rarely mentioned in the contexts where he is cited as an authority on financial regulation.[116] We have already mentioned his role in the *Squam Lake Report*; subsequently, Johnson reports he was paid $50,000 by SIFMA (Securities Industry and Financial Markets Association, a lobbyist organization) to produce a paper opposing certain forms of derivatives regulation by the CFTC. It seems pretty clear that Duffie allows the Stanford trademark to mask his role as paid apologist:

> Why should we take such work seriously—or any more seriously than other paid consulting work, for example, by a law firm or someone else working for the industry?
>
> The answer presumably is that Stanford University is very prestigious. As an institution, it has done great things. And its faculty is one of the best in the world. When a professor writes a paper on behalf of an industry group, the industry benefits from—and is, in a

sense, renting—the university's name and reputation. Naturally, the banker at the CFTC roundtable stressed "Stanford" when he cited the paper.[117]

The Dean of Columbia's Business School, Glenn Hubbard, came off as petulant in *Inside Job* when questioned concerning his corporate ties; but only long afterward did the public catch a glimpse of the sorts of shenanigans he was loathe to disclose. In a leaked set of depositions from a suit by monoline insurers against Bank of America, it was revealed that Hubbard was paid $1200 an hour to testify on behalf of Countrywide, conceded by all and sundry as one of the worst fraudulent mortgage pushers in the run-up to the crisis. Hubbard testified Countrywide's mortgages were not fraudulent with a straight face. The econometric exercise produced by Hubbard was so full of holes that the opposing counsel easily pointed out that it could not demonstrate that Countrywide did not engage in mortgage fraud; and that, in fact, Hubbard knew little about underwriting. This was the kind of work regularly undertaken for pay by the person who was once rumored to be Mitt Romney's choice for Treasury Secretary.[118] Or take Richard Clarida, an economist at Columbia University, and assistant treasury secretary under George W. Bush. Clarida has often been invited to testify on various aspects of government debt, but did not disclose he was also executive vice president at Pimco, the world's largest bond investment fund, until he was caught out by a *New York Times* reporter.[119] A little more digging uncovered more ties, such as positions at Credit Suisse and Grossman Asset Management.

The shadow banking sector has performed a minor séance, and conjured a shadow economist sector. We now have a better idea just who the Americans are who currently inhabit this shadow economist finance sector. Charles Ferguson, in his book *Predator Nation*, describes many of the key players by name: he covers Glenn Hubbard, Larry Summers, Fredric Mishkin, Richard Portes, Laura Tyson, Martin Feldstein, Hal Scott, and John Campbell.[120] The University of Massachusetts economist Gerry Epstein has taken a different tack, with a somewhat different roster. Epstein and his collaborators have collated two data sets linked to economists regularly summoned to pronounce upon financial regulation during the crisis, comparing the positions taken in their academic work and their "outside" positions and consultancies (derived entirely from public sources). Since it would be a daunting task to subject the entire profession to audit, he chose to pursue the prosopography of the manageable subset of financial economists who had presented themselves as "faceless" representatives of the orthodox economics discipline, either through the Squam Lake group (covered above) or the Pew Economic Policy Group Financial Reform Project.[121] By keeping the target group limited to nineteen prominent economists, his team was able to explore the nature of ties to financial firms in somewhat greater depth than one encounters in the news media. However, working only from open sources, the report depends entirely upon some manifestation of self-disclosure turning up in some public context; therefore, it necessarily underrepresents the true nature of financial connections. His summary report concluded:

> We find that 15 of 19 economists had private financial affiliations over 2005–09. The norm for economists was to not identify their private financial affiliations, establishing the need for a code of ethics prescribing disclosure guidelines.
>
> These same economists who mostly failed to warn of the increasing financial fragility and impending crisis also have developed a basic consensus view that favours more market-based reforms and relatively less government regulation as a way of preventing future financial meltdowns.[122]

This work documents a number of facts on a somewhat larger scale than the previous collection of individual anecdotes.[123] It reveals that ties to the financial sector are extensive and pervasive among those economists who specialize in the technicalities of finance, and that they are closely correlated with intellectual positions that actively absolve the financial sector of all responsibility for the crisis. Furthermore, these economists rarely disclose these patent conflicts of interest when they perform in the media and in political hearings their pronouncements upon what we should do about the crisis. They are invaluable for the industry because they appear in public as an independent academic elite, when they are something else besides. They are the same people we encounter throughout this book: Alan Blinder, Charles Calomiris, Richard Herring, John Taylor, Jeremy Stein, Andrew Bernard, John Campbell, John Cochrane, Douglas Diamond, Darrell Duffie, Kenneth French, Anil Kashyap, Frederic Mishkin, Raghuram Rajan, David Sharfstein, Robert Shiller, Hyun Song Shin, Matthew Slaughter, and Rene Stulz.[124]

We could go on and on in this vein, but there is little point in

choreographing this virtual economists' perp walk. There are further
European and Asian economists who would need to be added to the
list, because of their affiliations with international banks and other
central banks. London is another special hive of this activity. Well
before the census of these ranks was even partially populated, I expect
my audience would have thrown in the towel. Charles Ferguson's
Inside Job has just scratched the surface of paid-but-not-quite-disclosed
behavior by prominent economists; what is now needed is some
comprehension of the aggregate systemic character of what has become
a conventional career path. If you are lucky enough to write a few
macrofinance papers that attract the attention of people that matter,
and then garnish a plum political job such as under-assistant-subsecre-
tary of the Treasury/Council of Advisors, touching the right political
bases, then it just follows that you will in the fullness of time become
absorbed into the corporate/financial sector in some reasonably lucrative capacity, and even perhaps later on become a regional Fed
governor, all the while speaking out as an "independent" academic
voice for the public commonweal. This career trajectory has been a
conveyor belt for some time now, at least back to 1970, when Paul
Samuelson helped found the hedge fund Commodities Corporation.
The issue is not possible compromise of personal virtue of this or that
individual in the face of tempting blandishments; it is rather that the
proud pretense of "independent expertise" has become thoroughly
undermined within the current economics profession. This has been
the bane of academic economics, but also, after the crisis, the vessel of
its deliverance.

Because this is a book intently focused on the interplay of the crisis
and economics, in this section and elsewhere we have devoted the
bulk of attention to the subterranean connections of economists to the
financial sector. However, we would be remiss if we neglected to point
out that hidden ties to other private firms on the part of those who
purport to speak for "the public good" are in fact ubiquitous, wherever neoliberal doctrine has inspired initiatives to reengineer markets
with the help of state power. For instance, neoclassical "experts" on
global warming who promote emissions trading as the solution to
environmental degradation have been demonstrated to have extensive
ties to private for-profit firms benefiting from permit trading, which
they rarely acknowledge.[125] Indeed, one can understand the co-opta-
tion of climate activism by pollution permits as the engulfment of
science by the financial sector, ever in search of new fields to securitize. Much the same has happened in health economics. It is not just

macroeconomists who have succumbed to the siren song of paid advocacy: it is the entire economics profession.

To recap: the academic-governmental-financial complex has had profound intellectual consequences. Because the banks, hedge funds, and ratings agencies all dodged the bullet in the crisis, this enabled and empowered the economics profession to do likewise.

The Immunity Conveyed by the Neoliberal Restructuring of Universities

It was not just the turbocharged finance sector that provided cover for economists. Another major factor in the maintenance of the untouchable reputation of the orthodox economics profession has been the progressive commercialization of the totality of university research since the 1980s. This is a very large topic, and I have dealt with it in detail elsewhere.[126] The central observation for our present purposes is to realize that, if one wholeheartedly subscribes to the neoliberal doctrine of the market as über–information processor, then "reform" of the university prescribes the monetization of knowledge in all its forms. Since the 1980s, the most prominent academic prophets of this reform have been members of the economics profession. Indeed, so zealous were the boards of trustees and state governments to bring about this change that neoclassical economists were frequently installed as presidents of many major universities: Summers at Harvard, Hugo Sonnenschein at Chicago, Harold Shapiro at Princeton, Richard Levin at Yale, and more at lesser schools.[127] Summers, in particular, was brought on board at Harvard to induce what was perceived as a relatively recalcitrant bunch of pampered faculty to become more responsive to market signals.[128] These captains of erudition then set out to shrink the footprint of the humanities and expand the natural sciences at their institutions, since that was where the money was purportedly to be found. But a little-noted subsidiary trend was to further expand the representation of economists within the academic walls.

Curiously enough, there are no good aggregate time series of proportions of distinct disciplines' representations within any national university system. There have been a few stabs at performing a retrospective census at a few key junctures for limited geographical areas. For instance, one paper documents the recent incursion into law schools: Of the 1,338 faculty members at the top twenty-six American law schools, beyond the J.D., 27 percent had PhDs, with economics the most common concentration at 7 percent. Another 13 percent had PhDs in some social science other than economics, while 7 percent had PhDs in a non-social-science discipline. This is a substantial increase from merely a generation ago. Another work attempts to break down faculty representation across a sample of British Commonwealth universities in a few selected years over a century concludes: "Although it is good to understand why university economics prospered more than psychology over the 20th century, it would also be good to know why at the end of the century economists were ten times more common on average in the world's universities than psychologists." Marion Fourcade estimates that economics grew from roughly 1 percent of all university faculty in 1900 to about 4 percent by 2000. While all of these gauges are impressionistic to varying degrees, they do point to an important trend in academe, which is the expanding proportional representation of PhD economists in universities, especially over the last three decades.[129]

Any generalizations in this area are bound to be controversial, so let me simply suggest how this issue impinges upon the question at hand. Let us take as given that economists have come to occupy proportionally more positions and more strategic positions within the modern university; and let us also accept that the Great Transformation of the modern university since 1980 has followed the imperative to restructure research so it becomes more responsive to commercial imperatives. It remains to be demonstrated beyond a reasonable doubt, but there is plenty of circumstantial evidence to suggest that these two trends have been intimately related to one another. Economists have theorized and promoted the benefits of the commercialization of knowledge; and in turn, universities have hired more economists for their expertise to both preach and effectuate this commercialization outside the standard compartmentalization of departmental organization.

This goes some distance in explaining why economists would not readily be punished by universities for their undistinguished track record in the crisis. Within universities, economists have rendered themselves indispensable as the new arbiters of human-capital bestowal and commercial validation. Harvard's Rakesh Khurana has written, "As the Academy Award winning documentary *Inside Job* finds, highly reputable business schools and university economic departments now perform the same functions as college football or basketball programs: bringing in large dollars for the university and individual faculty, but increasingly divergent from the overall educational, intellectual, and societally oriented ideals of the university."[130] They occupy key posts in business schools, law schools, and medical schools, propounding doctrines both mathematical and cultural. When an academic economist ventured beyond the ivy walls to retail her expertise and preach the virtues of the marketplace, she was simply foreshadowing for other faculty members the behavior that would be required in the twenty-first-century university. Their sometimes shadowy positions in the financial-governmental-academic complex were occasions for pride and pomp in the eyes of university trustees, not of intellectual compromise or culpability. It would be a tremendous repudiation of everything the university had striven to become after 1980 to downsize or close an economics department as a cost-saving measure, unlike (say) the odd department of geography, or philosophy, or astronomy, or area studies.

Hence any academic status degradation of the economics profession on its home ground would entail an implicit repudiation of the trajectory of university restructuring, which had three decades of impetus behind it. In other words, absent the world being turned upside down, or another great wave of university restructuring, the economics profession would continue to enjoy shelter from the impecunious storm within the modern university.

Neoclassical Economic Theory Denies That Academic Markets Can Ever Be Corrupt

Essentially, the indictment by *Inside Job* and many commentators was that the crisis had revealed that the economics profession was rife with intense conflicts of interest, and this, in turn, had so corrupted the actual orthodox doctrines of the profession that its analyses of the crisis had become untrustworthy. What was missing from these screeds was an appreciation for a major escape hatch: that immersion in neoclassical training produced adherents who lived by the motto that the very notion of conflict of interest was unprepossessing, and that corruption of market-based research was essentially impossible. Rephrasing the insight, economists were fortified to dodge the bullet because they denied the bullet had ever taken flight.

The literature on the prevalence and management of conflicts of interest in the modern university is huge, and getting bigger by the hour.[131] Much of it has been centered upon the sphere of biomedical research, for the reason that biomedicine was one of the earliest research fields to become thoroughly commercialized in the modern university, and consequently a plethora of debacles in the arenas of lethal drugs, abused human subjects, botched pharmaceuticals, and outlandish expenses have drawn the attention of many to search for the explanation of such corruption of the research enterprise in the midst of largesse. Within the perimeter of university research, "financial conflict of interest" has come to be defined as the actual conduct of research in an environment where relevant financial interests of the researcher and/or his institution might conceivably influence the outcome, embedded in a larger societal context where impartiality is expected or presumed. Interestingly, sophisticated observers realize that even this definition is conditional upon a presumed list of goals of the research enterprise: in biomedicine, should the objective be simply to increase the stock of human knowledge, or is it the promotion of human health and welfare, or is it much more narrowly just to make money?

Confining conflicts of interest to a circumscribed set of phenomena is like herding cats; but that has not stopped medical journals from striving mightily to control it, the National Institutes of Health to legislate its permissible boundaries, and science-studies scholars to characterize its effects. The empirical literature reveals that instances of such conflicts are pervasive in biomedicine, and, not surprisingly, "Strong and consistent evidence shows that industry sponsored research tends to draw pro-industry conclusions."[132] Perhaps because of its ubiquity in the modern commercialized university, bureaucratic approaches to conflicts of interest in biomedical research tend to congregate in the area of risk management—that is, formal protection of the university from the lethal fallout from conflicted research—rather than proactive attempts to control bias and corruption in the research itself. If one detects certain affinities with the concepts of risk in the banking sector, one would not be too far off.

If academic biomedicine provides one pole of an institutional approach to conflicts of interest, then the financial community anchors the opposite pole. In finance, conflicts of interest are deemed so pervasive that they are generally ignored. Financial services professionals have little in the way of standardized legal or moral obligations to avoid such conflicts, except when their behavior rises to the level of fraud, or violates insider trading laws.[133] This is one very salient reason why Goldman Sachs was widely excoriated for essentially betting against its own clients in the sale of CDOs and the simultaneous offerings of credit default swaps on those CDOs it knew were more likely to fail, for instance as detailed in the U.S. Senate crisis inquiry, but was treated on Wall Street as nothing exceptional, and therefore morally unremarkable.[134] Similarly, when the LIBOR rate-setting scandal broke in 2012, the reaction of the Street was that everyone knew Barclays, JP

Morgan, and all the rest were lumbered with conflicts of interest in reporting interbank lending rates; no insiders were shocked that the "truth" was a flexible concept. This attitude can be traced back to the expectation that if, as a client, you wanted safeguards against such conflicts, then it was incumbent upon you to negotiate them before-hand into your contract.

Another major reason the economics profession has managed to dodge the bullet of the crisis is that its default stance toward conflicts of interest is much closer to that of the financial industry than academic biomedicine in the grand continuum of professional governance. Orthodox economists tend to see nothing wrong with conflicts of interest, since they have generally subscribed to the precept that market arrangements are capable in principle of monitoring, restricting, and resolving any such conflicts in the course of normal operation. Read-ers of this volume will recognize this as a corollary of the basic neoliberal precept that the market is a superior information processor to any other human or institutional intermediary when it comes to the revelation of knowledge. This has the curious implication that, when-ever the economic orthodoxy has written about the "problem of corruption," it parsed the problem as besetting *only* those individuals working in the public sector. Since everyone else employed in the private marketplace is known to be motivated by private gain, and the market turns that into public welfare, then by definition, there are no conflicts of interest in the private sector, only lax imposition of contractual protections. As usual, MPS economist Gary Becker boiled this down to a pithy epigram in his *Business Week* column: "if we abol-ish the state, we abolish corruption."[135]

Whenever neoclassical economists then reflexively apply these core theoretical principles to themselves, and it comes to issues of conflict of interest, they come off sounding a bit Pecksniffian. Conveniently, George DeMartino has collected together the whole litany of excuses that orthodox economists proffer as to why a code of ethical conduct should not apply to themselves; I urge the reader to consult it himself during an interval when his blood pressure might be a little sluggish.[136] However, DeMartino devotes only a page to the notion that contemporary neoclassical theory, and especially the vari-ant known as "public choice" theory, tutors them that conflicts of interest are best dealt with by the market, and that they stand exoner-ated to the extent they pledge their troth to said market. The financial sector and the economic orthodoxy are melded not only in personal roles, but in convictions as well.

The blogger Yves Smith has wonderfully parodied this, by slightly amending the language of public-choice theory of the neoliberal Virginia School to address the code of the economist:

What would you identify as the central insights of Academic Choice theory?
The theory begins by identifying three principal ways in which economists try to maximize their utility. First, they receive salaries from universities, which can be increased if their course enrollment increases. Course enrollment is primarily driven by students with future careers in business and the financial sector, so an economist has an incentive to propound theories that CEOs and financial institutions find attractive. Even if adoption of these theories leads to substantial public costs, these costs will not be shouldered by the economist personally. Second, by developing such theories an economist can open the door to future wealth as a lobbyist or consultant. Third, the support of economists is critical to creating and maintaining special privileges for the financial services industry and for top corporate officers. By threatening to withdraw this support, economists can engage in rent-seeking. I call this last practice academic entrepreneurship.
Is it really plausible that economists threaten top banks that in the absence of some kind of payoff, they will change the theories they teach in a direction that is less favorable to the banks?
There are certainly cases in history of the following sequence:

a. Economist E espouses views that are less favorable to certain special interest groups S. Doing so threatens the ability of S to extract rent from the public.
b. Later, E changes his view, thereby withdrawing the prior threat.
c. Still later, E is paid large amounts of money by representatives of S in exchange for services that do not appear particularly onerous.

For example, let E = Larry Summers and let S = the financial services industry. In 1989 E was (a) a supporter of the Tobin tax, which threatened to reduce the rent extracted by S. This threat was apparently later withdrawn (b), and in 2008 E was paid \$5.2 million (c) in exchange for working at the hedge fund D. E. Shaw (an element of S) for one day a week.

However, it is naturally more difficult to witness the negotiations in which specific threats were appeased with specific future payouts. This is a problem that also bedevils Public Choice theory, in which it is likewise difficult to show exactly how a particular politician is remunerated in exchange for threatening businesses with anti-business legislation. The theory assures us that such negotiations occur, although they are difficult to observe directly. Perhaps further theoretical advances will help us to close this gap.[137]

This was the very same Larry Summers who a decade before the crisis had been quoted as saying: "Financial markets don't just oil the wheels of economic growth—they *are* the wheels."[138]

It should now become apparent that the way in which these deep conceptual commitments get translated into public advocacy helps ward off brickbats hurled by those offended by the role of economists in the crisis. Economists, the prophets of incentives, quite logically respond to their own incentives to service their various constituencies, and as they never cease to insist, life is nothing but a sequence of trade-offs. Whenever they make reference to the "public good" or "general welfare" in the course of their endeavors, they frequently mean nothing more than the brute fact of *caveat emptor*. Thus, when some rude outsider—say, Charles Ferguson in *Inside Job*—gets all steamed up about "conflicts of interest" while uncovering their prognostications, they react in a way resembling the Harvard economist John Campbell in the film; insiders are nonplussed, really at a loss to see what all the fuss is about. (There is also the barely disguised sneer: stop your cheap rabble-rousing and riling up the groundlings. *We are Harvard.*) There will be no perfervid eleventh-hour conversions, no dark nights of repentance, no rending of garments and gnashing of teeth for the economics profession. And this, in turn, fortifies their inclinations to mount a united front to mollify the greater public already familiar with Freakonomic insouciance, no matter what their personal politics might be. There has materialized no better way to face up to the rebuke of the crash.

This dynamic explains why the push to get the American Economics Association (AEA) to adopt a professional code of ethics in response to the crisis was totally unavailing.[139] The AEA set up a committee to respond to the embarrassment of *Inside Job*, but it was met with a great wall of indifference. Neoliberal economists immediately argued to their own satisfaction that, within their worldview, there was no point to the AEA issuing a professional code:

Until "Inside Job," the most serious ethical debate that I know of within the profession was over advising Chile's Pinochet regime. One view was that providing advice to any regime that abused human rights was wrong. Another view was that providing economic advice was ethical, because it would improve the lives of the people living under the regime.

If the A.E.A. took either view on this thorny topic, the organization would have weakened itself dramatically, by creating conflict and alienating a significant fraction of its members. Another danger, which seems more likely, is that it might craft an excessively mild code of conduct that angers no one but sets too low a bar. That might be worse than no code of conduct at all, providing shelter to people who engage in inappropriate behavior but assert they are abiding by the A.E.A. code. . . .

What about disclosure in other contexts, such as non-refereed publications, speeches or comments to reporters? In these cases, universities—not the American Economic Association—are the natural ethical authority. (Full disclosure: I am just starting to serve on Harvard's university-wide Standing Committee on Individual Financial Conflict of Interest).

Universities have the resources to develop ethical guidelines and the power to enforce them. They are the employers of academic economists, and ethical lapses damage them, too. They are the natural institutional guardians of their employees' professional behavior.[140]

And, conveniently, universities also have been the staunch natural defenders of the Divine Right of economists to do whatever they please.

A year later, the AEA predictably declined to produce a code of ethics for its membership. It did issue a new disclosure policy for conflict-of-interest-reports for papers submitted to the AEA-sponsored economics journals—which are only a small subset of the universe of ranked economics journals.[141] Since the same body had earlier promulgated a code of provision of all econometric data sets for all submitted articles to AEA journals, which it then promptly proceeded to neglect and ignore, the prospects for any major changes of behavior are slim at best.

Agnotology Is the Economics Profession's Best Friend

Here we return to the most important "double truth" broached at the end of chapter 2: The major ambition of the Neoliberal Thought

Collective is to sow doubt and ignorance among the populace, because it helps foster the "spontaneous order" that is the object of all their endeavors. This is an extrapolation of the point stressed above: from this perspective, it is perfectly justifiable that paid experts should behave as apologists for the interests that hire them, insist the neoliberals, because that is how the marketplace of ideas works.

Although the neoliberal approach to knowledge bears profound consequences for nearly all aspects of human inquiry, it holds special salience for the contemporary economics profession. This is where the histories of neoliberalism and the economic orthodoxy collide in the most spectacular fashion. Yet, in the most unexpected fashion, the ensuing dynamic ended up providing still another layer of protection for economists.

My primary thesis here, and in the rest of this volume, is that the crisis has revealed a severe epistemological contradiction that festers at the heart of the modern economics profession; this has dovetailed with a new set of practices and institutions that have developed since 1980 to paper over the contradiction. It began when the economics profession tended to grow more neoliberal over the past few decades. We will take that proposition as given here, because we aim to explore one of its most important implications: namely, that it sets up a treacherous dynamic interplay between the economics profession and the general public, awkwardly brought closer to the surface by the crisis. In a word, neoliberal theory in the context of economic crisis creates problems for economists' self-image as public intellectuals.

In the neoliberal playbook, intellectuals are inherently shady characters precisely because they sell their pens-for-hire to private interests: that is their inescapable lot in life as participants in the marketplace of ideas. It is the market as superior information processor that ultimately sorts out what the masses should deem as truth, at least in the fullness of time. This constitutes the gist of the Robert Barro position that, as long as they keep paying us, we must be right. This stance creates a problem for the economics profession, because it drives a wedge between *trusting economists* to clarify issues of great public import, and *trusting the market* to arrive at time-tested knowledge. This epistemic tension becomes a full-blown contradiction when the issue becomes the possibility of the breakdown of the market itself. If one adopts the hard neoliberal horn of the dilemma, then the intricate operation of the market is truly inscrutable, unknowable by any individual person, and thus economists are despicable charlatans who keep pretending to know what they can never truly know. From this perspective, the market has never actually failed, even in the current crisis; all that has happened is that economists have befogged our understanding of the necessary accommodations that must occur in order for it to come to terms with current events. Clearly, in this special neoliberal frame, economists (with few exceptions) end up looking like part of the problem, not generally part of the solution. Yet, if one instead occupies the more "moderate" horn of the dilemma, then orthodox economics theory was never fundamentally falsified, because it was the markets themselves that bore inherent flaws, which only the economists can be trusted to rectify. However, this bumps up hard against the empirical phenomenon apparent for all the public to see: the orthodox profession was blindsided by the depth and pervasiveness of the crisis, and has been perplexed and befuddled as to any consensus diagnosis of the crisis, much less appropriate measures to rectify it. And worse, there is no limit to how "deep" the market failures go. Thus there is no reason not to think that "market failure" itself betokens failure of the orthodox economics profession as well.

Neither horn of this dilemma is very tolerable, so in the aftermath of economic collapse the economics profession has sought to have it both ways: the lesson they would want to draw from the crisis is that the public should trust *both* the market and the economics profession to rescue it from economic disaster.[142] This happened on both the notional left and the notional right. *Pace* Robert Barro, this contradiction has proven a source of growing dissatisfaction with economists on the part of the public. The purpose of the next chapter is to document how some elements within the economics profession have sought to sustain this impossible straddle, mainly by cooperating with new arbiters of public discourse such as think tanks, banks, and corporations, in order to modulate between the two opposed horns of the dilemma. The fallout from trying to have it both ways is that it is no longer possible for the heroic public intellectual to personally embody a shining beacon of rationality amid the rough and tumble of political discourse, at least in economics. Instead, orthodox economists tend to waver between two incompatible positions, depending upon which appears more convenient for the entity that provides their institutional identity (as explored in this chapter); but *the only way they can manage to accomplish this is by fostering greater ignorance among the public, their primary audience.* Indeed, the think tanks and corporations that employ economists frequently explicitly seek to foster ignorance as part of their business plans: that is the postmodern phenomenon of agnotology. Economists, witting or no, have become the vanguard of the purveyors of ignorance in matters pecuniary, precisely because they cannot face up to their own epistemic dilemma. The crisis only highlights the divergence between "Trust us" and "Trust the neoliberal market."

The most important part of the history of the crisis that has been neglected by the mass of commentary cited herein is that there have surfaced in the crisis some relatively systematic attempts to pump doubt and confusion into public discourse; in other words, some "explanations" of manifestations of the crisis and its aftermath have been launched as trial balloons *not* expressly for purposes of further test, judicious development, and elaboration by sanctioned professional economists or other intellectuals, but rather as calculated interventions in public discourse in order to buy time and frustrate any shared impressions of a few sharply delineated positions on a contentious issue. Think global-warming denialism, but now extended to the question of the causes and meaning of the economic crisis. And it is not some fringe anomaly, but built into the very conceptual structure of the contemporary economics profession.

The orthodox economist cannot help but try to get his audience to simultaneously trust markets and trust economists. As we have seen, he is also inextricably woven into the financial sector. Older notions of the role of the "public intellectual" referred to someone who served to both personify and clarify positions of great import in public debate;[143] but one of the signal contemporary postmodern developments has been the genesis and nurture of intellectuals poised and primed to muddy up the public mind and consequently foil and postpone most political action, and hence to preserve the *status quo ante*. This has been one of the objectives of the financial sector since the crisis, and economists are in the front lines of the disinformation project. John Dewey is most likely spinning in his grave, but the complex of neoliberal think tanks and corporations has sure control over what it is doing, and has sometimes even admitted its motives. The economists play along to maintain their untenable straddle between trusting the market and trusting the economists.

The literature that discusses this feature of public discourse travels under the rubric of agnotology.[144] It is not the study of ignorance and doubt under all their manifestations, as sometimes mistakenly asserted, but rather the focused study of the intentional manufacture of doubt and uncertainty in the general populace for specific political motives. This literature is very different from an older "sociology of propaganda," which was an artifact of Cold War theories of totalitarian societies.

Agnotology instead studies a pronounced market-based set of procedures, as opposed to propaganda, which tends to emanate from a single
source. It rather situates the practice of the manufacture of doubt as
rooted in the professions of advertising and public relations, with close
connections to the organization of think tanks and lobbying firms. Its
essence is a series of techniques and technologies to both *use* and *influence* independently existing academic disciplines for the purposes of
fostering impressions of implacable controversy where actual disputes
are marginal, wreaking havoc with outsider perceptions of the configuration of orthodox doctrines, and creating a parallel set of spokespersons
and outlets for ideas that are convenient for the behind-the-scenes funding interests, combined with the inflation of disputes in the name of
"balance" in order to infuse the impression in outsiders that nothing has
been settled within the core research community. The ultimate purpose
in erecting this Potemkin controversy is to stymie action. The earliest
instances of agnotology were focused upon instances deployed in the
natural sciences, most specifically, on the political controversies over the
cancer consequences of tobacco smoke, Star Wars antimissile systems,
the theory of evolution, the efficacy of pharmaceuticals, and the causes
and consequences of global warming.[145]

The advance of agnotology beyond propaganda is lodged in the fact
that its hallmark techniques thrive off a hermeneutics of suspicion,
with the result that the populace can maintain the comfortable fiction
that it is not being manipulated by the obscure interests funding the
initiatives. In this, it is similar to advertizing that makes use of the
general conviction of the target populace that they are immune to the
blandishments of advertising.[146] As the famous Frank Luntz memo to
the Republican Party stated:

> The scientific debate remains open. Voters believe that there is no
> consensus about global warming. Should the public come to believe
> that the scientific issues are settled, their views about global warm-
> ing will change accordingly. Therefore, you need to continue to
> make the lack of scientific certainty a primary issue in the debates.[147]

For many, this may sound like a feckless procedure of elevating the
marginal and the discredited in the interests of promoting spurious
science and dubious intelligence; but more recent historical work has
demonstrated that think tanks also have managed to recruit very
prominent scientists, from Nobel winners to presidents of the National
Academy, to lend their name to serial instances of agnotology.[148] In

many cases, these figures were willing to participate precisely because of their ideological commitments: namely, they regarded established science as helping foster illegitimate government intervention in the marketplace, or as perhaps providing support for political opponents, and that political considerations were sufficient to deem the existing consensus wanting. It is important to note that these recruits are not misrepresenting or lying about their deepest scientific beliefs; rather, they have come to embrace a different conception of "truth." In other words, the think-tank thought collective has been able to recruit esteemed members of the scientific community in good standing to volunteer in various agnotological projects, to better cultivate the ignorance that lies at the foundations of the neoliberal conception of social order. At the risk of venturing into thorny questions concerning individual motives, we reprise a quote from Hayek's *Constitution of Liberty*: "There is not much reason to believe that, if at any one time the best knowledge which some possess were made available to all, the result would be a much better society. *Knowledge and ignorance are relative concepts*" (my italics).[149]

Many professional economists, and perhaps even the reader, may have been predisposed to argue that agnotology is an inquiry bereft of subject matter—that is, there is no such thing as the conscious manufacture and promotion of ignorance. All that exists, they insist, are people of differing opinions, and some groups that may, from time to time, provide them with support for their own purposes. People just say what they believe: full stop, end of story. I have heard some economists opine that "agnotology" is just another left-wing curse word, roughly on a par with "neoliberalism," particularly back in the era when it was fashionable to bemoan a Republican "war on science."[150] Others might not go that far, but instead regard the public face-off of eminent intellectual figures as a matter of "intellectual capture," say, after the fashion of Simon Johnson. Admittedly, journalists exhibit an unfortunate tendency to treat a proposition as "true" as long as someone in a position of ostensible authority is willing to be quoted saying it, mitigated by the defensive codicil that no one seems willing to sue the journalist over it; or perhaps they confuse objectivity with presenting "two sides" to an issue, pitting jousting authorities against each other. The signal characteristic of agnotology is that it makes use of these journalistic inclinations to venture beyond simple difference of opinion in order to promulgate artificial "authorities" and calculated deception, not just to sway public opinion, but to foster the widespread attitude that there is so much unfocused controversy rattling around in the rarified world of intellectuals that the poor average citizen might as well believe whatever he pleases. It is the predicament of the hapless consumer of modern news: one study tells me red wine is good for my health, and another insists it is unhealthy! John Cochrane says the crisis is all the fault of the government, while Joe Stiglitz blames it all on the banks! By a simple jujitsu move, the mechanical journalist's appeal to objective presentation of "both sides" is turned into an imprimatur for the public to believe whatever their guts tell them is correct, at least until the marketplace of ideas delivers its final verdict. The aim of agnotology is not so much to convince the undecided, but to fog the minds of anyone lacking the patience to delve into the arguments in detail (which is pretty much everyone).

If we define agnotology to be the analysis of this phenomenon of the intentional production and promotion of ignorance, then it has been the Fourth Horseman of the Absolution from Apocalypse for economists. Whether it be in the context of global warming, oil depletion, "fracking" for natural gas, denial of Darwinism, disparagement of vaccination, or derangement of the conceptual content of Keynesianism, one unprecedented outcome of the Great Recession has been the redoubled efforts to pump massive amounts of noise into the mass media in order to discombobulate an already angry and restive populace. Much of this emanates from the outer think-tank shells of the neoliberal Russian doll, as I have already argued.[151] The techniques range from alignment of artificial echo chambers and special Potemkin research units to co-opting the names of the famous for semisubmerged political agendas; from setting up astroturfed organizations to misrepresenting the shape and character of orthodox discourse within various academic disciplines.

Agnotology takes many forms, as we point out in the next chapter. One of the major techniques of agnotology is to simultaneously fund both "legitimate" and illegitimate research out of the same pot, in order to expand the palette of explanations as a preliminary to downplaying the particular subset of causes that is damning for your client. As Robert Proctor explains:

> "It is less well known, but tobacco companies also spent large amounts subsidising good quality biomedical research in fields such as virology, genetics and immunology. They funded the work of several Nobel prize winners," Proctor says. "But they only encouraged this research to serve as a distraction. The idea was to build up

a corpus of work on possible causes of diseases which could not be attributed to cigarette-smoking. In court cases involving the industry, its lawyers always highlighted viral risks, the pre-disposition of certain families and so on to play down tobacco-related risks."[152]

Simply replace "disease" with "Great Recession," "cigarette-smoking" with "financial innovation," and "biomedical" with "economics," and one rapidly begins to grasp the parallels.

It might seem that agnotological interventions in an academic discipline could be greeted as an unwelcome source of meddling; for instance, many a climate scientist might ruefully wish that he had never drawn the attentions of the NTC. But in this, as in so many other respects, economics has been the outlier, because one might argue that the corporate body of orthodox economists has actually benefited enormously from the escalation of cacophony, rendering it relatively more immune to the wrath of a disillusioned populace. Precisely because of the material and intellectual conditions identified above, economists generally are not so very offended by the gush of tainted money and dubious activity pouring into the various extremities of the professional citadel of economics since the crisis. In short, the promotion of doubt over "what orthodox economists really believe" has proven a convenient smokescreen behind which the profession can evade the pitchfork-wielding populace, all the while pursuing its conventional practice of telling its patrons what they want to hear.

Causality and intentionality are notoriously hard to prove when one deals with such large and diffuse hypotheses. In this volume, I approach this claim by means of a couple of exercises: one, relating a truncated narrative of the utter confusion that surrounded the initial passage of the Emergency Economic Stabilization Act of 2008 here, combined with descriptions of the crucial role of some economists in promoting paralysis around the understanding of the TARP in the next chapter; also in the next chapter, I shall recount a few more substantial instances of neoliberal application of the techniques of agnotology to the economics profession in the ensuing three years, especially with regard to the most successful red herring of the Neoliberal Thought Collective, that it was all the fault of Fannie Mae and Freddie Mac.

Laying Down the TARP

The intense sequence of events that transpired during the government takeover of Freddie Mac and Fannie Mae, the failure of Lehman Brothers, and the passage of the widely disparaged "bailout" or TARP legislation on October 3, 2008, has been related in fair detail in a number of books and articles;[153] but one overlooked aspect has been the curious role of economists during its initial phases. Because it was largely conceived in haste in the crisis-consumed Treasury Department of Hank Paulson, the initial draft of a plan to purchase mortgage-backed securities, or, as we now know, the "toxic assets" of journalist parlance, the Treasury needed congressional approval to purchase up to $700 billion of these securities in the Paulson plan, so Paulson and Ben Bernanke sought to frighten the congressional leadership into hastily granting them this authority just before September 19, presenting them with a bald three-page proposal and Hobson's choice: this, or the collapse of Western Civilization.

Many members of Congress balked at the proposal, as explained in detail in the histories cited. But it is of equal interest to observe the reactions of the economics profession. One informant suggests that in the first hours of confusion, a couple of economists with close congressional connections were called in to canvass possible grounds for opposition to the plan: for instance, Jamie Galbraith was summoned by some Democrats led by Congressman Brad Sherman; the Skeptics' Caucus on the Republican side conscripted Bill Isaacs, former Reagan head of the FDIC. Issacs suggested that no expenditure was necessary, and that the crisis could be averted merely by changing a few rules. Staffers started making cold calls to economists down the list on Sunday, September 28, and another conscript was David Levy of George Mason University and the Mercatus Institute. Levy was not an expert on finance, so could not provide an alternate plan, but did talk to some staffers about the role of the ratings agencies. But Mercatus and George Mason were destined to play a more significant role in the weeks to come.

We need to wait for the verdict of future historians to get some sort of standard narrative, but it seems that the first vote on TARP was conducted in the face of sketchy and incomplete economic notions. My point in this section is to suggest that economists did not help clarify the situation, but instead swooped in to pump more doubt into an already baffling predicament—and that is the essence of agnotology. Clearly, most orthodox economists were flummoxed by the mere onset of the crisis, but a few neoliberal economists at the University of Chicago had the presence of mind to gear up the think-tank network of the thought collective in order to sign a petition calling for a flat-out rejection of the rescue package, and counseling pure delay on taking any action whatsoever. (Delay and stasis was a major agnotological objective in disputes over CFCs, tobacco smoke, and global warming.) The petition, arranged by the Chicago economists John Cochrane and Luigi Zingales, essentially preached delay, due to the precept that, as the text stated, "Investors who took risks to earn profits must also bear the losses. Not every business failure carries systemic risk. The government can ensure a well-functioning financial industry, able to make new loans to creditworthy borrowers, without bailing out particular investors and institutions whose choices proved unwise." The capacity of the Russian doll to mobilize the thought collective was demonstrated by the ability of the organizers to deliver the petition with the signatures of more than one hundred economists to the media on September 24.[154]

Senator Richard Shelby then went before the cameras on September 25, waving the petition and claiming that most prestigious economists at our leading universities were united in opposition to the bailout. As per usual, this was a bit misleading. Most (but not all) of the signatories were denizens of the financial–think tank nexus we have been describing in this chapter, and some were MPS members. It was not so clear that they so uniformly opposed a bailout, so much as they felt the need to head off the political dangers of government takeover of the financial sector. One might speculate that the banking sector wanted something like TARP that week, so there is no sense that the signatories were directly responding to any immediate bidding or specific objectives of the banks. The real practical effect of the petition was twofold: (1) to provide a list of whom in the economics profession might be available to be mobilized by Republicans in Congress, in the eventuality they might need to gin up opposition; and (2) to provide retrospective justification for the vilification of TARP, which is what happened once the Republicans suffered their rout. I doubt anyone had the foresight to imagine that this in turn would provide a basis for the reversal of the Democratic tide in 2010, so that the banks could get their cake and eat it, too. Rather, mostly it was the unceremonious jockeying for position in a highly fluid and confusing situation, with the neoliberals opting for the default position of cunctation and dissimulation. But of course, that is precisely when sharply drawn contraries can potentially have their greatest impact.

What is noteworthy about subsequent events is the way in which agnotological activity rushed in to fill the apparent intellectual vacuum around the bailout bill, both prior to passage and for long thereafter. One node of activity became centered upon John Cochrane and his Chicago colleagues Luigi Zingales, Gary Becker, and Raghuram Rajan. Cochrane was explicitly identified by National Public Radio as the ringleader of economists in opposition to the Paulson plan, while the quartet were ubiquitous in sympathetic outlets like the *Wall Street Journal*, *The Economist*, and even PBS.[155] However, in those contexts he was almost never publicly linked to his affiliation with the Cato Institute, one of the hardest-core shells of the Russian doll. A reliable bellwether, by October 14, Cochrane had already signed on to the incipient preferred story being developed by the NTC (more on this in the next section) in the *Wall Street Journal*:

> Most of all, I think it [the TARP bill] will "work" well enough to put a stop to the escalating political panic and the contagion of bail-outs. My biggest fears, and those of the markets, I think, have been that some new "plan" comes along every two days which can wreck everything . . . If I were in charge I would announce loudly "and we're going to sit on our hands for a whole week no matter what happens to daily stock prices."
>
> But there are lots and lots of problems with it. Most obviously, now the government has stock in banks. OK, it's preferred and nonvoting, but still, it is stock. And the government doesn't need to vote its shares in order to profoundly influence how banks are run! There are lots of good practical reasons to fear government-run banking systems; governments inevitably use control over the banking system for political ends. Already ours has shown a wonderful track record in pushing Fannie Freddie and banks to make and hold bad subprime loans.

Cochrane changed his tune in minor ways in subsequent months as it became increasingly apparent that the financial sector would be left more or less intact. He even was caught in an unguarded moment admitting one of the principal tenets of agnotology in an interview: "The business of advice remains what it was . . . You have to be willing to become a sort of media person. You have to tailor your advice to what people want to hear, and then shade it in the direction of common sense."[156] In the same period, Cochrane pursued agnotology most directly by denying that his Cato-blessed position was ideologically right wing, or that it unsubtly served as a shill for the financial sector: "Milton Friedman stood for freedom, social, political, and economic. He realized that they are inextricably linked. If the government controls your job or your business, dissent is impossible. He championed economic freedom as much as a means to political freedom as for its own sake. He favored, among other things, legalizing drugs, school choice, and volunteer army. To call him or his political legacy 'right wing' is simply ignorant, and I mean that also as a technically accurate description rather than an insult."[157] Agnotology delights in preaching everything you thought you knew about politics was wrong. Cochrane, as already mentioned, went on to become president of the American Finance Association in 2010.

The other major agnotological juggernaut in the immediate crisis was the Mercatus Center at George Mason University (GMU), just a short drive up Route 66 from Washington, D.C. The precursor to Mercatus at George Mason dates back to the early 1980s, when Richard Fink was on the economics faculty at GMU.[158] Fink was also highly connected to the many firms and foundations associated with Charles and David Koch, the infamous billionaire funders at the center of many neoliberal organizations, including Cato.[159] Koch funded Fink's Center for Market Processes at GMU, which was transformed into the Mercatus Center by the later 1990s, after Fink became vice-president of Koch Industries. Although GMU was nominally a state university, Mercatus was targeted by the Russian doll to become the premier one-stop shop for hard neoliberal economics in the nation's capital. For instance, in 2001, the Charles G. Koch Charitable Foundation gave GMU $3 million to hire the neoliberal Nobel economist and MPS member Vernon Smith; although that did not work out as planned, Koch gave another $2.5 million to Mercatus in 2009. Public sources suggest Mercatus has benefited to the tune of $30 million from Koch over the last two decades. Its general director is Tyler Cowen, another neoliberal we have already encountered.

Reuters has reported that this foresight proved prescient in helping deflect the interpretation of the "consensus" pronouncements of economists in testimony to Congress:

The House Financial Services Committee and Senate Banking Committee heard from academic economists linked to the Mercatus Center about a dozen times during the financial regulatory reform debate. That is roughly the same number of testimonies by academics hailing from both Harvard's business and law schools.

According to a 2009 ranking of 31 economics programs at US universities by US News and World Report, Harvard ranked No.1. George Mason didn't place.[160]

The objective here is not to praise or exult Harvard (especially in this chapter), nor to excoriate the laziness of resort to local talent, but rather to highlight the economics profession as the agonistic field it has become in the war over the interpretation of the crisis. Political expediency dictated the need for speed and cohesion in response to the numerous calls to understand what had happened in the crisis hard on the heels of 2008. The hubbub over the TARP revealed a field in discombobulation and disarray. Not least was there confusion over what it was supposed to accomplish, the topic of the next chapter. There was no luxury of waiting a generation for a synoptic account to emerge. The Koch brothers (and a rogues' gallery of others) have redoubled their attempts to skew the economics profession in a more neoliberal direction, precisely in order to broadcast in a timely fashion the notion that neoliberals bore no responsibility for the crisis, and indeed, come fully equipped with everything that is needed to remedy it. This book documents an astounding level of achievement in that regard.

Love for Sale

Even though the Russian doll has developed elaborate recruitment strategies and a farm team to keep live candidates on tap, it clearly has become an imperative for neoliberals such as the Koch brothers to further transform the economics profession by further dispersing their influence. Indeed, precisely because of their avidity, a few intrepid reporters picked up on Koch donations to universities such as Clemson, Utah State, University of West Virginia, and most notoriously, Florida State, to have direct say in hiring new economists, as well as a veto in blackballing those with insufficient "appreciation for academic freedom."[161] Donors often wish to exert personal control over how their money is spent at a university; what makes Koch different is its depth of expertise in making this happen while maintaining a thin veneer of university independence. At Florida State (FSU), Koch gave $1.5 million to the economics department in 2008, in exchange for staffing an advisory board that would approve faculty hires, and vested a Koch representative with sole veto power, which it proceeded to exercise in the first 2009 hiring round. A

Koch representative also prescreened candidates at the ASSA job meetings. Koch also stipulated as a condition a new course featuring the writings of Ayn Rand. The chairman of FSU's economics department, Bruce Benson, had close connections to Koch, and signed the agreement without a departmental vote. When asked why the faculty had abdicated curriculum control to such a degree, Benson answered, "Students will ultimately choose."[162]

The world has clearly changed since 1980. I reproduce below an ad from the current *Job Openings for Economists*, the Craigslist for academic positions in economics:

The Department of Economics at the University of Texas at Austin invites applications from distinguished senior scholars for the tenured position of the Murray S. Johnson Chair in Economics. Applicants should be an authority on the American free enterprise system. Preference will be given to scholars focusing on conservative economic philosophy. The position will be available in Fall 2012.

I don't recall politics being so openly for sale before 1980; but maybe I am being naïve. After all, the Volker Fund paid for Friedrich Hayek's chair at the University of Chicago in 1950.

When such deals were exposed in the media, the thought collective produced various talking heads suggesting that the Koch deals were no different than George Soros funding INET to alter the economics profession. This, of course, was a bit of agnotological intervention in itself. Soros, whatever his faults, has restrained himself from direct intervention in INET; and indeed, one of the striking things about that organization is the substantial representation of noteworthy neoliberals in its meetings and, to a certain extent, its educational programs. The major difference between Soros and the Kochs is that the latter have an entire half-century of doctrinal development of the thought collective to finely discriminate what should count as "sanctioned" knowledge. As Representative Brad Sherman of California so memorably complained, "The public is very angry at Wall Street. But they are told by all the respected voices that if we don't protect and preserve the institutions on Wall Street, we'll be fighting for rat meat in the streets." The role of economists, in the view of the Kochtopus (a term coined by disillusioned right-wing intellectuals), seemed to be to cheer on the big established forces intent on maintaining the *status quo ante* from before the crisis. Soros, from my limited perspective, is not very clear about what "New Economics" could conceivably be; if anything his financial persona seems at odds with his intellectual pretensions.[163]

One thing you have to concede to the Kochs: they know what they want to buy, and they go after it single-mindedly.

5

The Shock of the New: Have Neoclassical Economists

Learned Anything at All from the Crisis?

Picking Up the TINA Pieces

I can sympathize with those who feel that the last thing they want to do in the aftermath of the current crisis is revisit the corpus of ideas emanating from the neoclassical orthodoxy. Picking over the bones of the decrepit doctrines that inspired one misstep after another would seem the very height of bathos, if not specious distraction. In any event, serious foraging would teeter on the edge of yet another stripped-down history of orthodox macroeconomics, a massive undertaking better conducted by others.[1] Here we aim at something different. Given our ultimate objective is to understand the unreasonable resilience of the neoliberal *Weltanschauung*, and the role of the economists in fortifying it, I propose to concentrate on aspects of economics that have confused or otherwise obscured specific components of economic knowledge in the heat of the crisis and thereafter. In this, we further explore the phenomenon of "agnotology" raised in the previous chapter, growing out of the fundamental internal contradiction between trusting the economists to point the way out of the crisis, and trusting the markets to right themselves. Of course, in the midst of global crisis and upheaval, some economists might have become disoriented, and say some things that they might regret in quieter times. We have already raised the specter of cognitive dissonance and the Festinger effect; henceforth we just take it for granted that a substantial proportion of true believers would opt for a state of denial. A certain modicum of sympathetic indulgence (or at least, impartial spectatorship) is indispensable, or else the intellectual history of the crisis would degenerate into a serious of pointless "gotcha" exercises.

In that spirit, we might divide the reactions of the economics profession to the crisis into three broad categories: one, *the orthodoxy was right all along* and nothing that has transpired in recent events impugns the fundamental soundness of basic theory; two, the orthodox have made some unfortunate conceptual choices in the recent past, but the crisis has sobered us up, and *we are working hard to rectify them*, while maintaining fealty to all that was legitimate, timeless and dependable in neoclassical economics; and three, the best response would be to renounce neoclassical economics altogether, *and start anew with some other tradition of economic thought*. The first response was primarily dealt with in chapter 4. The second response is more difficult to characterize through any brief summary, and is the topic of the present chapter. The third response is the project of which this volume serves as preamble: it derives from a conclusion that renunciation of neoclassical economics is the only serious way forward to oppose the zombie fortification of modern neoliberalism. Precisely because the third option is such a disparaged minority position, we first have more work to do to improve its appeal.

To prepare the ground, we shall have to deal with the contemporary majority view that opposition to neoliberalism does not require throwing out baby with bathwater; that there is every reasonable expectation that neoclassical macroeconomics can be "fixed," and continuity with the current orthodox economics profession can be maintained. This is the conviction of many figures on the left, as currently constituted: it is the opinion of John Quiggin (sketched in chapter 1), as well as Joseph Stiglitz, Simon Johnson, Paul Krugman, and, perhaps more incongruously, the bulk of the participants in attendance at INET. This opinion should be expected to have been grounded in very detailed aspects of current economic theory, as one would anticipate from such illustrious adherents, and has assumed multiple formats.

It is astounding for a discipline so obsessed with exhibiting consensus over orthodoxy that genuflection to continuity in macroeconomics itself so rapidly unravels:

> Simon Wren-Lewis argues against the many people insisting that the crisis means that we must rebuild macroeconomics from the ground up; he argues, on the contrary, that the crisis doesn't require a fundamental rethink of macro. And I am very much in agreement there. Basic sensible macro—what we learned from Keynes and Hicks—has actually held up very well in the crisis. To the extent that we have a crisis in macroeconomics as practiced, it comes from

the way many economists chose to reject sensible macro. The crisis should (but won't) kill fresh-water, equilibrium macroeconomics; but IS-LM is looking pretty good.

... But macro as I understand it isn't what Wren-Lewis is describing when he talks about "the intertemporal optimising framework that is the heart of modern macro."

Um, it's not at the heart of MY macro. Or maybe I should say, it's not at the HEART of my macro. I'm willing to do models with intertemporal optimization, but the optimization is never the core of the story. Instead, it's just a gadget.[2]

In the heat of crisis, one man's gadget turns out to be another's dogma. Hence, by contrast with much of the rest of this volume, we will be brought into intimate confrontation with a few specifics of recent ideas about macroeconomics. The reason this may be significant for a larger audience outside of the cognoscenti of the economics profession is that, after the crash, very few economists have been willing to seriously entertain and evaluate the prospect that the dominant macroeconomic theory helped cause the crisis, by masking the buildup of instabilities before the crisis, and frustrating repair activity afterward.[3] This underappreciated phenomenon has been then further confounded when journalists have been prompted to repeat a fair number of fallacies about the current state of economics, under the tutelage of a select coterie of informants. The shape of things is rarely as solid as they have been there portrayed, and this, too, has direct bearing upon the Nine Lives of Neoliberalism.

The mantra that "There Is No Alternative" (colloquially, TINA) has been a very powerful incantation in the neoliberal rucksack; as we have already suggested in chapter 2, the role of ignorance looms quite large in formal neoliberal theory. Although there exist an infinite number of potential ways to revise and repair neoclassical economics (since there are an uncountable infinity of flaws), what has been striking about the crisis is the relatively small number of such revisions that have dominated the discourse concerning "what is to be done" about economics (outside of stubborn denial). Furthermore, one might imagine that, as the profession responded, the roster of proposed conceptual revisions to orthodoxy would have broadened and expanded with the passage of time; but this has not happened. Hence, there is something intriguing and very significant about the "version two" option that itself needs explanation: Why has the movement to "repair" orthodox economics been so ineffectual since the crash?

There are at least two immediate responses to this question: first, one might posit that there are aspects of the neoclassical intellectual tradition that are intrinsically incompatible with serious confrontation with the shape of the current crisis, such that engagement with the real causes is blocked; and second, that much of the profession suffers a "trained incapacity" to come up with really novel theoretical departures. Both of these propositions will be accorded attention in the rest of this chapter. However valid they might seem, these two particular explanations do not have much directly relevant to say about the particular role of the economics profession in fortification of the defenses of neoliberalism. That opens up the possibility that there is, furthermore, a third contributing explanation of the feeble success in the contemporary reconstruction of orthodox macroeconomics, which owes a debt to a long-standing subterranean affiliation with the Neoliberal Thought Collective.

The hypothesis I propose is to pursue a possibility raised in the previous chapter, that there have surfaced in the crisis some relatively systematic attempts to pump doubt and confusion into public discourse; in other words, some "explanations" of manifestations of the crisis and its aftermath have been launched as trial balloons *not* so much for purposes of further test and elaboration by sanctioned professional economists, but rather as calculated interventions in public discourse in order to buy time and frustrate any shared impressions of clearly delineated positions on a contentious issue. In other words, I am suggesting that the economics profession adopted a page from the neoliberal playbook, widely promoting the notion that intrepid economists were busy gestating all sorts of "new economic theory" to explain the crisis, when in fact they had mostly dug themselves into a defensive crouch where nothing about the orthodoxy was being sloughed off, and no errors would be freely conceded.

As chapter 2 argued, the relation of the control of knowledge to political power has been a neoliberal specialty. Evidence that such attitudes had become ingrained in some precincts of the NTC was exemplified by a notorious quote extracted from a Bush administration official in the summer of 2002:

> The aide said that guys like me were "in what we call the reality-based community," which he defined as people who "believe that solutions emerge from your judicious study of discernable reality." I nodded and murmured something about enlightenment principles

and empiricism. He cut me off. "We're an empire now, and when we act, we create our own reality. And while you're studying that reality—judiciously, as you will—we'll act again, creating other new realities, which you can study too, and that's how things will sort out. We're history's actors . . . and you, all of you, will be left just to study what we do."[4]

The creation of such alternate realities has by now become quite familiar in areas such as Iraqi "weapons of mass destruction" and in global-warming denialism. As the climate crisis worsens, the general populace appears to recoil from the worsening news, fleeing the facts, preferring to disdain the science rather than confront the crisis. In one instance, the Harris polling organization claimed that in 2007, 71 percent of Americans said they believed that continued combustion of fossil fuels resulted in climate change, whereas by June 2011 it had dropped to 41 percent. Further, Gordon Gauchat has demonstrated that the only group to express severely diminished trust in science in surveys from 1974 to 2010 were self-identified conservatives, with university-educated conservatives displaying the steeper decline. Gauchat points out, "the emergence of 'neoliberal science' as an alternative to regulatory regimes has coincided with increasing distrust of science among conservatives."[5]

The stance adopted in this chapter is that if agnotological procedures can be found regularly deployed in politics and biology, then we should not think it beyond the pale that they can be found in economics as well.[6] Indeed, given the neoliberal drift in the profession in the last three decades, it would be more surprising if the agnotological manufacture of doubt had somehow bypassed economists altogether. In particular, the elaborate staged debate between the true believers in good old neoclassical theory and the advocates of judicious macroeconomic revision provides us with yet another paradigm example of pointless dissention and manufactured doubt, which only serves the purpose of maintaining the larger populace in a state of suspended animation: the audience only grows further skeptical of the economics profession if it becomes apparent that (as they see it) the neoclassical orthodoxy does not speak with one voice concerning the crisis, and consequently, no particular reform policy can gain much in the way of activist traction. Economists fiddle with their models, Rome (and Athens) burns, and the Neoliberal Thought Collective just grows stronger.

I am not the first to suspect this. Even a few respected orthodox economists have sometimes entertained notions that "there is the possibility that moneyed interests could manufacture controversy through think tanks, as has happened with aspects of climate change debate."[7] Unfortunately, they then underestimate the extent to which the economics profession has become beholden to neoliberal institutions, and indeed, the possibility that garden-variety disagreement, which might happen under any other circumstances, gets amplified and phase-shifted to produce its real objective, the paralysis of serious reform of the economy. The beauty is that the economics profession as a corporate entity need not consciously *will* the resulting manufacture of doubt. Just add the reflex conservatism which kicks in with cognitive dissonance, and we have a perfect prescription for agnogenesis.

Agnotological fomentation of ignorance occurs on many different scales: incidents at the individual level are much easier to document and understand than those that happen at the scale of (let us say) the bulkier subset of the profession devoted to macroeconomic theory. For instance, take the individual case of Joseph Stiglitz having to undergo a bit of targeted agnotology. Big money cascaded into financial economics in order to defend the sector from threats of regulation of derivatives in 2010–11. Many think tanks and public relations firms produced "position papers" arguing that any attempt to reign in derivatives would be disastrous. One such contract research house issuing papers was Keybridge Associates. Their report drew attention because of some very high-profile names attached to the document as "advisors": Prof. Stiglitz for one, David Laibson of Harvard for another. The only problem was that, when the report was brought to the attention of those worthies, they felt impelled to go on record as repudiating the report.[8] What Keybridge had done was pay them a prior retainer for some other purposes, and then gone ahead and attached their names to documents that they would not normally endorse, without notifying them of its activities. Now, was Keybridge attempting to influence the positions of Joseph Stiglitz? No; rather, it was pursuing the standard agnotological procedure of the manufacture of ignorance and confusion over what Stiglitz stood for in the minds of the public. The fact that this was just one element of a full-service agnotological offensive is demonstrated by another concurrent parallel activity, the manufacture of an astroturfed letter campaign to the CFTC opposing rule changes to bank control of derivatives markets, which emanated from similar entities.[9] These are all standard practices from the agnotological playbook, orchestrated by firms located somewhere "outside" the academic sphere but "inside" the Beltway. And, when it came to the regulation of derivatives, money talked, and never shut up.

There have been a plethora of similar agnotological initiatives over the past few years: the artificial brouhaha over whether spending austerity can produce economic growth, the trope that extension of unemployment benefits in the United States after the crash caused the persistently high unemployment rate, the meme that the TARP procedure was totally successful and cost the taxpayer not a penny, and so on. Rather than document a further ragbag sequence of micro-level agnotological interventions in the crisis, having little common denominator from one instance to the next, the aim of this chapter is to assay a more macro-level account of intellectual (in)activity. Clearly, there are two agendas to be satisfied in this chapter: (1) demonstration that the intellectual content of the proposed amendments to neoclassical macroeconomics in response to the crisis has been comparatively minimal, inconsequential, and ineffectual; and (2) evidence that the Potemkin dispute set up between the fundamentalist defenders of orthodoxy and the supposed reformers of orthodoxy has sported some connections to the neoliberal collective. Chapter 4 suggested that the economics profession has emerged from the crisis relatively unscathed in part thanks to its often subterranean neoliberal support system. Chapter 5 reverses the causal arrow: it will suggest that the paltry ineffectual intellectual amendments to neoclassical macroeconomics prompted by the crisis exist, in part, serve the agnotological purposes of the NTC.

This particular approach transcends a false dichotomy concerning economists found in Reay[10] and elsewhere: either the contemporary economics profession enjoys such a tight consensus around its unified orthodoxy that it is capable of imposing neoliberal policies on all manner of clients, or else the doctrines of neoclassical economics are so very fragmented and diverse that it is ridiculous to assert that the orthodox economists have fostered and sustained any political position whatsoever.[11] This ignores the pivotal fact that modern political economy is the product of the *interactions* of two different groups, the Neoliberal Thought Collective and the academic economics orthodoxy, over the last half century. Some diversity may indeed exist in orthodox neoclassical economic doctrine, but it has been pruned in bonsai fashion by the growing strength of the NTC, and shoots were also grafted back onto the collective itself. This process has homed in on the precept that a certain amount of faux-dispute is actually beneficial for all concerned, within a narrow perimeter.

As Thomas Pynchon wrote in that great twentieth-century classic *Gravity's Rainbow*, "If you have them asking the wrong questions, you don't have to worry about the right answers." Just as in advertising, the media are full to the brim trumpeting the shock of the new, when all that really happens is that you are being sold the same old jalopy under a new brand name. Thus the economics profession and the Neoliberal Thought Collective have attained coadjuvancy in a mutually beneficial symbiosis, whose product is the maintenance of an economic system and a financial sector essentially unaltered by the greatest global breakdown since the 1930s.

"Prediction of the Crisis" as a Useless Distraction[12]

Easily the Number One Topic on the tip of everyone's cursor in the immediate aftermath of the financial crisis of 2008 was: Why didn't the economists see it coming? For the median layperson, this was an extrapolation of the frequent and widespread misconception that the primal raison d'être of the economics profession is to give investment advice. For journalists, it simply reprised the way they had been treating economics professionals all along as soothsayers on the cheap. But beneath the surface, this conviction that it was the professional responsibility of economists to predict such calamities in fact conjured deep unresolved philosophical issues concerning the very essence of economics, which were triggered when many members of the profession felt impelled to respond to the cascade of derision.

The journalists' complaint was broadcast from a number of platforms in normal times more respectful and subservient to economists, such as *Business Week*:

> Economists mostly failed to predict the worst economic crisis since the 1930s. Now they can't agree how to solve it. People are starting to wonder: What good are economists anyway? . . .
>
> To be fair, economists can't be expected to predict the future with any kind of exactitude. The world is simply too complicated for that. But collectively, they should be able to warn of dangers ahead. And when disaster strikes, they ought to know what to do. Indeed, people pay attention to economists at times like this precisely because of their bold claim that they know how to prevent the economy from sliding into a repeat of the Great Depression. But seven decades after the Depression, economists still haven't reached consensus on its lessons.[13]

At first, a few candid members of the profession opted to second the judgment of the journalists with respect to the crisis. One of the most heartfelt, because cast in the format of an apology, was by Uwe Rein-hardt at Princeton:

> If, like every university, the American Economic Association had a coat of arms, its obligatory Latin banner might read: *"Est, ergo opti-mum est, dummodo ne gubernatio civitatis implicatur."* ("It exists, therefore it must be optimal, provided that government has not been involved.") . . .
>
> These thoughts occurred to me as I attended the American Economic Association's annual conference in San Francisco over the weekend. It offered a humongous smorgasbord of eloquent theory, clever econometric tricks, illuminating empirical insights and a few standing-room-only panel discussions on the shocking surprises the real economy served up as the economics profession was otherwise preoccupied during the past two decades or so.
>
> Fewer than a dozen prominent economists saw this economic train wreck coming — and the Federal Reserve chairman, Ben Bernanke, an economist famous for his academic research on the Great Depression, was notably not among them. Alas, for the real world, the few who did warn us about the train wreck got no more respect from the rest of their colleagues or from decision-makers in business and government than prophets usually do.[14]

Far from merely echoing the antipathy of the man in the street, this refrain that the profession had suffered devastating failure by not predicting the crisis bore some emotional resonance among the rank and file for three substantive reasons. The first derived from the existence of the only self-identified methodological paper most contemporary economists had ever heard of, Milton Friedman's "Methodology of Positive Economics" (1953). It was not irrelevant that it was the work of one of the icons of postwar neoliberalism. Even those who had never actually read it nonetheless were possessed of some vague notion that Friedman had stated that the truth of assumptions didn't matter, just the success of predictions that the models emitted. We bypass whether that was the "real" or correct reading of Friedman's message; the point here is, rather, that the Friedman dispensation had become one expedient in the lazy econ-omists' playbook, in the odd situation they actually had to defend the "scientific character" of what they were doing to a semiliterate audi-ence. So the failure to predict the crisis tended to discomfit the last vestiges of what passed for philosophy in the training of the modern economist; concurrently, it also made "Chicago" look bad. No one wanted to reopen the old "unrealism of assumptions" debate, which the profession believed to have relegated to the dust heap of doctrinal history long ago. Hence, making a big deal of failed predictions summoned up a submerged world of humiliation that most economists would rather just avoid.

And then there was the second nagging source of relevance. It was a little-discussed attribute of the economics profession that, even in the last decade, many economists made their livings by producing predictions of one sort or another. Although it had become de rigueur in the commanding heights of reputable academic ivory towers to sneer at the very possibility of successful prediction (see below), the truth of the matter was that down in the trenches, where most economists lived, dealing in prediction was a bread-and-butter activity.[15]

"Prediction" had become the stereotypical outcome of most quotidian economic research, even though most players realized it merely signified a stylized denouement. As one MIT student reported:

> There is a sentiment here from people I have talked to that if they want a model we can give them a model. We sit down and make up a model, and we play with it until it gives us the empirical result that we find, even though you could as easily have written down a model that would have given a different result. We have even had seminar speakers say, "Oh, I worked on a model that predicts it; of course I could have written down a model that predicts the opposite, but why would I do that?" In general, you can write down a model that predicts just about anything.[16]

If you worked for a firm or the government, you were simply expected to produce predictions like clockwork, and with a straight face. The Federal Reserve Bank of Philadelphia regularly surveyed "professional" economic forecasters; not unexpectedly, their forecasts for GDP growth and the unemployment rate for the year 2008 tended to bunch together in November 2007: their mean predicted GDP growth of 2.5 percent and an unemployment rate of 4.9 percent, even though the financial collapse by then had already begun. If you had aspirations to be a public intellectual, then one could not write op-eds or appear on television or radio without being importuned to predict something or other. If you didn't comply, you wouldn't be invited back; there were hundreds lined up, willing to prognosticate. This was captured in some interview responses: "it's a Darwinian process in this case where people who are willing to say something without hedging it can get on the news . . . my optimal strategy is to make interesting predictions."[17] The entire quotidian public discourse of professional economists continuously revolved around predictions, whatever they might say to one another in university seminars or academic papers. It is significant that careful inquiry into economists' predictions had revealed a rather dismal track record long before the crisis had hit:

- The forecasting skill of economists is on average about as good as uninformed guessing. Predictions by the Council of Economic Advisors, Federal Reserve Board, and Congressional Budget Office were often worse than random.
- Economists have proven repeatedly that they cannot predict the turning points in the economy.
- No specific economic forecasters consistently lead the pack in accuracy.
- No economic forecaster has consistently higher forecasting skills predicting any particular economic statistic.
- Consensus forecasts do not improve accuracy (although the press loves them. So much for the wisdom of crowds) .
- Finally, there's no evidence that economic forecasting has improved in recent decades[18]

Again, if this track record was widely known already to have been so very poor, then missing the onset of the crisis should not have caused such consternation on its own. Or conversely, the profession could set about writing down little models that could "retrospectively" have predicted the crisis, doing whatever worked in the past. While a few commentators dallied with one or the other, neither of those eventualities got to the heart of the uproar about "failures of prediction" in the public press. Rather, the crisis brought to consciousness for the lay public the portent that there was a *specific bias* in the orientation of the profession, a bias that ruled out of bounds predictions of the sorts of global system-wide breakdowns that had galvanized those living through 2008–11. Hence what the clientele thought they were buying—a sort of neutral reconnaissance of the near future, a species of early-warning insurance—did not correspond very well with what the economists had been proffering.[19]

And that leads us to the third Pandora's Box opened by the mortification of failed prediction. Skipping over detail, it is sufficient to point to the fact that orthodox theories of macroeconomics since the

1980s had grown obsessed with the issue of prediction. Whereas earlier models in American Keynesianism had been constructed to be backward-looking (distributed lags, moving averages, etc.), both orthodox finance theory and the new macroeconomics adopted the neoclassical position that bygones are bygones, and from the "permanent income hypothesis" onward, therefore all relevant decisions were based upon agent expectations of the future. Furthermore, the rational-expectations school and the later dynamic stochastic general equilibrium models insisted that expectations were formed with the very same neoclassical models and econometric techniques that the orthodoxy endorsed. Thus the orthodoxy had effectively conflated the prediction of the economist with the predictions of the agent, and elevated it as a central theme of modern economic theory. There had always been pockets of resistance to this audacious theoretical move, but the crisis brought the qualms out into the open by suggesting that agents *should not* rely so heavily on the clones of the "rational" economists to ground their expectations. It wasn't intentional, but the hue and cry over failed prediction tore the scabs off a number of repressed and forgotten wounds in the philosophy of the "rational economic agent." This may explain why the journalists were so keen to indict the leaders of the "rational expectations" movement hard on the heels of the financial collapse.

The best evidence that the accusations of failed prediction were so rebarbative that they provoked a triumph of indignation over complacency can be found in the wildly bipolar reactions of economists to the indictment: one coterie insisted that economists were vindicated by the successful predictions of the few and the canny; whereas another insisted instead that good economists never claimed to be able to predict the economy in the first place. Viewed as a totality, this exemplified a larger tendency for the profession as a whole to simultaneously assert A and not-A in response to calumny.

The gambit to search for "successful predictors" among the economists seemed to have originated with journalists. Economists sat up and took more notice of the rebukes published in *The Economist* than the other news magazines, if only because those articles softened the condemnation with various potential excuses that the complaints found elsewhere had gone "too far," and that the allegations only had partial validity.[20] With regard to the accusation that "most economists failed to see the crisis coming," *The Economist* averred that some had indeed issued warnings, and explicitly named Robert Shiller, Nouriel Roubini, and the "team at the Bank for International Settlements."

This set off the starting gun for a veritable silly season of all manner of economists being proposed as vindicated prophets and unappreciated soothsayers, as though the prescience of the few would redeem the dimwittedness of the many. This race to populate the Nostradamus Codex continued for more than a year, encompassing even an online ballot to vote for the best crisis prognosticator.[21] A motley cavalcade of economists then jostled in an unseemly fashion to put themselves forward as having somehow anticipated the crisis, across not just from the orthodoxy, but spanning the political gamut from paleo-libertarians to left post-Keynesians.[22] But worse, the scrum began to dissipate the definition of the moving object that stood as the appropriate target for prediction. In the rush to judgment, anyone who said or wrote anything about some kind of bubble or imbalance or financial instability sometime in the 2000s suddenly sought to be credited as rivaling the Oracle at Delphi, engaging in the most exquisite augury. Some Nobel winners in particular pushed this ploy well beyond the breaking point, eliding prediction proper, and instead suggesting that anyone who had ever produced a mathematical model mentioning bank runs or financial fraud or irrational expectations or debt deflation or (fill in the blank) was proof positive that the economics profession had not been caught unawares.[23] It helped if the interlocutor stopped paying attention to what had been *taught* in the macroeconomics classes across the most highly ranked economics departments. It got so bad after a while that any mention of market failure or departure from equilibrium was supposed to function as a "get out of jail free" card in 2009. Here is one illustrative example:

Q: There's been lots of criticism, for example from Paul Krugman, that the economics profession did not foresee the crisis. But from the way you're talking, it seems there are existing models that predict that these crises will happen, and it's a question of how you respond. A: I don't accept the criticism that economic theory failed to provide a framework for understanding this crisis. Indeed, the papers we're discussing today show pretty clearly why the crisis occurred and what we can do about it. The sort of economics that deserves attack is Alan Greenspan's idealized world, in which financial markets work perfectly well on their own and don't require government action. There are, of course, still economists—probably fewer than before—who believe in that world. But it is an extreme position and not one likely to be held by those who understand the papers we're talking about.[24]

Of course, the unstated lesson was that no one possessing a gold-plated Ivy union card (Greenspan was awarded a belated PhD by NYU in 1977) who acknowledged the "best journals" as revealed doctrine was caught unawares by the crisis. This whole quest to identify the predictive elect among the economists was therefore very rapidly driven to Bedlam, partly because it was so mendacious, but also because it twisted the meaning of predictive success beyond all recognition. In a sort of Protestant Reformation, everyone was sanctioned to read and interpret the Revealed (Journal) Scripture and the crisis portents in their own idiosyncratic manner, and then enjoy absolution, so long as they pledged their troth to the One True neoclassical economics.

Lest the reader get the impression that this was the only retort to the accusation that economists had failed in predicting the crisis, they should be apprized that there was also a counterreformation movement. Primarily it was located among those economists found at the sharp end of the journalists' stick, the high-profile leaders of the rational-expectations macroeconomics movement. In the heat of the downdraft, magazines such as *Business Week* and *The Economist* were not shy in naming names: "Count Harvard's Robert Barro in this camp, along with Chicago's Robert E. Lucas, Arizona State's Edward C. Prescott, and the University of Minnesota's Patrick J. Kehoe and V. V. Chari."[25] It was seconded in a broadside from Willem Buiter:

> Most mainstream macroeconomic theoretical innovations since the 1970s (associated with such names as Robert E. Lucas Jr., Edward Prescott, Thomas Sargent, Robert Barro, etc., and the New Keynesian theorizing of Michael Woodford and many others) have turned out to be self-referential, inward-looking distractions at best. Research tended to be motivated by internal logic, intellectual sunk capital and aesthetic puzzles of established research programmes rather than by a powerful desire to understand how the economy works . . . the manifest failure of the EMH in many key asset markets was obvious to virtually all those whose cognitive abilities had not been warped by a modern Anglo-American Ph.D. education.[26]

Their intellectual leader, Robert Lucas, was quick to respond in the pages of *The Economist*: you critics are holding us to a standard that our own theories tell us we could never meet. In other words, economics tells us that economists will never be good predictors:

One thing we are not going to have, now or ever, is a set of models that forecasts sudden falls in the value of financial assets, like the declines that followed the failure of Lehman Brothers in September. This is nothing new. It has been known for more than 40 years and is one of the main implications of Eugene Fama's "efficient-market hypothesis" (EMH), which states that the price of a financial asset reflects all relevant, generally available information. If an economist had a formula that could reliably forecast crises a week in advance, say, then that formula would become part of generally available information and prices would fall a week earlier . . . *The Economist's* briefing also cited as an example of macroeconomic failure the "reassuring" simulations that Frederic Mishkin, then a governor of the Federal Reserve, presented in the summer of 2007. The charge is that the Fed's FRB/US forecasting model failed to predict the events of September 2008. Yet the simulations were not presented as assurance that no crisis would occur, but as a forecast of what could be expected conditional on a crisis not occurring.[27]

Patently, in the counterreformation, economists should never have been expected to predict the really bad stuff: that was the sole province of the market, the greatest information processor known to humanity. Furthermore, you in the bleachers don't appreciate what it means when we offer you a "model": it only "predicts" in limited situations that resemble the ones the model was built for. *Caveat emptor.*

One index of the extent of disruption within the profession induced by the crisis was that economists no longer felt compelled to humbly defer to the Nobelist Robert Lucas as they had before 2008, but rushed to go on record to dispute this "defense" of the profession and distance themselves from the Curia. *The Economist* was happy to provide a special blog on which they could register their dissent.[28] Some insisted that the heart of the problem was the efficient-markets hypothesis. Brad de Long suggested Lucas was changing his tune as the crisis evolved. Others, like Harvard's Robert Barro, propounded the proposition that the proof of the pudding was not in the success of the prediction, but instead what the clientele would pay for: "Like Bob Lucas, I have a hard time taking seriously the view that the financial and macroeconomic crisis has diminished economics as a field. In fact, the crisis has clearly raised the demand for economic services and economists. There is no more counter-cyclical occupation than economist." This only served to pour gasoline on the blogosphere.

The line quickly hardened within the counterreformation that the orthodox efficient-markets hypothesis had been confirmed by the crisis, and that economists had never borne the onus of predicting much of anything at all. This comes out quite clearly in the *New Yorker* interviews with Chicago economists:

> *I asked Fama how he thought the theory, which says prices of financial assets accurately reflect all of the available information about economic fundamentals, had fared.*
>
> Eugene Fama: I think it did quite well in this episode. Stock prices typically decline prior to and in a state of recession. This was a particularly severe recession. Prices started to decline in advance of when people recognized that it was a recession and then continued to decline. There was nothing unusual about that. That was exactly what you would expect if markets were efficient.
>
> *Many people would argue that, in this case, the inefficiency was primarily in the credit markets, not the stock market—that there was a credit bubble that inflated and ultimately burst.*
>
> I don't even know what that means. People who get credit have to get it from somewhere. Does a credit bubble mean that people save too much during that period? I don't know what a credit bubble means. I don't even know what a bubble means. These words have become popular. I don't think they have any meaning. . . .
>
> *Back to the efficient markets hypothesis. You said earlier that it comes out of this episode pretty well. Others say the market may be good at pricing in a relative sense—one stock versus another—but it is very bad at setting absolute prices, the level of the market as a whole. What do you say to that?*
>
> People say that. I don't know what the basis of it is. If they know, they should be rich men. What better way to make money than to know exactly about the absolute level of prices.
>
> *So you still think that the market is highly efficient at the overall level too?*
>
> Yes. And if it isn't, it's going to be impossible to tell.[29]

And then there is the Cassidy interview with the Cato neoliberal John Cochrane:

> *The two biggest ideas associated with Chicago economics over the past thirty years are the efficient markets hypothesis and the rational expectations hypothesis. At this stage, what's left of those two?*

John Cochrane: I think everything. Why not? Seriously, now, these are not ideas so superficial that you can reject them just by reading the newspaper. Rational expectations and efficient markets theories are both consistent with big price crashes. If you want to talk about this, we need to talk about specific evidence and how it does or doesn't match up with specific theories.

In the United States, we've had two massive speculative bubbles in ten years. How can that be consistent with the efficient markets hypothesis?

Great, so now you know how to define "bubbles" for me. I've been looking for that for twenty years.[30]

If one imagines the faint echoes of the Seekers after they were left stranded by the flying saucers, then perhaps you begin to comprehend how complaints that economists didn't predict or foresee the crisis are not going to change anyone's mind in economics.[31]

Abortive Attempts to Close the Barn Door After the Horses Have Bolted

As opposed to the out-and-out denial of a John Cochrane or a Eugene Fama or a John Taylor or a Robert Lucas, many neoclassical econo-mists were sufficiently chastened or blindsided by events in the economic crisis to concede that "something" about orthodox theory needed to be changed.[32] Of course, given the years that have elapsed, candidates for revision have tended to multiply. It would be a thankless task to track down and document each and every proposal, much less immerse oneself in the literature surrounding that option in order to assess its prospects and implications. Yet another reason to hesitate before this vast beehive of economist activity is the fact that a compre-hensive history of the desire to "fix" macroeconomics would have to wait long after crisis events had transpired, if only because an appre-ciation of which specific amendments and ideas really mattered would tend to become apparent with the fullness of time. Nevertheless, five years on, there is no consensus School of Reformed Orthodoxy in sight. And then there is the prospect that, all things considered, most readers of this volume probably are not all that hopeful about the chances for a revived and fortified economic orthodoxy. Consequently, a survey of proposed amendments to the corpus of macroeconomics will be conducted with relatively limited purview, tethered to a more tendentious set of objectives.

It is important to realize that, in the heat of the immediate crisis, a subset of economists was fully aware that a stance of implacable intransigence would play rather poorly in the public arena, so when journalists came around pleading to be enlightened on which aspects of economic orthodoxy would be revamped, these crafty economists saw an opportunity to promote lines of research that they had already been pursuing. Although many such options were potentially on offer, it can be reported that only a few were chosen, in the sense that only a small subset of revisions tended to get repeated and elaborated upon and promoted to the public. In fact, only three tended to get puffed up into full-blown paladins of deliverance: naming them in decreasing order of ambition, they were (1) behavioral economics; (2) repudiation of the efficient-markets hypothesis; and (3) fixing the DSGE macro model. All three were extensively discussed in the blogosphere and in generalist books, newspapers, and magazines; yet incongruously, all three were hopelessly ineffectual when it came to understanding the crisis. It is their power to mesmerize combined with their impotence that warrants their discussion in this chapter. Returning once more to our insistence on the importance of agnotology, it takes some diligence and not a little digging to come to understand why the populace was being led up the garden path; those seeking enlightenment were lured to waste their time in dalliance with ideas that did little more than divert attention from the deeper structural causes of the crisis. Daron Acemoglu's curious notion that "the crisis has increased the vitality of economics" was premature, to say the least.[33]

1) Getting a Little Irrational: Paradoxes of Ditching "Rationality" in Economics

It has become fairly common in the annals of economic history to observe that in the wake of serious financial crises, observers tended to bewail a certain weakness in human cognition, attributing pecuniary disaster to an endemic "madness of crowds."[34] In the current neoliberal era entranced with proclaiming the "wisdom of crowds," venturing to insist that the average man was a few sandwiches short of a picnic often appeared one easy way to register dissent from neoliberalism. Eventually, eschewing structural explanations, all serious problems would conventionally tend to be traced back through intermediate "bad choices" to moral or character flaws in particular individuals. Thus, it was no surprise that a pervasive and immediate response to 2008 was to blame the entire mess on a rabid outbreak of irrational exuberance.

Unfortunately, madness often lodged in the eye of the beholder. When it came to orthodox economics, the term "rationality" bore a very narrow and curious interpretation as the maximization of a utility function subject to constraints by an otherwise cognitively thin and emotionally deprived "agent." This unsatisfactory version of rationality had been the perennial subject of complaint and criticism from within and without economics since the 1870s; numerous defenses had been developed over the decades to supposedly neutralize those concerns.[35] I am not concerned here to rehearse familiar complaints that economists misconstrue or otherwise misrepresent that notoriously protean concept. All that is needed for current purposes is to point out that in orthodox economics, repudiation of "rationality" meant in practice tinkering with the utility function and/or its maximization. The latest forays at accommodation dated from the 1990s, introducing some amendments from narrow subsets of psychology (mostly decision theory) while keeping the basic maximization of utility framework: this had come to be called "behavioral economics." Some psychologists suggested these amendments were governed more by an imperative to save the previous neoclassical economics than to explore actual reasoning in the wild; but economists ignored them.[36] This purported "enrichment" of simpler concepts of rationality had even established a beachhead in the study of financial economics prior to the crisis; its most prominent advocate in the prelapsarian era was Lawrence Summers, which might begin to signal that its revolutionary potential may not have been all that transformative. Mostly, in finance it fostered models predicated upon the posited existence of a two-class world consisting of (a) stupid people, sometimes more charitably known as "noise traders," who performed certain functions in financial markets (liquidity, smoothing of reactions to shocks) so that the (b) neoclassically "rational" agents could more readily find the "true" or "fundamental" values dictated by the prior orthodox theory. Nothing here substantially impugned the basic orthodox model. As Jovanovic reports, "There exists as yet no unified theory of behavioral finance."

Once the crisis hit, journalists predictably turned to accusing Wall Street of behaving irrationally (in the looser vernacular meaning), and economists of investing too much credence in the rationality of their agents. Two best-selling books were especially effective in broadcasting this line: John Cassidy's *How Markets Fail* and Justin Fox's *Myth of the Rational Market*. Some economists who had been strong advocates of behavioral approaches prior to the crash, such as Robert Shiller and Robert Frank, leaped in with op-eds essentially blaming the entire crisis on native cognitive weaknesses of market participants.[37] This line became entrenched with the appearance of George Akerlof and Robert Shiller's *Animal Spirits*: displaying an utter contempt for the history of economic thought, they "reduced" the message of Keynes's *General Theory* to the proposition that people get a little irrational from time to time, and thus push the system away from full neoclassical general equilibrium.[38] They wrote:

> The idea that economic crises, like the current financial and housing crisis, are mainly caused by changing thought patterns goes against standard economic thinking. But current crisis bears witness to the role of such changes in thinking. It was caused precisely by our changing confidence, temptations, envy, resentment, and illusions . . . In Keynes' view these *animal spirits* are the main cause for why the economy fluctuates the way it does. They are also the main cause of involuntary unemployment.[39]

Nevertheless, in the few instances when journalists actually read the book, the first thing they noticed is that it said very little that was substantive about the current crisis, for much of it had been written well before 2008. Brought up short, they began to doubt its pertinence. The second thing they noticed was it was full of overweening claims, but contained very little in the way of causal mechanisms. "Animal spirits" boiled down to such timeworn neoclassical expedients as changing the utility function over time and calling it "confidence" (while Chicago called it "time-varying rates of discount"), appealing to sticky wages and prices while attributing them to "money illusion" and concerns over fairness (which the neoliberals modeled as "envy"), and suggestions that corruption would grow over the course of a long expansion (the Chicago theorist Gary Becker theorized this as the "rational choice approach to crime"). Far from some brave venturesome foray into the unexplored thickets of real psychology by open-minded economists unencumbered by entrenched dogmas, this was just more of the same old trick of tinkering with the "normal" utility function to get out the results you had wanted beforehand—something falling well short of the trumpeted dramatic divergence from standard economic theory.

This portmanteau utility function raised an objection that had long been a subject of discussion in the methodology literature: Wasn't "irrationality" in the neoclassical lexicon an oxymoron, since the moment one formalized it in the utility function, didn't it effectively get subsumed under some perverse version of meta-rationality?[40] Richard Posner, an especially perceptive critic from the right, pushed this point home in a review of *Animal Spirits*.[41] The Akerlof-Shiller reply, deficient in philosophical sophistication, proved unable to confront this debility:

> When Posner asserts that it is not always easy to rule out that people are acting rationally—even if they seem not to be—he is of course right, for this is what most academic economists have thought. It is hard to disprove such a theory that people are completely economically rational because the theory is somewhat slippery: It doesn't specify what objectives people have or what their information really is.[42]

The problem with behavioral economists going gaga over "irrationality" was that they conflated that incredibly complex and tortured phenomenon with minor divergences from their own overly rigid construct of pure deterministic maximization of an independent invariant "well-behaved" utility function. Akerlof and Shiller could only condone an incongruously rationalist framing of their irrational exuberance. Two decades of such behavioral research certainly has not resulted in any consensus systematic revisions of *microeconomics*, much less macroeconomics. Perhaps even more damning, the conventional sadomasochistic excuse that individuals would learn under pain of loss to behave like neoliberal agents was also unavailing: "almost no empirical evidence exists documenting that individuals who deviate from economic axioms of internal consistency (e.g., transitive preferences, expected utility axioms, and Bayesian beliefs) actually suffer any economic losses."[43] Beyond wishful thinking, why should one even think that the appropriate way to approach a macroeconomic crisis was through some arbitrary set of folk psychological mental categories? Again, they had to admit that Posner had caught them stuffing the rabbit into the hat:

> Posner makes the interesting point that most behavioral economists—who study the application of psychology to economics—did not predict the economic crisis either. We would put this somewhat differently: There were very few behavioral economists who made forceful public statements that a crisis may be imminent. That is

because there are very few behavioral economists who even specialized in macroeconomics, and so virtually none was willing to take
the risk of making any definitive forecast.[44]

The plea that in the eventuality behavioral economics had more
adherents, it would have done more of the things Akerlof promised,
is hardly a compelling reason to get enthused about that line of
research. Akerlof and Shiller were loathe to admit that they had not
proffered any good conceptual reasons to believe behavioral economics was even particularly relevant to the crisis. What this literature
had to do with the genesis of credit default swaps, the rise of the
shadow banking sector, and the collapse of the manufacturing sector
was entirely opaque. And however much Akerlof and Shiller protested
that their politics were diametrically opposed to neoliberals like
Reagan and Bush, what was their version of "animal spirits" but
tantamount to simply blaming the victims for the macroeconomic
contraction? (This was the option entertained by MIT's Andrew Lo,
described in the previous chapter.) Shiller's previous books did
indeed identify the housing bubble as a potential problem, but his
"solutions" always involved even more baroque securitizations of the
assets in question, as well as getting more people invested in Wall
Street even deeper than ever.[45] He finally revealed his true colors
soon thereafter in his unabashed apologetics for financial-sector
jiggery-pokery in his *Finance and the Good Society*. In this, he rivaled
the most avid Reaganite in his belief in the superior power of the
market to fix any problem.

The unbearable lightness of Akerlof's behavioral theory is nicely
exemplified by the one paper that was repeatedly cited by bloggers
and journalists during the crisis, his and Paul Romer's "Looting:
The Economic Underworld of Bankruptcy for Profit." From reading the title, one would suspect it might deal with the phenomenon
of running a financial institution into the ground given the tempta-
tions of short-term trading profits, like, say, Bear Stearns or Lehman
Brothers. Few of its enthusiasts actually bothered to go so far as to
peruse the model, however. In the MIT tradition, it was a purely
deterministic little toy model of a single firm over three periods,
where assets are not bought or sold after the first period, and a little
maximization exercise which argues that if the owners of the firm
could pay themselves more than the firm is worth and then declare
bankruptcy in period three, then they will do so. Accounting
manipulation and regulatory forbearance (which were not described

in any level of detail) are asserted to make this outcome more likely. Deposit insurance permits owners to offload costs of autodestruction onto the government. This was then asserted to "explain" the savings-and-loan crisis of the 1980s.

This displays all the hallmarks of the behavioral program touted by Akerlof and Shiller. First, a reputedly irrational behavior (looting and destruction of banks by their owners) is rendered "rational" through the minor amendment of a simple orthodox maximization exercise by tinkering with the utility function of bank owners. Insights from professional psychology are absent. The prospect that such behavior would bring the capitalist system to its knees is simply ignored. Macroeconomic phenomena are reduced to isolated individual choices in a manner far less sophisticated than in the reductionist rational-expectations movement. Predictably, the model adds nothing to what simple intuition would suggest, given the problem has been artificially restricted to a rudimentary cost-benefit exercise beforehand. Indeed, the model does not particularly illuminate the situation that nominally inspired it, since it does not encompass any of the specific institutional detail pertinent to the phenomenon; that is, it bypasses consensus factors that precipitated the crisis at that particular juncture. It ignores the breakdown of Depression-era walls between depository and investment institutions, and neglects the spread of baroque securitization at the behest of finance economists. But more to the point, their supposedly left-liberal approach ends up backhandedly reproducing the conventional neoliberal story, as was pointed out by Gregory Mankiw in his published commentary:

> Although the two authors from Berkeley did not intend this paper to be a defense of Ronald Reagan and his view of government, one can easily interpret it in this way. The paper shows that the savings and loan crisis was not the result of unregulated markets, but of overregulated ones ... The policy that led to the savings and loan crisis is, according to these authors, deposit insurance.[46]

Paul Romer, the other author of this paper, revealed his own neoliberal leanings when questioned concerning the crisis in 2011. "Every decade or so, any system of financial regulation will lead to systemic financial crisis."[47] Note well that for Romer it was not private financial sector "corruption" that produced instability, but rather government snafus in regulation, the standard public-choice account. His grasp of economic history was not very profound, either.

Hence, when some economists speculated that the orthodoxy would give way to a "more realistic" behavioral economics in reaction to the crisis, it was primarily a symptom of the general unwillingness to entertain any serious departure from conventional arguments.[48] If anyone had bothered to actually read any of the leaders of the behavioral "movement," they would have quickly realized that those economists went out of their way to renounce any ambitions to displace the orthodoxy. In one spectacularly badly timed compromise, in 2005 Andrew Lo had sought to reconcile the findings of behavioral finance with the efficient-markets hypothesis. And most behavioral economists couldn't care less about the layered complexity of the human soul.[49] Indeed, one needn't look far to encounter their contempt for the academic psychology profession:

> I think we strive for parsimonious, rigorous theoretical explanations; this distinguishes us from the psychologists . . . Economists want a theory that provides a unifying explanation of these results whereas psychologists are much more willing to accept two different theories to explain these "contradictory" results . . . I don't like the argument that everything is context dependent. That view lacks any grounding. In this regard, I really like the strong theoretical emphasis of economics and our desire for unifying explanations. It distinguishes us a lot from biologists and psychologists, and provides us with a normative anchor.[50]

If you asked behavioral economists what all this tinkering with conventional neoclassical utility functions was supposed to portend, they would tell you in no uncertain terms that so-called behavioral economics "is based not on a proposed paradigm shift in the basic approach of our field, but rather is a natural broadening of the field of economics . . . [it is] built on the premise that not only mainstream *methods* are great, but so too are mainstream economic *assumptions.*"[51]

So wherever did the vast bulk of lay commentators derive the unfounded impression that behavioral economics was poised to deliver us from the previous errors of orthodoxy when it came to the economic crisis? Partly, it was the fault of a few high-profile economists such as Shiller, Akerlof, Krugman, and Lo, whose "behavioral" credentials within the community were, shall we say, less than robust. Partly it was due to some political appointees in the Obama administration such as Cass Sunstein who claimed (falsely, as it turned out) that behavioral economics could be used to "nudge" people into behaving more like neoclassical agents.[52] Partly, it was the fault of a few bona fide behavioral finance economists (like Andrei Shleifer), who quickly whipped up a couple of toy models after the crisis, purportedly demonstrating that all agents are beset with a peculiar character flaw that causes them to ignore unlikely disastrous events, causing them to whipsaw around the true fundamental determinants of asset prices as defined by the orthodox rational-expectations model, in the face of securitization and tranching.[53] But it also emanated from the vast scrum of journalists, primed to believe that once economists would just abjure "rational choice theories," then all would become revealed. It got so bad that two bona fide behavioralists felt impelled to pen an op-ed for the *New York Times* absolving themselves of any responsibility to explain the crisis:

> It seems that every week a new book or major newspaper article appears showing that irrational decision-making helped cause the housing bubble . . . It's becoming clear that behavioral economics is being asked to solve problems it wasn't meant to address . . . Behavioral economics should complement, not substitute for, more substantive economic interventions [of] traditional economics.[54]

Ultimately, the more perceptive journalists acknowledged this: "While behaviorists and other critics poked a lot of holes in the edifice of rational market finance, they haven't been willing to abandon that edifice."[55] It's not even clear they have been all that willing to bring themselves to look out the window. The primary benefit of behavioral economics was conjuration of the warm glow that came from feeling like you had changed your economic stripes without having to change your mind, or even your models. Like the Seekers.

2) Renunciation of the Efficient Markets Hypothesis

For those riding the roller coaster of 2008, and retrospectively searching for previous wrong turns, it seemed obvious to focus on the sector wherefrom disasters cascaded one after another like clowns piling out of an auto: namely, Wall Street. Not only had finance become the four-hundred-pound gorilla of the U.S. economy, accounting for 41 percent of all corporate profits in 2007, but it was also the arena where economic theory had seemed to matter to a greater degree than elsewhere, given recourse to formal models to "justify" all manner of activities, from securitization and options pricing to risk management.[56] Thus it was fairly predictable that some economists would look to finance theory as the prime locus of error, and rapidly settled upon a single doctrine to scapegoat, the one dubbed the efficient-markets hypothesis (EMH). Paul Krugman became a prominent spokesperson for this option in his notorious "How Did Economists Get It So Wrong?":

> By 1970 or so, however, the study of financial markets seemed to have been taken over by Voltaire's Dr. Pangloss, who insisted we live in the best of all possible worlds. Discussion of investor irrationality, of bubbles, of destructive speculation had virtually disappeared from academic discourse. The field was dominated by the "efficient markets hypothesis" . . . which claims that financial markets price assets precisely at their intrinsic worth given all publicly available information . . . And by the 1980s, finance economists, notably Michael Jensen of the Harvard Business School, were arguing that because financial markets always get prices right, the best thing corporate chieftains can do, not just for themselves but for the sake of the economy, is to maximize their stock prices. In other words, finance economists believed that we should put the capital development of the nation in the hands of what Keynes had called "a casino."

Journalists found the EMH irresistibly seductive to ridicule, with John Cassidy and Justin Fox attacking it at length. The journalist Roger Lowenstein declared, "The upside of the current Great Recession is that it could drive a stake through the heart of the academic nostrum known as the efficient-market hypothesis."[57] There was more than sufficient ammunition to choose from to rain fire down on the EMH, not least because it had been the subject of repeated criticism from within the economics profession since the 1980s. But what the journalists like Cassidy, Fox, and Lowenstein and commentators like Krugman neglected to inform their readers was that the back and forth, the intellectual thrust and empirical parry, had ground to a standoff *more than a decade before the crisis*, as admirably explained in Lo and MacKinlay, *A Non-Random Walk Down Wall Street*:

> There is an old joke, widely told among economists, about an economist strolling down the street with a companion when they come upon a $100 bill lying on the ground. As the companion reaches down to pick it up, the economist says, "Don't bother—if it were a real $100 bill, someone would have already picked it up." This

humorous example of economic logic gone awry strikes dangerously close to home for students of the Efficient Markets
Hypothesis, one of the most important controversial and well-
studied propositions in all the social sciences. It is disarmingly
simple to state, has far-reaching consequences for academic pursuits
and business practice, and yet is surprisingly resilient to empirical
proof or refutation. Even after three decades of research and literally
thousands of journal articles, economists have not yet reached a
consensus about whether markets—particularly financial markets—
are efficient or not.

What can we conclude about the Efficient Markets Hypothesis?
Amazingly, there is still no consensus among financial economists.
Despite the many advances in the statistical analysis, databases, and
theoretical models surrounding the Efficient Markets Hypothesis,
the main effect that the large number of empirical studies have had
on this debate is to *harden the resolve of the proponents on each side*
[my italics]. One of the reasons for this state of affairs is the fact
that the Efficient Markets Hypothesis, by itself, is not a well-
defined and empirically refutable hypothesis. To make it
operational, one must specify additional structure, e.g., investors'
preferences, information structure, business conditions, etc. But
then a test of the Efficient Markets Hypothesis becomes a test of
several auxiliary hypotheses as well, and a rejection of such a joint
hypothesis tells us little about which aspect of the joint hypothesis
is inconsistent with the data. Are stock prices too volatile because
markets are inefficient, or is it due to risk aversion, or dividend
smoothing? All three inferences are consistent with the data.
Moreover, new statistical tests designed to distinguish among them
will no doubt require auxiliary hypotheses of their own which, in
turn, may be questioned.

This imperviousness of an isolated hypothesis to definitive empirical
rejection, and the crucial role of auxiliary hypotheses in serving as a
protective barrier, is familiar in the philosophy of science literature
as Duhem's Thesis. The mere fact of deflecting disconfirmation
onto harmless auxiliary hypotheses is not prima facie an illegitimate
ploy; it occurs in all the natural sciences. The issue was not that
immunizing stratagems had been resorted to in this instance; rather,
it was that the EMH had proven so rabidly tenacious within orthodox economics and in business schools, occupying pride of place for
decades within both macroeconomics and finance, that economists

had begun to ignore most modern attempts to disprove it. The lesson for crisis watchers that we shall entertain is that the EMH cannot be killed easily, and maybe not at all within the neoclassical parameters of the current economics profession. That is one reason noneconomists need to be suspicious of claims such as the pronunciation of the economist most famous for the "reject the EMH" option, Joseph Stiglitz:

> [A] considerable portion of [blame] lies with the economics profession. The notion economists pushed—that markets are efficient and self-adjusting—gave comfort to regulators like Alan Greenspan, who didn't believe in regulation in the first place . . . We should be clear about this: economic theory never provided much support for these free market views. Theories of imperfect and asymmetric information in markets had undermined every one of the "efficient market" doctrines, even before they became fashionable in the Reagan-Thatcher era.[58]

Pace Stiglitz, each blow just seemed to leave it a little stronger. One of the characteristics of the EMH that rendered it impervious to refutation was the fact that both proponents and critics were sometimes extremely cavalier about the meaning and referent of the adjective "efficient." Both Krugman and Stiglitz, for instance, in the above quotes simply conflate two major connotations of efficiency, namely, "informational efficiency" and "allocative efficiency." The former is a proposition about the efficacy and exactitude of markets as information-conveyance devices; the latter is a proposition that market prices correctly capture the "fundamentals" and maximize the benefits to market participants by always representing the unique arbitrage-free equilibrium. It is sometimes taken for granted that the former implies the latter; this is the gist of the comment that one will never find loose hundred-dollar bills on the sidewalk. However, if one rephrased the claim to state that no one will ever find valuable unused information on the sidewalk, then the fallacy starts to become apparent.[59] In order to respect the significance of that distinction, in this section we deal with those reformers who propose that the orthodoxy shed the information-processing version of the EMH in reaction to the crisis; while in the next section we consider those who seek to dispense with allocative efficiency altogether.

The key to the EMH is to insist that there are some rock-solid "fundamentals" that determine equilibrium price. If one accepts that premise, then orthodox finance economists assert that the EMH "simply comprises the testable implications of arbitrage." Even Chicago economists such as Luigi Zingales would concede that under certain circumstances asset prices might diverge from these fundamentals; but quickly add that economists had come up with theoretical reasons why these divergences assumed the trajectories we observe. "Thus far, the recent crisis has not provided any critical new evidence on the deviations of markets from fundamentals, only evidence of the costs of these deviations." The Fed chairman, Ben Bernanke, would concur, adding only that the EMH informs us that we can identify these divergences as "bubbles" only after the fact, so the only "rational" monetary policy should be to clean up the mess afterward. Conveniently, the EMH was then elevated to a self-reflexive theory of the economics profession: they are still paying us after the crisis, so we must be doing something right! "When the definitive history of the EMH is written, the 2007–8 financial crisis will not emerge as a major turning point."[60]

The journalist and blogger Felix Salmon posed the critical question during the crisis: Why did the EMH become Dulcinea in the destructive love affair that the economics profession seemed unable to shake off?[61] To appreciate the question, one must become acquainted with a little bit of history. The role of the EMH should be situated within the broader context of the ways that neoclassical economics has changed over time.[62] In a nutshell, neoclassical economics looks very different now than it did at its inception in the 1870s. From thenceforth until World War II, it was largely a theory of the allocation of scarce means to given ends. Although trade was supposed to enhance "utility," very little consideration was given to what people knew about commodities, or how they came to know it, or indeed, about how they knew much of anything else. The Socialist Calculation Controversy, running from the Great Depression until the Fall of the Wall, tended to change all that. In particular, Friedrich Hayek argued that the true function of the market was to serve as the greatest information processor known to mankind. Although Hayek was not initially accorded very much respect within the American economics profession before the 1980s, nonetheless, the "information processing" model of the market progressively displaced the earlier "static allocation" approach in the preponderance of neoclassical theory over the second half of the twentieth century. As one can appreciate, this profoundly changed the meaning of what it meant to assert "the market works just fine," at least within the confines of economics.[63] "Efficiency," a slippery term in the best of circumstances, had come increasingly to connote the proposition that the market could package and convey knowledge on a "need to know" basis in a manner that could never be matched by any human planner.

Once one recognizes this distinct trend, then the appearance of the EMH in 1965 in Samuelson and Fama, and its rapid exfoliation throughout finance theory and macroeconomics, becomes something more than just a fluke. Indeed, the EMH served as the first bedrock theoretical tenet of the nascent field of "financial economics" in the late 1960s. Almost every trademark model, from CAPM to the Black-Scholes model of option pricing, has it built in. Most academic financial engineers treat it as an inviolate premise. The notion that all relevant information is adequately embodied in price data was one incarnation of what was fast becoming one of the core commitments of the neoclassical approach to markets, not to mention the First Commandment of models of financial assets. It has subsequently been built into the models that inform and conduct trading on all the world's major exchanges. Of course, the fact that numerous ineffectual attempts were made along the way to refute the doctrine in specific instances (variance bounds violations, the end-of-the month effect, January effect, small-cap effects, mean reversion, and a host of others) did not impugn the EMH so much as quibble over just how far the horizon would be extended. The EMH spawned reams of econometric empiricism, but surprisingly little alteration in the base proposition. The massive number of papers published on the EMH merely testified to the Protean character of the idol of "market efficiency," which grew to the status of obsession within the American profession.[64]

One recent instance of EMH denial that has attracted the endorsement of reformers such as Adair Turner in Britain and Ezra Klein in the United States is the already-mentioned work of the Harvard economist Andrei Shleifer.[65] Shleifer is a neoliberal who passes as a left-liberal economist in America, in the Lawrence Summers mold. Shleifer's model initially "seems" to call into question the validity of certain classes of dubious artificial derivatives by suggesting someone is being misled by the market; but as usual, the devil is in the details. Shleifer combines some "behavioral" themes with a standard neoclassical model to blame the crisis on the investors, who unaccountably ignore the extreme tail risk of newly invented derivatives when they are minted. In other words, the crisis happens because the suitably adjusted agents are blind to its possibility. (Rabbit in hat; rabbit out.) Actually, the EMH is not "refuted" so much as reinforced in the model, since "the market" still emits the correct signals (which really do come out of nowhere in the mathematics); as in most neoliberal scenarios, the crash is the fault of the victims beset with "local think- ing" (Shleifer's terminology) rushing to dump their wonky assets all at the same time. Everything that actually happened, from the waves of neoliberal deregulation to the ratings hand jive to the whitewash of crude evasion of existing rules as financial "innovation" to accounting travesties to outright fraud leave no trace in the model: when in doubt, blame the victims. This is trumpeted to the world as neoclassical economics getting more true to the facts on the ground.

In the *Odyssey*, Proteus assumed a plethora of shapes to escape Menelaus; in the EMF, "information" had to be gripped tight by neoclassical theory, because it kept squirming and changing shape whenever anyone tried to confine it within the framework of a standard neoclassical model. Few have been sensitive enough to the struggle to attend to its twists and turns, but for present purposes it will be sufficient that three major categories of cages to tame the beast have been information portrayed as "thing" or object, informa- tion reified as inductive index, and information as the input to symbolic computation.[66] For numerous considerations here bypassed, they cannot in general be reduced one to another. The reason this matters to journalists' convictions that the crisis has invalidated the EMH is that the detractors mostly conform to the literature that treats information like a commodity, whereas the defenders repulse them from battlements of legitimation built largely from information as an inductive index. This may seem a distinction that only a pedant could love, but once clarified it goes a long way to demonstrating that the crisis will never induce the majority of neoclassical econo- mists to give up on the EMH.

The most prominent standard-bearer for the denial of the *Kennt- nisnahme über alles* EMH has been Joseph Stiglitz. Here it is important to acknowledge that Stiglitz is treated by the mainstream media as a stalwart of the American left because he has repeatedly taken politi- cal positions that have not ingratiated him with those in power; he often has been steadfast in his pessimistic evaluations of the crisis, when all the journalists wanted to hear was how the crisis was done, dusted, and under control. In stark contrast to most of the figures encountered in this history, he has repeatedly gone on record stating that economists should bear some responsibility for the crisis. He even said complimentary things about French demonstrations in October 2010 against raising the age of retirement. By these lights, Stiglitz has been an exemplary contrarian economist. Nonetheless, Stiglitz has simultaneously been a major defender of neoclassical economics, suggesting that the EMH is not all that central to the core doctrines of orthodoxy:

> Normally, most markets work reasonably well on their own. But this is not true when there are externalities . . . The markets failed, and the presence of large externalities is one of the reasons. But there are others. I have repeatedly noted the misalignment of incentives—bank officers' incentives were not consistent with the objectives of other stakeholders and society more generally. Buyers of assets also have imperfect information . . . The disaster that grew from these flawed financial incentives can be, to us economists, somewhat comforting: our models predicted that there would be excessive risk-taking and shortsighted behavior . . . In the end, economic theory was vindicated.[67]

It can sometimes be hard for outsiders to detect just where Stiglitz is coming from, since in the course of the very same lecture he can lead with a rousing call to battle like "There ought to be a crisis in economics" and yet follow with the oxymoronic "fortunately, we don't need to rewrite the textbooks."[68] Stiglitz has been known to make very insightful comments about how to judge crisis narratives, such as the observation that the crisis was not the consequence of "shocks" impinging on the system, but rather was man-made; the stretch comes in understanding how one was supposed to know this from the standard neoclassical model.[69]

This is what Krugman has called "flaws-and-frictions" economics, and it propounds the bromide that "we already had models that told us the crisis was coming." It follows that outsiders should ask: So why weren't these models well represented in macro *or* micro textbooks and graduate pedagogy? Stiglitz is fully aware there exists a tradition of oxymoronic "New Keynesianism" that reprised a boring old pre-Keynesian story of sticky wages and prices in a neoclassical equilibrium, but he suggests there exists something else on offer more compelling. In Stiglitz's case, there is a special caveat: the models he has in mind are found mostly in his own previous publications. While there could be no academic prohibition against tooting your own horn, there is something less than compelling about claiming a grand generality for some idiosyncratic models where the novelty quotient is distinctly low. While Stiglitz has certainly earned his Nobel, he has not effectively staunched the intellectual trend of treating markets as prodigious information processors; nor has he provided a knock-down refutation of the EMH. This has led to the distressing spectacle of Stiglitz, the great hope of the "legitimate left," openly defending the neoclassical approach to the crisis, while not really changing it all that much.

Stiglitz has admitted that his mission all along was to undermine free-market fundamentalism from within:

> [I]t seemed to me the most effective way of attacking the paradigm was to keep within the standard framework as much as possible . . .While there is a single way in which information is perfect, there are an infinite number of ways that information can be imperfect. One of the keys to success was formulating simple models in which the set of relevant information could be fully specified . . . the use of highly simplified models to help clarify thinking about quite complicated matters.[70]

The way he sought to do this is to produce little stripped-down models that maximize standard utility or production functions, with a glitch or two inserted up front in the setup. He has been especially partial to portraying "information" as a concrete thing to be purchased, and "risk" as standard density function with known parameters. There is no canonical Stiglitz "general model," but rather a number of specialized dedicated exercises, one for each flaw and/or friction explored. Macroeconomics then simply becomes microeconomics with the subscripts dropped. This distinguishes Stiglitz from the small cadre of researchers in the third section below, who are convinced that this "representative agent" trick does not constitute serious macroeconomic theory.[71]

In Stiglitz's academic writings, he stakes his claim to have refuted the EMH primarily on two papers, one co-authored with Sanford Grossman in 1980, the other with Bruce Greenwald in 1993.[72] The takeaway lesson of the first was summarized in his Nobel lecture:

> When there is no noise, prices convey all information, and there is no incentive to purchase information. But if everybody is uninformed, it clearly pays some individual to become informed. Thus, there does not exist a competitive equilibrium.[73]

The second is proffered as the fundamental cause of the crisis:

> It perceives the key market failures to be not just in the labor market, but also in financial markets. Because contracts are not appropriately indexed, alterations in economic circumstances can cause a rash of bankruptcies, and fear of bankruptcy contributes to the freezing of credit markets. The resulting economic disruption affects both aggregate demand and aggregate supply, and it's not easy to recover from this—one reason that my prognosis for the economy in the short term is so gloomy.[74]

Both of his crucial "findings" are in fact based upon very narrow versions of what is a much more diversified neoclassical orthodoxy. It would indeed have been noteworthy if Stiglitz or his co-workers had provided a general impossibility theorem, say, along the lines of Gödel's incompleteness theorem or Turing's computability theorem, but Stiglitz has explicitly rejected working with full Walrasian general equilibrium, or Chicago's resort to transactions costs, and doesn't seriously consider the game theorists' versions of strategic cognition. Indeed, it seems a rather heroic task to derive any blanket general propositions from any one of his individual toy models. Stiglitz himself admits this when he is not engaged in wholesale promotion of his information program.[75]

Take, for instance, the famous Grossman–Stiglitz model. The text starts out by positing information as a commodity that needs to be arbitraged, but claims in a footnote that the model of knowledge therein is tantamount to the portrayal of information as inductive index, which is not strictly true, and then defines its idiosyncratic notion of "equilibrium" as equivalence of plain vanilla rational expected utilities of informed and uninformed agents. Of course, "for simplicity" all the agents are posited identical; how this is supposed to relate to any vernacular notions of divergences in knowledge is something most economists have never been poised to address. Many economists of a different political persuasion simply ignored the model, because they deemed that Stiglitz was not taking into account their (inductive, computational) version of "information." When Grossman offered his own interpretation of their joint effort, he took the position that the rational expectations model was identical to the approach in Hayek, that "when the efficient markets hypothesis is true and information is costly, competitive markets break down," and that "We are attempting to redefine the Efficient Markets notion, not destroy it."[76] That seems closer to the median interpretation of Stiglitz's work in the profession as a whole.

Perhaps the most distressing aspect of Stiglitz's designated models that he believes starkly refuted neoliberalism has been that, when you really take the trouble to understand them, they end up having nothing cogent to say about the current crisis whatsoever. Start with Grossman and Stiglitz.[77] The problems with the financial system in 2007 had nothing to do with participants lacking correct incentives to purchase enough "information" that would have revealed the dodgy nature of the CDOs and other baroque assets which clogged the balance sheets of the financial sector. Rather, the reams of information they did purchase, from ratings agency evaluations to accounting audits to investment advice, was all deeply corrupted by being consciously skewed to mislead hapless clients and evade the letter of the law. Perhaps the "information" was corrupted by the mere fact of being bought and sold. Since Stiglitz never comes within hailing distance of confronting epistemology in any of his models—he disdains philosophy as much as the next neoclassical economist—he never really deals with matters of truth and falsehood. Agents are just machines buying unproblematic lumps of information (or not).

Stiglitz often mentions the complaints of heterodox economists (mostly without citing them), but curiously, he seems to have no appreciation for the extent to which no amount of mathematical tweaks could adequately reconcile them with any version of neoclassical theory. He concedes that non-ergodicity pervades real-world random variables (ignoring Paul Davidson), but offers no insights as to how they might be shoehorned into a neoclassical model. He allows that the Sonnenschein-Mantel-Debreu results banish the representative agent, but neglects to point out that they also render all aggregation (and hence all macroeconomics) under neoclassical general equilibrium groundless. More tellingly, he admits that the mere fact that prices for the "same" goods might be set in structurally different market formats would by itself account for destabilizing price dynamics; but passes over in silence the fact that this would delegitimize the entire neoclassical approach to pricing and risk, including his own work.[78]

And worse, the "market failure" that he repeatedly diagnoses has nothing to do with what people mean by "failure" in the vernacular. Stiglitz (and Krugman and Solow and other guest stars in the *New York Review of Books*) identify "market failure" with not realizing the full measure of utility that might have occurred in the standard neoclassical model—this is called Pareto optimality in the trade—and exists in an imaginary universe utterly devoid of markets freezing up and the implosion of the assignment of credible prices across the board. Likewise, the Stiglitz-Greenwald paper has nothing whatsoever to do with the collapse of the financial sector in 2008. Using their own words, "we showed that there were essentially always simple government interventions that could make some individuals better off without making anyone worse off. The intuition behind our result was that whenever information was imperfect, actions generated externality-like effects."[79] Stiglitz persistently conflates "welfare loss" with system-wide economic failure and market breakdown: this travesty stands in stark contrast to the model-free occasions wherein Stiglitz perceptively analyzes the inconsistencies of concrete practices in real world institutions, linking them to palpable dire outcomes. Pareto optimality was the last thing one needed to consult in trying to understand the utter confusion and disarray accompanying the mad improvisations at the Fed and the congressional TARP appropriation in the depths of the crisis; it certainly would be impotent to clarify the types of "government intervention" required to stem the collapse. Incredibly, the Greenwald–Stiglitz model *doesn't even explicitly have any money in it*, even though one core phenomenon of the 2008 meltdown was a financial credit crisis. Instead, their model identifies the central weakness of the capitalist system as a rational contraction of investment on the part of firms, not financial system collapse.[80]

Stiglitz repeatedly pronounces last rites over the EMH, but has little sway on the profession because he cannot see what is sauce for the goose is sauce for the gander. "The Chicago School and its disciples wanted to believe that the market for information was like any other market." Yet, that is the fundamental initial premise of his own models. "The widespread belief in the EMH played a role in the Federal Reserve's failure. If that hypothesis were true, then there were no such thing as bubbles." But this just displays a deficiency of hermeneutic attention. Both the Fed and the profession can accept that the EMH, properly understood, and bubbles are entirely compatible—you just won't know you are in one till it bursts. And paraphrasing Bill Clinton, it all depends what you mean by "bubble." Yet Stiglitz never *really* repudiates the neoliberal doctrine of the Marketplace of Ideas. "The price mechanism is at the core of the market process of gathering, processing and transmitting information." There is nothing autodestructive about the Marketplace of Ideas. But then, who in the elite of the orthodox economics profession ever thought otherwise?[81]

The endless quest to delete the EMH from the Ten Commandments of Neoclassicism almost constitutes the definition of "empty gesture" within orthodox economics.

3) Abandon the DSGE Model

A third reaction to the crisis is to refrain from indictment of the global orthodoxy, and instead suggest that since the crisis was eminently a "macroeconomic" event, the onus for failure must be narrowly restricted to that subset of the profession tasked with study of the macroeconomy; and furthermore, the correct response is to simply jettison the paradigmatic model found in contemporary macroeconomic textbooks, the so-called Dynamic Stochastic General Equilibrium (DSGE) model. The crisis, for this cadre, does not portend anything remotely like the "death of economics," but just a garden-variety "model failure": so replace the model. Now, I can imagine my audience rolling their eyes—even those willing to put up with the modicum of technical issues raised so far are not going to countenance a tedious discussion of a specific mathematical model, no matter how crucial to the self-image of the economics profession. And it is true that there is almost no commentary in the general press on the DSGE model, compared with breathless denunciations of "rational economic man" and the EMH. But this option does even more directly call into question the commonplace notion that economists can learn from their mistakes.

This is exemplified by an event in 2010 that was literally unprecedented in the history of economic thought in America. Congressional testimony is regularly convened on all manner of issues of applied economics, and economists are regularly enjoined to testify. But never before, to my knowledge, has an entire session been convened to hold public hearings on criticism of a mathematical model produced by economic theory, not on its purported applications. Yet, on July 20, 2010, a kind of Star Chamber was convened to pillory the DSGE model.[82]

This is how the committee staff described the DSGE model for a lay audience:

The dominant macro model has for some time been the Dynamic Stochastic General Equilibrium model, or DSGE, whose name points to some of its outstanding characteristics. "General" indicates that the model includes all markets in the economy. "Equilibrium" points to the assumptions that supply and demand balance out rapidly and unfailingly, and that competition reigns in markets that are undisturbed by shortages, surpluses, or involuntary unemployment. "Dynamic" means that the model looks at the economy over time rather than at an isolated moment. "Stochastic" corresponds to a specific type of manageable randomness built into the model that allows for unexpected events, such as oil shocks or technological changes, but assumes that the model's agents can assign a correct mathematical probability to such events, thereby making them insurable. Events to which one cannot assign a probability, and that are thus truly uncertain, are ruled out.

The agents populating DSGE models, functioning as individuals or firms, are endowed with a kind of clairvoyance. Immortal, they see to the end of time and are aware of anything that might possibly ever occur, as well as the likelihood of its occurring; their decisions are always instantaneous yet never in error, and no decision depends on a previous decision or influences a subsequent decision. Also assumed in the core DSGE model is that all agents of the same type—that is, individuals or firms—have identical needs and identical tastes, which, as "optimizers," they pursue with unbounded self-interest and full knowledge of what their wants are. By employing what is called the "representative agent" and assigning it these standardized features, the DSGE model excludes from the model economy almost all consequential diversity and uncertainty—characteristics that in many ways make the actual economy what it is. The DSGE universe makes no distinction between system equilibrium, in which balancing agent-level disequilibrium forces maintains the macroeconomy in equilibrium, and full agent equilibrium, in which every individual in the economy is in equilibrium. In so doing, it assumes away phenomena that are commonplace in the economy: involuntary unemployment and the failure of prices or wages to adjust instantaneously to changes in the relation of supply and demand. These phenomena are seen as exceptional and call for special explanation.

While skepticism concerning the DSGE is worn openly in this précis, it was nowhere near as scathing as the disparagement of the model that one hears in private and reads on blogs. Incredulity often focuses upon the presumption of a single immortal representative agent capturing the entire economy. For instance, at the April 2010 meetings of the Institute for New Economic Thinking, I witnessed one famous economist compare coordination failures in DSGE models with the right hand losing track of what the left hand was doing, and the treatment of uncertainty in DSGE as tantamount to diagnosing the onset of Alzheimer's. You can just imagine the bizarre shapes that "information" assumes in this solipsistic portrait: What can it mean for this godlike agent to learn anything? A good DSGE joke current on the blogs is: "Based on all available information, I rationally expect DSGE models to suck for an infinite number of future periods; and because I am a representative agent, everybody agrees with me."

So maybe economist jokes are not all that funny, but there are a few philosophical points to be extracted from the imbroglio. The first is that, within the profession, seeking out the Golden Mean does not guarantee intellectual credibility. The DSGE model was the product of a long series of compromises resulting in what was conceived as best-practice consensus, following a period in which participants had endured what they felt was three decades of bickering, discord, and wrangling over the correct way to theorize in macroeconomics.[83] In the middle of the noughties, embrace of the Great Moderation was coupled with declaration of the Great Macro Accord, and the DSGE model was its offspring. Complacency in the world of ideas replicated complacency in the world of policy. In another instance of bad timing, Olivier Blanchard, chief economist of the IMF, decreed: "The state of macro is good . . . macroeconomics is going through a period of great progress and excitement, and there has been, over the past two decades, convergence in both vision and methodology." "DSGE models have become ubiquitous. Dozens of researchers are involved in their construction. Nearly every central bank has one, or wants to have one."[84] And more astoundingly, all central banks *still* have one. Indeed, this is an illustration of the thesis proposed in the previous chapter, that the Federal Reserve (and central banks in general) have a much larger influence upon the configuration of the economics profession than often thought. But perhaps it better illustrates the fact that the DSGE model was an attempt to be all things to all sides, a détente imposed from above, emitted from a very few "top-ranked" economics departments rather than a voluntary truce taking hold organically. This had something to do with its clueless setup for its vertiginous fall.

While there are some good historical summaries of how the rational expectations movement and the so-called Lucas critique killed off the previous Keynesianism of the 1960s and '70s, there are very few sociological meditations on how economics got from there to the DSGE model. Starting out under the banner of "consistency," it was insisted that neoclassical microeconomics and macroeconomics had to be fully interchangeable. Second, orthodox macroeconomists came to conflate "being rational" with thinking like an orthodox economist. What this implied was that agents knew the one and only "true model" of the economy (which conveniently was stipulated as identical with neoclassical microeconomics); and since they all knew the same thing, for practical purposes of the model, they were all alike in most relevant respects. Hence, far from congealing an intellectual travesty, it seemed plausible (not to mention mathematically convenient) to portray the entire economy as playing out between the ears of a single person. Thus the "representative agent" fiction in fact constitutes a projection of deep commitments of the existing elite of the orthodox economics profession. That is why it became a shared presumption of neoliberals who believe in the natural healing powers of the market, as well as New Keynesians looking for reasons why the economy falters.

Consensus is often mistaken for groupthink within the DSGE model, and this tends to mirror a sociological characteristic of the economics profession. Both the "agent" in the DSGE model and in the American profession could not imagine an effective search for truth emerging out of substantial persistent disagreement over fundamentals. Agents in orthodox models are enjoined from "agreeing to disagree"; and economists in good standing must knuckle under as well. The utter revulsion for anything smacking of real heterodoxy, combined with a fear of appearing "unscientific" to outsiders, eventually led to a donnybrook far more drastic than any embarrassment or compromised legitimacy that might have otherwise previously arisen from strident disagreement in the court of public opinion. Indeed, the effect of the crisis has been to bring those repressed disputes out into the open.

Once the presumption of omniscience broke down, then the consequences of the banishment of methodological self-scrutiny began to be felt. Both the criticisms and defenses of DSGE, at the congressional hearings and elsewhere after the crisis onset, were distressingly unsophisticated, as one might expect as fallout from the ostracism of methodological thought. Robert Solow testified in Congress that DSGE models "didn't pass the smell test," introducing a novel olfactory standard for scientific model choice. The defense of DSGE by V. V. Chari at the hearings equally reveals the paucity of resources (and rhetorical skills) possessed by contemporary economists:

So, any interesting model must be a dynamic stochastic general equilibrium model. From this perspective, there is no other game in town. Modern macroeconomic models, often called DSGE models in macro share common additional features. All of them make sure that they are consistent with the National Income and Product Accounts. That is, things must add up. All of them lay out clearly how people make decisions. All of them are explicit about the constraints imposed by nature, the structure of markets and available information on choices to households, firms and the government. From this perspective DSGE land is a very big tent. The only alternatives are models in which the modeler does not clearly spell out how people make decisions. Why should we prefer obfuscation to clarity? My description of the style of modern macroeconomics makes it clear that modern macroeconomists use a common language to formulate their ideas and the style allows for substantial disagreement on the substance of the ideas. A useful aphorism in macroeconomics is: "If you have an interesting and coherent story to tell, you can tell it in a DSGE model. If you cannot, your story is incoherent."[85]

The rational-expectations crowd tended to take one of two opposed positions: either you couldn't think rationally without DSGE, or else you couldn't think about the crisis *with* it: "These models were designed to describe aggregate economic fluctuations during normal times . . . they are not designed to be theories of financial crises."[86] Perhaps they chose one or the other depending upon the character of their audience.

It is one thing to assert that you personally cannot imagine any other possible way to discuss the macroeconomy than the DSGE; it is quite another (in public, before a tribunal) to insist no one else can either, without babbling incoherently. And then there is the willful zombie response, which can acknowledge the point of all the dissent, but nevertheless retorts that once they have elected to become undead economists, there is no point whatsoever in having intellectual ambitions. Alan Kirman relates the following incident:

There was this young economist, I think he was at UCLA, who wrote to me when I published this paper called "Whom or What Does the Representative Agent Represent?" (Kirman, 1992). He said: Dear professor, I really agree with what you said. I think it is intellectually absolutely right. Unfortunately, I am a young macroeconomist who is an assistant professor. I build models based on a representative agent. I know how to do that, and I know how to publish that. And I need to get tenure. Once I have got tenure, maybe I will then be able to turn around and start to think about the sorts of models that do not use the representative agent, but unfortunately, what I think will happen is that by then I will have got into the habit of doing it. I will publish my articles, get a decent reputation, I will get a promotion, and I will probably never think about this again. But anyway, thank you very much for the insight![87]

What has been odd given the waves of incredulous disbelief cascading over the economics profession is just how scarce serious rationalizations of steadfast fealty to the DSGE model have been, emitted by orthodox macroeconomists after 2008. One of the very few instances came in a long review of John Quiggin's *Zombie Economics* by the monetarist economist Stephen Williamson.[88] Although he grumbles that complaints about the uselessness of DSGE models are a "cheap shot," he nonetheless grudgingly deigns to explain to the madding crowd why macroeconomists circle their wagons around the DSGE. With touching candor, he begins his defense by appealing to "efficiency," by which he means "It would be silly for macroeconomists to turn down the gifts [neoclassical] theorists have given us." Why not search where it is easiest? He then points to the trademark "Lucas critique," which states that for purposes of policy, we need to differentiate causal factors that remain invariant through interventions from those that are altered by them.[89] The DSGE model is lauded because it purportedly respects this separation. The amazing aspect of this justification resides in the fact that Lucas and friends unaccountably conflate things that are taken as independent primitives for the mathematical purposes in Arrow-Debreu theory—preferences, endowments, technology—with things that are actually invariant *in the world* for purposes of macroeconomic policy: a non sequitur if there ever was one. Next, because Williamson thinks the Kydland-Prescott (1977) notion of time inconsistency is one of the deepest insights into the politics of economic policy conceived in the last half-century, he insists only DSGE models encourage the casting of the problem of government versus the private sector as a game where the former attempts to outwit the latter. (As an aside: Amazing how little effort is expended to model firms swindling the government and the public in macroeconomics.) Besides, Williamson says with a yawn, we have already thought of all your picky quibbles, and someone somewhere in the literature has already addressed them. We orthodox make simplifying assumptions (representative agent, rationality, unique equilibrium) because we deem them useful, not because we believe any of this stuff. Anyway, you ask too much of the DSGE model—the purposes that motivate us orthodox macroeconomists rarely intersect with the issues you rabble think we should address: "Prediction need not always be the criterion of success of an economic model . . . By nature, a financial crisis is an unpredictable event . . . The basic real business cycle model was not designed for the purpose of understanding financial crises." While he sneers at everyone else's epistemic criteria and explanatory demands, it is significant that Williamson never once feels impelled to make explicit his own nonnegotiable litmus test for legitimate purposes in construction of models. Yet, looking back over his defense, it becomes clear: it is *political*, in the sense that if a particular model helps reify the neoliberal worldview, than it passes muster *a fortiori*. Williamson is subconsciously aware of this, since he turns swiftly to indict Quiggin for believing that proponents of DSGE, and zombie economics more generally, are "complicit in the conspiracy to make the rich richer by robbing the poor." His refutation of this notion comes in the format that some Minneapolis Fed economists (recall: the incubator of rational-expectations theory) made some noises about the dangers of too-big-to-fail, and that some critics of DSGE—he cites an old paper by Larry Summers—often get implicated in the financial crisis. This is a direct quote: "So does Quiggin think Summers is a good guy or a bad guy?"

The Williamson review reveals the longueurs and lacunae that ensue when an orthodox macroeconomist is forced to bring out into the open what has been drilled into him as prerequisite for obtaining his certificate of congruity with the sanctioned profession.

This even happens with key critics like Joseph Stiglitz. In a long meditation on the flaws of macroeconomics, he suggests the DSGE was the wrong place to start to formalize macroeconomics, and that even when well-meaning Keynesians tinker with it to address the chorus of complaints, "the improved macro-performance is accompanied by an increased arbitrariness in at least certain specifications . . . the DSGE models have made the wrong trade-offs, focusing on some complexities which are of less importance than those they ignore"; and yet, in the very same paper, he reveals his own ambivalence, writing, "no one can object to models that approximately model the general   equilibrium   properties   of   dynamic   economies facing endogenous and exogenous shocks, so on one level DSGE is unobjectionable." No one, that is, except those who trace the disease to the neoclassical model itself.[90]

But of course there were alternatives studded throughout the literature, ones that had been proposed repeatedly by those seeking to exit the "big tent" of orthodox macroeconomics. The immediate task is instead to ask, Why are so many economists so loathe to let go of the DSGE? All the usual considerations of inertia and sunk costs of intellectual commitment come into play; but there is something else, as well. One way to understand such intransigence is to explore the possibility that excision of the DSGE cannot staunch the bleeding of the American economics profession; for these economists, renunciation of the DSGE is a slippery slope to the dissolution of the entire economic orthodoxy. *Après DSGE, la déluge.*

There were a few economists who had proposed that the monolithic coherence of macroeconomics and neoclassical microeconomics was a sham, but there were not accorded much respect, and were notably absent from the congressional hearings. Perhaps the most prominent was the European economist Alan Kirman. He headed a group of scholars who issued the "Dahlem report" excoriating the economics profession early on in the crisis, and explained his own position in a widely read blog post.[91] Kirman suggested that the root problem with macroeconomics was really philosophical: the vaunted foundations of the DSGE model in full neoclassical general equilibrium were illusory. First, he cited some technical results dating from the 1970s stating that full general equilibrium analysis does not allow one to make much of any aggregate generalizations from the behavior of a diverse group of neoclassical agents; and furthermore, except under some strained special circumstances, one cannot guarantee the existence of a unique or stable general equilibrium.[92] The reason that DSGE models could pretend there was a full macroeconomic equilibrium was that the fiction of a one-person economy was one of the few cases where (obviously) the individual is identical to the aggregate economy, and that existence proofs were available in that case for a unique stable equilibrium. To put it more bluntly, DSGE models were predicated upon *the sole arbitrary special case* where neoclassical microeconomics and macro could be logically reconciled. This is a conceptual sticking point that runs so deep in the orthodoxy that they rarely can openly acknowledge it. Almost every single generalization about "demand" is obviated in a truly general equilibrium model; and worse, almost all welfare statements are rendered nugatory once the existence of truly heterogeneous agents are admitted.[93] Since all orthodox macro depends heavily upon Pareto comparisons of alternative equilibria as benchmarks, such generalization would make it entirely disappear in a puff of smoke.

Instead of drawing the conclusion that the marriage of micro and macro was doomed, and the DSGE a stillbirth, the profession had chosen to pledge its troth to an *outré* mutant case and call it the whole world. It would be as though a religious fanatic arranged to live in a hermetic world composed only of Christian Scientist cyborgs, so that he need never encounter anyone who might call his faith in natural healing into question. As Kirman wrote, "both the development of the DSGE model and the efficient markets hypothesis share a common feature—despite the empirical evidence and despite their theoretical weaknesses, their development proceeded as if the criticism did not exist."[94] But isn't that the very definition of a self-confident orthodoxy?

If there had been a sophisticated outside observer, they might have insisted that all the brouhaha about jettisoning the DSGE model was a weary sideshow, since the gnawing problem the economic orthodoxy was intent on avoiding was gauging to what extent the crisis had voided the legitimacy of neoclassical microeconomics. Legions of macroeconomists were mobilized into action by the crisis not to address its dire consequences, but instead to obscure this threatening conclusion through smoke, mirrors, and legerdemain. No one who wanted to maintain their position in academia would countenance the possibility that amputation of the DSGE would result in the patient bleeding to death. So instead they promoted endless expensive consultations over the health of the DSGE—and even Congress was snookered into the pointless game.

This argument would begin by characterizing the two options promoted after the crisis hit by economists who thought of themselves as orthodox macroeconomists. The first was to insist that all that ridicule of the DSGE model was simply ignorant: all those aspects of the crisis that critics said couldn't be accommodated by the model had in fact been fully taken into account somewhere in the journal literature.[95] You want heterogeneity of agents—we've already done it. We've got models with frictions galore, and we have even coquetted with bounded irrationality. You claim there are big political divisions within macro, and that DSGE describes only neoliberal fantasies of self-regulating markets; but the "freshwater/saltwater" divide is just an illusion. The orthodoxy comes equipped with DSGE models to conform to all ideologies. We even have some versions of the model here and there that mention banks and credit.[96] All those carping complaints are baseless, and mired in an outdated impression of real business-cycle theory back in the 1980s.

This option, while commonplace, is utterly unavailing. Some of the orthodox are beginning to notice this.[97] A philosophically grounded economist would point out that the canonical DSGE assumes its canonical outlandish format in order to "save" its microfoundations, viz., the nonnegotiable prescription that macro and neoclassical microeconomics constitute one big unified theory. All these current fragmentary amendments to render the DSGE model more "realistic," or perhaps more politically acceptable to the New Keynesians, turn out to be self-contradictory, since they attempt to mitigate or "undo" the microfoundations that had been imposed from the outset. It ends up being yet one more instance of economists blithely asserting both A and not-A simultaneously. By thrusting the rabbit into the hat, then pulling it back out with a different hand, the economist merely creates a model more awkward, arbitrary, and unprepossessing than if he had just started out explicitly to model confused heterogeneous agents, dodgy banks, consciously duplicitous CDOs, informationally challenged markets, and all the rest of the usual suspects for the crisis, minus the neoclassical window dressing and professions of fealty to "equilibrium." If you allowed freedom of amendment to the DSGE in this manner, you would end up with models that violated the Lucas critique in a more egregious fashion than the earlier Keynesian models these macroeconomists love to hate. And there are the nagging worries that, as in the case of undermining existence of equilibria and welfare indicies, one ends up driving the formalism into Bedlam. Thus, a "more realistic DSGE" ends up a contradiction in terms.

The second option, the one favored by the high-profile economists dismissive of the DSGE tradition such as Robert Solow and Paul Krugman, was to roll back the clock to 1969, and pretend like the whole sequence of sordid developments leading up to DSGE never happened. Sometimes this was bruited about as a "return to Keynes," although a historian might aver that the American profession was never all that enamored of the actual Keynes and his writings.[98] Nevertheless, this latter group was extrapolating from the heady days of late 2008, when all thoughts of DSGE were nowhere to be found. As the economic historian Greg Clark put it, "The debate about the bank bailout, and the stimulus package, has all revolved around issues that are entirely at the level of Econ I. What is the multiplier from government spending? Does government spending crowd out private spending? . . . If you got an A in college Econ I, you are an expert in this debate: fully an equal of Summers and Geithner."[99]

This proposal was, if anything, even more implausible than the revision of the DSGE. Most macroeconomists would rather abandon the field than admit all their technical sophistication was superfluous, and forget the lessons they learned at the feet of Robert Lucas and Thomas Sargent. The entire field was populated by people drilled in contempt for reading Keynes, and confirmed in their convictions that those 1960s-era models, like the old-fashioned IS-LM and Phillips Curve, fully deserved to be tossed on the trash heap of history. Yet, even if some magic wand waved away generations of inertia, there was no guarantee that if you reran the tape of history one more time, starting in 1969, the neoclassical orthodoxy wouldn't just end up rejecting all those 1960s-era models all over again. For Lucas and Sargent had a point: the earlier "Keynesian" macroeconomics as it existed back then *was* logically incompatible with neoclassical microeconomic theory; and if something had to give, it would be Keynes, and not the theory of general equilibrium, at least in America. Hence, by a circuitous route we arrive once more at the lesson of this section: the real bone of contention is not the DSGE model per se, but rather the preeminence of legitimacy of neoclassical microeconomics.

One of the places where the 2010 congressional hearing missed an opportunity at gaining an understanding of the true character of the path to dominance of the DSGE was in not inviting a historian/methodologist to provide metacommentary upon the curious testimony offered by the invited participants. Not only would the missing ghost witness have provided some context for the seemingly orthogonal positions voiced by Solow, Chari, Page, and Winter, and pointed out it was no accident that no substantial alternative to neoclassical theory had a place at the table; but she might have also suggested that the Congress (or its delegated agencies) itself deserved its own fair share of the blame for the rise to intellectual monopoly of the DSGE. To suggest where such testimony might have ventured, we here cite another occasion of testimony before the *same House committee* dating back to March 1981. Then the issue was a Reagan administration drive to cut the funding of economic research from the National Science Foundation. The speaker was the Harvard economist Zvi Griliches:

It is ironic and sad that whoever came up with these cuts does not even recognize that most of the recent "conservative" ideas in economics—the importance of "rational expectations" and the impotency of conventional macroeconomic policy, the disincentive effects of various income-support programs, the magnitude of the regulatory burden, and the arguments for deregulation—all originated in, or were provided with quantitative backing by NSF supported studies.[100]

Griliches was merely stating the obvious: "legitimate" economists produce the sorts of knowledge that their patrons desire, within the trajectory of their accumulated intellectual heritage; that list of patrons includes neoliberal elements within the government, with their allies in selected ranked economics departments and think tanks. Congressmen today should not act as though the DSGE model and its precursors were somehow foisted upon unsuspecting regulators and an innocent public by imperious economists. Mostly, Americans just got what they paid for.

High Theory to the Rescue

So perhaps all those attempts to "fix" orthodox neoclassical theory that were trumpeted by journalists after the crisis really didn't actually amount to much. Whether or not it was intentional, its effect was to foster the mistaken impression in the general populace that neoclassical economists were dutifully atoning for their sins by rethinking their past premises, even though no such thing was happening. Given the very notion that Nobel winners in economics were especially or ideally primed to fundamentally transform economic thinking once they had been anointed by the glittering prize bordered on delusional, and since those very same Nobel winners loomed large in journalists' accounts for reasons already discussed, this abortive outcome was more or less a foreordained conclusion. Behavioral economics, divestment of the EMH, and tinkering with the DSGE have all been abysmal failures. Yet something agnotological was achieved: the blogosphere was set all a-twitter on irrelevant pointless topics, while journalists were set off on wild goose chases. However, I expect that readers familiar with recent economics will tend to object: How about the best and brightest of the orthodox profession who are perched a bit lower down in the hierarchy, and therefore escape the public eye? What about their ideas?

One must concede it is at least more likely that any revitalization of the neoclassical tradition would come from below, a younger and less lionized cohort, if it were to happen at all. Journalists have been misled, barking up the wrong cedar. This, I believe, is also the current attitude of the effective leaders of the orthodox profession. Hence the dance card both lengthens and becomes a bit more obscure, with numerous potential candidates for the title of Prophet of the Reformation put forth from different corners. Indeed, there are already starting to appear dedicated surveys in the form of laundry lists that simply array any "cause" someone, somewhere managed to publish; and more pertinent to current concerns, surveys of all the different ways casts of hundreds have sought to stuff finance and "failure" into orthodox macroeconomic models.[101] Fear not, dear reader; I will not attempt anything remotely approaching that here, for the following reason.

Eric Maskin, whom we have encountered previously insisting that the orthodoxy was robust, convened a "Summer School" in Jerusalem in June 2011 to showcase what he considered to be the finest exemplars of orthodox explanations of the crisis. I would ask the reader to glance at the video online;[102] and if her patience is tried by the technical lectures, just sample the roundtable identified in the footnote. What you will quickly learn from the experience is that when these Princes of Theory were forced to summarize in ten minutes their take on the causes of the crisis, all the subtle models and technical details were soon left behind, and those economists reverted to fairly simple explanations already found in the more popular press. Nobel winners generally come off comparably worse than people who actually have had some relevant experience. There are moments of clarity, when someone realizes that generalizations turn out to be much less valid and more rare than theorists often presume. Furthermore, in the period of give-and-take, one august economist bemoaned that "we" really do not know the true causes of the crisis, and another counseled humility, since five participants there were seen to proffer eight or more different causes.[103]

I believe that particular panel gets to the heart of something important about the profession: building neoclassical mathematical models in the twenty-first century is a pursuit attuned to appeal to a narrow coterie of refined tastes; one should never confuse it with providing explanations of economic events. Indeed, more often than not, it tends to appear as a post-hoc rationalization for positions/explanations often arrived at elsewhere, and by alternative avenues. That doesn't mean the models are utterly superfluous; but mostly, what they manage to demonstrate is that it is nearly impossible to shoehorn vernacular conceptions of cause into legitimate neoclassical models, and at the same time obey the orthodox "norm of closure," which means you must demonstrate existence of an equilibrium, and preferably, a unique equilibrium. Since the vernacular causes of crisis sometimes championed by these orthodox economists are themselves interesting and potentially illuminating, it might repay some brief consideration of one or two of these cases, so as not to seem that the neoclassical project is being dismissed out of hand.

A) The Leverage Cycle of John Geanakoplos

Once we realize that numerous high-status academic economists enjoy a shadow life on Wall Street, then the question presents itself: Doesn't direct hands-on experience count for anything in the economics profession? While many such economists prize theoretical fidelity over practical acuity, there are a few more venturesome souls. One such person is John Geanakoplos, James Tobin Professor of Economics at Yale. Geanakoplos is known for his broad tastes in theory, having spent substantial intervals at the Santa Fe Institute, which was at one time a stomping ground for the avant-garde in mathematical economics. But more pertinently, he has enjoyed a long stint on Wall Street as well, serving first as a managing director at Kidder Peabody from 1990 to 1995, and then as one of the founding partners of the hedge fund Ellington Capital Management from 1995 to the present. (Again we observe the tight coupling of finance and the commanding heights of the economic profession described in chapter 4.) Ellington Capital is a hedge fund that specialized in mortgage-backed securities, so it seems safe to say Geanakoplos had a ringside seat at the grand defalcation that led to the current crisis. And indeed, when he talks in the vernacular about what has gone wrong in the financial industry, he tends to sound a bit like Hyman Minsky, which means he makes a fair bit of sense.[104] However, his academic persona is one of the elite among general-equilibrium theorists of the purest water: so the aspect of his personality that draws our attention is—how does he manage to reconcile the two?

Geanakoplos had a leg up on other economists because he did notice some pathologies of the mortgage market earlier on, and therefore had begun to concoct models well before the debacle of Bear Stearns and Lehman. Indeed, his Street connections were so good that when the crisis broke, the *Wall Street Journal* was quick off the blocks to anoint him with the title of New Orthodox Seer. Mostly, he did not tread the well-worn paths we have already summarized, such as awkward representative agent models, or retread neoclassical synthesis models. Interestingly, he eschews much of existing finance theory: "I don't believe in fundamental value; I think different people may have different views about the value of an asset." As we might expect from a consistent neoclassical, he also repudiates his Yale colleague Robert Shiller's appeals to irrational exuberance and the madness of crowds, suggesting Shiller did not avail himself of exploration of what was going on "beneath" the mortgage bubble. What this means is he is willing to consider market structure as a candidate causal mechanism; this is combined with a penchant for having heterogeneous agents in his models, which sometimes just means the old trick of inserting "noise traders" to jostle the über-rational neoclassical agents, but in other work, agents that have substantially different utility functions.[105] Because the models are still of the "general equilibrium" genus, tractability is imposed in all sorts of arbitrary fashions: there is only one "consumption good" but many "financial assets," time is finite but ticked off in discrete periods with "information" arriving between the ticks, news is either "good" or "'bad," expectations are old-fashioned von Neumann-Morgenstern expected utility . . . These are the sorts of jury-rigged assumptions we have come to expect to make the jerry-built neoclassical model give determinate results. What renders his models of the so-called leverage cycle of some passing interest is his explicit attempt to render both the interest rate and the degree of leverage as endogenous to the model, such that leverage degree and asset prices exhibit positive covariance.[106] This permits him to tell a story where control of the interest rate turns out to be insufficient to control the aggregate magnitude of borrowing in an economy, much less the degree of financial fragility, obviating the usual simplistic neoclassical models of savings and investment. The reason that prices go up when leverage goes up in the Geanakoplos model is that "optimists" always borrow up to the hilt, so in the eventuality they can increase their leverage, they will unreservedly use it to purchase more assets. In his model, "the leverage cycle simply asserts there is too much leverage in normal times and therefore too high asset prices and there is too little leverage in crisis times and therefore too low asset prices. The cycle recurs over and over again."[107] In his view the mortgage bubble was only half the story; the rise of shadow banking provides the necessary other half. Geanakoplos believes this permits him to reconcile the ahistorical laws of Walras with the historical specificities of the last few decades.

While the focus on procyclical movement of leverage and asset prices is an important departure from much of orthodox models, the commitment to Walrasian general equilibrium so hampers the formalism that good intentions ended up in Bedlam. Geanakoplos likes to phrase his commentary in terms of "cycles," but in fact, general equilibrium forces him to posit separate and unconnected sequential states of equilibrium, driven in a Rube Goldberg fashion by the arbitrarily sequenced arrival of asset issuance→"news"→valuation. Each state along the way is in "equilibrium," as defined by constrained optimization and market clearing. Because everything is *always already* in equilibrium, the only reason anything changes is the deus ex machina imposed from outside by the model builder. Worse, the sequence itself is completely arbitrary, dictated more by the math than by anything that happens in the world: for instance, each player has only one chance to issue assets, is proscribed from trading them on secondary markets, and consumption can happen only at the initial issuance and at the end of time.[108]

It seems that, however proud he may be of hewing to Walrasian heuristics, the suite of models he has constructed rarely do much to actually illuminate the actual crisis and aftermath. After all, if the different configurations of leverage and asset prices are each in "equilibrium," then there is no warrant for recourse to the language of prices and leverage being "too high" or "too low." At each Goldilocks state of the world, they are "just right" for all participants. Geanakoplos seems to have forgotten that there is no "unemployment," no unused resources, and no distress in Walrasian general equilibrium. The market always perfectly reflects the desires of all the agents; the only reason anything ever changes is that the godlike puppetmaster forces parameter alterations from another astral plane. Further, at least Minsky proposed a reason why leverage would increase over time: big players tend to shade or violate previous rules. Nobody ever breaks a rule in a Geanakoplos model. The closest he ever gets to realizing this is when he moves his comments outside the formalism to discuss actual institutional events in the history of the crisis: "the market engineered its own negative shock by creating credit default swaps, which started [MBS] prices down. Had the CDS been actively traded from the beginning, prices might never have got so high."[109] In effect, he finally defaults to the hoary old Arrow-Debreu excuse for "market failures": markets were unaccountably incomplete, and then they suddenly weren't. With a full complement of high-tech financial wizardry, the crisis would presumably never have happened, or so he seems to suggest.

There is one more reason Geanakoplos should be a little more wary about his own model. In public presentations, he suggests that it was the lenders who bore the onus of responsibility for the leverage cycle this time around; and consequently, in a just world, they should submit to substantial writedowns of principal to reboot the economy back to sustainable leverage levels. But he forgets that his model tells us excessive leverage is a product of supply *and* demand; keeping that in focus, it can just as easily underwrite the NTC story that it was as much the fault of irresponsible shady deadbeat borrowers who discovered a way to game the system and wallow in debt. The model is incapable of fingering culprits: no one here but us blameless Walrasian agents. As Markus Brunnermeier once is reported to have said about Geanakoplos, "His work assumes that the leverage cycle is bad, but gives little guidance to what extent regulators should control it."[110] And nothing in his model acknowledges that once Bernanke rescued the banks, they would end up essentially owning the government, rather than the other way around. The commitment to adhere to Walrasian heuristics can easily undermine his leftish politics, whatever the inclination of the particular economist.

B) Paul Krugman Conjures the Shade of Hyman Minsky

In this next model presentation, I cheat a little bit by returning to Paul Krugman via his younger collaborators. For the most part, my previous characterization of Krugman as someone who wishes to return to 1969 as if nothing else had happened in macro in the interim is basically correct, with the minor proviso that he has intermittently seemed to begrudgingly reach out to some strains of heterodox thought, under the guideline that the enemy of my enemy should be treated as a friend (although maybe in the way "friend" is treated as a verb in Facebook). Of course, he has always been candid about which side of the divide he really belongs:

> I like to think I am more open-minded about alternative approaches to economics than most, but I am basically a maximization-and-equilibrium kind of guy. Indeed, I am quite fanatical about defending the relevance of standard economic models ... I won't say I am entirely happy with the state of economics. But let us be honest: I

have done very well within the world of conventional economics. I have pushed the envelope, but not broken it, and have received very widespread acceptance for my ideas. What this means is that I may have more sympathy for standard economics than most of you . . . Methodological individualism is of the essence . . . I guess it is no secret that even John Kenneth Galbraith, still the public's idea of a great economist, looks to most serious economists like an intellectual dilettante who lacks the patience for hard thinking.[111]

In an era proud of its fearless "hard thinking," where heterodox economics is being stifled, it would perhaps become a bit more understandable that a few younger economists, seeking to construct models that would better address aspects of the crisis than those we have covered above, might gravitate toward collaboration with Krugman as a way to preserve some orthodox credentials. What is even more interesting is the way Krugman, given all his open allegiance to the orthodoxy, has apparently felt impelled to grapple with the legacy of Hyman Minsky since 2008. The first sign that something like this was going on was in a lecture series Krugman delivered at the LSE in June 2009, the third of which was titled "The Night they Re-read Minsky."[112] Paraphrasing, Krugman there aired his opinion that what had been done in macroeconomics over the past thirty years had been "spectacularly useless at best, positively harmful at worst." However, many journalists had been pointing to Minsky's work as an alternative, and Krugman conceded his core insight had been spectacularly right, concerning the dynamic of progressively increased leverage setting the stage for crisis. Nevertheless, Krugman raised what he saw as a definitive objection: Minsky had rejected neoclassical micro theory, and Krugman highlighted his rejection of marginal productivity theories of distribution as particularly unforgivable. Then he began to pine for a day when his favorite Men in White Hats, the behavioral economists, would ride into town and do what Minsky did, but in a more acceptable idiom.

Of course, as we have suggested above, it was a forlorn hope that day would ever arrive. Perhaps Krugman realized something similar, because in the subsequent year he teamed up with Gauti Eggertsson to author what he advertised as a "Fisher-Minsky-Koo" model. The problem Krugman hoped to address was to convince the reader that in the throes of a deleveraging crisis, when financial failures induced everyone to try to shed debt, there was room for the government to improve the situation by taking on substantial volumes of new debt. In his books, this supposed "Keynesian" solution had to map into the old-fashioned IS-LM model of a "liquidity trap," something he had long trumpeted as the paradigm for "depression economics," which he interpreted to mean that the supply and demand for loanable funds could be equilibrated only at a negative interest rate. Eggertsson and he sought to render these ideas more acceptable to the orthodoxy through resort to a standard New Keynesian model with the wrinkle that there were posited two different agents, and the "impatient agent borrows from the patient agent, but is subject to a debt limit. If this debt limit is, for some reason, suddenly reduced, the impatient agent is forced to cut spending; if the deleveraging required is large enough, the result can easily be to push the economy up against the zero lower bound . . . [This is appended to] a sticky-price model in which the deleveraging shock affects output instead of, or as well as, prices." Recall, "New Keynesians" get unemployment out of their neoclassical models by throwing a little sand in the gears—something Keynes himself rejected.[113]

There are a number of ironies about this paper. The first is, after saying such rude things about contemporary macroeconomics, Krugman ends up writing down a set of equations not so very different from those he had disparaged. Two simple log utility equations, Euler equations, divergences from long-run steady states, Taylor rules, the natural rate of interest, nominal prices but nary a bank or fiat money to be seen; perhaps one would be forgiven in thinking they were reading John Taylor, not Paul Krugman! Only the glaring absence of rational expectations (which would serve to neutralize all the results he strove so hard to derive) is a signal that someone is not completely toeing the line. Second, the only function of the interest rate in the model is to equate saving and investment, possibly carried out by two different people. This is a construct Keynes explicitly repudiated in the *General Theory*—so much for steadfast fealty to the Master. Finally, and most egregiously from our current perspective, none of this has any relationship to what Hyman Minsky wrote. Minsky wanted to identify a systematic source of instability in the capitalist economy in the financial sector, involving the need to continuously augment leverage in order to realize profit over time. By contrast, Krugman portrays the crisis as an unfortunate glitch due to flaws and frictions in an otherwise ideally functioning system, which are made manifest as a thoroughly arbitrary debt limit imposed upon the "impatient" agent by (God? The model fairy? The meddling government? Impetuous insufficiency of agent imagination? Too much sludge in the pipes?).

Our purpose is not to take the model apart, but rather to ask: Why pretend that truly heterodox ideas are becoming incorporated into the orthodoxy, when patently they are not? Why drag Minsky's name into this, demeaning the deceased? Why not just call a spade a spade: here is one more little toy model that wouldn't pass muster among the macroeconomic elite of the orthodoxy, and struggles mightily to derive what you could get just as easily out of an undergraduate IS-LM model, with pretty much the same level of disdain for logical consistency. Even with the Krugman imprimatur, no one will ever use this model as the basis for a "new economics," much less policy justification. No, it seems the only point of the exercise is to insist that there is nothing worth paying attention to outside the neoclassical orthodoxy; "we the elect" have said everything there is worthwhile to say, and absorbed every idea worth considering. There Is No Alternative.

Of course, if the profession expels anyone who takes Minsky seriously, and never publishes them in any ranked journal, soon there will be no one left who can credibly challenge TINA, or perturb the complacency of Krugman's self-congratulatory stance on his catholic tastes. The citadel is impregnable.

Hard-core Neoliberal Agnotology

I have just frog-marched the reader through some turgid conceptual critique of the last few years of orthodox neoclassical models of the crisis. It has not been pretty. Perhaps you have come to suspect that much of the sound and fury over the intellectual response of the economics profession to the crisis has been bootless and counterproductive. Even if you think that the history of economic thought should pertain to an assessment of the crisis, you might be inclined to wonder: Why bother with this mainstream stuff? Possibly you recognize that I have consciously chosen as candidates for consideration those vanguard deviations among the orthodox that have been most widely taken up by journalists and the blogosphere in the aftermath of the crisis; these, therefore, are the Potemkin controversies that have sucked up most of the intellectual oxygen in the public agora. However, what may have been felt missing from this tale of woe is evidence of the causal story proffered at the beginning of the chapter, namely, that the ensuing confusion serves the purposes of the Neoliberal Thought Collective in fostering doubt and confusion in pursuit of its political objectives. Sure, we may have encountered some individual MPS members and think tank denizens in the course of this chapter; but, after all, the odds of that happening are pretty high whenever one perambulates among the contemporary orthodox economics profession. The impartial spectator interjects: there are no Wizards lurking behind the curtain orchestrating this *ballet mécanique*, or so it seems. Perhaps what we have encountered here instead is just the garden-variety wishful thinking, stodgy cognitive conservatism, and discombobulated ripostes of any corporate entity that has endured a shock of the magnitude of the current crisis.

Decorum and prudence dictate we should invariably extend charitable interpretations to our opponents, avoid fractious and wanton approbation, and abjure from conspiracy theories. Yet the reason we need to invoke agnotology here is that even some figures in the mainstream media have come around to openly speculate that economic analyses of the crisis have been manipulated for dark motives for quite some while now. I shall here quote two impeccable sources. The first is the *New York Times* financial reporter Joe Nocera:

> So this is how the Big Lie works. You begin with a hypothesis that has a certain surface plausibility. You find an ally whose background suggests that he's an "expert"; out of thin air, he devises "data." You write articles in sympathetic publications, repeating the data endlessly; in time, some of these publications make your cause their own. Like-minded congressmen pick up your mantra and invite you to testify at hearings. You're chosen for an investigative panel related to your topic. When other panel members, after inspecting your evidence, reject your thesis, you claim that they did so for ideological reasons. This, too, is repeated by your allies. Soon, the echo chamber you created drowns out dissenting views; even presidential candidates begin repeating the Big Lie.[114]

My second exhibit comes from Paul Krugman:

> Basically, Joe is arriving where I've been since 2000: what's going on in the discussion of economic affairs (and other matters, like justifications for war) isn't just a case where different people look at the same facts but reach different conclusions. Instead, we're looking at a situation in which one side of the debate just isn't interested in the truth, in which alleged scholarship is actually just propaganda.
>
> Saying this, of course, gets you declared "shrill," denounced as partisan; you're supposed to pretend that we're having a civilized

discussion between people with good intentions. And you're supposed to match each attack on Republicans with an attack on Democrats, as if the mendacity were equal on both sides. Sorry, but it isn't. Democrats aren't angels; they're human and sometimes corrupt—but they don't operate a lie machine 24/7 the way modern Republicans do. Welcome to my world, Joe.[115]

Now, these people are not your usual blowhard bloggers. However, their recriminations do tend to resemble the earlier hubbub about a "Republican War on Science," and are deficient in many of the same respects.[116] The phenomenon they excoriate and try to pin on the Republican Party is far more elaborate and profound than any party-political dispute or local Machiavellian turn: how can there be a "Republican" plot when it is a worldwide phenomenon? Indeed, many NTC members reserve their purest disdain for card-carrying Republican Party figures. Surely a few think tanks inside the Beltway cannot, of themselves, paralyze our minds 24/7! The resort to the language of the Big Lie also suggests comparison with Cold War propaganda; but we have repeatedly insisted herein that conventional notions of propaganda do not begin to grasp the current phenomenon.

The understanding of politics displayed by these writers is far too parochial to stand up to the pervasive character of the global crisis. It is distressing that these writers, frequently champions of hard-nosed, tough-minded "analysis of reality," fall short when it comes to serious analysis of the multipronged efforts to steer public discourse in certain targeted directions, the incongruous swerves that so vex their sensibilities. Perhaps worse, it seems evident someone like Krugman might be more than a little disconcerted to be told that he is as much a cog in this larger machine as John Cochrane, or any other bête noire. That is why we had to insist in chapter 2 that the central doctrine of neoliberalism is the unquestioned superiority of the marketplace of ideas, but conjoined to a notion of the market that requires *endless vigilance and interventions*; sequentially that in chapter 4 that neoclassical economics has progressively come under the sway of neoliberalism, whether it can acknowledge it or not; and even in the previous parts of this chapter, that Krugman's economic analysis offers little respite from the run-of-the-mill superficial responses to the crisis found in the rest of the profession. We now need to consult the tenets of agnotology to begin to understand how the Neoliberal Thought Collective efficiently manufactures both knowledge and ignorance concerning the crisis.

Agnotology takes many forms. Sometimes, it is little more than a minor sideshow at the grand cacophony of the Interwebs. For instance, in 2011, Sarah Palin got caught on video confusing Paul Revere with some cartoon figures mimicking the Founding Fathers, and it rapidly went viral; some of her Tea Party acolytes then got into the act, revising the Paul Revere entry on Wikipedia to conform to her garbled recollections. This is the poor man's pocket version of the neoliberal creation of alternate realities. Other times, it involves descent into accusations of conflicts of interest in ways that serve only to distract the audience from the actual interests at play in the particular incident: here one might point to Gretchen Morgenson and Josh Rosner, authors of *Reckless Endangerment*, insinuating that Joseph Stiglitz was paid by Fannie Mae and Freddie Mac in order to defend their activities.[117] But the practice of agnotology that has long-term consequences operates at a much deeper level of intellectual activity. It ventures far beyond the discrediting of this or that individual; it seeks to destabilize the things we were predisposed to take for granted, and insinuate a sharply targeted narrative explanation as one of those default presumptions. This does not appear to the public as overt strident propaganda; rather, it presents itself as liberating, expanding the cloistered space of sanctioned explanation in an era of wrangling and indecision. There are two steps to this procedure: one is the effort to pump excess noise into the public discussion of appropriate frames within which to approach the controversy; the second is to provide the echoic preferred target narrative as coming from many different sanctioned sources at once; ubiquity helps pave the way for inevitability. To make this work, one must do both: amplify the impression of indecision and doubt on the part of the elect, while sharpening the preferred narrative as making a demand upon our attention. Doubt is their product, but eventual manufactured consensus is their profit.

It is therefore my contention that there is method to the madness, goal orientation behind the gallimaufry laid out in this chapter. I would suggest that much of the brouhaha documented above ends up being subservient to the first movement of the agnotological playbook. Whatever the individual motivations, the plangent exculpations of the orthodox economists serve mostly to ratchet up the levels of doubt and skepticism in the public mind, and lure unsuspecting bloggers into ineffectual disputes that lead nowhere fast. The folderol over the DSGE model or rationality or the EMH just prepares the ground for the implantation of one or more clear and simple neoliberal alternatives, covered in the remainder of this chapter. Of course, most of the technical topics covered herein do not lend themselves to direct affiliation between abstract theory and the special pleading of a particular powerful cadre (although the relation of the DSGE model to the patronage of the Federal Reserve and European central banks might be a counterexample). These sagas of the ineffectual "reform" of orthodoxy might be contrasted with instances where the unabashed promotion of the doctrine that the manufacture of ever more baroque derivatives must be framed as abstract "financial innovation," a force of nature on a par with more conventional technological innovation in the physical sphere, deserving utter freedom and profound obeisance, a meme stridently promoted by the Ewing Marion Kauffman Foundation, an openly certified neoliberal outfit.[118] There the lifelines are visible for all to see. Theoretical departures like behavioral economics or fortified DSGE are rather more obscure in their determinations. The connections might instead operate at a few steps' remove, such as the EMH indirectly expressing the worldview of the neoliberals, because it translates Hayek's central doctrine of the marketplace of ideas into the stochastic formalisms of neoclassical finance theory. However, behavioral economics and the DSGE model and Krugman's "Fisher-Minsky" model are not generally the sort of ideas that, on their face, readily lend themselves to special pleading and shady sponsors; they may not even initially appear especially neoliberal in orientation.

Agnotological precepts suggest that the orthodox economics profession has been useful for neoliberal projects because it fills the sphere of public discourse concerning the crisis with excess noise and doubt. As long as it promulgates ineffectual "revisions" to core doctrine and keeps people distracted, looking for novelty (that will assuage their fears) where none is to be found, confusing even insiders about whether the crisis warrants changing the orientation of economics, then the NTC is getting value for money. The only thing that would give them pause is the genesis of a serious antineoliberal doctrine that began to draw the allegiance of significant numbers of economists, posing a real challenge to the neoliberal ascendancy. So far, nothing of the sort has happened.

What might be the evidence for the orthodox economics profession fulfilling this agnotological function? One place to look would involve the question of the grounds upon which the orthodox economics profession has managed to widen the pay gap between itself and almost every other discipline in the modern university during a period of

Discipline	1980–81	1985–86	1991–92	1996–97	2001–02	2005–06	2009–10
Fine arts: visual and performing	-8.8%	-9.6%	-7.9%	-9.7%	-11.1%	-12.2%	-12.4%
Education	-4.0%	-8.0%	-1.2%	-0.8%	-2.5%	-3.8%	-4.3%
Foreign language and literature	0.9%	-1.8%	-1.5%	0.5%	-3.9%	-4.5%	-4.1%
Communications	-3.3%	-6.7%	2.6%	1.9%	-2.9%	-3.3%	-3.2%
Philosophy	2.3%	-4.8%	2.0%	1.1%	-2.9%	0.0%	2.1%
Library science	-1.5%	-0.6%	9.9%	6.6%	3.5%	-2.1%	3.6%
Mathematics	7.6%	4.4%	11.0%	11.5%	6.8%	6.8%	7.2%
Psychology	5.0%	1.6%	9.5%	9.7%	8.3%	9.0%	8.9%
Physical sciences	7.7%	8.0%	14.9%	14.5%	12.8%	12.1%	12.9%
All-discipline average (including medical)	4.8%	5.1%	13.3%	13.9%	12.2%	12.0%	13.4%
Social sciences	4.8%	3.2%	9.0%	8.7%	9.2%	14.1%	16.8%
Health professions and related sciences	20.3%	19.8%	34.3%	36.4%	31.3%	18.1%	18.9%
Engineering	8.1%	14.3%	29.0%	27.8%	24.0%	24.3%	25.2%
Computer and information sciences	13.4%	17.6%	32.2%	28.1%	28.7%	27.5%	28.4%
Economics	13.9%	11.3%	28.4%	25.7%	26.4%	32.4%	41.2%
Business administration and management	11.4%	15.2%	33.8%	38.7%	40.8%	46.5%	50.9%
Law and legal studies	33.2%	41.0%	54.2%	58.4%	53.5%	54.0%	59.5%

Table 5.1: How Much More (or Less) Full Professors Earned, by Discipline, than Average Full Professor of English Language and Literature, 1980–81 to 2009–10

Source: "Faculty Salary Survey by Discipline", Office of Istitutional Research and Information Management, Oklahoma State University retrenchment and austerity following the 2007–2008 crash, as demonstrated in Table 5.1. How can it be a straightforward return to human capital? If the economics profession has exhibited a glaring deficit of inventiveness concerning crisis explanations, recycling decrepit themes as novel insights, as we have argued here, then what can account for the lavish expanding remuneration? Is the marginal orthodox economist really that much more valuable than one more molecular biologist? It can't be inertia, plus the veiled threat that they could always abscond to the (contracting) private sector for a better salary . . .

The most plausible answer lies instead in the passive recruitment of the profession for agnotological purposes. Whether they realize it or not, the kabuki of ineffectual disputations over irrelevant models is one of the more effective interventions in the public sphere, because it distracts attention from far more threatening prospective explanations. These include: the possibility that the financial sector has evolved to the point of cannibalization of the rest of the economy; or that the economics profession played an enabling role in inventing and justifying the most Rube Goldberg of securitizations and alterations of regulations; that neoliberal agnotology has filtered down to the very statistics everyone consults in order to make sense of economic events; that there is no such thing as the market, but only an array of different markets of varying capacities; that this ecology of markets bears inherent tendencies toward niche collapse that undermine system operation; and that "free trade" is the cover story for the policies of a class of the cosmopolitan rich who believe they can evade all local consequences of system breakdown. Perhaps it even exists to facilitate the full-spectrum neoliberal approach to policy discussed in chapter 6.

Thus the injection of surplus noise into public discourse concerning the crisis is Phase One of the agnotological project, and its performance is a substantial justification for the otherwise unaccountable contemporary bounty of the bulk of the orthodox economics profession. But that is only half the story. The other half is amenable to being documented much more precisely.

Phase Two materializes when economists openly struggle with the contradiction between beseeching the public to place their Trust in the Market and insisting the public Trust the Economists. It was made starkly manifest in at least two incidents during the crisis: the public justification of the TARP bailout, and the subsequent whitewash of the Federal Crisis Inquiry Commission.

In both instances it involved the fabrication and promulgation of an alternative narrative concerning the crisis; nicely honed and simplified so it can fit on a placard, or a stump speech teleprompter; one that has the fingerprints of the NTC all over it.

Of course, it was all the government's fault.

Repent, Harlecons, Cried the History Man

Chapter 2 made some effort to insist that neoliberals don't really hate the government; it is just politically convenient for them to demonize it when it suits their purposes. It turns out to be doubly convenient for them to tar and feather government when some prior governmental/market innovations that have gone awry may have grown out of their earlier neoliberal occupations of the very same government—say, for instance, the privatization of some previously nonprofit governmental entity; in such instances, politics means never having to say you are sorry. This suggests that neoliberal stories concerning the crisis don't develop organically out of any particular economic theory, but instead grow out of the proleptic (but dependable and time-tested) neoliberal playbook: attack the legitimacy of government→assume power→impose various neoliberal market/government "reforms"→wait for failures→rinse→repeat. Phase One of the whitewash cycle therefore sets the perimeters within which any neoliberal crisis explanation must operate; but that still leaves the details open for negotiations. As we observed in chapter 1, the New York meeting of the Mont Pèlerin Society was an early arena for negotiations over what shapes the party line might assume; evidently there was little agreement or focus at that stage. Perhaps this had something to do with the wise Mont Pèlerin precept that general principles often have to be tailored and adjusted to fit local political circumstances. Nevertheless, a full-spectrum response was collated and normalized, based on previous doctrines enumerated in chapter 2. The lyrics might be different, but the hymn remains the same.

We shall now set about to observe the catechism in action in the genesis of the now-dominant neoliberal accounts of the crisis. Not unexpectedly, "government" was fingered as the culprit in all successful variations; but the detailed narratives have been recast to appeal to particular nations or geographical areas. In the United States, the neoliberal touchstone has become "Blame it all on Freddie Mac and Fannie Mae," whereas in Europe the cry has become "Blame it all on the PIIGS and Brussels bureaucrats." If tempers grow heated, blame it all on technological change and its rancid doppelganger, financial innovation. When all else fails, blame it on a dead man (John Maynard

Keynes) or blame it on China (global imbalances). Never, never, ever concede for a moment that the crisis was created and nurtured by market participants themselves.

A) Flipping Over the TARP[119]

We have briefly recounted the preliminary response of the neoliberal wing of the economics profession to the Troubled Asset Rescue Plan in the United States in the previous chapter; but here we subject the technical rationale of the program to scrutiny. In particular, we shall examine the circumstances surrounding the promotion (and subsequent demise) of the idea that the government could deliver us from financial calamity by devising a novel auction to remove "toxic assets" from the balance sheets of large banks. Most relevant from the present perspective was that the role of volunteer hazmat team was to be played by a small band of "market designers"—game theorists and experimental economists who were experts in the construction and deployment of specialized auctions.

The basic narrative goes like this in summary: In a little-noted sideshow to the catastrophe, economic theorists were called in to assist with the justification and passage of the Troubled Asset Relief Program in the confusion of late 2008. However, the U.S. Treasury rapidly decided it did not require their services, and in response, they turned their wrath against the TARP, all the while insisting it always lay within their power to rectify the whole bloody crisis, for a fee. In order to execute this reversal, market designers needed to modulate their public message, initially stressing the need to trust the market designers to correct flaws or imperfections with markets, yet subsequently, they altered their stance to insist upon the need to trust markets themselves as against the inept government. While speaking as public intellectuals, in retrospect they were persistently misrepresenting the nature of the problems involved, primarily due to strategic considerations of their own private profit. The net result turned out to be an infusion of surplus public confusion in an already chaotic situation. This is what agnotology in the crisis looks like.

The plan to run an auction for toxic assets originated in the immediate aftermath of the March 2008 Bear Stearns collapse, and from the conviction among market participants and some Treasury and Fed staff that it would be wise to have a plan to "pull off the shelf" in the case of another Bear Stearns–type emergency. Following several rounds of discussion between staff at the Treasury and the New York and D.C.

Feds, Neel Kashkari and Phillip Swagel drafted a memo entitled "Break the Glass: Bank Recapitalization Plan."[120] In this memo, Kashkari and Swagel identified alternative emergency measures, argued in favor of using asset auctions to remove mortgage-related assets from bank balance sheets, and set forth a timeline for completing the asset purchases. Secretary of the Treasury Henry Paulson would eventually second their judgment to purchase on ideological grounds, but at that juncture essentially ordered that the plan be set aside.[121]

So when the emergency did eventually arrive, following the September collapse of Lehman Brothers, breaking the glass was something Paulson and the Federal Reserve chairman, Ben Bernanke, attempted to do. They began to make rounds to convince members of congress of the need for an emergency asset purchase plan, solicited an auction plan from the New York Fed, and approached academic market designers to fill in the details.[122] But they almost immediately began to encounter difficulties. Bernanke gave a performance at Congress for which he was "much ridiculed": during a hearing on the impending asset purchase plan, Bernanke laid out a plan to purchase troubled assets from banks at "close to the hold-to-maturity price," a slippery magnitude that was highly disputable, but certainly meant paying prices much higher than currently prevailed on asset markets.[123] Serious criticisms immediately surfaced: Didn't this purchase plan just boil down to giving Wall Street a bailout? Then why bother with the circumlocutions? Given the nature of the emergency, was it realistic to believe that a relatively small asset purchase plan would do the job? While these objections were gaining intensity in the press, the Treasury worked behind closed doors to craft the original "Break the Glass" memo into a legislative proposal. The initial effort, which totaled only about 2⅔ pages, was viewed by many as so insubstantial as to be insulting; the House voted down the initial bill based on the proposal. Clearly the plan was in jeopardy.

It was in this context—with skepticism about the asset auctions abounding, and financial disaster looming—that market designers were recruited to fulfill a public role in the debate over TARP. Market designers soon found themselves in the public spotlight when Bernanke and Swagel referred to market designers' expertise when fielding concerns about the prices to be paid in their plan, and in short order two of the academic mechanism designers approached by the Treasury, Lawrence Ausubel and Peter Cramton, emerged publicly to defend the legitimacy of the asset purchase plan.[124] They publicly claimed they could design an auction that would improve upon the Treasury's approach in the sense of establishing lower "competitive market prices," a prospect that did not sound very salubrious from the standpoint of Bernanke, Paulson, and the bevy of Wall Street lobbyists who had already gone on the record with their concerns about the consequences of driving prices too low.[125] If these microeconomists were to be politically useful, they had better manage to get on the same page as the Treasury officials and the Fed. Ausubel and Cramton responded by creatively interpreting "competitive market prices" to mean prices that were "reasonably close to value," by which they meant basically the same thing as Bernanke's "hold-to-maturity" prices.[126] The plan purported to allow for the Treasury to manipulate its demand for securities, thereby manipulating the price paid, while preserving the ability to claim that the prices paid were still "market" prices, at least in some sense, an intention that has been subsequently acknowledged:

> A concern of many at the Treasury was that the reverse auctions would indicate prices for MBSs so low as to appear to make other companies appear to be insolvent if their balance sheets were revalued to the auction results. This could easily be handled within the reverse auction framework, however . . . we could experiment with the share of each security to bid on; the more we purchased, the higher, presumably, would be the price that resulted.[127]

The claim that, armed with the right technique, the Treasury could in effect "go the market one better," while not baldly implausible, did look like they were claiming that the circle could, in fact, be squared: the government could pay greater than market prices, and yet the act of doing so could be rendered "transparent" by the notional market setup.[128] But to the extent that it was possible to ignore this little detail, that would pave the way toward accepting the Treasury's position: issues ranging from executive compensation to reform of the structural composition of the financial sector to direct banishment of certain formats of derivatives immediately fell by the wayside. At a time when the many well-organized economists were arguing against the TARP, as documented in chapter 4, the endorsement of these market designers was surely welcome.[129]

According to the market designers, if you understood the crisis from the correct microeconomic perspective you would come to realize how necessary their intervention was. Market designers claimed the problem stemmed from an absence of liquidity, not—crucially— pervasive insolvency. In their frame, banks possessed a variety of assets,

some worthless but most others pretty valuable, and it was the inability
to distinguish between the two that caused the crisis. By purchasing
these assets, the government would reestablish liquidity, not merely by
removing toxic assets from the banks' balance sheets, but by releasing
information that would establish the assets' true values. One immediate consequence of this view was that the imposing magnitude of the
toxic asset problem was not necessarily worrisome, nor was the possibility that the TARP program would be unable to remove the vast
majority of the toxic assets from banks' balance sheets:

> The "losers" are not left high and dry. By determining the market
> clearing price, the auction increases liquidity . . . The auction has
> effectively aggregated information about the security's value. This
> price information is the essential ingredient needed to restore the
> secondary market for mortgage backed securities.[130]

What mattered, they insisted, was "information": information would
summon forth funds from private actors, thereby thawing frozen
secondary markets. The basis for this claim was that the assets to be
purchased were "common," or objectively, valued. According to
conventional theory, one should expect in such cases that purchasers of
such assets should find themselves misjudging this objective value,
resulting in a kind of undesirable behavior called the "winner's curse."
Market designers believed they could mitigate such problems by
designing markets that efficiently aggregate information, and thereby
assist market participants to discover the true value of items being sold.
Although one way of reading the market designers' argument was that
one should generally trust existing markets to do the best job of aggregating information about assets, there were specific flaws (resulting
from the nature of the commodity exchanged) that necessitated a suitably trained economist to provide a helping visible hand. In
circumstances like these, with the largest financial firms in the nation
perched on the precipice of default, the stakes were dangerously high,
making their participation all the more crucial.

However, in practice, the auction design process would encounter
serious difficulties. The Treasury had initially selected as a baseline
auction a design that "although undoubtedly sub-optimal in the
formal mechanism design sense, it was deemed simple, transparent,
and robust enough to be implemented rapidly and effectively."[131] In a
crisis, especially important was the speed of deployment, since from
the perspective of the "Break the Glass" memo, the Treasury had

already lost a week due to the House's rejection of the first version of TARP. Unfortunately, the market designers responded to the Treasury's call for assistance by submitting widely incompatible designs for the auctions, necessitating the Treasury to decide between the rival analyses. By itself, the presence of rival proposals was not an insuperable obstacle, but complicating matters was that from the perspective of the Treasury one could not tell on paper what the best auction form was.[132] For example, one dispute broke out over whether to run an "open" or "sealed bid" auction. This had historically been one of the most basic issues that market designers grapple with, and, yet, one proposal called for an "open" auction, yet another for a "closed" auction. Which one was to be preferred was supposed to turn on which mechanism did the best job of aggregating information, but theory provided neither guidance about which form was better, nor guidance about whether either form would bring new bits of useful information into the market. There were an enormous number of distinct heterogeneous securities (more than 23,000 types), but apparently there was no reliable price information from either markets (which had ground to a halt) or standard simulation methods (which had proved unreliable). Therefore, there was no reason for any market participant to generalize from information released by getting the price "right" for one security to the thousands of others available. The market designers placed in charge of implementing the auction acknowledged, "the relevant issues could not be addressed directly with economic theory."[133] So much for the bracing clarification of microeconomics. The dispute over auction forms raised a second, more serious problem: there was no good reason to believe that the auctions would do what the market designers had said they would: namely, summon a chain of events that would eventually bring the economy out of crisis by, in the first place, aggregating dispersed information. After all, no work had been done previously by market designers on how to fix a collapsing economy.

Since market designers could identify no single optimal auction, the Treasury decided to set up two teams and asked them to more fully develop their proposals. Whereas the "Break the Glass" memo called for announcement of auction terms within two weeks of TARP's passage, followed by the commencement of auctions in another two weeks, it took until the end of October to even manage to narrow down the candidates to two alternatives. Projections at that point had the first auctions beginning no earlier than December. Some of the Treasury staff became increasingly nervous about performance, regarding the auction design process as a "science experiment" run amok: market designers had always insisted that the performance of the auctions was sensitive to even seemingly minor changes in rules, and yet they could not even agree about how rule changes would affect performance. They wanted to implement both of the alternative auction forms and use the first set of auctions as trial runs, a prospect that surely failed to inspire confidence. And this in the midst of a collapsing world economy.

Meanwhile, markets themselves had turned against the TARP plan. Things initially had started out well for the Treasury. The first announcement of the toxic asset purchase plan led immediately (on September 18) to a gain on the Dow of 410 points, followed by another 369 points the very next day. Paulson observed that the Treasury's plan had "acted like a tonic to the markets." Unfortunately, matters went from bad to worse to catastrophic over the course of the next two weeks, at least if one was guided by the stars of markets. The Dow plummeted, and credit markets remained frozen. While it was tempting to attribute the declines to the initial failure to pass the TARP, its passage on Friday, October 3, made this a difficult position to maintain, since the declines continued unabated. When the declines resumed the following Monday and spread across the world, Paulson interpreted financial markets as having judged that "TARP would not provide a quick enough fix." But by then the handwriting was on the wall: Bernanke and various Treasury staff had been for at least a week expressing doubts that the asset purchase program would work; Paulson himself intimated to President Bush that the Treasury would probably need to purchase equity in the banks on October 1, *two days before TARP's passage.* On October 13, Paulson informed the CEOs of Citigroup, Wells Fargo, JP Morgan, Bank of America, Merrill Lynch, Goldman Sachs, Morgan Stanley, Bank of New York Mellon, and State Street Bank that the Treasury now intended to emphasize capital injections—and he instructed these nine banks to accept them. By the end of October, Paulson canceled the auctions and instructed his staff to concentrate on capital injections instead. When markets judged the prospective market-based program to be faulty, the Treasury heeded the markets, not the economists.[134]

To the Treasury, it ultimately didn't much matter whether it resorted to boutique auctions or capital injections: to be sure, Paulson and his staff might lose face through their reversal, but Paulson had been considering such action well before the TARP passed. What mattered was political efficacy, not austere academic notions of "efficiency." The

main policy objective was to stop the market free fall without succumb-
ing to bank "nationalization," and the capital injection program
basically accomplished that. But to the economist market designers, it
made all the difference in the world. The market designers still under
contract responded to the Treasury's volte-face in emphasis by insisting that there was no good reason the Treasury could not use auctions
to purchase bank shares in addition to toxic assets, a position they
maintained until the Treasury made it clear they had no intention to
seek release of any additional TARP funds, therefore foreclosing any
prospect for using auctions.[135]

Once that happened, things turned ugly: the market designers for
hire themselves became some of the most fierce critics of the TARP,
denouncing Cash for Trash. In an interview for NPR, Ausubel
complained, "Instead of conducting transparent auctions, the Treasury
is going to instead distribute suitcases of cash"; for Cramton, "It really
is moving down the path to crony capitalism, in my mind, where the
government is picking winners and losers in a nontransparent way."[136]
This turnabout, however turncoat, was easy to pull off because both
the market designers and the anti-TARP petitioners now claimed to
have shared very similar assumptions about the economic role of
government. At times these shared views became apparent: during the
period of the most heated disagreement, Charles Calomiris (a Cato-
based member of the NTC) stated to NPR, "If Larry [Ausubel] can
convince me that he's got the right mechanism, that's great"; Calomiris went on to point out that he and Ausubel actually agreed on
many things.[137] And so the neoliberals welcomed the market designers.

In hopes of getting auctions back on the agenda for the incoming
Obama administration, they publicly promoted what appeared to be
a scientific demonstration that the Paulson Treasury had taken the
wrong approach. Cramton claimed that his study had demonstrated
"the auction was a success. The banks traded their toxic assets for
solid capital, and the taxpayers got a fair deal." The fact that these
"banks," "taxpayers" and "assets" were only sketchy constructs in a
laboratory did not necessarily detract from the lesson, and might
even have served to highlight the difference between the naked politics governing Paulson's Treasury and the calm impartial science of
the market designers. One can institute real markets in laboratories,
removed from the noise of the real world, and these real markets
deemed the market designers to have been correct. But what did
getting a "fair deal" have to do with the market designers' theory of
the crisis? At most it seemed only to address the issue of whether one

could consider the price generated to be a legitimate "market" price—a matter that really could not be settled by an experiment, anyhow. This was a far different claim than the one they had originally made to the Treasury: in their initial submission, Ausubel and Cramton argued not for the aggregation ability of markets in general, but instead for a very specific kind of "clock auction." While their early public statements did take care to portray their auctions as marketlike, they tended to emphasize to the Treasury how their clock auction improved upon other designs:

> A frequent motivation for the use of dynamic auctions is reducing common-value uncertainty. In this setting there is a strong common-value element. A security's value is closely related to its "hold to maturity value," which is roughly the same for each bidder. Each bidder has an estimate of this value, but the true value is unknown. The dynamic auction, by revealing market supply as the price declines, lets the bidders condition their bids on the aggregate market information. As a result, common-value uncertainty is reduced and bidders will be comfortable bidding more aggressively without falling prey to the winner's curse—the tendency in a procurement setting of naïve sellers to sell at prices below true value . . . A principal benefit of the clock auction is the inherent price-discovery feedback mechanism that is absent in any sealed-bid auction format. Specifically, as the auction progresses, participants learn how the aggregate demand changes with price, which allows bidders to update their own strategies and avoid the winner's curse . . . Efficiency in the clock auction always exceeded 97%.[138]

This passage corresponds to the point made above, that market designers viewed the toxic assets as "common" or objectively valued, and that such cases posed for the market designer the task of figuring out how to aggregate information. It also makes explicit the mandate of Bernanke's warning to avoid selling assets at too-low prices (although market designers offered a different rationale for doing so—avoiding the "winner's curse"). But what is most notable about this passage is that it advocates a very specific type of auction—a clock auction—and does so on the basis of its ability to avoid the "winner's curse," as evident by its demonstrably superior "efficiency." The reason this claim is so notable is because it is incoherent on its own terms: it only makes sense to attribute "97 percent efficiency" in the case of private valued auctions.[139] If toxic assets are common valued, then all distributions are

efficient *by definition*, and therefore the efficiency criterion is useless, or
at best, irrelevant. While the criterion does make sense in the case of
private valued auctions, one can never suffer from the winner's curse
in such cases, again *by definition*, and therefore the argument to prefer
the clock auction on the grounds of information aggregation is
nonsense. Since the market designers' claim that one could avert the
crisis by increasing information about the value of assets implied that
the assets must be common valued (or else the link between auction
performance and crisis aversion is severed), the "efficiency" evidence
was especially misleading.

Now, experts in game theory during the past decade should immediately recognize that the claim advanced by Ausubel and Cramton to
the Treasury in support of their "clock auction" was misleading. But
perhaps the point of the exercise was never to get the particulars of the
economics justification correct, but instead to get the Treasury to
purchase their "clock auction." Sifting through all the coverage of the
TARP plan, one comes across an acute observation made by a *Newsweek* reporter:

> [Ausubel and Cramton] hope to convince officials that not only
> does a reverse auction work, but, in the event the Treasury conducts
> one, to run it off their patented software platform . . . Ausubel and
> Cramton own two auction-services companies, Power Auctions
> and Market Design, each of which handle the back end of auctions
> for companies and foreign governments. They've already helped the
> French government sell electricity off its grid and Dutch energy
> companies auction off natural gas.[140]

In fact, Power Auctions and Market Design, Inc., held the patents for
the stipulated clock auction. But the presentation delivered by Ausubel
and Cramton for the Treasury listed several additional "Typical Auction
Related Activities" (product design; definition of detailed auction
rules; auction software specification, development and testing; bidder
training; establishment of an auction "war room"; operation of auction;
post-auction reports on success of auction and possible improvements
for future auctions) for which Power Auctions and Market Design,
Inc., could provide assistance.[141] Of course one can't know the exact
provisions that would have been contracted between the parties, since
the Treasury scrapped the plan, but given the previous record of market
designers, it is entirely reasonable to believe that they shaped their
claims with an eye on landing lucrative contracts.[142] For years, market

designers had made all sorts of fantastic claims for newfangled markets—They can reverse global warming! Improve access to health care! Redress racial and gender discrimination, without committing "reverse discrimination!" Even achieve "free lunch redistribution!"—so long as you hire their firms to build them to your exacting specifications (after all: "details matter"). They have almost always directed the pitch at cash-strapped governments, urging them in particular to sell off public assets to private oligopolistic concerns; in the case of toxic asset auctions one need only invert the logic.

Unfortunately, no one could much be bothered to scrutinize the claims of market designers. After all, there was a crisis a-brewing. Only a relatively small coterie of market designers ever got invited to participate in market design exercises, and most were partners in a small set of firms with interlocking directorates. In the case of the toxic asset auctions, the job of judging the proposals was assigned to Jeremy Bulow and Paul Milgrom, both partners with Ausubel and Cramton in Market Design, Inc. So much for Chinese Walls and plausible deniability. It doesn't verge on the wildly conspiratorial to suggest that such arrangements create some perverse incentives when it comes to reining in some of the more fantastical claims (gaining popular acceptance for them improves the firm's prospects), a fact that has seemed only to encourage ever more extravagant claims:

> The crisis was caused by mispricing: investment bankers were able to sell poor securities for full value based on misleading ratings. This mispricing was supported by the absence of a transparent secondary market for these mortgage-related securities. If we had transparent prices, a lot of the bad things that happened would not have happened. In particular the housing bubble would have been much less, and the investment bankers would not have been able to make such clever use of the rating agencies and create tens-of-thousands of senseless securities obfuscating prices. Even a tiny bit of good market design would have averted the financial crisis by preventing its root cause: the sale of subprime mortgages as near-riskless securities.[143]

> . . . Calls for sensible regulation and market design were met with condescension before the credit crisis, a condescension that is being reevaluated now.[144]

> Good auction design in complex environments . . . requires exploiting the substantial advances that we have seen in market design over

the last fifteen years. The recent financial crisis is another example where the principles of market design, if effectively harnessed by regulators, could have prevented or at least mitigated the crisis.[145]

Of course, there is no record of any market designers having actually successfully intervened to prevent the crisis, or helped anyone else to ameliorate it, but historical accuracy was never the name of the game. And at a 2012 meeting of the Southern Economic Association, Peter Cramton repeated his claim that market design could have solved the economic crisis; the officer in charge of NSF funding for economics was a co-panelist; her response to Cramton's claim was to hold out market design as a perfect example of the kind of work the NSF likes to fund: referring to work done with the FCC, she gushed: "he made the government billions!"[146]

To understand what elevates the public activities of market designers from the realm of mere puffery and self-promotion to the level of agnotology it is necessary to review how their public statements changed over the course of the crisis. Initially, market designers provided public defense of the Treasury plan in both its particulars (the decision to use reverse auctions) and its generalities (they signed a petition to congress in support of the proposition that government could act beneficially to correct for market failures). Especially important was the seeming independence of the academic support—as Swagel rightly noted, Wall Street economists were cheerleaders for the TARP as well, but no one would pay attention to them. Inevitably, market designers had to walk a tightrope in order to participate, at times stressing their ability to deliver competitive (low) market prices, at others, higher than fire-sale prices. But in the short term, the academics gave the Treasury the arguments it wanted for instrumental ends—to get the TARP passed. Market designers then persisted with their advocacy for auctions even after the Treasury insiders had themselves dismissed the plan as unrealistic; once the Treasury changed its plans, the market designers now devolved into free agents, turned on a dime, and attacked the Treasury. Their complaints, rendered loudly and often in the public sphere, resembled nothing so much as those being made by the *opponents* of the TARP. If the public was tracking the record of the economists (which it wasn't—there was a crisis on), they would be justified in wondering: Did these market designers have any clear idea of what might have *caused* the crisis in the first place? Did they even have any expertise regarding the financial sector? What made this about-face so confusing is that the phantom public could not trace it to any major shift in the Treasury's position: the market designers had registered no dissent about the Treasury's plan to inject capital into the banks, at least so long as it was poised to use their auctions to do so. But once they were out of the running for any auction contracts, and kicked out into the cold, market designers merely flipped and adopted the rhetoric of the TARP opponents. So how much of their analytical stance can be traced to the icy slopes of logic, and how much to the fickle fiduciary considerations of their patrons?

One of the main arguments for the ultimate irrelevance of the market designers was that it was not so much "the market" that mattered when it came to the actual valuation of the wonky assets—it was rather a concerted political push to change the accounting rules, so that banks could proceed to assert that the values of the assets were whatever they wanted them to be. Under pressure from the White House, the Treasury, and the banking lobbyists, the Financial Accounting Standards Board was induced to change rule FASB 157-e in April 2009, against the explicit disapproval of the American Institute of Certified Public Accountants and the Center for Audit Quality.[147] Mortgage-backed assets could now be listed as enjoying elevated values in bank and SIV balance sheets, without all that muss and fuss of the excessive complexity of boutique auctions.

B) Fannie Mae and Freddie Mac Did It

You have to give them credit: it didn't take too many all-nighters for the Neoliberal Thought Collective to come up with what would become the single most popular story on the right in America, wrapping the entire crisis up in a neat tidy package. In this meme, the crisis was first and foremost a housing bubble, which, when it burst, had some other unpleasant side effects; loans were extended to a bunch of deadbeats who should never been given a shot at home ownership in the first place; the reason that happened was the ill-conceived Community Reinvestment Act passed by the Democrats in 1977; and then the mortgage loans to the deadbeats were enabled by the Government Sponsored Entities (GSEs) Fannie Mae (actually: Federal National Mortgage Association) and Freddie Mac (Federal Home Loan Mortgage Corporation). Hence, on both the demand and supply sides, the government had polluted the mortgage market, first causing the housing bubble, and then the subsequent collapse. It was all the fault of the government. Full stop.

It is indisputable that Fannie and Freddie had become untenable as vague "public-private" financial entities in the early phases of the crash as the prices and collateral value of mortgage-backed securities tanked, and as such were nationalized in September 6, 2008, by the Bush administration. Their previous status as purely governmental entities was therefore dubious, a minor glitch in the neoliberal demonization of the government. What is a bit more stunning is that the story that Fannie and Freddie had *caused the crisis* was first put forth a little more than a month later by the neoliberal collective members Charles Calomiris (Hoover, Cato) and Peter Wallison (American Enterprise Institute [AEI]) in the *Wall Street Journal*.[148] As a trial balloon, it initially appeared rather unpromising, both to those with ringside seats at the subsequent collapse of Wall Street giants like ninepins and to various pundits on both sides of the political divide in 2008. For instance, in testimony at the October 23, 2008, session of the House Committee on Oversight and Government Reform, Alan Greenspan explicitly ruled out the hypothesis that Fannie and Freddie were the "primary cause" of the financial crisis, as did Christopher Cox, then chair of the SEC. Paul Krugman, smelling a rat, came out fairly early against the whole idea:

> Fannie and Freddie had nothing to do with the explosion of high-risk lending a few years ago, an explosion that dwarfed the S&L fiasco. In fact, Fannie and Freddie, after growing rapidly in the 1990s, largely faded from the scene during the height of the housing bubble. Partly that's because regulators, responding to accounting scandals at the companies, placed temporary restraints on both Freddie and Fannie that curtailed their lending just as housing prices were really taking off. Also, they didn't do any subprime lending, because they can't.[149]

Here is where considerations of agnotology kicked in. The NTC does not abandon a delicious hypothesis simply because it appears to come a cropper on a few facts and encounters strenuous opposition. Instead, they are flush and primed to send up multiple trial balloons, observe which way the prevailing winds are blowing, and then invest in further inflation for those that appear to take flight and festoon their political allies. The Fannie/Freddie meme was not the only causal narrative explored by the collective, but it sure looked good in crisis-aftermath America, especially after the Tea Party movement was itself commandeered by various Koch-funded front organizations. The Cato Institute seconded the analysis with alacrity. The AEI then threw its weight behind the Freddie/Fannie story, with Wallison as point man, and the trusty echo chamber was revved up. Professional economists were recruited to bolster the narrative. The public-choice crowd was quick to chip in. Mark Calabria from Cato was brought in to fluff up the numbers. Dependable fellow travelers such as David Brooks, George Will, and Tyler Cowen chimed in in the columns and blogs. Douglas Holtz-Eakin signed on, in a way to soon become important in the Financial Crisis Inquiry Commission. Edward Pinto at AEI was brought on board to crunch some numbers. Raghuram Rajan promoted a more fuzzy-tinged and humanized version of the story in his *Fault Lines*. But the real agnotological breakthrough came when a respected journalist seemingly positioned outside of the Russian doll (indeed, hailing from within that brimstoned Mordor for the right, the *New York Times*) was somehow induced to write a book also casting Fannie and Freddie as the evil twins behind everything that went wrong in the crisis: Gretchen Morgenson and Josh Rosner's *Reckless Endangerment*. This sparsely sourced and footnote-free book clearly depended heavily on Pinto for the few vague numbers it cited; it was much more expansive when it pursued searing indictments of political figures such as Barney Frank, Robert Zoellick, and Andrew Cuomo. A few obscure economists at the Fed came in for especially vituperative comment. At this juncture the NTC had hit a home run: Michael Bloomberg was caught repeating the meme in his hissy fits provoked by the Occupy Wall Street movement. Persistence and repetition and emoluments had paid off—the Fannie/Freddie "explanation" had become embedded in the blogosphere and the cultural landscape, spread far and wide by the Republican presidential candidates and beyond. When the SEC brought charges against six former Fannie and Freddie executives in December 2011, Wallison was accorded column inches in the *Wall Street Journal* to crow that he and his comrades had been vindicated.[150]

It was this sequence of events that prompted Joe Nocera, also of the *Times*, to bemoan the spread of the Big Lie:

> Thus has Peter Wallison, a resident scholar at the American Enterprise Institute, and a former member of the Financial Crisis Inquiry Commission, almost single-handedly created the myth that Fannie Mae and Freddie Mac caused the financial crisis. His partner in crime is another A.E.I. scholar, Edward Pinto, who a very long time ago was Fannie's chief credit officer. Pinto claims that as of June 2008, 27 million "risky" mortgages had been issued—"and a lion's share was on Fannie and Freddie's books," as Wallison wrote recently. Never mind that his definition of "risky" is so all-encompassing that it includes mortgages with extremely low default rates as well as those with default rates nearing 30 percent. These latter mortgages were the

ones created by the unholy alliance between subprime lenders and Wall Street. Pinto's numbers are the Big Lie's primary data point.[151]

The literature attempting to refute this meme was even more prodigious than the usual crisis lit standards; it nearly defies cogent summary.[152] The vulnerability of those skeptical of the GSE meme was the fact that attack on the neoliberal Freddie/Fannie story was often confused with defense of the behavior and structure of Fannie and Freddie, something no politically saavy person of almost any stripe would countenance. Even its supposedly spineless regulator accused Fannie of accounting fraud in 2005.[153] At the end of the day, Fannie and Freddie had made money through heavily promoted ambiguity concerning whether or not as a privatized entity it had enjoyed a government guarantee of its debt; of course the government takeover settled that question, but only at the expense of debilitating the rest of the banking sector. The fact that it was a cesspit of party political slush funds, machine cronyism, and cooked books did not dispel the undeniable stench of corruption, something Morgenson and Rosner made much of. The other drawback in refuting the neoliberal meme was that almost no one wanted to get bogged down in the minutiae of the extended history of the GSEs, nor in endless picky fights over the numbers, and other subtleties that often eluded the journalists and bloggers. For instance, it was demonstrably the case that Fannie and Freddie were the initial loci of the invention of securitization of mortgages decades ago; but that hardly saddled them with responsibility for every baroque development of securitization thereafter, many of which it avoided. A crisis story that could fit on a three-by-five card, yet revealed multiple layers of slippery ramification just below the surface, was the holy grail for the Neoliberal Thought Collective. Yet, in the end, their three-by-five slogan was a ruse.

There are two pincers of the attack on the Freddie/Fannie meme: the first, concerning the Community Reinvestment Act (CRA), and the second, the weaknesses in the proposition that Fannie and Freddie somehow caused or motivated the housing bubble and subsequent crisis. With regard to the CRA, the largest players in the subprime market were private-sector firms that were not subject to CRA stipulated rules and regulations. Therefore, for the story to work, the bulk of the subprime action had to happen in the GSEs, but as we shall see, it did not. Furthermore, in institutions subject to the CRA, not all loans fell under the CRA guidelines; so the proportion of loans affected were quite small. Then the timing seems a little off, since the CRA came into effect in 1977, but the housing boom dates from much later. It has become commonplace to point out that housing bubbles happened in many countries in the first decade of the millennium; but none of those other countries had any legislation similar to the CRA. And finally, Democrats and Republicans alike basked in the warmth of CRA-style hosannas to the "ownership society," at least until the whole shebang went south. Thus it is not clear that the CRA was much more than background static in the great pell-mell rush to push mortgages off onto all manner of persons ill-equipped to maintain and service them. Some politicians were avid cheerleaders for what had happened; but they did not actually create the elaborate set of mechanisms and legal puffery that constituted the housing bubble.

The primary riposte to the Fannie/Freddie meme is that Fannie and Freddie lost market share in the subprime market to private-sector firms from 2002 until late 2006; and the reason that happened was that it was the private-label "originate and securitize" machine that was the main driver behind subprime mortgages and the housing boom in the last decade. Here is where the real pitched battles were fought between the neoliberal think tanks and their opponents.

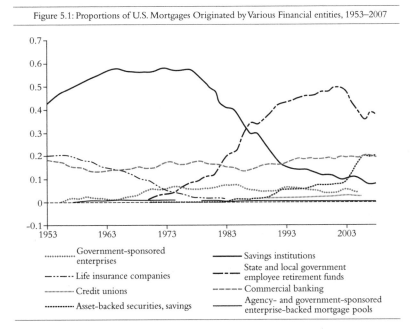

Figure 5.1: Proportions of U.S. Mortgages Originated by Various Financial entities, 1953–2007

The evidence on the face of it seems unequivocal: Figure 5.1 (proportions of mortgages originated by various financial institutions) shows the exit from mortgage finance of savings and loans after 1975;

the rise of securitizations by government sponsored entities from 1972 onward; the loss of market share by Fannie and Freddie beginning in 2002; and the twofold rise of private mortgage-backed securities and finance companies in the early 1990s and the acceleration in 2002. Most analysts by 2006 had been noticing that Fannie and Freddie had been losing market share because they had been avoiding the dicier "subprime" side of the mortgage market, in part due to their own government guidelines, avoiding nonconforming loans. Indeed, Ben Bernanke before the crisis was arguing that the CRA had been ineffectual precisely because less than 30 percent of Fannie and Freddie's portfolio consisted of mortgages that could be generously asserted to be based upon "affordable" or low-income properties.[154] As Moody's reported in 2006, just as the bubble was about to burst:

> Freddie Mac has long played a central role (shared with Fannie Mae) in the secondary mortgage finance market. In recent years, both housing GSEs have been losing share within the overall market due to the shifting nature of consumer preferences towards adjustable-rate loans and other hybrid products. For the first half of 2006, Fannie Mae and Freddie Mac captured about 44% of total origination volume—up from a 41% share in 2005, but down from 59% in 2003. Moody's would be concerned if Freddie Mac's market share (*i.e.*, mortgage portfolio plus securities as a percentage of conforming and non-conforming origination), which ranged between 18% and 23% from 1999 through the first half of 2006, declined below 15%. To buttress its market share, Freddie Mac has increased its purchases of private label securities.[155]

The GSEs had been getting prodded by members of Congress to purchase more subprime; but mostly, the "advice" came too close to the pricking of the housing bubble. There has been substantial dispute over just how much subprime and Alt-A loans Fannie and Freddie hoovered up in this narrow window; but a major riposte to the neoliberal story "The Democrats Made Them Do It" is that neither GSE touted a change in policy, but if anything, tended to underreport these activities. This is one primary reason most outside analysts trace the housing bubble to the private sector, and in particular, specialized subprime originators such as Countrywide and Ameriquest and the banking firms that repackaged them into baroque securities; it even corrupted profitable subsidiaries of "industrial firms" such as GMAC and GE Capital; consequently, "the biggest factor contributing to the subprime boom was securitization."[156] Another argument against the neoliberal story is that there was in parallel a bubble in commercial real estate, which had nothing whatsoever to do with the GSEs.[157] This trend dovetailed with another trend in the big banks, a transition from deriving much of their profit from loans to deriving it from fees for packaging mortgages (and other loans, such as credit card, auto loan, and student debt) into asset backed securities (ABS), selling ABSs and MBSs, creating dummy Structured Investment Vehicles (SIVs) to further reprocess MBSs into CDOs, and so forth. One estimate suggests that income from fee-related activities at commercial banks increased from 24 percent of total revenue in 1980 to 31 percent in 1990 to 48 percent in 2003.[158] Combined with stunning increases in concentration in the mortgage origination market, such that the top 25 mortgage originators controlled 90 percent of the market in 2007, the consensus interpretation of events was that the mortgage boom was an adjunct to bigger changes in the private financial sector, and not prompted by some outbreak of rabid mendacity amongst the newly conniving population of home purchasers.

For the neoliberal meme "Fannie and Freddie Did It" to work, it would be necessary to refute and reject this emergent consensus narrative. One major arena in which this happened was the Congress-mandated Financial Crisis Inquiry Commission.

C) Financial Crisis Inquiry Commission

The function of the Financial Crisis Inquiry Commission in the United States was purportedly to do for our Great Crisis what Ferdinand Pecora's investigation did for the Great Depression: provide trenchant research and a communal teaching experience concerning the causes of the crisis. On a public stage, our best and brightest would bring all the possibilities to the table, so that America might come to grips with its tragedy. Or at least that's the way it was sold to the public when it was included in the Fraud Enforcement and Recovery Act of 2009. But after a year and a half of hearings, many of which were made available online,[159] including questioning of more than eight hundred witnesses and expenditure of $6 million on staff, the whole pretence of a definitive archive of explanations broke down even before the report was formally issued in January 2011. The four Republican members of the supposedly bipartisan ten-person panel issued a preemptive-strike "Report" in December 2010, which sought to torpedo the main event (even before the final version had come up for a vote). That sketchy counterstory was more or less included as one of two "dissenting reports" appended to the final published report, the first under the names of Keith Hennessy, Douglas Holtz-Eakin, and Bill Thomas; the latter under the name of Peter Wallison. Wallison's appendix made the case for the neoliberal "Fannie/Freddie did it" line summarized above.

What one would derive from reading the document was the concurrent posit of A and not-A as causes of the crisis. The six-person endorsed body of the report pinned the crisis on "failure to effectively rein in excesses in the mortgage and financial markets," which then got parsed as a laundry list of usual suspects: credit-rating agencies, failures of regulators, OTC derivatives, crappy mortgages repackaged as sweets, Greenspan, executive compensation, Bernanke, shadow banking, etc. However, the majority went out of their way to reject one cause: "we examined the role of the GSEs . . . We conclude these two entities contributed to the crisis, but were not a primary cause . . . The GSEs participated in the expansion of subprime and other risky mortgages, but they followed rather than led Wall Street." In other words, it went out of the way to insist everything contained in the Wallison appendix was false. The other minority appendix endorsed the Wallison line in passing, but seemed more concerned to absolve Wall Street of any culpability, proclaiming, "derivatives did not in any meaningful way cause or contribute to the crisis," and denying that "shadow banking" was even a coherent concept.[160] Consequently, it was exceedingly vague about what did cause the crisis, although it did coquette with the notion that it was all China's fault. The first Republican dissent did not even bother with much in the way of evidence.

It must be conceded that Wallison did preface his dissent with the right question: "why Congress bothered to authorize [the FCIC] at all? Without waiting for the Commissioners' insights into the causes of the financial crisis, Congress passed and the President signed the Dodd-Frank Act."[161] Of course, the obvious answer was that the FCIC was set up to fail from the outset; but that might reflect badly on Wallison's willing participation. So instead he opted for an answer that shed some light on agnotology. He began by quoting Rahm Emmanuel saying "Never let a good crisis go to waste," and then suggested that the real purpose of the report was to gain some control over the "first draft of history." Wallison's behavior demonstrated that the NTC appreciated the importance of venturing beyond the mere short-term partisan bickering of the first dissent, or the sloppy endless laundry list of the majority report, to providing a simple pithy narrative to contrast with the general cacophony of noise concerning the crisis.

I do not propose to go into detail here why Wallison's own narrative indicting the GSEs is fatally flawed, although I believe it is.[162] If there is any truth to the notion that the GSEs were much more heavily invested in subprime than in the consensus narrative, especially 2006 and after, it would have to do with the backdoor bailout manipulation of Fannie and Freddie purchases to prop up private label securities by the Treasury, which of course hastened their insolvency. The point here is rather to suggest that economists from both sides of the (narrowly conceived) political spectrum have conspired to divert attention from serious analysis of the crisis, each for their own respective agnotological purposes. The Bloomberg journalist Jonathan Weil best captured the brazen impudence of pretence behind the FCIC report:

> This, in journalistic parlance, is what we call a clip job. And that's the trouble with much of the commission's 545-page report. There's lots of breezy, magazine-style, narrative prose. But there's not much new information. You can tell the writers knew they were sprinkling MSG on a bunch of recycled material, too, by the way they described their sources. The text and accompanying notes often seem deliberately unclear about whether the commission had dug up its own facts, or was rehashing information already disclosed in court records, news articles or other congressional inquiries . . .
>
> The FCIC's failure was predictable from the start. To examine the causes of the financial crisis, Congress created a bipartisan panel of 10 political appointees led by Democrat Phil Angelides, a former California state treasurer. What was needed was a nonpartisan investigation directed by seasoned prosecutors (like Pecora was) who know how to cross-examine witnesses and get answers. Whereas Pecora had no fixed deadline, Congress gave the crisis commission until December 2010 to complete its inquiry. Witnesses who didn't want to cooperate fully could simply milk the clock. The panel got a budget of less than $10 million to investigate all the causes of the financial crisis. Lehman's bankruptcy examiner got $42 million to produce a 2,200-page report on the failure of a single company.[163]

Having watched some of the hearings online, I can attest that witnesses were tossed one whiffle ball after another. Yves Smith reported the disgust of one of the FCIC staff, who complained, "I am still getting the stink out of my clothes." He understood that both the majority line that it was all the fault of wicked deregulation, and the Wallison line of "Fannie/Freddie did it," were equally unavailing. Both versions conspired to help perpetuate a myth that Wall Street financial firms were as much the victim of the crisis as everyone else, and existed to keep the proceedings from tripping up the sausage machine that eventually became the Dodd-Frank act.[164] Supposedly neutral economists participated in this travesty. Anat Admati of Stanford wrote, "Peter Wallison in his dissent attributes blame solely to the government housing policy of earlier administrations. While he is right to identify this as important, he misses other critical ingredients."[165] Jeffrey Miron of Harvard muddied the waters further by introducing the Rogoff Reinhart neoliberal line: "In asking whether the recent financial crisis could have been avoided, the crucial fact is that crises of various flavors have occurred for centuries in countries around the world. Thus, any explanation based mainly on recent factors—subprime lending, derivatives trading, or financial deregulation—cannot be the whole story. A full account must identify factors that have been present widely, and for centuries."[166] How the Dutch Tulip craze would help illuminate the structural deficiencies of a CDO-squared was left for someone else to figure out. I cannot find an example of an orthodox economist who came right out and said that the entire exercise was a cynical whitewash, although many bloggers came close.

The Democrat electoral debacle of November 2010 only exacerbated the tensions underlying the jousting agnotologies within the FCIC, as Rep. Darryl Issa subsequently convened an investigation into the mismanagement of the Inquiry to settle scores in Spring 2011. His subpoenas then unintentionally delivered another lesson in agnotology: it seems Peter Wallison had broken a number of confidentiality rules while serving on the FCIC, leaking secret Fed data to the AEI, while co-chair Bill Thomas secretly prepped many of the representatives of the banks on the level of questions they might expect.[167] The purpose overtly had never been to find new things out, so much as it was to make the preset narrative look good in public. Journalists yawned—so what else is new on the Hill?—but few pulled back to reconsider what this meant about the ongoing miasma that surrounded discussions of the crisis. Here, years after the crisis hit, and millions of dollars thrown at the economics profession, people were still no closer to a richer and more plausible understanding of the crisis than in its immediate aftermath. Worse, this was the unapologetic bottom line of some of the economic orthodoxy as well![168] Where was the bracing lucidity born of years of training in the most difficult technicalities of theory, or the ballast of reams of numerical data at our fingertips?

Where was the clarifying steel of econometric technique, or the glassy grand transparency of axiomatic method?

None of that seemed to have had any influence whatsoever. Instead, it was the dogged persistence of the Neoliberal Thought Collective that had overcome the vast tidal wave of analysis, and the endless vistas of economists' mumble jumbo, and occupied the public mind. Is it any wonder that the most common impression among people who have not bothered to read up on the crisis is that it has been the fault of the government, and that Fannie and Freddie are somehow behind it all?

6

The Red Guide to the Neoliberal Playbook

For someone who has just spent a few hundred pages arguing that the economics profession has been proven hopelessly corrupt by virtue of its behavior during the crisis, and that the Neoliberal Thought Collective has managed to weather the crisis by expanding to fill the entire space of political discourse left void by the dereliction of the economists, I am now going to do something a little counterintuitive: I am going to start by agreeing (in a limited way) with one famous Mont Pèlerin member, Hernando de Soto. In a retrospective on the crisis, he insisted, "the recession wasn't about bubbles but about the organization of knowledge."[1] Of course, this was not entirely unexpected, coming from a member of the NTC: it has persistently been an outlier in the history of reactionary movements, a political formation built upon a realization that their own core foundational commitments were epistemological, rather than simply "conservative" or capitalist or traditionalist;[2] but I think it is more revealing than perhaps he himself would concede. For it gestures toward the key question that has been raised by the neoliberal ascendancy: What is it that the opponents of neoliberalism believe that markets are capable of "knowing," and conversely, what is it that humans can know that falls outside the precinct of markets and their supposed omniscience and information-processing capacities? How much of any forward-looking political program can be premised upon a set of faculties and competences with regard to the economy that are not reducible to simple profit-seeking?

It has become a trite habit of the thousands of books and articles discussing the crisis of 2007–? to wind up their final chapter with a set of bullet points on what is to be done about our predicament. In this, as in other ways, this book breaks with precedent. The time has come to acknowledge that this obligatory genre of pithy programmatic statements has been sadly ineffectual, if not cringingly jejune. Heartfelt exhortations of "End This Depression Now!" have become sure signs of chicanery, the half-disguised theurgy of an often shadowy clique of economists. The neoliberals have triumphed in the face of this cacophony, at least in part, because their nominal opponents and their nostrums have proven so clueless. The resistance to the neoliberal tide has repeatedly looked to orthodox economics for succor, and it has betrayed them time and again. Beyond orthodoxy, even the intellectual case for a return to Keynes, or Marx, or Minsky as a panacea for the crisis has proven thin and insubstantial. Not only does the left lack a clear agenda for their own political objectives, but they have repeatedly mistaken or misunderstood the nature of the neoliberal political project, and consequently found themselves co-opted into it, or worse. This book preaches a simple message: Know Your Enemy before you start daydreaming of a better world. In this one particular respect, Carl Schmitt was right.

The Privatization of Protest and the Occupy Movement

The current problem of left political movements, whatever that benighted term might encompass nowadays, is that they have fallen into the trap where discussions of the crisis end up being hopelessly backward-looking: perhaps preaching "restoration" of proper "regulation," reenergizing mid-twentieth-century configurations of state power, or returning to a more "fair and equal" income distribution, or redeeming and making debtors whole through debt forgiveness, refurbishing an economy less beholden to and less composed of financialized corporate entities, resembling that which reigned during the immediate postwar period. Some have waxed openly nostalgic about the New Deal; others idealize the 1960s. Yet this ignores a basic truism learned by conservatives long ago: "To preserve the regime, the conservative must reconstruct the regime."[3] The superior insight of the neoliberals, in particular, is that you can never go home again, largely because they have sought to build intentional irreversibilities into their previous political interventions. To take but one telling example, if the hundreds of lobbyists and millions of dollars of campaign contributions were not sufficient to neuter all attempts at financial reform in the United States, such as the so-called Volcker Rule, then the banksters were not subtle in summoning their second line of defense, insisting that any such rule would violate NAFTA and other international "free trade agreements" instituted under prior transnational neoliberal regimes.[4]

Although it seems impolite to mention it, the collapse of the "Occupy" movement over 2011–12 was largely due to the long-discredited notion that political action could be sustained and effective in the absence of any sort of theoretical guidance and hierarchical organization of short- to longer-term goals. The Tea Party had Ayn Rand; the closest thing to an Occupy inspiration seemed to be John Stewart. People seem to have forgotten that the initial Occupy Wall Street encampment on September 17, 2011, was sparked by a call from Adbusters, a "global network of culture jammers" based in Vancouver, built around a media collective and a glossy magazine. Its founder, Kalle Lasn, has asserted, "What we're trying to do is pioneer a new form of social activism using all the power of the mass media to sell ideas rather than products"; its website proclaims, "The purpose of life is not to find yourself, but to lose yourself."[5] More neoliberal sentiments would be hard to find. The website also has a set of pages devoted to economics; under the rubric "Meet the Mavericks" it profiled Paul Samuelson, George Akerlof, Joseph Stiglitz, and Herman Daly. Kalle Lasn Associates has also published an anti-textbook entitled *Meme Wars: The Creative Destruction of Neoclassical Economics* which contains contributions by George Akerlof and Joseph Stiglitz. At least the graphics were radical. Similar ideas were promoted in the curiously titled *Occupy Handbook*, which included chapters by Raghuram Rajan, Tyler Cowen, Martin Wolf, David Graeber, Jeffrey Sachs, and Robert Shiller.[6] Besotted by the millenarian idea of starting anew, and lacking any sense of the history of protest and political organization, both neoliberals and neoclassical economists rapidly addled whatever political curiosity and radical inclinations that the well-intentioned protestors might have had. Rebels railed against corporate power, but apparently had no idea how it actually worked. The result was predictably utter failure. For instance, the protestors never actually managed to "Occupy Wall Street," since Zuccotti Park was four blocks away. Once the security apparatus was mobilized across more than eighteen different sites across the country in the space of a few days, Zuccotti Park was cleared on November 15, 2011, and the movement essentially collapsed.

While brave activists had proven willing to invent new forms of civil disobedience, much of their tweeting and blogging tended to reveal a reversion to themes already promulgated by the usual suspects covered in this volume. When not openly appealing to a lost world, like the "Take Back the American Dream" motif, they would propose "reforms" dating back to the 1980s, such as the Tobin tax on financial transactions, or a "fairness doctrine" for political ads, or an ineffectual public financing scheme for election campaigns. Mostly in the heat of Occupy, disputations over the crisis and financial sector were dominated by backward-looking ambitions and nostalgia for a happier and more prosperous time. Slogans like "We are the 99%" seemed to be calculated so as to be overly inclusive, confusing expansiveness with democracy, and therefore ineffectual. But even those wistful recollections were selective. The Occupiers were disdainful of close ties to trade unions, only to witness their own dreams of a General Strike fizzle in May 2012. Obsessed with dangers of being hijacked by existing organized political entities that might be sympathetic to their energy and fervor, they eventually found themselves utterly abandoned instead. Contemptuous of government, existing government returned the favor, eavesdropping on their communications and swooping down to arrest protestors while neutralizing press presence. Heavily informed by libertarian, "anarchist," and neoliberal elements, the belief that nothing more than endless General Assembly discussion and finger-waggling would lead to sustained political success was brought up short by police raids, harassment through the legal system, organizational breakdown, and the fleeting fickle attentions of the media. Quickly they were poleaxed that their pledges of allegiance to some political version of "spontaneous order" had come to grief.[7] They apparently held fast to their conviction that their primary role in life was to express themselves, especially with cameras nearby, rather than to work patiently for a thought-out political project. As one journalist observed about Occupy Wall Street (OWS), "They saw themselves as a counterculture; and to continue as such they had to remain uncontaminated by the culture they opposed . . . The ambitions of the core group of activists were more cultural than political, in the sense they sought to influence the way people think about their lives."[8] But that would presume they had a firm grasp of what it meant to inhabit a neoliberal persona in the first place. The trademark shout of "mike check" revealed their orientation pointed toward mimicry of media technologies as opposed to concerted political mobilization. The fascination with Twitter, Facebook, and other social media components of neoliberal technologies of the self revealed their lack of acquaintance with the ideas of their nominal opponents.

Indeed, I would suggest that the palpable failure of the Occupy movement demonstrates the relevance of the thesis of chapter 3: the neoliberal worldview has become embedded in contemporary culture to such an extent that when well-meaning activists sought to call attention to the slow-motion trainwreck of the world economic system, they came to their encampments with no solid conception of what they might need to know to make their indictments stick; nor did they have any clear perspective on what their opponents knew or believed about markets and politics, not to mention what the markets themselves knew about their attempts at resistance. With the generous assistance of economists, libertarians, and a raft of pundits, all their incipient neoliberal tendencies were amplified and encouraged, while their nascent attempts at political organization that might effectively challenge the NTC were quashed.[9]

People do not generally imagine themselves trapped in a world that is upside-down relative to what they think they know; indeed, persistent faith in the reliability of our own epistemic capacities is one of the more touching frailties of the human race. But when people on the left are rousted to action, the first qualm they must confront is that, at least in the contemporary world, most conventional notions of political protest themselves have been transformed and subverted by privatization and commercialization. This begins with their opponents, but does not end there.

The Tea Party is one of the prime examples of the metamorphosis of protest movements through the revamping of politics in a commercial privatized direction. Not only was the movement largely professionally astroturfed by a few large shadow private organizations, such as Americans for Prosperity, American Majority, the Tea Party Express, and FreedomWorks, but it derived much of its energy on the ground through open encouragement of small-bore entrepreneurs to make money in whatever ways they might imagine off the cascading sequence of rallies, bus tours, self-publication of pamphlets, conferences, disruption of town meetings, and other public gatherings.[10] In a sort of chain-letter Ponzi scheme, or better yet, an Amway franchise, the disgruntled were first financed and regimented through large quasi-corporations, made to feel empowered by encouragement to do the same on a smaller scale with their own venture-capital start-ups, then themselves motivated to recruit others to join the movement.[11] For instance, 41 percent of the booths at the Tea Party convention in Phoenix in February 2011 were manned by for-profit groups; an additional 35 percent were large business interests such as Philip Morris and Exxon Mobil. The top-down direction was thoroughly obscured by the groundswell of profit-making activities. Although the crisis might seem a horribly complicated phenomenon, the organizations at the core of the Tea Party franchise kept trumpeting simple "explanations" for the economically challenged, like "It was all the fault of the government, and especially, Fannie and Freddie," covered in the previous chapter, as well as stranger notions for the economically challenged and memory-impaired, such as the notion that Obama's election precipitated the crisis. All the while, they would guilelessly repeatedly testify that the entire movement was a wonderful example of "spontaneous order" (if they had read a little Hayek) or else the indomitable populist spirit of bottom-up American democracy, like that of the Founding Fathers (if they had read almost nothing).[12]

When the Occupy movement sat down in Zuccoti Park, they set out to wrest the title for Purity of Populist Expression away from the Tea Party, but almost instantaneously revealed a dearth of appreciation of what might materialize that could render them different. Indeed, many of the obsessions and even some of the language disturbingly mirrored those of their purported opponents. True, they did not immediately set about selling T-shirts, cocked hats, and placards, but the attempt to convince the masses that they should reinterpret their victimhood as a form of empowerment was an agenda without a narrative. In their quest for a more pure democracy, they renounced the existing structures of government, and consequently, abandoned the rafts of state and local unionized workers who were right then being shed by cash-strapped states and municipalities. The disparagement of government was one script practically plagiarized from the Tea Party. The gutting of government employment was an active political battleground (in places such as Ohio and Wisconsin resisting union-stripping and decertification) contemporaneous with OWS, but because it concerned unions, the Occupiers tended to act like it didn't exist. But more to the point, the Tea Party was consciously organized to give its recruits things to do and upbeat political identities to inhabit, all revolving around the commercialization of protest. All OWS offered were endless feints toward an oxymoron of an anarchist powwow, complete with tents. It was a murketing ploy, only bereft of anything to sell. OWS did not sufficiently appreciate the topography and extent of its opponent's political organization coupled with its cultural scripts, and for that reason made no coherent attempts to craft and supply an alternative. Or, to phrase it more cruelly, Occupy believed in the bedtime stories of the power of spontaneous order welling up from below, but was in the dark about the realpolitik of the modern privatization of protest.

I believe this was true even for more relatively modest attempts at protest, such as various undertakings to mobilize public support for federal regulators to more seriously discipline the banks. I choose here one example at random, the effort by the economist Simon Johnson to petition the Fed Board of Governors to remove JP Morgan's CEO, Jamie Dimon, from the Board of Governors of the New York Federal Reserve Bank.[13] Without meditating upon the sheer improbability of the Fed actually rebuking the heads of the banks that own and control it, we will focus here instead on the pedestrian mechanics of this attempt at the promotion of the simplest form of political protest. Johnson couldn't organize the petition himself, so he outsourced it to a new-media website, change.org. The qualms begin when one learns that this is a private for-profit corporation, or as it states, "Change.org is a social action platform that empowers anyone, anywhere to start, join, and win campaigns to change the world. We're proud to be a certified B Corp, using the power of business for social good."[14]

Qualms turn to disquiet when the fine print informs anyone who uses the site that their personal information may be passed on to the person/organization initiating the petition; further, it may also be shared with third parties, may be disclosed to authorities or other legal petitioners, and may even be sold under certain circumstances. In other words, perhaps unwittingly, Simon Johnson is exposing those who sign on to his petition to all the usual dangers of data aggregation, surveillance, and analysis familiar from the long history of high-volume for-profit direct mail operations. Johnson's "protest" orchestrates the harvesting of information for private profit and political machinations, precipitating an asymmetry, weakening the movement in the name of symbolic action. Furthermore, although Jamie Dimon will never ever be ousted by any such petition, or similar symbolic political activity,[15] thousands of people will enter their names into a database archiving the expressed hostility to the banksters, and someone, somewhere, is making a profit.

In the topsy-turvy world of neoliberalism, you may think that you are busily expressing your innate right to protest the cruel and distorted state of the world; but in most cases, you are echoing scripts and pursuing an identity that has already been mapped out and optimized beforehand to permit the market to evaluate and process knowledge about you, and convey it to the users with deepest pockets. Protest has been *murketed*. You get to express yourself; they get to make money. If you are smart, the neoliberals anticipate you might just realize you could eliminate the middleman, and end up commercializing your protest on your own.

Never forget: for neoliberals, the preordained answer to any problem, economic or otherwise, is more markets.

The Full-Spectrum Approach to Neoliberal Political Mobilization

The potent combination of top-down funding and organization with bottom-up incubation of commercial activity within the very same protest movement is certainly one very important explanation why the neoliberals have outclassed their opponents in political organization in the crisis, at least in the United States. But there is another, more comprehensive handicap that gives the neoliberals a crucial edge. Perhaps because of its Russian doll structure, the NTC has managed to provide not just isolated individual single-issue political proposals to respond to the various controversies (say, privatize Social Security, "incentivize" the National Health Service, hobble public-sector unions, undermine public schools with voucher schemes), but in the really big instances of political donnybrooks, they have been able to promote and coordinate interlocking full-spectrum braces of alternative policies that expand until they entirely fill the public space of perceived alternatives. The genius of the Neoliberal Thought Collective has been to appreciate that it is not enough to dangle a utopian vision just beyond reach as eventual motivation for political action; the cadre that triumphs is the side that can simultaneously mount a full set of seemingly unrelated political proposals that deal with the short-, medium-, and long-term horizons of action, combining regimes of knowledge and interim outcomes, so that the end result is the inexorable movement of the *polis* ever closer to the eventual goal. The shrewd strategy of simultaneously conducting both a short game and a long game, superficially appearing to the uninformed to be in mutual conflict but united behind the scenes by overarching theoretical aims, is probably the single most significant explanation of the triumph of neoliberal policies during a conjuncture where their opponents had come to expect their utter refutation. The left, clinging to an obsolescent vision of pragmatism and committed to rational compromise, has seen rings run around its meager attempts to come up with remedies for the crisis.

Since any analytical statements that delve into neoliberal practice have to avoid the Scylla of conspiracy theories as well as the Charybdis of endorsement of their trademark notions of spontaneous order, it will be necessary to insist that their contemporary full-spectrum approach to politics has not been comprehensively described anywhere by any of the major neoliberal thinkers. The approach instead grows directly out of their hallmark organization of the thought collective, in conjunction with their specific theoretical commitments concerning the role of knowledge in markets. In other words, the Russian doll organization of Mont Pèlerin, affiliated think tanks, dedicated funding agencies, academic units, and astroturf operations is nicely suited to promote seemingly alternative policies emanating from different compass points within the hierarchy of the NTC; what melds this policy entrepreneurship into a monolithic agenda is precisely the sociology of knowledge that grows out of their core epistemological commitments. A few historians have begun to glimpse the larger mechanisms at work here, although incongruously, this has occurred far more often in the history of science and technology, rather than in the seemingly more germane areas of political science or sociology.[16] Precisely for that reason, it will be more convenient for expository purposes to make the case for a full-spectrum neoliberal offensive first in the case of a political controversy in the natural sciences—here, the other major crisis of our time, the threat of global warming due to the human-initiated emissions of carbon dioxide into the atmosphere since the Industrial Revolution.

The outline of the neoliberal response to global warming over the last three decades may seem an ill-considered detour from the current topic of the global economic crisis, but rest assured, it is not. Starting with notions of the Natural is one efficient way to get to the heart of neoliberal philosophy.[17] The objective of the rest of this chapter is to describe the template of neoliberal policy response in an area where it has been coming to be understood in perhaps the most elaborate detail, and then to demonstrate that the pattern has been essentially the same as that found in the responses to the economic crisis covered in this book. Contrary to the raft of writers who insist that modern neoliberalism is far too variegated, contingent, flexible, and local to constitute any sort of unified political movement, I shall insist that there indeed has been a standard-issue Neoliberal Playbook in responding to big political challenges; and furthermore, its scripts constitute the major reason that the NTC has come through the economic crisis unscathed. The full-spectrum mobilization strategy can then retrospectively begin to clarify some of the incidents recounted in previous chapters. What at the micro level might appear chaotic and wavering turns out to have been a canny stratagem from an altitude of 10,000 feet.

The Neoliberal Response to Global Warming

Neoliberals depart from the simplistic dichotomies of distinct spheres of State vs. Market inherited from classical liberalism along two rather obvious axes: they have a very different conception of what a market does, and a novel doctrine of what the role of the state should be in their ideal utopia. Recapitulating chapter 2, neoliberals more or less reject the older notion of a market as a physical allocation device; instead, they invest the market with superhuman qualities of information processing—the Ultimate Cyborg—in that it is literally taken to be smarter than any human being, and further, to convey just the right information to those who need it in real time. The market is still treated as one special aspect of nature—no one is ready to renounce that particular cultural obsession[18]—but nature itself is portrayed as ineffably complex, after notions developed in cybernetics and systems theory: evolving, adaptive, nonlinear, chaotic. This ontology constitutes the core of the neoliberal critique of socialism: no human intelligence could ever understand itself, much less the roiling appearance of chaos which constitutes its natural environment, to a degree sufficient to plan the economy, because the reasons it musters are always less complex than the phenomena it would wish to master. However, contrary to their libertarian fellow travelers, neoliberals also subscribe to the doctrine of a strong state, one poised and willing to build and maintain the world of markets, which in their view conforms to their vision of ever greater freedom. The neoliberals concede that it may appear that the existing market system sometimes fails; but the answer to these hiccups is to impose more markets, since nothing else can ever begin to cope with the complexity of evolution. The prescription for market failures is always more markets; however, that prescription can only reliably and successfully be imposed by a strong state. Moreover, since democratic electorates are always clamoring for bread and circuses, which threatens to thwart the telos of economic improvement from their perspective, a strong state must vigilantly strive to keep them in line; ideally, a state controlled by neoliberal politicians. This sometimes appears confusing to outsiders, who cannot understand how neoliberals can so blithely demonize the state and simultaneously concede its necessity.

Jeremy Walker and Melinda Cooper have done us the service of outlining how the neoliberal political project has taken substantial inspiration from modern scientific disciplines such as ecology, in portraying social systems as complex adaptive systems. They particularly highlight the notion of "resilience" promoted in the systems ecology literature, starting with the papers of Crawford Holling. As they put it:

> Hayek defines the radical freedom of the market by its indifference to all external limits and transcendental laws . . . The laws of the market rest on no pre-existent foundation: their very resilience serves as proof of concept, in the same way that the law of natural selection constantly proves or disproves the viability of chance mutations in nature.[19]

What they do not stress sufficiently, however, is that Hayek and his followers have been able to endow the market with such transcendental legitimacy because they subscribe to a seldom-examined ontological tenet: rules (which Hayek equates with "society") do evolve, as does nature; but the market is treated as both uniform and invariant. This commitment has been seconded by the Chicago School of economics. The market can dependably sanction success or failure of human endeavor because it is the Rock upon which the complex chaotic maelstrom dashes; the market is the zero point from which all motion and change is measured. The market itself is never chaotic, because it exists outside of time. The market must be generic and unwavering, because if it were completely embedded in historical time (like society, like nature), then it could in principle be just as clueless about the true telos of human striving as any deluded human being; in other words, *it could get things wrong*.

Here we observe how neoliberals depart substantially from orthodox neoclassical environmental economics. The neoclassical economists tend to approach problems in the biosphere as symptoms of a glitch in the market—granted, a stunted and inarticulate notion of market failure, but market malfunction nonetheless—whereas neoliberals will never countenance that approach. We have previously mentioned how the so-called Coase Theorem was an intentional intervention to undermine and dissolve the whole neoclassical notion of "externalities," and the theory of public goods built around it. In a slogan: for neoclassical economists, nature is simple and eternal, while markets seize up due to market flaws (external commodity definitions) rooted in that very same nature; the neoclassical solution is for the state to mimic the way an ideal market should have performed, in order to rectify these unfortunate lacunae. Conversely, for neoliberals, problems in the biosphere arise because of the intrinsic complexity and chaotic trajectories of both nature and society, which will never be adequately comprehended by human science. Those problems, they insist, are never the fault of the market. Understandably, people will always seek to respond to some perceived biosphere crisis by attempting to tinker with and reform economic activity, but they are deluded, and must be shunted into harmless pursuits. In a slogan, for neoliberals, humans can never be trusted to know whether the biosphere is in crisis or not, because both nature and society are dauntingly complex and evolving; therefore, the neoliberal solution is to enlist the strong state to allow the market to find its own way to the ultimate solution. It can accomplish this only if the invariant character of the market is allowed to manifest itself in all its glorious resilience.

The role of the neoliberal state is therefore threefold: to becalm and mollify the restive public who are provoked to constrain or neutralize the market in response to problems; to reiterate and deploy the Neoliberal panacea that the way to address any (falsely) perceived market failures is to introduce more markets; and finally, to facilitate the market in discovering its own eventual transformations of nature and society which will transcend any biosphere crisis. By contrast with orthodox neoclassical economics, this entails not one, but a whole panoply of diverse "policy" responses, the sum total of which are jointly attuned to bring about the final end of capitulation to the greater wisdom of the ineffable market. I should like to argue here that one of the reasons that the neoliberals have come to triumph over all their ideological rivals in recent decades is that they have managed to venture beyond any simplistic notion of a single "fix" for any given problem, but always strive instead to invent and deploy a broad spectrum of different policies, from the most expendable short-term expedients to medium-term politics to long-horizon utopian projects, all of which may appear to outsiders as distinct and emanating from different quarters, but in fact turn out inevitably to be nicely integrated so as to produce the eventual capitulation of nature and society to the market. Certainly the left has produced nothing that remotely compares in terms of sophistication—either in this case, or as later, concerning the global economic crisis.

This notion of a full-spectrum neoliberal pharmacopoeia suitable for any malady is fairly hard to grasp in the abstract, particularly when nature is being treated as slippery as society. Furthermore, one cannot extract a comprehensive example from any single neoliberal author or Hayekian encyclical: for instance, Hayek merely expressed an opinion that market processes would deal with environmental problems in the fullness of time;[20] it took legions of specialists in the think-tank thought collective to come up with the component interlocking policies over multiple decades. Perhaps the easiest way to illustrate the neoliberal playbook is to briefly survey its deployment in the concrete case of global warming.

I think most people on the left don't fully realize that the phenomena of "science denialism," "carbon permit trading," and the nascent science of "geoengineering" are not three unrelated or rival panaceas, but together constitute the full-spectrum neoliberal response to the challenge of global warming. The reason this array qualifies as neoliberal is twofold: initially, they were all proposals originating from within the array of think tanks and academic units affiliated with the Neoliberal Thought Collective; and then, if and when they come to be deployed in tandem, the net consequence is to leave the entire problem to be solved, ultimately not by the state, but rather by the market. The promotion of denialism buys time for the other two options; the financialization of carbon credits gets all the attention in the medium term, while appeals to geoengineering incubate in the wings as a techno-utopian deus ex machina to swoop down when the other options fail. At each step along the way, the neoliberals guarantee their core tenet remains in force: the market will arbitrate any and all responses to biosphere degradation, because it knows more than any of us about nature and society. As a bonus from the neoliberal vantage point, perhaps some segments of the left, operating under the quaint impression they can effectively oppose one or more of these options they find anathema by advocating another—say, aiming to defeat science denialism or geoengineering by taking up advocacy of carbon trading—end up being recruited as unwitting foot soldiers for the neoliberal long march.

Each component of the neoliberal response is firmly grounded in neoliberal economic doctrine, and as such, has its own special function to perform. As we have already learned from historians of the tobacco strategy such as Richard Proctor and historians of climate denialism such as Naomi Oreskes, the purpose of science denialism has been to quash all immediate impulses to respond to the perceived biosphere crisis, and to buy time for commercial interests to construct some other eventual market solutions to global warming. Denying the very existence of global warming is cheap and easy to propagate, can be fostered quickly, and tends to draw attention away from issues of appropriate responses to crisis. The neoliberal think tanks behind the denial of climate change don't seriously believe they are going to win the war of ideas within academic science in the long run, just as the tobacco strategy never envisioned disproving the smoking-cancer link. Yet, nevertheless, even the existing denial of the science displays its neoliberal bona fides. The first response to a political challenge should always be epistemological, in the sense that the marketplace of ideas has to be seeded with doubt and confusion. This is the core of the agnotological project. Furthermore, human science will never fully comprehend nature in real time. Neoliberals have assumed the equivalent stance hostile to intellectuals dating back to Hayek's attack in 1949, and no one gets more aggrieved about the lack of deference shown by the intelligentsia than your median neoliberal.[21] Bashing pointy-headed elites lends them a certain populist caché; and it plays to an incipient fondness among the uneducated for the fuzzy conviction that wishing can make anything so. This is short-term politics in pursuit of short-term aims. Neoliberal doctrine maintains that anyone should be free to propound any wonky falsehood they may wish, because the final arbiter of truth is the market, and not some clutch of experts who represent sanctioned science. If it just so happens to resonate with the commercial propaganda interests of the oil companies, well, so much the better.

The project to institute markets in pollution permits is a neoliberal mid-range strategy, better attuned to appeal to neoliberal governments, NGOs, and the more educated segments of the populace, not to mention the all-important FIRE sector of the economy. In effect, this strategy is an elaborate bait-and-switch, where political actors originally bent upon using state power to curb emissions are instead diverted into the endless technicalities of the institution and maintenance of novel markets for carbon permits, with the not unintended consequence that the level of emissions continues to grow apace in the interim. Furthermore, professional economists are brought in to shill for this strategy, largely because they enjoy conflicts of interest in this area of a magnitude commensurate with those they have nurtured with the financial sector in general. The neoliberal genealogy of this approach is conventionally traced back to the MPS member Ronald Coase, who first proposed that pollution could be optimized by submitting it to a market calculus.[22]

The chequered history of traded carbon permits and their mind-numbing technicalities of the ways in which these markets were foisted upon well-meaning reformers has been explained in a number of excellent papers by Larry Lohmann, which deserve to be much better known among environmentalists and the left in general. For purposes of brevity, I will just summarize the case that trading carbon permits doesn't work, and was never intended to do so.[23] The major intentional stratagem is that, once the framework of permit trading is put into place, the full force of lobbying and financial innovation comes into play to flood the fledgling market with excess permits, offsets, and other instruments, so that the nominal cap on carbon emissions never actually stunts the growth of actual CO_2 emissions.[24] This, in turn, leads to persistent falls in prices of the permits, which continually trend toward utter collapse. This has happened a number of times in the European Emissions Trading System since its inception in 2005.[25] Indeed, prices of the ETS dropped to zero in the first phase in 2007, and have been falling again, as demonstrated in Figure 6.1, even though concurrently emissions have risen more or less continuously, with a hiccup during the early phases of the financial crisis. But wild swings in the markets do not perturb neoliberals, since they take the longer view.

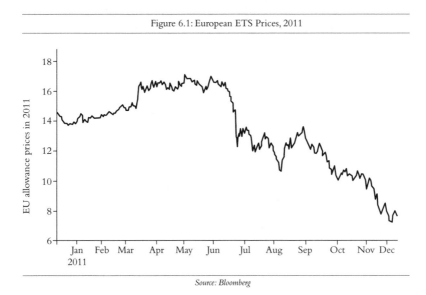

Figure 6.1: European ETS Prices, 2011

Source: Bloomberg

The engineered glut of permits is not temporary, since in this system, unused permits can be "banked" for use in future years, although it might not be the most prudent course to hoard an asset of falling value. Indeed, trading systems tend to reinforce oligopoly power, since they always grandfather in the largest emitters, and tend to penalize new entrants. And it is well understood that trading systems tend to stifle further technological measures to curb emissions. Money that might have been used productively to alter the energy infrastructure instead gets pumped into yet another set of speculative financial instruments, leading to bubbles, distortions of capital flows, and all the usual symptoms of financialization.[26]

So "cap-and-trade" does not work at ameliorating global warming, primarily because it was never really intended to do so. But as that intentional consequence becomes clear, it gets displaced by the long-game neoliberal solution. The final neoliberal fallback is geoengineering, which derives from the core neoliberal doctrine that entrepreneurs, unleashed to exploit acts of creative destruction, will eventually innovate market solutions to address dire economic problems. This is the whiz-bang futuristic science fiction side of neoliberalism, which appeals to male adolescents and Silicon Valley entrepreneurs almost as much as do the novels of Ayn Rand. Geoengineering is a portmanteau term covering a range of intentional large-scale manipulations of the earth's climate, often proposed to counteract existing man-made climate change, such as global warming. It proudly flaunts the neoliberal precept that if the economy screws up, just double down on the same sorts of things you have been doing already. It encompasses such phenomena as Earth albedo enhancement through "solar radiation management" (injecting reflective particles into the stratosphere, space mirrors, desert covering); CO_2 sequestration (through ocean seeding or churning, burying biochar, introduction of special genetically modified organisms, or CO_2 extraction at point of emission); and direct weather modification (hygroscopic cloud seeding, storm modification).

Geoengineering has close ties to the Neoliberal Thought Collective. The American Enterprise Institute has a full-time geoengineering project, and a number of other neoliberal think tanks, such as Cato, the Hoover Institution, and the Competitive Enterprise Institute, have produced studies. Chicago School SuperFreakonomics has come out in hearty open endorsement. Of course, it might seem a bit tactless for units that have prior histories of support for climate denial now getting behind geoengineering; but that simply demonstrates that this is another component of a full-spectrum neoliberal project. The real objective is to get the idea injected into general political discourse; and one indication that they are succeeding is an article that appeared in *The New Yorker* in 2012, which actually treats the idea as a serious prospect.[27] Unfortunately, this article somehow managed to skip over all the daunting reasons why the entire program is sheer lunacy: that there is no way it could be tested ahead of time; that it involves unilateral actions that violate many international treaties; that it imagines a few corporations might hold the entire globe hostage for the sake of some short-term profit; and last but not least, all of the variants of interventions could at best be short-term expedients, since none actually could rectify the true underlying problem, which is the careening acceleration of CO_2 emissions worldwide. It gleefully diverts attention to Band-Aids while the patient is dying of heat exhaustion. But maybe that is the point of the exercise.

Like most neoliberal prescriptions, the most important fact concerning this tortured marriage of science and corporate commodification is that it often doesn't work to ameliorate its stated target problem, although it does permit further amplification of the larger neoliberal political project. Permit me to relate one recent incident that illustrates this fact. For some inexplicable reason, the British Royal Society has been one of the biggest "insider" boosters of geoengineering. Partly for that reason, one of the earliest consortia of scientists seeking to mount a pilot program for injecting particles into the stratosphere has been the British Stratospheric Particle Injection for Climate Engineering project, or SPICE, headquartered at Bristol and Cambridge universities. SPICE announced in 2011 that it would use a weather balloon to lift a one-kilometer-high hose to spray an aerosol, as proof of concept.[28]

This provoked a great hue and cry in Britain, with more than fifty scientific organizations opposing even this limited test project. In the current neoliberal circumstances, mere political opposition resorting to reasoned arguments that this sort of "experimentation" was dangerous and ill-conceived was nowhere sufficient to stop a well-funded scientific cadre with some ceremonial credibility and political clout. No, what got the experiment canceled before it was finally carried out was a dispute among the team over *intellectual property*: two members of SPICE, Hugh Hunt and Peter Davidson, had filed for a patent for an "apparatus for transporting and dispersing solid particles into the Earth's stratosphere by balloon, dirigible or airship" without informing the other members of the team. Other participants, learning of this, called the experiment to a halt. Just like in so many other areas of modern science, faculty here occupied dual roles as academic researchers and CEOs of their own startup firms: not just Hunt and Davidson, but the other participants as well. This speaks louder than any public relations claims about the nominal public-spirited character of the project: geoengineering is not really about saving the planet; it is instead mostly about laying claim to privatization of the global troposphere.

Once the relevant corporations and scientists get all their legal property claims in a row, and unless environmentalists can mount some further serious obstacles, I have no doubt something like SPICE will go forward. But in the meantime, temporary failure of this or that particular geoengineering project is entirely consistent with the success of the neoliberal political project. For the ultimate objective of the exercise is to rely upon the market, the only dependable source of knowledge concerning the roiling chaos of evolving nature, in the face of similar complexity of its interaction with society.

Note well that each neoliberal component of the full-spectrum strategy does not by itself actually ameliorate global warming. Denialism postpones the issue; carbon permit trading does not actually reduce CO_2 emissions in actual practice; and geoengineering just treats the symptoms of global warming without curtailing emissions. What might at first seem to be a serious defect of the neoliberal strategy is, in fact, the crux of its ultimate rationale. If nature and society evolve in complex and impenetrable ways, then humanity should be prevented from joining together to impose unilateral policies to deal with the perceived root problem. For which humans can actually understand where the market is taking us? Better to defer all political action to the market, which will come to some eventual accommodation to the transformation of nature in good time. But this would never happen under pure passive laissez-faire. Instead, neoliberals must mobilize to capture the state and impose the spectrum of interim "solutions" so that people can come to believe that something is being done to stem the crisis, even if, strictly speaking, no such thing has occurred.

The full-spectrum neoliberal response is the double truth doctrine in action.

B) The Neoliberal Response to the Economic Crisis

The fundamental contrast between the dynamic chaotic character of nature and society and the immutable solidity of the market turns out to be the Rosetta Stone for understanding the response of neoliberals to the Great Economic Crisis of the twenty-first century, as well as explaining their response to climate change. To a first approximation, it accounts for their often eccentric position that the crisis cannot be understood as revealing any flaws in markets whatsoever. For neoliberals, the manifestation of an economic crisis is never traceable to any defects in their own previous policies (say, the deregulation of finance, or the quasi-privatization of the securitization function with regard to newer classes of debt, the breakdown of private-label debt issuance, or deindustrialization); rather, it is a consequence of the unstoppable evolution of nature and society (of which their interventions are a significant component), which can never be fully comprehended by mere human intelligence. The demonization of the government becomes one salient corollary of this fundamental precept: in their version of events, nothing was ever intrinsically wrong with the mortgage market or CDOs or the megabanks or the shadow banking sector or trade imbalances between China and the rest of the world; the snafu came when governments sought to rein them in, encourage them, or call them to account. The bureaucrats had presumed to control something they could never fully comprehend. Nothing about the market had changed, it was only the hubris of the governing class that brought the system to the precipice of collapse. The changes that had occurred in the run-up to 2007 were deemed eminently natural; all that was required was the humility to realize that evolution often appears chaotic to the informationally challenged and preternaturally impetuous, and the patience to wait for the market to come to adequate accommodation of the trends.

But, of course, when it looks to all the world like the global economy is collapsing, the public wants action, and wants it *now*, not passive acquiescence.[29] Fools rush in, say the neoliberals, and therefore a full-spectrum response is needed to counter the palliatives of their opponents. And, with benefit of hindsight, that is precisely what happened in the five years following the crash. Conveniently, the spectrum of policies can be arrayed more or less in parallel with the spectrum of responses to global warming outlined above, because *the rough structure of short-, middle-, and long-term responses are essentially the same.* Indeed, pointing out the similarities suggests that the neoliberal political project has by now attained a kind of efficient stability and coherence, rolling out many of the same time-tested responses in widely varying contexts. In the case of the global economic crisis, they comprise *denialism, market-based rescue of banks, and financial innovation.* This full-spectrum neoliberal response can serve to organize and clarify many of the ideas and incidents related in previous chapters into a single narrative that ultimately answers the question: How did the neoliberals emerge from the crisis stronger than when it began?

The phenomenon of denialism as regards the profession of economics in the crisis has been surveyed in detail in chapter 4. In the case of global warming, think tanks mobilized various protagonists to deny the science, which had suggested that global average temperatures were increasing and that human carbon emissions were the primary cause. In the case of the economic crisis, the spin was slightly different: economists had noted that nothing in their orthodox theories had anything whatsoever to say about the global crash, but nevertheless, various protagonists were encouraged to deny that this implied that the theories were contravened or impugned in any fashion. In the former case of climate change, the suggestion was floated that existing science did not correctly comprehend nature; in the latter of economic crisis, the suggestion was that, contrary to all evidence of the senses, economists did nonetheless understand the crisis. The former was fomenting denial on the part of outsiders, the latter emboldened denial on the part of insiders. While the valence of the claims was reversed, it is important to frame the phenomenon in both instances as a commensurate political intervention on the part of the neoliberals. The purpose of denialism in both cases has been not actually to influence the relevant science over the long run—recall that most neoliberals of a Hayekian persuasion have never been terribly enamored of neoclassical economic theory—but rather to sow doubt and confusion in the general public concerning the causes and significance of the crisis in question. The mantra here, from Ezra Klein to Andrew Haldane to Gary Gorton, is that it is just all too complex to understand.[30] If tense issues are presented in a nominally "fair and balanced" manner as rife with uncertainty, then most of the tyro public will just tune out. The deployment of agnotology is a major hallmark of the neoliberal collective, as we have repeatedly argued throughout this volume.

From this perspective, the crisis is, in the first instance, an epistemological phenomenon. The beauty of the manufacture of ignorance is that it has proven an ideal short-term response to unanticipated surprises: when disaster hits, and reformers propose to strike while the iron is hot with their nostrums and antidotes, the Neoliberal Thought Collective can stymie them and can buy time by filling the public sphere with fog. Since the orthodox economics profession had ventured quite some distance down the road to being co-opted by the neoliberals prior to the crash, if anything, the latter brand of denial was just easier to gin up in the aftermath of the economic crisis. The newspapers bayed for economists' blood; and economists spat back all manner of excuses. With enough fog emitted, almost anything becomes possible. Glenn Hubbard, subjected to scathing ridicule in the movie *Inside Job*, could be rehabilitated as a major economic advisor to the Mitt Romney campaign in 2012. Gary Gorton, inventor of the CDS instruments that sank AIG, could be rehabilitated as one of the primary experts in the economics literature concerning the causes of the crisis. Ben Bernanke, booster of the Great Moderation, could be rehabilitated as the Savior of the American Economy. The busier the economists were in drawing all sorts of red herrings across the landscape, and the more the think-tank tokens stoked the controversy, the better the neoliberals liked it. It didn't hurt that the fog also rendered them better able to insert their utterly implausible meme ("Fannie and Freddie did it") into the mix, such that it became one of the top three "explanations" of the crisis among hoi polloi.

The promotion of denialism may have bought time, but only subordinate to the bringing into play of the replacement middle-term policy response of the market-based rescue of the banks covered in chapter 5. In the case of global warming, the medium-term instrumentality was to have the state construct new markets for emissions permits. Interestingly, as described in above, during the crisis a very close analogue was also floated to create new markets to sell off the so-called toxic assets that the government would "temporarily" take off the balance sheets of the faltering banks. Market designers were initially brought in to help concoct boutique auctions to somehow actualize and validate the ramshackle expedient of the TARP. As previously noted, that specific project rapidly turned abortive, but for comparative purposes it is instructive to inquire just how much of the original plan remained as the premier approach to rectifying the financial crisis as the rescue unfolded. True, the market designers were themselves cashiered by fast-moving political events; but the shell of the approach persisted, only now embedded within the rapidly proliferating government asset purchase programs.

In the scramble to quickly implement the TARP, a motley collection of various "programs" with impenetrable acronyms such as TALF, HAMP, and P-PIP were mounted to "leverage" government money with participation of specially induced private investors to vacuum up all manner of distressed assets.[31] Of course, in the initial phases, the exact means chosen may have been dictated more by crude political calculus along the lines of a "Paulson Put"—an improvised attempt to stave off the worst of the collapse and bailouts until after the 2008 election—than by any coherent strategy.[32] Nevertheless, the obvious prescription of the government taking over the failing banks and forcing their restructuring, deleveraging, and downsizing was ruled permanently out of bounds; but instead, under the proliferation of program acronyms (post-Lehmann), no major stakeholder in the FIRE sector was forced to suffer a write-down of assets or even change of personnel. The template of "market-maker of last resort" began with the Paulson-Geithner improvisation of having the New York Fed assume $30 billion of the worst assets from Bear-Stearns before selling the firm cheaply to JP Morgan, and then hiring Black Rock to supervise and manage the scheme.[33] This set the pattern for what became the "market based rescue," or what might be deemed a newfangled privatization of government rescue of the financial sector. Indeed, many of the programs were not only outsourced, but even *designed* by private firms such as Black Rock and Trust Company of the West. What happened was that initially the federal government, and later the Federal Reserve, provided "loans" and guarantees and purchased vast amounts of dodgy securities at prices favorable to the insolvent banks and some firms (such as the auto industry), all subordinate to the principle that government should facilitate a "market-based" rescue by having private interests manage and carry out the investments to the greatest extent possible. Under P-IPP, for instance, private firms needed only to put up $1.67 to purchase $100 retail of "toxic assets"; further, the taxpayer provided a promise to cover 93 percent of any potential losses.[34] "Shadow" or hidden bailouts were also pursued through the Federal Home Loan Bank system, stepping up Fannie and Freddie purchases, and unconventional expansion of the Fed balance sheet. In effect, the government acted to directly or indirectly provide a price floor for selected investors for all manner of financial assets, no matter how dubious or damaged. In a pinch, the central banks were brought in to do much the same thing under the euphemism of "quantitative easing." In the few instances when the government was forced to take an equity stake as well, it did so with the proviso that it would not actually "nationalize" the companies in question, and would endeavor to sell off the stake as soon as feasible. This pattern was followed with minor variations in the United Kingdom and throughout the European Union as the financial crisis spread.

It is important to perceive that this middle-term response was the locus of the Schmittian moment of the neoliberal program. In normal times, none of these governmental entities would ever have had the authority or sovereignty to farm out massive government subsidies and waivers to other third-party private firms at the stroke of a pen: in a sense, the "privatization" of a financial rescue was more or less unthinkable. Indeed, Treasury Secretary Paulson and Fed Chairman Bernanke had been known to repeatedly deny that they had the statutory authority to do any number of things during the crisis. Yet, precisely here, in the midst of the collapse, these neoliberal leaders took upon themselves the right to arrogate the power of defining the "exception," to anoint themselves as the true political sovereigns in time of emergency; and right at that juncture, they imposed the neoliberal prescription that creating more and different "markets" would serve to rescue the economy. Here lay the deep neoliberal provenance of the seeming potpourri of bailouts, rule suspensions, windfalls, forced mergers, and all the rest.

One way to describe this unprecedented array of practices was to gloss it as the prevention of rolling bankruptcy through the instrumentality of the central government and the central banks taking much of the risks and bad paper onto their own balance sheets, either directly or virtually through loans and guarantees to private interests. Rather than create a new market in "carbon-style permits," the government and central banks jury-rigged a novel market in quasi-public, quasi-private debt. As has often been bemoaned, in practice profits remained privatized while all the downside risk was nationalized. It has been less frequently noticed that most of these activities didn't actually "solve" the financial crisis in any lasting or definitive way; all they did was shift it onto the balance sheets of governments, who then subsequently found their own public debt ballooning and their central banks becoming market-makers of last resort.[35] This ramshackle contraption of the government backstopping corporate failure through disguised asset "purchases" on a grand scale has morphed into a mutant form of capitalism, one that sports its origins in the neoliberal precept that the solution to supposed market failures is more markets.

This mechanism of "market-maker of last resort" as a neoliberal analogue of the carbon-trading schemes has had a felicitous political effect from the perspective of the neoliberals, of shifting attention away from the original insolvency of the banks and firms who securitized the impossible and proliferated the debt in the first place, and displacing it onto the sovereign federal governments, who found their public debt growing perilously out of control. One might regard this innovation as co-opting the very idea of nationalization of business firms from the history of the left, but turning it on its head, lumbering the state with only the failed assets off the crippled private balance sheets, while leaving the remainder of the firm in private hands, to enjoy revived profitability. As the Manchester CRESC group observed, "Leverage was the driving force behind the privatization of gains and the socialization of losses."[36]

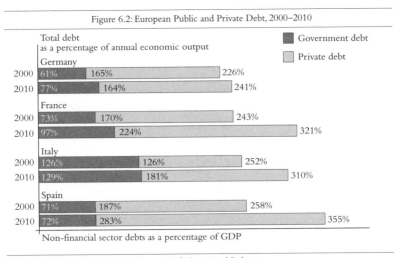

Figure 6.2: European Public and Private Debt, 2000–2010

Source: Bank for International Settlements

Alternatively, one might discern in its vaulting ambition the financial logic of the Structured Investment Vehicle used to hide crushing liabilities, only now being imposed on the state itself. In the meantime, as bond vigilantes conduct their attacks and government insolvency looms, states are forced by neoliberal parties and international agencies to engage in myriad forms of "austerity," which include fire sales of viable legacy state assets and crude attempts to lower wages and renege on social insurance schemes. Indeed, this narrative that the crisis is all the fault of the government conforms so faithfully to the standard neoliberal script, trumpeted relentlessly from the think-tank shell of the Russian doll since early in the crisis, that it is hard to imagine that the tactical political economy of market-maker of last resort was not engineered to conjure this outcome. Its provenance dates back to Milton Friedman's account of the errors of the Great Depression of the 1930s, and its outlines have been implemented by Friedman's acolyte Ben Bernanke during the current crisis.[37] The beauty of the dynamic is that other segments of the NTC could then exercise their hostility toward both the federal government and the Federal Reserve with seeming justification, thus filling up most of the political space churning around reactions to the crisis. For instance, the Tea Party could not have existed without this "market-based" practice of shifting the onus of business-induced leverage onto the state, then having private interests run the bailout, and then, as a consequence, precipitating a

crisis of state legitimacy. Once set in motion, it has been a juggernaut that moves of its own accord. In parallel with carbon trading,
the medium-term failure of the policy turns into long-term political success for the neoliberals.[38]

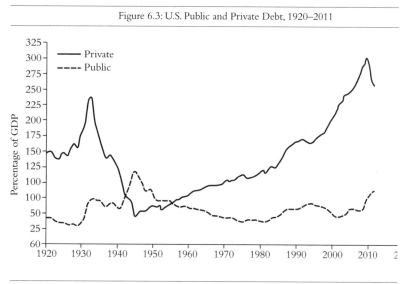

Figure 6.3: U.S. Public and Private Debt, 1920–2011

Source: debtdeflation.com/blogs

Just as cap-and-trade in permits exists primarily to thwart serious
reduction of carbon emissions, contemporary "last resort" market
policies that set up the state as dumping ground for financial detritus,
only then to have it managed behind the scenes by private interests,
mostly exist to thwart any serious intervention–cum–nationalization
and subsequent writedown of insolvent firms in a crash. Hobbled
firms may therefore continue to soldier on and make a profit, but the
underlying load of unsustainable debt in the society as a whole has not
been addressed. In this it resembles nothing so much as the "private
equity" model of business predation. Whatever it was about unsustainable levels of private debt and irredeemable backlogs of dubious
financial instruments that may have led up to the crisis, government-
based market policies have done almost nothing to rectify the
elemental flaws in the instruments themselves. Thus, postcrisis,
enhanced leverage proceeds apace. This is demonstrated in Figure 6.2
in data for levels of public and private debt as a percentage of GDP for
a selection of European countries before and after the crisis, and in
Figure 6.3, time series of public and private debt percentages for the

United States over the twentieth century. Soon governments, having opted for the privatized market-maker model, are then forced by political shifts to somehow curtail spending. Austerity programs only make most attempts to deleverage less effective, all in the name of restoration of fiscal prudence. If anything, the private sector has managed to resume most of the practices that were acknowledged to have inflated the bubble in the first decade of the 2000s. Although there is no reliable gauge of the world trading volume of over-the-counter credit default swaps, the industry trade group provides data suggesting that gross exposure of such derivatives topped $5 trillion in December 2008, and was around $3 trillion in 2011.[39] However, it has been various interest-rate contracts among the various financial derivatives that have expanded to the greatest degree, both before and after the crisis, as revealed in Figure 6.4.

The prospect of the government serving as market-maker of last resort presumably cannot be extended indefinitely, which brings us to the final long-game component of the full-spectrum brace of policies: the crisis analogue of geoengineering for neoliberals is the equally science-fiction prospect of financial innovation as the mode of ultimate deliverance from economic stagnation. Just as with geoengineering, the policy consists more of insubstantial promise than in demonstrated capabilities; but it plays an important pivotal political role nonetheless. The prophets of financial innovation are at pains to portray the invention of new pecuniary instruments, practices, and products as on a par with the science-based innovation of new physical technologies; in other words, it is the very apotheosis of the market coming to terms with an evolving nature. Indeed, one of the first people to promote the notion of financial innovation as a phenomenon commensurate with technological change was the Chicago neoliberal economist Merton Miller, again demonstrating direct affiliations with the thought collective.[40] Miller himself admitted that much of the motive for this innovation was to avoid or circumvent prior regulations; but later discussions tended instead to stress purported improvements in general welfare, on the same footing as welfare gains from enhanced solar cells or combustion engines. While the terminology has been percolating around the edges of the economics profession ever since then, it really rose to public consciousness only in the crisis, as revealed in the Google Trends compendium of Google searches (top) and mentions in the news media (bottom), displayed in Figure 6.5. It is the rollout of the concept from discussion internal to the economics profession to its uses in the larger public sphere that is central to its strategic function within the neoliberal full-spectrum policy response.

Figure 6.4: Total Over-the-Counter Outstanding Derivatives ($trillions)

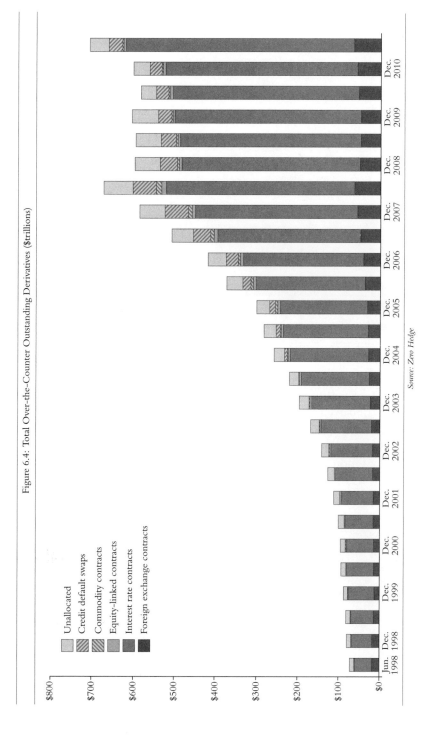

Unallocated
Credit default swaps
Commodity contracts
Equity-linked contracts
Interest rate contracts
Foreign exchange contracts

Source: Zero Hedge

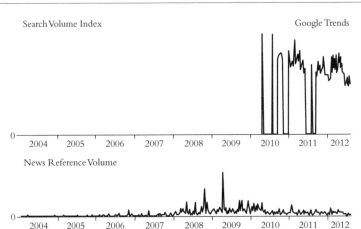

Figure 6.5: Google Trends for Term "Financial Innovation"

The conflation of options pricing with the ophthalmoscope made great semiotic play with the connotations of technological "improvements," which somehow enhanced efficiency and efficacy; and soon thereafter one began to hear of dedicated "financial engineers" (aka "quants") tinkering and fine-tuning the machinery of Wall Street and London. One conflation soon spawned another: denizens of "science studies," accustomed as they were to description of technological artifacts, conceived of the notion that they could just as readily apply their expertise to these financial phenomena, since, after all, they were just another species of technological innovation. Thus appeared a whole series of monographs on the "social studies of finance," most of which tended to recapitulate the accounts of finance already current among the orthodox economists and practitioners in the area; perhaps inadvertently, they tended to reinforce the cultural *Geist* that the banking sector sported a teleology of internal scientific logic of development.[41] It then comes as no surprise that it was a sociologist of science who came up with a thoroughly internalist and technical account of the causes of the crisis, devoid of all political economy.[42]

It should be noted that another neoliberal phenomenon came into play to reinforce the equation of physical technology and finance. As described in detail in *ScienceMart*, the expansion of the patent system to encompass all sorts of previously unpatentable phenomena occurred in the 1980s. One of the major classes of newly minted intellectual property was precisely "business methods," particularly those which were inscribed within computer programs. Almost immediately, a wave of financial algorithms were newly patented;[43] and this, in turn, rendered financial manipulations conceptually more on a par with technologies that had been previously subject to being reduced to intellectual property. What was posited as a newly valid classification ended up as real in its consequences.

It was one thing to reduce the tortured history of finance to a science-fiction narrative of the technological sublime; it has been quite another to turn it into the ne plus ultra of the full-spectrum neoliberal response to the crisis. As in the case of geoengineering, it has been necessary to recruit scientists who concede that they will never rectify the underlying crisis debility, so they must turn their efforts instead to fashioning Band-Aids to treat the symptoms. As the economist Paul Romer is reported to have said, "Every decade or so, any finite system of financial regulation will lead to a systemic financial crisis."[44] Never mind the history of the agent practices or the neoliberal capture of politics (or economic history, for that matter); the market will always periodically experience indigestion. Options, CDOs-squared, credit default swaps, high-frequency trading, dark pools, repo, rehypothecation, shadow banking, SIVs: you can't hold back the ocean. Financial complexification is as inevitable as the tides. If nature will never be thoroughly tamed, then it behooves us to at least develop instrumentalities to ride its chaotic complexity. And it follows that the response to apparent market glitches is to double down with even more markets.

The appeals to nature are rather unself-conscious and aboveboard in the writings of the contemporary proponents of financial engineering, such as Robert Litan, Barry Eichengreen, and Robert Shiller.[45] Because Shiller had become anointed by the media as the exemplar of an economist who had presciently warned of the housing bubble before it burst, the public has imbibed a seriously mistaken impression of him as some sort of economic maverick of the left. While he diffidently renounces the Efficient Markets Hypothesis, in all other matters Shiller is about as orthodox an economist as one can find nowadays. Shiller has been insisting upon the literal interpretation of finance as a technology for some time now;[46] and given the opportunity, he reaches for the physical equivalent in order to render his utopian vision more tangible. Here, for instance, he responds to a question about the banks, not understanding the full implications of the instruments they peddled during the bubble:

That is a problem, and I would say that it's a problem with technology in general. When someone designs an airplane, if it gets too complicated then the engineers don't understand what's happening. This is to do with systems, so if you're designing an air traffic control system and it's too complicated, there's going to be a catastrophe. But on the other hand I'm thinking that modern civilisation with modern computers can create some pretty complicated things. I'm thinking of, for example, the automobile. It's got more and more complicated over the years and it's getting harder and harder for the backyard mechanic who wants to fix the car. So you take it out to a dealer who has a computerised diagnostic system and so on. That's the kind of society we're living in. We always have to be mindful of some catastrophe that could result from our not understanding the complexity, definitely. But on the other hand I think we're on a secure trend to more complexity, and computers are an important reason why we are. Life is going to get more and more complex and specialised, that's pretty inevitable while civilisation advances.[47]

Thus what we confront in this sphere is very similar to what we encountered in the case of geoengineering: since no one can staunch carbon emissions, we might as well spew sulfur dioxide into the troposphere to attempt to reflect back a little more infrared, and provoke runaway algae blooms in the ocean to soak up a little more CO_2. There may be unanticipated feedbacks, and further disruptions, but complexity be damned. Likewise, since no one will ever staunch the roiling financialization of the modern economy, we might as well concoct even more new "financial instruments" and baroque trading procedures to make people feel a bit more that the market is really on their side. Some wet blankets such as Nouriel Roubini, Simon Johnson, and Richard Bookstaber may denounce certain aspects of securitization; but they just don't understand:

> The Occupy Wall Street and Occupy London people say "We are the 99%." There's an increasing concern with unequal distribution of wealth, and finance is perceived as the villain in all of this. But I'm thinking it can't be the villain; finance is a technology that can, if it's properly applied, help reduce inequality if it's applied to everyone. So I think that people who are in finance today have a moral obligation to help advance the trend toward democratisation of finance.[48]

So how will more financial engineering help us out of the hole left by the global crisis? Some say the working-class "democratization" was just feedstock so that Wall Street and the City could securitize ever-expanding volumes of debt (while getting it graded AAA and foisting it off onto gullible money-market funds) as inadequate compensation for the dismantling of the welfare state; but people like Shiller say that the poverty and inequality could actually be mitigated by further financial engineering. The detailed examples provided in above turn out to be a little underwhelming, such as a "social impact bond" that pays a return if a particular social goal is met, or crowdfunding of public investment projects. But, just as with geoengineering, the nitty-gritty specifics are secondary: what really matters is that we learn to outsource our biggest social problems to entrepreneurs, who are the only people capable of using the market to discover really big solutions. In this respect, the promotion of financial engineering is a willfully ideological project.

> There are a lot of people who think that I am defending bad behavior. In no way am I defending corrupt behavior and my book contains a plea for inclusiveness, that all people are created equal. The criticism that Karl Marx advanced of capitalism, in a nutshell, he said the capitalists dominate because they own the capital. And the other people, the working class, have no access to capital. But as modern society becomes more inclusive, everyone who becomes knowledgeable about finance can have access to capital. You don't have to be born rich; we have a mechanism that allocates capital, that's the financial system at its best use. So what you have to know is: How do I get into that? You have to know how you can, for example, develop a business plan and present it to a venture capitalist, and in the modern economies I think they really don't care what social class you came from. You could be very working-class and, before you know it, you have millions of pounds to allocate, and that is the way that it's increasingly working. That is the fundamental flaw in Marx's thinking. He thought that these social classes were permanent and hopeless. We're learning that it's not. We should seek more progress, more democratisation of finance in the future.[49]

Having trouble with those student loans? Just incorporate yourself, and get some venture capitalist to stake your latest bright idea (should you have one), and maybe you can finance your very own way out of the bind. Certainly that's what Shiller did, by monetizing his ideas as chief economist of MacroMarkets LLC![50] Readers of chapter 3 will recognize the provenance of this particular moral tale.

Why They Have Won, Preliminary Version

The purpose of this book has been to attempt to answer this question: Why did the neoliberals come through the crisis stronger than ever? Precisely for that reason, we have passed lightly over some other highly contentious collateral issues, such as:

What were the key causes of the crisis?

Have economists of any stripe managed to produce a coherent and plausible narrative of the crisis, at least so far? What role have heterodox economists played in the dispute?

What are the major political weaknesses of the contemporary neoliberal movement?

What is the current topography of the Neoliberal Thought Collective?

What lessons should the left learn from the neoliberals, and which should they abjure?

What would a vital counternarrative to the epistemological commitments of the neoliberals look like?

Is there a coherent alternative framework within which to understand the interaction of the financialization of the economy with larger ebbs and flows of political economy in the global transformations of capitalism?

These are serious inquiries, demanding lavishly documented advocacy and lengthy disputations (and maybe a different species of Mont Pèlerin Society to hash them out?), which should be on the agenda of the left. Of course, there may not be the luxury of decades of time similar to that available to the neoliberals back in the 1940s (with tipping points looming for world climate and corporate domination). However, I do believe the current volume does dispel some commonplace notions that have gotten in the way of that project. The neoliberals have triumphed in the global economic crisis because:

1) Individual neoliberals reacted to cognitive dissonance precisely in the ways that social psychology has suggested they would. Contrary evidence did not dent their worldview.

2) Far from withdrawing from the intellectual agonistic field, after brief disarray they redoubled their efforts to influence and capture the economics profession, which has also benefitted economists in weathering the crisis. The preemption of the breaking up of the financial sector in reaction to its insolvency in almost every country has been the single most important event that has bolstered both the

transnational orthodox economist profession and the Neoliberal Thought Collective. Absent the maintenance of the previous leisure class and the further subsidy of the wealthy, the politics of the situation would potentially have been strikingly different. The relationship between the immunity of finance and the imperviousness of change in economic ideas has been direct.

3) Since economists were caught off-guard during the onset of the crisis, both journalists and the general public had initially to fall back on vernacular understandings of the disaster, as well as cultural conceptions of the economy then prevalent. Hence the prior decades of "everyday neoliberalism" that had taken root in the culture provided a bulwark until the active mobilization of the Neoliberal Thought Collective could mount further responses.

4) The thought collective has resorted to industrial-scale manufacture of ignorance about the crisis, based upon the time-tested model of the "tobacco strategy." The excuses generated by economists for defending their profession were a major component of this activity. This in turn deems that the burgeoning resistance to doing anything substantive about global warming should be paired as symmetric with the burgeoning resistance to doing anything about the global economic crisis, with orthodox economists playing a comparable role in each, for purposes of strategic analysis. Agnotology has proven an effective and cheap short-term strategy to paralyze political action.

5) The neoliberals have developed a relatively novel way to co-opt protest movements, through a combination of top-down hierarchical takeover plus a bottom-up commercialization and privatization of protest activities and recruitment. This is the extension of the practice of "murketing" to political action itself. Pop fascination with the role of social media in protest movements only strengthens this development.

6) Finally, the Neoliberal Thought Collective has displayed an identifiable repeating pattern of full-spectrum policy responses to really pervasive crisis, which consists of short-run denialism (see 4, above), medium-term imposition of state-sponsored markets, and long-term recruitment of entrepreneurs to explore scientific blue-sky projects to transform human relationships to nature. Different components might seemingly appear to emanate from different sectors of the thought collective, and often appear on their face to contradict one another, which helps to inflate characteristically neoliberal responses to fill up the space of public discussion during the crisis, pushing other options to the margins. Furthermore, the different components often

operate in tandem (in time, in co-opting opponents) to produce the ultimate result, which is to allow the market to come to its own inscrutable accommodation to the crisis.

Many of the components of the full-spectrum response can only be imposed in those special moments of "emergency" by a strong state, when all standard rule-governed activity is suspended. The neoliberals may preach the rule of law, and sneer in public about the ineptitude of government, but they win by taking advantage of "the exception" to introduce components of their program unencumbered by judicial or democratic accountability. We observe this happened during the global economic crisis, and fully expect to see it again upon onset of further climate catastrophe. It is here that it is most obvious that they take their Schmittian heritage to heart. They know what it means to never let a serious crisis go to waste.

Notes

1. One More Red Nightmare

1 For those with access to a film library, I would suggest *The Descent* (2006); or for something closer to the current topic, Adam Curtis's *The Trap* (2007). Just when I had begun feeling proud of my little trope, a friend pointed me to Wendy Brown's "American Nightmare: Neoliberalism, Neoconservatism, and De-democratization." Originality is an overrated virtue.

2 Video recordings of much of the proceedings are available on the Web at www.ineteconomics.org.

3 Kay, "The Map Is Not the Territory."

4 Tankersley and Hirsh, "Neo–Voodoo Economics."

5 Tiago Mata, at History of Economics Playground, at http://historyofeconomics.wordpress.com/2011/04/10/inet-bw-of-history-repeating/#more-2002.

6 Stephan Richter, www.theglobalist.com/storyid.aspx?StoryId=9096. See also the account by Yves Smith at www.nakedcapitalism.com/2011/04/page/3, which suggests that the video available at the INET website may have been redacted. I can vouch that in the Q&A, Summers called Smith's suggestion "socialism."

7 Brad DeLong, "Economics in Crisis," www.project-syndicate.org/commentary/delong113/English. As we shall see below, DeLong frequently used his blog to defend orthodox figures like Larry Summers and denounce heterodoxy, thus raising the issue of what this quote really was intended to convey.

8 This was brought home with the news in 2011 that the European Court for Human Rights refused to overturn Soros's 2002 French conviction for insider trading (Colchester, "Setback for Soros in Paris"). The Advisory Board at INET is studded with a number of neoliberals, and even a Mont Pèlerin member or two! See the roster at http://ineteconomics.org/about/leadership.

9 The list of speakers at INET Bretton Woods included two out of four of those anointed by the *Economist* magazine that same year as having "the most important ideas in a post-crisis world": Raghuram Rajan, Robert Shiller, Kenneth

Rogoff, and Barry Eichengreen. That magazine neglected to inform its readers that all four served as apologists for the orthodoxy. The doctrines of each are covered in this volume. At the conference there was, however, a substantial contingent from the Austrian School heterodoxy at INET. The Tea Party demonstrators outside the New Hampshire conference thus demonstrated once again that their grasp of the practical politics of Soros and his organization was less than sound.

10 Speakers included Deepak Lal, Amity Shales, John B. Taylor, Peter Boettke, Steve Forbes, Niall Ferguson, Hannes Gissurarson, Timothy Congdon, Martin Wolf, and Gary Becker. The papers, once available on the Mont Pèlerin website, have since been removed. For some further description, see Plehwe, "Neoliberal Think Tanks and the Crisis." The dominant neoliberal narrative of the crisis, which had stabilized by 2010, blaming it entirely on government policies, is described below in chapter 5.

11 Lehmann, "Let Them Eat Dogma."

12 This statement takes into account the numerous assertions of "reform," from the Dodd-Frank bill in the U.S. to the Basel III international bank regulations. On these issues, see R. Lee, *Running the World's Markets*; Konzelman et al., "Governance, Regulation and Financial Market Instability"; and Konczal, *Will It Work? How Will We Know?* "I am surprised—more than surprised, shocked even—that all that's transpired since 2007–8 has produced as little as it has" (the historian Steve Fraser quoted in Chan, "Dissenters Fault Report on Crisis in Finance"). This point is reprised in chapter 6, which proposes that this was a conscious outcome.

13 This story is still developing: www.huffingtonpost.com/2013/03/12/aig-hank-greenberg-lawsuit-bailout_n_2862195.html

14 Tabulated and graphed at www.dailystaghunt.com/markets/2012/1/12/the-correlation-of-laughter-at-fomc-meetings.html#entry14562168.

15 Adam Curtis, "The Economists' New Clothes," www.bbc.co.uk/blogs/adamcurtis/2010/02/the_economists_new_clothes.html.

16 Tkacik, "Journals of the Crisis Year."

17 The quote is from Ezra Klein, "What 'Inside Job' Got Wrong." Yves Smith at nakedcapitalism.com immediately responded to this attack on the movie with a riposte that will be expanded upon in this book: "This is worse than useless, since Klein incorrectly throws up his hands and effectively says no one can understand what happened and therefore there's no answer. One of the reasons the crisis has been so 'difficult to understand' is that the government and banking elites have been taking extraordinary efforts to obscure the truth. The AIG bailout, the GSE bailouts, the alphabet soup of Fed facilities, the con game of the 'stress tests,' the refusal to release information, the ridiculous government programs to 'restart' the market, the efforts to deny the mortgage crisis, HAMP,

the ongoing efforts to prop up the banks even though they are insolvent, they are all massive efforts at obscuring what really happened and what is still going on. This is not a coincidence; it is a deliberate effort orchestrated by the banks, the Fed, and the Treasury." Compare Klein's position with the neoliberal attack on *Inside Job*: see Kling, "Economics: A Million Mutinies Now."

18 John Kenneth Galbraith started out his PBS series *The Age of Uncertainty* with this quote from Keynes. It did not bode well for the rest of the series.

19 Crouch, *The Strange Non-Death of Neoliberalism*, p. 179.

20 Far and away the best systematic account of how the entire system of finance had become corrupted, beginning with the mortgage loan originators, extending through the rating agencies and regulatory agencies, and ending up at financial behemoths such as Goldman Sachs, is the U.S. Senate's Subcommittee on Investigations, *Wall Street and the Financial Crisis*, available at: www.hsgac.senate.gov. It is far superior to the final report of the Financial Crisis Inquiry Committee, archived at http://cybercemetery.unt.edu/archive/fcic/20110310173538/http://www.fcic.gov/report; this latter report was itself torpedoed by neoliberal attempts to neuter its findings, as I describe in chapter 5. The website nakedcapitalism .com has performed a valuable service in tracking down numerous technical aspects of the crisis. Other superior accounts of the crisis can be found in Taibbi, *Griftopia*; Engel and McCoy, *The Subprime Virus*; Buckley, *Financial Crisis*; and Ferguson, *Predator Nation*. Characteristically, none of these are covered in the orthodox economist's "survey" of crisis literature (Lo, "Reading About the Financial Crisis").

21 "'In the US,' Alan Blinder told me weeks later, a little bleakly, a little apologetically, 'there is no left left'" (quoted in Wallace-Wells, "What's Left of the Left"). Of course, most Europeans would surely disqualify such Americans from claiming that mantle of the left; but I think the generic debility runs much deeper. This notion of the intellectual capitulation of the left to neoliberal dominance is a frequent topic on such blogs as *Naked Capitalism*, *Crooked Timber*, and *Slack Wire*.

22 In a review of Simon Johnson and James Kwak's *13 Bankers*, the economist Guillermo Calvo ("Yes, the Rich Will Drive Recovery") neatly summarized the neoliberal case: "The authors detail at prolix length the oscillation between Team Greed and Team Regulation, each of which perpetually insists it has brought systemic problems to heel, and each of which is inevitably embarrassed. . . . The authors seem, in that instant, on the verge of realizing that the problem is the dynamic itself—that the choice between greed and regulation is a false one, that the dance of bankers and regulators is exactly what ends in a tangle on the floor, with the markets a shambles."

23 The latest to insist upon this is Bernard Harcourt (*The Illusion of Free Markets*); even he admits the central observation dates back to Karl Polanyi (*The Great*

Transformation) and even earlier to the American Institutionalists (Samuels, *Essays in the Economic Role of Government*; "The Economy as a System of Power") and the early legal realists. For other clear statements from historians and political scientists, see Roberts, *Victorian Origins of the British Welfare State*; Campbell and Pedersen, *The Rise of Neoliberalism and Institutional Analysis*.

24 This precept is made explicit in a recent Graeber interview: "I first was putting it together in a piece for *Mute* in the immediate wake of 2008, and I began by saying that when you're in a crisis, the first thing you have to do is ask, What is the larger rhythmic or temporal structure in which these events are taking place? So I decided to cast my net as widely as possible, to say, What if this was part of a genuinely world-historic breaking point, the sort of thing that happens every 500 years or so—my idea of a long oscillation between periods of credit" (in R. Jones, "Bookforum Talks with David Graeber"). Here we observe that Graeber serves as the Ken Rogoff of the left, insisting, "The very notion that we exist in a totalizing system is itself the core ideological idea we need to overcome." Rogoff and Reinhart's headline generalization that economic growth generally turned negative when the ratio of public debt/GDP breached the 90 percent barrier was later shown to have been an artifact of suspicious data "errors' in those authors' analyses by Herndon, Ash and Pollin, "Does High Public Debt . . ." Not only did Rogoff misrepresent the history, but he also indirectly revealed the extent to which he approached it as a malleable truth subservient to neoliberal imperatives.

25 Friedrich Hayek, "Why I Am Not a Conservative," in *The Constitution of Liberty*, pp. 397–411); James Buchanan, *Why I, Too, Am Not a Conservative*.

26 This is one place where I must demur from the otherwise perceptive Jamie Peck ("Zombie Neoliberalism and the Ambidextrous State"). Surely neoliberalism is beset with internal contradictions; but it is also important to have some appreciation for the lack of identity between the neoliberal program and the statecraft that can often fail in its implementation. This may also be a problem with some of the work of David Harvey.

27 John Quiggin at http://crookedtimber.org/2007/06/01/heterodoxy-is-not-my-doxy/. The footnote (*) to the text reads: "I guess the big exception to this is if you want to discard methodological individualism altogether, but the theoretical enterprises that took this route (such as structuralism) don't seem to me to be prospering."

28 Quiggin, *Zombie Economics*, p. 83, 129, 121, 87.

29 Paul Krugman blog, http://krugman.blogs.nytimes.com/2010/11/26/the-instability-of-moderation/#more-14713, November 26, 2010.

30 See, for instance, the letter of Paul Samuelson to Assar Lindbeck, February 14, 1977, in Box 4, Folder "Nobel Nominating Committee," Paul Samuelson Papers, Perkins Library, Duke University.

31   This literature became so prevalent that this footnote offers just a representative
     sampling: Backhouse, *The Puzzle of Modern Economics*; Brock and Colander,
     "Complexity, Pedagogy, and the Economics of Muddling Through"; Colander,
     "The Death of Neoclassical Economics"; Colander, Holt, and Rosser, "Live
     and Dead Issues in the Methodology of Economics" and "The Changing Face
     of Economics"; J. Davis, "The Turn in Economics," "The Turn in Recent
     Economics and the Return of Orthodoxy" and "The Change In and Recent
     State of Economics"; Eichengreen, "The Last Temptation of Risk."

32   Arnsperger and Varoufakis, "What Is Neoclassical Economics?"

33   Bowmaker, *Economics Uncut*; Lehrer, "Can We Prevent the Next Bubble?";
     Camerer et al., "Neuroeconomics"; Mirowski, *ScienceMart*; Akerlof and Kran-
     ton, *Identity Economics*; Benabou and Tirole, "Identity, Dignity and Taboos."

34   "But we have a Chicago economy, not a neoclassical one." (Crouch, *The Strange
     Non-Death of Neoliberalism*, p.122). While the spirit of this observation is mostly
     correct, the situation is far more complicated than the "Privatized Keynesian-
     ism" described by Crouch.

35   Quiggin, *Zombie Economics*, p. 122.

2. *Shock Block Doctrine*

1   Some representative instances: Barnett, "The Consolations of Neoliberalism";
    Caldwell, "The Chicago School, Hayek, and Neoliberalism"; Boas and Gans-
    Morse, "Neoliberalism"; Kingfisher and Maskovsky, "Introduction." Even
    stranger is the assertion that we have entered upon a period of "postneoliberal-
    ism" (Brand and Seckler, *Postneoliberalism*). The economist's refrain of "this time
    is never different" (Rogoff and Reinhart, *This Time Is Different*) is taken to an
    extreme by Kean Birch, "Have We Ever Been Neoliberal?": "If financial crises
    have happened before—and they have, repeatedly [see Roubini and Mihm,
    Crisis Economics]—then this would suggest that neoliberalism has and does not
    necessarily play a consequential role in the current crisis."

2   "Bruce Caldwell . . . said he hoped that we were experiencing, partly through
    [Paul] Ryan's ascendancy, the first stage of a slow but steady embrace of Hayek's
    philosophy" (Davidson, "Prime Time for Paul Ryan's Guru"). As if it hadn't
    been happening well prior to the 2012 election—but one neoliberal trick is to
    insist they are the perennial underdogs, even as they overrun one intellectual
    citadel after another.

3   Dean, "Rethinking Neoliberalism."

4   Some examples: Saad-Filho and Johnston, *Neoliberalism*; Calhoun and Derlu-
    guian, *The Deepening Crisis*; Harvey, *A Brief History of Neoliberalism*. Indeed, the
    otherwise very interesting book by the Manchester group on the reaction of the
    financial sector to the crisis abjures recourse to the concept of Neoliberalism,

because it emphasizes cross county similarities of processes that the authors wish to call into question (Engelen et al., *After the Great Complacence*, p. 33).

5   Some of the most important sources will be Cockett, *Thinking the Unthinkable*; Mirowski and Plehwe, *The Road from Mont Pèlerin*; Walpen, *Die offenen Feinde und ihre Gesellschaft*; Burgin, "The Political Economy of the Early Mont Pèlerin Society" and *The Return of Laissez Faire*; Amable, "Morals and Politics in the Ideology of Neoliberalism"; Jackson, "At the Origins of Neo-liberalism"; Harcourt, *The Illusion of Free Markets*; O'Neill, *The Market*; Ban, *Neoliberalism in Translation*; Wacquant, "Three Steps to an Historical Anthropology of Actually Existing Neoliberalism"; Zuidhof, *Imagining Markets*; Dean, "Rethinking Neoliberalism"; D. Jones, *Masters of the Universe*.

6   George Monbiot, "How Did We Get into This Mess?" *Guardian*, August 28, 2007; available on his website, www.monbiot.com.

7   Kunkel, "On Your Marx."

8   Peck, Theodore, and Brenner, "Postneoliberalism and its Malcontents," p. 94.

9   Birch and Mykhnenko, *The Rise and Fall of Neoliberalism*, p. 255. Kean Birch has come to repudiate this verdict in an interesting manner, as discussed in "Have We Ever Been Neoliberal?"

10   Judt, *Ill Fares the Land*, p. 7.

11   Duménil and Dominique Lévy, *The Crisis of Neoliberalism*, pp. 1, 9.

12   Wilby, "All of Us Live by the Logic of Finance."

13   Gusenbauer, "La Strada on Wall Street."

14   Charles Mudede, in a review of DeAngelis's *The End of History* at http://slog. thestranger.com/slog/archives/2011/05/13/the-end-of-neoliberalism-explained.

15   Stiglitz, "The End of Neoliberalism."

16   http://news.infoshop.org/article.php?story=20081017213027248. This interview was published in *Berliner Zeitung*, October 9, 2008. Stiglitz grew more circumspect in outlets that were print-based: see Stiglitz, *Freefall* .

17   Saskia Sassen, "Too Big to Save," www.opendemocracy.net, April 1, 2009.

18   www.counterpunch.org/harvey03132009.html.

19   Konzelmann et al., "Governance, Regulation and Financial Market Instability."

20   For the specifics see Nik-Khah, "Chicago Neoliberalism and the Genesis of the Milton Friedman Institute." There are some subsequent indications that this fund drive did not go well.

21   Campbell, "Neoliberalism in Crisis."

22   See, for instance, Callinicos, *Bonfire of Illusions*; Cassidy, *How Markets Fail*; Fox, *The Myth of the Rational Market*; Westbrook, *Out of the Crisis*; Yves Smith, *Econned*; Mason, *Meltdown*; Kaletsky, *Capitalism 4.0*; Stiglitz, *Freefall*.

23   The various approaches to social epistemology within the philosophy literature are fascinating; without endorsing any specific position, one can sample the options in Goldman and Whitcomb, *Social Epistemology*; Kourany, *Philosophy of*

Science after Feminism; Kusch, *Knowledge by Agreement*; Longino, *The Fate of Knowledge*; Solomon, *Social Empiricism*; Fuller, *Social Epistemology*; Harding, *Can Theories Be Refuted?*.

24 Festinger et al., *When Prophecy Fails*, p. 3.

25 Lord et al., "Biased Assimilation and Attitude Polarization"; Fischer et al., "The Theory of Cognitive Dissonance."

26 D. Jones, *Masters of the Universe*, p. 7.

27 Nicholls, *Freedom with Responsibility*, p. 96; Hartwell, *A History of the Mont Pèlerin Society*, pp. 84, 93; Walpen, *Die offenen Feinde und ihre Gesellschaft*, pp. 1072, 1074.

28 Thanks to Anette Nyqvist and Jamie Peck for the translation of this document from the Norwegian.

29 See, for instance, Hulsmann, *Mises*: "We find a clear expression of the neo-liberal world view in a paper Hayek wrote in 1935" (p. 710); "The exchange between Mises and his neo-liberal opponents set the tone in the Mont Pèlerin Society for years to come" (p. 871); "In the 1960s Austro-libertarianism came to be largely supplanted . . . [by] the takeover of the Mont Pèlerin Society by Chicago School neoliberals in the 1960s, and the emergence of an organized Randian or 'Objectivist' movement" (p. 989). Other general historians of the larger conservative movement use the term in the same way, e.g., Nash, *The Conservative Intellectual Movement in America*, p. 32.

30 Nash, *The Conservative Intellectual Movement in America*; Phillips-Fein, *Invisible Hands*; Gross et al., "The Contemporary American Conservative Movement."

31 Even historians sympathetic to neoliberalism have concluded that Hayek's approach to knowledge preclude a direct genealogy rooted in Hume (Kukathas, *Hayek and Modern Liberalism*; Petsoulas, *Hayek's Liberalism and Its Origins*). That Smith would never have accepted neoliberal politics is a hallowed theme in the history of economic thought.

32 Quoted in Hartwell, *A History of the Mont Pèlerin Society*, p. 33.

33 Friedman, "Interview," 1995.

34 Milton Friedman, "Economic Freedom behind the Scenes" (2002), at www.cato.org/special/friedman/friedman/friedman4.html. A nice introduction to hard libertarian doctrines of Hoppe and others is Dittmer, "Journey into a Libertarian Future."

35 This key point repeatedly trips up otherwise perceptive historians of the movement. For instance, "transatlantic Neoliberalism, as used in this book, is the free market ideology based on individual liberty and limited government that connected human freedom to the actions of the rational, self-interested actor in the competitive marketplace" (D. Jones, *Masters of the Universe*, p. 2).

36 Brown, *Edgework*, p. 40.

37 See, for instance, Brown, *Edgework*; Campbell, "Neoliberalism in Crisis";

Jackson, "At the Origins of Neo-liberalism"; Zuidhof, *Imagining Markets*; Plehwe et al., *Neoliberal Hegemony*; Mirowski and Plehwe, *The Road from Mont Pèlerin*; Peck, *Constructions of Neoliberal Reason*; Walpen, *Die offenen Feinde und ihre Gesellschaft*.

38 See Jackson, "At the Origins of Neo-liberalism," p. 135 et seq.; Dardot and Laval, *La nouvelle raison du monde*. Hayek in *The Road to Serfdom* notoriously opined, "Probably nothing has done as much harm to the liberal cause as the wooden insistence of some liberals on certain rough rules of thumb, above all the principle of *laissez-faire*" (p. 71). Wacquant ("Three Steps to an Historical Anthropology of Actually Existing Neoliberalism") points out that neoliberals advocate laissez-faire only for the rich and powerful, not for the subalterns.

39 James Buchanan, "Man and the State," MPS Presidential talk, August 31, 1986, pp. 2, 11. LAMP, 1986, Saint Vincent, Italy, meeting records. Henceforth, all primary source material from Mont Pèlerin meetings is quoted with permission from the Liberaal Archief, Ghent, Belgium, and will be cited in this chapter as [LAMP, date]. The hand list for this collection can be consulted at www.liber aalarchief.be/MPS2005.pdf.

40 Quoted in Burgin, *The Return of Laissez Faire*, p. 203.

41 To avoid testing the reader's patience, I will not deal here with more recent academic works that pursue obfuscation to ever greater degrees, such as Bockman, *Markets in the Name of Socialism*, which argues that the origins of neoliberalism should be traced to Eastern European socialist intellectuals. Worse is Zingales, *A Capitalism for the People*, which attempts to argue that neoliberalism is pro-capitalism, but hostile to the elite rich and their political power. This latter work is an exemplar of the neoliberal practice of the manufacture of ignorance, discussed later in this chapter.

42 Later, one might add "Virginia public choice theory" as a fourth. For an insider's attempt at discrimination between the Hayekians and the Chicago School, see Skousen, *Chicago and Vienna*. For an overview of the Ordoliberals, see Nicholls, *Freedom with Responsibility*. For some history of public choice, see Amadae, *Rationalizing Capitalist Democracy*.

43 Hayek to Arthur Seldon, May 13, 1985, quoted in Hennecke, *Friedrich August von Hayek*, p. 316.

44 Howard and King, *The Rise of Neoliberalism in Advanced Capitalist Economies*, p. 11.

45 Jones, *Masters of the Universe*.

46 Peck, *Constructions of Neoliberal Reason*, p. 72.

47 Zuidhof, *Imagining Markets*.

48 In Burgin, *The Return of Laissez Faire*, p. 180.

49 Hayek to de Jouvenel, October 4, 1950, quoted in Burgin, *The Return of Laissez Faire*, p. 206.

50 Hartwell, *A History of the Mont Pèlerin Society*, p. 44.

51 See the letter from Smedley to Anthony Fisher dated June 25, 1956, quoted in Cockett, *Thinking the Unthinkable*, p. 131: "[I]t is imperative we should give no indication in our literature that we are working to educate the Public along certain lines which might be interpreted as having political bias . . . it might enable our enemies to question the charitableness of our motives." For Leonard Read admitting the same thing, see Burns, *Goddess of the Market*, p. 116.

52 Burgin, *The Return of Laissez Faire*, p. 306.

53 Some important examples: the Heritage Foundation (USA), the Manhattan Institute (USA), the Mercatus Center (USA), the Fraser Institute (Canada), Stiftung Marktwirtschaft (Germany), Center for a New Europe (Brussels). There are even specialized neoliberal think tanks devoted to science policy, such as the George Marshall Institute, the Annapolis Center, the Heartland Institute, and the Ethics and Public Policy Center—note the anodyne names, hiding the political orientation.

54 For more on Atlas and Antony Fisher, see www.atlas.org and Frost, *Antony Fisher*; Hoplin and Robinson, *Funding Fathers*, chap. 6; Burton, "Atlas Research Foundation."

55 The byzantine politics of the Murdoch empire is discussed in an interesting fashion by Adam Curtis at www.bbc.co.uk/blogs/adamcurtis/2011/01/rupert_murdoch_-_a_portrait_of.html.

56 Covington, "Moving Public Policy to the Right," pp. 91–92; also Medvetz, *Think Tanks in America*.

57 The various ways in which fake local grass-roots movements are co-opted by neoliberal organizations has become the subject of some journalistic interest. One telling example in the arcane technical area of environmental sciences was the subject of a PBS program reporting on the investigations of the journalist Paul Thacker (see *American Investigative Reporting*, program 11, November 10, 2006, accessed at www.pbs.org. For another perspective, see *(Astro)Turf Wars* (2010).

58 Davidson, "Prime Time for Paul Ryan's Guru."

59 Max Thurn, 1964 meeting records, LAMP, emphasis added.

60 Insistence upon this point has been one of the great strengths of the Foucault-inspired tradition of analysis of neoliberalism, an argument made with great effect by Donzelot, "Michel Foucault and Liberal Intelligence." It was also a major theme of Brown, *Edgework*.

61 Quoted in Cockett, *Thinking the Unthinkable*, p. 112.

62 The complaint that this construction is too narrow (D. Jones, *Masters of the Universe*) confuses its use to *define* neoliberalism, and other uses in tracking the political activities of neoliberals. This chapter is engaged in the former; the remainder of the book with the latter.

63 This point is nicely made by Dean, "Rethinking Neoliberalism."

64 Van Horn and Mirowski, "The Rise of the Chicago School and the Birth of Neoliberalism"; Van Horn and Klaes, "Chicago Neoliberalism Versus Cowles Planning."

65 Kaiser, *How the Hippies Saved Physics*; Kragh, *Higher Speculations*.

66 One interesting meditation can be found in Brenner et al., "Variegated Neoliberalization," where they take the governmentality literature to task for imagining a "context-drenched, haphazardly mobile, radically fluid and infinitely mutable" portrait of neoliberalism. The extent to which the neoliberal project is "top down" or "bottom up" is something that has been transcended by the Russian doll structure, in my view. Another is Zuidhof (*Imagining Markets*), who finds neoliberal discourse is more deeply "statist" in the Netherlands than in the United States. One might aver this is due to the greater salience of ordoliberalism in Holland.

67 Peck, *Constructions of Neoliberal Reason*, p. 30.

68 Brenner, Peck, and Theodore, "Variegated Neoliberalization"; Klein, *The Shock Doctrine*.

69 In this volume I will avoid detailed specification of what actual persons would or would not subscribe to each individual tenet, mainly because such detailed historical work would take us too far away from our focus on the crisis. However, this should not be taken to imply in any way that I deem such work unimportant.

70 Foucault, *Naissance de la Biopolitique*, p. 137, my translation; Wolin, *Politics and Vision*, p. 314; Peck, *Constructions of Neoliberal Reason*, p. 3; Wacquant, "Three Steps to an Historical Anthropology of Actually Existing Neoliberalism."

71 See Wiseman, *Cost, Choice and Political Economy*; Buchanan and Vanberg, "Constitutional Choice, Rational Ignorance and the Limits of Reason." This is the version that comes closest to Ayn Rand and the "Objectivists," although Rand herself found Hayek anathema. In Burns, *Goddess of the Market*, p. 104, she is quoted as saying, "The man [Hayek] is an ass, with no conception of a free society at all."

72 This is discussed in greater detail in Caldwell, *Hayek's Challenge*; Mirowski, *Machine Dreams*, "Naturalizing the Market," and in my forthcoming lectures, "The History of the Economics of Information."

73 Ptak, "Neoliberalism in Germany"; Bonefeld, "Freedom and the Strong State."

74 The similarities to Christian notions of the Godhead are perhaps not altogether accidental. "In the Ordo-liberal scheme, the market does not amount to a natural economic reality, with intrinsic laws that the art of government must bear in mind; instead, the market can be constituted and kept alive only by dint of political interventions" (Lemke, "The Birth of Biopolitics," p. 193).

75 This is further discussed by Mirowski in Van Horn et al., *Building Chicago Economics*. See also Vroman, "Allusions to Evolution," and Mirowski, *Machine Dreams*, on the origins of the "cyborg sciences."

76 Cooper, *Life as Surplus*; Nadesan, *Governmentality, Biopower and Everyday Life*.

77 See, for instance, McKinnon, *Neo-liberal Genetics*; Ridley, *The Agile Gene* and *The Rational Optimist*; Pickering, *The Cybernetic Brain*; and my review of the latter book in *Technology and Culture*, 2012.

78 Cooper, "Complexity Theory after the Crisis"; Walker and Cooper, "Genealogies of Resistance."

79 This subtle ontological move and its relationship to political action is best illustrated by the neoliberal response to global warming, discussed in chapter 6.

80 Peck, *Constructions of Neoliberal Reason*, p. xiii.

81 Neoliberals tend to perceive democracy as desirable only insofar as democratic institutions encourage the development of the economic system they advocate. This was noted as far back as Friedrich, "Review: The Political Thought of Neo-Liberalism," and the topic of many commentaries on the neoliberal project. See Brown, *Edgework*; Plehwe et al., *Neoliberal Hegemony*; Robison, *The Neoliberal Revolution*; Turner, *Neo-liberal Ideology*; Dean, "Rethinking Neoliberalism".

82 Hayek, *Studies in Philosophy, Politics and Economics*, p. 161.

83 Power, *The Audit Society*; Lane, *New Public Management*.

84 It was an early clear signal of the unwillingness of the Obama administration to clean up the financial sector that he appointed Mary Schapiro as his new chair of the Securities and Exchange Commission, previously the chair and CEO of FINRA in 2009, long an advocate of the position that the financial sector had suffered overregulation.

85 On the modern trend toward privatized military functions, see Singer, *Corporate Warriors*; Scahill, *Blackwater*. The constant bewailing of the size of government is a win-win situation for neoliberals: they complain about recent growth of government, which they have themselves fostered, use the outrage they fan to "privatize" more functions, which leads only to more spending and a more intrusive infrastructure of government operations. The same dynamic is now at play in the further privatization and "rationalization" of European state health care systems.

86 Hayek, "The Moral Element in Free Enterprise."

87 In this regard, the nominally left-liberal tradition of "social-choice theory" (Kenneth Arrow, Amartya Sen, John Rawls) by this criterion is virtually as neoliberal as the right-wing tradition of the "public-choice theory" of Buchanan and Tullock and the Virginia School. See Amadae, *Rationalizing Capitalist Democracy*; Arnsperger, *Critical Political Economy*.

88 Plant, *The Neoliberal State*.

89 Foucault, *The Birth of Biopolitics*, p. 226.

90 Davis, *The Theory of the Individual in Economics* and *Individuals and Identity in Economics*.

91   Milton Friedman in Friedman and Samuelson, *Discuss the Responsibility of Government*, p. 5.

92   "Neoliberalism figures interest as both a psychology that drives rational choices, and as the good achieved by those choices. Subjective and objective interests are thus rendered neatly compatible: questions of false consciousness on the one hand, or of a 'real interest' that exceeds what people can realize by means of price-taking choices on the other, are not so much answered as they are rendered unintelligible" (Mathiowetz, *Appeals to Interest*).

93   Hayek, *The Constitution of Liberty*, p. 81; Plant, *The Neoliberal State*, p. 67; Friedman, "Economic Freedom Behind the Scenes."

94   On "negative" rather than "positive" definitions of freedom, see Berlin, "Two Concepts of Liberty"; Smith, "Friedman, Liberalism, and the Meaning of Negative Freedom." Even Berlin, not often considered a supporter of neoliberals, suggests that positive freedom leads inexorably to totalitarian systems. Hayek insists positive freedom violates the rule of law (Plant, *The Neoliberal State*, p. 38). The neoliberal subject is not supposed to be "free" to meditate upon the nature and limits of her own freedom—that is the dreaded "relativism" which neoliberals uniformly denounce.

95   Behrent, "Liberalism Without Humanism." This is discussed in the next chapter, in the section on governmentality.

96   See Kristol, "Socialism, Capitalism, Nihilism," LAMP, Montreux meeting, 1972: "And what if the 'self' that is 'realized' under the conditions of liberal capitalism is a self that despises liberal capitalism, and uses its liberty to subvert and abolish a free society? To this question, Hayek—like Friedman—has no answer."

97   There are exceptions to this generalization. For instance, the MPS member Gary Becker has proposed to solve illegal immigration by "selling" the rights to citizenship. This reduces state services to the ultimate commodity. It is significant that few other neoliberals have endorsed this complete dissolution of nationalist identity, although one could argue it follows logically from the other tenets of the program. What can nationality mean for a person without a stable identity?

98   See Helleiner, *States and the Re-emergence of Global Finance*; Weller and Singleton, in Plehwe et al., *Neoliberal Hegemony*; Thirkell-White, in Robison, *The Neoliberal Revolution*.

99   In Mirowski and Plehwe, *The Road from Mont Pèlerin*. See also Chwieroth, *Capital Ideas*.

100   Hayek, *Studies in Philosophy, Politics and Economics*, p. 172.

101   See the papers and data available for download at http://elsa.berkeley.edu/~saez/.

102   Rajan, *Fault Lines*.

103   See Van Horn and Mirowski, "The Rise of the Chicago School and the Birth of Neoliberalism."

104 Nace, *Gangs of America.*

105 Jensen and Meckling, "Theory of the Firm."

106 Nik-Khah, "A Tale of Two Auctions."

107 On the ill-fated DARPA "policy analysis market" project, see www.sfgate. com/cgi-bin/article.cgi?file=/c/a/2003/07/29/MN126930.DTL (accessed December 2, 2006) and Justin Wolfers and Eric Zitzowitz, "Prediction Markets in Theory and Practice," www.dartmouth.edu/~ericz/palgrave.pdf.

108 For unabashed examples of this neoliberal argument, see Litan, "In Defense of Much, but Not All, Financial Innovation" and *The Derivatives Dealer's Club*; Shiller, *Finance and the Good Society.* A more skeptical summary is Engelen, et al., *After the Great Complacence.* This constitutes a major component of the full-spectrum political response of the NTC to the crisis, as described in chapter 6.

109 Harcourt, *The Illusion of Free Markets*, p. 147.

110 Posner, quoted in ibid., p. 149.

111 Hayek, *The Constitution of Liberty*, p. 68, 69; Hayek, *Studies in Philosophy, Politics and Economics*, p. 155; Hartwell, *A History of the Mont Pèlerin Society*, p. 47. Modern neoliberals more or less echo these sentiments: "Our opponents have every right to contend that economists are unwisely idolizing liberty, but they err by saying we sail without a moral North Star" (Glaeser, "The Moral Heart of Economics").

112 Hayek, "The Moral Element in Free Enterprise."

113 Buchanan, *Ideas, Persons and Events*; Amable, "Morals and Politics in the Ideology of Neoliberalism."

114 See, for instance, Linker, *The Theocons*; S. Diamond, *Roads to Dominion*; Eecke, "Ethics in Economics." Hayek tipped his hand on his own approach to a general philosophy of neoliberalism when he said in the discussion of the MPS session on April 4: "Does liberalism presuppose some set of values which are commonly accepted as faith and in themselves not capable of rational demonstration?" (MPS archives, 1947 meeting). It seems clear from his later writings that he believed this was true about belief in the superiority of market organization itself.

115 Smith, *Cambridge Companion to Leo Strauss*, p. 18.

116 Davies, "The Emerging Neo-communitarianism."

117 Oliver, "German Neoliberalism."

118 From unpublished speech by Friedrich Hayek, "The Prospects of Freedom," quoted in Burgin, *The Return of Laissez Faire*, p. 180. The Burgin thesis has a nice discussion of the struggles of the early MPS with the incongruity of its character as a closed society; as he says, "an organization which forced members to hold a liberal point of view would be, in its very structure, illiberal" (p. 187).

119 Popper to Hayek, January 11, 1947. Karl Popper papers, Hoover Institute, Stanford California, Box 305, folder 13.

120 See, for instance, his 1954 speech "Towards a Liberal Theory of Public Opin-
     ion," quoted in Burgin, *The Return of Laissez Faire*, pp. 186-87.

121 Maurice Allais to Friedrich Hayek, May 12, 1947, quoted in Burgin, p. 189.

122 Hartwell, *A History of the Mont Pèlerin Society*, chapter 5.

123 For the clash of Popper and Hayek, see Vernon, "The Great Society and the
     Open Society"; Kukathas, *Hayek and Modern Liberalism*; for the rejection of
     Popper on science and knowledge, see Lakatos, *Criticism and the Growth of
     Knowledge*. This question has some bearing upon the attempt by George Soros
     to profess Popperian principles in his new organization INET and its response
     to the crisis.

124 Popper, *The Open Society and Its Enemies*, p. 265; Popper, *After the Open Society*,
     pp. 137, 239.

125 Quoted in Hartwell, *A History of the Mont Pèlerin Society*, p. xiv.

126 Buchanan, *Ideas, Persons and Events*, p. 211.

127 See Friedman and Friedman, *Free to Choose* and *Two Lucky People*; Friedman,
     Bright Promises, Dismal Performances. The position of James Buchanan (*Ideas,
     Persons and Events*, pp. 210–20) was only a slightly different variant, suggesting
     that the populace had to be tutored in the "elementary principles of [economic]
     science" to embrace the neoliberal position.

128 *Friedman and Samuelson Discuss the Responsibility of Government*, p. 13, gives a nice
     short example of his style: "I have often challenged audiences to name a significant
     program of government intervention intended to distribute income from high to
     low incomes, which succeeds in so doing." The television series funded by the
     Neoliberal Thought Collective on PBS, *Free to Choose*, provides many more.

129 Mirowski, *ScienceMart*; Thorpe, "Political Theory in STS".

130 Hayek, "The Intellectuals and Socialism"; Burgin, *History*, p. 194; Hayek, *Law,
     Legislation and Liberty*, chapter 2.

131 The response of Caldwell, "The Chicago School, Hayek, and Neoliberalism,"
     to this criticism is a good example of the unwillingness to explore this issue.

132 Hayek, *Law, Legislation and Liberty*, pp. 45–46.

133 Ibid., p. 51.

134 Zingales, *A Capitalism for the People*.

135 Conversation among Friedman, Director, and Craig Freedman, August 1997;
     reported in Freedman, *Chicago Fundamentalism*, p. 12.

136 Stigler, "The Intellectual and His Society," p. 312.

137 "The large mass of the public does not find it economically worthwhile to
     become well acquainted with the effects of policies which have small harmful
     effects upon each non-beneficiary." (George Stigler, unpublished paper "Schools
     in Science," quoted in Nik-Khah, "George Stigler, the Graduate School of
     Business, and the Pillars of the Chicago School," p. 140)

138 Some evidence supports Stigler's position: in a number of countries, it was

explicitly socialist parties that introduced some of the most critical neoliberal reforms. See Ban, *Neoliberalism in Translation*; Zuidhof, *Imagining Markets*.

139 Nik-Khah, "George Stigler." See also his forthcoming work on the role of Stigler in building a defense of the pharmaceutical sector against the FDA.

140 Parts of this section have previously appeared in Mirowski, *ScienceMart*.

141 Hayek, *The Constitution of Liberty*, p. 29.

142 Ibid., p. 110.

143 Ibid., p. 3; Arnsperger, *Critical Political Economy*, p. 90.

144 Hayek, *The Road to Serfdom*, p. 164.

145 Hayek, *The Constitution of Liberty*, p. 376; Hayek, *The Road to Serfdom*, p. 77, 30, 290–91. What is regarded as wickedly radical in science studies, is propounded as eminently conservative by the Hayek wing of neoliberalism.

146 Hayek, *The Constitution of Liberty*, p. 378, my italics. This explains why neoliberals tend to diverge from their predecessors: "most nineteenth century liberals were guided by a naïve overconfidence in what mere communication of knowledge could achieve" (p. 377).

147 Hayek, *The Road to Serfdom*, pp. 204–5.

148 Hayek reveled in the tough-minded stance of the scholar who disparaged any recourse to the Third Way, most notoriously in his denunciation of the welfare state as just the slippery "Road to Serfdom." This sets him apart from his contemporary figures like Walter Lippmann, or Keynes, or their modern epigones like Cass Sunstein or Joseph Stiglitz.

149 Hayek, *The Constitution of Liberty*, p. 377, 112, 110, 22.

150 Schneider, "The Role of the Category of Ignorance in Sociological Theory," p. 498.

151 Ibid., p. 500.

152 Hayek entertained the possibility of blaming "the engineers" for the frustration of the neoliberal project in his *Counterrevolution of Science* (1952), but subsequently came around to the position that it was politically unwise to demonize such a powerful constituency in the twentieth-century economy. See Mirowski, "Naturalizing the Market."

153 Hayek, *Road to Serfdom*, p. 162.

154 Hayek, *Studies in Philosophy, Politics and Economics*, p. 178. Attacks upon "intellectuals" were a common refrain in the history of Mont Pèlerin, and not restricted to Hayek. See, for instance, Hartwell, *A History of the Mont Pèlerin Society*, p. 161; Friedman, *Capitalism and Freedom*, p. 8. But of course the neoliberals don't renounce *all* expertise—just the stuff they don't like.

155 Hayek, *Studies in Philosophy, Politics and Economics*, p. 169; Christi, "Hayek and Schmitt on the Rule of Law," p. 532; Scheuerman, *Carl Schmitt: The End of Law*, chapter 8.

156 Hayek, *Studies in Philosophy, Politics and Economics*, p. 161.

157 Hayek, *The Constitution of Liberty*, p. 13.

158   Hayek, *Individualism and Economic Order*, p. 24.

159   Interestingly, here is where Hayek rejected the maximization of utility as the standard equilibrium concept in neoclassical economic theory. Markets don't maximize happiness, rather, "the use of the market mechanism brings more of the dispersed knowledge of society into play than by any other [method]" (*Studies in Philosophy, Politics and Economics*, p. 174).

160   Scheuerman, *Carl Schmitt*, p. 216.

161   Davies, "When is a Market Not a Market?" p.24

162   Quoted in Christi, *Carl Schmitt and Authoritarian Liberalism*, pp. 31, 34n7; Hayek, *The Constitution of Liberty*, p. 32.

163   Christi, *Carl Schmitt and Authoritarian Liberalism*, p. 23.

164   Milton Friedman, in an interview transcript posted at www.thecorporation. com/media/Friedman.pdf.

165   Arnsperger, *Critical Political Economy*.

166   The Graph and data courtesy of Gilles Christoph.

167   Consult my discussion "Why Is There a Nobel Prize in Economics?" at www. youtube.com/watch?v=dLtEo8lplwg.

168   Davidson, "Prime Time for Paul Ryan's Guru"; Lahart, "The Glenn Beck Effect."

3. Everyday Neoliberalism

1   Wallace, *Consider the Lobster and Other Essays*, p. 288.

2   McGuigan, "Neoliberalism, Culture and Policy," p. 229; Sandel, "What Isn't for Sale?"

3   Konings, "Social Scientists and Economic Life at the Start of the 21st Century," pp. 715–16. One indication that it is short-sighted to restrict neoliberal movements strictly to the sphere of the "governmental" is the historical fact that "privatization" movements preceded the birthdate of neoliberalism: the Italian Fascist government instituted a broad program of large-scale privatization in 1922–25 (Bel, "The First Privatisation").

4   Walzer, *Spheres of Justice*; Radin, *Contested Commodities*; Satz, *Why Some Things Should Not Be for Sale*; Sandel, "What Isn't for Sale?"

5   Shteyngart, *Super Sad True Love Story*, pp. 90–92.

6   Or, as Foucault put it in the manuscript of his first lecture of January 1979, "Studying Liberalism as the General Framework of Biopolitics" (*The Birth of Biopolitics*, p. 328). However, few have noted that this is a free translation of the ordoliberal term *Vitalpolitik*, which hints at its National Socialist genealogy (Deuber-Mankowsky, "Nothing Is Political, Everything Can Be Politicized," p. 141).

7   Foucault, *The Birth of Biopolitics*, p. 131.

8   Ibid., p. 241.

9   Ibid., pp. 268, 270; Moreton, *To Serve God and Wal-Mart*, p. 156.

10 The following quote may seem contrary to this claim, but I believe it sets the stage
    for it: "Economics is an atheistic discipline; economics is a discipline without
    God; economics is a discipline without totality; economics is a discipline that
    begins to demonstrate the pointlessness, but also the impossibility of a sovereign
    point of view" (Foucault, *The Birth of Biopolitics*, p. 282).

11 In Payne, *The Consumer, Credit and Neoliberalism*, p. 91; Hackworth, *Faith Based*, p. 9.

12 Foucault, *The Birth of Biopolitics*, p. 228.

13 Ibid., pp. 252–53.

14 Ibid., pp. 279, 280, 283.

15 Or better yet, *The Island of Doctor Moreau*.

16 Some of the better examples of literature that explores this possibility: Tellmann,
    "Foucault and the Invisible Economy," "The Economic Beyond Governmental-
    ity"; Behrent, "Liberalism Without Humanism"; Barnett, "The Consolations
    of Neoliberalism"; Deuber-Mankowsky, "Nothing Is Political, Everything Can
    Be Politicized"; Brocking et al., *Governmentality*.

17 "The analysis of wealth is to political economy what general grammar is to
    philology and what natural history is to biology" (*The Order of Things*, p. 168).

18 Foucault, *The Birth of Biopolitics*, p. 31, 17, 13, 92.

19 Behrent ("Liberalism Without Humanism," pp. 545 et seq.) points to the sali-
    ence of the 1973 economic crisis in France, in conjunction with Foucault's
    previous antihumanism and suspicions concerning state power—both resonant
    themes for the neoliberals. Paras (*Foucault 2.0*) raises his support for the Iranian
    Revolution. Cooper ("Foucault, Neoliberalism and the Iranian Revolution")
    argues that he fused neoliberal ideas with admiration for Islamic repression of
    feminine sexuality. Donzelot and Gordon ("Governing Liberal Societies") refer
    to his break with French Socialist Party figures.

20 Tellmann, "Foucault and the Invisible Economy," p. 22. One example of an
    author "more Foucauldian than Foucault" would be Bernard Harcourt ("Radi-
    cal Thought from Marx, Nietzsche and Freud through Foucault, to the
    Present"), who argues that the idea of a small limited government hemmed in
    vis-à-vis the market is itself a spurious construct, "'false,' but not because its
    opposite is 'true'" (ibid., p. 15). In this reading, Foucault himself was a cog in the
    neoliberal regime of truth, promulgating the notion that "government" was in
    fact being limited by neoliberal interventions, when in fact it was expanding in
    both size and power.

21 Barnett, "The Consolations of Neoliberalism."

22 Foucault, *Discipline and Punish*, p. 194.

23 Jacques Donzelot has admitted this in a backhanded fashion: "In Anglo-Saxon
    countries where Neoliberalism was imposed from the start of the 80s, Foucault
    studies provide the means of a sophisticated critique, albeit one which is visibly

lacking a capacity to propose alternatives. Does this political ambivalence in the notion of governmentality not condemn it to serving an ideological function?" (Donzelot and Gordon, "Governing Liberal Societies," pp. 55–56).

24 Foucault, *Dits et Ecrits*, vol. 3, p. 991; translation in Deuber-Mankowsky, "Nothing Is Political, Everything Can Be Politicized," p. 160).

25 These were not concocted out of thin air. Honestly. I witnessed them on ABC News the evening of December 18, 2008. The reporter, Gigi Stone, ambivalently presented these options as real solutions to economic distress.

26 Cowen, *Create Your Own Economy*.

27 Frank, *What's the Matter with Kansas?* p. 136. Or even better: "Because some artist decides to shock the hicks by dunking Jesus in urine, the entire planet must remake itself along the lines of the Republican Party." You have to admit, Frank can turn a phrase.

28 Ehrenreich, *Bait and Switch*; Schulman and Zelizer, *Rightward Bound*; Frank, *What's the Matter with Kansas?* p. 245.

29 See, for instance, Bartels, "What's the Matter with *What's the Matter with Kansas?*"; Ansolabehere et al., "Purple America." Some of these were members of the "rational choice" strain of political science, which had become the neoclassical economics outpost in that discipline. Of course, given the freedom in defining the "economic," which we described in chapter 1, these academics had tremendous leeway in defining their categories in such a way that their assertion of the primacy of the economic was not impugned. But more to the point, this type of argument dates back to the neoliberal denial that advertizing could ever bamboozle anyone into buying something they didn't want (Dunn, *The Economics of John Kenneth Galbraith*).

30 Frank, *Pity the Billionaire*, pp. 9–10, 154.

31 Frank, *One Market Under God*, p. 15; Hackworth, *Faith Based*; Foucault, *The Hermeneutics of the Subject*, p. 252.

32 Frank, *Pity the Billionaire*, pp. 35–36, 101, 127.

33 See, for instance, Kingfisher and Makovsky, "Introduction: The Limits of Neoliberalism"; Ong, *Neoliberalism as Exception*; Clarke, "Living with/in and without Neoliberalism"; and authors cited in Gershon ("Neoliberal Agency").

34 Radin, *Contested Commodities*, pp. 58, 60.

35 Some instances that document this tendency: Emily Martin, *Flexible Bodies* and "Designing Flexibility"; Swan and Fox, "Becoming Flexible"; Swan, *Worked-up Selves*; Urciuoli, "Skills and Selves in the New Workplace"; Gershon, "Neoliberal Agency"; Moreton, *To Serve God and Wal-Mart*.

36 Vaidhyanathan, "Planet of the Apps."

37 Hochschild, *The Outsourced Self*.

38 Urciuoli, "Skills and Selves in the New Workplace," p. 217; Martin, *Flexible Bodies*; Ehrenreich, *Bait and Switch*, p. 79.

39 Swan, *Worked-up Selves*, p. 140.

40 Ehrenreich, *Bait and Switch*, p. 103; ibid., chapter 5; Moreton, *To Serve God and Wal-Mart*, p. 94.

41 Some of the better ethnographies exploring these issues are Turkle, *Life on the Screen* and *Alone Together*; Gershon, "Un-friend My Heart."

42 Gershon, "Un-friend My Heart."

43 Turkle, *Alone Together*, p. 273.

44 Frank, *One Market Under God*, p. 244.

45 Bowmaker, *Economics Uncut*; Lipman, "Why Is Language Vague?"

46 This argument is made with great perspicuity by John Davis in his *The Theory of the Individual in Economics* and *Individuals and Identity in Economics*.

47 It seems to have escaped most economists that these resorts to tautology in economic theory have leached the Prime Imperative of Pareto Optimality of any meaning whatsoever. In any event, the supposedly fixed repertoire of roles and types to be emulated by the agent has also been eroded by the neoliberal ascendancy. This is yet another example of the Zombie Neoclassical Economist lurching aimlessly across the landscape.

48 Davis, *Individuals and Identity in Economics*; Mirowski, *Machine Dreams*, pp. 443–52.

49 There are a fair number of books written by MPS members denying any salience to class. For instance, Lord Peter Bauer wrote a pamphlet, *Class on the Brain: The Cost of a British Obsession* (1997), which asserted, "for about eight centuries Britain has not been a closed society, much less a caste society," that there have been few class barriers to wealth in Britain, and that to the extent that Britain became less open and flexible in the postwar years, "it needed the reforms of Mrs. Thatcher's governments to re-open the road of opportunity."

50 O. Jones, *Chavs*, p. 167.

51 Data from http://quickfacts.census.gov/qfd/states/00000.html. Last consulted August 7, 2011. The mean was so far below the median because the distribution of income had become so skewed to the bottom, and expanded labor force participation: see the data presented at http://elsa.berkeley.edu/~saez/.

52 Linden, "Addictive Personality?"

53 Ailon, "The Discursive Management of Financial Risk Scandals," pp. 264–65.

54 Ibid., p. 267.

55 The narrative that blamed the crisis on Fannie Mae and Freddie Mac and improvident home owners is covered below in chapter 5. However, even Payne admits that parts of this story comes perilously close to that propounded by the American Enterprise Institute and Peter Wallison (Payne, *The Consumer, Credit and Neoliberalism*, p. 169).

56 Gravois, "Too Important to Fail."

57 "The only problem is that, in all likelihood, such a world would be one where banks only get more sophisticated, powerful, and centralized. And herein lies

the main philosophical shadow lurking over the bureau. By setting out to match the analytical prowess of the financial industry, the CFPB is implicitly giving its assent to a world where finance is governed by complicated models, big data, and the statistical masters of the universe who command them—as opposed to an older world where finance was governed by the personal relationship between a borrower and a lender." (Gravois, "Too Important to Fail")

58 For the video, consult www.huffingtonpost.com/2010/09/20/rick-santelli-i-sparked-t_n_731249.html. See also Frank, *Pity the Billionaire*, pp. 44–45. This attack on the poor for taking on the debt foisted upon their neoliberal selves is explored in the next section.

59 Lanchester, "Once Greece Goes . . . ," p. 6.

60 For a general discussion of the issues, see Quinn, "The Transformation of Morals in Markets." Some dedicated viatical firms, which sold investment shares in units dedicated to monitoring the deathwatch of their policies, such as Mutual Benefits and Kelco, Inc., have been the subject of prolonged lawsuits.

61 Quinn, "The Transformation of Morals in Markets," p. 771.

62 In practice, the three largest consumer rating agencies in the United States—TransUnion, Equifax, and Experian—all use somewhat different scoring algorithms, although all are treated as comparable because they are issued under the FICO brand label.

63 See www.washingtonpost.com/wp-dyn/content/article/2006/06/09/AR2006 060900027.html.

64 Poon, "From New Deal Risk Institutions to Capital Markets."

65 I am assured it was not an attempt to revive or promote the Dead Kennedys song from 1979. And it is noteworthy that the limo was not cruising Harlem or the Bronx. For the relationship of such contempt for the poor to the origins of the Tea Party, see note 58 above.

66 I can't make this stuff up. See www.tednugent.com/news/newsDetails.aspx? PostID=940937.

67 Nietzsche, *Genealogy of Morals*, p. 64.

68 Veblen, *Theory*, p. 40.

69 Couldry, "Reality TV, or the Secret Theatre of Neoliberalism."

70 http://tpmdc.talkingpointsmemo.com/2011/08/nebraska-ag-jon-bruning-compares-welfare-recipients-to-scavenging-racoons.php.

71 "Today, we face an unsustainable trajectory of government spending that is accelerating the nation toward a ruinous debt crisis. Mounting debt also threatens our poorest and most vulnerable citizens, because those who depend most on government would be hit hardest by a fiscal crisis. Harsh austerity would be the only course left. A broke government unable to finance its spending commitments would be forced to make indiscriminate cuts affecting current

beneficiaries of government programs—without giving them time to prepare or adjust." Paul Ryan, *Christian Science Monitor*, May 18, 2011, archived at http://budget.house.gov/News/DocumentSingle.aspx?DocumentID=241970. It is astounding that, implicitly, Ryan is allowed to state in a national newspaper that mounting debt does not threaten the rich.

72 www.thedailyshow.com/watch/thu-august-18-2011/world-of-class-warfare---the-poor-s-free-ride-is-over. See this meme repeated by Stephen Schwartzman, CEO of Blackstone Group, in Lofgren, "Revolt of the Rich"; and also Weigel, "Republicans for Tax Hikes," for how this entire echo chamber meme was concocted by one of the outer layers of the neoliberal Russian doll, the so-called Tax Foundation.

73 Rivlin, *Broke, USA*, pp. 27, 30.

74 Rivlin, *Broke, USA*.

75 Diamond, "The Return of Debtor's Prisons."

76 Konings, *The Great Credit Crash*.

77 Ibid., pp. 120–21.

78 Ehrenreich, "Turning Poverty into an American Crime."

79 See www.indybay.org/newsitems/2010/02/05/18637084.php.

80 Knight, "Gary Lures Hollywood with a Bounty of Decay."

81 Lieber, "Last Plea on Student Loans."

82 Hacker and Dreifus, "The Debt Crisis at American Colleges."

83 One must acknowledge that there have been various "epicycles" proposed to the neoclassical model to supposedly cover these phenomena, from "search costs" to "'asymmetric information" to "lemon models" and beyond; but two observations render them moot. First, they really are epicycles, and have never been incorporated into the core microeconomic model. One reason may be that there is no consensus technique to correctly incorporate "information" into the model of the economic agent (Mirowski, "Why There Is (as Yet) No Such Thing as an Economics of Knowledge"). But second, it has proven almost impossible to maintain a neoclassical model where someone is "bamboozled" into belief in an untruth, and justified in acting upon it. This has something to do with the colonization of neoclassical theory by neoliberal doctrine (Mirowski, *ScienceMart*, chapter 7). Both considerations bear consequences for orthodox accounts of the crisis.

84 Galbraith, *New Industrial State*, p. 206.

85 Ibid., p. 219.

86 Dunn, *The Economics of John Kenneth Galbraith*, chapter 9.

87 R. Walker, *Buying In*, pp. 64, 104.

88 Wallace, *Oblivion*, p. 61.

89 Walker, *Buying In*, pp. 168–73, 179.

90 Marazzi, *The Violence of Financial Capitalism*; Ross, "A Capitalist's Dream."

91 Pinch and Kessler, "How Aunt Ammy Gets Her Free Lunch." "The sale of

the *Huffington Post* to AOL in February 2011 prompted a sharp reaction from the hundreds of bloggers whose unpaid work had built up the site's cachet. It provoked outrage (and a class-action lawsuit) because the owner, Arianna Huffington, had made so much money out of the bloggers' work: AOL paid $315 million for the site." (Ross, "A Capitalist's Dream")

92 "An auction market has even sprung up to sell these [intern] positions to the highest bidder. A Versace internship fetched $5,000 at auction, temporary blogging rights at the *Huffington Post* went for $13,000, and someone paid $42,500 for a one-week stint at *Vogue*. At one Californian outfit, Dream Careers, 2,000 internships all over the world are sold annually. You can buy an eight-week summer position for $8,000 (a placement in London will set you back $9,500)." (Perlin, *Intern Nation*).

93 Quoted from http://brianholmes.wordpress.com/. Also consult Preston, "Foreign Students in Work Visa Program Stage Walkout at Plant" and "Pleas Unheeded as Students' US Jobs Soured."

94 Lohmann, "The Endless Algebra of Climate Markets"; Richey and Ponte, *Brand Aid*.

95 Haight, "The Problem with Fair Trade Coffee."

96 See www.transfairusa.org/about-fair-trade-usa. The neoliberal character of the marketing appeal is revealed in another quote: "We're a nonprofit, but we don't do charity. Instead, we teach disadvantaged communities how to use the free market to their advantage."

97 Daviron and Ponte, *The Coffee Paradox*; Fridell, "Fair-Trade Coffee and Commodity Fetishism," pp. 92, 97.

98 Haight, "The Problem with Fair Trade Coffee."

99 Giridharadas, "Boycotts Minus the Pain."

100 Arrow, "Invaluable Goods" (p. 761), an essay review of Radin, *Contested Commodities*. Arrow is regarded within the profession as progenitor of the Arrow-Debreu model, an inventor of neoclassical "health economics" and someone as far removed from neoliberal beliefs as it is possible for a respected orthodox economist to be; which just goes to illustrate the assertion in chapter 1 that the profession has become unself-consciously neoliberal, and also thoroughly compromised in its ability to conceptualize the main problems of the current era. See also how his position anticipated that of the self-identified neoliberals in Becker and Elias, "Introducing Incentives in the Market for Live and Cadaveric Organs."

101 Rose, "The Neurochemical Self and Its Anomalies" and *The Politics of Life Itself*.

102 Frazzeto and Anker, "Neuroculture."

103 See Camerer et al. "Neuroeconomics"; Ariely, *Predictably Irrational*; Akerlof and Shiller, *Animal Spirits*. By most accounts, this attempted reconciliation has been an *ignis fatuus*. This dynamic has resulted in one analytical dead-end in discussions of the causes of the crisis: see chapter 5 below.

104 Hutheesing, "Better Trading Through Science."

105 Talbot, "Brain Gain."

106 Ibid., p. 43.

107 See Havinghurst, "Trafficking in Human Blood"; Healy, *Last Best Gifts*; Washington, *Deadly Monopolies*, chapter 7; Arrow, "Gifts and Exchanges." A history of the debate can be found in Fontaine, "Blood, Politics and Social Science"; Sheper-Hughes and Wacquant, *Commodifying Bodies*; Krawiec, "Show Me the Money."

108 Spar, *The Baby Business*; Thernstrom, "Meet the Twiblings."

109 "'Experts are not certain what it means to a child to discover that he or she is but one of 50 children—or even more [due to IV fertilization]. Experts don't talk about this when they counsel people dealing with infertility,' Ms. Kramer said. 'How do you make connections with so many siblings? What does family mean to these children?'" (Mroz, "One Sperm Donor").

110 Krawiec, "Show Me the Money," p. xii.

111 Bess, "Blurring the Boundary Between Person and Product."

112 Ibid., p. 63.

113 Cowen, *Create Your Own Economy*, p. 117.

114 This has been the last refuge of the scoundrel contingent of the economics profession, which includes Ben Bernanke ("The US Economic Outlook").

4. Mumbo Jumble

1 Along with Sorkin, *Too Big to Fail*; Krugman, "The Return of Depression Economics"; and Morgenson and Rosner, *Reckless Endangerment*, as of 2011. As someone who has spent an inordinate amount of his life with the tsunami of crisis books over the past three years, I have to once again report that the marketplace of ideas seems an unreliable tutor, since these books are, in my estimation, some of the least informative sources on the causes and consequences of the crisis. Moe Tkacik ("Journals of the Crisis Year") provides a similar assessment. See www.amazon.com/s?ie=UTF8&rh=n%3A283155%2Ck%3Afinancial%20crisis%20best%20sellers&page=1.

2 Cohen, "Ivory Tower Unswayed by Crashing Economy."

3 One book that more or less acknowledges the incongruity, only to then attempt to justify it, is *Backhouse: The Puzzle of Modern Economics*. Some better meditations are Spaveneta, "Economists and Economics"; Westbrook, *Out of the Crisis*; Basen, "Economics Has Met the Enemy, and It Is Economics"; Chakrabortty, "Angry Economists Can't Answer my Criticism," and Palley, *From Financial Crisis to Stagnation*. "None of [the orthodox] economists are losing their jobs. In fact, it is unlikely that many are even missing out on a scheduled promotion as a result of having failed to see the largest financial

bubble in the history of the world" (Baker, "Creating Political Space for Effective Financial Regulation," p. 72).

4   Portions of this section appeared previously in different format in the Hedgehog Review, vol. 12, 2010.

5   Sometimes I am suspected of hyperbole in my generalizations, so I need to document this one here, with regard to Joseph Stiglitz: "We should be clear about this: [neoclassical] economic theory never provided much support for these free-market views. Theories of imperfect and asymmetric information in markets had undermined every one of the efficient market doctrines, even before they became fashionable" (Stiglitz, "The Non-existent Hand"). For a number of examples on the right, see the Chicago interviews of John Cassidy ("Rational Irrationality") or Taylor, "How Government Created the Financial Crisis." History is always the first casualty in any economics dispute.

6   See www.britac.ac.uk/events/archive/forum-economy.cfm. The Queen's question is also discussed in Kay, "The Map Is Not the Territory."

7   See, for instance, Jane Smiley's novel *Moo*, or Olivier Assayas's film *Summer Hours*.

8   Sorman, "The Free Marketers Strike Back."

9   Thoma, "What Caused the Financial Crisis?"

10 Here is the economist David Levine: "I was reading your article 'How Did Economists Get It So Wrong.' Who are these economists who got it so wrong? Speak for yourself kemo sabe. And since you got it wrong—why should we believe your discredited theories?" (www.huffingtonpost.com/david-k-levine/an-open-letter-to-paul-kr_b_289768.html?view=print). In a different register, Jagdish Bhagwati accused his Columbia colleague Joseph Stiglitz of being one of "capitalism's petty detractors" (www.worldafairsjournal.org/articles/2009-Fall). Eugene Fama in an interview with John Cassidy of *The New Yorker*: "Krugman wants to be czar of the world. There are no economists that he likes [laughs]. And Larry Summers? What other position could he take and still have a job?" (www.newyorker.com/online/blogs/johncassidy/chicago-interviews). Brad de Long on John Cochrane: "No one could be that ignorant . . . to fail to have noticed that commercial banks are more tightly regulated than investment banks. . . . Cochrane may be completely ignorant about the macro literature except for that recently written somewhere near a great lake, but he must know that investment banks suffered more dramatically than commercial banks" (October 9, 2009, at http://delong.typepad.com/sdj/). Paul Krugman: "Eugene Fama, at least, and perhaps Cochrane too, began this debate from a position of complete ignorance—not understanding at all the logic of Keynesian models (even for the purposes of debunking), and imagining that the savings-investment identity necessarily implies 100-percent crowding out. There was no deeper logic. And since then, what we've been witnessing is a simple matter of digging

in, refusing to admit a mistake. I do not believe that Cochrane has, in his head or on the back of his envelope, a maximization-and-equilibrium model that justifies what he's saying" (http://krugman.blogs.nytimes.com/, February 23, 2010). Brad de Long criticized Robert Lucas: "Last March—when the only reason Mr. Lucas could think of why Mrs. Romer and Mr. Bernanke were saying the stimulus was likely to be effective was that they were corrupt, and when he just 'didn't really get' any piece of Mr. Bernanke's major contributions to economics" (www.economist.com/blogs/freeexchange/lucas_roundtable). "Sorry, Art, but aside from the foolish and intellectually lazy remark about mathematics, all of the criticisms that you have listed reflect either woeful ignorance or intentional disregard for what much of modern macroeconomics is about and what it has accomplished" (Sargent, "Modern Macroeconomics Under Attack").

11 James Galbraith, "Who Are These Economists, Anyway?" p. 95. I should note that this passage had been written long before the crisis, in 2000. It is indicative that no one had stepped forward to reprimand any of the bad behavior documented in the last footnote, but as soon as Galbraith actually outed the general intolerance within the orthodox economics profession, then he himself was immediately reprimanded. See Hedoin, "Towards a Paradigm Shift in Economics?" This audacious evasion of accountability in the economics profession is the Great Unmentionable in any gathering of the faithful.

12 Y. Smith, *Econned*, p. 19.

13 Some brand-name economists, such as Simon Johnson, Tyler Cowen, Richard Posner, Steven Levitt, Mark Thoma, and Paul Krugman, greatly expanded and extended their influence through their blogs. The *New York Times* gave many previously obscure economists a soapbox on the Economix blog; similar things happened at the *Financial Times* and *Economist* sites. The right wing of the profession ended up generally more successful in amplifying its message through these devices than the left, in my estimation. Some of the better quasi-anonymous independent blogs turned out to be more informative in general, such as Yves Smith's nakedcapitalism.com, and the blog of my colleague David Ruccio at http://anticap.wordpress.com/. Some of the greater disappointments have been figures like Mark Thoma, who has written critical things from time to time on his blog, but turned more orthodox than the Pope when pressed: see http://thebrowser.com/interviews/mark-thoma-on-econometrics.

14 See Robert Barro in www.economist.com/blogs/freeexchange/lucas_round table, which was itself an online discussion of Lucas, "In Defense of the Dismal Science."

15 Abate, "After Calamity, Economics Leaders Rethink Strategy"; Rajan, "Bankers Have Been Sold Short by Market Distortions." On Greenspan's close relationship with the Randroid cult, see Burns, *Goddess of the Market*; Kinsey, "Greenspan

Shrugged." On the attempt to pin the crisis on Greenspan soon after it broke, see Goodman, "Taking a Hard Look at the Greenspan Legacy." But even there, Very Serious Economists sprang to his defense: "'The notion that Greenspan could have generated a totally different outcome is naïve,' said Robert E. Hall, an economist at the conservative Hoover Institution, a research group at Stanford."

16 I have quoted Brad de Long ("Economics in Crisis") already in the first chapter: "But what astonishes me even more is the apparent failure of academic economics to take steps to prepare itself for the future." See also Hirsh, "Our Best Minds Are Failing Us"; Kay (all); Baker, *The End of Loser Liberalism*.

17 A random sample: Eichengreen, "The Last Temptation of Risk"; Litan, "In Defense of Much"; Cochrane, "Lessons from the Financial Crisis"; Zingales, "Learning to Live with Not-So-Efficient Markets"; Saint-Paul, "A Modest Intellectual Discipline"; Sorman, "The Free Marketers Strike Back"; Sargent, "Modern Macroeconomics Under Attack." An especially fervid advocate of nothing-to-see-here has been John B. Taylor: "And so getting back on track is the way I put it, but the theory itself—the basic theory of economics is just fine" at http://findarticles.com/p/news-articles/analyst-wire/mi_8077/is_20100803/john-taylor-raymond-professor-economics/ai_n54673887/.

18 Here is not the place to document this trend, but see Paul Samuelson's setting the tone for the community in the 1970s: "Those who can, do science; those who can't, prattle on about its methodology" (quoted in Holcombe, Economic *Models and Methodology*). I survey Samuelson's attitudes toward intellectual history and philosophy of economics in "Did the Victor Enjoy the Spoils?"

19 Klamer and Colander, *The Making of an Economist*; N. Smith, "What I Learned in Grad School."

20 This dynamic is described from various vantage points in Weintraub, *The Future of the History of Economics*; Lee, *A History of Heterodox Economics*; and Haring, "Economics Is Losing Its Memory."

21 Available for viewing at www.aeaweb.org/webcasts/assa2010.php.

22 For a video admission by Alan Blinder, see www.cengagesites.com/academic/?site=5322&secID=5312. And for that of John Taylor: www.cengagesites.com/academic/?site=5724&SecID=7344.

23 The texts were "The Methodology of Positive Economics" in Friedman, *Essays in Positive Economics*, and Thomas Kuhn, *The Structure of Scientific Revolutions*. See, for instance, http://economistsview.typepad.com/economistsview/ 2009/08/why-this-new-crisis-needs-a-new-paradigm-of-economic-thought.html#more; or www.voxeu.org/index.php?q=node/3210; or www.rieti.go.jp/en/rieti_report/ 108.html. It was instructive how economists instinctively and unselfconsciously turned to the writings of members of the Mont Pèlerin Society such as Friedman and Popper when they were forced to access "philosophy."

Neoliberalism thus came as naturally to them as the air they breathed.

24 Mata, "Reckonings."

25 Eichengreen and O'Rourke, "A Tale of Two Depressions." I thank Professor O'Rourke for generously providing the updated data.

26 Rogoff and Reinhart, *This Time Is Different*.

27 For the 1870s see Mirowski, *More Heat Than Light*; for World War II see Mirowski, *Machine Dreams*. "The intellectual history of economics might be understood as a succession of ways to socialize conceptions of nature" (Westbrook, *Out of the Crisis*, p. 78); MacFarquahar, "The Deflationist."

28 More unexpected, it comes from his most cited work, *The General Theory of Employment, Interest and Money*, pp. 32–33.

29 One would begin with Joan Robinson, then proceed up through Axel Leijonhufvud and Robert Clower, and then to the French Regulationist school. Robert Lucas more or less agrees with this point: "I think that in writing the General Theory, Keynes was viewing himself as a spokesman for a discredited profession. . . . He was writing in a situation where people are ready to throw in the towel on capitalism and liberal democracy and go with fascism or corporatism, protectionism, socialist planning. . . . [Keynes] was a political activist from beginning to end. What he was concerned about when he wrote the General Theory was convincing people there was a way to deal with the Depression that was forceful and effective but didn't involve scrapping the capitalist system" ("My Keynesian Education," p. 24).

30 Or its parallel universe, the American Finance Association, which had the spectacular gall to appoint Cochrane as its president in 2010. See Cochrane, "Presidential Address."

31 Eaton, "Osborne's Supporters Turn on Him."

32 This petition provides a quick roster of the hard-right membership of the Neoliberal Thought Collective: www.speaker.gov/UploadedFiles/Economists-11-8-11.pdf. A few notables: Michael Boskin (Stanford), Charles Calomiris (Columbia), Eugene Fama (Chicago), Douglas Holtz-Eakin, Jeffrey Miron (Harvard), and Barry Keating (Notre Dame). Events surrounding this incident are discussed further in chapter 5.

33 John Cochrane's own connections to both neoliberal think tanks (Cato) and the place where large hedge funds intersect with the Tea Party wing of the Republican Party have been documented by journalists (Crabtree, "Paul Ryan's $700-Wine-Sipping Buddies"). Here Paul Ryan was observed dining in Washington, D.C. with John Cochrane and a hedge fund manager.

34 Quote from Bowman et al., *Scapegoats Aren't Enough*. Neoliberals, feeling the heat perhaps getting nearer, are quick to dismiss this as "conspiracy theories" ("Economics: A Million Mutinies Now").

35 See, for instance, Imperia and Maffeo, "As If Nothing Were Going to Happen";

Baker, "The Soft Bigotry of Incredibly Low Expectations." There is a big difference between warning of a housing bubble, as did Robert Shiller, for instance, and warning of global system breakdown over a long horizon. Shiller's intellectual role in the crisis has been misunderstood, as we argue in chapter 6. (This generalization would also have to take into account the subsequent popularity of a few serial Cassandras such as Nouriel Roubini and Marxists such as David Harvey and Robert Brenner: they exist outside the ambit of this book, dealing as it does with the orthodox neoclassical profession.)

36 Buiter, "The Unfortunate Uselessness of Most State of the Art Academic Monetary Economics." Buiter then wrote: "The Bank of England in 2007 faced the onset of the credit crunch with too much Robert Lucas, Michael Woodford and Robert Merton in its intellectual cupboard. A drastic but chaotic re-education took place and is continuing." Chapter 5 reveals that, in this instance, another economist's prediction has since bitten the dust.

37 Ibanez, *The Current State of Macroeconomics*, p. 180.

38 Blanchard, "The State of Macro."

39 They are available online at www.newyorker.com/online/blogs/johncassidy/chicago-interviews. One wishes more business journalists would emulate this practice of providing full transcripts.

40 Kroszner and Rajan, "Is the Glass Steagall Act Justified?" p. 811.

41 Although this chapter deals with economists, and not the theories, I want to insist here that none of these components is plausible on its own terms. The "savings glut" appeals to a discredited theory of "'loanable funds," the mortgage story is dismissed in chapter 5, and the financial-innovation trope is discussed in chapter 6. See also Palley, *From Financial Crisis to Stagnation*, pp.117–21.

42 For example, C. Ferguson, *Predator Nation*, p. 271, and Byrne, *Occupy Handbook*, p.79 et seq.

43 "We have seen the triumph of sensible ideas and reaped the rewards in terms of macroeconomic performance. The costly wrong turn in ideas and macropolicy of the 1960s/70s has been righted, and the future of stabilization looks bright" (Romer, 2007, quoted in DeMartino, *The Economist's Oath*, p. 165).

44 Westbrook, *Out of the Crisis*, p. 60; D. MacKenzie, *An Engine, Not a Camera* and "The Credit Crisis as a Problem in the Sociology of Knowledge"; Mehrling, *Fischer Black and the Revolutionary Idea of Finance*.

45 MacKenzie, *An Engine*; O'Neill, "Black Scholes and the Normal Distribution"; Sherman, "Revolver."

46 Bullock, "Friedman Economics"; Khademian, "The Pracademic and the Fed," p. 142; Bernanke, congressional testimony, 2006.

47 The phrase was actually first coined by the Harvard economists James Stock and Mark Watson in 2002.

48 Bernanke, "The Great Moderation."

49 Bernanke, congressional testimony, 2007; Leonard, "Alan Greenspan's Housing Bubble Coffee Break"; Olivier Coibion and Yuri Gorodnichenko, "Did the Great Recession Mean the End of the Great Moderation?" at www.voxeu.org/index.php?q=node/4496.

50 Khademian, "The Pracademic and the Fed"; Lowenstein, "The Villain."

51 Although one might want to insist upon the doctrinal differences between Randian libertarians and the Chicago School for some conceptual purposes, it is noteworthy that Milton Friedman was a vocal supporter of the Greenspan record in the press (Auerbach, *Deception and Abuse at the Fed*, p. 246n54).

52 Khademian, "The Pracademic and the Fed," p. 146.

53 Bullock, "Friedman Economics."

54 Partnoy, "Sunlight Shows Cracks in Crisis Rescue Story"; Chan and Protess, "Cross Section of Rich Invested with Fed"; Ivry, Keoun, and Kuntz, "Secret Fed Loans Helped Banks Net $13 Billion."

55 Bernanke has changed his tune a few times over just why the Fed had to let Lehman fail. See John Cassidy, "Bernanke Changes Story on Lehman Collapse," September 2, 2010, at www.newyorker.com/online/blogs/johncassidy/2010/09.

56 "Christy [Mack] and her pal Susan [Karches] launched their investment initiative called Waterfall TALF. Neither seems to have any experience whatsoever in finance, beyond Susan's penchant for dabbling in thoroughbred racehorses. But with an upfront investment of $15 million, they quickly received $220 million in cash from the Fed, most of which they used to purchase student loans and commercial mortgages. The loans were set up so that Christy and Susan would keep 100 percent of any gains on the deals, while the Fed and the Treasury (read: the taxpayer) would eat 90 percent of the losses. Given out as part of a bailout program ostensibly designed to help ordinary people by kick-starting consumer lending, the deals were a classic heads-I-win, tails-you-lose investment." (Taibbi, "The Real Housewives of Wall Street"). TARP and TALF are further discussed in chapter 5.

57 Lowenstein, "The Villain"; Krugman, "Return of Depression Economics."

58 U.S. Government Accounting Office, "Opportunities Exist to Strengthen Policies and Processes for Managing Emergency Assistance."

59 Johnson, "An Institutional Flaw"; Sanders, "Jamie Dimon Is Not Alone."

60 Bernanke, congressional testimony, 2007.

61 Bernanke, "On the Implications of the Financial Crisis for Economics."

62 Bernanke, "Global Imbalances."

63 This has been seconded by Yves Smith ("New York Fed Brownshirt"): "The prestigious staff roles relate to the central banking functions: economic research, macro modeling, and of course, monetary policy. PhD monetary economists rule the roost. And there is considerable group think. The organization is very

vertical, with little lateral hiring except at the very top levels. The result is intellectual inbreeding. I'm told the public rejection of perspectives that ruffled the Fed's world view, such as Robert Shiller being pushed off the New York Fed's economic advisory board after he suggested that there was a housing bubble pre crisis and the dressing down of Raghuram Rajan at Jackson Hole in 2005 is consistent with an internal posture of ignoring people who don't fall in with the party line."

64 Baker, *The End of Loser Liberalism*, p. 59.

65 "The Reserve Banks issue shares of stock to member banks. However, owning Reserve Bank stock is quite different from owning stock in a private company. The Reserve Banks are not operated for profit, and ownership of a certain amount of stock is, by law, a condition of membership in the System. The stock may not be sold, traded, or pledged as security for a loan; dividends are, by law, 6 percent per year." At www.federalreserve.gov/faqs/about_14986.htm.

66 There are some further stipulations of three "classes" of governors, one-third of whom are supposed to represent the public interest; but given that most are economists or bankers, that is mostly window dressing. There is some rotation of regional bank presidents on the Federal Reserve Open Market Committee, which votes every six weeks on monetary policy; but the details are moot for our current purposes.

67 The ability to act subservient to the banking sector while posing as a regulator has been a major factor in the trajectory of the current crisis. For instance, the Fed dictated to AIG that it must keep all details of the bailout secret, even from the SEC (Walsh, "Fed Advice to AIG Scrutinized"). This was done to hide what was arguably one of the most corrupt aspects of Fed behavior in the early phases of the crisis, namely, pretending the system of credit default swaps had any integrity whatsoever. Moreover, the Fed has persistently used underhanded tactics, like having the private banking lobby block most scrutiny of Fed actions, to consolidate its lack of political accountability (Auerbach, 2008, pp. 5, 157–59). It fought the Freedom of Information Act request of Bloomberg to disclose its actions during the crisis retrospectively all the way to the Supreme Court through surrogates from the banking industry.

68 Adams, "Who Directs the Fed?" Duchin and Sosyura ("The Politics of Government Investments") find that banks with Fed directorships were more likely to receive TARP funds during the crisis. Someone needs to do a similar study with the Bloomberg release of Fed data on previously secret loans. Westbrook, *Out of the Crisis*, p. 134.

69 Auerbach, *Deception and Abuse at the Fed*; White, "The Federal Reserve System's Influence on Research in Monetary Economics"; Grim, "Priceless."

70 Auerbach, *Deception and Abuse*, p. 141. This made the Fed one of the largest employers of economists within the federal government, above the

Department of Agriculture (525) and below the Department of Labor (1,076) in the year 2000. White (p. 325) gives a figure of 495 full-time staff, which for a decade later is suspiciously too close to the 1992 figure to be entirely credible. In another attempt to gauge Fed employment, but relying solely on BLS data, DeMartino (*The Economist's Oath*, p. 25) estimates only 310 economists working there in 2008. This, most likely, is an undercount. DeMartino gives a rough estimate of 28,000 persons employed as economists in the United States in 2008.

71 White, "The Federal Reserve System's Influence," pp. 325–26.

72 Grim, "Priceless"; DeMartino, *The Economist's Oath*, p. 25; Auerbach, *Deception and Abuse*, p. 145.

73 Information provided in a presentation by Warren Young at a talk delivered in Tel Aviv in December 2010.

74 See http://netrightdaily.com/2011/06/150-economists-call-for-spending-cuts-that-exceed-debt-limit-hike/. The Nobelists were Robert Mundell and Vernon Smith. Not unexpectedly, the petition was arranged by a neoliberal think tank. "The absence of a clear mainstream is one underappreciated reason for the standoff between the Obama administration and Congressional Republicans over raising the debt limit" (Appelbaum, 2011).

75 Suskind, *Confidence Men*, pp. 56–57.

76 Gerardi, Foote, and Willen, "Reasonable People Did Disagree."

77 Subramanian, "How Economics Managed to Make Amends."

78 *Economist*, "Influential Economists."

79 http://makemarketsbemarkets.org/. It was one of the earliest programs of finance reform from the center-left.

80 Johnson and Kwak, *13 Bankers*, p. 51; For some documentation of the failure of the FDA, see Mirowski, *ScienceMart*; Angell, *The Truth About the Drug Companies*; Washington, Deadly Monopolies; and Murray and Johnston, *Trust and Integrity in Biomedical Research*.

81 Available at www.cfr.org/publication/19540/reforming_global_finance.html and published as French et al., *The Squam Lake Report*.

82 The Squam Lake papers are archived on the Greenberg website, www.cfr.org/thinktank/cgs/index.html. Of course, where the money for the exercise really came from remains unreported. However, the financial backgrounds of the individual Squam Lake members is covered in Epstein and Carrick-Hagenbarth, "Financial Economists, Financial Interests and the Dark Corners of the Meltdown," and below. The Council on Foreign Relations is chaired by Robert Rubin, which further cements the behind-the-scenes Wall Street influence, not to mention the Rubin effect on the Democratic Party administrations (Suskind, *Confidence Men*).

83 This is the interpretation found in many reviews not emitted from the economics

journals controlled by the Squam Lake cabal: see Goodhart, "The Squam Lake Report," and Mike Konczal at http://rortybomb.wordpress.com/2011/05/13/darrell-duffie-on-regulating-foreign-exchange-swap-moderate-1990s-republican-style-financial-reform/. The latter writes: "You can take the Squam Lake report on what financial reform should look like as a kind of moderate Right/moderate Republican view of financial reform post–financial crisis. Dodd-Frank is conceptually similar in theory and very similar in practice to the Squam Lake report . . . when it is compared to Dodd-Frank, Squam Lake was weaker on consumer protection, conceptually stronger on derivatives (with a purposeful eye towards eliminating regulation arbitrage, hence Duffie's no exemptions for foreign-exchange and little emphasis on end-user exemptions), and focused on coco bonds as the major companion piece to resolution authority."

84 Independent Commission on Banking, Vickers Report. As Sir John Vickers is reported to have said in the rollout news conference: "The too big to fail problem must not be recast as a too delicate to reform problem." This itself was a sharp departure from the Squam Lake document. But eventually, the Tory government could not bring itself to implement the recommendations.

85 Dash, "Feasting on Paperwork."

86 Mirowski, *The Effortless Economy of Science?*

87 See, for instance, the discussion on Paul Krugman's blog, March 19, 2011, http://krugman.blogs.nytimes.com/2011/03/19/disagreement-among-economists/; or that of Peter Dorman, http://econospeak.blogspot.com/2011/08/its-political-economy-stupid.html.

88 Blinder, *Hard Heads, Soft Hearts*, p. 1.

89 Orthodox economists are simply incapable of admitting that the crisis impugns their microeconomics as drastically as their macroeconomics. "There is a sense in which times like these are what economists are for, just as wars are what career military officers are for. OK, maybe I can let microeconomists off the hook" (Krugman, "The Profession and the Crisis," p. 307).

90 The preliminary SEC report can be consulted at www.sec.gov/sec-cftc-prelim-report.pdf. The final attempt at imposing consensus came out five months later as U.S. SEC, *Findings Regarding the Market Events of May 6, 2010*, but the dispute nevertheless continues. See Kirilenko et al., "The Flash Crash"; Easley et al., "The Microstructure of the Flash Crash".

91 This attitude is almost too ubiquitous to document properly. For selected examples, see Coyle, "The Public Responsibilities of the Economist"; Krugman, *End This Depression Now!*; and Quiggin, *Zombie Economics*.

92 One rather unapologetic example is Eric Maskin at http://thebrowser.com/interviews/eric-maskin-on-economic-theory-and-financial-crisis. Maskin is domiciled at the Institute for Advanced Study, and is a specialist in game theory, which may go some distance in explaining the intellectual bubble he inhabits.

Another is Sargent, "Modern Macroeconomics Under Attack."

93 See Zeleny, "Financial Industry Paid Millions to Obama Aide"; Skomarovsky, "Evidence of an American Plutocracy"; Ferguson, "Larry Summers and the Subversion of Economics"; Cohan, "Endless Summers"; and Story, "A Rich Education for Summers."

94 Schmitt, "Prophet and Loss"; Skomarovsky, "Evidence of an American Plutocracy"; Mirowski, *ScienceMart*, pp. 343–49.

95 David Warsh suggested there may have been a conflict of interest, even this early: "Summers had consulted for a hedge fund, Taconic Capital Advisors, from 2004 until 2006, while president of Harvard. Its founders, Kenneth Brody and Frank P. Brosens, had earlier been Goldman Sachs partners. . . . Professors report their outside consulting income to their deans, and deans report theirs to the president. Presumably the president reports his outside earnings to the Harvard Corporation, of which he is a member. Summers is going to have some explaining to do to his Harvard colleagues when he returns" (www.economic principals.com/issues/tag/lawrence-summers).

96 Suskind, *Confidence Men*.

97 '*Inside Job* had essentially all its facts wrong,' replies Summers, unbelievably, resorting to an argument based on timing: because he didn't work in financial services before he was Treasury secretary, and because he waited a few years before taking that job at DE Shaw, Summers says it's 'absurd' to blame the revolving door for any of his actions. It's weird that Summers, who loves debate, generally refuses to sit down in some public forum and answer serious, informed questions about the legacy of his tenure at Treasury; it might well be that this single interview is the closest we'll ever get. And on the basis of this interview, it's clear that, far from apologizing for his actions, Summers is going Full Bluster, denying any culpability, and choosing instead to violently reject and belittle any suggestion that he holds any responsibility for the crisis at all." www.cjr.org/the_audit/summers_inside_job_had_essenti.php?page=all. Summers's assertions here have been challenged (Ferguson, *Predator Nation*, p. 252).

98 Summers, "The Great Liberator."

99 The role of government spending and borrowing in the full-spectrum neoliberal response to the economic crisis is described in chapter 6.

100 Summers, Interview, 2011.

101 Ferguson, *Predator Nation*, chapter 8.

102 Henderson, "AIG Scandal Could Hurt Official's Chances."

103 Ferguson, *Predator Nation*, p. 260.

104 In Mollenkamp et al., "Behind AIG's Fall, Risk Models Failed to Pass Real World Test."

105 "Mr. Gorton's work helped convince [Joe] Cassano that these things were only gold . . . because AIG would never have to make payments to cover actual

defaults . . . However, Mr. Gorton's work didn't address the potential write-downs or collateral payments to trading partners." (Mollenkamp et al., "Behind AIG's Fall")

106 Corkery, "Ben Bernanke's Labor Day Reading List"; Gorton, Interview, 2010, p. 1; Suskind, *Confidence Men*, pp. 86–91.

107 Gorton and Metrick, "Getting Up to Speed"; Rogoff and Reinhart, *This Time is Different*.

108 I have to enter the demurrer that I think the claims of Rogoff and Bernanke are essentially wrong, and that Gorton misportrays the nature and role of the shadow banking sector. He is especially dense on the causes of the financialization of the economy as a whole. The role of the Federal Crisis Inquiry Commission as explanatory cover-up is dealt with in the next chapter.

109 Gorton and Metrick, "Getting Up to Speed," p. 150.

110 Gorton, Interview, 2010, p. 16.

111 The trope of natural financial innovation, shared by many other economists of similar inclination, such as Robert Shiller, is discussed in chapter 6.

112 Lo, "Reading About the Financial Crisis."

113 See the NSF's Science360: "Are Mathematical Models the Cause for Financial Crisis in the Global Economy?" at http://science360.gov/obj/tkn-video/86c73a5e-4710-4c7d-ac76-ff635dc93937.

114 Lo, "Reading About the Financial Crisis."

115 See Epstein and Carrick-Hagenbarth, "Dangerous Interconnectedness." The incident gained notoriety because Duffie's belated admission was captured on YouTube: www.youtube.com/watch?=OSBgfYrL9fs.

116 Johnson, "Predators and Professors."

117 Ibid.

118 Taibbi, "Glenn Hubbard Leading Academic."

119 Chan, "Academic Economists to Consider Ethics Code."

120 Ferguson, *Predator Nation*, chapter 8; kapur "Academics Have More to Declare."

121 The membership of the Pew Group can be examined at www.pewfr.org; its major publications at www.financialreformtaskforce.org.

122 Carrick-Hagenbarth and Epstein, "Dangerous Interconnectedness," p. 59.

123 Out of the nineteen academic economists chosen, thirteen had identifiable ties to some private financial firm, while eight served on boards of directors, and two were co-founders. When writing for the public (with the interesting partial exception of business advice proffered on Bloomberg), very rarely did any of these figures self-report their financial affiliations; rather, they did identify their affiliation with the NBER or the Fed. In academic papers published from January 2005 through October 2009, with one exception, the financial affiliations were never mentioned. They also noted "the stronger the economists' alliance with the private sector the weaker would be their calls for regulation."

124 Carrick-Hagenbarth and Epstein, "Dangerous Interconnectedness."

125 Lohmann, "The Endless Algebra of Climate Markets."

126 Mirowski, *ScienceMart*.

127 Of course, many of these particular economists have subsequently been succeeded by noneconomist presidents. But having just concluded numerous interviews with technology transfer officers recently, it seems clear to me that economists have successfully seeded their vision of the purpose of the university throughout its administrative structures.

128 Bradley, *Harvard Rules*, p. 67.

129 Hersch and Viscusi, "Law and Economics as a Pillar of Legal Education"; Frank and Gabler, *Reconstructing the University*, pp. 202–3; Fourcade, "The Construction of a Global Profession."

130 Khurana, "Why Are There Business Schools in Universities?"

131 Some representative samples: Cook et al., "Reporting Science and Conflicts of Interest in the Lay Press"; Bekelman et al., "Scope and Impacts of Financial Conflicts of Interest in Biomedical Research"; Sismondo, "Pharmaceutical Company Funding and Its Consequences"; Slaughter et al., "U.S. Research Universities' Institutional Conflict of Interest Policies"; Murray and Johnston, *Trust and Integrity in Biomedical Research*; Moore et al., *Conflicts of Interest*; Mirowski, *ScienceMart*, pp. 233–39; M. Epstein, "How Will the Economic Downturn Affect Academic Bioethics?"

132 Bekelman et al., "Scope and Impacts," p. 43.

133 Murray and Johnston, *Trust and Integrity*, p. 138.

134 U.S. Senate, *Wall Street and the Financial Crisis*.

135 Hodgson and Jiang, *The Economics of Corruption and the Corruption of Economics*, 2008.

136 DeMartino, *The Economist's Oath*, chapter 5.

137 The longer version can be consulted at www.nakedcapitalism.com/2011/04/blacklisted-economics-professor-found-dead-nc-publishes-his-last-letter.html.

138 Larry Summers quoted in *Wall Street Journal*, December 8, 1997.

139 The movement was spearheaded by DeMartino (*The Economist's Oath*) and supported by Carrick-Hagenbarth and Epstein, "Dangerous Interconnectedness." The tepid response of the profession is documented in Cooke and Flitter, "Economists Display Little Interest in Ethics Code." I leave it to some future historian to document the deliberations of the Ad Hoc Committee headed by Robert Solow, first convened in January 2011. Instead of carrying out its deliberations in public, as per normal, the AEA committee discussions were themselves secret.

140 Edward Glaeser, "Where to Draw a Line on Ethics," Economix blog, April 1, 2011, at http://economix.blogs.nytimes.com/2011/01/04/where-to-draw-a-line-on-ethics/. This confession of administrative responsibility for

neutralizing conflict-of-interest policies is another example of how neoliberal economists actively push universities such as Harvard in a more neoliberal direction.

141   For the text, see www.aeaweb.org/aea_journals/AEA_Disclosure_Policy.pdf.

142   Davies and McGoey, "Rationalities of Ignorance," p. 77.

143   Posner, *Public Intellectuals*.

144   Proctor and Scheibinger, *Agnotology*. It should be sharply distinguished from agnoiology, "the doctrine of things of which we are necessarily ignorant" (p. 27).

145   For some telling examples, see Oreskes and Conway, *Merchants of Doubt*; Michaels, *Doubt Is Our Product*; and Sismondo, "Corporate Disguises in Medical Science."

146   Walker, *Buying In*. This was analyzed in chapter 3.

147   Quoted in Proctor and Scheibinger, *Agnotology*, p. 74.

148   Oreskes and Conway, *Merchants of Doubt*. For some quick summaries of this very important work, see www.youtube.com/watch?v=jOnXL8ob_js.

149   Hayek, *Constitution of Liberty*, p. 378.

150   Mooney, *The Republican War on Science*.

151   Mirowski, *ScienceMart*, chapter 7.

152   Foucart, "When Science Is Hidden Behind a Smokescreen."

153   See Sorkin, *Too Big to Fail*; Swagel, "The Financial Crisis"; and Ferguson and Johnson, "Too Big to Bail." The key source on economists' behavior used here is Glenn, "In Dismal Times, Economists Try to Shape Financial Debates."

154   The text of the petition and the signatories can be found at http://faculty.chicago booth.edu/john.cochrane/research/Papers/mortgage_protest.htm.

155   The sequence of interventions is conveniently documented at www.chicago booth.edu/news/2008-09-29_voicegsb.aspx. The NPR interview identifying Cochrane as ringleader can be accessed at www.npr.org/blogs/money/2008/09/ economist_leads_push_against_t.html.

156   Glenn, "In Dismal Times."

157   In John Cochrane, "Comments on the Milton Friedman Institute Protest" at http://faculty.chicagobooth.edu/john.cochrane/research/Papers/friedman_ letter_comments.htm.

158   The close connections between George Mason and numerous appendages of the neoliberal Russian doll are explored in Tkacik, www.daskrap.com/.

159   Mayer, "Covert Operations"; Gordon, "The Kochtopus vs. Murray Rothbard."

160   Flitter et al., "For Some Professors, Disclosure Is Academic."

161   Some major sources here are Hundley, "Billionaire's Role in Hiring Decisions at Florida State University Raises Questions"; Berrett, "Not Just Florida State"; and Jaschik, "Who Controls a Grant?"

162   Hundley, "Billionaire's Role in Hiring Decisions."

163 Sherman quoted in David Corn, "Thank You, Wall Street. May We Have Another?" *Mother Jones*, January 2010; Soros, "My Philanthropy."

5. *The Shock of the New*

1 Some of the best recent attempts include Snowdon and Vane, *Modern Macroeconomics*; Laidler, "Lucas, Keynes and the Crisis"; King, "Microfoundations for Macroeconomics?"; and Duarte, "Recent Developments in Macroeconomics." For a truncated seven-bullet version of the history from Krugman's perspective, see http://krugman.blogs.nytimes.com/2011/09/26/lucas-in-context-wonkish.

2 Paul Krugman blog, July 13, 2012, at http://krugman.blogs.nytimes.com/2012/07/13/gadgets-versus-fundamentals-wonkish/.

3 For an important exception, see Stiglitz, "Rethinking Macroeconomics," p. 593; "Needed").

4 Suskind, "Faith, Certainty, and the Presidency of George W. Bush."

5 Gauchat, "Politicization of Science in the Public Sphere," p. 183.

6 I have sought to make this case in greater detail in *ScienceMart*. Both that previous and this current book exist to contravene the conventional wisdom within the profession that, "although some economists within the Mont Pèlerin Society became very influential within economics, changes in the academic arena were driven by other forces" (Backhouse, *The Puzzle of Modern Economics*, p. 143).

7 Simon Wren-Lewis blog, "Mainly Macro," February 18, 2012, at http://mainlymacro.blogspot.com/2012/02.

8 Sorkin, "Vanishing Act."

9 Brush and Benson, "Forged Comment Letters Sent to U.S. Regulators Writing Derivative Rules."

10 Reay, "The Flexible Unity of Economics."

11 For examples of the former, see the "performativity" school (Callon, *The Laws of the Markets*; MacKenzie et al., *Do Economists Make Markets?*) and authors such as Chwieroth, *Capital Ideas*; for the latter, see Prasad, *The Politics of Free Markets*; Fourcade, *Economists and Societies*.

12 A previous version of this section appeared as a contribution to Hands and Davis, *The Elgar Companion to Recent Economic Methodology*.

13 Coy, "What Good Are Economists Anyway?"

14 Reinhardt, "An Economist's Mea Culpa."

15 Sherden, *The Fortune Sellers*.

16 Colander, *The Making of an Economist Redux*, p. 241.

17 FRB Philadelphia, *Survey of Professional Forecasters*; Reay, "The Flexible Unity of Economics," p. 71.

18 Sherden, *The Fortune Sellers*.

19 "It's not just that they missed it, they positively denied that it would happen"

(Knowledge@Wharton, "Why Economists Failed to Predict the Financial Crisis"). Compare this with an unfounded apologetic version of events: "It is impossible to predict a stock market collapse . . . [yet] there were many economists who did see that something was seriously wrong: they anticipated that a crash was virtually inevitable" (Backhouse, *The Puzzle of Modern Economics*, p. 94). Backhouse, a historian, declines to name any of those prescient souls.

20   *Economist,* "What Went Wrong with Economics?"

21   I refer to the so-called Revere Prize organized by the *Real World Economic Review*. The winners are described at http://rwer.wordpress.com/2010/05/13/keen-roubini-and-baker-win-revere-award-for-economics-2/.

22   See, for candidates from the left, Galbraith, 2009; for candidates from the far right, consult www.freedomfest.com/2009/home.htm.

23   Lucas and Stokey, "Liquidity Crises"; Warsh, "Last Week in Jerusalem."

24   Maskin, "Economic Theory and the Financial Crisis."

25   Coy, "What Good Are Economists Anyway?"

26   Buiter, "The Unfortunate Uselessness of Most State of the Art Academic Monetary Economics."

27   Lucas, "In Defense of the Dismal Science."

28   See www.economist.com/blogs/freeexchange/lucas_roundtable. All quotes in this paragraph come from this source.

29   Cassidy, "Rational Irrationality."

30   Ibid.

31   "[T]his inability to predict does not concern me much. It is almost tautological that severe crises are essentially unpredictable" (Caballero, "Macroeconomics After the Crisis," p. 85).

32   S. Johnson, "The Economic Crisis and the Crisis in Economics."

33   Acemoglu, "The Crisis of 2008," p. 3.

34   This tendency dates back to Mackay, *Memoirs of Extraordinary Popular Delusions and the Madness of Crowds,* if not all the way back to the South Sea Bubble.

35   Hands, "Economics, Psychology, and the History of Consumer Choice Theory."

36   Berg and Gigerenzer, "As-if Behavioral Economics"; Harford, "Why We Do What We Do." "There is no question that economics has been improved by being reminded of the heterogeneity of economic behavior, and the fact that much of the behavior observed does not fit well with existing models. . . . However, now begins the more serious task of restating, re-applying and extending the tools of traditional economics" (Harrison, "The Behavioral Counter-revolution," p. 56). Concerning such diktats, Berg and Gigerenzer ("As-if Behavioral Economics," p. 148) observe: "The odd tension between descriptive openness and normative dogmatism is interesting . . . [it] served as compensation for the out-and-out skeptics of allowing psychology into economics."

37   Shiller and Frank, "Flaw in Free Markets."

38 Although calling themselves Keynesians, their understanding of what Keynes wrote was so tenuous that they were called to account in this regard by Posner, "Shorting Reason," and Nuti, "Akerlof and Shiller." That is not to say no historians tended to promote an interpretation of Keynes friendly to the supposed behavioral insights (Backhouse and Bateman, "Methodological Issues in Keynesian Macroeconomics," p. 447).

39 Akerlof and Shiller, *Animal Spirits*, pp. 4, ix.

40 "Irrationality is the great copout, and simply represents a failure of imagination. Rationality is so weak a requirement that the set of potential explanations for a particular phenomenon that incorporate rationality is boundless" (S. D. Williamson, "A Defense of Contemporary Economics").

41 Posner, "Shorting Reason."

42 Akerlof and Shiller, "Disputations."

43 Berg and Gigerenzer, "As-if Behavioral Economics," p. 148.

44 Akerlof and Shiller, "Disputations."

45 Shiller, *Irrational Exuberance*. Donald Westbrook (*Out of the Crisis*, p. 41) captures the incongruity: "if [Shiller], a tenured superstar at Yale with a reputation for intellectual originality, feels constrained to be orthodox, it seems a safe bet that most of what passes for financial policy is merely recycled." Lo ("Reading About the Financial Crisis") summarizes: Shiller proposes "democratizing finance—extending the application of sound financial principles to a larger and larger segment of society." This follows from his theoretical premise: if bubbles are caused by the contagion of mistaken beliefs about economic outcomes, then the cure must be inoculation against further mistaken beliefs and eradication of currently mistaken ones. Much as the government plays a vital role in public health against the spread of contagious disease, Shiller recommends government subsidies to provide financial advisors for the less wealthy, and greater government monitoring of financial products, analogous to the consumer product regulatory agencies already in existence in the United States. More speculatively, he also suggests using financial engineering to create safer financial products and markets." The fundamental neoliberal character of Shiller's work is discussed in chapter 6.

46 Comment by Greg Mankiw appended to Akerlof and Romer, "Looting", p. 65.

47 Norris, "The Crisis Is Over, but Where's the Fix?"

48 "What's probably going to happen now—in fact, it's already happening—is that flaws-and-frictions economics will move from the periphery of economic analysis to its center. There's a fairly well developed example of the kind of economics I have in mind: the school of thought known as behavioral finance" (Krugman, "How Did Economics").

49 Lo, "Reconciling Efficient Markets with Behavioral Finance"; Caplin and Schotter, *The Foundations of Positive and Normative Economics*; Harrison, "The Behavioral Counter-revolution."

50 Ernst Fehr interview in Rosser et al., *European Economics at a Crossroads*, pp. 72–73.

51 Rabin, "A Perspective on Psychology and Economics," p. 659. Yet even this divergence went too far for the Old Guard of the orthodoxy, such as Kenneth Arrow. The dividing line between the postwar generation of neoclassical economists and the post-1980 cohort is that the former believed they could abjure all dependence on academic psychology, whereas the latter believed they could pick and choose among psychological doctrines to elevate those that seemingly reinforced the neoclassical orthodoxy.

52 Foer, "Nudge-ocracy."

53 Gennaioli, Shleifer, and Vishny, "Neglected Risks, Financial Innovation and Financial Fragility." Of course, since this is an orthodox model, fluctuations are relative to a rational-expectations equilibrium, and *not* of employment, income, and output. This is compounded by the fact that rational-expectations forecasts of identical agents are replaced by identical inaccurate forecasts. Whoever doubted neoclassical equilibrium would fail in a world populated by identical wonky forecasters?

54 Loewenstein and Ubel, "Economics Behaving Badly."

55 Fox, *The Myth of the Rational Market*, p. 301.

56 Stiglitz, *Freefall*, p. 7. The impression that economists were in some sense responsible for the existence of these markets became the pretense for the burgeoning literature on "performativity" in the sociology of finance. See MacKenzie et al., *Do Economists Make Markets?*

57 *Washington Post*, June 7, 2008.

58 Stiglitz, "The Non-existent Hand."

59 This distinction has been a crucial component in some contemporary defenses of the EMH. See, for instance, Szafarz, "How Did Crisis-Based Criticisms of Market Efficiency Get It So Wrong?" or the Cassidy interview with Richard Thaler: "I always stress that there are two components to the theory. One, the market price is always right. Two, there is no free lunch: you can't beat the market without taking on more risk. The no-free-lunch component is still sturdy, and it was in no way shaken by recent events: in fact, it may have been strengthened" ("Rational Irrationality").

60 S. D. Williamson, "A Defense of Contemporary Economics"; Zingales, "Learning to Live with Not-So-Efficient Markets," p. 1, 9.

61 http://blogs.reuters.com/felix-salmon/2009/08/11/why-the-efficient-markets-hypothesis-caught-on/: "Economists *are* scientists, after all. That which they can't explain, they turn into an axiom."

62 The following three paragraphs are ridiculously telegraphed summaries of narratives found in Mirowski, *Machine Dreams* and "Why There Is (as Yet) No Such Thing as an Economics of Knowledge."

63 Since the notion that the market is uniquely better at information processing than any human mind is a core tenet of neoliberalism, as explained in chapter 2, this trend is another bit of evidence for the claim that the economic orthodoxy has become more neoliberal, and hence more conservative, over time.

64 Samuelson, "Proof That Properly Anticipated Prices Fluctuate Randomly"; Fama, "The Behavior of Stock Market Prices"; Mehrling, "A Tale of Two Cities"; Bernstein, *Capital Ideas*; Jovanovic, "Finance in Modern Economic Thought"; Lo, "Reading About the Financial Crisis"; MacKenzie, *An Engine, Not a Camera*.

65 See Gennaioli, Shleifer, and Vishny, "Neglected Risks, Financial Innovation and Financial Fragility." The endorsement of Turner is described in www.bbc.co.uk/news/mobile/business-12679947; Klein in http://voices.washington post.com/ezra-klein/2010/04/how_financial_innovation_cause.html.

66 Mirowski, "Why There Is No Such Thing."

67 Stiglitz, *Freefall*, pp. 150, 153.

68 Both quotes are from the Stiglitz lecture to the Lindau Nobel Conference 2011, at www.mediatheque.lindau-nobel.org/#/Video?id=622.

69 Stiglitz, "Rethinking Macroeconomics," p. 593.

70 Stiglitz, "Information and the Change in Paradigm in Economics," pp. 613, 583, 577.

71 Stiglitz has been known to pillory the representative agent model in some cases ("Rethinking Macroeconomics"); but since his entire oeuvre is built upon them (*Selected Works*), it is hard to know what to make of this.

72 These are reprinted in *Selected Works* as chapters 21 and 26, respectively. Stiglitz identifies these as the key papers in his *Freefall* and "The Non-existent Hand."

73 Stiglitz, "Information and the Change in Paradigm in Economics," p. 395.

74 Stiglitz, "The Non-existent Hand."

75 Stiglitz, "Information and the Change in Paradigm," pp. 573, 580, 620. "Unfortunately, we have not been able to obtain a general proof of any of these propositions. What we have been able to do is analyze an interesting example" (Grossman and Stiglitz, "On the Impossibility of Informationally Efficient Markets," p. 395).

76 Grossman and Stiglitz, "On the Impossibility of Informationally Efficient Markets," pp. 393, 397; Grossman, *The Informational Role of Prices*, p.108.

77 Grossman and Stiglitz, "On the Impossibility of Informationally Efficient Markets."

78 Stiglitz, "Rethinking Macroeconomics," p. 596, 618. This point is made in greater analytical detail in Mirowski, "Markets Come to Bits" and "Inherent Vice."

79 Stiglitz, *Selected Works*, p. 557.

80 "While Keynes was willing to let animal spirits serve as the *deus ex machina* to retrieve an explanation of investment variability, our theory provides a more

plausible explanation of variability in investment" (*Selected Works*, p. 647). "Talking up animal spirits can only take you so far" (*Freefall*, p. 256). These quotes exemplify why Stiglitz does not belong in our previous category of "behavioral economics."

81   Stiglitz, *Freefall*, p. 268, 269, 266.

82   The Hearing Charter (quoted above) of the House Committee on Science and Technology and sworn testimony of the economists Sidney Winter, Scott Page, Robert Solow, David Colander, and V. V.Chari can be found at http://democrats.science.house.gov/publications/hearings_markups_details.aspx?NewsID=2876. David Colander (e-mail dated 12/21/2010) informs me his connections to the committee staff member Ken Jacobson may have played a role in the idea of convening a session devoted to the DSGE.

83   This is not the place to run through the tortured history of orthodox neoclassical macroeconomics, from the "neoclassical synthesis" through Friedman's monetarism to "New Classical" to "real business cycles" to "New Keynesians," and thus finally to DSGE. Two good sources on this massive literature are Quiggin, *Zombie Economics*, and Mehrling, "A Tale of Two Cities." As usual, the history is frequently accompanied by utterly naïve methodological statements: "the field looked like a battlefield. Researchers split in different directions, mostly ignoring each other, or else engaging in bitter fights or controversies. Over time however, largely because facts have a way of not going away, a largely shared vision of fluctuations and of methodology has emerged" (Blanchard, "The State of Macro," p. 2).

84   Blanchard, "The State of Macro," pp. 2, 26, 24.

85   V. V. Chari, testimony before the Committee on Science and Technology, Subcommittee on Investigations and Oversight, U.S. House of Representatives, July 20, 2010. For a similar argument, see Kocherlakota, *Modern Macroeconomic Models as Tools for Economic Policy*.

86   Sargent, "Modern Macroeconomics Under Attack," p. 29.

87   Kirman, "The Economic Entomologist," p. 63.

88   S. D. Williamson, "A Defense of Contemporary Economics."

89   Lucas, "Econometric Policy Evaluation."

90   Stiglitz, "Rethinking Macroeconomics," pp. 606–7, p. 597n7.

91   Colander et al., "Beyond DSGE Models"; Kirman, "Economic Theory and the Crisis."

92   For the curious, he was referencing the Sonnenschein-Mantel-Debreu theorems in microeconomics. See Kirman, "Whom or What Does the Representative Agent Represent?"; Rizvi, "The Sonnenschein-Mantel-Debreu Results After 30 Years."

93   Brunnermeier et al., "Macroeconomics with Financial Frictions," p. 38.

94   Kirman, "Economic Theory and the Crisis."

95 This position is almost exactly repeated in the Chari testimony, and in Kocher-lakota, *Modern Macroeconomic Models as Tools for Economic Policy*; De Grauwe, "The Scientific Foundation of DSGE Models"; Maskin, "Economic Theory and the Financial Crisis"; Caballero, "Macroeconomics After the Crisis"; S. D. Williamson, "A Defense of Contemporary Economics"; and Sargent, "Modern Macroeconomics Under Attack." All reactions in this paragraph are paraphrases of DSGE defenses found in these sources.

96 See, for instance, Brunnermeier et al., "Macroeconomics with Financial Frictions." We shall indulge in just one example of how such protests were so misleading as to border on misrepresentation. The notion that DSGE models, which rarely incorporated money, much less a banking sector, could indeed handle a financial crisis, is often motivated by citation of the Diamond and Dybvig model (1983), which is a model of a run on a solvent bank (Krugman, "The Profession and the Crisis," p. 309). Since most of the main institutions in the current crisis were insolvent, and not merely illiquid, this model turns out to be utterly irrelevant. Furthermore, since most DSGE models encompass a presumption of the EMH at base, and accept the Modigliani-Miller theorem, there are no functions for finance to perform in the models.

97 Although he does not fully concur with the points made here, one example could be Ricardo Caballero ("Macroeconomics After the Crisis," p. 90): "We are digging ourselves, one step at a time, deeper and deeper into Fantasyland, with economic agents who can solve richer and richer stochastic general equilibrium problems containing all sorts of frictions."

98 See, for instance, Mirowski, "The Cowles Anti-Keynesians" for American hostility to Keynes. Robert Skidelsky is the most prominent prophet of the Old-Time Religion when it comes to Keynes.

99 Clark, "Where's My Money, Idiot?"

100 Quoted in Scheiding and Mata, "National Science Foundation Patronage."

101 Buckley, *Financial Crisis*; "Financial Plumbing," *Journal of Economic Perspectives*, Winter 2010; Brunnermeier et al., "Macroeconomics with Financial Frictions."

102 For the 22nd Jerusalem Summer School in Economic Theory, table of contents, see http://iasmac31.as.huji.ac.il:8080/groups/economics_school_22/search/; See the roundtable video at www.youtube.com/watch?v=6NkBODcJSX4. David Warsh's summary of the conference ("Last Week in Jerusalem") provides a short precis of events there.

103 Warsh, "Last Week in Jerusalem."

104 Geanakoplos, "Managing the Leverage Cycle."

105 Whitehouse, "Crisis Compels Economists to Reach for New Paradigm"; Geanakoplos, "Managing the Leverage Cycle," p. 90; Thurner et al., "Leverage Causes Fat Tails and Clustered Volatility."

106 Geanakoplos collapses the concept of "collateral" and the concept of "leverage"

in his models by assuming "no-recourse collateral": the borrower must put up a percentage of the asset value as collateral, and lose the entire amount if payments are reneged upon. Abstractly, no-recourse collateral is portrayed as a plain put option for the borrower.

107 Geanakoplos, "Managing the Leverage Cycle," p. 90.

108 Geanakoplos and Fostel, "Leverage Cycles and the Anxious Economy," p. 1239.

109 Geanakoplos, "Managing the Leverage Cycle," p. 97.

110 Brunnermeier quoted in Whitehouse, "Crisis Compels Economists."

111 From an unpublished address of Paul Krugman to the European Association for Evolutionary Political Economy, November 1996, at www.mit.edu/~krugman/evolute.html. He rather touchingly concedes there: "As you probably know, I am not exactly an evolutionary economist." I owe a debt to Steve Keen ("Like a Dog Walking on Its Hind Legs") for this, and some other ideas covered in this section.

112 See Krugman, "The Return of Depression Economics." This talk has disappeared from its original site, and was never published; it can be found at www.youtube.com/watch?v=5N35mq4_gIw.

113 Eggertsson and Krugman, "Debt, Deleveraging, and the Liquidity Trap," p. 3.

114 Nocera, "The Big Lie."

115 Paul Krugman blog, December 24, 2011, at http://krugman.blogs.nytimes.com/2011/12/24/joe-nocera-gets-mad/#postComment.

116 For the original claim, see Mooney, *The Republican War on Science*. The misguided tendency of blaming "Republicans" for the transformation of academic science in the United States is covered in Mirowski, *ScienceMart*, pp. 35 et seq.)

117 Interview with Josh Rosner, *PBS NewsHour*, August 1, 2011; "Fannie was shrewd enough to understand that in order to push their agenda on Capitol Hill they needed to be supported by economists as well and so they started a series of papers where they would hire notable Conservative economists like Glenn Hubbard or progressive economists like Joe Stiglitz and Peter Orszag to justify various aspects of Fannie and Freddie's mission, or dispel concerns about their safety and soundness, and really used those as lobbying points on Capitol Hill," said Rosner. For Stiglitz's response see www.pbs.org/newshour/rundown/2011/07/-rep-barney-frank-d-mass.html. This issue is parsed in the next section. We might note in passing that both Morgenson and Nocera reign over the financial pages of the *New York Times*, and yet seem perched on opposite sides of the agnotological divide.

118 See, for instance, Litan, "In Defense of Much, but Not All, Financial Innovation" and *The Derivatives Dealer's Club and Derivates Markets Reform*. This is discussed further in chapter 6. The Kauffman Foundation website opens with a

quote from Hayek: www.kauffman.org. They have also funded their own Haye-kian critiques of the economics profession: see Frydman and Goldberg, *Beyond Mechanical Markets*, which was distributed *gratis* to participants at the 2011 meet-ing of INET at Bretton Woods.

119   This section is joint work with Edward Nik-Khah.

120   Swagel, "The Financial Crisis"; Sorkin, *Too Big to Fail*; "Break the Glass Bank Recapitalization Plan," dated 4/15/2008, available at www.scribd.com/doc/ 21266810/Too-Big-To-Fail-Confidential-Break-the-Glass-Plan-from-Treasury (accessed 2/21/2012).

121   "Secretary Paulson's intent to use TARP to purchase assets reflected a philo-sophical concern with having the government buy equity stakes in banks: he saw it as fundamentally a bad idea to have the government involved in bank ownership" (Swagel, "The Financial Crisis," p. 50).

122   Oliver Armantier and James Vickery of the N.Y. Fed delivered the baseline auction proposal on September 20; during the following week, the Treasury and the N.Y. and Washington Feds reached out to the academic market designers Lawrence Ausubel, Peter Cramton, Jacob Goeree, Charles Holt, Paul Milgrom, Jeremy Bulow, and Jonathan Levin. See Armantier et al., "A Procurement Auction for Toxic Assets with Asymmetric Information"; Klemperer, "The Product-Mix Auction."

123   Ferguson and Johnson, "Too Big to Bail," pp. 28–29; Prasch, "After the Crash of 2008." See "Bernanke's Comments on Asset Auction Process," dated 9/23/2008, available at www.reuters.com/article/2008/09/23/financial-bailout-bernanke-auctions-idUSN2338396920080923. The concern was with "mark to market" accounting rules, under which low prices might make banks (incor-rectly) appear insolvent.

124   For example: "Treasury is talking with the experts you would expect—promi-nent academics who have designed auctions. . . . Treasury is committed to get the market price as best it can." Swagel, quoted on Greg Mankiw's blog, dated 9/25/2008, http://gregmankiw.blogspot.com/2008/09/defense-of-paulson-plan .html (accessed 2/20/12). Whereas the quote is unattributed on this blog entry, Swagel has subsequently made clear that he was its author (Swagel, "The Finan-cial Crisis," p. 47).

125   For an example of the latter, see Tim Ryan, "Lesson from Saving and Loan Rescue," *Financial Times*, September 24, 2008, available at www.ft.com/cms/s/ 0/8e19c058-8a35-11dd-a76a-0000779fd18c.html#axzz1oOrqY4OO. Tim Ryan was the president and CEO of the Securities Industry and Financial Markets Asso-ciation, a lobbying group.

126   Ausubel and Cramton, "Auction Design Critical for Rescue Plan." Cramton makes clear in an NPR interview with David Kestenbaum that he shared Bern-anke's concern: "If the price [for a toxic asset] was too low then the banks would collapse and we would still have a mess." See "Complicated Reverse

Auction May Aid In Bailout," October 10, 2008, available at www.npr.org/templates/story/story.php?storyId=95591129.

127 Swagel, "The Financial Crisis," p. 56.

128 Promoting confusion about what markets are supposed to be has become standard operating procedure among market designers. To wit: "In addition to markets, there is also the market, an abstraction as in 'the market economy' or 'the free market' or 'the market system.' The abstract market arises from the interaction of many actual markets" (McMillan, *Reinventing the Bazaar*, p. 6).

129 The fact they were *academic* economists was significant. Swagel noted that Wall Street economists were also in favor of the TARP, but acknowledged that people would be suspicious of their judgments. (Swagel, quoted on Mankiw's blog, September 25, 2008, at http://gregmankiw.blogspot.com/ 2008/09/defense-of-paulson-plan.html).

130 Ausubel and Cramton, "Auctions for Injecting Bank Capital," p. 2.

131 Armantier et al., "A Procurement Auction for Toxic Assets with Asymmetric Information," p. 6.

132 Ausubel and Cramton, "Auctions for Injecting Bank Capital"; Klemperer, "The Product-Mix Auction"; Armantier et al., "A Procurement Auction"; Swagel, "The Financial Crisis"; Armantier et al., "A Procurement Auction."

133 Ausubel and Cromtom, "Auctions for Injecting Bank Capital," p. 4. More specifically, Ausubel et al. have since acknowledged, "there is no Bayesian Nash equilibrium bidding strategy for a similar auction that we can use as a benchmark. The reference price auction is beyond current theory" ("Common-Value Auctions with Liquidity Needs").

134 Paulson, *On the Brink*, pp. 258, 264, 334, 363–68, 389; see also Swagel, "The Financial Crisis," pp. 50–52, 58.

135 Ausubel and Cramton, "Auctions for Injecting Bank Capital."

136 "Study Suggests Buying Toxic Assets Could Work," *NPR*, November 18, 2008, available at www.npr.org/templates/story/story.php?storyId=97161786. Ausubel and Cramton ("No Substitute for the 'P'-Word in Financial Rescue," p. 1) repeat the "suitcase approach" charge.

137 "Complicated Reverse Auction May Aid in Bailout," *NPR*, October 10, 2008.

138 Ausubel and Cramton, "A Troubled Asset Reverse Auction," p. 10.

139 And, indeed, the studies that Ausubel and Cramton draw upon to get their 97 percent figure (Kagel and Levin, "Implementing Efficient Multi-Object Auction Institutions") provided experimental treatments of *private value* auctions.

140 Matthew Philips, "Gaming the Financial System," *Newsweek*, November 18, 2008, available at www.thedailybeast.com/newsweek/2008/11/17/gaming-the-financial-system.html.

141 Lawrence Ausubel and Peter Cramton, "Auction Design for the Rescue Plan," presentation dated October 5, 2008, available at www.cramton.umd.edu/

papers2005-2009/ausubel-cramton-auction-for-rescue-plan-slides.pdf (accessed March 6, 2012).

142 Nik-Khah, "A Tale of Two Auctions."

143 Cramton, "Auctioning the Digital Dividend," p. 1.

144 "The Credit Crisis and Market Design," Alvin Roth's Market Design Blog, January 3, 2009, at http://marketdesigner.blogspot.com/2009/01/credit-crisis-and-market-design.html.

145 Cramton, "Market Design," p. 2.

146 Session on "Research Funding for Economists." See www.etnpconferences.net/sea/seaarchive/sea2011/User/Program.php?TimeSlot=4#Session11.

147 Prasch, "After the Crash of 2008," p. 161.

148 Sorkin, *Too Big to Fail*, pp. 227–29; Calomiris and Wallison, "Blame Fannie Mae and Congress for the Credit Mess."

149 Krugman, "Fannie, Freddie and You."

150 White, "The Federal Reserve System's Influence on Research in Monetary Economics"; Wallison, see all; Congleton, "On the Political Economy of the Financial Crisis and Bailout 2008–9"; Calabria, "Fannie, Freddie and the Subprime Mortgage Market"; Pinto, "ACORN and the Housing Bubble"; Paybarah, "Bloomberg: Plain and Simple."

151 Nocera, "The Big Lie."

152 For the best examples, consult Engel and McCoy, *The Subprime Virus*; Muolo and Padilla, *Chain of Blame*; Fligstein and Goldstein, "A Long Strange Trip"; Avery and Brevoort, "The Subprime Crisis"; Madrick and Partnoy, "Did Fannie Cause the Disaster?"; and Levitin and Wachter, "The Commercial Real Estate Bubble." See also http://motherjones.com/kevin-drum/2011/12/housing bubble-and-big-lie.

153 Morgenson and Rosner, *Reckless Endangerment*, p. 121.

154 Bernanke, congressional testimony, 2007.

155 www.freddiemac.com/investors/pdffiles/fm2006_moodys.pdf. This evidence also calls into question the curious claims by Morgenson and Rosner that in 1993 "the new Fannie and Freddie [Alternative Qualifying] program institutionalized the endorsement of untested underwriting criteria [for mortgages]" (*Reckless Endangerment*, p. 53). This and similar locutions attempt to bypass or evade the fact that Fannie and Freddie neither pioneered nor engineered the spread of subprime practices; and that the timing of events is off for them to bear responsibility.

156 Engel and McCoy, *The Subprime Virus*, p. 17, 40; Muolo and Padilla, *Chain of Blame*; Roubini and Mihm, *Crisis Economics*.

157 See, for instance, Levitin and Wachter, "The Commercial Real Estate Bubble" and "Explaining the Housing Bubble"; Palley, *From Financial Crisis to Stagnation*, pp. 83–85.

158 Fligstein and Goldstein, "A Long Strange Trip."

159 These disappeared suspiciously soon from the Web after the FCIC was wound up, but were then archived at http://fcic.law.stanford.edu/hearings.

160 Financial Crisis Inquiry Commission, *Final Report*, pp. xxvi, xxxvi, 414, 427. Wallison's dissent reprised this point: "Wall Street was not a significant participant in the subprime PMBS market between 2004 and 2007, or at any time before" (p. 504). This does border on Orwellian doublethink.

161 *Final Report*, p. 443.

162 See the work by David Min at www.americanprogress.org/issues/2011/07/wallison.html. These are the basis for the complaints of Nocera, Barry Ritholtz, and Paul Krugman. The short version is that Wallison and Edward Pinto have played fast and loose with what counts as "subprime" in the GSE balance sheets. This complaint is then extended to Morgenson & Rossner, *Reckless Endangerment*.

163 Weil, "Wall Street's Collapse to Be Mystery Forever."

164 This comes from a posting by Yves Smith on Nakedcapitalism.com of January 26, 2011: www.americanprogress.org/issues/2011/07/wallison.html.

165 Room for Debate, *New York Times*: www.nytimes.com/roomfordebate/2011/01/30/was-the-financial-crisis-avoidable/address-excessive-leverage.

166 Room for Debate, *New York Times*, www.nytimes.com/roomfordebate/2011/01/30/was-the-financial-crisis-avoidable/more-than-just-greed.

167 U.S. House Committee on Oversight, *An Examination of Attacks Against the Financial Crisis Inquiry Commission*.

168 Lo, "Reading About the Financial Crisis."

6. The Red Guide to the Neoliberal Playbook

1 De Soto, "The Destruction of Economic Facts."

2 While one can readily endorse Corey Robin's insistence that the historical common denominator of conservatism has been that "the conservative favored liberty for the higher orders and constraint for the lower orders" (*The Reactionary Mind*, p. 8), there is indeed something more that sets the neoliberals apart, and helps explain their successes in the face of economic circumstances that should have shredded their credibility.

3 Robin, *The Reactionary Mind*, p. 24.

4 Sorkin, "Volcker Rule Stirs Up Opposition Overseas."

5 Fleming, "Adbusters Sparks Wall Street Protest"; Lasn quote in Motavalli, "Cultural Jammin'"; Adbusters website at adbusters.org. It is full of upbeat slogans such as: "As the #S17 anniversary of Occupy Wall Street nears, an art war against capitalism grows."

6 Byrne, *The Occupy Handbook*.

7 "Occupiers should not worry about liberal institutions or advocacy

organizations hijacking their movement right now. What they should worry about is how they characterize what they are inspiring. For example, the 'Take Back the American Dream' campaign is more likely to achieve its agenda because there are people out in the streets demonstrating and creating the climate for people to care about this project. It will likely receive more attention from media and politicians because there is a social movement inspiring discussion about the American economy. There doesn't need to be a choice between supporting the campaign or an occupation but what people do need to be conscientious of is the fact that conferences, summits, advocacy campaigns, petitions and Internet activism have all been tried and hasn't had a measurable impact in the past ten years. What hasn't been tried is the kind of resistance on display in Liberty Park" (http://dissenter.firedoglake.com/2011/10/03/occupy-wall-street-doesnt-need-to-issue-any-demands-yet/). See also Kunkel, "Forgive Us Our Debts," on the anarchist-inspired concept of "direct action," which openly conflates means and ends.

8   Greenberg, "What Future for Occupy Wall Street?" p. 47.

9   "[Jackie DiSalvo] hoped that OWS would run candidates in 2012, as the Tea Party did in 2010. But again, she admitted, 'OWS would never endorse them'" (Greenberg, "What Future for Occupy Wall Street?" p. 47).

10 These observations frequently arise in descriptions of the Tea Party from the left, such as Frank, *Pity the Billionaire*, and DiMaggio, *The Rise of the Tea Party*, but they never make the next analytical step to realize this is a signal characteristic of neoliberal political mobilization. The best short introduction to astroturfing in its relation to the Tea Party is the film, Taki Oldham's *(Astro) Turf Wars*.

11 The historical connection of Amway to the NTC is discussed by Maureen Tkacik at www.daskrap.com/2012/8/mont-pèlerin-society-john-birch-society-society-pages%E2%80%A6.

12 DiMaggio, *The Rise of the Tea Party*, pp. 212, 76.

13 Johnson, "Predators and Professors."

14 At the website www.change.org.

15 This was made clear in a 2012 interview with Dimon: "But when I ask if this episode has made him regret being such an outspoken defender of the banking industry, he looks at me point blank. 'I'm an outspoken defender of the *truth*,' he corrects me. 'Everyone is afraid of retaliation and retribution. We recently had an event with a hundred small bankers here, and 85 percent of them said they can't challenge the regulation because of the potential retribution. That's a terrible thing. Okay? This is not the Soviet Union. This is the United States of America. That's what I remember. Guess what,' he says, almost shouting now. 'It's a *free. Fucking. Country*'" (Pressler, "122 Minutes with Jamie Dimon").

16 I am thinking here specifically of Oreskes and Conway, *Merchants of Doubt*;

Proctor, *Golden Holocaust*; and Walker and Cooper, "Genealogies of Resistance."

17 As Congressman Paul Ryan said in his speech accepting the vice presidential candidacy in August 2012, "Our rights come from Nature and God, not from the government."

18 Friedrich Hayek's own repudiation of his midlife attempt to hang all the problems of the world on "scientism" in favor of an embrace of his own idiosyncratic understanding of cybernetics and evolutionary theory is a case in point. See Mirowski, "Naturalizing the Market."

19 Walker and Cooper, "Genealogies of Resistance," p. 150. Melinda Cooper in particular has been exploring the neoliberal appropriation of nature to construct its modern politics (*Life as Surplus*).

20 See Aarons, *Market Versus Nature*, pp. 62–63.

21 "The Intellectuals and Socialism" (1949), reprinted in Hayek, *Studies in Philosophy, Politics*.

22 Coase, "The Problem of Social Cost."

23 See Lohmann (all); Friends of the Earth, *The EU Emissions Trading System*; and Jung, "The EU's Emissions Trading System Isn't Working."

24 This occurred, for instance, in the cap and trade bill which passed the U.S. House in 2009, before it was killed in the Senate. The bill as passed gave away 83 percent of permits for free, with an excess subsidy to the worst polluters of $134 billion (Goodell, "As the World Burns").

25 "The first carbon trading trial phase in 2005–2007 was an abject failure. At 2298 million tons of CO_2, the 2007 cap was actually 8.3% *higher* than verified 2005 greenhouse gas emissions. Businesses were therefore free to increase emissions—or set emission permits aside for the next EU-ETS phases. Anxious to avoid having to make short-term investments in emissions reductions, industry lobbying against higher, effective targets has been extremely effective. In the current 2008–2012 phase, the average CO_2 cap is 2% lower than 2005 emissions. But in seventeen out of twenty member states—including France, Poland and the UK—2012 caps are still higher than measured emissions in 2005. Overall, twenty-one out of twenty-seven member states sought 2012 emissions caps that were higher than 2005 emissions (with the richest EU member state, Luxembourg, pushing for a 52% increase). There are now so many unused permits that most industries covered by the Emissions Trading System (responsible for almost 50% of EU emissions) can legally avoid making any cuts before at least 2016. What's more, there is no obligation to reduce emissions in Europe. Through the United Nations' Clean Development Mechanism, EU-ETS sector businesses may invest in projects outside Europe. Known as offsetting, this avoids domestic cuts, frequently even fails to reduce emissions in developing countries, and may also cause significant social and environmental problems" (Friends of the Earth, *The EU Emissions Trading System*).

26 According to UBS Investment Research, the ETS system has cost $287 billion till 2011 with "almost zero impact" on overall emissions in the European Union, and the money could have resulted in over 40 percent reduction if used in a targeted way, e.g., to upgrade power plants (Maher, "Europe's $287 Billion Carbon Waste").

27 Specter, "The Climate Fixers."

28 This is covered in Cressy, "Geoengineering Experiment Cancelled Amid Patent Row," with some background information provided by Specter, "The Climate Fixers." One might regard this incident as another illustration of the themes adumbrated in Mirowski, *ScienceMart*.

29 This was nicely captured in a cartoon that came out around the time of the Occupy movement. A stereotyped banker is looking out the window at a protester with a sign, "The Sky Is Falling!" The banker spins around and shouts, "Buy the Sky!"

30 Recall Klein's attack on *Inside Job* discussed in chapter 1; or see Andrew Haldane's speech at Jackson Hole in August 2012, "The Dog and the Frisbee."

31 The best description of such programs (as P-PIP and Term Asset-Backed Securities Loan Facility) and their dodgy nature can be found in Barofsky, *Bailout*; but see also the various Special Inspector General for TARP reports at www.sigtarp.gov and U.S. Government Accountability Office, *Opportunities Exist to Strengthen Policies and Processes*.

32 This is the interpretation of Ferguson and Johnson, "Too Big to Bail," for instance. It was later denied in Paulson, *On the Brink*.

33 Ferguson and Johnson, "Too Big to Bail: Part II," p. 16.

34 Barofsky, *Bailout*, pp. 129–31.

35 Perry Mehrling (*The New Lombard Street*) has been one of the few to highlight these recent alterations in functions, only to praise them as an obvious extension of Bagehot's principle of central banks acting as lenders of last resort. He might be less pleased to regard them as one integral component of the neoliberal policy response.

36 Engelen et al., *An Alternative Report on UK Banking Reform*, p. 112.

37 Friedman and Schwartz, *A Monetary History of the United States*.

38 It goes without saying that I am not the first to notice the perverse genius of this strategy. See, for instance, Chang, "The Revival—and the Retreat—of the State?"

39 See MacKenzie and Demos, "Credit Default Swap Trading Drops." This estimate may be limited in its geographic range, and is probably too low.

40 Miller, "Financial Innovation."

41 Some examples of the "social studies of finance" are MacKenzie, *An Engine, Not a Camera*; MacKenzie et al., *Do Economists Make Markets?*; and Preda and Knorr-Cetina, *Handbook of the Sociology of Finance*. The critique of the role of science

studies in helping reify this interpretation of financial innovation can be found in Engelen et al., "Reconceptualizing Financial Innovation."

42 I refer here to a paper by Donald MacKenzie ("The Credit Crisis as a Problem in the Sociology of Knowledge"), who argues that a shift in cultures of evaluation within the ratings agencies, from older corporate collateralized debt obligations to the newer CDOs composed of mortgage-backed securities, accounted for a number of "slips" when it came to evaluation of the dangers posed by the latter. Of course, MacKenzie realized that the narrative of "technological error" seems on its face implausible (pp. 1830–32); but by focusing so intently upon the narrowly confined world of the low-level analysts and traders, he misses most of the action surveyed in this volume.

43 Shiller, *Finance and the Good Society*, p. 13.

44 In Norris, "The Crisis Is Over, but Where's the Fix?"

45 See Litan, "In Defense of Much, but Not All, Financial Innovation" and *The Derivatives Dealer's Club and Derivates Markets Reform*; Litan and Wallison, *Competitive Equity*; Eichengreen, "The Crisis in Financial Innovation"; Shiller, "Radical Financial Innovation," "In Defense of Financial Innovation," and *Finance and the Good Society*.

46 Shiller, "Radical Financial Innovation" and "In Defense of Financial Innovation."

47 Shiller, Interview on *Finance and the Good Society*.

48 Ibid.

49 Ibid.

50 The fact that Shiller has a conflict of interest in promoting the Case-Shiller index and his other financial contraptions is revealed by the mission statement of his company, at www.macromarkets.com/index.shtml. He also is part-owner of Case Shiller Weiss, Inc. Some may object that Shiller is not a card-carrying member of the Neoliberal Thought Collective. While true, many other comparable proponents of financial innovation are, such as Robert Litan, research director of the Kauffmann Foundation, and co-author of Litan and Wallison, *Competitive Equity*. I use Shiller's quotes in the text because he has been such a high-profile commentator on the crisis.

Bibliography

Aarons, Eric. *Market Versus Nature: The Social Philosophy of Friedrich Hayek* (Melbourne: Australian Scholarly Publishing, 2008).

Abate, Tom. "After Calamity, Economics Leaders Rethink Strategy," *San Francisco Chronicle*, December 20, 2010.

Acemoglu, Daron. "The Crisis of 2008: Structural Lessons for and from Economics," *CEPT Policy Insight* no. 28 (2009).

Adams, Renee. "Who Directs the Fed?" SSRN working paper, 2011.

Ailon, Galit. "The Discursive Management of Financial Risk Scandals," *Qualitative Sociology* 35 (2012): 251–70.

Akerlof, George, and Rachel Kranton. *Identity Economics* (Princeton: Princeton University Press, 2010).

Akerlof, George, and Paul Romer. "Looting: The Economic Underworld of Bankruptcy for Profit," *Brookings Papers on Economic Activity* no. 2 (1993): 1–73.

Akerlof, George, and Robert Shiller. *Animal Spirits* (Princeton: Princeton University Press, 2009).

Akerlof, George, and Robert Shiller. "Disputations: Our New Theory of Macroeconomics," *New Republic* (2009), www.tnr.com/article/books-and-arts/disputations-our-new-theory-macroeconomics.

Akerlof, George, and Joseph Stiglitz. "Let a Hundred Theories Bloom" (2009), www.project-synciate.org.

Alterman, Eric. "The Professors, the Press, the Think Tanks—and Their Problems," *Academe*, May-June, 2011.

Amable, Bruno. "Morals and Politics in the Ideology of Neoliberalism," *Socio-Economic Review*, 2010.

Amadae, Sonja. *Rationalizing Capitalist Democracy* (Chicago: University of Chicago Press, 2003).

Andersen, Camilla. "Rethinking Economics in a Changing World," *Finance and Development*, June 2011: 50–52.

Andrews, Suzanna. "Larry Fink's $12 Trillion Shadow," *Vanity Fair*, April 2010.

Angell, Marcia. *The Truth About the Drug Companies* (New York: Random House, 2005).

Ansolabehere, Stephen, Johnathan Rodden, and James M. Snyder. "Purple America," *Journal of Economic Perspectives* 20 (2006): 97–118.

Appelbaum, Binyamin. "Politicians Can't Agree on Debt? Well, Neither Can Economists," *New York Times*, July 17, 2011.

Ariely, Daniel. *Predictably Irrational*, rev. ed. (New York: HarperCollins, 2010).

Armantier, Olivier, Charles Holt, and Charles Plott. "A Procurement Auction for Toxic Assets with Asymmetric Information," *CalTech Social Science Working Paper 1330R*, 2011.

Arnsperger, Christian. *Critical Political Economy* (London: Routledge, 2008).

Arnsperger, Christian, and Yanis Varoufakis. "What Is Neoclassical Economics?" *Post-Autistic Economics Review* 38 (2006): 2–12.

Arrow, Kenneth. "Gifts and Exchanges," *Philosophy and Public Affairs* 1 (1972): 343–62.

Arrow, Kenneth. "Invaluable Goods," *Journal of Economic Literature* 35 (1997): 757–65.

Auerbach, Robert. *Deception and Abuse at the Fed* (Austin: University of Texas Press, 2008).

Ausubel, Lawrence, and Peter Cramton. "Auction Design Critical for Rescue Plan" *The Economists' Voice* 5 (5) (2008).

Ausubel, Lawrence, and Peter Cramton. "Auctions for Injecting Bank Capital (Addendum to 'A Troubled Asset Reverse Auction')" (2008), Working Paper, University of Maryland. Available at http://works .bepress.com/cramton/8.

Ausubel, Lawrence, and Peter Cramton. "No Substitute for the 'P'-Word in Financial Rescue," *The Economists' Voice* 6 (2) (2009).

Ausubel, Lawrence, and Peter Cramton. "A Troubled Asset Reverse Auction" (2008), Working Paper, University of Maryland. Available at http://works.bepress.com/cramton/9/.

Ausubel, Lawrence, et al. "Common-Value Auctions with Liquidity Needs: An Experimental Test of a Troubled Assets Reverse Auction" (2011), available at www.cramton.umd.edu/papers/finance/.

Avery, Robert, and Kenneth Brevoort. "The Subprime Crisis: Is Government Housing Policy to Blame?" Federal Reserve Board of Governors, Finance and Economics Discussion Paper #36 (2011).

Backhouse, Roger. *The Puzzle of Modern Economics: Science or Ideology?* (Cambridge, U.K.: Cambridge University Press, 2010).

Backhouse, Roger, and Bradley Bateman. "Methodological Issues in

Keynesian Macroeconomics," in John B. Davis and D. Wade Hands, eds., *The Elgar Companion to Recent Economic Methodology*.

Baker, Dean. "Creating Political Space for Effective Financial Regulation," *Dialogue on Globalization* 42 (2009): 66–72.

Baker, Dean. *The End of Loser Liberalism* (Washington: Center for Economic and Policy Research, 2011).

Baker, Dean. "The Soft Bigotry of Incredibly Low Expectations: The Case of Economists," September 15, 2010, available at http://rwer .wordpress.com/2010/09/15.

Ban, Cornell. *Neoliberalism in Translation: Economic Ideas and Reforms in Spain and Romania*. Ph.D thesis, University of Maryland, 2011.

Barnett, Clive. "The Consolations of Neoliberalism," *Geoforum* 36 (1) (2005): 7–12.

Barofsky, Neil. *Bailout* (New York: Free Press, 2012).

Bartels, Larry. "What's the Matter with *What's the Matter with Kansas?*" *Quarterly Journal of Political Science* 1 (2006): 201–26.

Basen, Ira. "Economics Has Met the Enemy, and It Is Economics," *Toronto Globe and Mail*, October 15, 2011.

Becker, Gary. *Human Capital* (Chicago: University of Chicago Press, 1964).

Becker, Gary, and Julio Elias. "Introducing Incentives in the Market for Live and Cadaveric Organs," *Journal of Economic Perspectives* 21 (2007): 3.

Behrent, Michael. "Liberalism Without Humanism: Foucault and the Free Market Creed," *Modern Intellectual History* 6 (2009): 539–68.

Bekelman, Justin, Yan Li, and Cary Gross. "Scope and Impacts of Financial Conflicts of Interest in Biomedical Research," *Journal of the American Medical Association* 284 (2003): 454–65.

Bel, Germa. "The First Privatisation: Seeling SOEs and Privatizing Public Monopolies in Fascist Italy," *Cambridge Journal of Economics* 35(5) (2011): 937-956.

Benabou, Roland, and Jean Tirole. "Identity, Dignity and Taboos," CEPR Discussion Paper 6123 (2007), available at www.vwl.tuwien.ac.at/ hanappi/AgeSo/rp/Benabou_2007.pdf.

Benabou, Roland, and Jean Tirole. "Self-Knowledge and Self-Regulation: An Economic Approach," in I. Brocas and J. Carillo, eds., *The Psychology of Economic Decisions*, vol. 1 (Oxford: Oxford University Press, 2003), pp. 137–67.

Benabou, Roland, and Jean Tirole. "Willpower and Personal Rules," *Journal of Political Economy* 112 (2004): 848–86.

Berg, Nathan, and Gerd Gigerenzer. "As-if Behavioral Economics: Neoclassical Economics in Disguise?" *History of Economic Ideas* 18 (2010): 133–65.

Berlin, Isaiah. "Two Concepts of Liberty," in *Four Essays on Liberty* (Oxford: Oxford University Press, 1969 [1958]).

Bernanke, Ben. Congressional testimony, July 20, 2006.

Bernanke, Ben. Congressional testimony, March 28, 2007, available at www.federalreserve.gov/newsevents/testimony/bernanke20070328a .htm.

Bernanke, Ben. *Essays on the Great Depression* (Princeton: Princeton University Press, 2004).

Bernanke, Ben. "Global Imbalances: Links to Economic and Financial Stability" (2011), available at www.federalreserve.gov/newsevents/speech/ bernanke20110218a.htm.

Bernanke, Ben. "The Great Moderation" (2004), www.federalreserve. gov/Boarddocs/Speeches/2004/20040220/default.htm.

Bernanke, Ben. "On the Implications of the Financial Crisis for Economics," September 24, 2010, available at www.federalreserve.gov/newsevents/ speech/bernanke20100924a.htm.

Bernanke, Ben. "The US Economic Outlook" (2011), available at www .federalreserve.gov/newsevents/speech/bernanke20110908a.htm.

Bernanke, Ben, and Mark Gertler. "Agency Costs, Net Worth and Business Fluctuations," *American Economic Review* 79 (1989): 14–31.

Bernstein, Peter. *Capital Ideas* (New York: Free Press, 1992).

Berrett, Dan. "Not Just Florida State," *Inside Higher Ed*, June 28, 2011.

Bess, Michael. "Blurring the Boundary between Person and Product: Human Genetic Technologies," *Hedgehog Review*, Summer 2011, 56–67.

Beucke, Dan. "BATS: The Epic Fail of the Worst IPO Ever," *Business-Week*, March 23, 2012.

Bini, Piero, and Luigino Bruni. "Intervista a Gerard Debreu," *Storia del Pensiero Economico* 35 (1998): 3–29.

Birch, Kean. "Have We Ever Been Neoliberal?" (2011), available at www.iippe.org/wiki/images/c/cd/Working_Paper_Ever_Neoliberal .pdf

Birch, Kean, and Vlad Mykhnenko, eds. *The Rise and Fall of Neoliberalism: The Collapse of an Economic Order?* (London: Zed, 2010).

Blackburn, Robin. "The Subprime Crisis," *New Left Review* 50 (2008): 63–106.

Blanchard, Olivier. "The State of Macro," NBER Working Paper 14259 (2008).

Blanchard, Olivier, Giovanni Dell'Ariccia, and Paolo Mauro. "Rethinking Macro Policy," February 16, 2010, available at www .voxeu.org

Blinder, Alan. *Hard Heads, Soft Hearts* (Reading: Addison-Wesley, 1987).

Blundell, John. *Waging the War of Ideas*, 2nd ed. (London: Institute of Economic Affairs, 2003).

Boas, Taylor, and Jonas Gans-Morse. "Neoliberalism: From New Liberal Philosophy to Anti-Liberal Slogan," *Studies in International Development* 44 (2) (2009): 137–61.

Bockman, Johanna. *Markets in the Name of Socialism* (Stanford: Stanford University Press, 2011).

Boltanski, Luc, and Eve Chiapello. *The New Spirit of Capitalism* (London: Verso, 2005).

Bonefeld, Werner. "Freedom and the Strong State," *New Political Economy* 17 (2012): 633-656.

Bookstaber, Richard. *A Demon of Our Own Design* (New York: Wiley, 2007).

Bourdieu, Pierre. "The Essence of Neoliberalism," *Le Monde Diplomatique*, December 8, 1998.

Bowmaker, Simon, ed. *Economics Uncut: The Complete Guide to Life, Death and Misadventure* (Cheltenham, U.K.: Elgar, 2005).

Bowman, Andrew, Mick Moran, and Karl Williams. "The (Mis)rule of the Econocrats," OpenDemocracy blog, April 19, 2012.

Bowman, Andrew, et al. *Scapegoats Aren't Enough: A Leveson for the Banks?* CRESC policy brief, July 2012, available at www.cresc.ac.uk/sites/default/files/LEVESON%20FOR%20THE%20BANKS%202012%2007%2001.pdf.

Boyes, Roger. *Meltdown Iceland* (New York: Bloomsbury, 2009).

Bradley, Richard. *Harvard Rules* (New York: HarperCollins, 2005).

Brand, Ulrich, and Nicola Seckler, eds. *Postneoliberalism—A Beginning Debate*. Special Issue of *Development Dialogue*, no. 51 (2009).

Brenner, Neil, Jamie Peck, and Nik Theodore. "Variegated Neoliberalization: Geographies, Modalities, Pathways," *Global Networks* 10 (2010): 182–222.

Brenner, Robert. "What Is Good for Goldman Sachs Is Good for America" (2009), http://escholarship.org/uc/item/0sg0782h.

Brock, William, and David Colander. "Complexity, Pedagogy, and the Economics of Muddling Through," in Alan Kirman and M. Salzano, eds., *Economics Complex Windows* (Berlin: Springer Verlag, 2005).

Brocking, Ulrich, Susanne Krasmann, and Thomas Lemke, eds. *Governmentality: Current Issues and Future Challenges* (London: Routledge, 2011).

Brown, Wendy. "American Nightmare: Neoliberalism, Neoconservatism, and De-democratization," *Political Theory* 34 (2006): 690–714.

Brown, Wendy. *Edgework* (Princeton: Princeton University Press, 2005).

Brunnermeier, Markus. "Deciphering the Liquidity and Credit Crunch 2007–8," *Journal of Economic Literature* 23 (2009): 77–100.

Brunnermeier, Markus, Thomas Eisenbach, and Yuliy Sannikov. "Macroeconomics with Financial Frictions: A Survey," paper presented to 22nd Jerusalem Summer School in Economic Theory, 2011.

Brush, Silla, and Clea Benson. "Forged Comment Letters Sent to U.S. Regulators Writing Derivative Rules," *Bloomberg News*, November 30, 2010 at www.bloomberg.com/news/2010-11-30/forged-comment-letters-sent-to-u-s-regulators-writing-derivatives-rules.html.

Buchanan, James. *Ideas, Persons and Events*, vol. 19 of *Collected Works* (Indianapolis: Liberty Fund, 2001).

Buchanan, James. *Why I, Too, Am Not a Conservative* (Cheltenham, U.K.: Elgar, 2005).

Buchanan, James, and Viktor Vanberg. "Constitutional Choice, Rational Ignorance and the Limits of Reason" (1991), in Viktor Vanberg, *Rules and Choice in Economics* (London: Routledge, 1994).

Buckley, Adrian. *Financial Crisis: Causes, Context, Consequences* (Harlow, U.K.: Financial Times Prentice Hall, 2011).

Buiter, Willem. "The Unfortunate Uselessness of Most State of the Art Academic Monetary Economics" (2009), at www.voxeu.org/index.php?q=node/3210.

Bullock, Penn. "Friedman Economics," *Reason Magazine*, September 2009.

Burgin, Angus. "The Political Economy of the Early Mont Pèlerin Society," paper presented to History of Economics Society, 2007.

Burgin, Angus. *The Return of Laissez Faire*, Harvard PhD thesis, 2009.

Burns, Jennifer. *Goddess of the Market* (New York: Oxford University Press, 2009).

Burton, Bob. "Atlas Research Foundation: The Think Tank Breeders," *PR Watch* vol. 11, no. 3, 2004.

Byrne, Janet, ed. *The Occupy Handbook* (Boston: Back Bay, 2012).

Caballero, Ricardo. "Macroeconomics After the Crisis," *Journal of Economic Perspectives* 24 (2010): 85–102.

Calabria, Mark. "Fannie, Freddie and the Subprime Mortgage Market," Cato brief #120, 2011, at www.cato.org/pub_display.php?pub_id=12846.

Caldwell, Bruce. "The Chicago School, Hayek, and Neoliberalism," in Van Horn et al., *Building Chicago Economics*.

Caldwell, Bruce. *Hayek's Challenge* (Chicago: University of Chicago Press, 2004).

Calhoun, Craig, and Georgi Derluguian, eds. *The Deepening Crisis:*

Governance Challenges After Neoliberalism (New York: New York University Press, 2011).

Callinicos, Alex. *Bonfire of Illusions* (Cambridge, U.K.: Polity, 2010).

Callon, Michel. *The Laws of the Markets* (New York: Blackwell, 1998).

Calomiris, Charles, and Peter Wallison. "Blame Fannie Mae and Congress for the Credit Mess," *Wall Street Journal*, October 23, 2008.

Calvo, Guillermo. "Yes, the Rich Will Drive Recovery," *Economist*, September 6, 2010, available at www.economist.com/economics /by-invitation/guest-contributions.

Camerer, Colin, George Loewenstein, and Darzen Prelec. "Neuroeconomics: How Neuroscience Can Inform Economics," *Journal of Economic Literature* 43 (2005): 9–64.

Campbell, John. "Neoliberalism in Crisis: Regulatory Roots of the U.S. Financial Meltdown," *Research in the Sociology of Organizations* 30B (2010): 65–101.

Campbell, John, and Ove Pedersen, eds. *The Rise of Neoliberalism and Institutional Analysis* (Princeton: Princeton University Press, 2001).

Campos, Nauro, and Jeffrey Nugent. "Why Has This One Been Such a Disappointing Crisis?" July 10, 2011, at www.voxeu.org.

Caplin, Andrew, and Andrew Schotter, eds. *The Foundations of Positive and Normative Economics* (Oxford: Oxford University Press, 2008).

Carey, Mark, and Rene Stulz, eds. *The Risks of Financial Innovations* (Chicago: University of Chicago Press, 2006).

Carrick-Hagenbarth, Jessica, and Gerald Epstein. "Dangerous Interconnectedness: Conflicts of Interest, Ideology and the Financial Crisis," *Cambridge Journal of Economics* 36 (2012): 43–63.

Cassidy, John. *How Markets Fail* (New York: Farrar, Straus and Giroux, 2009)

Cassidy, John. "No Credit: Timothy Geithner's Financial Plan Is Working," *The New Yorker*, March 15, 2010.

Cassidy, John. "Rational Irrationality," Chicago Interviews, *The New Yorker*, January 21, 2010, at www.newyorker.com/online/blogs/john cassidy/chicago-interviews/.

Cecchetti, Stephen, and Enisse Kharroubi. "Reassessing the Impact of Finance on Growth," Bank for International Settlements Working Paper, 2012.

Cerny, Philip. "Embedding Neoliberalism: The Evolution of a Hegemonic Paradigm," *Journal of International Trade and Diplomacy* 2 (2008): 1–46.

Chakrabortty, Aditya. "Angry Economists Can't Answer My Criticism That There's Too Little Analysis of Our Current Crisis" *Guardian*, May

7, 2012, at: www.guardian.co.uk/commentisfree/2012/may/07/academics-cant-answer-criticism-analysis.

Chan, Sewell. "Academic Economists to Consider Ethics Code," *New York Times*, December 30, 2010.

Chan, Sewell. "Bernanke Defends Fed's Ability to Supervise Banks," *New York Times*, February 26, 2010.

Chan, Sewell. "Dissenters Fault Report on Crisis in Finance," *New York Times*, January 26, 2011.

Chan, Sewell, and Ben Protess. "Cross Section of Rich Invested with Fed," *New York Times,* December 2, 2010.

Chang, Ha-Joon. "The Revival—and the Retreat—of the State?" *Red Pepper*, June 2011.

Christi, F. R. "Hayek and Schmitt on the Rule of Law," *Canadian Journal of Political Science* 17 (1984): 521–35.

Christi, Renato. *Carl Schmitt and Authoritarian Liberalism* (Cardiff: University of Wales Press, 1998).

Chwieroth, Jeffrey. *Capital Ideas: The IMF and the Rise of Financial Liberalization* (Princeton: Princeton University Press, 2010).

Clark, Gregory. "Where's My Money, Idiot?" (2009) at *Atlantic* magazine blogs: http://business.theatlantic.com/2009/02/wheres_my_money_idiot.php.

Clarke, John. "Living with/in and without Neoliberalism," *Focaal* 51 (2008): 135–47.

Coase, Ronald. *Essays on Economics and Economists* (Chicago: University of Chicago Press, 1994).

Coase, Ronald. "The Problem of Social Cost," *Journal of Law and Economics* 3 (1960): 1–44.

Cochrane, John. "Lessons from the Financial Crisis," *Regulation*, Winter 2009.

Cochrane, John. "Presidential Address: Discount Rates," *Journal of Finance* 66 (2011): 1047–1108.

Cockett, Richard. *Thinking the Unthinkable: Think Tanks and the Economic Counter-revolution, 1931–83* (London: Fontana, 1995).

Cohan, William. "Endless Summers," *Vanity Fair*, December 2009.

Cohen, Patricia. "Ivory Tower Unswayed by Crashing Economy," *New York Times*, March 5, 2009.

Colander, David. "The Death of Neoclassical Economics," *Journal of the History of Economic Thought* 22 (2000): 127–43.

Colander, David. "How Did Macroeconomic Theory Get So Far off Track?" in E. Hein, T. Niechoj, and E. Stockhammer, eds. *Macroeconomic Policies on Shaky Foundations* (Marburg, Germany: Metropolis Verlag, 2009).

Colander, David. *The Making of an Economist Redux* (Princeton: Princeton University Press, 2007).

Colander, David, Rick Holt, and Barkley Rosser. "The Changing Face of Economics," *The Long Term View* 7 (1) (2008): 31–42.

Colander, David, Rick Holt, and Barkley Rosser. "Live and Dead Issues in the Methodology of Economics," *Journal of Post Keynesian Economics* 30 (2007): 303–12.

Colander, David, et al. "Beyond DSGE Models," *American Economic Review, Papers and Proceedings* 98 (2) (2008): 236–40.

Colander, David, et al. *The Financial Crisis and the Systemic Failure of Academic Economists* ["Dahlem Report"] (2009), at www.debtdeflation. com/blogs/wp-content/uploads/papers/Dahlem_Report_EconCrisis 021809.pdf.

Colchester, Max. "Setback for Soros in Paris," *Wall Street Journal*, October 7, 2011.

Congleton, Roger. "On the Political Economy of the Financial Crisis and Bailout 2008–9," *Public Choice* 140 (2009): 287–317.

Cook, Daniel, Elizabeth Boyd, Claudia Grossman, and Lisa Bero. "Reporting Science and Conflicts of Interest in the Lay Press," *PLoS One* 12 (December 2007): e1266.

Cooke, Kristina, and Emily Flitter. "Economists Display Little Interest in Ethics Code," Reuters, July 8, 2011, at http://ca.reuters.com/article /newsOne/idCATRE7673XK20110708.

Cooper, Melinda. "Complexity Theory after the Crisis: The Death of Neoliberalism or the Triumph of Hayek?" *Journal of Cultural Economy* 4 (2011): 371–85.

Cooper, Melinda. "Foucault, Neoliberalism and the Iranian Revolution," in Vanessa Lemm and Miguel Vatter, eds., *The Government of Life: Michel Foucault and Neoliberalism* (New York: Fordham University Press, 2012).

Cooper, Melinda. *Life as Surplus* (Seattle: University of Washington Press, 2008).

Corkery, Michael. "Ben Bernanke's Labor Day Reading List," *Wall Street Journal*, September 2, 2010.

Couldry, Nick. "Reality TV, or the Secret Theatre of Neoliberalism," *Review of Education, Pedagogy and Cultural Studies* 30 (2008): 3–13.

Covington, Sally. "Moving Public Policy to the Right," in Daniel Faber and Deborah McCarthy, eds., *Foundations for Social Change* (Lanham, Md.: Rowman & Littlefield, 2005).

Cowen, Tyler. *Create Your Own Economy* (New York: Dutton, 2009).

Cowen, Tyler. "Why Everything Has Changed: The Recent Revolution in Cultural Economics," *Journal of Cultural Economics* 32 (2008): 261–73.

Coy, Peter. "What Good Are Economists Anyway?" *Business Week*, April 16, 2009.

Coyle, Diana. "The Public Responsibilities of the Economist," Tanner Lectures, 2012, at www.enlightenmenteconomics.com/blog/index.php/2012/06/a-macroeconomist-tells-me-off/.

Crabtree, Susan. "Paul Ryan's $700-Wine-Sipping Buddies," *Talking Points Memo*, July 9, 2011.

Cramton, Peter. "Auctioning the Digital Dividend" (2008), available at www.cramton.umd.edu/papers2005-2009/cramton-auctioning-the-digital-dividend.pdf.

Cramton, Peter. "Market Design: Harnessing Market Methods to Improve Resource Allocation," *American Economic Association, Ten Years and Beyond: Economists Answer NSF's Call for Long-Term Research Agendas* (2010), available at http://papers.ssrn.com/sol3/papers.cfm?abstract_id=1888577.

Cressy, Daniel. "Geoengineering Experiment Cancelled Amid Patent Row," *Nature* 15, May 2012.

Crouch, Colin. *The Strange Non-Death of Neoliberalism* (Cambridge, U.K.: Polity, 2011).

Dardot, Pierre, and Christian Laval. *La nouvelle raison du monde. Essai sur la societé néolibérale* (Paris: La Decouverte, 2009).

Dash, Eric. "Feasting on Paperwork," *New York Times*, September 9, 2011.

Davidson, Adam. "Prime Time for Paul Ryan's Guru (the One That's Not Ayn Rand)," *New York Times*, August 21, 2012.

Davies, William. "The Emerging Neo-communitarianism," *Political Quarterly* 83 (2012): 767-776.

Davies, William. "When is a Market Not a Market?" *Theory, Culture and Society*, forthcoming 2013.

Davies, William, & Linsey McGoey. "Rationalities of Ignorance: On the Financial Crisis and the Ambivalence of Neoliberal Epistemology," *Economy and Society* 41 (2012): 64–83.

Daviron, Benoit, and Stefano Ponte. *The Coffee Paradox* (London: Zed, 2005).

Davis, John. "The Change In and Recent State of Economics," *The Long Term View* 7 (1) (2008): 7–13.

Davis, John. *Individuals and Identity in Economics* (New York: Cambridge University Press, 2011).

Davis, John. *The Theory of the Individual in Economics* (London: Routledge, 2003).

Davis, John. "The Turn in Economics: Neoclassical Dominance to Mainstream Pluralism?" *Journal of Institutional Economics* 2 (2006): 1–20.

Davis, John. "The Turn in Recent Economics and the Return of Ortho-doxy," *Cambridge Journal of Economics* 32 (2008): 349–66.

Davis, Mike, and Daniel Monk, eds. *Evil Paradises* (New York: New Press, 2007).

Dean, Mitchell. "Rethinking Neoliberalism," *Journal of Sociology* (2012), at: http://jos.sagepub.com/content/early/2012/04/19/1440783312442 256.abstract

De Grauwe, Paul. "The Scientific Foundation of DSGE Models," *Public Choice* 144 (2010): 413–43.

DeLong, Brad. "Economics in Crisis" (2011), www.project-syndicate.org.

DeMartino, George. *The Economist's Oath* (New York: Oxford University Press, 2011).

Denord, Francois. *Néo-Libéralisme version francais* (Paris: Demopolis, 2007).

De Soto, Hernando. "The Destruction of Economic Facts," *Business Week*, April 28, 2011.

Deuber-Mankowsky, Astrid. "Nothing Is Political, Everything Can Be Politicized: On the Concept of the Political in Michel Foucault and Carl Schmitt," *Telos* 142 (2008): 135–61.

Diamond, Douglas, and Philip Dybvig. "Bank Runs, Deposit Insurance and Liquidity," *Journal of Political Economy* 91 (1983): 401–19.

Diamond, Marie. "The Return of Debtor's Prisons" (2011), at http://thinkprogress.org/justice/2011/12/13/388303/the-return-of-debtors-prisons-thousands-of-americans-jailed-for-not-paying-their-bills/.

Diamond, Sara. *Not by Politics Alone* (New York: Guilford Press, 1998).

Diamond, Sara. *Roads to Dominion* (New York: Guilford Press, 1995).

Dickinson, Tom. "How Roger Ailes Built the Fox News Fear Factory," *Rolling Stone*, May 25, 2011.

DiMaggio, Anthony. *The Rise of the Tea Party* (New York: Monthly Review Press, 2011).

Dittmer, Andrew. "Journey into a Libertarian Future" (2011), at www.nakedcapitalism.com/2011/11/journey-into-a-libertarian-future-part-i-%E2%80%93the-vision.html.

Donzelot, Jacques. "Michel Foucault and Liberal Intelligence," *Economy and Society* 37 (2008): 115–34.

Donzelot, Jacques, and Colin Gordon. "Governing Liberal Societies—the Foucault Effect for the English-speaking World," *Foucault Studies* 5 (2008): 48–62.

Duarte, Pedro. "Recent Developments in Macroeconomics: The DSGE Approach to Business Cycles," in Hands and Davis, *The Elgar Companion to Recent Economic Methodology*.

Duchin, Ran, and Denis Sosyura. "The Politics of Government Investments," *Journal of Financial Economics*, 106 (2012) 24-48

Duffie, Darrell. *Dark Markets* (Princeton: Princeton University Press, 2011).

Duffie, Darrell. "The Failure Mechanics of Dealer Banks," *Journal of Economic Perspectives* 24 (2010): 51–72.

Duggan, Lisa. *The Twilight of Equality?* (Boston: Beacon Press, 2003).

Duménil, Gérard, and Dominique Lévy. *The Crisis of Neoliberalism* (Cambridge, Mass.: Harvard University Press, 2011).

Dunn, Stephen. *The Economics of John Kenneth Galbraith* (New York: Cambridge University Press, 2011).

Easley, David, Marcos De Prado, and Maureen O'Hara. "The Microstructure of the Flash Crash," *Journal of Portfolio Management* 37 (Winter 2011): 118-28

Eaton, George. "Osborne's Supporters Turn on Him," *New Statesman*, August 15, 2012.

Economist. "Influential Economists," *The Economist*, February 10, 2011.

Economist. "What Went Wrong with Economics?" *The Economist*, July 18, 2009.

Eecke, Wilfred ver. "Ethics in Economics: From Classical Economics to Neoliberalism," *Philosophy and Social Criticism* 9 (1982): 145–68.

Eggertsson, Gauti, and Paul Krugman. "Debt, Deleveraging, and the Liquidity Trap: A Fisher-Minsky-Koo Approach" (2010), at www.frbsf.org/economics/conferences/1102/eggertsson.pdf.

Ehrenreich, Barbara. *Bait and Switch* (New York: Henry Holt, 2005).

Ehrenreich, Barbara. "Turning Poverty into an American Crime," *The Nation*, August 9, 2011.

Eichengreen, Barry. "The Crisis in Financial Innovation," address to International Schumpeter Society, 2010, available at http://emlab.berkeley.edu/~eichengr/crisis_finan_innov.pdf.

Eichengreen, Barry. "The Last Temptation of Risk," *National Interest*, April 28, 2009.

Eichengreen, Barry, and Kevin O'Rourke. "A Tale of Two Depressions" (2010), www.voxeu.org/index.php?q=node/3421.

Elliott, Douglas, and Martin Baily. "Telling the Narrative of the Financial Crisis: Not Just a Housing Bubble" (2009), at www.brookings.edu/research papers/2009/11 23-narrative-elliott-baily.

Engel, Kathleen, and Patricia McCoy. *The Subprime Virus: Reckless Credit, Regulatory Failure and Next Steps* (New York: Oxford University Press, 2011).

Engelen, Ewald, et al.. *After the Great Complacence* (Oxford: Oxford University Press, 2011).

Engelen, Ewald, et al. *An Alternative Report on UK Banking Reform* (2009), CRESC: www.cresc.ac.uk/publications/an-alternative-report-on-uk-banking-reform.

Engelen, Ewald, et al. "Reconceptualizing Financial Innovation: Frame, Conjuncture and Bricolage," *Economy and Society* 39 (2010): 33–63.

Epstein, Gerald, and Jessica Carrick-Hagenbarth. "Avoiding Group Think and Conflicts of Interest: Widening the Circle of Central Bank Advice," *Central Bank Journal*, May 2011.

Epstein, Gerald, and Jessica Carrick-Hagenbarth. "Financial Economists, Financial Interests and the Dark Corners of the Meltdown," PERI working paper #239, 2010.

Epstein, Miran. "How Will the Economic Downturn Affect Academic Bioethics?" *Bioethics* 24 (2010): 226–33.

Fama, Eugene. "The Behavior of Stock Market Prices," *Journal of Business* 38 (1965): 34–105.

Federal Reserve Bank of Philadelphia. *Survey of Professional Forecasters.* Fourth quarter, 2007.

Ferguson, Charles. "Larry Summers and the Subversion of Economics," *Chronicle of Higher Education*, October 3, 2010.

Ferguson, Charles. *Predator Nation* (New York: Crown, 2012).

Ferguson, Thomas, and Robert Johnson. "Too Big to Bail: Parts I & II," *International Journal of Political Economy* 38 (2009) (1): 3–34; (2): 5–45.

Feser, Edward, ed. *Cambridge Companion to Hayek* (Cambridge, U.K.: Cambridge University Press, 2006).

Festinger, Leon, Henry Riecken, and Stanley Schachter. *When Prophecy Fails* (Minneapolis: University of Minnesota Press, 1956).

Fischer, Peter, Dieter Frey, Claudia Peus, and Andreas Kastenmüller. "The Theory of Cognitive Dissonance: The State of the Science," in Muesburger et al., eds, *Clashes of Knowledge.*

Fleming, Andrew. "Adbusters Sparks Wall Street Protest," *Vancouver Courier*, September 27, 2011.

Flew, Terry. "Michel Foucault's Birth of Biopolitics and Contemporary Neo-liberalism Debates," *Thesis Eleven* 108 (2012): 44–65.

Fligstein, Neil, and Adam Goldstein. "A Long Strange Trip: The State and Mortgage Securitization, 1968–2010," in Preda and Knorr-Cetina, *Handbook of the Sociology of Finance.*

Flitter, Emily, Kristina Cooke, and Pedro DaCosta. "For Some Professors, Disclosure Is Academic," Reuters special report, 2010, at http://link. reuters.com/heq72q.

Foer, Franklin. "Nudge-ocracy," *New Republic*, May 6, 2009.

Fontaine, Philippe. "Blood, Politics and Social Science," *Isis* 93 (2002): 401–34.

Forrester, Katrina. "Tocqueville Anticipated Me," *London Review of Books*, April 26, 2012.

Foucart, Stephane. "When Science Is Hidden Behind a Smokescreen," *Guardian Weekly*, June 28, 2011.

Foucault, Michel. *The Birth of Biopolitics* (New York: Palgrave Macmillan, 2008).

Foucault, Michel. *Discipline and Punish* (New York: Vintage, 1977).

Foucault, Michel. *The Hermeneutics of the Subject* (New York: Palgrave Macmillan, 2005).

Foucault, Michel. *The Order of Things* (New York: Vintage, 1973).

Fourcade, Marion. "The Construction of a Global Profession," *American Journal of Sociology* 117 (2006): 145–94.

Fourcade, Marion. *Economists and Societies* (Princeton: Princeton University Press, 2009).

Foust, Dean, and Aaron Pressman. "Credit Scores: Not So Magic Numbers," *Business Week*, February 7, 2008.

Fox, Justin. *The Myth of the Rational Market* (New York: HarperCollins, 2009).

Frank, David, and Jay Gabler. *Reconstructing the University* (Stanford: Stanford University Press, 2006).

Frank, Robert. "Flaw in Free Markets: Humans," *New York Times*, September 14, 2009.

Frank, Thomas. *One Market Under God* (New York: Anchor, 2000).

Frank, Thomas. *Pity the Billionaire* (New York: Henry Holt, 2012).

Frank, Thomas. *What's the Matter with Kansas? How Conservatives Won the Heart of America* (New York: Henry Holt, 2004).

Frank, Thomas. "The Wrecking Crew," *Harper's*, August 2008, 35–45.

Frazzetto, Giovanni, and Suzanne Anker. "Neuroculture," *Nature Reviews Neuroscience* 19 (2009): 815–21.

Freedman, Craig. *Chicago Fundamentalism: Ideology and Methodology in Economics* (Singapore: World Scientific, 2008).

French, Kenneth, et al. *The Squam Lake Report* (Princeton: Princeton University Press, 2010).

Fridell, Gavin. "Fair-Trade Coffee and Commodity Fetishism: The Limits of Market-Driven Social Justice," *Historical Materialism* 15 (2007): 79–104.

Friedman, Milton. *Bright Promises, Dismal Performances* (Sun Lakes, Ariz.: Thomas Horton & Daughters, 1983).

Friedman, Milton. *Capitalism and Freedom* (Chicago: University of Chicago Press, 1962).

Friedman, Milton. "Economic Freedom Behind the Scenes" (2002), at www.cato.org/special/friedman/friedman/friedman4.html.

Friedman, Milton. *Essays in Positive Economics* (Chicago: University of Chicago Press, 1953).

Friedman, Milton. "Interview," with Brian Doherty, *Reason Magazine*, June 1995.

Friedman, Milton. "Neoliberalism and Its Prospects," *Farmand*, February 17, 1951, 89–93.

Friedman, Milton, and Rose Friedman. *Free to Choose* (New York: Harcourt Brace, 1980).

Friedman, Milton, and Rose Friedman. *Two Lucky People* (Chicago: University of Chicago Press, 1998).

Friedman, Milton, and Paul Samuelson. *Friedman and Samuelson Discuss the Responsibility of Government* (College Station, Tex.: Center for Education and Research in Free Enterprise, 1980).

Friedman, Milton, and Anna Schwartz. *A Monetary History of the United States, 1867–1960* (Princeton: Princeton University Press, 1963).

Friedrich, Carl. "Review: The Political Thought of Neo-Liberalism," *American Political Science Review* 49 (1955): 509–25.

Friends of the Earth Europe. *The EU Emissions Trading System: Failing to Deliver* (2010), at http://ec.europa.eu/clima/consultations/0005/registered/982555 3393-31_friends_of_the_earth_europe_en.pdf.

Frost, Gerald. *Antony Fisher, Champion of Liberty* (London: Profile Books, 2002).

Frydman, Roman, and Michael Goldberg. *Beyond Mechanical Markets* (Princeton: Princeton University Press, 2011).

Fukuyama, Francis. "The End of History," *National Interest* 16 (1989): 3–18.

Fuller, Steve. *Social Epistemology*, 2nd ed. (Bloomington: Indiana University Press, 2002).

Galbraith, James K. "Who Are These Economists, Anyway?" *Thought and Action*, Fall 2009, 85–97.

Galbraith, John Kenneth. *The New Industrial State* (New York: Houghton, 1967).

Galbraith, John Kenneth. "Power and the Useful Economist," *American Economic Review* 63 (1973): 1–11.

Gali, Jordi, and Luca Gambetti. "On the Sources of the Great Moderation," *American Economic Journal: Macroeconomics* 1 (2009): 26–57.

Gauchat, Gordon. "Politicization of Science in the Public Sphere: A Study of Public Trust in the United States, 1974–2010," *American Sociological Review* 77 (2012): 167–87.

Geanakoplos, John. "The Leverage Cycle," in D. Acemoglu, K. Rogoff, and M. Woodford, eds., *NBER Macroeconomics Annual* 24 (2009): 1–64.

Geanakoplos, John. "Managing the Leverage Cycle," in *Dopo la Crisi*, (Milan: Giuffre Editione), 2010 http://dido.econ.yale.edu/P/cp/p13a/p1306.pdf.

Geanakoplos, John, and Ana Fostel. "Leverage Cycles and the Anxious Economy," *American Economic Review* 98 (2008): 1211–44.

Gennaioli, Nicola, Andrei Shleifer, and Robert Vishny. "Neglected Risks, Financial Innovation and Financial Fragility," NBER Working Paper 16068, 2010.

Gerardi, Kristopher, Christopher Foote, and Paul Willen. "Reasonable People Did Disagree," Boston Fed working paper (2010), at www.bos.frb.org/economic/ppdp/2010/ppdp1005.htm.

Gershon, Ilana. "Neoliberal Agency," *Current Anthropology* 52 (2011): 537–55.

Gershon, Ilana. "Un-friend My Heart: Facebook, Promiscuity, and Heartbreak in a Neoliberal Age," *Anthropological Quarterly* 84 (4) (2011): 867–96.

Giridharadas, Anand. "Boycotts Minus the Pain," *New York Times*, October 11, 2009.

Glaeser, Edward. "The Moral Heart of Economics," NY Times Economix blog, January 1, 2011, at http://economix.blogs.nytimes.com/2011/01/25.

Glaeser, Edward, Joshua Gottlieb, and Joseph Gyourko. "Did Credit Market Policies Cause the Housing Bubble?" Harvard Kennedy School Policy Briefs, May 2010.

Glenn, David. "In Dismal Times, Economists Try to Shape Financial Debates," *Chronicle of Higher Education*, October 10, 2008.

Goldman, Alvin, and Dennis Whitcomb, eds. *Social Epistemology: Essential Readings* (New York: Oxford University Press, 2011).

Goodell, Jeff. "As the World Burns," *Rolling Stone*, January 21, 2010.

Goodhart, Charles. "The Squam Lake Report: Commentary," *Journal of Economic Literature* 49 (2011): 114–19.

Goodman, Peter. "Taking a Hard Look at the Greenspan Legacy," *New York Times*, October 8, 2008.

Gordon, David. "The Kochtopus vs. Murray Rothbard" (2008), at www.lewrockwell.com/gordon/gordon37.htm.

Gorton, Gary. "The Big Short Shrift," *Journal of Economic Literature* 49 (2) (2011): 450–53.

Gorton, Gary. Interview, *Minneapolis Federal Reserve Report*, December 2010, at www.minneapolisfed.org.

Gorton, Gary. *Slapped by the Invisible Hand* (New York: Oxford University Press, 2010).

Gorton, Gary, and Andrew Metrick. "Getting Up to Speed: A One-Weekend Reader's Guide," *Journal of Economic Literature* 50 (2012): 128–50.

Graeber, David. *Debt: The First 5,000 Years* (Brooklyn, N.Y.: Melville House, 2011).

Gravois, John. "Too Important to Fail," *Washington Monthly*, July 2012.

Greenberg, Michael. "What Future for Occupy Wall Street?" *New York Review of Books*, February 9, 2012, pp. 46–48.

Grim, Ryan. "Priceless: How the Federal Reserve Bought the Economics Profession" (2009), at www.huffingtonpost.com/2009/09/07/priceless-how-the-federal_n_278805.html.

Gross, Neil, Thomas Medvetz, and Rupert Russell. "The Contemporary American Conservative Movement," *Annual Review of Sociology* 37 (2011): 325–54.

Grossman, Sanford. *The Informational Role of Prices* (Cambridge, Mass.: MIT Press, 1989).

Grossman, Sanford, and Joseph Stiglitz. "On the Impossibility of Informationally Efficient Markets," *American Economic Review* 70 (1980): 393–408.

Guess, Andy. "Who You Calling Heterodox?" *Inside Higher Ed*, October 3, 2007.

Gusenbauer, Alfred. "La Strada on Wall Street" (2008), www.project-syndicate.org.

Hacker, Andrew, and Claudia Dreifus. "The Debt Crisis at American Colleges," *The Atlantic*, August 2011.

Hackworth, Jason. *Faith Based: Religious Neoliberalism and the Politics of Welfare in the United States* (Athens: University of Georgia Press, 2012).

Hacohen, Mordechai. *Karl Popper: The Formative Years* (New York: Cambridge University Press, 2002).

Haight, Colleen. "The Problem with Fair Trade Coffee," *Stanford Social Innovation Review*, Summer 2011, at www.ssireview.org/articles/entry/the_problem_with_fair_trade_coffee/.

Haldane, Andrew. "The Dog and the Frisbee" (2012) at www.bankofengland.co.uk/publications/Documents/speeches/2012/speech596.pdf.

Hands, D. Wade. "Economics, Psychology, and the History of Consumer Choice Theory," *Cambridge Journal of Economics* 34 (4) (2010): 633–48.

Hands, D. Wade, and John Davis, eds. *The Elgar Companion to Recent Economic Methodology* (Cheltenham, U.K.: Elgar, 2011).

Hanke, Steven. "Abolish the IMF," *Forbes*, April 13, 2000.

Harcourt, Bernard. *The Illusion of Free Markets* (Cambridge, Mass.: Harvard University Press, 2011).

Harcourt, Bernard. "Radical Thought from Marx, Nietzsche and Freud through Foucault, to the Present," Chicago Public Law and Legal Theory Working Paper no. 355, 2011.

Harding, Sandra, ed. *Can Theories Be Refuted? Essays on Duhem's Thesis* (Boston: Reidel, 1976).

Harford, Tim. "Why We Do What We Do," *Financial Times*, January 30, 2011.

Haring, Norbert. "Economics Is Losing Its Memory" (2011), at http://olafstorbeck.com/2011/03/25/how-economics-is-losing-its-memory/.

Harrison, Glenn. "The Behavioral Counter-revolution," *Journal of Economic Behavior and Organization* 73 (2010): 49–57.

Hartwell, R. M. *A History of the Mont Pèlerin Society* (Indianapolis: Liberty Fund, 1995).

Harvey, David. *A Brief History of Neoliberalism* (Oxford: Oxford University Press, 2005).

Havinghurst, Clark. "Trafficking in Human Blood," *Law and Contemporary Problems* 72 (2009): 1–16.

Hayek, Friedrich. "Capitalism and Freedom," *New Individualist Review* 1 (April 1961), no. 1.

Hayek, Friedrich. *The Constitution of Liberty* (Chicago: University of Chicago Press, 1960).

Hayek, Friedrich. *Individualism and Economic Order* (Chicago: Regnery, 1972 [1948]).

Hayek, Friedrich. "The Intellectuals and Socialism," *University of Chicago Law Review* 16 (1949): 417–33.

Hayek, Friedrich. *Law, Legislation and Liberty*, vol. 1 (Chicago: University of Chicago Press, 1973).

Hayek, Friedrich. "The Moral Element in Free Enterprise," *The Freeman* 12 (7) (1962): 44–51.

Hayek, Friedrich. *The Road to Serfdom* (Chicago: University of Chicago Press, 1944).

Hayek, Friedrich. *Studies in Philosophy, Politics and Economics* (New York: Simon & Schuster, 1967).

Healy, Kieran. *Last Best Gifts: Altruism and the Market for Human Blood and Organs* (Chicago: University of Chicago Press, 2006).

Hedoin, Cyril. "Towards a Paradigm Shift in Economics?" April 6, 2009, at www.laviedesidees.fr.

Helleiner, Eric. "A Bretton Woods Moment? The 2007/8 Crisis and the Future of Global Finance," *International Affairs* 86 (2010): 619–36.

Helleiner, Eric. *States and the Re-emergence of Global Finance* (Ithaca, N.Y.: Cornell University Press, 1994).

Henderson, Nell. "AIG Scandal Could Hurt Official's Chances," *Washington Post*, May 12, 2005.

Hennecke, Hans Jorg. *Friedrich August von Hayek: Die tradition der Freiheit* (Dusseldorf: Verlagsgruppe Handelsblatt, 2000).

Herndon, Thomas et al., "Does High Public Debt Consistently Stifle Economic Growth? A Critique of Reinhart and Rogoff," PERI Working Paper 332, April 2013.

Hersch, Joni, and Kip Viscusi. "Law and Economics as a Pillar of Legal Education," Vanderbilt discussion paper, 2011.

Hirsh, Michael. "Our Best Minds Are Failing Us," *Newsweek*, September 16, 2010.

Hochschild, Arlie. *The Outsourced Self* (New York: Metropolitan, 2012).

Hodgson, Geoffrey. "The Great Crash of 2008 and the Reform of Economics," *Cambridge Journal of Economics*, 33 (2009): 1205-1221.

Hodgson, Geoffrey, and Shuxia Jiang. "The Economics of Corruption and the Corruption of Economics," *Revista de Economía Institucional* 10 (2008), No. 18.

Holcombe, Randall. *Economic Models and Methodology* (New York: Greenwood, 1989).

Holling, Crawford. "Resilience and Stability of Ecological Systems," *Annual Review of Ecology and Systematics* 4 (1973): 1–23.

Holmstrom, Bengt. "Ignorance Is (Almost) Bliss," Arrow Lecture, 28 June 28, 2011, 22nd Jerusalem Summer School, at http://iasmac31.as.huji.ac.il:8080/groups/economics_school_22/weblog/9a883/.

Hoplin, Nicole, and Ron Robinson. *Funding Fathers: Unsung Heroes of the Conservative Movement* (Washington: Regnery, 2008).

Howard, Michael, and J. E. King. *The Rise of Neoliberalism in Advanced Capitalist Economies* (London: Palgrave Macmillan, 2008).

Howitt, P. "Macroeconomics with Intelligent Autonomous Agents," in R. Farmer, ed., *Macroeconomics in the Small and the Large: Essays on Microfoundations, Macroeconomic Applications and Economic History in Honor of Axel Leijonhufvud* (Cheltenham, U.K.: Edward Elgar, 2008), 157–77.

Howitt, P. "The Microfoundations of the Keynesian Multiplier Process," *Journal of Economic Interaction and Coordination* 1 (2006): 33–44.

Hulsmann, Jorg. *Mises: The Last Knight of Liberalism* (Auburn, Mass.: Mises Institute, 2007).

Hundley, Kris. "Billionaire's Role in Hiring Decisions at Florida State University Raises Questions," *St. Petersburg Times*, May 9, 2011.

Hunt, Louis, and Peter McNamera, eds. *Liberalism, Conservatism and Hayek's Idea of Spontaneous Order* (New York: Palgrave Macmillan, 2007).

Hutheesing, Nikil. "Better Trading Through Science," Bloomberg News, August 31, 2011, at www.bloomberg.com/news/2011-08-31/better-trading-through-science.html.

Ibanez, Carlos. *The Current State of Macroeconomics* (Basingstoke, U.K.: Macmillan, 1999).

Imperia, Andrea, and Vincenzo Maffeo. "As If Nothing Were Going to Happen: A Search in Vain for Warnings about the Current Crisis in Economics Journals with the Highest Impact Factors," paper presented to World Economy in Crisis conference, October 31, 2009.

Independent Commission on Banking. *Vickers Report*, 2011, at http://bankingcommission.s3.amazonaws.com/wp-content/uploads/2010/07/ICB-Final-Report.pdf.

Ivry, Bob, Bradley Keoun, and Phil Kuntz. "Secret Fed Loans Helped Banks Net $13 Billion," *Bloomberg Markets*, November 27, 2011, at http://www.bloomberg.com/news/2011-11-28/secret-fed-loans-undisclosed-to-congress-gave-banks-13-billion-in-income.html.

Jackson, Ben. "At the Origins of Neo-liberalism: The Free Economy and the Strong State, 1930–1947," *The Historical Journal* 53 (1) (2010): 129–51.

Jaschik, Scott. "Who Controls a Grant?" *Inside Higher Ed*, May 11, 2011.

Jensen, Michael, and William Meckling. "Theory of the Firm: Managerial Behavior, Agency Costs and Ownership Structure," *Journal of Financial Economics* 3 (1976): 305–60.

Jickling, Mark. "Causes of the Financial Crisis," Congressional Research Service, R40173, 2009.

Johnson, Robert, and Erica Payne, eds. *Make Markets Be Markets* (New York: Roosevelt Institute, 2010).

Johnson, Simon. "Big Banks Have a Big Problem," NY Times Economix, blog, at http://economix.blogs.nytimes.com/22013/03/14/. March 14 2013.

Johnson, Simon. "The Economic Crisis and the Crisis in Economics," Presidential Address to Association for Comparative Economics, 2009, at http://baselinescenario.files.wordpress.com/2009/01/aces-presidential-lecture-jan-6-2008-for-posting.pdf.

Johnson, Simon. "An Institutional Flaw at the Heart of the Federal Reserve," NY Times Economix blog, June 14, 2012, at http://economix.blogs.nytimes.com/2012/06/14/an-institutional-flaw-at-the-heart-of-the-federal-reserve/.

Johnson, Simon. "Predators and Professors" (2012), at http://www.project-syndicate.org/commentary/predators-and-professors.

Johnson, Simon, and James Kwak. *13 Bankers* (New York: Pantheon, 2010).

Jones, Daniel Stedman. *Masters of the Universe: Friedman, Hayek and the Birth of Neoliberal Politics* (Princeton: Princeton University Press, 2012).

Jones, Owen. *Chavs: The Demonization of the Working Class* (London: Verso, 2011).

Jones, Rachel. "Bookforum Talks with David Graeber" (2012), at www.bookforum.com/interview/9154.

Jovanovic, Franck. "Finance in Modern Economic Thought," in Alex Preda and Karin Knorr-Cetina, eds., *Handbook of the Sociology of Finance*.

Judt, Tony. *Ill Fares the Land* (London: Penguin, 2010).

Jung, Alexander. "The EU's Emissions Trading System Isn't Working," *Der Spiegel*, February 15, 2012.

Kagel, John, and Dan Levin. "Implementing Efficient Multi-Object Auction Institutions: An Experimental Study of the Performance of Boundedly Rational Agents," *Games and Economic Behavior* 66 (2009): 221–37.

Kaiser, David. *How the Hippies Saved Physics* (New York: Norton, 2011).

Kaletsky, Anatole. *Capitalism 4.0* (New York: Public Affairs Press, 2010).

Kaptur, Devesh. "Academics Have More to Declare than Their Genius," *Financial Times*, June 24, 2009.

Kates, Steven. *The Global Financial Crisis: What Have We Learnt?* (Cheltenham, U.K.: Elgar, 2011).

Kay, John. "Economics: Rituals of Rigor," *Financial Times*, August 25, 2011.

Kay, John. "The Map Is Not the Territory," October 4, 2011, at www.johnkay.com/2011/10/04/the-map-is-not-the-territory-an-essay-on-the-state-of-economics.

Kay, John. "Why Economists Stubbornly Stick to their Guns," *Financial Times*, April 15, 2011.

Keen, Steve. "Like a Dog Walking on Its Hind Legs: Krugman's Minsky Model," March 4, 2011, at www.debunkingeconomics.com.

Keynes, John Maynard. *The General Theory of Employment, Interest and Money* (New York: Harcourt Brace, 1964 [1936]).

Khademian, Anne. "The Pracademic and the Fed," *Public Administration Review* 70 (2010): 142–50.

Khurana, Rakesh. "Why Are There Business Schools in Universities?" (2011), at http://publicsphere.ssrc.org/khurana-why-are-there-business-schools-in-universities/.

King, J. E. "Microfoundations for Macroeconomics? The Pre-history of a Dogma, 1936–75" (2010), at www.hetsa.org.au/aigaion2/index.php/attachments/single/78.

Kingfisher, Catherine, and Jeff Maskovsky. "Introduction: The Limits of Neoliberalism," *Critique of Anthropology* 28 (2008): 115–26.

Kinsey, Michael. "Greenspan Shrugged," *New York Times*, October 14, 2007.

Kirilenko, Andrei, Albert Kyle, Mehrad Samadi, and Tugkan Tuzun. "The Flash Crash: The Impact of High Frequency Trading on an Electronic Market" (2011), at http://papers.ssrn.com/sol3/papers.cfm?abstract_id=1686004.

Kirman, Alan. "The Economic Entomologist," *Erasmus Journal for Philosophy and Economics* 4 (2) (2011): 42–66.

Kirman, Alan. "Economic Theory and the Crisis" (2009), at www.voxeu.org/index.php?q=node/4208.

Kirman, Alan. "Whom or What Does the Representative Agent Represent?" *Journal of Economic Perspectives* 6 (1992): 117–36.

Kirschner, Suzanne. "From Flexible Bodies to Fluid Minds: An Interview with Emily Martin," *Ethnos* 27 (1999): 247–82.

Klamer, Arjo, and David Colander. *The Making of an Economist* (Boulder: Westview, 1990).

Klein, Ezra. "What 'Inside Job' Got Wrong," *Washington Post*, June 22, 2011.

Klein, Naomi. "Capitalism vs. the Climate," *The Nation*, November 9, 2011.

Klein, Naomi. *The Shock Doctrine* (New York: Henry Holt, 2007).

Klemperer, Paul. "The Product-Mix Auction: A New Auction Design for Differentiated Goods," *Journal of the European Economic Association* 8 (2–3) (2010): 526–36.

Kling, Arnold. "Economics: A Million Mutinies Now," *The American* (AEI), February 2012.

Knight, Meribah. "Gary Lures Hollywood with a Bounty of Decay," *New York Times*, August 21, 2011.

Knowledge@Wharton. "Why Economists Failed to Predict the Financial Crisis" (2009), at http://knowledge.wharton.upenn.edu/article.cfm?artcleid=2234.

Kocherlakota, Narayana. *Modern Macroeconomic Models as Tools for Economic Policy* (Minneapolis: Federal Reserve Bank, 2010).

Konczal, Michael, ed. *Will It Work? How Will We Know? The Future of Financial Reform* (New York: Roosevelt Institute, 2010).

Konings, Martijn. *The Great Credit Crash* (London: Verso, 2010).

Konings, Martijn. "Rethinking Neoliberalism and the Subprime Crisis," *Competition and Change* 13 (2009): 108–27.

Konings, Martijn. "Social Scientists and Economic Life at the Start of the 21st Century," *Australian Journal of Political Science* 45 (4) (2010): 713–18.

Konings, Martijn. "The Ups and Downs of a Liberal Consciousness, or, Why Paul Krugman Should Learn to Tarry with the Negative," *Ephemera* 9 (4) (2009): 350–56.

Konzelmann, Sue, Frank Wilkinson, Marc Fovargue, and Duncan Sankey.

"Governance, Regulation and Financial Market Instability," *Cambridge Journal of Economics* 34 (2010): 929–54.

Kourany, Janet. *Philosophy of Science After Feminism* (New York: Oxford University Press, 2010).

Kragh, Helge. *Higher Speculations* (Oxford: Oxford University Press, 2011).

Krawiec, Kimberly. "Show Me the Money: Making Markets in Forbidden Exchange," *Law and Contemporary Problems* 72 (2009): i–xiv.

Krishnamurthy, Arvind. "How Debt Markets Malfunctioned in the Crisis," *Journal of Economic Perspectives* 24 (2010): 3–28.

Kroszner, Randall, and Raghuram Rajan. "Is the Glass Steagall Act Justified? A Study of US Experience with Universal Banking," *American Economic Review* 84 (1994): 810–32.

Krugman, Paul. "Economics in the Crisis," lecture delivered to University of Lisbon, February 27, 2012.

Krugman, Paul. *End This Depression Now!* (New York: Norton, 2012).

Krugman, Paul. "Fannie, Freddie and You," *New York Times*, July 14, 2008.

Krugman, Paul. "How Did Economics Get It So Wrong?" *New York Times Magazine*, September 6, 2009.

Krugman, Paul. "Memories of the Carter Administration," September 19, 2009, at krugman.blogs.nytimes.com/.../memories-of-the-carter-administration.

Krugman, Paul. "The Profession and the Crisis," *Eastern Economic Journal* 37 (2011): 307–12.

Krugman, Paul. "The Return of Depression Economics," LSE lectures, June 2009, at www.youtube.com/watch?v=5N35mq4_gIw.

Krugman, Paul. *The Return of Depression Economics and the Crisis of 2008* (New York: Norton, 2009).

Kukathas, Chandran. *Hayek and Modern Liberalism* (Oxford: Oxford University Press, 1989).

Kunkel, Benjamin. "Forgive Us Our Debts," *London Review of Books*, May 10, 2012.

Kunkel, Benjamin. "On Your Marx," *n+1*, Issue 8, 2010.

Kusch, Martin. *Knowledge by Agreement: The Programme of Communitarian Epistemology* (Oxford: Oxford University Press, 2002).

Kuttner, Robert. "History's Missed Moment," *American Prospect*, September 28, 2011.

Kydland, Finn., and Edward. C. Prescott. "Rules Rather than Discretion: The Inconsistency of Optimal Plans," *Journal of Political Economy*: 473–492, 1977.

Lahart, Justin. "The Glenn Beck Effect: Hayek Has a Hit," *Wall Street Journal*, June 17, 2010.

Lahart, Justin. "Stung by *Inside Job*, Economists Pen a Code of Ethics," *Wall Street Journal*, October 12, 2011.

Laidler, David. "Lucas, Keynes and the Crisis," *Journal of the History of Economic Thought* 32 (2010): 39–62.

Lakatos, Imre. *Criticism and the Growth of Knowledge* (Cambridge, U.K.: Cambridge University Press, 1970).

Lanchester, John. "Once Greece Goes . . . ," *London Review of Books* 33 (July 14, 2011): 3–7.

Lane, Jan-Erik. *New Public Management* (London: Routledge, 2000).

Langley, Paul. *The Everyday Life of Global Finance: Saving and Borrowing in Anglo-America* (Oxford: Oxford University Press, 2008).

Lasn, Kalle. *Meme Wars: The Creative Destruction of Neoclassical Economics.* London: Penguin, 2012.

Latsis, Spiro, ed. *Method and Appraisal in Economics* (Cambridge, U.K.: Cambridge University Press, 1976).

Laux, Christian, and Christian Leuz. 2010. "Did Fair-Value Accounting Contribute to the Financial Crisis?" *Journal of Economic Perspectives* 24 (2010): 93–118.

Lee, Frederic. *A History of Heterodox Economics* (London: Routledge, 2009).

Lee, Ruben. *Running the World's Markets: The Governance of Financial Infrastructure* (Princeton: Princeton University Press, 2011).

Lehman, Chris. "Let Them Eat Dogma," *The Baffler*, January 2010.

Lehrer, Jonah. "Can We Prevent the Next Bubble?" *Wired*, June, 2011.

Lemke, Thomas. "The Birth of Biopolitics: Michel Foucault's Lecture at the College de France on Neoliberal Governmentality," *Economy and Society* 30 (2001): 190–207.

Leonard, Andrew. "Alan Greenspan's Housing Bubble Coffee Break," Salon.com, January 14, 2011.

Lerner, Josh. "The Litigation of Financial Innovations," Harvard Business School Working Paper, 09-027, 2008.

Levine, Ross. "An Autopsy of the US Financial System: Accident, Suicide, or Negligent Homicide?" *Journal of Financial Economic Policy* 2 (2010): 196–213.

Levitin, Adam, and Susan M. Wachter. "The Commercial Real Estate Bubble," Georgetown University Law Center Working Paper, 2012. At www.fdnpro.com/pleadings/documents/2012-Levitin-Wachter-Commercia-RE-Bubble-WorkingPaper.pdf.

Levitin, Adam, and Susan M. Wachter. "Explaining the Housing Bubble," *Georgetown Law Journal* 100 (2012) 1177–258.

Levitt, Steven, and Stephen Dubner. *SuperFreakonomics* (New York: Morrow, 2009).

Lewis, Michael. *The Big Short* (New York: Norton, 2010).

Lieber, Ron. "Last Plea on Student Loans: Proving a Hopeless Future," *New York Times*, September 1, 2012.

Linden, David. "Addictive Personality? You Might Be a Leader," *New York Times*, July 23, 2011.

Linker, Damon. *The Theocons* (New York: Doubleday, 2006).

Lipman, Barton. "Why Is Language Vague?" Boston University working paper, 2009.

Litan, Robert. *The Derivatives Dealer's Club and Derivates Markets Reform: A Guide for Citizens* (Washington: Brookings, 2010).

Litan, Robert. "In Defense of Much, but Not All, Financial Innovation" (2010), at www.brookings.edu/papers/2010/0217_financial_innovation_litan.aspx.

Litan, Robert, and Peter Wallison. *Competitive Equity: A Better Way to Organize Mutual Funds* (Washington: American Enterprise Institute, 2007).

Lo, Andrew. "Reading About the Financial Crisis," *Journal of Economic Literature*, 50 (2012): 151-178.

Lo, Andrew. "Reconciling Efficient Markets with Behavioral Finance: The Adaptive Markets Hypothesis," *Journal of Investment Consulting* 7 (2005): 21–44.

Lo, Andrew, and Craig MacKinlay. *A Non-Random Walk Down Wall Street* (Princeton: Princeton University Press, 1999).

Loewenstein, George, and Peter Ubel. "Economics Behaving Badly," *New York Times*, July 14, 2010.

Lofgren, Mike. "Revolt of the Rich," *American Conservative*, September 2012.

Lohmann, Larry. "Carbon Trading: A Critical Dialogue," *Development Dialogue* no. 48, September 2006.

Lohmann, Larry. "Carbon Trading, Climate Justice, and the Production of Ignorance," *Development* 51 (2008): 359–65.

Lohmann, Larry. "The Endless Algebra of Climate Markets," *Capitalism Nature Socialism* 22 (2011): 93–116.

Lohmann, Larry. "Neoliberalism and the Calculable World," in Birch and Mykhnenko, *The Rise and Fall of Neoliberalism*.

Lohmann, Larry. "Toward a Different Debate in Environmental Accounting: The Cases of Carbon and Cost-Benefit," *Accounting, Organization and Society* 34 (2009): 499–534.

Longino, Helen. *The Fate of Knowledge* (Princeton: Princeton University Press, 2002).

Lord, Charles, Lee Ross, and Mark Lepper. "Biased Assimilation and Attitude Polarization: The Effects of Prior Theories on Subsequently Considered Evidence," *Journal of Personality and Social Psychology* 37 (1979): 2098–109.

Lowenstein, Roger. "The Villain," *The Atlantic*, April 2012.

Lucas, Robert. "Econometric Policy Evaluation: A Critique," in *Carnegie-Rochester Conference Series on Public Policy* 1 (1976): 19–46.

Lucas, Robert. "In Defense of the Dismal Science," *The Economist*, August 6, 2009.

Lucas, Robert. "My Keynesian Education," in Michel De Vroey and Kevin Hoover, eds., *The IS-LM Model: Its Rise, Fall and Strange Persistence* (Durham, N.C.: Duke University Press, 2004).

Lucas, Robert, and Nancy Stokey. "Liquidity Crises" *Minneapolis Economic Policy Papers* 2011. At www.minneapolisfed.org/publications_papers/ pub_display.cfm?id=4670.

Maasen, Sabine, and Barbara Sutter, eds. *On Willing Selves: Neoliberal Politics vis-à-vis the Neuroscientific Challenge* (Basingstoke, U.K.: Palgrave Macmillan, 2007).

MacFarquahar, Larissa. "The Deflationist: How Paul Krugman Found Politics," *The New Yorker*, March 1, 2010.

Mackay, Charles. *Memoirs of Extraordinary Popular Delusions and the Madness of Crowds* (London: Robson, Levey, 1852).

MacKenzie, Donald. "The Credit Crisis as a Problem in the Sociology of Knowledge," *American Journal of Sociology* 116 (2011): 1778–841.

MacKenzie, Donald. *An Engine, Not a Camera: How Financial Models Shape Markets* (Cambridge, Mass.: MIT Press, 2006).

MacKenzie, Michael, and Telis Demos. "Credit Default Swap Trading Drops," *Financial Times*, May 1, 2012.

MacKenzie, Donald, Fabian Muniesa, and Lucia Siu., eds. *Do Economists Make Markets?* (Princeton: Princeton University Press, 2008).

Madrick, Jeff, and Frank Partnoy. "Did Fannie Cause the Disaster?" *New York Review of Books*, October 27, 2011.

Maher, Sid. "Europe's $287 Billion Carbon Waste," *The Australian*, November 23, 2011.

Maki, Uskali, ed. *The Methodology of Positive Economics* (New York: Cambridge University Press, 2009).

Mallaby, Sebastian. *More Money Than God* (New York: Penguin, 2010).

Marazzi, Christian. *The Violence of Financial Capitalism* (Los Angeles: Semiotext(e), 2010).

Martin, Emily. "Designing Flexibility: Science and Work in an Age of Flexible Accumulation," *Science as Culture* 6 (1997): 327–62.

Martin, Emily. *Flexible Bodies* (Boston: Beacon Press, 1994).

Martin, Randy. *The Financialization of Everyday Life* (Philadelphia: Temple University Press, 2002).

Mas-Collel, Andrew, Michael Whinston, and Jerry Green. *Microeconomic Theory* (New York: Oxford University Press, 1995).

Masini, Fabio. 2012. "Designing the Institutions of International Liberalism: The Interwar Period," *Constitutional Political Economy* 23 (2012): 45–65.

Maskin, Eric. "Economic Theory and the Financial Crisis" (2009), at http://five-books.com/interviews/eric-maskin.

Mason, Paul. *Meltdown: The End of the Age of Greed* (London: Verso, 2009).

Mata, Tiago. "Reckonings," *Fortnight Journal*, February 12, 2012.

Mathiowetz, Dean. *Appeals to Interest: Language, Contestation and the Shaping of Political Agency* (State College: Pennsylvania State University Press, 2011).

Mayer, Jane. "Covert Operations: The Billionaire Brothers Who Are Waging a War Against Obama," *The New Yorker*, August 30, 2010.

McCarthy, James. "The Financial Crisis and Environmental Governance 'after' Neoliberalism," *Tijdschrift voor Economische en Sociale Geografie* 103 (2012): 180–95.

McGuigan, Jim. "Neoliberalism, Culture and Policy," *International Journal of Cultural Policy* 11 (2005): 229–41.

McKinnon, Susan. *Neo-liberal Genetics* (Chicago: Prickly Paradigm Press, 2005).

McMillan, John. *Reinventing the Bazaar*. New York: W.W. Norton, 2002.

Medvetz, Thomas. *Think Tanks in America*. (Chicago: University of Chicago Press, 2012).

Meeusen, Wim. "Whither the Microeconomic Foundations of Macroeconomic Theory?" (2010), at http://webcache.googleusercontent.com/search?q=cache:FqRtjNQ9ZMcJ:www.wise.xmu.edu.cn/Master/News/NewsPic/20106309239228.pdf+Microeconomic+Foundations+%22Wim+Meeusen%22&cd=2&hl=en&ct=clnk&gl=us.

Megay, Edward. "Anti-Pluralist Liberalism: The German Neoliberals," *Political Science Quarterly* 85 (1970): 422–42.

Mehrling, Perry. *Fischer Black and the Revolutionary Idea of Finance* (New York: Wiley, 2005).

Mehrling, Perry. *The New Lombard Street* (Princeton: Princeton University Press, 2011).

Mehrling, Perry. "A Tale of Two Cities," *History of Political Economy* 42 (2010): 201–20.

Meusburger, Peter, Michael Welker, and Edgar Wunder, eds. *Clashes of Knowledge* (Berlin: Springer, 2008).

Michaels, David. *Doubt Is Our Product* (Oxford: Oxford University Press, 2008).

Miller, Merton. "Financial Innovation: The Last 20 Years and the Next," *Journal of Financial and Quantitative Analysis* 21 (1986): 459–71.

Mirowski, Philip. "The Cowles Anti-Keynesians," in Pedro Duarte and Gilberto Lima, eds., *Microfoundations Reconsidered: The Relationship of Micro and Macroeconomics in Historical Perspective* (Cheltenham, U.K.: Elgar, 2012).

Mirowski, Philip. "Defining Neoliberalism," in Mirowski and Plehwe, *The Road from Mont Pèlerin.*

Mirowski, Philip. "Does the Victor Enjoy the Spoils? Paul Samuelson as Historian of Economic Thought," *Journal of the History of Economic Thought* 35 (2013): 1–17.

Mirowski, Philip. *The Effortless Economy of Science?* (Durham, N.C.: Duke University Press, 2004).

Mirowski, Philip. "The Great Mortification," *Hedgehog Review* 12 (2) (Summer 2010): 28–41.

Mirowski, Philip. "Inherent Vice: Minsky, Markomata, and the Tendency of Markets to Undermine Themselves," *Journal of Institutional Economics* 6 (2010): 415–43.

Mirowski, Philip. *Machine Dreams: Economics Becomes a Cyborg Science* (New York: Cambridge University Press, 2002).

Mirowski, Philip. "Markets Come to Bits," *Journal of Economic Behavior and Organization* 63 (2007): 209–42.

Mirowski, Philip. *More Heat Than Light: Economics as Social Physics* (New York: Cambridge University Press, 1989).

Mirowski, Philip. "Naturalizing the Market on the Road to Revisionism: Caldwell on *Hayek's Challenge*," *Journal of Institutional Economics* 3 (2007): 351–72.

Mirowski, Philip. *ScienceMart: Privatizing American Science* (Cambridge, Mass.: Harvard University Press, 2011).

Mirowski, Philip. "Why There Is (as Yet) No Such Thing as an Economics of Knowledge," in Harold Kincaid and Don Ross, eds., *Oxford Handbook of Philosophy of Economics* (Oxford: Oxford University Press, 2009), pp. 99–156.

Mirowski, Philip, and Dieter Plehwe, eds. *The Road from Mont Pèlerin: The Making of the Neoliberal Thought Collective* (Cambridge, Mass.: Harvard University Press, 2009).

Mollenkamp, Carrick, Serena Ng, Liam Pleven, and Randall Smith. "Behind AIG's Fall, Risk Models Failed to Pass Real World Test," *Wall Street Journal*, October 31, 2008.

Mooney, Chris. *The Republican War on Science* (New York: Basic, 2005).

Moore, Don, Daylian Cain, George Loewenstein, and Max Bazerman, eds. *Conflicts of Interest* (New York: Cambridge University Press, 2005).

Moore, John. "Leverage Stacks and the Financial System," Ross Prize Lecture to the Foundation for the Advancement of Research in Financial Economics, Boston, October 2011, at http://bit.ly/LeverageStacksOctober2011.

Moreton, Bethany. *To Serve God and Wal-Mart* (Cambridge, Mass.: Harvard University Press, 2009).

Morgenson, Gretchen, and Josh Rosner. *Reckless Endangerment* (New York: Times Books, 2011).

Morley, James. "The Emperor Has No Clothes," *Macroeconomic Advisors Macro Focus* 5, no. 2 (June 24, 2010).

Motavalli, Jim. "Cultural Jammin'" *E—The Environmental Magazine* 7 (1996) (3): 41.

Mroz, Jacqueline. "One Sperm Donor, 150 Offspring," *New York Times*, September 5, 2011.

Muolo, Paul, and Matthew Padilla. *Chain of Blame* (New York: Wiley, 2008).

Murray, Thomas, and Josephine Johnston, eds. *Trust and Integrity in Biomedical Research: The Case of Financial Conflicts of Interest* (Baltimore: Johns Hopkins University Press, 2010).

Nace, Ted. *Gangs of America* (San Francisco: Berrett-Koehler, 2003).

Nadesan, Majia. *Governmentality, Biopower and Everyday Life* (London: Routledge, 2008).

Nash, George.. *The Conservative Intellectual Movement in America* (Washington, D.C.: ISI Books, 2006 [176]).

Nelson, Maggie. *The Art of Cruelty: A Reckoning* (New York: Norton, 2011).

Nicholls, A. J. *Freedom with Responsibility* (Oxford: Oxford University Press, 1994).

Nienhaus, Lisa. "What Went Wrong? Economists in Identity Crisis," *Frankfurter Allgemeine Zeitung*, April 5, 2009.

Nietzsche, Friedrich. *Genealogy of Morals* (New York: Vintage, 1969).

Nik-Khah, Edward. "Chicago Neoliberalism and the Genesis of the Milton Friedman Institute," in Van Horn. et al, *Building Chicago Economics*.

Nik-Khah, Edward. "George Stigler, the Graduate School of Business, and the Pillars of the Chicago School," in Van Horn, et al. *Building Chicago Economics*.

Nik-Khah, Edward. "A Tale of Two Auctions," *Journal of Institutional Economics* 4 (2008): 73-97.

Nocera, Joe. "The Big Lie," *New York Times*, December 23, 2011.

Noeth, Bryan, and Rajdeep Sengupta. "Is Shadow Banking Really Banking?" *Minnesota Federal Reserve Regional Economist*, October 2011.

Norris, Floyd. "The Crisis Is Over, but Where's the Fix?" *New York Times*, March 11, 2011.

Nuti, Dominico. "Akerlof & Shiller, Animal Spirits" (2009), http://dipe codir.it/upload/sn/5.pdf

O'Brien, Ellen. "How 'G' Got into the GNP," in K. I. Vaughn, ed., *Perspectives on the History of Economic Thought*, vol. X (New York: Edward Elgar Press, 1994).

Oliver, Henry Jr. "German Neoliberalism," *Quarterly Journal of Economics* 74 (1960): 117–49.

O'Neill, Cathy. "Black Scholes and the Normal Distribution," March 14, 2013, at: www.nakedcapitalism.com/2013/03/cathy-oneil-black-scholes-and -the-normal-distribution.html.

O'Neill, John. *The Market: Ethics, Knowledge and Politics* (London: Routledge, 1998).

Ong, Aihwa. *Neoliberalism as Exception* (Durham, N.C.: Duke University Press, 2006).

Oppenheimer, Mark. "Christian Economics Meets the Antiunion Movement," *New York Times*, April 29, 2011.

Oreskes, Naomi, and Erik Conway. *Merchants of Doubt* (New York: Bloomsbury, 2010).

Palley, Thomas. *From Financial Crisis to Stagnation* (New York: Cambridge University Press, 2012).

Paras, Eric. *Foucault 2.0: Beyond Power and Knowledge* (Boston: Other Press, 2006).

Partnoy, Frank. "Sunlight Shows Cracks in Crisis Rescue Story," *Financial Times*, December 3, 2010.

Patterson, Scott. *Dark Pools: High Frequency Trading and the Threat to the Global Financial System* (New York: Crown, 2012).

Paulson, Henry. *On the Brink* (New York: Business Plus, 2010).

Paumgarten, Nick. "The Death of Kings," *The New Yorker*, May 18, 2009.

Paybarah, Azi. "Bloomberg: Plain and Simple, Congress Caused the Mortgage Crisis, Not the Banks," *Capital New York*, November 1, 2011.

Payne, Christopher. *The Consumer, Credit and Neoliberalism: Governing the Modern Economy* (London: Routledge, 2012).

Peck, Jamie. *Constructions of Neoliberal Reason* (Oxford: Oxford University Press, 2010).

Peck, Jamie. "Zombie Neoliberalism and the Ambidextrous State," *Theoretical Criminology* 14 (2010): 104–10.

Peck, Jamie, Nik Theodore, and Neil Brenner. "Postneoliberalism and its Malcontents," *Antipode* 41 (2009): 94–116.

Perino, Michael. *The Hellhound of Wall Street* (New York: Penguin, 2010).

Perlin, Ross. *Intern Nation* (New York: Verso, 2011).

Petsoulas, Christina. *Hayek's Liberalism and Its Origins* (London: Routledge, 2001).

Phillips-Fein, Kim. "Conservatism: The State of the Field," *Journal of American History* 98 (3) (2011): 723–43.

Phillips-Fein, Kim. *Invisible Hands: The Making of the Conservative Movement from the New Deal to Reagan* (New York: Norton, 2009).

Pickering, Andrew. *The Cybernetic Brain* (Chicago: University of Chicago Press, 2010).

Pinch, Trevor, and Filip Kesler. "How Aunt Ammy Gets Her Free Lunch: A Study of the Top Thousand Customer Reviewers at Amazon.com" (2011), http://lammgl.files.wordpress.com/2011/03/how-aunt-ammy-gets-her-free-lunch-final.pdf.

Pinto, Edward. "ACORN and the Housing Bubble," *Wall Street Journal*, November. 12, 2009.

Plant, Raymond. *The Neoliberal State* (Oxford: Oxford University Press, 2010).

Plehwe, Dieter. "Neoliberal Think Tanks and the Crisis," paper presented to SGIR Pan-European International Relations Conference, Stockholm, 2010.

Plehwe, Dieter, Bernhard Walpen, and G. Neunhoffer, eds. *Neoliberal Hegemony: A Global Critique* (London: Routledge, 2006).

Plickert, Philip. "Cheating in the Economy," *Frankfurter Allgemeine Zeitung*, May 8, 2012.

Polanyi, Karl. *The Great Transformation* (Boston: Beacon Press, 1944).

Poon, Martha. "From New Deal Risk Institutions to Capital Markets: Consumer Risk Scores," *Accounting, Organization and Society* 34 (2009): 654–74.

Popper, Karl. *After the Open Society*, Jeremy Shearmur and Piers Turner, eds. (London: Routledge, 2008).

Popper, Karl. *The Open Society and Its Enemies*, 5th ed. (London: Routledge & Kegan Paul, 1966).

Posner, Richard. *A Failure of Capitalism* (Cambridge, Mass.: Harvard University Press, 2009).

Posner, Richard. *Public Intellectuals: A Study of Decline* (Cambridge, Mass.: Harvard University Press, 2003).

Posner, Richard. "Shorting Reason," *New Republic*, April 15, 2009.

Power, Michael. *The Audit Society* (Oxford: Oxford University Press, 1997).

Prasad, Monica. *The Politics of Free Markets* (Chicago: University of Chicago Press, 2006).

Prasch, Robert. "After the Crash of 2008: Financial Reform in an Age of Plutocracy," in Kates, *The Global Financial Crisis*.

Preda, Alex, and Karin Knorr-Cetina. *Handbook of the Sociology of Finance* (Oxford: Oxford University Press, 2012).

Pressler, Jaime. "122 Minutes with Jamie Dimon," *New York*, August 2012.

Preston, Julia. "Foreign Students in Work Visa Program Stage Walkout at Plant," *New York Times*, August 17, 2011.

Preston, Julia. "Pleas Unheeded as Students' US Jobs Soured," *New York Times*, October 16, 2011.

Proctor, Robert. *Golden Holocaust* (Berkeley: University of California Press, 2012).

Proctor, Robert. *Value Free Science?* (Cambridge, Mass.: Harvard University Press, 1991).

Proctor, Robert, and Londa Scheibinger, eds. *Agnotology: The Making and Unmaking of Ignorance* (Stanford: Stanford University Press, 2008).

Ptak, Ralf. "Neoliberalism in Germany," in Mirowski and Plehwe, *The Road from Mont Pèlerin*, pp. 98–138.

Quiggin, John. "Six Refuted Doctrines," *Economic Papers* 28 (2009): 239–48.

Quiggin, John. *Zombie Economics* (Princeton: Princeton University Press, 2010).

Quinn, Sarah. "The Transformation of Morals in Markets: Death Benefits and the Exchange of Life Insurance Policies," *American Journal of Sociology* 114 (2008): 738–80.

Rabin, Matthew. "A Perspective on Psychology and Economics," *European Economic Review* 46 (2002): 657–85.

Radin, Margaret Jane. *Contested Commodities: The Trouble with Trade in Sex, Children, Body Parts, and Other Things* (Cambridge, Mass.: Harvard University Press, 1996).

Rajan, Raghuram. "Bankers Have Been Sold Short by Market Distortions," *Financial Times*, June 2, 2010.

Rajan, Raghuram. *Fault Lines* (Princeton: Princeton University Press, 2010).

Reay, Michael. "The Flexible Unity of Economics," *American Journal of Sociology* 118 (2012): 45–87.

Reinhardt, Uwe. "An Economist's Mea Culpa," NY Times Economix blog, January 9, 2009, at http://economix.blogs.nytimes.com/2009/01/09.

Rich, Andrew. *Think Tanks, Public Policy, and the Politics of Expertise* (New York: Cambridge University Press, 2004).

Richey, Lisa, and Stefano Ponte. *Brand Aid: Shopping Well to Save the World* (Minneapolis: University of Minnesota Press, 2011).

Richland, Justin. "On Neoliberalism and Other Social Diseases," *American Anthropologist* III (2009): 170–76.

Ridley, Matt. *The Agile Gene* (New York: HarperCollins, 2003).

Ridley, Matt. *The Rational Optimist: How Prosperity Evolves* (New York: HarperCollins, 2011).

Rivlin, Gary. "America's Nastiest Lender," Daily Beast, June 25, 2011, at www.thedailybeast.com/articles/2011/06/25/america-s-worst-subprime-lender-jared-davis-vs-allan-jones.html.

Rivlin, Gary. *Broke, USA* (New York: HarperCollins, 2010).

Rizvi, Abu. "The Sonnenschein-Mantel-Debreu Results After 30 Years," in P. Mirowski and W. Hands, eds., *Agreement on Demand: Consumer Theory in the 20th Century* (Durham, N.C.: Duke University Press, 2006).

Roberts, David. *Victorian Origins of the British Welfare State* (New Haven: Yale University Press, 1960).

Robin, Corey. *The Reactionary Mind* (New York: Oxford University Press, 2011).

Robison, Richard. *The Neoliberal Revolution: Forging the Market State* (London: Palgrave, 2006).

Rogoff, Kenneth, and Carmen Reinhart. *This Time Is Different* (Princeton: Princeton University Press, 2009).

Roncaglia, Alessandro. *Why Economists Got It Wrong: The Crisis and Its Cultural Roots* (London: Anthem, 2010).

Rose, Nikolas. *Inventing Our Selves: Psychology, Power and Personhood* (Cambridge, U.K.: Cambridge University Press, 1996).

Rose, Nikolas. "The Neurochemical Self and Its Anomalies," in R. Ericson, ed., *Risk and Morality* (Toronto: University of Toronto Press, 2003), pp. 407–37.

Rose, Nikolas. *The Politics of Life Itself* (Princeton: Princeton University Press, 2006).

Ross, Andrew. "A Capitalist's Dream," *London Review of Books* 33 (10) (2011): 33–35.

Rosser, J. B., Richard Holt, and David Colander. *European Economics at a Crossroads* (Cheltenham, U.K.: Elgar, 2010).

Roubini, Nouriel, and Stephen Mihm. *Crisis Economics* (New York: Penguin, 2010).

Rudd, Kevin. "The Global Financial Crisis," *The Monthly*, February 25, 2009.

Saad-Filho, Alfredo, and Deborah Johnston, eds. *Neoliberalism: A Critical Reader* (London: Pluto Press, 2005).

Saint-Paul, Gilles. "A Modest Intellectual Discipline" (2009), at www. voxeu.org.

Samuels, Warren. "The Economy as a System of Power: Legal Economics of Robert Lee Hale," *University of Miami Law Review* 27 (1973): 261–371.

Samuels, Warren. *Essays in the Economic Role of Government* (New York: New York University Press, 1992).

Samuelson, Paul. "Proof That Properly Anticipated Prices Fluctuate Randomly," *Industrial Management Review* 6 (1965): 41–49.

Sandel, Michael. "What Isn't for Sale?" *The Atlantic*, April 2012.

Sanders, Bernard. "Jamie Dimon Is Not Alone," Office of the U.S. Senator Bernard Sanders, 2012.

Sargent, Thomas. "Modern Macroeconomics Under Attack," Minneapolis Federal Reserve, 2010, at www.minneapolisfed.org/pubs/region/10-09/sargent.pdf.

Satz, Deborah. *Why Some Things Should Not Be for Sale* (Oxford: Oxford University Press, 2010).

Scahill, Jeremy. *Blackwater: The Rise of the World's Most Powerful Mercenary Army* (New York: Nation Books, 2007).

Scheiding, Tom, and Tiago Mata. "National Science Foundation Patronage of Social Science, 1970s/80s," *Minerva* 50 (2012): 423-449.

Scheuerman, William. *Carl Schmitt: The End of Law.* (Lanham: Rowman & Littlefield, 1999).

Schliesser, Eric. "Inventing Paradigms, Monopoly, Methodology, and Mythology at Chicago," *Studies in the History and Philosophy of Science* 43 (2012): 160–71.

Schmitt, Rick. "Prophet and Loss," *Stanford Magazine*, March 2009.

Schneider, Louis. "The Role of the Category of Ignorance in Sociological Theory," *American Sociological Review* 27 (1962): 492–508.

Schulman, Bruce, and Julian Zelizer, eds. *Rightward Bound* (Cambridge, Mass.: Harvard University Press, 2008).

Sent, Esther-Mirjam. *The Evolving Rationality of Rational Expectations* (New York: Cambridge University Press, 1998).

Shaxson, Nicholas. *Treasure Islands: Uncovering the Damage of Offshore Banking* (New York: Palgrave Macmillan, 2011).

Shearmur, Jeremy. *Hayek and After* (London: Routledge, 1996).

Sheper-Hughes, Nancy, and Loic Wacquant, eds. *Commodifying Bodies* (London: Sage, 2002).

Sherden, William. *The Fortune Sellers* (New York: Wiley, 1998).

Sherman, Gabriel. "Revolver," *New York*, April 2011, at http://nymag.com/news/business/wallstreet/peter-orszag-2011-4/index6.html.

Shiller, Robert. *Finance and the Good Society* (Princeton: Princeton University Press, 2012).

Shiller, Robert. "The Future of Capitalism: A Failure to Control Animal Spirits," *Financial Times Magazine*, May 12, 2009, 14–16.

Shiller, Robert. "In Defense of Financial Innovation," *Financial Times*, September 27, 2009.

Shiller, Robert. Interview on *Finance and the Good Society* (2012), www.voxeu.org/vox-talks/finance-and-good-society.

Shiller, Robert. *Irrational Exuberance*, rev. ed. (New York: Broadway, 2006).

Shiller, Robert. "Radical Financial Innovation," Cowles Foundation discussion paper #1461, 2004.

Shiller, Robert. "The Use of Volatility Measures in Assessing Market Efficiency," *Journal of Finance* 36 (1981): 291–304.

Shteyngart, Gary. *Super Sad True Love Story* (New York: Random House, 2010).

Singer, P. W. *Corporate Warriors* (Ithaca, N.Y.: Cornell University Press, 2003).

Sismondo, Sergio. "Corporate Disguises in Medical Science: Dodging the Interest Repertoire," *Bulletin of Science, Technology and Society*, 2011.

Sismondo, Sergio. "Pharmaceutical Company Funding and Its Consequences: A Qualitative Systematic Review," *Contemporary Clinical Trials* 29 (2008): 109–13.

Sissoko, Carolyn. "The Legal Foundations of the Financial Collapse," *Journal of Financial Economic Policy* 2 (1) (2010): 5–34.

Skidelsky, Robert. *John Maynard Keynes: Economist as Saviour* (London: Penguin, 1994).

Skidelsky, Robert. *John Maynard Keynes: Hope Betrayed* (London: Penguin, 1983).

Skomarovsky, Matthew. "Evidence of an American Plutocracy: The Larry Summers Story" (January 10, 2011), at http://blog.littlesis.org/2011/01/10.

Skousen, Mark. *Chicago and Vienna* (Washington, D.C.: Capital Press, 2005).

Slaughter, Sheila, Maryann Feldman, and Scott Thomas. "U.S. Research Universities' Institutional Conflict of Interest Policies," *Journal of Empirical research on Human Research Ethics* 4 (2009): 3–20.

Smith, Noah. "What I Learned in Grad School," April 29, 2011, at http://noahpinionblog.blogspot.com/2011/04.

Smith, Steven, ed. *Cambridge Companion to Leo Strauss* (Cambridge, U.K.: Cambridge University Press, 2009).

Smith, Vardaman. "Friedman, Liberalism, and the Meaning of Negative Freedom," *Economics and Philosophy* 14 (1998): 75–94.

Smith, Yves. *Econned* (London: Palgrave, 2010).

Smith, Yves. "New York Fed Brownshirt Jason Barker Urges Police to Crack Skulls of #OWS" (November 2011), at www.nakedcapitalism .com/2011/11/22811.html.

Snowdon, Brian, and Howard Vane. *Modern Macroeconomics: Its Origins, Development and Current State* (Cheltenham, U.K.: Elgar, 2005).

Soederberg, Susan, George Menz, and Philip Cerny, eds. *Internalizing Globalization: The Rise of Neoliberalism* (London: Palgrave, 2005).

Solomon, Miriam. *Social Empiricism* (Cambridge, Mass.: MIT Press, 2001).

Solow, Robert. "Hedging America," *New Republic*, January 12, 2010.

Sommer, Jeff. "The Slogans Stop Here," *New York Times*, October 30, 2011.

Sorkin, Andrew. *Too Big to Fail* (New York: Viking, 2009).

Sorkin, Andrew. "Vanishing Act: 'Advisers' Seek Distance from a Report," *New York Times Dealbook*, February 14, 2011, at http://dealbook. nytimes.com/2011/02/14/vanishing-act-advisers-seek-distance-from-a-report/.

Sorkin, Andrew. "Volcker Rule Stirs Up Opposition Overseas," *New York Times Dealbook*, January 20, 2012.

Sorman, Guy. "The Free Marketers Strike Back," *City Journal* (Manhattan Institute), Summer 2010.

Soros, George. "My Philanthropy," *New York Review of Books* (June 23, 2011), pp. 12-16.

Spar, Debora. *The Baby Business* (Cambridge, Mass.: Harvard Business School Press, 2006).

Spar, Debora, and Anna Harrington. "Building a Better Baby Business," *Minnesota Journal of Law, Science and Technology* 10 (2009): 41–69.

Spaveneta, Luigi. "Economists and Economics: What Does the Crisis Tell Us?" *Real-World Economics Review* 50 (September 2009).

Specter, Michael. "The Climate Fixers," *The New Yorker*, May 14, 2012.

Springer, Simon. "Neoliberalism and Geography: Expansions, Variegations, Formations," *Geography Compass* 4/8 (2010): 1025–38.

Stigler, George. "The Intellectual and His Society," in Richard Selden, ed., *Capitalism and Freedom: Problems and Prospects* (Charlottesville: University Press of Virginia, 1975).

Stigler, George. *The Intellectual and the Marketplace* (New York: Free Press, 1963).

Stigler, George, and Gary Becker. "De Gustibus non est Disputandum," *American Economic Review* 76 (1977): 76–90.

Stiglitz, Joseph. "An Agenda for Reforming Economic Theory," ms. distributed at INET Conference, King's College, Cambridge University, April 2010.

Stiglitz, Joseph. "The Book of Jobs," *Vanity Fair*, January 2012.

Stiglitz, Joseph. "The Contributions of the Theory of Information to 20th Century Economics," *Quarterly Journal of Economics* 140 (2000): 1441–78.

Stiglitz, Joseph. "The End of Neoliberalism," *Project Syndicate* (2008), at www.project-syndicate.org/commentary/the-end-of-neo-liberalism-.

Stiglitz, Joseph. *Freefall* (New York: Norton, 2010).

Stiglitz, Joseph. "Information and the Change in Paradigm in Economics," in R. Arnott, B. Greenwald, R. Kanbur, and B. Nalebuff, eds., *Economics in an Imperfect World* (Cambridge, Mass.: MIT Press, 2003).

Stiglitz, Joseph. "Knowledge in the Modern Economy," in Romesh Vaitilingham, ed., *The Economics of the Knowledge Driven Economy* (London: Department of Trade and Industry, 1999).

Stiglitz, Joseph. "Needed: A New Economic Paradigm," *Financial Times*, August 19, 2010.

Stiglitz, Joseph. "The Non-existent Hand," *London Review of Books*, April 22, 2010.

Stiglitz, Joseph. "Reflections on Economics," in Arnold Heertje, ed., *Makers of Modern Economics*, vol. 1 (Hemel Hempstead, U.K.: Harvester Wheatsheaf, 1993).

Stiglitz, Joseph. "Rethinking Macroeconomics: What Failed, and How to Repair It," *Journal of the European Economic Association* 9 (2011): 591–645.

Stiglitz, Joseph. *Selected Works* (Oxford: Oxford University Press, 2009).

Stiglitz, Joseph, and Bruce Greenwald. "Financial Market Imperfections and Business Cycles," *Quarterly Journal of Economics* 108 (1993): 77–114.

Story, Louise. "Income Inequality and Financial Crises," *New York Times*, August 21, 2010.

Story, Louise. "A Rich Education for Summers," *New York Times*, April 5, 2009.

Subramanian, Arvind. "How Economics Managed to Make Amends," *Financial Times*, December 28, 2009.

Summers, Lawrence. "The Great Liberator," *New York Times*, November 19, 2006.

Summers, Lawrence. Interview, Ezra Klein blog, 2011, at www.washington post.com/blogs/ezra-klein/post/larry-summers-i-think-keynes-mistitled-his-book/2011/07/11/gIQAzZd4aI_blog.htm.

Suskind, Ron. *Confidence Men: Wall Street, Washington, and the Education of a President* (New York: HarperCollins, 2011).

Suskind, Ron. "Faith, Certainty, and the Presidency of George W. Bush," *New York Times Magazine*, October 17, 2004.

Suter, Susan. "Giving In to Baby Markets," *Michigan Journal of Gender and Law* 16 (2009): 217.

Swagel, Phillip. "The Financial Crisis: An Insider's View," *Brookings Papers on Economic Activity*, Spring 2009: 1–63.

Swan, Elaine. *Worked-up Selves* (New York: Palgrave Macmillan, 2010).

Swan, Elaine, and Stephen Fox. "Becoming Flexible: Self-flexibility and Its Pedagogies," *British Journal of Management* 20 (2009): S149–59.

Szafarz, Ariane. "How Did Crisis-Based Criticisms of Market Efficiency Get It So Wrong?" 2009.

Taibbi, Matt. "Glenn Hubbard Leading Academic" Rolling Stone blog, December 12, 2012 at: www.rollingstone.com/politics/blogs/taibblog/glenn-hubbard-leading-academic-and-mitt-romney-advisor-took-1200-an-hour-to-be-countrywides-expert-witness-20121220.

Taibbi, Matt. *Griftopia: Bubble Machines, Vampire Squids, and the Long Con* (New York: Spiegel & Grau, 2010).

Taibbi, Matt. "The Real Housewives of Wall Street," *Rolling Stone*, April 12, 2011.

Talbot, Margaret. "Brain Gain," *The New Yorker*, April 27, 2009.

Tankersley, Jim, and Michael Hirsh. "Neo-Voodoo Economics," *National Journal*, May 20, 2011.

Taylor, John. "How Government Created the Financial Crisis," *Wall Street Journal,* February 3, 2009.

Tellmann, Ute. "The Economic beyond Governmentality," in Brockling et al., *Governmentality*.

Tellmann, Ute. "Foucault and the Invisible Economy," *Foucault Studies* 6 (2009): 5–24.

Tett, Gilian. *Fool's Gold* (New York: Free Press, 2009).

Thernstrom, Melanie. "Meet the Twiblings," *New York Times Magazine*, December 29, 2010.

Thoma, Mark. "A Great Divide Holds Back the Relevance of Economists," with comments by Dean Baker, Lawrence Summers, and Paul Krugman (July 26, 2011), at http://blogs.reuters.com/great-debate/2011/07/26/a-great-divide-holds-back-the-relevance-of-economists/.

Thoma, Mark. "What Caused the Financial Crisis? Don't Ask an Economist," *Fiscal Times*, August 30, 2011, at www.thefiscaltimes.com/Columns/2011/08/30/What-Caused-the-Financial-Crisis-Dont-Ask-an-Economist.

Thompson, Helen. "The Limits of Blaming Neoliberalism: Fannie Mae, Freddie Mac, and the Financial Crisis," *New Political Economy* 17 (2012): 399-419

Thorpe, Charles. "Political Theory in STS," in Ed Hackett et al., eds., *Handbook of Science and Technology Studies* (Cambridge: MIT Press, 2008).

Thurner, Stephan, Doyne Farmer, and John Geanakoplos. "Leverage Causes Fat Tails and Clustered Volatility," Cowles Foundation Discussion Paper 1745, 2009.

Tkacik, Moe. "Journals of the Crisis Year," *The Baffler* no. 18, 2010.

Turkle, Sherry. *Alone Together* (New York: Basic Books, 2011).

Turkle, Sherry. *Life on the Screen: Identity in the Age of the Internet* (New York: Simon & Schuster, 1995).

Turner, Rachel. *Neo-liberal Ideology* (Edinburgh: Edinburgh University Press, 2008).

Urciuoli, Bonnie. "Skills and Selves in the New Workplace," *American Ethnologist* 35 (2008): 211-28.

U.S. Federal Crisis Inquiry Commission. *Final Report*, 2011, at http://cybercemetery.unt.edu/archive/fcic/20110310173538/http://www.fcic.gov/report.

U.S. Government Accountability Office. *Opportunities Exist to Strengthen Policies and Processes for Managing Emergency Assistance*, 2011, at www.gao.gov/new.items/d11696.pdf.

U.S. House Committee on Oversight and Governmental Reform. *An Examination of Attacks against the Financial Crisis Inquiry Commission*, July 13, 2011, at http://democrats.oversight.house.gov/images/stories/MINORITY/fcic%20report/FCIC%20Report%2007-13-11.pdf.

U.S. Securities and Exchange Commission. *Findings Regarding the Market Events of May 6, 2010*, at www.sec.gov/news/studies/2010/market-events-report.pdf.

U.S. Senate, Permanent Subcommittee on Investigations. *Wall Street and the Financial Crisis: Anatomy of a Financial Collapse* (Washington, D.C.: U.S. Government Printing Office, 2011); also at www.hsgac.senate.gov.

Vaidhyanathan, Siva. "Planet of the Apps," *Bookforum*, June 2012.

Van Horn, Robert, and Matthias Klaes. "Chicago Neoliberalism Versus Cowles Planning: Perspectives on Patents and Public Goods," *Journal of the History of the Behavioral Sciences* 47 (2011): 302-21.

Van Horn, Robert, and Philip Mirowski. "The Rise of the Chicago School and the Birth of Neoliberalism," in Mirowski and Plehwe, *The Road from Mont Pèlerin*.

Van Horn, Robert, Philip Mirowski, and Thomas Stapleford, eds. *Building Chicago Economics* (New York: Cambridge University Press, 2011).

Veblen, Thorstein. *The Theory of the Leisure Class* (New York: Mentor, 1953).

Vernon, Richard. "The Great Society and the Open Society: Liberalism in Hayek and Popper," *Canadian Journal of Political Science* 9 (1976): 261–76.

Vroman, Jack. "Allusions to Evolution," in Van Horn et al., *Building Chicago Economics*.

Wacquant, Loic. "Three Steps to a Historical Anthropology of Actually Existing Neoliberalism," *Social Anthropology* 20 (2012): 66–79.

Walker, Jeremy, and Melinda Cooper. "Genealogies of Resistance," *Security Dialogue* 42 (2011): 143–60.

Walker, Rob. *Buying In* (New York: Random House, 2008).

Wallace, David Foster. *Consider the Lobster and Other Essays* (Boston: Back Bay, 2007).

Wallace, David Foster. *Oblivion: Stories* (Boston: Back Bay, 2004).

Wallace, David Foster. *A Supposedly Fun Thing I'll Never Do Again* (Boston: Little Brown, 1997).

Wallace-Wells, Benjamin. "What's Left of the Left: Paul Krugman's Lonely Crusade," *New York*, April 2011.

Wallison, Peter. "Slaughter of the Innocents," *AEI Financial Services Outlook* (November 8, 2010), at www.aei.org/files/2010/11/08/FSO-2010-10-11-g.pdf.

Wallison, Peter. "The True Origins of the Financial Crisis," *AEI on the Issues*, February 19, 2009.

Wallison, Peter. "The True Story of the Financial Crisis," *American Spectator*, May 2010.

Walpen, Bernhard. *Die offenen Feinde und ihre Gesellschaft* (Hamburg: VSA, 2004).

Walsh, Mary. "Fed Advice to AIG Scrutinized," *New York Times*, January 8, 2010.

Walzer, Michael. *Spheres of Justice* (New York: Basic, 1983).

Warsh, David. "Last Week in Jerusalem" (2011), at www.economicprincipals.com/issues/2011.07.03/1276.html.

Washington, Harriet. *Deadly Monopolies: The Shocking Corporate Takeover of Life Itself* (New York: Doubleday, 2011).

Weigel, David. "Republicans for Tax Hikes," *Slate*, August 22, 2011, at www.slate.com/id/2302131/.

Weil, Jonathan. "Wall Street's Collapse to Be Mystery Forever," Bloomberg News, January 27, 2011, at www.bloomberg.com/news/2011-01-28/

wall-street-s-collapse-to-be-mystery-forever-commentary-by-jonathan-weil.html.

Weintraub, Roy, ed. *The Future of the History of Economics*, Supplement to HOPE, vol. 24 (Durham, N.C.: Duke University Press, 2002).

Westbrook, Donald. *Out of the Crisis* (Boulder: Paradigm, 2010).

White, Lawrence. "The Federal Reserve System's Influence on Research in Monetary Economics," *Economics Journals Watch* 2 (2005): 325–54.

Whitehouse, Mark. "Crisis Compels Economists to Reach for New Paradigm," *Wall Street Journal*, November 4, 2009.

Wilby, Peter. "All of Us Live by the Logic of Finance," *New Statesman*, February 9, 2009.

Williamson, John. "What Washington Means by Policy Reform," in John Williamson, ed., *Latin American Adjustment: How Much Has Happened?* (Washington, D.C.: Institute for International Economics, 1990).

Williamson, Stephen D. "A Defense of Contemporary Economics: John Quiggin's *Zombie Economics* in Review," *Agenda* 18 (3), 2011.

Wiseman, Jack. *Cost, Choice and Political Economy* (Cheltenham, U.K.: Elgar, 1989).

Wolin, Sheldon. *Politics and Vision* (Princeton: Princeton University Press, 2004).

Woodford, Michael. "Convergence in Macroeconomics: Elements of the New Synthesis," *American Economic Journal: Macroeconomics* 1 (2009): 267–79.

Wren-Lewis, Simon. "Lessons from Failure: Fiscal Policy, Indulgence and Ideology," *National Institute Economic Review* 217 (2011): R31–46.

Yates, Luke. "Critical Consumption," *European Societies* 13 (2) (2011): 191–217.

Zeleny, Jeff. "Financial Industry Paid Millions to Obama Aide," *New York Times*, April 4, 2009.

Zingales, Luigi. *A Capitalism for the People* (New York: Basic, 2012).

Zingales, Luigi. "Learning to Live with Not-So-Efficient Markets," *Daedalus*, Fall 2010, 1–10.

Zuidhof, Peter-Wim. *Imagining Markets: The Discursive Politics of Neoliberalism*, Ph.D. thesis, Erasmus University, Rotterdam, 2012.

Films and Video

Assayas, Olivier. *Summer Hours* (2010).

Curtis, Adam. *The Trap* (2007).

Estrada, Luis. *Un Mundo Maravilloso* (2006).

Ferguson, Charles. *Inside Job* (2010).

Klarlund, Anders Rønnow. *How to Get Rid of the Others* (2006).

LaBute, Neil. *The Shape of Things* (2003).

Marshall, Neil. *The Descent* (2006).

National Science Foundation. Andrew Lo lecture: "Are Mathematical Models the Cause for the Financial Crisis in the Global Economy?" (2009).

Nolan, Christopher. *Memento* (2001).

Oldham, Taki. *(Astro)Turf Wars* (2010).

Index

connection between economics profession
and, 159
"conservatism," 106
"constructivism" in, 53
core insight of, 104
on crime, 66
current topography of, 356
defense mechanisms of, 34
doctrines for, 52, 68
on economic crisis, 296, 298, 301, 358
emergency executive committee meeting, 7
on equality, 116
exercising hostility toward federal
government and Federal Reserve, 348
on Fannie Mae and Freddie Mac, 313, 314,
315
Foucault on, 94
on freedom, 107
Friedman on, 60
function of, 77, 83, 84, 85, 87
geoengineering and, 340
"good society," 69
major ambition of, 224
membership of, 385n32
on neuroenhancers, 151
normalization of everyday sadism, 130
orthodox macroeconomics and, 242, 243,
245, 246
parallels between Seekers and, 36
persistence of, 323
on personhood, 121
political mobilizations of, 142, 145
Radin on, 91
on "risk," 119
Russian doll structure of, 43, 49, 55, 57–58,
332, 333
sociological structure of, 89
success stories, 184
think tanks affiliated with, 337
Thirteen Commandments, 67
writings of members of, 97
Neoliberalism
Alternatives to, 101
Crisis response, 343–355
Defined, 27–70, 367
Distinguished from neoclassical econimics,
26, 36–37, 335–336
Left epithet, 37
Premature obituaries for, 31–32
Netflix, 143
New Age, 52
New Deal, 326
New Disrespect, 163

New Economic Thinking, 3, 4, 5, 160, 237
New Industrial State (Galbraith), 139
"New Keynesianism," 270
New Keynesians model, 278, 293
New Knowledge Economy, 79
New Labour, 117
New Orthodox Seer, 289
New Right, 39
New Statesman, 177
New York Federal Reserve Bank, 186, 196,
211, 302–303, 331, 346, 387–388n63,
403n122
New York Review of Books, 273
New York Times, 144, 158, 160, 213, 263, 295,
315, 383n13
New York University (NYU), 252
New Yorker, 179, 204, 254, 340, 382–383n10
Newbery, David
on "investments," 177
News Corporation, 45
Newshour, 176, 204, 402n117
Newsnight, 204
Newsweek, 74, 117, 310
Nietzsche, Friedrich, 129, 130, 135, 170
"The Night they Re-read Minsky," 292
Nik-Khah, Edward, 364, 403
Nine Lives of Neoliberalism, 241
Nobel Prize, 87, 161, 228, 230, 251, 271, 286, 287
Nobelists, 389n74
Nocera, Joe, 295, 315, 406n162
Nolan, Christopher, 163
A Non-Random Walk Down Wall Street (Lo
and MacKinley), 264
Northern Rock, 30
Nostradamus Codex, 251
Notre Dame, University of, 159
NPR (National Public Radio), 233, 308
NSF (National Science Foundation), 212,
285, 286, 312
NTC. *See* Neoliberal Thought Collective
(NTC)
Nugent, Ted, 129
NYU (New York University), 252

O
Obama, Barack, 4, 118, 181, 183, 207, 262,
308, 389n74
Occam's Razor, 30
Occupiers, 328
Occupy Handbook, 327
Occupy London, 355
Occupy Movement, 204, 315, 326–332, 355,
406–407n7